Electronic Media and Industrialized Nations

A Comparative Study

Electronic Media and Industrialized Nations

A Comparative Study

Donald R. Browne

IOWA STATE UNIVERSITY PRESS / AMES

Once again, to Kathy
And to her niece Kim Stephanie

Donald R. Browne is professor and chair of the Department of Speech-Communication at the University of Minnesota. He has written extensively about broadcast systems, drawing on professional experience in over 30 countries as a teacher, overseas correspondent for the Voice of America and as an international broadcast consultant.

Iowa State University Press
2121 South State Avenue, Ames, Iowa 50014

Orders: 1-800-862-6657
Office: 1-515-292-0140
Fax: 1-515-292-3348
Web site: www.isupress.edu

♾ Printed on acid-free paper in the United States of America

First edition, 1999

This book replaces *Comparing Broadcast Systems: The Experiences of Six Industrialized Nations* by the same author, © 1989, Iowa State University Press.

International Standard Book Number: 0-8138-0422-1

Library of Congress Cataloging-in-Publication Data

Browne, Donald R.
Electronic media and industrialized nations: a comparative study / Donald R. Browne. —1st ed.
p. cm.
Includes bibliographical references and index.
ISBN 0-8138-0422-1
1. Broadcasting—Europe. 2. Mass media—Europe. I. Title.
PN1990.6.E85B76 1999
384.54'094—dc21 98-55110

The last digit is the print number: 9 8 7 6 5 4 3 2 1

Contents

3. The Netherlands: *Plurality in an Era of Competition,* 157

4. Germany: *States' Rights, National Goals and Unification,* 215

6. What's Comparable, What Isn't And What It May Mean, 397

Preface

There's an old popular song title: "What a Difference a Day Makes!" A song couldn't begin to describe what has happened to the electronic media in industrialized nations over the past decade. When I wrote the book *Comparing Broadcast Systems,* on which the present text is based, most systems around the globe were just beginning to experience the pressures of media diversification that have revolutionized the media world. Monopolies were the dominant structures, with a few duopolies (Japan, Great Britain) and a scattering of commercially oriented systems (the United States, certainly, with Australia and Canada featuring strong commercial structures). As of 1998, the systems of most industrialized nations are far more commercially oriented than they were a decade ago, to the point where some observers have expressed doubts that the old public service model typical of monopoly structures will live much longer. While I find that an extreme position, I must agree that life certainly has changed for the public service broadcasters.

What I hope for readers to see is that there are many different ways to finance, supervise and program the electronic media, but also that there is very little that is inevitable about media history and structure. With any luck, that should lead readers to reconsider the functions of the mass media in the United States and elsewhere. And that in turn may lead to the realization that national characteristics help to determine only a part of any one nation's experience with the media. Furthermore, as channels proliferate, as satellites act as global antennae, and as the Internet penetrates even tightly closed societies, industrialized nations increasingly are influenced by one another's experiences, sometimes for good, sometimes for ill. The developing nations sometimes have erected novel structures and have made innovative uses of the electronic media, but they, too, have been influenced heavily by the experiences of the industrially developed nations, several of which were their colonial rulers when broadcasting began.

The nations represented in the nation-specific chapters were chosen on the basis of three characteristics: their influence on the systems of other nations, their adoption of unusual approaches to the structure and use of the electronic media, and the relative scarcity of material on them in English (but I'm pleased to see just how much more is available now). Great Britain, Canada, New Zealand and Australia present many interesting examples of uses and structures, and I refer to them in the opening and closing chapters. They have also been influential in other parts of the world. But all four have already been covered in many books, monographs and articles in English.

It will quickly become evident that I have a strong historical orientation. That's because of my conviction that, to borrow the old adage, those who refuse to learn from history are bound to repeat its mistakes. Also, I feel that a historically based account of an electronic media system throws into sharper relief just how dynamic the electronic media are, and shows how political, cultural, demographic/linguistic, geographic, technological and economic forces, singly and in combination, affect their development over time. Such an account also underscores one of my long-held beliefs: that there's nothing inevitable about the form that those media take in any nation. History, especially when we see it at work in a number of broadcast systems, shows us that external as well as internal developments shape systems over time, often for different reasons and with varying degrees of power and duration.

I cannot claim to have a citizen's appreciation for the effects of the electronic media in the nations covered here, but I have a certain amount of outsider's acquaintance: two periods in the Soviet Union (1970, 1985), and six or more in divided and united Germany, the Netherlands and France, from 1956 through 1996. I completed work on the manuscript in December 1997, with some additions in 1998.

I have received great encouragement, assistance and cooperation from hundreds of individuals but wish to give particular thanks to the following: Harrie Bos, Kees van der Haak, Ed Klute, Jonathan Marks, and Bert Steinkamp (the Netherlands); Antoine de Tarlé, Claude-Jean Bertrand, Pierre Braillard, and Rouget L'Estaire (France); Jochen Zimmer, Wolfgang Hoffmann-Riem, Klaus Schoenbach, Manfred Jahnke, and Hans Bausch (Germany); Eric Johnson, Nick Hayes, Ellen Mickiewicz, Joe Adamov, Gene Parta, Henrikas Yushkiavitshus, and Burton Paulu (the Soviet Union and Russia); Tadao Nomura, Chosei Kabira, and Hiroko Nishida (Japan); Chris Sterling (bibliography); and Douglas Boyd (general). I'm also grateful to the Department of Speech-Communication, the Office of International Programs, the McMillan Fund, and the Graduate School, all of the University of Minnesota, and to the Fulbright-Hays Program and the North Atlantic Treaty Organization for various forms and amounts of financial assistance over the years, making 20 overseas trips possible.

The organization of the chapters that follow coincides with the organization of my course on comparative electronic media systems at the University of Minnesota: I begin with a consideration of elements that will serve as the structural backbone of a comparative consideration. I follow that with the

French system (reasonably clear-cut); the Dutch system (quite complex, and as societally responsive as the French system is not); the systems of the various Germanies that have existed over the decades (which also provide a good contrast between noncommunist and communist approaches for the period 1945–90); and the Soviet system (communist, and thus related to the East German system), succeeded (and to some extent imitated) by the Russian system.* I conclude with a summation of what we may learn through a comparison of experiences, followed by speculation on what an ideal system of broadcasting might look like, and then a bit of forecasting.

You'll note that the more detailed illustrations of programming practices come from the mid-1990s. They are based largely on my personal viewing of programs, which has allowed me to provide what I feel is a fuller and more lively portrait of what audiences see and hear. There are two websites that I've found useful for tracking overall schedules (mostly from European nations) and for obtaining brief sketches of some programs. They are *http://www.ultimatetv.com* and *http://www.buttle.com*. There also are many websites operated by broadcasters, e.g., *http://www.ard.de* for Germany's ARD stations.

I hope and trust that this book will bring readers to consider more carefully what the electronic media were, are and could be to society. I want to show not just the whats of media experiences, but the whys and hows, as well. The Underground Grammarian of November 1987 contained a fascinating article entitled "The Age of Outformation." After presenting the need for the establishment of an ordering principle, the (anonymous) author decried the mindless devotion to facts and observed,"Cluttered will better describe the mind that is full of bits of news of this and that, a junkyard in which everything lies where it fell." If I have avoided the junkyard syndrome, I shall be content.

---

* *Comparing Broadcast Systems* also contained a chapter on Japan. Regrettably, the large amount of additional information that has become available on the nations covered as case studies, along with the need to hold the current book to a page limit that would keep the price at a reasonable level, necessitated cutting the Japan chapter. It is available directly from me as revised through the end of 1997, if your written request specifies classroom use only, and if you will cover the costs of duplication (single-sided), packaging and mailing. Please address your inquiries to *brown003@umn.edu*.

Electronic Media and Industrialized Nations

A Comparative Study

1 Comparing Electronic Media Systems

No two electronic media systems are absolutely alike. All have been influenced to greater or lesser degrees by other systems, and all have been influenced by geographic, demographic, linguistic, economic, cultural, political and technological forces in their own and neighboring countries. Nor is there a perfect model for an electronic media system. Even if there were, changing circumstances soon would render it invalid. The electronic media—radio, television, cable and satellite, audio- and videodiscs and cassette recordings, the Internet—are as dynamic as society itself, although they may not change at the same pace. They may lead or be accused of leading (or following) public taste, or they may be "just about right." But for which publics? The concept of a single "mass public" has been dead for some time now, and the expansion of electronic media services in all industrialized nations (and in increasing numbers of developing nations) has led to predictions that society may become even more fractionated.

The electronic media are shaped by more forces than are most other institutions, in part because they are so closely interlinked with society. By the same token, the nature and process of that shaping may be even less predictable than it would be for an institution more removed from such daily and highly visible (and audible) contact with the public. I do not present what follows with the idea that it will lead to precise models or highly predictive formulas. Rather, I intend it to aid in understanding the electronic media more clearly by considering the elements that characterize them and the factors that influence them, and then presenting, chiefly through the experiences of five nations, the ways in which those elements and factors appear in and affect specific electronic media systems. I draw those experiences together in the final chapter, but in the spirit of offering points that may be worth considering whenever there's discussion of the possible reform of the electronic media. That same spirit leads me to conclude with thoughts on the ideal electronic media system, if one could in fact exist.

THE COMPARATIVE STUDY OF SYSTEMS

Since this is a *comparative* study, I begin by considering *why* we should compare the approaches that various industrialized nations have taken to introducing, developing, controlling and using the electronic media. Comparative studies exist in a number of academic fields, but probably are most common in political science, where they've served to illustrate and analyze the varied experiences of cities, states and nations in their political practices: How are election campaigns run? How do legislatures legislate? How do heads of state function? Through such comparisons, we expect to learn not only how things are done, but why they're done in particular ways, and, perhaps, whether certain ways seem better than others. That qualitative dimension—"better"—is considerably more difficult to articulate and assess than are the descriptive dimensions implied in the "How do's" of the preceding questions. Difficult it may be, but many scholars who undertake comparative research are drawn to it because they hope, if not expect, that they will arrive at something resembling that holy grail of comparative researchers: the perfect system.

As you'll see when you finally arrive at my description of the ideal system, I didn't find one specific national example that embodied something like perfection; rather, I found a number of examples of different aspects of the component parts of electronic media systems that seemed to be better than others of like nature. In turn, they became the components of my ideal system. But I must remind myself that it's *my* particular ideal system; that is, I inevitably bring my own value system into any such consideration.

I see two dimensions to this—and, I would claim, every—comparative study: the more or less objective structural elements that systems hold more or less in common; and the subjective value judgments that lead comparative scholars to emphasize one element more than another, both through the amount of time they spend in researching it, the space they use when writing about it, and the importance they confer upon it through their choice of evaluative terms ("most important," "chief reason for," etc.) when describing it. Even the order in which they present each element may indicate its relative importance, at least in their minds.

I've attempted to understand my particular biases as I wrote this book, and have sought to keep them in check, chiefly by acknowledging them. My greatest, most all-encompassing bias is that the electronic media are important elements in shaping and reflecting society. To me, this means that those who govern, regulate, administer and produce for them have an obligation to take their responsibilities seriously, just as viewers and listeners have the obligation to understand how those media function and what they, the program-consuming public, can and even must do to ensure that those media function in ways that will support the development of healthy societies. I wouldn't have written this book if I did not believe that. But my bias certainly isn't universally held: more and more systems are turning in the direction of less regulation and more competition for the electronic media, which can mean greater freedom of speech and of choice for more people through more channels of communication, but which also can mean that the electronic media come to be thought of as business operations which differ little from auto plants, fast-food restaurants or life insurance companies, all of which are regulated, but none of which are expected to place *obligation* to society at the top of their lists of responsibilities.

So what is it that comparative studies can provide? A firmer basis for making comparisons, by providing articulations of specific elements common to most, perhaps all, systems. Stimulation to ask oneself why specific differences and similarities in those elements exist. And perhaps the inspiration to imagine how a better system might be developed out of what we can discover in existing systems.[1]

As for *systems,* I use the term to indicate that there are a number of attributes which characterize the presence of electronic media in all nations. I do *not* mean that the attributes will be equally important in all nations, or that they will interact in the same ways from nation to nation. I mean only that an identification and examination of attributes which appear in all nations (although some sub-attributes may not; e.g., unions—which are present in most industrialized nations, but may or may not be represented in the electronic media) will allow for more systematic comparisons of experiences. That in turn should encourage questions regarding why there are certain similarities and dissimilarities, which in my experience leads to a richer understanding of how the media and society interact.

I begin by considering six fundamental factors affecting the electronic media. Geography, demography/linguistics, economy, culture, politics and technology cannot fully explain the development of electronic media systems, but they do serve as common denominators and help to establish parameters for further comparisons. I treat them as distinct entities. However, as the chapters on specific nations soon will illustrate, they interact to varying degrees, and the nature and extent of interaction varies over time: some elements rise and fall in their influence, while others remain quite stable.

BASIC FACTORS

Geographic

The physical disposition of a nation has a major effect upon the development of its electronic media system. The ideal nation for broadcasting, from a geographic point of view, would be one that is circular in shape and either without mountains (if the country is small) or with a small core of mountains in the very center (if the country is of medium size). With radio transmitters placed in the center of either country, it should be possible to reach all parts of the small nation, while the mountainous core of a medium-sized country could increase the height of a transmitter tower and help extend the signal to the nation's borders.

Few nations have such geographic characteristics. The Netherlands is small, comes reasonably close to being circular, and certainly is flat. Sri Lanka is oval-shaped, not much bigger than the Netherlands, and has a central core of mountains; the Republic of China-Taiwan closely resembles it. Some Caribbean and Pacific island nations are similarly shaped, and even smaller than Sri Lanka or Taiwan. France has a mountainous core that is reasonably central, and the other French mountain ranges are at the borders. However, most small and medium-sized nations have hilly or mountainous terrain that runs across the landscape at various angles, leaving some viewers and listeners in hard-to-reach valleys, where it is extremely expensive to bring signals to them. Often nations will be long and fairly narrow, as well, which means that circular broadcast signals will spill into the sea or into neighboring countries unless elaborate and costly precautions are taken to shape the signal to a noncircular pattern. Nations such as Japan, Great Britain, Norway, Sweden and Finland, which face both problems, have to invest tremendous amounts of money in reaching all of their viewers and listeners, and even then coverage is not 100 percent for each and every broadcast service.

Communication satellites can overcome those problems, but they, too, are expensive, and only Japan, India, Canada, the former U.S.S.R., Indonesia, and possibly Australia, have made major efforts to use them on a full, national scale in order to overcome the effects of mountainous terrain, a widely scattered population, or a chain of islands strung out over a few thousand miles. Even then, the receiving equipment is expensive, due to the need for a special antenna and a signal converter, and it's often necessary to subsidize the cost of purchasing sets, especially if those living in difficult-to-reach areas are less well-off economically.

Size is an important variable here. On the whole, it would seem more feasible for a small to medium-sized nation to consider developing a national electronic media system rather than a set of regional or local services, because of economy of scale. Of course, not all such nations have developed national systems, but many European countries have, and two of the major colonizers among them—France and Great Britain—have left the same legacy with their former colonies in Africa and Asia.

Large nations might be expected to favor the development of regional and/or local services, particularly if, as is usually the case with such nations, there is an uneven distribution of the population to go along with the vast spaces and great topographical variety. Several of the world's largest nations display those characteristics and have at least partially adopted that solution. The United States, Canada, China (before the Communists assumed political power in 1949), Australia and Brazil all seemed fairly indifferent to the development of national systems during the early years of broadcasting in their countries, although by the late 1920s Australia and Canada had begun to give national services more serious attention, and the United States had developed a clear channel system of frequency allocation that would bring at least a few stations to even the most geographically isolated listeners during the nighttime.

Not that most systems started life at the national level. Up until the mid-

1920s, radio broadcasting generally was considered more of an amusement than anything else, and there was little interest on the part of governments in seeing it develop to serve the entire nation. The postmaster general's insistence that British companies wishing to broadcast band themselves together to provide a national service was a rarity in its time (1922), although it had a counterpart in the U.S.S.R., where Lenin encouraged the development of a national service.

Geographical neighbors also play a role in the development of domestic systems. An isolated island can broadcast slightly beyond its national borders without disturbing its neighbors; a nation such as Switzerland, if it were to do the same, would reach Germany, France, Italy and Austria. Even at that, Switzerland has the advantage of being fairly circular, whereas Austria, which is long and narrow, could not broadcast from a single central location without major spillover into five or six neighboring nations and minor spillover into two or three more. That can be turned into a virtue of sorts, as Luxembourg proves: Its radio service (in private hands, but with the government as a major controller) spilled over into many surrounding countries and in the early 1930s began to broadcast in the languages of those countries and to carry ads directed at their listeners.

Among the six factors presented here, geography may be the one that stands the greatest chance of becoming less relevant over the next few decades. Satellites have made it possible to bring services to remote locations within nations, to entire continents, to the world. Audio- and videocassettes have become less expensive and more compact with the passage of time, making it cheaper and easier to reproduce them and distribute them in other nations by the tens of thousands, in some cases. The Internet already girdles the globe, although the vast majority of human beings don't yet have access to it. But it's almost certain to become less expensive and more accessible in the coming years. Some even predict that the nation-state will vanish, in part because advances in communications technology have favored the growth of worldwide communities of interest whose importance may come to exceed—in certain instances, may already exceed—the importance of geographical communities.[2]

Demographic/Linguistic

Anyone who has traveled across the United States is well aware of its uneven distribution of population. The extremes are probably most vivid when approaching or leaving Phoenix, Salt Lake City or Denver, where population density changes dramatically within a range of 15 to 20 miles. The more uneven the distribution, the more difficult it becomes for most medium-sized to large countries to furnish broadcast services for everyone unless there is a commitment to some form of national service—something the United States, Canada, Australia and, much later, Brazil all eventually realized. Such a national service is far more costly per inhabitant than in a small, densely populated nation such as Belgium, the Netherlands, Kuwait, Hong Kong or Singapore. The existence of a highly urbanized population often has favored the development of local services, as in the 1920s in the United States, Canada, Australia and Brazil, and also in several European nations, among them France, Germany, Norway and Spain.

It isn't just a matter of how the population is distributed across the country; *where* it's distributed also matters. For example, major cities are found all across the United States. In Canada, most of them are within 50 miles of the U.S. border and thus are within easy reach of U.S. broadcasts, which have had major influences on the development of Canadian broadcasting. Most of the major cities in the Netherlands lie on a strip of land that is 30 miles wide, 90 miles deep and paralleling the seacoast; that made them easy targets for "pirate" (unauthorized) radio and TV broadcasts in the late 1950s to early 1970s. Similarly, most of the heavier concentrations of British listeners are on or close to the sea, which made them easily reachable by shipboard pirate radio broadcasts in the 1960s and again in the 1980s. In both cases, the pirates affected the development of the domestic broadcast systems. During the "cold war," radio and TV broadcasts in West Berlin carried far into the German Democratic Republic and vice versa: The city was a densely populated "island," or enclave, in the middle of the GDR. West Berlin broadcasts caused the GDR to make great efforts to produce high-quality entertainment programming, so as to compete more effectively for listeners and viewers in their own country, and to a lesser extent in West Berlin.

In all of those cases, influences from abroad would have been minimized if it had not been for the existence of a common language. French-language broadcasting in Canada is not all that heavily influenced by U.S. broadcasts, even though Montréal and many other cities and towns in Québec are near the U.S. border. That's because many Québec viewers and listeners prefer French-language broadcasts, and few U.S. stations broadcast in French. But the German spoken in the GDR was much the same as that spoken in West Berlin. The pirates off Great Britain were operated for the most part by Britons, Canadians, Irish and Americans, who spoke understandable, if accented, English.

Most of the industrially developed nations have the advantage (for the development of electronic media, at any rate) of a single, common language. That's true of most of the nations of Europe (Switzerland is an exception, as were the former Yugoslavia, U.S.S.R. and Czechoslovakia), the Arab world, Latin America, Japan and Australia. The situation is far worse for the nations of sub-Saharan Africa and for South Asia, where there may be a dozen or more languages spoken by sizable segments of the population. If a country is large, it may be possible to regionalize the broadcast service to some extent, as the People's Republic of China and India have done: There, most of the major linguistic groups fall into fairly neat geographical divisions. But if a country is small, as is the West African nation of Guinea, and has Guinea's dozens of tribal languages, all of roughly equal status, regionalization can be pretty expensive.

There's another consideration, as well: national unity versus regional or local identity. Most Americans have little trouble thinking of themselves as (forgive my parochialism!) Saint Paulites, Minnesotans and Americans simultaneously. It isn't always that easy for people in other countries, and they may have particular difficulty with the notion that the country as a whole has any meaning for them. The troubled situation in Lebanon probably stems in part from lack of any sense of national identity on the part of most Lebanese. Disturbances in India, Pakistan, Zaire and many other countries, not to mention the collapse of the U.S.S.R. and Yugoslavia and the division of Czechoslovakia, show that national unity often is very fragile. Should a broadcast system particularly encourage national identity as opposed to regional or local identity, or vice versa? Or should it seek some sort of balance, which often is more expensive than favoring either of the first two options? Guinea provides both a national radio service (in French, which few Guineans speak, but it was the language of Guinea's colonial ruler) and a tribal-language service. The latter features such short blocks of airtime per language that a listener has to know exactly which half-hour or so of the day her or his language will be on the air or miss out. The compromise is expensive and not particularly efficient, but the number of languages to be covered and the relative poverty of the country mean that there are few alternatives.

Even the industrially developed countries over the past two decades have become more aware of linguistic (often ethnic) minorities. The migration of "guest workers" within and to western Europe has brought Turks, Greeks, Portuguese, Spaniards, Italians, Indians and North Africans into the work forces of West Germany, France, the Netherlands and so on in considerable numbers. In turn, and as the numbers of "guests" increase, the resident majority population has become much more aware of them, not always with happy results. There have been indigenous movements, as well: the Welsh in Great Britain made a major case of their demands for a separate Welsh-language television service and finally achieved their goal in the late 1970s. Services in Sami (Lapp) have spread across northern Scandinavia. Australia and New Zealand feature Aboriginal- and Maori-operated radio and TV stations. Some of the French regional stations formed in the early 1980s began to broadcast in regional languages such as Breton. There's a Basque-language TV station in Spain. There are even brief bits of programming in Cornish over the British Broadcasting Corporation (BBC) Radio Cornwall, although probably no more than 200 to 300 people living there can speak it. Most of those linguistic pressures do not threaten national unity, although Basque and Corsican nationalist movements sometimes have become violent, and the Breton separatist movement has been a bit feisty at times.

Economic

Throughout most of their existence, the electronic media have been a fairly expensive venture. By that token, it stands to reason that wealthier nations would find it easier to support them than would poorer nations. However, poverty doesn't seem to have deterred any nation from establishing a broadcast service—even the tiniest, poorest Caribbean island nations have their own radio stations—although it may have kept those services modest. The economy and the media are directly related in other ways. Every major method of financing radio, TV, cable and satellites is dependent to some extent on the short-term and long-term economic health of the country. A recession generally means that there will be a tightening of the national budget; of individual and corporate donations, as well as advertising; of the purchase of radio and television receivers, VCRs and satellite dishes; and of subscription to cable, satellite and Internet services. Annual license fees probably won't be lowered, but they will not increase, either, despite increased costs for broadcasting, which must be met by revenues from somewhere if cuts in service are to be avoided.

The overall economic philosophy of a nation also may influence modes of financing the broadcast system. A communist economy ordinarily doesn't consider advertising to be a particularly desirable way to finance broadcasting, although many communist nations did, and China still does, advertise over radio and television. A capitalist economy sees advertising as normal business practice, and, where broadcast advertising is concerned, as a further stimulus to the economy, since ads induce people to spend more on goods and services. A socialist economy may take a middle road, although it seems more likely to generate money through an annual license fee assessed against households with radio and TV sets than do the communist or capitalist economies. It's also somewhat more tolerant of advertising than the former, but less likely to leave it uncontrolled or loosely regulated than the latter.

The ways in which the population earns its money also affect the media, in that certain sectors of the economy need, or are thought to need, the up-to-the-minute information that they can provide. Any economic activity directly affected by the weather—fishing, farming, recreational sports—will need timely weather forecasts. Livestock and grain farmers and dealers will want livestock and grain market reports. A free enterprise economy often demands regular stock market reports. Local or regional broadcast services may be more efficient in providing certain specialized information than are national services (what interest would most Londoners or New Yorkers have in hog market reports?) but national services usually may be obligated to carry them if there's no regional or local service to do so.

There's also the nebulous matter of how the electronic media may promote or discourage various economic philosophies by their programming. Books written by communists about capitalist media systems often conclude that those systems support the capitalist economic philosophy by various means: by giving little if any attention to the worker's point of view,[3] by giving prominence to statements made by the country's economic leaders in management and government, and even by carrying ads, which themselves seem to indicate that the economy makes plenty of goods and services available to everyone.[4] Critics of communist broadcast systems have noted their frequent use of individuals as economic models: farmers, factory workers and so on, who overfulfill work quotas, introduce more labor-efficient methods, overcome skepticism among fellow workers, and encourage group participation.

Finally, since most electronic media equipment is manufactured in the industrially developed nations, the developing, or Third World, nations must dig into their limited, precious reserves of "hard" (internationally convertible) currency to pay for its acquisition and maintenance. That condition can limit the expansion of the media; in extreme circumstances, it can even bring them to a halt until money can be found for imported replacement parts and/or imported technicians to install them. The same applies to the purchase of energy for powering broadcast transmitters: Many developing nations have little or no domestic energy-generating capacity and must import oil for the purpose—again, usually having to pay for it in hard currency.

Cultural

Cultural subdivisions are a part of every nation. Whether based on language, economic class, religious or political affiliation, education or a host of other elements, and whether existing singly or in various combinations, they are what give nations their "national character." They can serve as elements of national unity or division. Their strength may come from historical tradition, economic or political power, a sudden catastrophic event (e.g., assassination of a prominent figure), or sheer force of numbers. The media may help bring them to the attention of the general public, but they themselves may bring pressure on the media to devote more attention to their causes.

Most systems make provision for mirroring the interests of at least a few cultural groups. In some cases, there are designated language services; special programs or even entire stations to serve ethnic minorities; popular music stations; "high-culture" stations; stations promoting educational development; and specialized stations operated by political parties, the military, religious organizations or labor unions. However, with the exception of religious stations, most of the last-named group of stations carry broadcasts for members and nonmembers alike. Cable and satellite usually offer a number of highly specialized services, as well, and there are videocassettes to suit a wide range of tastes and languages. Some nations also permit the importation of program material from foreign countries, such as Turkish domestic radio and TV services via satellite and videocassette recordings of Turkish movies for Turks living in Germany and the Netherlands.

The French have attempted to discourage the satellite distribution of television services from Arabic-speaking nations in North Africa to North Africans living in France, apparently because French authorities fear that such broadcasts will stir up discontent. That's a possibility, given the high levels of poverty among North Africans living in France, but also given the fact that there's so little about their own situations, never mind in their own languages, that French electronic media carry. Even so, many North Africans rent Arabic-language videocassettes, listen to the few Arabic-language radio stations available in the country, and (increasingly) find the financial means to install dishes and bring in TV signals from North Africa.

Some of those groups will have sufficient economic strength that services in advertiser-supported systems find it profitable to cater to them, as many Spanish-language, black-oriented and (more rarely) classical music stations do in the United States. More often, however, it will be necessary for the nation's legislative body, the media system itself, or some governmental agency charged with the administration or regulation of the media, to encourage or require some forms of service to cultural groups. That could be done by reserving broadcast time for them on national, regional and/or local services, by authorizing the use of entire stations (e.g., Channel Four's Welsh-language service in Great Britain), by making it possible for them to acquire their own stations through the help of government grants and low-interest loans, or by providing them with access to transmitter facilities at low cost, but having them be responsible for financing their own program and administrative activities, for example the "närradio," or neighborhood radio, services of Norway, Sweden and Denmark.[5]

The granting of special media rights to various cultural groups can open Pandora's box in some cases. The creation of a popular music radio station by the Dutch broadcasting system in the late 1960s—itself an attempt to win back listeners from broadcast pirates beaming "nonstop pop" to Dutch audiences—resulted in the claim by high-culture advocates that their interests were being neglected; that in turn led to the creation of a "high-culture" radio service featuring classical music and original drama in the mid-1970s. U.S. educators staked their claim to reserved frequencies for FM broadcasting just before World War II and for television just after the war; their argument was that commercial broadcasters never would find it in their own interests to allow the educators much airtime over commercial stations. But the educators eventually ended up competing with other nonprofit groups, and religious groups in particular, for the use of those reserved frequencies, since those other groups could make the same argument for themselves. The development of broadcast services by and for Maori audiences in New Zealand starting in the late 1980s led South Pacific islanders resident in New Zealand to press for creation of services appropriate for their needs, and there are now three radio stations for that purpose, two of them supported in part with government funds.

The question of where the cultural subdivision of the electronic media should start or stop is a very difficult one to answer. It's more difficult for countries where there is but one national radio or TV service, little or no time or facilities available for regional or local broadcasting, and a society resembling a cultural crazy quilt tacked together by outsiders—in other words, the sort of situation that exists in so much of sub-Saharan Africa and in parts of South Asia. And even if time and facilities are available, is it conducive to national unity to mirror the many, diverse, and often conflicting interests of the various groups? The experiences of several nations which have made major commitments to media access for ethnic minorities—Australia for Aborigines, New Zealand for Maori, Norway for Sami, Ireland for Gaelic speakers, Great Britain for Welsh speakers—seem to indicate that it is, but specific evidence is not plentiful.[6]

Furthermore, cultural groups themselves seldom are monolithic entities. Most contain factions, and often the factions do not see eye to eye. If the administrators of the system are in charge of deciding who gets to use what amounts of airtime and when, which criteria will they employ in making those decisions? If the groups have to do it themselves, will this encourage a sort of gang warfare, as appears to have happened at times within the major political parties of West Germany, where radical groups within the parties once fought for airtime to present their particular points of view? If some governmental authority, whether legislature or regulatory agency, has to make such decisions, will party politics ultimately determine who gets what? And if budgets are tight when new services for minorities are being created, who will establish the budgetary priorities that are bound to end up seeming to favor one group over another?

No electronic media system anywhere in the world yet has found a formula for satisfying all of the people all of the time. Some have left it to economics—if the group has the money, it can develop a broadcast service. Some have imposed a few overall criteria for satisfying the largest or most vocal or most politically powerful groups and have left the rest up to fate or circumstance. (The development of the Channel Four Welsh Service is an interesting illustration of how circumstances can change.)[7] A few, as in the Netherlands and in much of Scandinavia, have established systems where it's reasonably easy for groups to gain access to the airwaves so long as all but the major groups don't ask for it very often. Cable television, with its multiple-channel capacity, has been hailed by some as the answer to the problem of limited airtime for cultural groups. It may be a technical answer, but who will pay for the productions? Satellites are of great potential benefit to minority groups whose members are scattered over a wide geographic area, as are Aborigines in Australia, but the cost of developing a satellite service, including hardware for signal reception, will be very high if measured by cost per thousand audience members. And if there are, to borrow from Chinese leader Mao Tse-Tung, "a hundred flowers blooming, a hundred schools of thought contending," how many of them will listeners and viewers make the effort to seek out? If and when they do, will societal cohesion increase or diminish?

Political

Just as economic philosophies can influence the nature of media systems, so can political philosophies make their mark. All broadcast and satellite systems fall under governmental jurisdiction in at least one sense: Any authorized use of the frequency spectrum for either must be licensed by the government as a condition of belonging to the International Telecommunications Union (ITU), a United Nations body that attempts to keep users of the spectrum from interfering with one another. All sovereign nations of the world belong to the ITU, although not all cooperate fully with it.[8] Membership in the ITU requires only that governments license use of the spectrum on a technical basis: broadcast or satellite frequency, time of day, power and direction of signal. It does not involve control of program content. However, very few governments have refrained from controlling program content to some degree, and since governments generally are made up of political parties (there are few absolute monarchies left in the world), politics and electronic media interact.

The political spectrum runs as broad a gamut as does the frequency spectrum but doesn't enjoy so clear a set of definitions. The categories I use have been influenced to some degree by the Siebert et al. four theories of the press, but more as a point of departure than anything else.[9] When Siebert and his co-authors set forth their theories, the world of the electronic media was a much simpler place: monopoly structures predominated, audiotape recorders were bulky and expensive, videocassettes didn't exist, cable TV was a rarity, and communication satellites were only one part of a 1945 proposal by British scientist Arthur Clarke. Their greatest utility for my purposes has been their establishment of links between political philosophies and media systems. But I feel that they are best understood as a set of points along a continuum of those philosophies, ranging from the anarchical to the absolute in terms of political control/involvement.

I cannot come up with examples of media systems in anarchical societies, any more than I can offer examples of media systems in societies with absolute, total political control. From what I've seen, neither has ever existed, although it could be interesting to consider what they might be like if they did exist. The four labels offered by Fred Siebert and his colleagues—Libertarian, Social Responsibility, Communist and Authoritarian—cover rather loose constructs. Once they're understood in that light, it's easier to see how the balance in relationships between politics and the media may change over time, although the overall categorical label may remain the same. In other words, I use a more dynamic, time-sensitive approach than the creators of the four theories may have intended—an approach that allows for movement back and forth across the philosophical continuum.

Libertarian (and Possibly Laissez-Faire)

The libertarian government is often associated with capitalist nations, and more particularly with "conservative" governments (here meaning those more favorable toward private enterprise and less favorable toward government regulation of its practices). This philosophy holds that interests (whether economic, philosophical or whatever) should be allowed to "fight it out" among themselves, and the public will decide which ones it favors. Many libertarians favor well-nigh unrestricted freedom of speech, as well. Laissez-faire governments generally are regarded as being even more permissive in those respects than are libertarian governments, especially in promoting economic competition.

It follows, then, that libertarian governments should be willing to license as many users of frequency spectrum space for electronic media services as the spectrum will hold, and to impose very few criteria for deciding who should receive frequencies. Few governments are that open-handed or nonjudgmental in practice, but many come close, as witness the 37 mediumwave (AM) stations licensed in Quito, Ecuador, or the 18 FM stations in Manila, the Philippines. If stations in such countries feel that they must alter their program mix in order to remain competitive, it's generally easy for them to do so, since regulation of program content is minimal. The attempt in the United States during the 1970s to give audiences some say in whether changes in broadcast formats were in their best interests seems to have been the exception that proves the rule, and that movement itself was short-lived.[10]

Libertarian and laissez-faire governments also are apt to take a dim view of governmental financial support for electronic media, or indeed of any form of financial support other than advertising. The governments of Latin America, most of which historically have been laissez-faire or dictatorial, have done little to promote the development of public broadcasting; even the educational services generally are financed by the Roman Catholic Church or some other institution that raises its own funds. U.S. government support for public broadcasting was almost nonexistent until passage of the Public Broadcasting Act of 1967, and the Reagan administration, notably more laissez-faire than its immediate predecessors, sought to cut back sharply on the annual congressional appropriation for public broadcasting.

Libertarian or laissez-faire governments aren't totally indifferent to program content, however. Most of them issue few if any formal rules or even guidelines on program content, but they feel perfectly free to step in when the occasion seems, in their view, to demand it. Many of the civilian and military governments of Latin America even have suspended or removed stations from the airwaves for being "overcritical" of the government. However, the many stations that stick to entertainment and to news from officially approved sources have little to fear from such governments.

Social Responsibility

Mixed capitalist-socialist political/economic systems often are thought of as promoters of "socially responsible" electronic media, regulating both physical access to the airwaves and program content. Social responsibility embodies the concept that, while the media may possess and exercise some degree of responsibility toward society on their own, they also need occasional or even more than occasional reminders of that responsibility, and possibly a set of requirements to encourage them to carry it out. Until quite recently, regulation by media law, administered by a designated unit of government, wasn't a common practice in social-responsibility systems. Instead, the media organizations themselves were expected to evolve their own written and/or unwritten codes of practice and to be under the scrutiny, if not the supervision, of a public body. That could be a board of governors and/or a media council, with members appointed by the government and/or public organizations (churches, labor unions, etc.) and/or the media organizations themselves. The board or council might or might not report to the public and the government. The national legislative body ordinarily would discuss media performance each year when budgets were approved. Even if income from license fees was earmarked by law for the support of broadcasting, that still required legislative approval.

A social-responsibility government also usually restricted the licensing of the media to one or two organizations. If there was more than one, usually it was because a "conservative" (pro-private industry) government permitted or encouraged the development of a second, commercially supported service, as occurred in Japan, Germany, France and Great Britain. Monopolistic services often were thought to better serve the needs of a wide spectrum of society: if there was only one service available, and if all listeners and viewers paid for it, that service should attempt to meet as many needs and tastes as possible. Also, a monopoly made it easy for governments to pinpoint responsibility, and to influence program decision-making.

Much of the above remains true today, but much has changed. In Europe, western and eastern alike, commercial broadcasting has emerged as a powerful competitor to the older public service broadcasting (PSB) operations, such as Germany's ARD and ZDF. Cable is growing quite rapidly in some nations (Germany, Switzerland, Sweden), more slowly in others. Direct-to-home satellite (direct broadcast satellite, or DBS) services in Great Britain and in Germany have subscriber rates of 15 percent and more. A majority of households in most western European nations now have VCRs, and some of the central and eastern European nations (Poland, the Czech Republic) aren't far behind. Even with that expansion in electronic media services, however, there are important elements of social responsibility in the laws that regulate them, ranging from obligations on the German private TV stations to present various religious points of view to pre-screening of videocassettes in Sweden in order to block the distribution of overly violent or sexual video material.

In earlier times, most of the social-responsibility broadcast systems carried advertising, but usually in restricted amounts. In some cases, ads came under the supervision of an autonomous or semiautonomous organization, such as the Netherlands' Stichting Ether Reklame (STER), to emphasize the separation between advertising and program content. Now that commercial broadcasting has become common, advertising faces fewer restrictions, although many social-responsibility governments place limits on amounts of advertising time and on what can be advertised (hard liquor, tobacco products and politicians/political parties usually are shut out). Social-responsibility governments also may approve special financial appropriations for specific needs—for example, the introduction of color television—if those needs exceed the budgetary resources of the broadcasters. Such appropriations, however, aren't a regular practice of those governments.

Most social-responsibility governments reserve for themselves the right to have access to the airwaves, and media laws usually contain provisions for this. However, the media outlets generally are free to make announcements stating that the government has requested airtime, which might reassure the listener or viewer that the service isn't playing political favorites by allowing such access.

Communist

While social-responsibility governments have some general notion of the roles that electronic media can and should play in serving society, they don't ordinarily go very far in defining the specific details of that role. Communist governments are more inclined to be specific about the role and the ways in which electronic media can, should, even *must,* fulfill it. To some degree, then, the communist and social-responsibility philosophies have common roots: both look to the media to serve society, but also to shape it. The chief difference is one of emphasis, with communist governments placing much greater (and far more obvious) stress on using the media to shape pro-social and avoid anti-social behavior; also, Communist Party members, and not society as a whole, decide what's pro- or anti-social. In other words, father knows best.

According to the communist philosophy, the media should promote certain behaviors and discourage others. Encouraged behaviors would include working for the common good, being ready to defend and extend the gains made under communism, having an appreciation of cultures (especially domestic) other than one's own, participating to varying degrees in the political process, and supporting the cause of the working classes in other countries. Types of behavior commonly discouraged would include criminal behavior, participation in organized religious activities, self-centeredness, and saying or showing anything favorable to noncommunist (but especially capitalist) governments. While programming doesn't deal exclusively with those themes, most of them appear frequently and in everything from newscast items to quiz shows.

Communist governments usually prefer to finance electronic media from annual government appropriations, although at one time the former Soviet Union had annual license fees. They seem to prefer to spread the cost among all who contribute to the national budget, whether everyone can receive the programs or not. Such a policy may help encourage people to buy receivers, since they're already paying for the service, and it certainly gets across the point that the media are for all the people, in theory if not in practice. Communist governments also permit advertising in limited amounts, not so much as a source of revenue (the money goes to the national budget and not to the media, although China's private radio stations are an exception), but as a way of promoting new products and encouraging the sale of those that are a glut on the market.

Media laws in communist countries usually are not very specific on program content and aren't really necessary anyway, as there's usually just one broadcasting organization and decision-making positions are occupied by Communist Party members who are well aware of what the party expects from the system. The public may be encouraged to write to or visit media organizations in order to voice complaints, but the legislative bodies (e.g., the Supreme Soviet in the former U.S.S.R.) as a rule don't debate media policy or review performance, and boards of governors or media councils drawn from among the general public are rare. That's almost certainly the result of the Communist Party's frequent assertion that the party and the people are indivisible; therefore, it isn't necessary to have boards or councils, since the party can be trusted to look after the people's interests.

There are few communist-ruled nations left in the world, at least in the more traditional sense of "communist." (Former communists have done quite well in elections held in many of the eastern European nations during the 1990s.) The People's Republic of China, the Democratic People's Republic of North Korea, the Democratic Republic of Laos, Vietnam and Cuba are the last bastions of the faith. And in two of those five nations, media practices are changing, with Laos, Vietnam and North Korea as the remaining examples of a more or less traditional communist approach to the electronic media. From the time (1960) that Fidel Castro declared that Cuba was a "Socialist" (here meaning Communist) nation, the country has always had to contend with Spanish-language broadcasts coming from parts of Central and South America and the Dominican Republic, and U.S.-originated radio broadcasts in Spanish and directed to Cuba. Because of that competition, Cuban broadcasting had to be somewhat more entertaining than were most communist stations at the time if it were to have much chance of attracting sizable audiences. However, the news and other informational programs were tightly controlled. China's media system faced little competition from abroad, but the more relaxed economic policies of the 1980s saw the country accepting a certain amount of western (including U.S.) entertainment and informational programming for rebroadcast over China Central Television and China National Radio. Vietnam and Laos, too, are changing, if not as rapidly as China. Western programs appear more and more frequently, and news programs aren't as harshly anticapitalist as they once were. North Korea remains the one "true believer" where doctrinaire communism is concerned.

Authoritarian

The three previous philosophies generally involve elected governments, but authoritarian governments usually exist where there's been a seizure or consolidation of power: often a military coup, but sometimes an elected government that subsequently has outlawed other political parties, perhaps suspended parts or all of the constitution, and occasionally has abolished elections altogether. The National Socialist (Nazi) government, which ruled Germany from 1933 to 1945, is a classic example of this form of government; so were (and in a few cases, still are) many military dictatorships in Latin America.

Authoritarian governments generally are very interested in the electronic media. While they don't often operate the systems themselves (a definite contrast with communist practices), they let it be known that stations are expected to refrain from criticism of the government, and that the government will use stations to broadcast whenever and whatever it feels is necessary. The media may or may not be expected to provide "socially responsible" programming, although it isn't unusual for an authoritarian government to ban certain types of entertainment that it considers "decadent influences," as the Nazis did when they banned the broadcasting of jazz in 1935.

The financing of the media probably will continue in the same form under an authoritarian government as under the previous government, with one exception: Annual license fees, if they exist, are likely to be abolished or reduced, due to a desire on the part of most authoritarian governments to increase listening and viewing and perhaps to gain favor with society (although it's doubtful that the existence of a license fee, at least in the last few decades, has kept most people from purchasing radio or TV sets). The Nazis, for example, exempted many groups, including World War I veterans and old-age pensioners (retirees), from paying license fees. Likewise, the administrative structures of media organizations probably won't change, although the Nazis eventually did incorporate all broadcast activities into the governmental structure.

If there's any one thing that characterizes the electronic media under an authoritarian government, it's the randomness, the unpredictability of governmental involvement. This seems particularly true when the previous government's philosophy had been laissez-faire and many competing stations were in operation. In Chile, which went from a laissez-faire, to a mild social-responsibility, to a mild communist, to an authoritarian government over the period 1965-73, most of the stations underwent few changes in programming policies, perhaps because the two middle governments were in power for too brief a period to effect widespread changes. But the authoritarian Pinochet regime was in power for over 15 years—ample time for changes—and yet there weren't many, probably because the programming offered by the vast majority of stations (mostly light entertainment) represented no particular threat or challenge and might even have served to keep the population pacified. Instead, governmental involvement took the form of occasional disciplinary measures against individual stations, often for vaguely defined offenses and seemingly as a way of reminding broadcasters that the government was ready to use its power when and where it chose.[11]

One of the ironies of many Latin American experiences is that broadcasting services have moved back and forth between authoritarian and laissez-faire governments in some countries without changing their character very much. But that only illustrates a fairly common feature of a continuum:

follow it to its end and you may find yourself at its beginning! In other words, there may not be all that much separating the program practices of electronic media under laissez-faire and authoritarian governments, aside from news and politically oriented informational programming: it tends to be quite tightly controlled by authoritarian governments. And here's yet another irony: a large number of the services operating in *both* laissez-faire and authoritarian situations offer little or no news and politically oriented informational programming.

Alternative Perspectives

There are other labels that scholars have proposed to supplement or modify the original four theories, but I find that most of them are variations on one or another of the four. William Hachten proposes *developmental*, which he uses to describe the practice of governments in many Third World nations when they use their media to mobilize society in various ways: developing a sense of national cohesion (nations with strong tribal traditions, as in much of Africa, often suffer a lack of cohesion); improving and modifying the economy (many Third World nations are almost totally dependent on one or two commodities suitable for export); and making education available to all (most colonial governments made some education available to people living in the cities, but neglected rural areas). Certain Third World media systems do provide program material that addresses those needs, but it's usually a small portion of the overall broadcast output, while a great deal of the programming provides uncritical coverage of the national leader (president, prime minister) and her or his political party.[12] I tend to think of those media experiences as far more authoritarian than developmental, although the latter certainly are worth acknowledging. Perhaps the clearest indication of the usual priorities of Third World governments is that they invest very little of their already modest annual budgets for the media in the production of developmental programs.

Other authors regard the four theories as having outlived their usefulness, but propose nothing very concrete to replace them. Perhaps that's only a reflection of what has happened throughout much of the world, where citizens have access to a larger and larger range of electronic media, and governments possess less and less power to control what those media present. There's little argument over the designation of the People's Republic of China as a Communist country, but the Chinese people are able to hear and see a much wider range of media content than they were 10 years ago. The Tienanmen Square massacre of 1989 shocked the world, the more so because much of it was carried by television (but not in China itself). The Chinese authorities probably were at least as shocked to discover just how many Chinese were able to learn about the massacre so quickly. However, bringing the Chinese electronic media back under tighter control has proven difficult, chiefly due to the fact that so many Chinese have access to material from outside the national borders, through e-mail, fax, satellite TV, videocassettes and other sources.

At one time, the Chinese authorities could block such access, since much of it came through international radio broadcasts that could be jammed. While it wasn't perfect, that electronic iron curtain did a fair job of keeping out unwanted information. Nowadays, the sheer multitude of media, and the ease with which some of them can pass through borders, have placed the Chinese government, and many other authoritarian governments, in the position of the Dutch boy using his finger to stop the hole in the dike: there aren't enough fingers to stop the many holes through which most of the newer electronic media can pass. That's another way of saying that the officially (governmentally) authorized electronic media systems of China and virtually all other nations account for only a portion of what the people themselves are able to, and choose to, hear and watch. Singapore, India, Malaysia and other nations have attempted to ban individually or group-owned satellite dishes, which has become increasingly difficult as the size of the dishes shrinks and as black-market distribution systems for copies of videocassettes of "banned" satellite-transmitted material grow. The rapidly spreading use of the Internet seems to have baffled the authorities, who often appear unable to understand it well enough to know how to control it, were that possible.

So I return to the continuum concept: a range of political approaches to the electronic media. On one end of the scale would be political systems where governments allowed and even encouraged a wide variety of largely commercial electronic media, and did little to control media content or audience access. The industrialized nations in North America, much of Europe, and Australia and New Zealand, would take their places toward that end of the scale. At the other end would be nations such as North Korea, Vietnam, the People's Republic of China, a number of African countries, and perhaps Singapore, but only North Korea seems bent on retaining tight control over every aspect of the electronic media. Proliferation of electronic media outlets, coupled with miniaturization of receiving equipment, have made it exceptionally difficult for the modern state to create and maintain a media shield for whatever reason, as the effort required becomes greater and accomplishes less.

That certainly doesn't mean that attempts to regulate media content and audience access have disappeared from the political scene. The U.S. Congress and president continue to discuss ways to regulate pornography on the Internet. Germany works to exclude neo-Nazi material from the Internet. The Canadian Parliament continues to work for tighter controls on violent TV content. The post-communist governments of central and eastern Europe continue to search for ways to open up licensing of radio and TV stations without opening up broadcasting to political forces on the right and/or left with which the new governments disagree. Policy debates (see Communications Policy below) still show much of their former intensity. However, they may be increasingly irrelevant in terms of dictating what the public hears and sees, unless governments are prepared to spend a great deal more time, money and effort in policing the electronic media. In the late 1990s, few governments care to even consider making such investments.

Technological

All electronic media systems are affected by technological development, and its impact on the global media landscape—Europe's in particular—over the past decade has been profound. The rapid pace and broad scope of technological change has been accompanied by a level of competition that has served to drive costs down to a point where corporations, groups and individuals of relatively modest means can afford them. Pirate (unlicensed) radio broadcasters purchase the bare essentials in studio and transmitter equipment for a few thousand dollars, or even less. Villagers in India pool their meager resources to purchase satellite dishes in order to receive a wide range of television programs. The Internet links schoolchildren in inner city schools thousands of miles apart. Videocassette recorders are so inexpensive that half or more of the households in most industrialized nations now have them. Satellites using compressed signal technology can deliver 150 or more television channels, and at subscription rates comparable to those of cable systems with less than half the channel capacity.

All of the basic factors covered here are interrelated to varying degrees, but technology may lead the way in that regard. Take the Belgian experience with cable as one example. Its *geography* and *demography*—flat, densely populated—favored the rapid growth of cable. Its *culture*—mostly bilingual, and fairly receptive to foreign cultures—made it potentially more receptive to the sorts of television services that could be easily and inexpensively brought in from other parts of Europe to fill cable channels. Its *economy* was strong enough that many households could afford to subscribe to cable, and many local entrepreneurs could invest in local cable companies. Its *political* situation, especially during cable's growth years (the 1970s and 1980s), became generally more encouraging to cable, in that it placed fewer and fewer regulatory conditions on the medium. By the end of the 1980s, the European Community (now Union), to which Belgium belongs, had begun to require its members to open their markets, television included, to one another. That helped to increase the amount of channel choice available through cable, and also stimulated outside (non-Belgian) investment in cable companies, which favored the rise of cable conglomerates and the decline of small, localized operations. And finally, *technological* developments, especially for satellites, made it easier to operate cable companies more attractively (a wider variety of channels) without increasing costs substantially. One might still argue that, because it's so very interrelated with the other factors, perhaps *technology* doesn't merit such a designation. But it has become so prominent in the growth and change of electronic media systems that it seems impossible to exclude it from the list.

Other Perspectives

There's another perspective on influential factors that I've found quite useful, and it pertains directly to programming. As I became more and more familiar with the electronic media experiences of a wide variety of nations, I began to realize that *all* of them, regardless of geography, culture or any of the other factors just covered, displayed certain elements in common in making and distributing programs:

All had to obtain program material, whether by producing their own or by using syndicated material from within or outside the country, or a mixture of the two.

All had to consider the nature of the audiences they hoped to attract to those programs.

All had to find ways to pay for the production or purchase of the programs.

All were careful not to anger the major sources of that money, whether governments, advertisers or whoever else.

All at least claimed to be aware of the influence of the media on society, which meant that they should be careful to act responsibly when deciding what to put out over the airwaves, through cable or satellite, or as videocassettes.

The case studies that follow this chapter will show that each of those five elements may appear in quite different guises in each nation and across time. However, they're always present, and they can be useful when examining the media experiences of other nations, because they should provide a clearer picture of the role and the limitations of the media in the exercising of power and influence in society.

I devote the rest of this chapter to a more specific consideration of several questions regarding the basic factors and programming elements just presented, among them: Where does the money come from? How are the media administered and influenced both internally and externally? What sorts of programming do they produce, and why? How are they regulated?

FINANCING

The old adage "whoever pays the piper calls the tunes" may or may not apply to the electronic media. It seems to depend a great deal upon whether there's more than one source of financial support and more than one electronic media organization in a country. If there is only one of each, financial support can usually be used to control the organization with relative ease. Similarly, if governments or advertisers are willing to be dictatorial enough, it really doesn't matter where the money comes from or how many media organizations receive it.

No system of financing can ensure freedom from outside interference, nor can any guarantee a steady supply of all the money a media organization might wish or need. There are advantages and disadvantages to each system, and some appear to complement each other better than do others. Briefly, the following are the major and minor modes of financing the electronic media.

Advertising

Advertising is used as the chief means of financing broadcasting in North, Central and South America and the Caribbean, and in the "non-PSB systems" of much of Europe, Japan, New Zealand and Australia. It's been a minor but increasingly important source in parts of Africa and Asia since the early 1920s. Broadcast advertising is one of the most controversial forms of financial support; many critics have linked it with catering to mass tastes, ignoring minority audiences and promoting a capitalist outlook on life by emphasizing competition, individualism and material gain.

It also is one of the more undependable forms of support, in that economic slumps may reduce ad revenues considerably. (This isn't inevitable, however; broadcast advertising actually increased markedly during the U.S. economic depression of the early 1930s.) Also, in a competitive market—and heavy reliance on advertising generally is associated with systems in which a large number of stations are licensed to broadcast—competition itself will cause unpredictable rises and falls in revenues for individual stations. In attempting to recover from such losses, stations may lower the quality of their services in order to cut costs and may drop programs that attract small audiences, no matter how devoted those audiences may be.

Nations differ in their approaches to regulating the amount and nature of advertising. Laissez-faire governments tend to leave regulation to "marketplace forces," and if a station can contract and carry, say, 30 or 40 minutes of ads per hour, as some Latin American stations do on occasion, that's perfectly all right. Nor does it seem to make much difference what the ads promote, whether smoking, astrology, patent medicines or dating services, so long as the product is not illegal. Other governments may encourage broadcasters to regulate themselves in these respects, as the United States, Canada, Japan and Australia do with regard to their private broadcasting sectors; however, those governments also may establish guidelines and even a few prohibitions (e.g., no tobacco product ads, no political advertising) and may charge government commissions or agencies with the responsibility of administering them.

Nations with only one or two media organizations generally don't expect or even desire advertising to furnish the major share of financial support. In such cases, the organizations generally establish their own bodies for the regulation of advertising, for example, the Advertising Control Division of Great Britain's former Independent Broadcasting Authority (IBA), although separate bodies may be created, too, as with the Netherlands' STER. In both cases, the government, usually through the legislative body or the minister responsible for broadcasting, generally establishes overall limits on amounts of advertising. Often this is 10 to 30 minutes a day for PSB television, sometimes slightly more for PSB radio, and frequently during designated time periods only, with no interruption of programs. As more and more commercial organizations take their places alongside the PSBs, the government may create new regulatory bodies or modify old ones, as did Great Britain when it developed the Independent Television Commission (ITC) in 1990; the ITC resembles the old IBA in many respects, and even has some of the same staff members.

Very few systems allowing advertising will permit sponsorship: the assumption of the costs of making a program and of its total airtime in return for named identification with the program, for example, "The Chevrolet Hour." Full sponsorship was linked with deceptive practices in U.S. quiz show scandals of the late 1950s,[13] and most sponsorship in the United States now involves several different sponsors per show, with the various sponsors exercising some influence and control over one another. But other countries seem either wary of the practice because of the influence sponsors might have over program policies or unconvinced that it's worth the extra investment; only in Canada, Japan, Australia and Latin America does sponsorship appear to any great extent, although it began to appear in some of the European countries starting in the late 1980s. Radio Luxembourg and some of the other commercial radio stations broadcasting to various parts of Europe in the 1930s also carried sponsored programs, and Radio Lux continued the practice after World War II.

There's also the question of whether advertising is more or less of a financial burden for listeners and viewers than are other means of support. As advertising costs are passed along to the consumer in the price of the product or service, obviously the audience does pay. But presumably not all of the audience pays equally: People's consumption habits differ, and costly items such as real estate and higher education rarely are advertised over radio and TV. Certainly the audience is less aware of paying for broadcasting in this way than it is with annual license fees or individual contributions.

Advertiser support does have the possible advantage of making the media organization very much aware of the size and composition of the audience, since both elements have great bearing on the rates to be charged for advertising time. That means that an ad-supported service is not likely to become the exclusive province of the intelligentsia or of a political or religious group, but instead will seek to reach the mass public at least some of the time. Also, many media organizations, including those in systems where ad support is minimal or nonexistent, believe that a commercial system will operate more efficiently and more cost-effectively than will systems supported principally by license fees or by the government. However, it's quite possible that cost efficiency comes as much from widespread competition as it does from reliance on ads; if there were a system in which a large number of stations competed for license fee money or annual government appropriations, that might induce more efficiency!

Cable- and satellite- (DBS) delivered services often earn money by carrying ads, as well, although they usually aren't the chief source of income. Still, they can bring in enough supplementary income to more than cover the cost of having an advertising department, and when the Australian government finally authorized cable and satellite companies to carry them in mid-1997, the companies were delighted at the prospect of increasing their revenues. The sorts of regulations just noted usually apply to them, as well, and often are administered by regulatory agencies already supervising broadcasters. Great Britain's ITC took over the supervision of cable and satellite services from the former Cable Authority. Videocassette recordings also may carry ads, but that activity often seems to escape the notice of regulators.

Annual License Fees

The annual license fee is based on a concept of broadcasting as a "luxury" service to society: something that no one absolutely has to have, and, in the infancy of the media, something that rather few had. Some countries assessed it from the earliest days of broadcasting, while others introduced it later in the 1920s or during the 1930s. It made particularly good sense when radio, and later television, didn't reach that many people (lack of sets, inadequacy of transmissions). Those who could hear and see paid; those who couldn't, didn't.

As ownership of radio and TV sets and extent of signal coverage approaches 100 percent of the population, which it does in the United States, Canada, Japan, Australia and much of western Europe, a user-based fee of this sort no longer makes quite so much sense in some respects, especially in efficiency of collection: Roughly 5-10 percent of the proceeds from license fees go to cover the costs of collection, which usually is done by the national postal, telephone and telegraph service (PTT). Furthermore, license fee money rarely goes directly to the broadcast organization; it first passes through the hands of the national legislative body, which sometimes sets aside a portion of it to cover transmission costs (some countries have transmitter systems operated by PTTs rather than by broadcasters) and possibly a portion to help reduce governmental deficits having nothing to do with broadcasting. In view of this, it would seem to make more sense to abolish the license fee and simply give the broadcast organization an annual governmental appropriation, as many nations do.

Defenders of the license fee have answers to that argument. For one thing, they claim, the fee is at least a rough indication of the amount of money that should be going into broadcasting and gives broadcasters some notion of what their budgets will be for the next fiscal year. Governments may be far more capricious with appropriations, especially during economic downturns, and besides, license fees rarely are reduced. For another, the license fee can act as a buffer between government and broadcaster: If the government does not appropriate the money as part of the national budget, it may have less say in how the money is spent (which doesn't prevent a determined government, as some in France have been, from telling broadcasters exactly what it expects, notwithstanding the presence of a license fee). For a third, the public may feel a greater sense of involvement with broadcasting, and vice versa, if both realize that the public is making specific payment for the service. License-fee-based broadcasting systems do seem more likely to establish and work through councils and committees drawn from among the audience, and to conduct more frequent and thorough qualitative studies of audience reactions to program content, than do systems based on other forms of support. They also offer a wider variety of programming for more subgroups of the population than do ad-supported broadcast systems.

But the license fee doesn't allow broadcasters much control over increasing their revenues. Unlike ad-supported systems, they cannot use sheer audience size per program or per week to justify higher rates. The size of license fees is proposed by broadcast organizations but almost always established by legislative bodies. Raising license fees, so most legislators reason, is almost certain to raise citizen ire, because there's a visible increase in what citizens have to spend. Broadcast organizations attempt to justify increases in several ways—through their own broadcasts, in press interviews, in public meetings held by them and through testimony before legislative bodies—but they rarely receive the full increase they request. Furthermore, any increase they do receive is likely to have to remain at that level for a three- to five-year period, regardless of the rate of inflation during that time.

There also are four problems of fairness associated with the license fee. First, not every viewer or listener pays it: most license-fee-based systems have 5-15 percent noncompliance rates, although Japan has claimed something closer to 3 percent. (Perhaps the Japanese are more law-abiding, or perhaps they're readier to pay because the Japan Broadcasting Corporation [the NHK] collects the fees itself and at the same time asks people to comment on the quality of the broadcast service.) It's very expensive to search out noncomplying households, although electronic set-detection equipment—virtually useless for tall apartment buildings—and payment of "fink fees" to people who disclose noncomplying neighbors, sometimes have been used to detect cheaters.

Second, some license-fee-supported organizations operate alongside ad-supported organizations. Many European nations, as well as Japan and New Zealand, are set up this way. Can listeners or viewers claim to listen to or watch only the ad-supported service, thus exempting themselves from paying the license fee? A few people have advanced such claims in British courts; the courts have dismissed them on the grounds that the license-fee-supported service is available to anyone in the household, and no member of that household can truly guarantee that no other member ever watches or listens to it. Furthermore, authorities can never really be certain that no one views or listens to it short of invading the privacy of the home.

Third, there are some areas in some countries so physically remote or isolated that broadcast service for them is poor to nonexistent, yet because many people living there do possess sets (they may be able to receive signals from neighboring countries), they are required to pay license fees. Some people count on their physical remoteness to keep fee collectors away; others criticize what they see as a form of taxation without representation. In turn, however, license-fee-supported systems generally have gone to great expense to ensure that all households have access to at least some of their broadcast services, and broadcast signal coverage in such systems is likely to be more complete than it is with other systems.

And fourth, there is the problem of equitability of services. As license fees are assessed and collected on a national basis, it can be extremely difficult to justify establishment of geographically specialized services, unless those services are for linguistic or ethnic minorities. One reason for the relative lack of development of local radio and TV services for major urban centers in Europe until fairly recently appears to have been the political problem of justifying the creation of an additional service for a portion of the national population—and a portion that often is viewed by small-town and rural dwellers as already privileged enough.

Subscriber Fees

Along with the commercial stations, cable and satellite services don't receive income from annual license fees. However, cable and satellite do collect initial hook-up fees and monthly subscriber fees (service charges) from their customers. Those services often enjoy considerable freedom in the frequency and amount of increases in service charges. If those charges seem unreasonable to enough subscribers, as they did with respect to cable TV service charges in the United States in the late 1980s, governments may step in: The only presidential veto that the U.S. Congress managed to override during the Bush administration (1989-93) was of an act that reinstituted some government control over the setting of monthly service charges by cable operators.[14]

Subscriber fees for cable and satellite services usually come in two forms: basic and supplementary. The basic monthly fee brings the subscriber an assortment of channels, ranging from news through entertainment. The supplementary fees may bring packages of several channels, or a single channel, but all of them will be entertainment—usually made-for-cinema movies without commercial interruptions and of fairly recent date. Special sports events, championship boxing matches in particular, may be made available on a pay-per-view basis, where the subscriber must contract with the cable or satellite company to receive the event and to pay a special fee for doing so. Both annual license fees and cable/satellite subscriber fees are forms of user fee, but the former differs from the latter in several important respects. First, the government sets the amount of the license fee, whereas most cable and satellite enterprises decide for themselves what their fee will be, and when and how much to raise it.[15] Since there rarely is direct competition between two cable companies serving the same locale, this gives a cable firm considerable leeway. Satellite-to-home services may find it easier to compete for the same audience, and there are four (but DirecTV is almost certain to acquire USSB by mid-1999) major commercial DBS services in the United States as of 1998, which charge roughly the same amount for comparable services. Most nations don't have such competition yet. Many services charge *rental* fees, where users of cable and direct-to-home satellite services pay monthly fees for the rental of equipment, although they must pay separate fees for the reception of pay-per-view programs or certain movie channels. As channel choice increases, the services often subdivide the channels, and group them as "tiers" of program services, with differentiated monthly charges for their use.

Cable fees may cover more than just the costs of providing the cable service itself. Many public access channels on cable operations in the United States, Canada, western Europe and Japan are supported by money from the fee. Sometimes the cable companies agree to provide that money from their gross receipts, as part of their licensing agreement with municipalities—a common practice in the United States. However, when economic times are tough for the companies, they may negotiate with the municipal government to get a reduction or even abolition in that obligation. A number of the German cable companies have a small surcharge ("Kabelgroschen," or cable penny) on the usual cable fee, and it supports the "Offenet Kanaele," or public access channels. Most of the technologically sophisticated cable operations have tiered systems, in which subscribers receive a number of channels for one basic fee, another set of channels for an additional fee, and certain individual channels (usually new to fairly new movies, but sometimes with additional entertainment, such as original, made-for-TV movies, variety shows and even stage plays). And finally, cable in the United States has done very well in recent years by offering sports events on a pay-per-view basis, where each viewing household must contract with the cable provider to bring in the particular event.

When movie channels first became widely available to cable subscribers in the United States, they were highly popular, and cable operators made a good profit on them. But VCRs became less expensive in the early 1980s, and video stores multiplied. Subscribers then began dropping their movie channel subscriptions in favor of renting the particular videocassettes they wanted at the times most convenient for them. As signal compression became a feature of communication satellites in the mid-1990s, cable operations and direct-to-home satellite services became capable of carrying 150 channels. The movie channels such as Home Box Office (HBO) then began to deliver their product over six or more channels, varying the time and day of showing so that subscribers had a much greater choice of when to see a particular movie. That seems to have helped to bring subscribers back; so has HBO's policy of commissioning original movies (some of them excellent) and premiering them through cable and satellite.

For a brief period in the late 1970s to early 1980s, there was another type of subscriber service in the United States: pay television through terrestrial stations. The stations transmitted regular signals for part of each day (usually morning and/or afternoon), and scrambled signals at other times. Customers would pay monthly fees to receive descrambled signals, and in return would receive feature-length, commercial-free movies (some stations included "soft pornography"), and, in many cases, sports, usually featuring the home team. Some of the stations got off to a fairly promising start, but the advent of inexpensive VCRs and video stores spelled their doom.

However, France's Canal Plus became a huge success with a very similar sort of operation. When it came on air in 1984, there were only three other TV services in France, and few French households owned VCRs. It has become so financially successful that it commissions many films, not just in France, but elsewhere in Europe and in the United States. It also has set up other Canal Plus operations in Germany, Spain and Belgium, and bought up the largest Dutch pay-TV company in 1996. Some of the other European and Japanese operations are following suit.

Annual Governmental Appropriations

The annual governmental appropriation treats electronic media as public services to be made available to the *general* public. It spreads the cost of furnishing the service over all members of society who "contribute" to the nation's annual budget through taxes, whether or not they choose to view or listen, or are even capable of viewing or listening. The annual appropriation may be the only practicable way to develop a media service in a country where there are too few viewers or listeners to permit raising much money through advertising or through annual license fees, and many developing nations have relied upon this means of financing their new or rapidly expanding services.

However, very few nations with annual government appropriations ever have dropped that system of financing in favor of an alternative system, once the audience has grown to a respectable size. The difficulty and expense of collecting license fees and the lack of strongly consumer-based economies that advertising requires may help to explain this seeming devotion to annual appropriations, but part of their attractiveness may lie in the degree of control that the government itself can exercise through them. The Canadian Broadcasting Corporation (CBC), the Australian Broadcasting Corporation (ABC), and the State (national) Radio and Television Service of the former Soviet Union at one time were supported by license fees, but that support was replaced by annual appropriations. All three countries are vast and unevenly populated, which meant that license fee collection was particularly expensive, as was the large transmission system needed to carry signals (especially television signals) to audiences throughout the land. However, politicians from the major Canadian and Australian political parties also seemed to favor the switch because it would remove the politically unpopular necessity of raising license fees, and because annual appropriations would make it easier to influence broadcast policies at the CBC and the ABC.[16]

Certainly the annual appropriation avoids the cost of license fee collection, and it also may allow the government to expand and improve broadcast facilities more quickly and thoroughly than would license fees or ad revenues. One also might expect that there would be a greater likelihood of an annual public (legislative and/or administrative) review of broadcast performance when the government must decide how much to spend on it. However, this is not true of the eastern European or Third World systems, where annual appropriations are most common. (It *is* the practice in Canada and Australia, however.) If the political system of the country is multiparty, the broadcast organizations may be able to get the major parties to outbid one another in appropriating money for a strong public broadcast service, while at the same time using interparty rivalry to help ensure that no one party becomes too influential where program policy is concerned.

But most eastern European and developing nations do not have strong multiparty systems, and most are careful to place the administration of broadcasting in the hands of people who belong to or are sympathetic toward the ruling political party. Somewhat surprisingly, this remains true in eastern Europe, whether the new ruling parties are communist or not. Top-level broadcast administrators generally are replaced when a new party gains power in a system based upon annual appropriations, while license-fee-based systems usually are far more stable in that respect. (France is a notable exception to the latter, and Canada and Australia to the former.) In fact, it's quite common for political leaders in appropriations-based systems to make "recommendations" (often tantamount to edicts) on broadcast policy through the ruling political party rather than through a government ministry in charge of broadcasting. There is every expectation that broadcasters will attempt to comply with those "recommendations," since the ruling political party usually will have great influence over the size of the appropriation, whatever the other parties (if there are any) may say or think.

As I noted earlier, annual government appropriations are subject to fluctuations in the national economy. If the electronic media aren't a terribly important part of national life, the government may feel little compunction in cutting back on the appropriation. Even if they are important, the government may urge the media to increase other sources of revenue, especially sales of programs abroad and advertising (if there is any). Such urging takes place almost every year when the Canadian Parliament discusses next year's appropriation for the CBC. The U.S. Public Broadcasting Service (PBS) is facing the same sorts of demands from the U.S. Congress as of the mid-1990s. With such budgetary unpredictability, it becomes very difficult to engage in long-term planning. All in all, media staff members who work in such systems treat the annual appropriation as a necessary evil, and some feel that it reduces creativity and investigative reporting while it increases inefficiency: if political influence is used to create and fill positions, those filling them often don't feel disposed to overwork themselves or to go out on any creative or investigative limbs.

Most annual appropriations are made at the national level, but there are a few instances of state (or province or district) and local government appropriations, especially in Canada and the United States. School districts in some parts of the United States also appropriate money for educational broadcasting. There even have been a few instances of city government-financed and -administered broadcasting stations in the United States, although New York

City sold its public television station in 1995, as part of an attempt to balance the city budget.

It's rare for cable and satellite services to receive governmental support, but the Japanese government provided a considerable amount of economic assistance to communication satellite development in the mid-to-late 1980s and early 1990s, and the French government did likewise for satellites and for fiber-optic cable development in the early to mid-1980s. When that occurs, it's usually because the government sees a potential long-term economic gain: development of a first-rate cable or satellite system will lead to development of an exportable cable or satellite technology, and the nation will gain both economically and psychologically (we're world leaders!).

Institutional Support

Institutional support stems from the democratic notion that, if you want something done, you should do it and pay for it yourself. It had its heyday early in broadcast history, but still appears in limited ways in certain countries, and in a major (but modified) form in the Netherlands. Most institutional support for the electronic media has come from educational and religious organizations, although there have been cases of stations and services supported by department stores, newspapers, labor unions, political parties and the military. (A military coup in a country doesn't necessarily mean that the military will run the broadcast services, and if it does, it won't run the service for the particular benefit of military audiences.)

Institutionally supported stations usually are found in countries with laissez-faire or libertarian governments, as in North, Central and South America, where a multitude of stations broadcast in almost every country of any size. They are few in number in Canada (which had problems with a religious station in the 1920s, but which has permitted educational stations) and in Australia (which has a few university student-run stations) and generally absent in license fee and annual appropriations systems elsewhere. The Swedish, Norwegian and Danish "närradio" services require that organizations using airtime pay their own programming costs, but government-appointed boards decide who will have access to airtime, and the airtime itself is quite limited for each group, since there are only a few public-authority-operated transmitters for "närradio" to use.

While institutionally supported stations do spare the government and the public a certain amount of expense, they also constitute a form of broadcasting that depends upon the organization's ability to continue to afford the cost. This has two implications. First, only the wealthier organizations can afford such an expensive activity and probably won't be tolerant enough to share their airtime with those less able to pay; and second, the organizations themselves may constitute an uncertain funding base, so that organizationally supported stations might decline in quality or even go off the air altogether in times of economic stress, as happened with many U.S. educational radio broadcasters during the economic depression of the early 1930s.

One other form of institutional support was used quite widely in the 1920s. Manufacturers and dealers in radio sets and parts, and sometimes phonograph record companies, developed stations to stimulate public purchase of their goods. The United States, Canada, Australia, Great Britain, France, Germany, the Netherlands and several other countries saw broadcasting develop largely or in part because the manufacturers and dealers set up stations. But most of them didn't see that line of work as an integral part of their business, and once the public had become numerous and steady consumers of radio, they were ready enough to get out of the programming business, so long as someone else would be sure to provide it.

Educational and religious organizations have been interested in operating their own stations or cable because they wish to reach audiences whom they consider ill-served, underserved, or not at all served by other stations. (There are exceptions: A few U.S. educational institutions operate commercial stations as revenue-generating enterprises.) Most other organizations operate stations either to produce revenue for the organization or as a public relations tool. Many U.S. newspapers and department stores that operated their own stations in the 1920s did so to remind people of their existence and to develop goodwill, which might translate into purchase of the newspaper or patronage of the department store; they didn't advertise their own goods and services in any specific way. As broadcast advertising became more common, such stations either began to accept advertising from a wide assortment of customers or went out of existence as the stores and newspapers found it cheaper to place ads about themselves on other stations rather than bear the costs of operating their own. Newspapers continue to be major investors in or even operators of stations in Japan, Australia, Canada, Germany and Great Britain, and many of them have gained a foothold in cable and pay-cable operations, as well as DBS services, throughout Europe.

Finally, there are limited numbers of "community-operated" stations (mostly radio) in New Zealand, the United States, Australia, France, Canada, Japan and a few other nations. These really are "community of cultural or social interest" stations. Funding usually comes from corporate or individual contributions, and costs are kept low through the use of volunteer or low-wage labor: Everyone from janitor to station manager works for little or no money. Programming usually is a mix of locally produced material (even the music often is locally produced) designed to cater to a wide range of needs and tastes of various cultural and social interest communities. Some of the Scandinavian "närradio" services are of the same nature. The high cost of television has meant that community TV stations are rare, although Australia has licensed five of them on an experimental basis. Those stations rely on individual community groups to produce their own videos and bring them to the operational headquarters, rather than furnishing studios. Accordingly, quality is uneven, but variety of subject matter is great, and some of the groups—particularly those connected with schools of art—turn out quite sophisticated productions while operating on very limited budgets.[17]

Corporate and Individual Contributions

Corporate and individual contributions treat the electronic media as a sort of charitable institution (in a few countries, such as the United States, contributions to certain types of public stations qualify as tax deductions). This form of support almost never occurs in isolation. Few stations would care to risk their existences on the possibility of receiving such funds, partly because they fluctuate so much due to changing tax laws and the state of the economy. There were stations that attempted to survive largely through listener contributions in the Netherlands and the United States during the early 1920s, but they didn't last.

In more recent times, corporate and individual contributions have become an important and even major source of income for public radio and television in the United States, as anyone who has had to sit through another "pledge week" (semiannual, or more frequent, broadcast campaign for contributions) can testify. Some U.S. stations even hold auctions of donated goods in order to raise money. Corporate givers receive a certain amount of mention (corporate name, brief description of nature of goods and services) on the air in return for their contributions. Very few other countries encourage or even permit corporate contributions, and very few allow solicitation of individual contributions, although the broadcast organizations in the Netherlands, New Zealand and Australia recruit paying members, and the radio clubs in Portugal and Spain and in their one-time colonies have or have had paying supporters.

Aside from the uncertainty of contributions, there's another problem. Corporate donors are very likely to want to support stations and programs that complement their own cultural and sometimes political perspectives. U.S. corporate donors such as Mobil Oil often have been criticized for supporting little besides high-culture programs that would appeal to an affluent white viewership and even for pressuring public broadcasting to carry certain programs that the broadcasters themselves might not have chosen (sports, certain British-produced TV dramas).[18]

Sales of Goods and Services

The sales of goods and services take the approach that the electronic media can generate some of their own revenue. This form of support appears in many systems but is a major contributor in none. Its most common manifestation is the sale of programs, domestically and abroad. The United States, Great Britain, Mexico, Brazil, Japan, Germany and Egypt all are major program exporters. Most U.S. programs are sold overseas by businesses organized for the purpose, often by production houses; the stations and networks themselves earn rather little this way. However, systems in other countries generally sell their own programs and may earn as much as 5 percent of their annual budgets through such sales. Many other countries have tried to break into the overseas sales market, and Mexico, Brazil, Great Britain, Canada, Japan and Australia have had some success in selling their material to foreign cable TV channels, as well as to the increasingly important European commercial TV market. (Brazilian and Mexican soap operas are quite popular in eastern Europe and Russia, perhaps because they're exotic, colorful and sexually explicit.) Still, as in so much else, it takes money to make money, and few broadcasters are willing to invest the substantial sums needed for successful overseas sales efforts. Some broadcasters, especially in Canada, Great Britain and the United States, see some commercial possibilities in selling original (made by the system, but not shown by it) programs to pay-cable systems in their own countries.

A number of broadcast systems sell weekly program guides, and in a few countries (Great Britain and the Netherlands), only the broadcasters were allowed to sell them until recently. In addition to generating income from newsstand and subscription sales, there's also income from the sale of advertising space in the guides. A few broadcasters publish other periodicals: The BBC's The Listener was a very prestigious literary weekly in its day. A number of broadcasters publish books and pamphlets to go along with their broadcasts, especially educational programs, but few of these do better than break even. And, since publishing anything costs a fair amount of money, publishing ventures run by broadcasters seldom earn more than 1 or 2 percent of the annual budget, over and above publishing costs themselves (editorial staff, printing and distribution).

As the newer media (cable, videotext, teletext, pay-cable, DBS) develop, many PSBs are attempting to ensure that they get a share of the new media action, or even all of it, although private industry seems to have gotten a foothold even in countries where only a single public broadcast system exists, as in the Netherlands. Since those newer services already are or will be paid for by individual users, they represent a potential revenue-generating source for broadcasters. The BBC and the stations which once were part of the IBA both have had teletext services for those British viewers who wish to pay for them. France introduced an independent pay-TV service (Canal Plus) in 1984, and other nations (e.g., the Netherlands, Germany, Spain, some of the Scandinavian nations) have decided to allow private industry to operate such services. Most of these new media require massive infusions of capital, and many PSBs lack sufficient financial reserves to begin to cover the costs, which is precisely why they must turn to private investment sources if they wish to support such services, as has the BBC (with the William Smith publishing giant). Government loans would be a possibility (several countries issued them in the 1960s to help cover the conversion to color TV), but much of western Europe, and indeed the rest of the world, is still feeling the economic pinch as of the mid-1990s. A number of the more conservative governments also prefer to see such services developed by private industry. Finally, conventional cable systems in many western European countries and in North America already are operated by private businesses and under local franchise agreements, although often there are national laws that apply to them, too.

Ownership of Closely Related Enterprises

The ownership of closely related enterprises is gaining in importance as a source of income. Some electronic media operations have begun to invest in cable and satellite services. France's A2 and Switzerland's Schweizer Rundfunk Gesellschaft (SRG) both have part ownership in cable channels.[19] The BBC, as noted, has coinvested with a commercial book publisher in the development of satellite channels. In some cases, governments have encouraged PSBs to develop such ventures; if they become profitable, that may make it less necessary to raise the license fee. However, there are almost certain to be challenges to such moves by other commercial enterprises, which can't see why electronic media supported by public money should also be allowed to compete with private industry. The European Union, too, has raised questions about such competition, for example with the BBC-William Smith venture. Also, PSBs might alienate audiences if the latter feel that the PSBs are paying too much attention to the revenue-generating services and not enough to the license-fee-supported services.

Public broadcasting services in the United States were encouraged by Congress to seek fresh sources of financial support when Congress cut its annual appropriation to the Corporation for Public Broadcasting in 1983. Some stations took up the challenge, and began to develop such enterprises as mail-order services, complete with catalogs listing a wide assortment of items which had little or nothing to do with public broadcasting per se. Minnesota Public Radio (MPR) soon began to make a tidy profit from its catalog service, and added a mail-order CD service through which listeners could order selections they had heard over MPR, but also other selections that they had heard or read about elsewhere. A Philadelphia public radio station, WHYY, also has developed a mail-order book service for books featured on its nationally syndicated discussion program, "Fresh Air." Such moves have led to criticism from commercial competitors; the stations could reply that the government, like the devil, told them to do it, but that wouldn't mute the criticism. MPR's manager found himself the target of criticism both by commercial enterprises and by members of the state legislature when the operation's catalog services came into public view.[20]

Odds and Ends

With no convenient title to describe some of the more exotic revenue-generating mechanisms, odds and ends will have to cover the lot! A few nations (e.g., Tunisia, Portugal) have placed a special broadcast tax on electricity bills, reasoning that consumers of electricity probably are using some of it to run radio and TV sets. A few nations (e.g., Canada, the former Soviet

Union) at one time imposed special purchase taxes on receivers, with the money generated going to help support broadcasting. The problem with such a tax was that there were boom and bust years for set sales, while broadcasting needed a steady, reasonably predictable flow of income. Very few nations today have such a tax, which also encourages smuggling in sets from outside the country.

In the early years, when equipment was primitive and inexpensive (many people made their own receivers and transmitters), and when some countries did very little to regulate broadcasting, it was possible for individuals to operate their own stations, often as a hobby and usually financed out of their own pockets. As broadcasting became more sophisticated, more expensive and more heavily regulated, personal ownership for the most part disappeared and is now found only in the form of very low-power, land-based and generally urban pirate (unauthorized) radio stations. Those stations number in the hundreds and possibly thousands in the United States, Japan and in several European countries (notably the Netherlands, France and Great Britain). Few of them last very long; either the operator tires of the hobby or is detected by authorities and put off the air. Some of them, especially in France, Great Britain and the Netherlands, have managed to keep alive by selling small amounts of airtime to advertisers.

Because of the growing costs of most of the electronic media,[21] many systems use a combination of sources of support to finance themselves. License fees and advertising often are found together, annual government appropriations and advertising less often, and license fees and annual appropriations almost never (that might amount to double taxation on a listener or viewer). Individual and corporate contributions usually come in combination with institutional support and government appropriations. And irrespective of the major form of support, most media systems would like to generate extra revenue by selling some of their services: primarily the programming they make, as I've already noted, secondarily their own staff expertise (training programs for foreign media personnel, which Great Britain, Germany, France and the Netherlands offer with some frequency), and even spare time in their production studios (many U.S. public TV stations make some extra income by producing advertisements and training tapes for various clients).

Whatever the financial sources, there is a set of questions that should be applied to them. Is financing continuous, or is it sporadic? Is it predictable in amount, or does it fluctuate? Is it easy or difficult to increase? Obviously, the more continuous, predictable and increasable, the better, but there remains a more fundamental question: What sorts of controls and influences does each bring from outside the broadcast system itself? How will they affect program decisions? Since many controls and influences are quite sporadic, subtle, undocumented and even sometimes unintentional (or not perceived as intentional), they are often difficult to detect. Still, every system has them, and how they manifest themselves will become more apparent after reading about the various national systems covered in later chapters.

SUPERVISION, CONTROL AND INFLUENCE

With the possible exception of the low-power, land-based pirate radio operations, most electronic media operations and systems are subject to supervision, control and influence, sometimes from within and sometimes from without. (Video production for VCR distribution is far less supervised and controlled, chiefly because the producers operate on a small scale and aren't involved with daily programming.) Media staff sometimes claim that they and they alone should make final decisions on what is to be programmed, when and how. They base this claim on the need for professional judgment: Hire the best person for the job, then invest her or him with the responsibility to carry it out. If she or he fails to do so, the administrative staff of the station or system should impose disciplinary measures—not the parliament, not a panel of listeners and viewers, not the courts.

If all administrators were professional program-makers themselves, and if they were 100 percent honest, thorough and omniscient, there might be more to that argument. After all, doctors and lawyers police themselves to a great extent. But there's some question as to whether broadcasting is a profession with an agreed-upon set of professional standards. Furthermore, the money needed to keep it operating often comes from public funds. And since media services (sometimes excluding cable, usually excluding Internet) must be licensed by the government in order to conform to ITU standards, it's a relatively small step for many governments to place program supervision, control or influence alongside technical control. For those and other reasons, it's almost impossible to find a station or system that doesn't have some outside forces that involve themselves in the program decision-making process. Some will be major forces,[22] some minor; few will operate all of the time or seek to influence all forms of programming. Some will be more effective at certain times than at others; some will try to enhance their effectiveness by combining forces with others. Some will come from within the media organizations, others from outside (particularly from government and public). Those presented here generally have one thing in common: They're carried out through established organizations and have a continuing existence (which means only that they aren't temporary or ad hoc).

Internal Controls and Influences

There are several possible levels and forms of internal control. In countries where there are large numbers of individually owned and operated stations and services, as there are in the United States, Canada, most of Latin America, Japan, Great Britain, New Zealand and Australia, there are likely to be networks and associations of broadcasters, and all levels will have controls of various sorts. In countries with one or two centralized broadcasting organizations, there's need for associations and little need for separate control at the local level, since most such countries either do not have local broadcasting or place it firmly under the control of the national organization.

Individual Stations

Very few individual stations have formal codes of conduct that guide their programming policies. Instead, the tendency is to leave program regulation to the network or national organization, since it is from those sources that much if not most of the individual station's programs come. However, individual stations sometimes do have advisory committees composed of people living within the station's coverage area. It's common for station administrators to appoint advisory committee members, and while there may be an attempt at "representativeness" by choosing members who are young, old, rich, poor and so on, the usual tendency is to choose people the administrators know to be interested in broadcasting but not severely critical of it. As the committees are advisory, their only power is that of moral force and of the presumed need for the administration to heed what they say at least some of the time, lest the members see the process as a waste of their time. The committees may or may not be required by law (they were for certain categories of public broadcasting stations in the United States in the late 1970s, but in most countries they are not), but few broadcasters would want to risk offending their members to the point of mass resignations and the attendant bad publicity.

Administrators must take responsibility for their programming, whether locally originated or coming from outside. There may be a certain amount of "buck-passing" if the offending material comes from a network or national organization, or through syndication, but it's expected that local administrators listen to and watch program material coming from the outside and make their own decisions as to whether anything in it is not suitable for local tastes. There are no precise laws or even guidelines to assist local administrators in making such decisions, however, aside from right of reply issues, which in some countries are governed by laws (e.g., the Netherlands) and doctrines (e.g., the United States, where the fairness doctrine was in effect until 1987). If there's a local advisory committee, it might be of some help, but usually such decisions must be made immediately.

Networks or National Organizations

Networks and national organizations are quite likely to have codes of conduct that influence their programming. If programs come to the network or organization from a variety of domestic sources, as is true in the United States and increasingly of western European systems (which sometimes are encouraged by their governments to have at least some productions made outside the system because that often ends up being less costly, and makes independent producers happy), such codes are necessary to ensure that outside productions are in line with network or organization program policy. Even if most productions are made within the network or organization, there will be a need for an overall set of standards, since the numbers of programming departments (drama, quiz shows, call-ins, etc.) and personnel involved are considerable. Standards usually deal with treatment of sexually explicit material, violence, ethnic minorities, religious and political groups, children and possibly the handicapped. Terms of reference often are not very specific, and the need for artistic integrity often can allow a producer to ignore certain aspects of the standards. Time of broadcast may be another mitigating circumstance, and a number of countries (e.g., Great Britain and Germany) are "looser" with standards governing sex and violence after 9 p.m. or so than they are before that hour. Germany also has a federal law regulating program content where the protection of children is concerned, and it applies to radio, TV, cable, satellite *and* videocassette material. The 1998 draft Broadcasting Act of Russia is similar.

The program standards and practices departments that preview scripts, rehearsals and tapings of entertainment programming in the U.S. commercial TV networks are a rarity; most systems around the world are far more informal in their previewing practices, and many have no systematic approaches. Instead, it's left up to the discretion of the head of the particular program service and to the central administrative staff to look in on productions if they wish. The U.S. commercial system features far more production of entertainment shows by independent producers (almost 100 percent, although that figure is dropping with recent changes in legislation allowing the networks to be co-owners of some of the shows) than do systems in other industrialized nations, many of which produce well over half of their own entertainment in the system's own studios; a few—e.g., NHK and the broadcasting system of the former Soviet Union—produce(d) nearly everything themselves. That may help to explain why prebroadcast supervision is more informal in other countries. Administrators may discuss programs once they have been aired, although that usually occurs only if there has been a highly publicized problem with a show or a major research report on audience reactions to it.

Many networks and national organizations, especially in smaller and/or poorer nations, rely heavily upon imported programming to fill sizable portions of their broadcast schedules. In some of these, there are various categories of forbidden material (sexual display and violence, or at least certain treatments of them, are most often taboo, but religion in some forms may be excluded, as well, particularly in Muslim nations), and "censors" working at the central station or from within the ministry of information audition incoming material. Entire shows may be rejected, although it is more common to select offending material and edit it out, resulting in awkward jump cuts and voiceless conversations. Many U.S. and other foreign TV series emerge from the process in a barely recognizable state in such countries as India and Saudi Arabia, where "sexually suggestive" dress can cover a wide area.

Councils and Boards

Broadcaster-appointed advisory councils are fairly common in license-fee-supported broadcast systems. Most western European PSBs have such councils, which may have very general or very specific mandates. Great Britain's BBC and ITC have both forms: general advisory councils to advise in theory on anything pertaining to broadcasting, and specialized advisory councils to deal with programming for such subject areas as education, religion and charities. The broadcasters do not have to heed the advice given by the councils, and the general bodies often have little to give on their own, preferring to respond to specific questions and issues put to them by the broadcasters. The specialized councils are more apt to expect to have some meaningful influence upon the decision-making process, however: Most of their members are experts (or at least persons of note) in the field covered by the particular council and are accustomed to being listened to.

Advisory council activities rarely receive much publicity, and it is doubtful that the general public knows much about their existence or their impact on the system. As with local advisory councils, members of the national councils often are chosen because they have shown some interest in broadcasting. They are not encouraged to think of themselves as representatives of the general public or of any particular interest group or profession. Most broadcast organizations protect their council members from becoming widely known to the public (unless of course a member wishes to become widely known) by revealing their identities only in annual reports and other less-than-widely-distributed documents. Council meetings and recommendations similarly receive little publicity in most broadcast systems, either through the printed press or through broadcasting itself.

A few media systems have appointed review boards through which the public may register complaints about programming, usually having to do with incorrect, misleading or incomplete information contained in a broadcast. Both the BBC and the IBA developed such bodies in the early 1970s, partly as a response to some public criticism alleging unfair broadcast treatment of people and institutions. The BBC review board was staffed by reputable individuals (e.g., a retired chief justice), while the IBA review board drew its members from its own administrative staff and the IBA general advisory council. Neither board meted out penalties, although both on occasion reached judgments critical of producers, directors or others involved in production. Those judgments were made available to the press, which sometimes printed them, and the BBC regularly printed its board's judgments in the BBC weekly magazine, *The Listener.*

The major problem with such boards is that the public, if it knows anything about them, may be inclined to doubt that the media services would appoint members who might be very critical of broadcasting. Furthermore, if there is no specific evidence of disciplinary action taken against broadcast staff who are found "guilty," that cynicism may increase. It's partly for those reasons that the BBC and IBA[23] boards were merged into one body with government-appointed members in 1982.

In 1988, the British government created a new supervisory agency, the Broadcasting Complaints Commission (BCC). Some critics initially felt that the BCC was forged as yet another weapon in Prime Minister Margaret Thatcher's ongoing campaign to bring the BBC and the IBA under tighter government control, especially as regarded moral standards in broadcasting. However, the combination of independence and evenhandedness displayed by the new body allayed some of the critics' worst fears. The broadcasters themselves were among those critics, but the BCC's first director, Colin Shaw, had had many years of experience with both the BBC and IBA, and he proceeded tactfully. Also, the broadcasters were allowed to decide what to do with the judgments rendered by the Commission; there were no specific legal penalties attached to those judgments, and no requirement that judgments be broadcast.

That changed in 1990, when Parliament passed a new broadcasting act. The BCC now gained the power to require stations to broadcast judgments involving their programs. What's more, its frequent meetings with public groups around the country, coupled with its commissioning and publication of research reports on issues such as language in broadcasting, treatment of minorities in programs, and several other topics of more or less general public interest, raised the public's level of knowledge and trust where the Commission was concerned. At the same time, broadcasters became more confident that the BCC wasn't involved in witch hunts, where broadcasters would be assumed guilty until proven innocent; instead, BCC judgments were as apt to be in the broadcaster's favor as they were against. Its success in working with the public and with broadcasters on issues such as violence and sexual display has led several nations, including Canada, to seek to develop similar bodies.[24]

Cable and satellite services in most nations lack review boards specific to their activities, although the various German "Laender" (states) have media councils that supervise such services and commercial radio and TV stations, in addition to the long-established broadcast councils for the public (PSB) radio and television stations; the British ITC, as noted above, supervises cable, satellite and commercial TV operations. Because cable and satellite services traditionally haven't produced much, if any, of the material they transmit, there appears to be the feeling that those services don't need close supervision, or perhaps any supervision at all. That may change if more nations follow the example of cable TV in the United States, where program origination by the cable services is becoming more common. On the other hand, the U.S. municipal councils that license such services rarely show great interest in supervising cable programming, unless there are allegations of indecent language or overly explicit sexual material.[25] In any case, thanks in part to concerns in the United States over freedom of speech, and in part to cable's unusual common carrier-like status, there are severe limits on the power of any supervisory body for cable, and much the same holds for satellite services.

Professional Associations

In most countries where there are national associations of broadcasters, cable operators, etc., there will be some sort of voluntary code of practices. Sometimes this is a brief, vaguely worded document speaking to the need for all broadcasters or cablecasters to remember their responsibilities to their audiences, but with no specification of how anyone who fails to remember those responsibilities might be penalized. Associations in the United States, Japan, Australia and Canada have more elaborate codes of practice, although the wording often may be just as vague and the penalties just as unspecified. The U.S. National Association of Broadcasters Television Code (suspended as of 1983 following a negative legal decision on one aspect of the code) contained various prohibitions against sexual display but added the statement "unless its portrayal is essential to the plot." The Japanese National Association of Commercial Broadcasters Television Code contains similar statements. Both countries feature a great deal of violent fare during prime-time hours, and there is little evidence that the codes have had much influence over the nature or amount of such programming.

Part of the reason may be lack of penalties, although codes can bring peer group pressure to bear on an individual operation which appears to be stepping out of line. Self-regulation, after all, is based at least in part on the idea that, if the industry regulates itself, the government will not have to regulate it, or at least not as much. But if excesses in programming, however a code may define these, are committed by the largest and most powerful members of the association, will the association itself have much force of moral suasion? And are media staff necessarily well-equipped to judge what might be excessive? Some national associations have appointed advisory panels for certain activities (children's advertising, medical products), but that is not a general practice. Still, national associations and their codes can have an impact on programming, as the U.S. National Association of Broadcasters (NAB) showed by keeping hard-liquor advertising off radio and television for over five decades.

Associations exist within organizations, as well. Several nations have associations of broadcast journalists, such as the United States Radio-TV News Directors Association and the British National Union of Journalists (which includes print and electronic journalists). They work for the improvement of professional standards and defend the integrity of their work when it's questioned through the nation's political or legal systems. They also may campaign for higher wages or better working conditions.

There also are associations of media-related organizations. Perhaps the best known of these, at least in countries where advertising is common, is the association of advertising agencies. Those in Great Britain, Canada, Australia, Japan and the United States have attempted to set general standards for advertising, including broadcast advertising. Occasionally such associations have allied themselves with associations of broadcasters by endorsing the broadcasters' codes and refusing to deal with stations that do not subscribe to those codes. For the most part, however, associations of advertisers face the same limitations as do their broadcasting counterparts.

The Influence of the Manager/Director

At one time, individual managers could be very influential in shaping the program output of stations and networks. Great Britain's John Reith, the managing director of the BBC from its birth in 1922 until 1938, was convinced of radio's potential ability to raise public taste, and confident of his own ability to make the BBC do so.[26] A much later (1960s) BBC director general, Hugh Green, did much to convert BBC Television from a rather stodgy and limited service into a diverse, innovative one, especially in the form of satire ("Monty Python's Flying Circus"; "That Was the Week That Was").[27] William Paley, who headed the CBS network in the United States for roughly five decades, had much to do with building the network's news division into a model of excellence for a commercial system. Sylvester "Pat" Weaver revolutionized NBC's approach to television entertainment by working for the inclusion of material that also would educate.[28] Italy's Silvio Berlusconi clearly set the programming policies of his several commercial TV networks in the 1970s and 1980s.[29] Germany's Leo Kirch has done much the same for his highly successful commercial TV service SAT1. But most of the larger electronic media operations have become so vast, diverse and expensive that very few important programming decisions would be left chiefly to one individual. Furthermore, as such operations are swallowed up in still larger commercial enterprises, as in the merger of ABC and Disney in 1995, profitability and the "bottom line" become even more important, and heads of media operations are more likely to find themselves overruled by their new super-bosses.

External Controls and Influences

National Governments

The traditional division of legislative, executive and judicial branches works well for an examination of government's role in controlling, supervising and influencing the electronic media. Most countries have legislative, executive and judicial bodies, and most of those bodies become involved with the media in one way or another. Administrative (regulatory) agencies, such as the U.S. Federal Communications Commission (FCC), were almost unknown in other parts of the world until the 1950s, when Japan and Great Britain introduced them in order to license their newly created commercial broadcast services. The Australian Broadcasting Control Board, however, goes back to 1948. The Australian commercial broadcasting sector had been present from the early days of radio in Australia, and has almost always attracted far larger audiences than does the nation's PSB, the ABC. Canada's Board of Broadcast Governors also came into being in the 1950s, in order to give commercial TV owners a better opportunity to compete with the CBC, which had licensed all Canadian TV services (and favored its own stations) up until 1958. Otherwise, monopoly services predominated and made administrative agencies unnecessary. However, as commercial broadcasting, satellite-to-home services and cable radio and TV became more common in Europe in the 1980s and early 1990s, the need for such agencies grew—not without problems, as will be evident in the case of France.

Legislative Bodies

Legislative bodies in most countries have three major methods for dealing with the electronic media: setting of annual license fees and appropriation of the annual budget; development and amendment of laws governing the media, as well as establishment and supervision of administrative agencies which regulate them; and appointment of committees to review the performance of the media. Where the budget is concerned, even countries with license-fee-based systems usually give the legislature responsibility for approving the annual budget, although rarely does that power extend to blocking or increasing expenditures on specific programs. Lawmaking and amending probably will not be as frequent an activity, and the tendency in most countries is to formulate laws that are quite general, rather than being loaded down with specifics that seek to regulate every possible programming contingency. Review committees may come from within or from outside the legislature; while there is a tendency for the former to be more political than the latter, most countries with such committees (Canada and many European nations) attempt to create bipartisan or nonpartisan bodies.

Great Britain is unusual in having a systematic approach to the formation of such committees: Originally they were to be appointed every 10 years, but the intervals have grown longer in the past few decades, notwithstanding which there is a commitment to their appointment at regular intervals. Most countries appoint them on a perceived need basis: Whenever a major problem or important technical development appears (or looks as if it is about to appear) on the scene, a committee is appointed. Both approaches have points in their favor, but periodic review does have the advantage of permitting the assessment of broadcasting in a noncrisis atmosphere.

Because review committees generally are expected to report on public satisfaction with the media, they usually take public testimony, whether in hearings conducted around the country or in invited written appraisals or both. That approach usually means that the work of the committee itself will receive considerable public attention, especially in the press, which loves to cover the trials and tribulations of a rival medium. In turn, there's a climate of expectation regarding the possible outcomes of a committee report, so that, even though the legislative body is free to ignore the report completely if it wishes, it isn't very likely to do so. If the political balance of power shifts between the time the committee is appointed and the time it reports, there may be some effect on what gets enacted, as there was in Great Britain in the early 1950s and again in the late 1970s, but even there the bipartisan or nonpartisan nature of the committee probably will mean that at least some of its recommendations will be heeded.

Legislative bodies also may conduct specific investigations of specific broadcasts, as the U.S. Congress and Australian and Canadian parliaments have done on occasion, but that's rare. It may be that legislatures simply are too unwieldy and too slow to respond to be able to exercise much control or influence over specific program decision-making.

Executive Bodies

Executive bodies (I include various types of chiefs of state and their cabinets) generally have three major means of exercising control and influence, as well: the proposal of budgets (in systems where there are annual government appropriations), the appointment of members to supervisory bodies (and even in some cases of top administrative officials in the broadcast system), and the systematic involvement of the ruling political party in the staffing of the broadcast service. Budgets may be passed by legislatures, but the executive branch often prepares them, and failure on the broadcaster's part to convince the executive body that more money is needed can make it awfully difficult to convince the legislature to approve any increase. The power of appointment likewise can give the executive body considerable access to decision-making bodies: An individual who is beholden to the executive branch for her or his prestigious position on the broadcasting system's board of governors is likely to listen when that body talks.

Some countries make such appointments a bipartisan matter (e.g., through a bipartisan committee or with the advice and consent of the legislature), while others have laws limiting membership on such supervisory bodies to certain numbers of individuals from the political parties, staggering terms of appointment so that they will not necessarily coincide with changes in political leadership, and so on. And in countries with one-party systems, membership in that party, and the endorsement of the party's leaders (who usually hold executive positions in government), may be necessary to win appointment to any position of responsibility in broadcasting. (That also may be true in multiparty systems, as it usually has been in France.)

Judicial Bodies

Judicial bodies usually limit their involvement in the electronic media to judging cases in which there are allegations of illegality in media practices. Some of those cases may arise under specific laws governing the media, while others may come from more general bodies of law, such as laws on libel, slander, misrepresentation and so on. The courts also may be called upon by various parties—the public, the government, media administrators—to review decisions made by administrative bodies or lower courts. Although courts make judgments on individual cases, these can influence the overall development of the media, as have U.S. Supreme Court decisions on network-affiliate station relations and on the legal validity of the FCC's power to penalize stations for carrying "indecent" programming.

Regulatory Agencies

Regulatory agencies were few in number until quite recently, but those that do exist generally are quite influential. The Canadian Radio-Television and Telecommunications Commission (CRTC), the Australian Broadcasting Tribunal and the U.S. FCC all are active in the control and supervision of the electronic media; the British ITC, the French Conseil Supérieure de l'Audiovisuel (CSA) and the various German "Land" (State) Media Councils are learning more and more about the setting and administration of standards as they develop. Regulatory agencies generally are developed by legislatures, which also finance them, so they're open to a certain amount of legislative influence. Their top officials often are appointed by the executive branch or office of the prime minister, which presents the opportunity for influence from that quarter. The judicial branch—the federal/national courts—usually is empowered to review their decisions, so that the agencies must be sensitive to the ultimate legality of their actions. Yet they are a means of ensuring that a specialized and potentially influential public activity will be supervised on a continuing basis, which the legislative, executive and judicial branches themselves never could find the time to do.

Such agencies make sense only in countries where there are relatively large numbers of individual broadcast stations, cable and satellite operations, etc., as is true of Australia, New Zealand, Canada, France, the United States, Great Britain and Germany. All of them have regulatory agencies. Yet Japan, which also has many stations, has no regulatory agency with any real power. (The U.S. occupation government tried to impose one after World War II, but it never took root; instead, the Ministry of Posts and Telecommunications [MPT] issues licenses and, nominally, supervises media operations.) Most of the Latin American countries and Italy have many stations, as well, but few regulatory agencies specific to the electronic media. (Perhaps regulatory agencies are largely Anglo-Saxon concepts?)

Regulatory agencies have various ways of dealing with electronic media. There are periodic renewals of licenses to broadcast in Canada, Australia and the United States. The public generally is invited to comment on station performance at license-renewal time, and in Australia and Canada the agencies often hold their hearings in the communities served by the stations. However, the laws, rules and regulations administered by the agencies often are complex, and in all three countries there are frequent criticisms of the way in which the system puts the public at a disadvantage, especially in terms of understanding the laws and the legal procedures accompanying them. Sometimes the agencies have attempted to educate the public, and in the United States specialized organizations have arisen to help citizen groups to hold their own before the FCC, but such organizations usually have been dependent upon the monetary support of foundations, and that support has vanished, for the most part. There also have been accusations in Australia and in the United States that the regulatory agencies are more sympathetic to the media operators than they are to the public because agencies and the media "understand one another," "talk the same language" and so on. Since the important positions in the agencies often are held by former broadcasters and communications lawyers, there may be some truth to that accusation. Certainly the agencies are not representative of the general public.

Another sort of agency—sometimes a full-blown ministry or government department—is the aforementioned PTT. This agency often has tremendous power to set rates for uses of a wide variety of communication services and even to determine whether further communication services (e.g., cable, DBS) should be allowed, and if so, under what conditions. It also may be the agency through which the national broadcast system reports to the government, as is Japan's MPT.

Municipal and State Governments

Most countries either do not have states or vest no political power in them, and their regulatory force in the electronic media generally is minimal or nonexistent. However, Germany's electronic media system is state, rather than federally, operated; provinces in Canada have established educational broadcast services; and some U.S. states provide or assist in financing public radio and television services, and at one time regulated cable TV.

Municipalities generally have been just as uninvolved in the regulatory process, although city governments occasionally finance their own radio stations. But cable television, when it appeared in the 1950s in the United States and Canada, and more recently in western Europe, often came under the partial control of city governments, perhaps because it was regarded as a utility, like telephone or mass transit service. City governments usually confine themselves to ensuring a certain standard of technical quality and specified numbers and types of channels of service, in addition to regulating the rates charged for service (a power that U.S. cities lost in January 1987). Rarely do they concern themselves with program content, although the provision of "soft-porn" channels on some cable systems has aroused the attention of city administrators.

Educational systems, which sometimes receive their financial support from municipal- and/or state-levied taxes, also may establish broadcast services and are responsible for controlling their output. Since such systems usually are operated by the system's own staff members, that control is easy to exercise.

Trade Unions

While trade unions may and often do act as an outside pressure group on electronic media systems, they also function in many countries as "insiders." Most of the industrialized nations of western Europe and North America have broadcast systems with some union membership. That is especially true of the highly centralized systems and of broadcast networks, where union membership may well extend from one end of the production process to the other, with higher administrative staff as the only really significant nonunion group.

Broadcast unions have several ways of bringing pressure to bear on broadcast systems, including soliciting the support of the larger union structures to which some of them belong, and which usually contain other, nonbroadcast unions. The French Confederation Generale de Travail is an example of such a structure. They may have access to the press (union-owned papers and periodicals still flourish in some countries), they may engage in work slowdowns, and of course they may strike. Broadcast unions in the United States generally have gone on strike for higher wages and improved physical working conditions; rarely do they strike to protest the content of broadcasts. However, TV directors, producers and writers did bring a "denial of First Amendment (freedom of speech) rights" case to court in the family viewing time controversy,[30] and once went to Congress to testify against heavy network use of reruns.

Western European unions generally have been more willing to threaten to strike over issues involving broadcast content and at times actually have gone out on strike for those issues. Perhaps the most famous example of that was the strike by French broadcast news personnel during the 1968 general strike in Paris and other parts of the country. They were protesting the government's refusal to allow them to report the strike in what they considered an unbiased manner; the government wanted coverage entirely favorable to itself and unfavorable to the general strikers. As a result, French TV screens were dark for some of the newscasts and carried government statements at other times. Most of the strikers never did get their jobs back following the strike.

There also has been an interesting movement in a few countries toward "editorial codetermination." Some broadcast journalists, frustrated with what they see as bias among their editors or higher administrators, have requested or demanded a voice in the editorial decision-making process. That movement appears to have been most powerful in Germany, where certain journalists have been disturbed at what they perceive as political bias among "higher-ups" and have sought to offset it (perhaps with their own biases) through codetermination. No German station has a policy allowing for this, but it has been the subject of occasional experiments, and a member of the news staff sits with the Broadcasting Council in Radio Bremen.

There have been a few instances where printers have refused to print issues of newspapers that they felt misrepresented union positions (that happened in Great Britain in the 1970s). So far, there has been no similar occurrence in broadcasting, but certainly it could happen, if technicians operating transmitters were to react negatively to a certain broadcast policy, or even to individual broadcasts. The transmitting equipment is in the hands of the post office in many countries, but technical personnel usually belong to unions, too.

Unions have one other possible effect upon programming. Usually they are zealous in the protection of job security for their members. In some western European countries, stringers and other part-time, occasional staff may receive full job security if they have been employed by the broadcast system for a certain period of time (usually over a number of years). That has made some broadcasters reluctant to use part-timers; however beneficial they might be in covering events that otherwise might not get covered, those broadcasters do not feel that it is worth the eventual cost of restricting the broadcaster's freedom of movement. Broadcast administrators also often are critical of the need to send four- or five-person crews out to cover events when experience (usually that of U.S. stations) has shown that two or even one could do the job. Union rules often call for such crews, but the unions would argue that the end result is a higher-quality product.

In general, the newer private commercial media services in Europe and

Asia feature even less union involvement than do the older PSBs. For one thing, unions were beginning to lose some of their power by the early 1980s, partly as a result of economically conservative governments coming to power in many European nations. When the commercial stations, cable and satellite began to appear in the mid-to-late 1980s, they and the governments seemed to assume that union involvement would not be, and should not be, at the same level as it had been for the PSBs. For another, those newer operations bought most or all of their program material, rather than producing it themselves, whereas most PSBs had large and active production units. That made the former a much less interesting proposition for the unions, since there were far fewer potential members per operation than there were with the PSBs. Even the various unions of journalists found little prospect for success in the newer operations, because most of them carried few or no newscasts, or relied on outside program suppliers for them.

As we enter the next millennium, union involvement and influence in the electronic media seem to be shrinking, although now and again there will be a strike of media union workers over issues of wages, job security, staffing, and, less often, editorial policies and control. Cost-effectiveness is the name of the game for the newer operations, and the older public service broadcasters have faced increasing pressures from government and public for tighter budgetary practices. That's not a climate in which unions are likely to flourish, although they may have some success in getting wage increases for their members at the PSBs.

The Public

As previously noted, the public may be involved in the supervision and control of electronic media through advisory committees and through governmentally appointed bodies. In both cases, however, the initiative is not the public's: Broadcast operations usually appoint advisory committees, and legislators or the executive branch usually choose the members or at least designate the categories for public participation. Broadcast systems in all countries have various devices for eliciting feedback from the public. Surveys, letter writing, telephone calling, public meetings, as well as fax and e-mail for certain specialized publics, all may serve as bridges between broadcaster and public. Telephone calls and mail may or may not be solicited by the broadcaster, but surveys and public meetings are the broadcaster's choice. Likewise, the governmentally appointed bodies develop their own rules for dealing with the public. It's rarer for cable and satellite operations to be required to have councils, in part because cable operations in most countries don't originate much, if any, programming. However, the German states have media councils, and their membership usually is public, at least to some degree.

There also are some examples of continuing activities aimed at controlling or influencing electronic media systems that are developed and operated *by* the public, or, more often, a specific public interest group. The United States has had public interest groups active in this field since the 1930s, and several of the groups have been able to achieve at least some of their aims, particularly during the heyday of citizen activism in the late 1960s to late 1970s. Action for Children's Television (ACT) perhaps was the most famous,[31] but the National Citizen's Committee on Broadcasting (NCCB), Accuracy in Media (AIM), the American Family Association and several others also have had an impact on broadcast legislation and broadcast programming.

Such groups generally have been less numerous in other parts of the world, although Canada had a very active Canadian Radio League from the late 1920s to the late 1930s, and it continued to function until the 1960s.[32] Australia also has had an active citizen's committee on children's broadcasting, generally acknowledged to have helped lead to the development of the Australian Children's Television Foundation (ACTF). The ACTF, a federal- and state-government-financed body, in turn has been given credit for developing and lobbying for an amendment to the Australian Broadcasting Act that set a minimum requirement for TV programming made specifically for children.[33]

Great Britain's National Viewer's and Listener's Association (VALA) has been in existence since the early 1960s. Led by a former girls' school headmistress, Mary Whitehouse, VALA has attempted to achieve a reduction in the amount and explicit nature of sex and violence in television entertainment. In more recent years, ethnic minorities in Great Britain have sought a more balanced portrayal of their members, and some have worked through the Local Radio Workshop to achieve this. The group Campaign for Better Television was active in lobbying the British Parliament to establish more rigorous programming standards in the Broadcasting Act of 1990.[34] German feminists have tried to get German television to alter the allegedly sexist nature of much TV advertising and many entertainment programs. Turks living in Germany have organized to protest their portrayal over German television. Japanese parents and teachers have been laboring for decades through parent-teacher associations to achieve a reduction in the amount and intensity of violent programming on Japanese commercial television.

These groups have certain features in common. They're almost perpetually short of money, they rely heavily upon volunteers for their staffing, and they are quite dependent upon the media (often print, rather than electronic) to bring wider public attention to their causes. Some also would claim that they have unrealistic views of how broadcasting works, but that varies a good deal: Many of the groups have enlisted the aid of producers, researchers and communications lawyers to help them in the formulation of realistic calls for change. Those groups that appear to have been most successful have been persistent, realistic in the sense of not expecting total transformation of the existing system, limited in their aims (usually restricting themselves to very specific types of programs, e.g., children's programming, morality, etc.), and resourceful, especially in knowing where to bring pressure for change, and when and how long to apply it. Unfortunately for these groups, money is a necessary element in their effectiveness, and public memberships do not seem to have generated much of it. Support by various foundations (e.g., Ford and Markle in the United States) has helped but cannot be relied upon from year to year.[35]

The groups often face one further problem: dealing with the regulatory systems of their respective countries. Media law, as with any specialized body of law, has its own jargon and its own sets of procedures. Usually the legal system hasn't been designed to make it easy for the public to become involved. The U.S. FCC set up a Consumer Assistance Office during the 1970s, but staffing was minimal and public knowledge of its existence not very high.[36] The Australian Broadcasting Tribunal appeared to have discouraged public involvement in its processes on occasion.[37] The many countries without administrative agencies for the electronic media virtually force their citizens to turn to the general legal system for addressing grievances, with the attendant time, money and effort involved in presenting a court case. Most citizens probably don't wish to go to the trouble. And, while one certainly can argue that it should not be possible for every citizen or citizen's group to demand the right to be heard by the legal system or the media system for every single element of programming that annoys or offends, it remains true that those citizens do pay for broadcasting in one way or another and are entitled to have at least some effective influence on the medium.

Cable and satellite operations rarely are the target of public protest, for one major reason: since each is a user-fee-based service, all that dissatisfied viewers need to do is to stop taking the service. The assumption is that, if they've subscribed voluntarily, they needn't watch the channels they don't like, and, if they're concerned parents, they can prevent their children from watching. Cable companies frequently offer their customers the possibility of blocking certain specific channels from even entering the home, but few parents seem to avail themselves of such services.

International Institutions

Certain international institutions, the ITU in particular, have had some degree of influence on the electronic media from early on. The ITU held its first international conference on broadcaster utilization of the frequency spectrum in 1929. Its record of keeping broadcasters on their frequencies and clear of other broadcasters has been quite good, on the whole. Its record of finding frequency spectrum space to accommodate the spectrum needs of the developing nations has been less stellar, mainly because there isn't a lot of unused frequency space, but also because nations which commandeered a lot of it in the days when much more was available aren't that willing to give up much of it to meet those more recent needs.

The ITU represents one form of involvement by international institutions: *technological.* A second form, *programmatic,* presents far more problems of regulation and cooperation, because of differing national standards in taste, differing traditions, differing laws and differing languages. However, two factors—programming costs and fears of cultural and informational imperialism—have given rise to a number of international institutions, especially within Europe.[38] The Council of Europe has worked to develop closer cultural cooperation among European nations since the 1950s, and that has included cooperation among the various electronic media systems. However, the Council has no real power over its member states—only the moral persuasion of "do unto others as you would have them do to you."

Europe also has led the way in developing news exchange systems: the European Broadcasting Union (EBU) created Eurovision in 1954, and it continues to facilitate the exchange of television news and sports material among European PSBs, but also to sponsor a modest number of cultural programs, e.g., the annual Eurovision Song Contest. Most other regions of the world have roughly similar structures, but only the Asian Broadcasting Union (ABU) and its Asiavision news exchange service have come close to matching the EBU's record. The EBU and the ABU face a common problem: what to do about private, commercial electronic media. Those media weren't much of a competitive factor until the past decade or so, and neither organization welcomed them as potential members. Now it seems to be too late for cooperation: The European private broadcasters have formed their own association, and their Asian counterparts may soon do so.

But Europe's most famous international institution is one that began life as a partnership of coal and steel producers and didn't become seriously involved in electronic media until 1984. The European Union (EU) includes as members most of the nations of western Europe (Norway and Switzerland don't belong, as of 1998), and seeks to strengthen economic ties among them. What's more, unlike the Council of Europe, it has the power to enforce the legislation it passes; it has used it to open some of the protected markets of its members, block mergers that might bring with them too much outside (non-EU member) influence, etc.

As communication satellites became more common in the 1970s, several European Economic Community (EEC, a predecessor to the EU) members could see that it wouldn't be long before television programming could be beamed from satellites to the whole of western and central Europe. However, a number of national laws dealing with foreign investment in domestic businesses, allowable forms and subjects of advertising, protection of minors, copyright, etc., made it unlikely that satellite transmissions of broadcast programming would flourish on a pan-European basis unless nations would agree to modify their laws and work together, as they had done with coal and steel.

By 1984, the European Community (EC, the *next* predecessor to the EU!) had worked out a draft agreement for facilitating the free flow of TV among its members. While programming was the most visible element, the EC was if anything even more interested in the *economic* dimension of the electronic media. Its 1984 report, "Television Without Frontiers," identified barriers to cross-national advertising, investment and other economic elements, and committed EC members to dropping them by the early 1990s. They should have disappeared by January 1, 1993, and many had, but copyright proved much more difficult to harmonize than did advertising standards; as of 1998, copyright remains a barrier.

Copyright protections vary from country to country within the EU, chiefly in terms of how they define the *creators* of intellectual products. Electronic media are particularly troublesome in that regard, since so many different creators may be involved: producers, directors, writers, actors, designers, etc. If EU members could agree upon just which creators merit copyright protection, that would help to reduce costs associated with distributing programs throughout the Union, by saving time and legal fees. But the differing ways in which nations define creativity often stem from some very deep nationalistic feelings about creativity and how it should be protected, so it may be one of those emblems of national sovereignty that EU member nations will defend in the face of any and all arguments about gains in economic efficiency.[39]

There was less of a problem with the establishment of quotas designed both to favor production and exchange of programming within Europe, and to keep non-EC programming (mainly U.S.) from dominating the European electronic media scene. Great Britain led those few EC members who didn't want quotas; France stood alone in wanting even higher ones. The Community finally settled on a limit of 50 percent for imported programming, which made the United States furious, but the final EC agreement made it possible for individual members to take some liberties in their imposition of the quota. That didn't satisfy the United States, which wanted *no* barriers to trade in programming (a field that the United States dominated), and which accused the EC of creating a "fortress Europe."

As things have turned out, the United States is doing very well in supplying European television with American programs. The many commercial services—cable, satellite, terrestrial, VCRs—provide the United States with far more customers than ever, and various U.S. production houses are entering into coproduction arrangements with their European counterparts, which is one way around the quota on imports. The many European "media barons" (Berlusconi, Murdoch, Kirch) and multinational commercial services (France's Canal Plus, Luxembourg's RadioTéléLuxembourg [RTL]) are flourishing, for the most part, and smaller versions are doing well in Scandinavia. Some are doing well enough to cause certain of the smaller EU member nations to fear cultural imperialism from Germany, Italy or Great Britain, and not just the United States. Ironically, most of the multinationals also use large amounts of U.S. television and movies, although Canal Plus has commissioned many French made-for-TV films, and has entered several coproduction deals or financed programs in other nations, including the United States.

While the EU is best known in the United States for its quotas, it has pursued one other line of cooperation that has both programmatic and economic dimensions: the stimulation of the European audiovisual production industry. U.S. imports enjoyed a fairly warm reception in Europe in part because they were inexpensive when compared with the costs of making similar original productions, but also because they were usually well-made and entertaining. They were inexpensive because of economies of scale: the U.S. market is large enough in itself that program producers have a fair chance of operating at a profit, even though most of them don't do so on the first runs of their programs. That enables them to sell cheaply to the overseas market. In Europe, the major program producers always had been the PSBs, and there was very little by way of an independent production sector.

The then-EC sought to remedy the situation by establishing a funding agency: MEDIA. All member states support it financially, since its budget comes through annual EU appropriations, and the EU budget comes from assessments on each member. MEDIA, formed in 1991, was to make "seed money" grants to applicants in a variety of fields: script-writing, production costs, program publicity, etc. Each grant was intended to develop the European production industry in one way or another, and would, whenever possible, support a multimember venture. That was the economic side of MEDIA, but there was a cultural angle, as well: the EU hoped to develop a better sense of what it meant to be European, and not simply Spanish or Dutch or Finnish, through the program content of MEDIA-supported productions. It's far too early to tell whether either goal will be met; in any event, the annual MEDIA budget of roughly 100 million dollars won't go far in supporting high-quality or elaborate productions, although MEDIA support may help to attract additional funding for some of the ventures. Identifying a European perspective, much less developing programs that reflect it, also will be an enormous undertaking.[40]

The EU also helps to support a European news program for television, Euronews. It is based in Lyon, France—a controversial choice, since a few other applicants had stronger claims in the form of existing facilities and personnel. But that reflects another problem the EU faces: when all members contribute to its budget, all expect to receive something from it, sooner or later, even when their claims might not be the strongest of the lot.

If the EU were prepared to invest considerably more in MEDIA, it might have a real impact on the development of a strong, competitive European production industry. The larger commercial ventures already are increasing their orders for European-made productions, and production houses such as Netherlands-based Endemol are more active as producers for other European outlets than they are for media in their own countries. But if U.S.-style productions continue to predominate, European television may come to resemble U.S. television rather more than it already does. Yet, if the European industry is to become truly competitive with U.S. producers, it has to find ways to penetrate the U.S. market—the world's largest and most prosperous where TV is concerned—and that almost certainly means developing a product that isn't too different from its U.S. counterpart.

Finally, the EU has shown increasing interest in certain "hot" topics involving program content. Its "Green Paper on the Protection of Minors and Human Dignity in Audiovisual and Information Services," issued in mid-1997, is a very thoughtful and thorough document on the subject (available through website *http://www.ispo.cec.be/infosoc/legreg/docs/protect.html*). While it places responsibility for some degree of control in the hands of the parents, it also speculates on various forms of cooperation between EU nations that would help to remind and even require electronic media outlets (including Internet providers) to exercise some responsibility in those domains.

There also are many international investors in electronic media enterprises. The U.S. "baby Bell" telephone companies have been very active investors in cable operations in Europe and elsewhere. The Japanese Sony electronics corporation is a highly visible investor, especially in the United States, but several other Japanese electronics and telecommunications corporations have become active in Asian and European markets. Such investors are looking for good financial returns, and have little direct interest in influencing program content, but their concern with the "bottom line" may mean that they will press for a lowering of production costs, which is likely to affect program quality and origin, since imported material in comparable genres is almost always considerably less expensive than locally produced material. That may make the major program-exporting nations—Brazil, Egypt, Japan, Mexico, the United States, followed by Great Britain and Australia—very happy, but it does little for national pride in the many nations that are heavy importers. Even there, however, nationally produced programming of any reasonable quality usually beats the imported material by a considerable margin. So, to paraphrase Jeremy Tunstall,[41] the media are not yet (all) American, or Japanese, or Brazilian, and national culture still fares reasonably well on TV, although it will face increasing competition from imported material in all but a few nations.

COMMUNICATIONS POLICY

The various agencies involved in control and supervision of electronic media function as part of an interconnected whole, but it's an uncoordinated whole, for the most part. As Krasnow et al. have pointed out in their study of the dynamics of the governance of U.S. broadcasting, those interconnections can be diagrammed, but the strength of specific interconnections fluctuates over time and varies according to the nature of the situation.[42] That also characterizes systems in other countries and is quite natural and even desirable for a medium of communication that both influences and is influenced by the society within which it functions.

However, some governments, citizens and media staff have wondered whether it might not be better to have a little more stability in this respect, particularly in planning for the future. With the expansion of possible uses for electronic media during the 1970s—cable, satellites, multipoint distribution services and so on—that approach seemed wise. Furthermore, many of the developing nations, feeling the need to expand their broadcast systems so as to better serve national development, were considering the possibility of doing so in a more orderly and more cost-efficient way than had most of the world's developed nations. In the early 1970s, UNESCO (United Nations Educational, Scientific and Cultural Organization) commissioned a set of studies of communications policy in several countries, about half of them developed, and half developing, nations. The organization's hope was to discover what already had been accomplished by way of communications policy, so that other countries about to consider the subject might be helped. Also, the attention on communications policy might inspire those nations that had no policy to consider whether they should.

What UNESCO actually discovered was that there were few common denominators in policy development and implementation. Most nations had evolved policies piecemeal, and few had stepped back to consider whether those policies still were relevant or whether they might profit from better coordination. Where the developed nations were concerned, the chief obstacle to orderly planning seemed to be that so many interests—business, government and public—were involved in the mass media, and that their involvement had continued over so many decades that it was impractical to redesign a total system along more rational lines. Some governments had studied communications policy from time to time, but often such studies examined only one segment of the whole, for example, cable TV or frequency spectrum use.[43]

With few examples of concerted attempts at the formulation of communications policy to guide them, and with little money of their own for implementation of such policies as they might devise, developing countries generally dabbled with the concept but did little to implement it. Indonesia and India, faced with common problems of large geographical areas, difficult climatic conditions, multilingual populations and widespread poverty, disease and illiteracy, did develop and attempt to implement wide-spanning communications policies, especially involving a high reliance on satellite technology and the expansion of broadcasting.[44] Few others followed their example.

Why have attempts at coordinated communications policy-making been so few in number and generally so abortive, when such policy-making would seem so economically, technologically, politically and culturally superior to a lack of coordination? The degree of financial investment in the older and more highly developed media systems is one explanation: It's one thing to argue that, with today's technology, one could have a far better system, but it's another to find the money to construct such a system and to protect the interests of those who have a stake in the present system. There's also the old adage, "Better the devil you know than the devil you don't." The media, governments and the public learn to live with imperfect systems and may feel threatened by proposals for change that look good on paper, but that are untested. And developing countries where the existing systems haven't been around long enough to have fossilized nevertheless face tremendous pressures from developed countries that want to sell them something less than state-of-the art equipment and something other than "culturally relevant" programming, usually at prices more in line with what the country feels it can afford.

There are several ways of considering communications policy-making, however, and many of them acknowledge that policy-making needn't necessarily be along the grand design lines that UNESCO seemed to favor. In fact, most nations can offer several examples of media policy-making along more modest, but nonetheless important, lines. For most purposes, policy-making can be considered as attempts to make more economical and/or socially desirable use of the electronic media. Usually this involves public deliberation and decision-making by the major parties that will be affected by changed or new policies: the government (national, state and/or local), the broadcast industry (broadcasters, advertisers and/or manufacturers), and the public (whether general or special interest groups), all may (and probably should) take part in the process. And finally, it may take the form of short-term, medium-term or long-term policy, although, as we shall see, short-term policies sometimes have a way of becoming long-term ones, and long-term policies may disappear from view in a year or so.

Short-Term Policies

Sometimes electronic media systems are faced with problems that must be addressed immediately with mechanisms that, once they have cleared up the problem, can be abolished. An example of that would be the intention of the U.S. Congress to create the Federal Radio Commission (FRC) as a body that would bring order to the chaotic conditions of U.S. radio broadcast licensing, then disappear, with responsibility for the further licensing of stations to be returned to the Department of Commerce, from whence it had come. The FRC had its term of service extended twice, after which the commission became a "permanent" administrative agency. It was enlarged and retitled in 1934, when passage of the Communications Act of 1934 saw the transformation of the FRC into the FCC, which certainly has the look of permanency! The chief advocates of this policy were the more professional (as opposed to amateur, or hobbyist) broadcasters, the Department of Commerce and the U.S. Senate. The public had little involvement or even apparent interest in the development of this policy.[45]

The French government developed a number of short-term policies aimed at protecting the nation's audiovisual industry, but perhaps the best known would be the government's 1983 decision to slow down the importation of Japanese videocassette recorders, so that French makes might have better chances in the market. The effort lasted only a few months: The Japanese agreed to allow a French firm to make Japanese VCRs. That resulted in additional French jobs and increased France's gross domestic product (GDP), but did nothing to help develop a truly competitive *French* audiovisual industry. This was a purely government-industry policy initiative; the public had nothing to do with it (except perhaps to complain about the temporary scarcity and higher cost of Japanese-made VCRs).

Medium-Term Policies

There are problems that may require several years to solve, thus necessitating medium-term policies. When their solution takes even longer than anticipated, or when attempts to solve them lead to new problems, the structures or approaches created by the policy may become more permanent. A possible example of a medium-term policy (although it's difficult to know whether it really was intended that way) is the FCC's policy toward the regulation of cable television, as set forth in three reports and orders in 1965, 1966 and 1972. It seems clear that the major purpose of this policy was to protect over-the-air broadcasting from cable; it also seems quite possible that the FCC saw this as a medium-term policy in that cable eventually would have to be given freer rein, but only after over-the-air broadcasting had had time to adjust to that likelihood and take measures necessary to deal with it. That particular policy thrust ended in the mid-to-late 1970s with a series of court decisions and FCC actions favoring the growth of cable. Chief advocates of the initial policy were the broadcast industry and the FCC; again, the public had little to do with its development.

When the French and British governments began to support the development of national cable and satellite systems in the 1980s, both conceived of them as potential moneymakers over the medium term, and possibly beyond. They saw cable and satellite in technological terms: if the national development of hardware—fiber-optic cable in France, communication satellites in France and Great Britain—resulted in top-quality product that came into the international market early enough, French and British industry would do well in both the national and international arenas. Several years of protection from foreign imports and, for cable in France, some government financial support, might be enough to do the trick. In neither case was the policy successful, thanks to a combination of insufficient private financing, faulty technology, poor marketing and bad luck.

Long-Term Policies

Most policy-making seems to be intended for long-term service, although changing governments, changing technologies and changing economic circumstances may bring a halt to a given policy. In the late 1970s Iran was developing an "open university" along British lines, with degree-related courses offered through a combination of radio, TV and correspondence. Then the Shah of Iran fled the country and the Ayatollah Khomeini's anti-western government took over. The open university, since it was associated with the Shah and with western technology and education, was dropped. (Its high cost probably told against it, as well.)

The FCC's development of the all-channel (VHF and UHF) TV receiver policy in the late 1950s and early 1960s was an attempt to set long-term policy that would promote use by broadcasters of a portion of the frequency spectrum that already was available but was underutilized because so few people had sets capable of receiving UHF. The FCC hoped that the all-channel receiver bill would lead to the growth of broadcast outlets, thus promoting competition. The bill was necessary because otherwise few investors would consider UHF stations profitable, whereas the guarantee of large numbers of VHF-UHF receivers within a few years would make such stations potentially lucrative. That has, for the most part, turned out to be the case. The FCC, the then-existing UHF station owners and certain manufacturers were the initial advocates of the policy; Congress eventually supported it. Once again, the public had little to do with the process, whether through ignorance of its implications, indifference to the outcome, lack of knowledge as to how to make its opinions known or some combination of these.[46]

Perhaps the most significant of long-term policies that have altered the media landscape in important ways is the widespread shift from monopoly or duopoly systems to highly competitive systems. That shift took place in different nations at different times, but the 1980s marked its starting point for many European nations. The U.S. move in the direction of deregulating the electronic media started in the late 1970s under Democratic President Jimmy Carter, and increased rapidly following the election of Republican President Ronald Reagan in 1980. Several western European nations saw more or less conservative political parties coming to power during that same period, and similar changes followed. Many conservatives had wanted to open the electronic media field to competition, or, in the case of Great Britain, more competition, for some time.[47] However, they either didn't win control, didn't hold control for very long or simply couldn't interest enough of the public or their own political leaders in making the change.

The political balance of power began to shift in the late 1970s. Kenneth Dyson and Peter Humphreys perceived another shift which worked in the conservatives' favor: "the erosion of the belief in a monopoly for public service broadcasting antedated ... technological changes. ... changing family structures and social habits have expressed themselves in demands for more 'home-based' leisure and greater consumer choice to meet the different interests of family members."[48] One by one, most European nations began to authorize competitive electronic media services; by the early 1990s, most of those nations not only had competitive services—terrestrial, cable and/or satellite—but the new terrestrial services were seriously challenging the older PSBs in terms of shares of audience.

While that particular long-term policy change was a political decision, it was helped along by strong pressures from would-be commercial investors, especially from the newspaper, magazine and film distribution and exhibition sectors; they were anxious to enter the electronic media market in part because they could see the increasing technological convergence of the mass media, and wanted to secure for themselves a prominent place at the table. They also had the advantage of understanding the media business, and often were prepared to risk their capital in a form of investment that frightened less knowledgeable financiers. Technological advances, particularly in communication satellites and fiber-optic cable, also looked promising in terms of their cost-effectiveness in delivering electronic signals over large areas at a relatively low cost per channel of service. For their part, conservative politicians welcomed the prospect of not having to raise license fees quite so often, since (hopefully) the new commercial services would show the PSBs how electronic media operations could be run less expensively. There also may have been politicians who subscribed to the notion that more radio and TV—and commercial programming in particular—might bring audiences to embrace a more conservative outlook on life, since advertising stimulates consumer desire, which in turn supposedly drives capitalist economies. A few governments—most notably Great Britain and France—also saw economic benefits arising from the creation or expansion of commercial electronic media; not only was there the prospect of encouraging greater "consumerism," but also the prospect of developing and selling one's own technological systems. Both France and Great Britain thought that they could encourage the domestic development and manufacture of communication satellites of world-class standard, although as already noted neither nation succeeded in fulfilling that ambition.

Finally, if Dyson and Humphreys are correct, this is one long-term policy that the public did influence, although very few politicians campaigned on the promise that they would open broadcasting to competition. (Oddly enough, as you'll see in the next chapter, the one really prominent example of such campaign promises came from the French Socialist Party in the 1981 election campaign.) Nor did public opinion polls reveal that the public was clamoring for more radio or television. Yet I sensed in my own visits to Europe during this period that there was an increasing interest on the part of the public in having a greater range of choice, or at least some alternatives to the PSBs. I suspect that part of the desire was fueled by newspaper and magazine articles describing the channel choice available in North America, Japan or even already heavily cabled Belgium and the Netherlands—and the print media did have an interest in fueling such desires.

Policy-Making Purposes

The nation-specific chapters that follow contain many examples of policy-making. Most of them fit into the long-term category. But policy-making of any sort ultimately comes down to *purpose.* That purpose can be "pro" or "anti," supporting a positive development or avoiding a negative one. While the list that follows isn't exhaustive, it should provide a good overall picture of the ways in which types of policies might fit into one or the other of these kinds of purposes. But any discussion of purpose must take into account the question "Pro (or anti) for *whom?*" Holding the rates charged for services such as cable TV as low as possible might be just fine for subscribers, but not necessarily for providers. Relaxing limits on multiple ownership of radio or TV stations probably will delight the companies which already own a number of them, might or might not result in better quality of programming and probably will work to the disadvantage of a company owning just one or two stations which isn't ready to expand for the moment, but hopes to be later on, *if* there are any stations left to purchase. Imposing limits on the use of "indecent" language will please those who feel that the electronic media are major contributors to the moral decline of society, but will likely be opposed by those who favor the greatest possible freedom for the content and form of expression of ideas.

Positive Purposes

- The greatest possible program diversity for the greatest number of people (this could include local and regional broadcasting; programs for children; multicultural programming; broadcasting by, to and from ethnic minorities; provision of minority language services; services for the handicapped, etc.).
- The greatest possible availability of clearly receivable broadcast signals, cable and satellite transmissions.
- The greatest possible opportunity for the expression of viewpoints.
- The greatest possible freedom for the expression of viewpoints.
- The greatest possible availability of broadcast receivers (this could include the removal or reduction of taxes and import duties on sets, the manufacture of inexpensive receivers, etc.).
- The greatest possible use of electronic media to provide positive guidance to society, e.g., through programming featuring positive role models.
- Encouragement of one's national, regional, local, ethnic, etc., cultures.
- The lowest possible rates on services.
- The largest possible numbers of competing broadcast, cable and satellite services.

Negative Purposes

- Protection from unfair or unbalanced reporting.
- Protection from possible harmful effects of programming, including advertising.
- Protection from excessive amounts of certain kinds of programming (usually advertising and imported material).[49]
- Protection from monopolization of broadcasting by governments, businesses, religious organizations or any other single entity.
- Protection from unfair competitive practices within the industry and between broadcasting and related media.
- Protection from "unfair" pricing of services, e.g., cable TV monthly fees.
- Protection from easy access to "undesirable" material by children, e.g., to X- or R-rated videocassettes at video rental shops, or to sexually explicit Internet services.

MEDIA-AUDIENCE INTERACTION

In the final analysis, the electronic media do not exist to serve governments, businesses or other abstract entities; they exist to serve listeners and viewers. If they fail to do so, governments, businesses and others will not have their particular purposes met. Furthermore, the audience pays in one way or another to receive the media. In fact, no broadcasting system anywhere in the world totally ignores its audience, although some appear to have precious little regard or respect for its opinions. (I once asked a researcher for the East German [Communist] broadcast service what would happen if research revealed that a program the government felt was very important attracted very few listeners or viewers, and furthermore, even their number were shrinking. She replied, "Somewhere this bargaining with the audience must stop!" What she meant was that, if the government felt that strongly, the show must and will go on, whether there's an audience or not!) However, cable and satellite services usually limit their public contact to the servicing of complaints about quality of signal reception, and only become involved in programming issues when a number of subscribers complain about "objectionable" material such as soft porn, or about the disappearance of a favorite channel from the lineup.[50]

You've already seen how the public may become involved through various committees, councils and groups, most of these established and appointed by broadcasters and governments. Aside from such mechanisms, electronic media providers usually have other methods for establishing contact with audiences, many of which also are initiated by providers and/or governments. Some are continuous, some are sporadic, some have permanency, some clearly are designed to deal with crises. These methods fall under the major categories of audience research; solicitation and/or reception of audience mail, telephone calls and visits; public meetings with the audience; and public use of the media.

Audience Research

Almost every broadcast system (but not necessarily every individual station, or most cable or satellite services) in the industrially developed world makes use of audience research. *Quantitative* research predominates; the United States, Canada and many European nations have conducted it on a regular basis since the mid-1930s. Survey research is its most frequent form. Surveys generally seek to discover how many of what kinds of people are watching or listening, but many European countries also want to know whether the audiences liked the broadcasts or not, so they employ a numerical "appreciation index," which invites listeners and viewers to rate programs on a letter-grade or a 1-to-10 scale (the latter is widely used in European schools for the grading of schoolwork, so audiences are very familiar—perhaps unhappily!—with it). The great advantage to appreciation indexes is that they yield data that allow programmers to argue for the continuation of programs that attract small but highly devoted audiences.

Appreciation indexes also can be considered a form of *qualitative* research, in that they tell those who wish to know (media staff, advertisers, advertising agencies and sometimes the public) something about audience reactions to specific programs. However, the term usually is reserved for more highly detailed, interview-based studies in which listeners and viewers are asked sets of general and specific questions about specific programs, categories of programs, the perceived influence of programs on their daily lives, uses made of the media, perceived accuracy of the media and so on. Such studies are widely and regularly conducted in most European and North American countries, Japan, Australia and New Zealand. Japan's NHK and Great Britain's BBC are famous for the number and quality of their research studies, and the public broadcast services of Germany, Italy, Sweden and Finland aren't far behind.

In the United States, however, qualitative research is far more likely to be conducted by social scientists at universities who are working with university, foundation or federal government financial support than it is by broadcasters. The latter seemed indifferent to the need for such research until the 1970s, with a rising tide of public opinion and congressional pressures concerning violence on TV and its effects. Some networks also claimed that they had little faith in the accuracy of existing methodologies. They also stated that, if they themselves supported or conducted such studies and the results turned out to be favorable to them, those results would not be accepted by the scientific community. Universities are important centers for audience research in Canada, Australia, Great Britain, Japan, the Scandinavian countries and Germany. Advertiser-supported broadcast systems in general seem far less likely to feature qualitative research than do license-fee-supported systems. (Great Britain's ITC is a notable exception.) Perhaps that's because advertisers do not really care what the audience thinks of a program, so long as it continues to watch or listen in large numbers; or perhaps the license-fee-supported systems feel a greater sense of obligation to know more about public reactions to programs when that public pays directly for them.

Solicitation/Reception of Audience Mail and Telephone Calls

Broadcasters vary in their practices of soliciting mail and phone calls from the audience, and cable and satellite services rarely do it, aside from encouraging calls on service problems. Some seem to think it beneath their dignity or worthless, while others engage in it regularly. Some use it to generate data with which to impress advertisers or government officials, while others analyze it carefully for such clues as it might yield to audience reactions and tastes (in which respect it may be used as a supplement to or substitute for survey-based qualitative research). Several of the old European communist systems had regularly scheduled programs in which broadcast staff reacted to letters, and some of the western European systems feature readings of excerpts from those letters, but usually not the reactions of media staff members. Many PSBs, especially radio stations, have regularly scheduled program segments featuring listener phone calls or mailed-in cassettes with critical comment on program material.

Such programs themselves serve to induce the public to write or call, but the public also may do so without any urging. Unsolicited mail and calls aren't likely to have much impact on programming policies, because, unlike most solicited feedback, they usually have no focal point and thus lack the force of numbers to carry any weight with broadcast staff. Sometimes, however, there are letter-writing campaigns generated by television critics writing in newspapers and/or by public interest groups, and sometimes those campaigns generate enough mail to influence policy-making: Several entertainment programs on U.S. commercial TV have been saved from elimination by such campaigns, which have given the broadcasters a further set of data with which to convince advertisers that there was an appreciative and sizable audience out there, and which also has allowed them to claim that they were responsive to public demand.

In any case, no social scientist is willing to accord audience mail or calls the scientific respect received by properly planned and executed surveys. On those rare occasions when audience characteristics can be discerned from the letters or calls, the writers and callers turn out to be unrepresentative of the audience as a whole. It takes a certain amount of drive and a certain level of confidence in one's ability to write or speak well to engage in such an act. It also requires a certain amount of leisure time and disposable income. Many audience members lack one or more of those characteristics, and in developing countries large segments of the audience often lack all four of them. Thus, while letters and calls may be a useful (not to mention interesting and colorful) form of audience feedback, one must bear in mind that that audience is a limited one.

The Internet may become a useful vehicle for feedback on media performance, and a number of newspapers which have gone on line also have experienced an increase in audience feedback from their new (in this technological format, at least) readers.[51] For anyone who has ever wished that she or he could talk back to a reporter, editor, program-maker, etc., immediately, the Internet has obvious appeal. So far, however, its user-cum-audience members hardly are representative of a broader public.

Public Meetings

Visits to media outlets share in the disadvantages just mentioned, and visits require transportation and even larger amounts of leisure time. However, license-fee- and government-appropriation-supported systems often feature regularly scheduled or specially arranged station tours, at the end of which the tour group members may gather in a room and share their views on programming with members of the staff. That was a fairly common practice in the European communist broadcast systems.

It's more common for such dialogues with the public to take place outside the station, in the form of general public or special group meetings. Many European PSB systems hold regular or irregular public meetings at which one to several broadcast staff members answer questions put to them by the public. More often than not, the "public" will take one of two forms: (a) a heterogeneous group made up of those who are anxious to have the opportunity to see what a particular broadcaster "really looks like" and those who have a particular complaint to voice; or (b) a very homogeneous group, for example, schoolchildren, old-age pensioners, factory workers and so on. Japan's NHK also has open meetings with the public, usually on a more frequent basis than do the European systems. The U.S. NAB also has held them on a few occasions.

Public meetings seem to function more as an arm of public relations than as a meaningful source of feedback. Meetings with the general public often are so brief (usually two hours or so) and so crowded (a few to several hundred people in the audience) that it's almost impossible to tell whether there is much agreement among audience members as to whether a given concern is widely shared or not. It's also quite easy for a few dominant individuals to concentrate their fire on one or two issues and to monopolize the meeting time with their concerns. But what often happens is that the audience wants the broadcast staff to tell them what "really" goes on in the making of programs, so that a fair amount of any given meeting may be taken up with informal talks by the staff.

A few broadcast systems require reports on the meetings, with precise indications of the sorts of concerns expressed by the group. More often, however, such reporting as occurs is limited to anecdotal statements shared with colleagues. There are few indications that feedback gathered through public meetings has any real impact upon the decision-making process, the more so because different sets of staff members usually preside at each meeting, which minimizes the possibility that any one staff member will acquire a broader sense of the issues that arise.

Program-Making by the Audience

To some individuals, the ultimate form of feedback is to permit and even encourage members of the audience to make their own programs. In theory, that would allow audiences to make the sorts of programs that they would want to see. In practice, such an approach seems unreasonable where the vast majority of programming is concerned: entertainment, sports and the news, at least as intended for the general public, are too expensive and too complex for most audience members to produce. However, it's possible to consider approaches that leave the actual production of programs to professional broadcasters but give members of the audience relatively free rein in determining program content.

In fact, participation in program-making usually is a group, rather than an individual, activity. Most individuals don't have the time or skill required to make a program, although the German Democratic Republic experimented in the early 1970s with radio "access booths," which allowed interested individuals to operate tape recorders and microphones capable of recording "broadcast-quality" statements, which might or might not be broadcast. Great Britain's IBA tried the same sort of thing with television in the mid-1980s: People could enter video booths (only three cities had them) and record statements, which were then edited and used in a sort of "voice of the people" TV program. (That "voice" sometimes included individuals making rude gestures and remarks, and, in a few cases, a couple having sexual intercourse, although the latter never found their way into a program.) Groups often have more time, as well as the motivation and resources required to prepare a program. But a program usually is what it amounts to, since either the airtime or the production facilities or both are limited and have to be shared among groups.

There's another factor that limits the growth of audience-produced programming: "professionalism." Most broadcasters in most countries look upon themselves as "professionals," which to them usually means that it takes a certain level of skill to produce a program worthy of being broadcast to the public. Skills demanded probably will include the ability to compose, present and record one's message in a professional manner, but the criteria for "professional manner" will be those set and defined by the professionals themselves. In some (perhaps even most) broadcast systems, that will include the use of "correct" speech (and many broadcast services look upon themselves as upholders of the proper standards of speech), "correct" dress, "correct" recording levels and balances and so on. Again, "correct" usually is defined by the broadcasters, and usually does not encompass what most members of the public might prepare. The September 1997 Russian draft Law on Broadcasting even contained a provision urging broadcasters to see to it that announcers follow correct standards of pronunciation for Russian and other languages.

A few systems, or stations within them, have taken a slightly different approach to the problem (if it is one) of helping elements of the public to express themselves through the electronic media. Professional staff have worked with groups, making programs about the groups, their perceptions of society, and their perceptions of society's perceptions of them, but guided through every step of the production process by the views of the group members themselves. In that way, the messages that emerged would be professional in their production techniques, yet reflective of the groups' self-perceptions. This has been done in Canada (with Native American peoples) and in the Netherlands (with day laborers), and it was proposed in Great Britain, albeit by some "concerned individuals," and not by the broadcasters themselves. Its failure to materialize in Great Britain is instructive: One of the chief sources of the failure was the very entity that in fact should have been speaking on behalf of the people, notably labor unions. Whether the unions had little knowledge of, or contempt for, broadcasting, or whether they regarded programs made with the active collaboration of their members as a threat to their own power, is hard to say.[52] It is true, however, that little of what appears over most national broadcasting services would inspire most special interest groups to feel that the mainstream media could render a true picture of either their activities or their views on society. National programming, especially on television, tends to generalize and simplify, doesn't feature too much uncertainty and avoids unhappy endings.

Cable operations, on the other hand, often have designated access channels. Cable systems in the United States, Canada, much of Europe, and, to a lesser extent, Japan furnish not only airtime, but also equipment and professional advice that enable individuals and groups to make their own programs, and make them well enough so that most of them won't be dismissed by the audience as too amateurish. It's usually a requirement of cable licensing that the cable operator furnish the financial support for the access channel service, although the municipal government also may contribute. Some of the access channels began life with hopes of becoming electronic media soap boxes, powerful voices of the people, etc. On occasion, their offerings do have some impact on public life, but more often they seem to create only slight ripples, if that. Their programming isn't well publicized, on the whole, and a lot of it is of the "talking heads" variety. Sometimes the program-makers seem interested only in speaking to their own followers. Sometimes, despite the efforts of the access channel production staff, the footage that the program-makers shoot *is* amateurish. And finally, very few access channel operations are well-funded, so the equipment gets older, underpaid staff members leave, and program publicity becomes almost nonexistent.

Many of those same problems afflict the very few community television stations that exist: Australia experimentally licensed several such stations in 1993; all have had to struggle to remain afloat financially. Most are in major metropolitan areas, where they can draw from educational institutions, ethnic groups and others eager to present their low-budget messages through television. Many of the groups are able to contribute to the upkeep of the stations, both with money and with volunteers, but general lack of program publicity has kept much of the potential audience in the dark as to their existence and purpose. Still, they often manage to present some highly original and controversial discussions, documentaries and even dramas.[53]

A few nations (e.g., New Zealand, Great Britain) authorize citizen-operated stations for brief periods of time (from a day to a month or more) and usually in conjunction with a local event, such as a fair or a festival. Such an approach should help citizens to gain more experience with broadcasting and at less cost than is the case with "närradio," where groups must commit themselves to the project for a full year.

As the Internet develops a more sizable subscriber base, it too may serve as an outlet for interest group-initiated programs. Most of the better-publicized uses thus far involve the creation of interactive TV soap operas such as Australia's "Friday's Beach," advertising aimed at younger viewers, sites for the discussion of TV programs, such as the Animation World Network, or even sites for creating one's own (and often rude or risqué) versions of existing programs.[54] For now, however, the "voiceless minorities" are almost totally absent, although many are involved in such activities as language preseravtion through the Internet.[54a]

PROGRAMMING

As one listens to and views the electronic media around the world, it's interesting to note that program genres, themes and styles often seem quite similar. News and public affairs, sports and game shows, "light" and "heavy" fictional entertainment, all are present in considerable quantity in television schedules around the world, and in radio schedules too, if television hasn't been introduced yet, or is still in its early stages of growth. The evening hours tend to include the most mass-oriented entertainment, and newscasts tend to come on the hour, albeit not every hour (although that, too, is becoming increasingly common in systems with several radio services, where one of them generally will provide brief newscasts hourly). Sports and action-oriented fictional entertainment tend to be most popular, but newscasts are not far behind in most countries. Quiz and game shows have spread rapidly in the wake of the expansion of commercial television, with French, Italian, etc. versions of U.S. shows such as "Dialing for Dollars" and "Wheel of Fortune" receiving high ratings. "Help the police find the missing criminal" shows such as Germany's long-running (it started in 1967) "Aktienzeichen XY ... ungelost" have their counterparts in many European nations, although we don't know just how and why those counterparts developed.[55] Even styles of presentation tend to resemble one another, whether because of the modeling effect of imported programming, the influence of broadcast training classes taught by foreigners, perceived limitations of the media themselves (how many ways can one manipulate a camera or microphone?), or some combination of those factors.

But there are differences, as well, and they take two forms: the balance between domestic and imported broadcast material; and the balance and timing of presentation of program types. Many studies have been conducted on patterns of program importation and exportation, the most notable being Nordenstreng and Varis (UNESCO, 1974); Guback and Varis (UNESCO, 1982); Varis (UNESCO, 1985); Chapman et al. (1986); Import/Export (1990); and Sepstrup and Goonasekera (1994).[56] None are definitive; gathering accurate data for such studies is extremely difficult. All suggest that most of the world's television stations and networks import more programming than they produce.

Those studies deal with TV only. If radio were to be studied in that manner, I suspect that it would reveal some quite distinct patterns of importation of popular music from the United States, Great Britain and perhaps France by other American and European systems, but also a fairly heavy reliance by most radio (and TV) news operations on three or four major wire services, all of them in the United States and Europe (including the U.S.S.R.'s Tass, until 1990).

Whether imported programs are good or bad is an unanswerable question. But if one were to attempt to answer it, one should take into account not only the quantity of such importation (which may be the least important factor), but also the types of shows imported, their placement on the schedule and the state of homogeneity/heterogeneity between the cultures of the exporting and importing systems, if that can be defined without reference to the influence of the electronic media. While the first three factors may be quantifiable, the fourth is not, which is what makes the question unanswerable.

But it *is* possible to make a rough estimate of homogeneity/heterogeneity by examining the cultural traditions of nations to see whether they include genres of entertainment, information and education that resemble or differ from those of other nations. For example, the cultures of many of the Arab world nations include a tradition of very physical comedy routines, much in the manner of slapstick comedy in the western world. Thus, the U.S. situation comedy "I Love Lucy" didn't violate many local cultural norms and was quite compatible with others when it was broadcast on Egyptian TV. Similarly, there's a tradition of physical comedy in Thai culture, and many U.S. situation comedies find ready acceptance there. Drama portraying extreme and very realistic violence, however, may find no domestic counterpart in nations such as China, where the portrayal of violence in drama doesn't occur all that often, and where its presentation on those occasions is highly stylized.

There's more than the presentation of basic themes involved here, however. One of the touchiest aspects of the debate over "cultural imperialism" is the possible role of television in contributing to the "revolution of rising expectations." Schiller, Wells, Nordenstreng and other writers have expressed the fear that TV programs imported from the western world (and from the United States in particular, since it exports more television entertainment than does any other country) will show viewers in developing nations a range of goods and services (dress, housing, diet, etc.) that are far beyond their personal or national means. Such portrayals may cause them to be dissatisfied with their lot in life, may bring them to reject much of what is good in their own traditions, and, in extreme cases, may lead them to revolution to address those perceived needs.[57]

Media systems in many nations have erected various barriers against what they consider cultural imperialism. The most common is refusing to purchase "offensive" programs in the first place.[58] That's not as simple as it sounds, however. First of all, imported programs almost always are much cheaper than those made by the domestic system. Second, neighboring countries may produce or import and then broadcast some of those offensive programs, which may attract many domestic viewers. And third, there is great pressure on a system to make programming available for as much of the day and night as possible; given their low cost, imported programs appear to be a logical answer to meeting that demand. Yet another barrier is internal censorship, which can be used to eliminate anything from a five-second glimpse of an improperly dressed (by domestic standards) actor or actress to an entire episode from a series. Such prescreening takes time, money and effort, as well as the guidance of a clearly articulated set of cultural standards, and some of the developing nations possess few or none of these.

A third barrier, seldom used, is the presentation of potentially offensive imported programs within a broader framework, where explanations before, during and/or after the program are intended to help the audience assimilate the program within the domestic cultural context. Some of the communist systems used to introduce certain U.S. programs at times with explanations that indicated that they were portrayals of present-day life in the United States, and worth seeing as examples of how materialistic or violent conditions were over there. There's even a story (perhaps apocryphal) that a Thai television station introduced the U.S. situation comedy "Laverne and Shirley" to its audience by stating that it took place in an insane asylum, which accounted for its off-the-wall style! The devising and presentation of such explanations takes time, money, effort and a set of cultural standards, as well. For all that work, it might or might not have the desired effect upon the audience.

Barriers notwithstanding, there's a great deal of imported programming on television stations, cable operations and satellites in most countries around the world—more in the developing nations, to be sure, but plenty in the smaller nations of western Europe and increasing amounts among the central and eastern European nations, especially where commercial TV has taken hold. Much of it is entertainment, but much of it is information, too, through the largest wire services and through special television services such as UPITN (United Press/Independent Television News) and all-news channels such as Turner's CNN, or through the Eurovision and Intervision news exchange services. Only educational programming seems largely domestic, and even there many developing countries import the "Let's Learn English" (French, German, etc.) types of series from the United States, Great Britain, France, Germany and so on, as well as other categories of in-school and adult education programs, the latter very often from their former colonial mentors, such as Great Britain or France.

Whether imported programs are "bad" or "good" is a personal value judgment and has been subjected to very little empirical testing. It's safe to say that such programs have brought images of a much wider world to viewers than most of them ever had seen before the advent of television. It is also safe to say that patterns of importation/exportation are unlikely to change much over the next decade or two, if only because the alternatives—more domestic production or shorter broadcast hours—seem unattainable or unthinkable to most broadcast systems, their financiers and/or their audiences. Once again, however, India has attempted to hold the line: In 1996, the Indian government reaffirmed earlier rulings that it still would not allow foreign media companies, including electronic media, to operate within the country—this despite pressures in India to open up the economy to foreign investors.[59]

Just as there are differences in patterns of importation and domestic production of programs, so are there differences in scheduling practices. If there's a norm for scheduling and for programming in North American broadcast systems, it's for a radio broadcasting day that begins at 6 a.m. and ends in the late afternoon or evening hours if a station is licensed to broadcast only during daylight hours, or a day that often does not end at all if the station is allowed to broadcast after dark. Television stations, none of which have "daylight hours only" restrictions, usually begin around 6 a.m. and stop around midnight or 1 a.m., although increasing numbers of stations in large cities are telecasting around the clock, too. Most cable and satellite channels are 24-hour-per-day services.

Most radio schedules are filled with popular music, and individual stations specialize in one category of popular music (e.g., country and western) and offer brief hourly newscasts, most of whose items come from the wire services. The U.S. radio stations that belong to National Public Radio or that operate noncommercially on limited power (community radio), as well as the Canadian CBC networks, NHK radio, Australia's ABC and many of the European PSBs, offer greater variety, although they, too, often play large amounts of music. Many of the PSBs offer two, three, four and even five separate national radio services, one of which probably will be a news and talk service, another a "high-culture" (classical music, drama, etc.) service, a third a teenager-oriented service (lots of popular music, some of it "cutting edge"), a fourth a service for various cultural, linguistic, ethnic and other minorities, a fifth educational. Unlike the United States, religious radio stations are rare in other industrially developed nations, although they're somewhat more common in Latin America, Asia and the Pacific, especially in places where Christian missionaries are well-established.

Most TV stations feature light entertainment during the daylight hours; even the two-hour-long information shows provided by the U.S. commercial networks at the beginning of the day, such as ABC's "Good Morning America," contain many entertaining items. Many of the newer commercial stations and some of the PSBs have developed roughly similar morning shows, and may feature daily horoscopes, weight-reduction contests and characters such as BBC's Roland the Rat. Quiz and game shows, soap operas, talk shows (e.g., the Oprah Winfrey show) and reruns of old network entertainment series abound on U.S., Canadian and Mexican commercial stations. Programming between midnight and 5 or 6 a.m. often takes the form of "infomercials," 30-minute or more programs that "inform" viewers about a product or service as they make their sales pitches. Grade B movies also fill some of the time. Educational material, sometimes directed to school, sometimes to adults at home, generally is relegated to the public stations (the CBC, Mexico's Television Cultural de Mexico and U.S. public TV), which sometimes aren't as widely available to the public as are the commercial stations.

It's hard for someone who never has seen television or heard radio outside North America or in those European nations with readily available cable and satellite services to realize that there's any other way of scheduling programs. In fact, there are a few systems in other countries whose practices do resemble those just presented. The European, Australian and Japanese commercial services look and sound a good deal like their North American counterparts. Some South American commercial services, especially Brazil's, also bear a close resemblance. In the developing countries, where money is in short supply and where a given system may have to supply broadcasts in a dozen or more languages, one wouldn't expect radio and TV schedules to resemble those in North America, and generally speaking, they don't. But Europe, one might think, would be a different proposition. Certainly people must want to have radio and television available most of the day and night.

It's quite possible that people do want more programming than they get. However, the prevailing philosophy among European broadcasters, most of them PSBs, and their governments prior to the 1980s generally was to provide programs on a more limited basis than what the public might want. That programming philosophy might have been dictated in part by insufficient funding to do more, but it also seemed to result from a conviction on the part of many broadcasters and some government leaders (e.g., Germany's chancellor, Helmut Schmidt) that the public should find other things to do with its time than simply sit around and watch TV. For many years, communist nations generally halted TV and radio broadcasts at 11 p.m. or midnight; the underlying philosophy was that people should be in bed early so that they'd be ready for a full day's work the next day. Malaysia still requires its broadcasters to halt their transmissions at midnight, for the same reason.

Round-the-clock radio services in most parts of the industrialized world outside of North America are largely a phenomenon of the past two decades (Radio Luxembourg and Radio Monte Carlo, both of them commercial enterprises, offered such services earlier than that). As for TV, the typical pre-1980s day in the European nations (then dominated by PSBs) offered little but educational programs in the morning, a brief newscast and possibly a talk show or a household hints program during the noon hour, programs for children in the late afternoon hours (and possibly some light entertainment, often syndicated U.S. situation comedies), news either at 6 p.m. or at 9 or 10 p.m., and a mixture of light entertainment, documentaries, interviews, serious drama, cultural productions (operas, symphonies, etc.) and the major newscast of the day during the evening hours. There were feature films on some nights, but often they were aired after 10 p.m. Advertisements were usually clustered and presented during an early evening hour; they didn't interrupt programs or, for the most part, appear between programs. Where there was only one national TV system, programs might begin and end at odd times, rather than on the hour or half-hour, since there was no need for a rigid schedule that would enable local stations to schedule their own commercials or insert their own programs.

All of that changed quite radically during the decade running from the early 1980s to the early 1990s. Great Britain's BBC and IBA introduced breakfast-time television in late 1982 and early 1983, respectively; "Good Morning Britain" and "The Breakfast Show" both showed strong resemblances to NBC's "Today" and comparable U.S. programs. Germany, France and Spain followed suit by the early 1990s. TV test patterns, once a common sight during certain mid-to-late morning and mid-afternoon periods, began to be replaced by repeat broadcasts and syndicated material, much of it from the United States.

The Programming Philosophy of Public Service Broadcasting

There were financial reasons for the earlier PSB programming practices, of course, but it would have been possible two or three decades ago for most of the European national systems to fill the gaps in the television day with more repeats and with syndicated material, which wouldn't have added that much to the cost. Something else was at work, and it appeared to be this: that the prevailing European public broadcasting philosophy of providing limited amounts of programming had an underlying social philosophy of providing what was best for the public. Best, of course, had different definitions among the various systems, but the idea was generally to provide a wide variety of programs and to present a good share of that variety at times when most people would be available to see it (or hear it, since the philosophy applies to certain types of radio services, too), whether they chose to do so or not. In that way, the public's cultural tastes and exposure to information might be broadened. Most European public broadcast administrators saw that as an essential function of broadcasting. It also was important for that wide variety of programs to be as well produced as possible, so that almost all programs would be roughly equal in quality of production. That in turn meant that financial resources and studio time probably wouldn't be sufficient to fill the entire broadcast day and night.

There also was the feeling among European public broadcasters that they should produce as much of their own material as possible, rather than rely upon imported programs, or even on programming produced by independent production companies operating in their own nations. That was linked with the assumption that most European PSBs should play roles as patrons of the arts, commissioning various original musical and dramatic works. Furthermore, they felt that it was important to use only as many program episodes as one needed to tell a story, or as one considered to be the maximum level at which acceptable production quality could be sustained. As a result, many PSBs produced dramas that ran for seven, 10 or some other finite number of episodes. And when shows *did* carry on from season to season, there might be only 10 or 12 episodes made within any one season. Finally, paternalistic as it might sound, most European public broadcasters felt that their audiences shouldn't depend upon broadcasting for an unending flow of programming, but should be able to find other leisure-time pursuits. (In other words, "Get a life beyond TV!")

For, in the final analysis, listening to radio and watching television usually *were* seen as leisure-time pursuits, first and foremost. National laws of broadcasting may call upon the media to inform, educate and entertain, and there are very few nations where any of the three is missing (although different parts of the overall system may serve as primary or exclusive channels for one or another of those functions). However, entertainment usually receives the lion's share of airtime. Of course, that entertainment also may inform, educate, shape peoples' understanding of prevailing social norms, convey some sense of social, political or cultural history, and so on, but at least one of its functions will be to allow people to relax, sit back and enjoy what comes out of the speaker and over the screen.

India started out with a very different view of the functions of television. For the initial years of TV, entertainment as such had no place. The medium was to be used to inform and educate; while information and education might be presented in an entertaining manner, that wasn't the primary purpose of the broadcasts.[60] As television signals covered more and more of the country, and as more and more people began purchasing sets, pressures mounted for longer broadcast days and more entertaining programs. The pressures also led to the licensing of a few commercial TV services, with still more broadcasting to India via satellite from outside the country. The result is that Indian television as of the late-1990s carries far more entertainment than anything else, although its use for educational purposes on India's PSB, Doordarshan, still receives governmental support. It may be that television is especially well-suited to the transmission of entertainment, but it also may be that the citizens of any country just beginning to develop the medium already know that it is being used for that purpose all around the globe and expect the same for themselves.

The Influence of Cable, Satellite and Commercial Services

The coming of cable TV and satellite services to most of Europe, along with the move to license private commercial broadcasting in a few nations—Italy, Germany and France in a major way, Greece, Spain, Scandinavia, the Czech Republic, Poland and Russia to a more modest degree—already has changed the shape of TV scheduling. Imported TV entertainment predominates on those services, and some of them are on air for 18 to 24 hours a day. Ads sometimes interrupt programs, and there are more of them. Cable and satellite also offer the usual assortment of specialized channels: movies, sports, children's, news and current affairs, music video. Those newer services have had considerable impact on the older national systems, especially in Germany and the Netherlands. (And in France, but that occurred chiefly because the leading public TV station, TF1, was "privatized"—that is, sold to commercial interests—so it started life as a commercial station with the built-in advantage of an existing [and sizable] audience.)

Videocassette recorders also are making their presence felt in many nations,[61] although their major impact in Europe seems to have been to slow the growth of cable. Some of the PSBs are fighting back, chiefly by making every effort to bring in the best of imported entertainment themselves, often at a hefty price and therefore at some cost to the overall budget for programming, which of course includes domestic programming. That also has a potential effect on the role of PSBs as patrons of the arts—a costly role, and therefore more difficult to justify as the PSBs themselves are expected to operate more and more economically (more in line with the costs of commercial broadcasting).

The land-based commercial services in particular have had considerable effect on how the PSBs schedule their material and on the length of the broadcast day. The former PSB opposition to filling the entire broadcast day is crumbling almost everywhere, and very few of the PSBs fail to offer at least some general interest program material during the morning and early afternoon hours, although some of it may take the form of repeats and/or of syndicated material, often imported. A number of PSB radio services are on air for 24-hour broadcast days. Prime-time schedules for PSBs used to include many programs for minority interests; that has become something of a rarity, although there may be specific PSB channels that specialize in minority-interest material, and the "mainstream" PSB channels often have a good share of minority-interest material in the periods just before and just after prime time. The frequent PSB practice of producing limited-run series (eight episodes of this drama, 12 episodes of that variety show) has diminished: in addition to the higher costs of such a practice, it's harder to sell such series in the international syndication market—and PSBs often face pressures from legislatures to earn more of their income in that way.

All of that doesn't mean that the PSBs have become indistinguishable from their commercial counterparts. Examples provided in the following chapters should show that there still are numerous differences between the two, both in overall scheduling and in what appears during prime-time hours. But there's little doubt on my part, after having watched TV and listened to radio in Europe, Japan, Australia, New Zealand and Canada over the decades, that PSB programming *is* less bold, original, stimulating, than it once was, and that the advent of meaningful commercial competition is a major reason for those changes. At the same time, the PSBs do seem to have become more aware of how to achieve high-quality production on slimmer budgets, just as many of them have tightened up their newscasts, often making them more informative and easier to follow without compromising on quality of reporting (and even sometimes improving on it). That, too, has been stimulated by commercial competition.

Minorities and Programming

As governments became more and more involved with radio in the 1920s, they had the opportunity to consider what sorts of publics this new medium should serve. A number of nations saw the development of educational broadcasts, formal and informal. (In the case of the BBC, the initiative to develop educational broadcasts came from the BBC's manager, John Reith, and not from the government. But visionaries such as Reith were and are few in number.) Some nations required stations to furnish newscasts. Some governments provided political indoctrination through radio. Many stations developed specific program formats on their own, for women, farmers, sports fans, etc. But few nations paid any attention to ethnic and linguistic minorities living within their borders.

Often that was because national governments wanted to encourage greater national unity, and were uncomfortable with the idea that citizens with different cultural traditions and languages should be encouraged to retain them. Sometimes the people with those different traditions and languages, especially if they were recent émigrés, didn't want to retain them, and didn't want their children exposed to them. Some of the minority groups were at the bottom of the economic ladder, and weren't attractive to advertisers over commercial stations. And some groups were too small to come to the attention of those in political or economic power.

By the late 1920s to early 1930s, some nations began to allow certain minorities some small bits of airtime, usually as a part of some commemorative occasion (the signing of treaties between "native" peoples and their new, usually European, colonizers) or for a touch of the exotic. It took World War II to bring minorities one step further, as nations enlisted them for the war effort, and attempted to both acknowledge and encourage them by carrying broadcasts that presented them, not as exotics, but as darker-skinned or less fluent members of the mainstream population.

That tendency carried through the 1950s and much of the 1960s, when the Vietnam War, civil rights and "power to the people" movements erupted in a number of countries in North America, western Europe, and Australia and New Zealand. Some of the mainstream broadcast services then began to cover minority issues and individuals in less stereotyped fashion, in part because leaders of minority groups often pushed them to do so. But some of the minorities began to wonder why they couldn't speak for themselves. That coincided with certain technological developments that made available low-cost transmitters and studio equipment, but also with an opening up of the FM band in many countries, which often brought with it the licensing of community radio services, including some run exclusively by minorities. The spread of cable and satellite services in the 1970s and 1980s gave rise to the creation of some minority-oriented (and occasionally minority-owned and -operated) TV services. By the 1990s, many industrialized nations had a variety of radio and TV services that were minority-oriented, but few that were minority-owned and -operated.

Even with that increase in minority service, there remain many complaints that some minorities get almost no attention, while others appear over the electronic media only when they're involved in something negative, or can play certain stereotyped roles. There are a number of reasons for those complaints, and they differ somewhat from nation to nation, as the next five chapters will show. But the chapters also will show that very few electronic media systems have done anything very substantial to increase minority exposure through the media, or to break down stereotypes, or to help them portray themselves. The Netherlands is something of an exception to that generalization, but the generalization itself remains valid.[62]

CONCLUSION

Is it possible to consider the host of elements presented in this chapter and select any that are especially helpful in understanding any and all electronic media systems? Certainly the basic factors of geography, population characteristics, economy, cultural and political makeup of the nation, and technological development, are influential everywhere, but their specific influence will vary over time and from country to country. The ways in which systems are financed, administered, governed and influenced also varies a good deal among nations, and while some individuals claim that their particular systems come as close to perfection as humans can expect, none of those claims has gone unchallenged. Interaction between media services and their audiences varies just as much, and so do approaches to programming, although there appears to be increasing homogeneity in television program scheduling.

In fact, all of the elements presented here should help to increase one's understanding of how the electronic media were, are and might be used to serve society. They also should make it easier to observe how and why systems resemble each other and differ, and what each might profitably learn from another's experiences. Some nations, faced with the challenge of reformulating a system or introducing a new form of service (television, cable, videotext, DBS, Internet) into the existing one, have examined other systems in order to avoid repeating their mistakes or to profit from their successes. The old adage that those who will not learn from history are doomed to repeat its mistakes applies just as well to the electronic media as it does to any other human venture. The systems presented in the following chapters don't run the entire gamut of experiences, but for various reasons they have had influences, good and bad, extending far beyond their national boundaries, and even far beyond the industrialized world. No nation, no society, is any longer immune to the influence of other systems; the larger, richer, more powerful the system, the stronger that influence is likely to be.

2 France

From Competition to Monopoly and Back Again

For many years the French broadcasting system was widely regarded as the mouthpiece of the government. That was primarily due to the often heavy-handed political interference with it by President Charles de Gaulle and his successors. However, the system underwent a number of rapid and fundamental transformations during the 1980s, and serves as a case study of how a change in political leadership can alter an established system in a major way. That, and France's use of the electronic media to promote French culture, make it well worth consideration.[1]

BASIC FACTORS

Geographic

France is the largest country in Europe, excluding Russia. It is about four-fifths the size of Texas. Most of the north is relatively flat, and the major mountain ranges lie on the eastern and southwestern borders. The French terrain in general presents no overwhelming problems for broadcasting. France has several neighbors, but three of the four larger ones lie behind barriers. Spain is almost completely screened off by the Pyrenees Mountains, Italy likewise by the Mediterranean Alps, and Great Britain by the channel. Germany, Luxembourg, Belgium and Switzerland all share relatively barrier-free borders, although the Swiss border is quite mountainous in places. The bulk of the country, excluding the Breton peninsula, fits quite nicely within a circle and includes little of the territory of its neighbors within that circle. Its geographical shape is conducive to broadcasting, and a powerful radio transmitter set up near the center of the country can reach its borders quite comfortably and without too much spillover into adjoining nations.

The country is not very densely populated by European standards. There are about 100 inhabitants to the square kilometer, far lower than Germany, Great Britain, Italy and certainly the Netherlands. While the vast majority of the French live in towns and cities, there are few really large cities: Only six had populations in excess of 500,000 as of the mid-1990s, and only one metropolitan area, Paris, was much over a million—about 10 million at the time. Those larger cities are scattered around the country, but they are linked with Paris far more efficiently than they are with one another. The major rail lines and the road and airline networks all converge on Paris, and often it's quicker to travel from one large city to another via Paris than it is to use a more geographically direct route. That centralizing tendency also has had its impact upon broadcasting.

Demographic

France has had one language and one basically universal manner of using that language for several centuries. It also has had relatively stable borders for a similar period, although wars at various times have brought foreign invaders onto French soil. Those two conditions help to account for France's ability to develop as a nation with a strong national language and widely shared national culture since the mid-1400s. That experience stands in strong contrast to Italy and Germany, and to a lesser extent Great Britain. Even if the French often are depicted as a highly individualistic people, they're very homogeneous in many respects.

In recent years, that homogeneity has been compromised somewhat by the influx of émigrés and their families, who now make up about 10 percent of the French population, and who largely come from North Africa and Portugal. Most are in the larger cities, where entire quarters may be virtually dominated by them. Little was done to provide them with broadcast services until the advent of local radio in the early 1980s, and even then there was little systematic encouragement. Much the same has been true for the country's minority-language speakers (Breton, Provençal and others), although virtually every speaker of Breton or Provençal speaks fluent French, as well.

Economic

Like most other west European nations, France has become heavily industrialized during the twentieth century. However, it continues to have a larger percentage of its population engaged in agriculture than is typical of western Europe: as of 1998, roughly 6 percent of the overall population. The agricultural sector may be inefficient, but it's jealously protected by the French government, which has engaged in countless battles with other European Union members over what those members see as agricultural protectionism. French broadcasting has served the agricultural community since the 1920s with market reports and information on new agricultural techniques and products, and France was a pioneer in utilizing television for rural development.[2]

Industrialization in France in the first half of the twentieth century took the traditional form of manufacturing: steel, automobiles, etc., some of it exported. In the 1950s, industrialization expanded into other spheres, and France shared in the generally booming European economy. More and more of the work force had to be recruited from outside the country, bringing cities such as Paris, Lyon and Lille their first sizable numbers of southern European and North African residents. Emigrés now account for nearly 10 percent of the population. With unemployment running around 12 percent (much higher among emigrés), various individuals and groups claiming to represent mainstream opinion have called for tighter limits on immigration and even at times for deportation of emigrés. However, it's doubtful that most mainstream French would take the heavy manual labor jobs—garbage collection, street-sweeping, now done by emigrés. France is not a heavily unionized country; less than 20 percent of the labor force belongs to unions, and that percentage is dropping.

Cultural

The French are justly proud of their cultural achievements, which include the work of some of the greatest artists in western civilization. They also are proud of their educational system, which is mandatory until the age of 16 and which includes a heavy emphasis on those cultural achievements—some would say to the point of cultural chauvinism. The educational system is highly centralized: for certain subjects, every student throughout France who is enrolled in a given course will be studying the same material on a given day of the week. It is not a system that encourages individualism or innovation, and critics such as J. J. Sevran-Schreiber have accused it of hindering French economic development in the postindustrial age.

France also possesses a rich regional and local cultural heritage. Folk dancing and singing still occur spontaneously, and there's been a revival of interest in regional languages and literatures, aided by the creation of a regional TV system and local radio stations.

Religion is a major force in French cultural life, thanks to the activities of the Roman Catholic Church, to which approximately 90 percent of the French belong. The church operates educational institutions, sponsors cultural activities, participates actively in political life and is engaged in various welfare enterprises. It operates few electronic media services and has no formal rights of participation in broadcast advisory councils, but station administrators are well aware of its presence and take its sensitivities into account in making programming decisions. For example, birth control was a virtual taboo subject for French broadcasters until the late 1970s, which accounted for the large audiences attracted by Radio Luxembourg's programs on sex education.

Political

France has been a parliamentary democracy for well over a century, but there have been periods of time when governments rose and fell several times a year, and others when a strong political leader largely ignored the parties. Since 1958, France has had a popularly elected president/chief executive. Before then, the prime minister was the chief executive, chosen by whichever party or coalition of parties could command a majority in the House of Deputies, the more powerful by far of the two branches of Parliament. (The other branch is the Senate.)

French politics features a number of political parties, most of which ally themselves with other parties in order to obtain enough votes on a given issue at least to make their voices heard, if not to pass or defeat the legislation. They display political philosophies that range from extreme right to extreme left. The ultra-nationalist Front Nationale under Jean Marie Le Pen received over 15 percent of the vote in the March 1998 local/regional elections, and could be moving up to a stronger showing in the next national election. Votes of no confidence can result in the dissolution of a government but would not result in the resignation of the president.

France is a highly centralized nation in political terms, and the regions and departments into which the country is divided have limited self-governance, although the Socialist government of François Mitterand increased their power in the early 1980s. It's possible for a politician to rise to prominence from a local or regional power base, and several mayors have done so, but that's been more a case of individual charisma and, quite often, the advantage of being mayor of a large city, with consequent media attention. Until the very late 1970s, however, that media attention would have been in the form of newspaper or magazine attention, because radio and television either were largely apolitical or were in the service of whichever political party was in power. The history of French broadcasting, as you'll see, is heavily influenced by politics, but the ways in which that political influence has manifested itself have varied a great deal over time.

A BRIEF HISTORY

The early history of French broadcasting closely resembles the early history of broadcasting in most industrialized nations: a good deal of activity on the part of radio amateurs using homemade equipment, little interest on the part of the government in setting up its own radio service, and considerable interest on the part of manufacturers of sets and parts in establishing their own stations. The first regularly scheduled radio broadcasts began in November 1922 from Radio Paris, operated by a company that manufactured radio equipment and saw the station as a way of promoting set sales. The station was licensed by the government through the PTT, had some very general program standards as a condition of its license, couldn't carry ads and had to pay an annual license fee to the government.

Several months later, the French government enlarged the scope of programming offered over its Eiffel Tower station (used previously for meteorological broadcasts), making it sound much more like Radio Paris: concerts, readings, interviews, sports, radio plays, and in 1924, a daily newscast. Radio Paris already had occasional news bulletins and in 1925 made an agreement with the French news agency Havas (also an investor in the station) giving the station and its parent corporation, the Companie Française de Radio (CFR), exclusive rights to use Havas material in their broadcasts. Thus there was competition between public and private radio almost from the beginning.

A government decree passed in 1923 granted concessions for private stations for a period of 10 years, but also mentioned the possibility that the government would take over those stations sometime during that period. A 1926 decree reaffirmed that limitation, but did permit private stations and the PTT station to carry ads, and most quickly did so. Private stations sprouted up in other parts of France—by 1926 Lyon, Toulouse, Bordeaux and several smaller cities had them—and CFR proposed the creation of a private network. Most of the other private stations were uninterested in or even hostile to the idea, but some French officials thought the government should consider it. They were intrigued by the possibility of making radio an instrument of national unity, and from the early 1920s on the various decrees made it a condition of licensing that stations use "proper" French in their broadcasts and avoid slang and regional dialects. However, the government wouldn't provide the PTT with much of a budget for radio (funding came directly from the government, and listeners paid no license fees). The private stations clearly had the upper hand in reaching listeners nationwide, since they were available in many places where the PTT station wasn't. But they weren't unified—indeed, many of their owners were bitter enemies—and eventually the PTT came out on top.[3]

During the 1920s, radio remained largely an entertainment outlet. Stations began to experiment with original newscasts by the late 1920s, but most attempts were short-lived. Where coverage of politics was concerned, the government discouraged it in several ways: by forbidding the broadcast of ministerial speeches to public groups, and, in 1928, by issuing a decree that forbade political broadcasts, including campaign speeches, during election campaigns. As there were few periods during the year when there *weren't* election campaigns of some sort taking place somewhere in the country, that was a significant limitation. On the rare occasions when someone broadcast an "alternative" viewpoint on a sensitive subject—for example, the performance of the French army during World War I—there was almost instant condemnation of the broadcast, even by the station carrying the speech. But in 1930, the government embraced radio as a means of bringing its views to the nation. As Brochard observes, "From now on the President of the Council (cabinet) doesn't push the microphone away. Quite the opposite: he accepts it, solicits it, even insists on having it."[4]

A major shift in the balance of power between public and private broadcasting came in 1933, a year when, as some previous decrees had stated, private broadcasting was to cease. In the early 1930s, the PTT had raided and closed a few of the smaller unauthorized private stations, most of which never were on the air for more than a few months, anyway. The PTT then used the decrees to justify its purchase of Radio Paris and to place further restrictions on the development of the remaining private stations (13 by this time). The PTT also acquired a new form of financial support: Starting in 1933, French listeners were required to pay annual license fees for the privilege of receiving broadcasts. None of the fee money went to private stations; none went directly to the PTT, either, but it could be used as a basis for requesting annual appropriations from the government. Those appropriations now increased and allowed the PTT to expand its services and create a genuine national network—something the private stations never had managed to achieve. In 1935 a new decree gave the private stations the exclusive right to carry ads but placed further restrictions upon them that would ensure the primacy of the PTT network.

Even with those limitations, a few of the private stations attempted to earn reputations as providers of news. One of them, Radio Cité, began a regularly scheduled newscast in 1935 that featured original (gathered by the station's own reporters) news stories, with broadcast vans to record material all around Paris, and that won some grudging praise from French newspapers.[5] However, more and more of the newspapers were becoming alarmed by radio's "intrusion" into their territory. In a move reminiscent of the U.S. Press-Radio "War" of the early 1930s,[6] the French newspapers forced an agreement on the radio stations. Radio news programs were to come on air after distribution of the morning and afternoon papers had hit the newsstands; news items were to be brief; and the newscast was to conclude with, "For more details, consult your usual newspaper." But the agreement didn't hold up very well, because many of the private stations had links with specific newspapers, which continued to supply them with sufficient news material for longer newscasts. Then the Spanish Civil War broke out (1936), and public demand for up-to-the-minute news about what was happening to France's western neighbor made broadcast journalism even more important.[7]

As the PTT system expanded, government officials began to take more interest in it. The director of the PTT radio station reported directly to the minister of posts, and there was a direct telephone link between the two offices, which high government officials did not hesitate to use—also a practice of the de Gaulle presidency, as we'll see later on. Some of the private stations were owned in part by leading politicians, who used the stations to support their own views and to ignore or oppose the views of other politicians and of the government. To prevent such usage, the PTT, which licensed all stations, placed a new condition on them in decrees issued in 1934 and 1935: Each would have to have a council of management directly elected by the listeners.

The councils would have some power in deciding broadcast policy. They rapidly became very political, and in 1937, elections to them became a straightforward contest between government and opposition parties.[8]

The mid-1930s saw some hotly contested national elections, and political parties sought more and more to express their views over radio. Both private and PTT stations broadcast speeches and news items about the campaigns, as well as election results. The use of radio during the 1936 election campaign was especially widespread at a local level. The party coalition that finally emerged victorious, with Socialist Léon Blum at its head, decided that henceforth it would be better if all radio news reporting were done from Paris, so the PTT decreed a ban on local news broadcasts. That was one more link in the centralization and consolidation of control over radio by the government, which was followed by a 1936 decree creating a council to supervise the preparation of network broadcasts from Paris.[9] The Blum government (1936-37) also tried to democratize radio by making it more open to trade unions, communists and "the people" in general, but it had only modest success.[10]

A 1938 decree established strict surveillance of programs on economic, financial and political topics. And in July 1939, radio was made a separate administrative operation under the direct supervision of the president of the council (prime minister), the better to function as a "powerful instrument of moral defense," presumably against Nazi propaganda. The private stations, now 12 in number, continued to function but had to broadcast official news bulletins at fixed times and saw a decrease in advertising revenue as the war drew near. One of them, Radio Normandie, was taken over by the French government in 1939 presumably to assist in the war effort but, according to René Duval, in part because of some personal grudges.[11]

In June 1940 the French government surrendered to the Nazis and the four-year occupation of France began. The country was divided in two, the northern half administered directly by the Germans and the southern half by a French government acceptable to the Germans. The German occupation government took over all stations in its area, using some for domestic broadcasts and others for broadcasts to other parts of Europe. The French had experimented with TV since 1935, and transmitted regularly scheduled broadcasts (vaudeville, variety programs, musical comedy, drama and classical music)[12] over a 455-line system by late 1937. When it went off the air at the outbreak of World War II, it was still available only in the Paris region, and to only a few thousand sets. The Nazi occupation force restarted it, and produced and regularly broadcast TV news and entertainment in the Paris region, both for their own personnel (in German) and to the French. There also was propaganda, including programs intended to recruit French workers to come and work in Germany. French personnel were heavily involved in the station, and many appeared to be very willing collaborators. The station went off the air shortly before the liberation of Paris in August 1944.[13]

The French government in the south (the Vichy government, named after its capital) continued to operate the PTT-founded system but became more and more involved with the private stations, as well: lacking sufficient ad revenue, private stations became more and more dependent upon government subsidies for their continued existence, and in 1943 the government bought up the hitherto private Société Financière de Radiodiffusion (SOFIRAD), which in turn bought up 50 percent of the shares in the newly created (largely by the Germans and Italians) Radio Monte Carlo. Furthermore, a law of November 1942 gave the national (government) radio operation the power to buy shares in private stations. The Vichy government made heavy use of radio to propagandize, and the only counterweights to its messages came from outside the country—London, Brazzaville, New York, Moscow, and, later in the war, North Africa. By 1944 the private stations had been absorbed completely into the national system. Their owners may have hoped for better things to come as the liberation of France began in May 1944, but if so those hopes soon were dashed.

Monopoly in the Fourth Republic (1944–1958)

The Allied forces liberated Paris in June of 1944, and most of the remaining parts of France were freed from the Germans by the end of the year. The new French government, under the leadership of Gen. Charles de Gaulle, began to bring order out of relative chaos. The Germans had left much destruction in their wake, and Allied air raids and ground attacks had added to it, but there remained a fairly viable nucleus of facilities, public and private. A March 1945 ordinance revoked all private licenses; some private station owners were compensated, others were not, and a few even were jailed as alleged collaborators with the Nazis—allegations that may have stemmed from personal grudges.[14] Vichy government laws pertaining to radio were abolished, but some elements from them began to appear in new legislative proposals. In November 1945, a decree established the Radiodiffusion-Télévision Française (RTF), but on a temporary basis. However, attempts of other groups to get the government to consider alternative approaches proved futile. De Gaulle himself, although hailed as a war hero, was out of power soon after the war ended. He quickly helped to organize an opposition party, but received very little broadcast time to present his views—and, between 1947 and 1951,[15] *no* airtime whatsoever.[16]

The various governments of the period seemed to become more and more conservative as time passed. Some of the leading, and often "radical," artists of the time—Camus, Sartre, Eluard—were quite heavily involved with radio in the late 1940s, but their broadcast appearances became less and less frequent in the 1950s, perhaps through fears of "communist infiltration."[17] The same spirit of conservatism hampered efforts to recreate a commercial broadcasting sector: Thomas indicates that there were more than a dozen statutes on alternative forms of broadcasting proposed between 1945 and 1958, but none received serious consideration. The government seemed satisfied to let the monopoly stand, and even coalitions that might have been expected to favor the rebirth of private broadcasting stuck with the RTF.[18]

Staff members of RTF found plenty of grounds to express their dissatisfaction, however. The period 1944-59 saw over 80 strikes, sometimes regarding salaries but at least as often over questions of editorial and artistic freedom. The RTF remained firmly under the government's control; the director general of RTF was selected by the French cabinet and reported directly to the minister of information (a wartime office that persisted in peacetime), while the director of radio news was directly appointed by that minister. The RTF operated as a civil service department, which meant that its annual budget was voted by Parliament and that its accounting practices had to follow civil service rules dating from 1862! Virtually all financial operations required prior consent of the Ministry of Finance. The structure was an administrative nightmare, and the modest budgets approved by Parliament added to the frustration.[19]

Governments came and went rapidly during the period, so almost none of them tried to use radio and, later in the 1950s, television to support their particular policies. Presumably none of them wanted other political coalitions to use radio to support their own positions, should they come to power. Instead, each government interfered chiefly by "asking" RTF not to cover or at least not to emphasize certain events, for example, North African resistance to French colonial rule there. As the conflicts in North Africa became more numerous and violent, the various governing coalitions clamped down on RTF even harder, but domestic events occasioned pressures from the top, as well: In 1957 the government suppressed a broadcast declaration by Fréderic Joliet-Curie against nuclear weapons, and an RTF interviewer faced threats of dismissal because he had interviewed politicians who opposed the then-prime minister, Guy Mollet.

Television mattered little to any political party at first. Television broadcasts resumed in 1947, though not on weekends, but by 1950 there still were only 4,000 sets in the entire country. By 1954 there were 60,000, and finally by 1958 over a million, in a nation of perhaps 12 million households. Television news at first was considered unimportant, and it was controlled by the director of television. By the mid-1950s, it had come under the control of the director of radio news, who reported directly to the minister of information. Henri Spade suggests that the practice of holding daily conferences between RTF and the Ministry of Information on the makeup of each day's TV newscast started then.[20] (The head of radio news had been conferring daily with government ministers on news content since 1948.)[21] Some producers resented what they saw as censorship, especially of news about developments in North Africa (Algeria in particular), and a few refused to continue producing their programs. There was no alternative source of television, either for producers to express their points of view or for audiences to receive them. Unlike radio, where stations from around the periphery of France (Radio Monte Carlo in Monaco, Europe No. One in the Saar, Radio Andorra, Radio Luxembourg) sometimes provided contrasting material, few foreign TV stations were receivable in France. Still, the government attempted to ensure that viewers in areas able to receive outside signals (Strasbourg from West Germany in particular) have French TV as soon as possible, and indeed the second TV transmitter outside of Paris was in Strasbourg (1953).

The Fifth Republic Begins (1958–1964)

A 1958 statement by a former director of RTF makes it quite clear that the state and those who run it are in the best position to judge how broadcasting should be used for the benefit of the people. After Gabriel Delaunay had attacked (foreign) television systems that were "over-responsive to immediate public demand," he went on to say, "A modern state has the duty to consider radio and television as an essential element of its domestic life, as a necessary expression of its radiance, as the best means of making last that which continues to give it its grandeur. France, and France more than any other nation, since it has an exceptionally radiant past to defend, would thus commit a serious error if, faced with a thing so exceptional and so revolutionary, it were to abandon itself to empiricism, being content to follow and imitate, not setting a policy and defining the means to realize that policy."[22] Complaints about the quality of broadcast services, and especially about the censored newscasts and the many dull discussion and talk programs, appeared regularly in the press, and listeners frequently turned to the peripheral services in Monaco, the Saar, Andorra and Luxembourg for alternatives to the RTF services. Those services also handled live reporting better than did the rather traditional and less-well-equipped RTF staff.[23] Occasionally RTF reporters appearing on the street were booed and hissed and even pelted with rotten fruit.

The coming to power of Charles de Gaulle in 1958 didn't bring with it any marked degree of liberalization. De Gaulle saw a need for a strong hand to "guide" (some would say "command") radio and TV, which could play important roles in reinforcing French culture at home and spreading it abroad. He also regarded them as politically useful, and soon set about using them to "personalize" the French presidency. Stiff and seemingly unsure of himself at first, de Gaulle evolved into a skilled performer, especially on television. He developed a more informal style of speaking, often delivering his remarks while seated (rare for a French politician on TV in those days). He didn't become directly involved in the administration of broadcasting; he left that to his chief ministers and close friends.[24]

The daily conferences involving RTF staff and ministerial representatives became a more formal institution soon after de Gaulle took office. The Interministerial Information Liaison Service (SLII), set up by and under the Ministry of Information, undertook the planning of each day's news programs. According to the then-assistant director of television, Jacques Thibau, the meetings centered on items that should not be covered and on inaugurations and ceremonies that should receive maximum coverage.[25] The new government passed a statute in 1959; under it, RTF became an autonomous public institution, but the government named its director general, and it would not have its own board of directors. If anything, the statute increased the degree of governmental control.

De Gaulle and his political followers ignored criticisms of their heavy-handed treatment of French broadcasting. He is alleged to have claimed on more than one occasion, "My opponents have the press. Why shouldn't I have television?" The 1962 election saw a tremendous imbalance between appearances on TV of the Gaullists and appearances of opposition candidates—not quite the reverse image of what had happened to de Gaulle himself in the late 1940s and early 1950s, but close enough. Criticism of that imbalance was widespread in the press and even within RTF, where there was a protest strike in October 1962. But the government dealt with such internal opposition by asking RTF management (itself thoroughly Gaullist by then) to suspend or dismiss protesters, and many had to leave.[26] When Alain Peyrefitte took over as minister of information in 1962, his predecessor showed him a row of buttons at his desk, which were to be used to call the heads of radio and TV news "just like calling in the cleaning woman" in order to eliminate whatever might be displeasing in the evening news.[27] Peyrefitte proved to be a quick study: he saw television as de Gaulle saw it, and stated during the local elections of 1965 that, "In certain regions [of France], the opposition holds a quasi-monopoly on the printed press ... it can be the role of television to re-establish some balance."[28]

There were some bright journalistic moments, particularly in the creation in 1959 of a monthly 90-minute current affairs program, "Cinq Colonnes à la Une" ("Five [newspaper] Columns on Page/Channel One"). It was far superior to any TV current affairs series yet attempted on TV, and had a top-notch staff of reporters and producers. Items came from France and abroad; a given program might contain a report on a strike in Belgium or a portrait of French pop singer Johnny Halliday, all in a personalized, fast-moving presentation. Bourdon points out that there was emphasis on foreign political events, but little on French domestic politics. Reports on Algeria during the war of independence (which ended in 1963) emphasized elements that would support de Gaulle's plan—not all that popular in France—to bring an end to the war and to negotiate independence with the Algerian Muslims. Stories on the French army's problems in Algeria, the increasing disillusionment of the French settlers there, etc., all served to support the logic of that plan.[29]

There was enough ill feeling over this abuse of power to lead the French National Assembly to pass a law in November 1962, followed by a decree in March 1964, which guaranteed opposition parties, as well as the parties involved in the governing coalition, the right to equal amounts of airtime in election campaigns. Furthermore, a national commission composed of senior magistrates was to supervise RTF's practices in order to ensure fairness. But some politicians felt that more sweeping reforms were necessary. In 1962, André Diligent proposed a new structure that would include an administrative council made up of members of the public and of the government, with the council selecting the director general of RTF. His proposal never got beyond the committee stage. Prime Minister Georges Pompidou promised Parliament in October of 1962 that the government would propose a new statute, but it didn't emerge until 1964.

The bill regarding broadcasting was debated intensely in May and June, and both houses of the Assembly passed numerous amendments; the Senate, the weaker of the two bodies but the one in which the opposition was in the majority, rejected most of the major points in the government's proposal. A joint committee worked out a compromise, but the government would not accept it and forced the Assembly to approve the original bill.[30] In late June 1964, the statute became law, the RTF was abolished and the new Office de Radiodiffusion-Télévision Française (ORTF) took its place. To the audience, the change would prove to be almost unnoticeable.

The ORTF (1964–1974)

The one change in the broadcast organization's initials—O for Office—was supposed to be significant. It would mean that there would be an administrative council and a director general. Furthermore, the administrative council would be made up half of representatives of the state and half of representatives of viewers and listeners, the press, ORTF itself, and "highly qualified persons" (usually people who were well-known artists, diplomats, etc.). The council would approve and supervise the ORTF budget, would examine the quality and moral tone of broadcasting, would assure objectivity and accuracy, and would see to it that "principal trends of thought" could find expression through ORTF broadcasts. On the surface, all of that sounded like André Diligent's 1962 proposal. Beneath the surface, the government was as involved as ever. It appointed all members of the council; "representative organizations" could submit lists of qualified nominees, but the government made the final choice, and it chose individuals who were favorably inclined toward its policies. The government also retained power of appointment of the director general and the two deputy directors general. In theory, the council and the director general shared power, but the arrangement was not clearly defined in the new law, and it soon became evident that the director general held the balance of that power.

The annual license fee continued to supply most of the annual budget, but it was still up to the minister of information and the National Assembly to decide the size of that budget, although the onerous system of control that had required prior approval of expenditures in the RTF was modified to cover "only" recruitment, pay and promotion of permanent staff; program expenditures themselves could be approved after the fact. Program advisory committees now were authorized, and covered music, science, literature and drama, and light entertainment. But their membership, too, was appointed by the government. As the old French saying goes, "*Plus ça change, plus c'est la même chose*" (the more things change, the more they remain the same).

It wasn't long before the implications of that saying became evident to viewers and listeners. A second TV channel came on the air in 1964, but it offered few real alternatives. There was a temporary flourishing of magazine programs, and some of them presented the views of political opponents of de Gaulle and dealt with hitherto little-covered subjects such as unemployment and prejudice (the ending of the Algerian War in 1963 saw an influx of French citizens living in Algeria and of Algerians who chose to leave their native land, but neither group found a very warm welcome in France). Already by 1965 there were governmental pressures on producers of those programs to tone them down. The 1965 presidential election campaign followed the principle of fair and equal division of airtime among the six main parties, but only to airtime set aside for political campaigning during the official election campaign. De Gaulle had decreed early in 1964 that broadcasting would be closed to all presidential candidates until two weeks before the election, but that limitation did not apply to himself.[31] Nor did it apply to other members of the Gaullist coalition when they ran for office: They were frequent guests on interview and talk shows. Television reporters covering opposition candidates were instructed to shoot them from the back, so that their faces wouldn't be visible.[32] Newscasts showed opposition party members in the Assembly stumbling over their words.[33]

There was a spate of current affairs programs in 1966 that showed some promise. Not only did the political opposition obtain frequent and fair coverage, but Gaullist politicians sometimes faced tough and even hostile questions from journalists. However, in November 1966 the cabinet decided that there would be an equal division of campaign broadcast time between the two Gaullist parties on the one hand and the four main and several smaller opposition parties on the other—hardly the sort of "equal time" principle covered in the 1962 and 1964 equal time statutes. Then, on the eve of the 1967 election day, after formal campaigning had closed, President de Gaulle came on TV to make a special appeal to the nation for its electoral support. Political parties from right to left, excepting of course the Gaullist parties, condemned the move—the Communist paper L'Humanité called it "a characteristic rape" and the leader of an extreme right-wing party called upon the ORTF technicians to strike (they didn't)—but their condemnations had no effect. The Gaullists won the election.[34]

As blatant as that interference was, it paled by comparison with what happened in May 1968. Ironically, the Senate had released a report by a special Senate commission on the ORTF only weeks earlier. The 1968 Diligent Report was highly critical of the ORTF, although it acknowledged that there had been some improvement. It saw the administrative council as largely ineffective because the Gaullists controlled it and because there were no clear lines of authority for it. The report also noted the increasing sense of professionalism within ORTF but added that that professionalism was coupled with a growing sense of frustration on the part of staff members, especially journalists. The report recommended that the ORTF function through the minister of culture rather than the minister of information, that the administrative council be appointed in a more democratic manner, and that a special council be created to ensure impartiality and to protect journalists against "unjustified sanctions." It condemned political interference and in particular the SLII.[35]

Then came what U.S. novelist James Jones called "the merry month of May." Student riots broke out early in the month, barricades went up, some workers joined with the students, and a confrontation with the government was joined. The ORTF waited for about a week, and then the "Panorama" program staff prepared a report on the riots. The ministries of information and education ordered it to be dropped from the program schedule, and it was. On May 11 a number of ORTF TV producers demanded a full documentary on the student problem. Instead, the assistant director of TV news broadcast an edited version of the "Panorama" report, but without the consent of the journalists involved. That led to a 24-hour strike at ORTF. On May 16 riot police took up positions around the ORTF headquarters. Personnel at ORTF set forth a list of demands, including resignations of the administrative council, director general, deputies and heads of TV news, and annulment of the 1964 statute that had created the ORTF, plus preparation of a new statute.[36]

Strikes at ORTF started in late May. One involved nearly a hundred TV journalists, angry with the director of television because he would not allow the airing of reactions from other political figures to de Gaulle's speech to the nation on May 24 (his first broadcast about the crisis). There were roughly 40 members of the news staff who did not go out on strike, most of them staunch Gaullists, and it was they who put together the news for the next few weeks. The strikers and the Ministry of Information negotiated for reform, but as they did, a group of radio news journalists who had been attempting to put out impartial news bulletins in the meantime went out on strike in response to a June 3 gag order by the minister of information. Splits then developed in union ranks. Radio journalists voted to return to work in late June, TV journalists in mid-July. Both groups were told by the ORTF administration to wait: Broadcast journalism was being "reformed." In August 1968, ORTF announced a "reduction in manpower," under which most of the striking TV journalists were suspended, transferred or dismissed—a violation of government promises of "no retaliation."[37]

What effect those events had on public opinion of ORTF credibility is uncertain, since the ORTF didn't conduct public-opinion surveys on any regular basis and rarely released any details from those it did conduct. But France's most popular weekly television magazine, *Télé-7 Jours,* asked its readers in late July about the need for reforms in broadcasting. Of the roughly 50,000 replying, nearly 90 percent wanted to see the statute governing ORTF modified, about 85 percent said that broadcast news should be more independent from the government, and almost 95 percent wanted more audience representation on the administrative council, which then had only one audience representative.[38]

The government announced its reforms on July 31. They included enlargement of the administrative council from 16 to 24 members. Audience representation didn't increase, but ORTF staff representation did, to five members. But the government still appointed 16 of the 24 members directly and chose the remaining eight from lists supplied by various organizations. The council thus got bigger (and somewhat younger), but not much more independent. The SLII was replaced by the Interministerial Information Committee, which was not to have any direct links with the ORTF. The director general also now became president of the administrative council; since council members were appointed for three-year terms, that could have given the president-director general a bit more job security, but it didn't: The government still could "unappoint" any council member that it had appointed whenever it wished.

The puny character of those reforms attracted some attention in the press, but another government reform move drew far more criticism. Various government officials had discussed the possibility of limited advertising on ORTF over the previous few years. In the spring of 1968, some of them began to mention it as if it were fait accompli. When the list of reforms came out, there it was. Advertising was to be limited to 20 minutes a day, on TV only, but many newspapers saw it as the opening wedge in the government's attempt to draw advertising revenue away from the press, especially from smaller, financially weaker newspapers that were more or less anti-Gaullist.

A referendum held in 1969 caused President de Gaulle to retire, since he had staked his political reputation on a strongly positive outcome, and saw the vote as a rejection of his leadership. That was followed by a presidential election, where all candidates made promises to develop a more objective ORTF and to abolish the Ministry of Information. Georges Pompidou, a Gaullist, won the election. He did abolish the Ministry (although it returned a few years later) and placed the ORTF under the prime minister, who soon announced plans to reform ORTF. The most notable aspect of the reform was the creation of two separate and competing news teams for the two television channels, one team to be headed by a noted Gaullist, the other by a noted liberal journalist.

The two-team concept indeed seemed to produce a more independent brand of TV news, although Gaullist political figures continued to find it easy to get on the air, while the opposition had far less opportunity. But it also proved to be very costly, with journalists from the two teams sometimes covering the same foreign news story, and not always with a discernible difference. A special governmental commission (the Paye Commission) reported in 1970 that more should be done to ensure objectivity and proposed some changes in the administrative structure, but the report never was taken up by the Assembly. President Pompidou stated in a press conference in July 1970 that the ORTF was the "voice of France," and that in itself meant that ORTF journalists had to accept some restraints. In December 1970, an ORTF staff directive indicated that politics should be kept out of entertainment programs. There had been a well-established tradition of political satire during the 1960s, especially as produced by Jean-Christophe Avérty in a program entitled "Les Raisins Vertes" ("Sour Grapes"), which for example lampooned government policy on birth control by putting on a modern version of Jonathan Swift's "A Modest Proposal." Since such programs had been regarded as entertainment, they either escaped the notice of sensitive government officials or were passed off as harmless diversion. Now they would receive closer attention.

Then in November 1971 a financial scandal broke. A number of ORTF staff were working with a state-operated advertising and public relations agency to insert commercials in noncommercial programs, generally by slipping in mention of brand names. Both houses of Parliament appointed commissions to look into the allegations. They found plenty of proof. The government reacted by discharging the director general of ORTF, and drew up a proposal for yet another reform.

The 1972 statute altered the composition of the administrative council. Listeners and viewers now would be represented by two individuals instead of one, and fewer council members would be appointed directly by the government. Council functions remained basically unchanged. The posts of council president and of ORTF director general were combined, but the new head still was appointed by the government. There was specific emphasis on ORTF's role as "guardian of the purest standards of the French language," and there was a new "right of reply" article—something long sought by reformers. However, right of reply was limited to persons as individuals, and not as members of groups or parties. There also was to be a new High Audiovisual Council to advise the government on the implications of new electronic media technologies, cable TV and satellite TV in particular.

Members of left-of-center parties were disappointed because the new statute did very little to encourage greater freedom of expression. Members of right-of-center parties were disappointed because the new statute didn't provide for private broadcasting, although one article in the statute raised the possibility of developing separate program services for "particular audiences." The government would decide whether to issue such permission, which would be temporary. The Senate voted down the statute, but the government pushed it through the Assembly anyway, and it became law.

One small element of the statute, Article 4, addressed an issue that many members of Parliament and some government officials had raised on several occasions, but especially following the 1971 advertising scandal. Those individuals saw the ORTF as overly centralized and felt that decentralization might make the organization more efficient financially, administratively and programmatically. Article 4 created a more subdivided ORTF, with various large units (e.g., radio) having slightly more autonomy, and with an indication that the degree of autonomy might be increased. This became the core of the next reorganization of the ORTF, scarcely two years later.

Meanwhile, it was business as usual, meaning that government officials still felt perfectly free to call ORTF studios directly to voice their objections to programs, even as those programs were being broadcast and even to the extent of demanding that they be cut off immediately. Journalists continued to be sacked, transferred or encouraged to leave, and a total of roughly 200 departed shortly after passage of the new statute. The new president-director general, Arthur Conte, once a Socialist but now seen by some of his former

Socialist colleagues as a turncoat for having accepted appointment by the Conservative government to such an influential post, appeared to be responsible for causing the departure of the liberal head of TV news on Channel 1, Pierre Desgraupes. Conte defended the action in indirect terms in a speech to the ORTF staff.[39] Conte also appeared to regard television as well suited to entertain but not to raise questions about troublesome issues in French society. His predecessor had forbidden ORTF to broadcast a documentary ("The Sorrow and the Pity") made for it by Marcel Ophuls, because it brought up the "taboo" subject of French collaboration with the Nazis during the occupation. When asked whether he planned to unearth the documentary, Conte was reported to have said, "I don't sense any impatience on the public's part to see it." That corresponded with the feelings of the minister of information, Philippe Malaud, to whom Conte reported: Malaud often had criticized French TV for its "pessimistic image of society."[40]

Beneath the surface, there were problems between Malaud and Conte, and they erupted when the authoritative newspaper Le Monde published excerpts from a letter from Malaud to an old friend who also happened to be assistant director at ORTF. Malaud called one of the radio services, France-Culture, a "permanent Communist pulpit," said that some TV news coverage had "a leftist bias," and accused Conte of financial irresponsibility. (There were rumors that there would be a deficit of Fr 150 million [roughly $35 million] for 1974.)[41] Conte replied publicly that the ORTF had been subjected to "intolerable political pressures" by Malaud. Conte was replaced in late October by a "nonpolitical" appointee, Marcel Long, and Malaud was demoted to a lesser ministerial post.

Long quickly announced that a certain amount of administrative reorganization was in order, and that it would take the form of greater autonomy for major units within ORTF: radio, the three TV channels (the third channel had come on the air in 1973, mainly to serve France's regions), possibly production, and the foreign radio service. The trade unions did not like the look of the new system, still felt concern over government pressures, and called a 24-hour strike on November 6. Journalists at ORTF called a three-hour sympathy strike. Further strikes came in ensuing weeks, but they did no good; Long's plan won cabinet approval in March 1974. Meanwhile, Conte attempted to tell his side of the story through publication of his memoirs,[42] but when he was scheduled to discuss those memoirs on television, the government barred him from appearing.[43]

One element in Conte's accusation was that President Pompidou was so ill that others were running the government, and with it the ORTF. Pompidou died in April 1974, forcing a new election and delaying consideration of the latest ORTF reform. The three major candidates all had different views on broadcasting. Giscard won the election, abolished the Ministry of Information, and promised that ORTF would display a more highly diverse set of viewpoints. But ORTF's financial situation was bleak, and in June there was a lengthy strike by technical and administrative staff over the issue of salary increases. There was speculation that TV Channel One might become semiautonomous and more heavily commercial. The speculation—and ORTF itself—ended when the government announced that, on January 1, 1975, the organization would be split into six separate establishments, each with its own administrative structure. Characteristically, the government rushed the bill through Parliament in late July, amid complaints that there was not enough time for proper consideration, that there were too few details on how the new system would function and so on. Still, both houses approved, and French viewers and listeners received their New Year's present with little expectation that the results would be much different. They were correct in most respects, but few could have anticipated the cost in terms of financial inefficiency.[44]

The Decentralized ORTF (1975–1981)

The new law actually came into effect on January 6, 1975, accompanied by 25 decrees (not subject to passage by the French Parliament) to flesh out its slender skeleton. In the place of the dismantled ORTF arose seven separate companies, each with its own president, administrative council and director. All of those individuals ultimately were chosen by the government, although many administrative council members were nominated by various groups, usually on lists of several possible candidates. Three companies dealt with television programming; two of them were responsible for the two national channels, the third for regional TV and France's few overseas territories. One company handled the four radio services. One company was responsible for major TV productions (drama, variety, etc.), and the three television program companies were to order their productions from it, although they also could place orders with private production companies. One company was in charge of certain common services: research, in-service training, archives. The seventh company took care of broadcast transmissions and the maintenance of the transmission system. There was to be a High Audiovisual Council with 40 members, six appointed by Parliament, 34 by the government, to advise the government on the development of audiovisual technology, but also on ethical issues and on right of reply.[45]

Such an organizational framework wasn't likely to make much sense in terms of administrative efficiency, but it did have the virtue (from the government's standpoint) of reducing the power of the trade unions, which now were split among seven companies. The government appointed the directors of each company, which probably helped to keep order in the ranks. Also, each company's administrative council contained a member of Parliament, who usually came from the majority party. As Jean Diwo explains, "Everything is decided by the Minister of State [for the Interior] and by his principal private secretary. ... Every name, down to the heads of department, has been carefully scrutinized. It is most unfortunate for anyone whose past record is not entirely reassuring."[46]

Still, matters improved to the point where major-party politicians, whether in the majority or in the opposition, found airtime much more readily available. Usually they appeared in current affairs programs, sometimes in debates. Minor political parties (extreme right, ecologists, etc.) had little opportunity to be seen or heard, although France Regions 3 (FR3), the regional TV service and probably the least widely viewed of the three TV services, carried a 15-minute "open forum" program five nights a week. A right of reply bill was passed in 1975 but, like the article in the 1972 statute, it applied only to individual persons; in 1976 the Socialist Party proposed a law that would give that right to trade unions and political parties as well, but it wasn't adopted.[47]

Some government officials continued in the long-established tradition of interfering with program decision-making when it suited their purposes. "Les Dossiers de l'Ecran," a popular program that covered sensitive topics, introducing them with a film and following the film with a debate, was pressured into dropping proposed programs on crime (1975) and on the army (1976) by the ministers of the interior and of defense.[48] Politicians from the opposition parties continued to claim that their views were underrepresented or distorted on TV.

There was an interesting provision in the new system with implications for program quality. Some members of the public and many newspaper critics had complained about poor production standards, especially in television entertainment. Imports from the United States may have struck the critics as deplorable on moral grounds or for their weak story lines, but critics also acknowledged that they were much more attractive to watch than was most of the homemade product. Now the distribution of license fee money to the program companies would be based on a formula that would take into account both the size of the audience and the quality of the programs. A committee "representing the geographical and social diversity of the country" would carry out the evaluation.[49]

The financing of the new system remained a problem. Indeed, in some respects the problem became far worse. Parliament continued to set the size of the license fee and exercised general supervision over its expenditure. It also had the power to vote for or against collection of the succeeding year's license fee, and in 1973 and again in 1975 the Assembly nearly refused to authorize the following year's collection because of its dissatisfaction with the fiscal management of broadcasting and with the broadcast administrators' incomplete and possibly even deceitful presentation of the budget. Budgetary matters went from bad to worse as the 1970s wore on. There were allegations of gross inefficiency in the "official" production company, Société Française de Production (SFP). (One French producer told me in 1981 that most major TV programs could be and sometimes were produced by private companies at a third of the cost that the official company charged—and were produced more skillfully, at that.) Furthermore, the three TV companies were expected to give a large share of their production business to SFP regardless of cost-effectiveness. Occasional license fee increases offset some of the budgetary losses, but the losses never disappeared.

The political opposition led the way in calling attention to the problems of the new broadcast setup, but there were no prospects for any real reform, since the government of the day didn't wish to relinquish its control over the system. (However, the SLII, according to Bourdon ["Haute Fidelité," 180] became far less powerful in 1975, when it was transformed into the SID, or Service d'Information et Documentation.) Public opinion concerning broadcasting remained something of a mystery, both because of a general absence of surveys and the tendency of the broadcasters not to release any data. Magazines, newspapers and various organizations conducted their own polls, most of which showed a fairly high degree of dissatisfaction with informational broadcasts (but some improvement in that respect compared with the pre-1974 era); however, most of those polls didn't use accepted survey techniques, and their questions sometimes were quite biased.

All during the 1970s, the system remained a monopoly in law, but less so in fact. In 1977, union groups and political parties began to experiment with "radio libre"—free, or pirate, radio (independent of government control, but also unauthorized). Steelworkers in the province of Lorraine set up Radio Coeur d'Acier, ecologists in Alsace Radio Verte Fessenheim, and there were several others, some of them on the air very briefly, others for years.[50]

Following a legal challenge to the government's licensing authority by a Montpellier commercial station, Radio Fil Bleue, in 1978, the government passed legislation later that year that specifically forbade such transmissions, as there had been an ambiguity in the 1974 law on that point. However, in most cases the inhabitants of the communities or districts from which the free stations broadcast alerted station staff whenever government inspectors came around. The Socialist Party, frustrated perhaps more than any other party by the Conservative coalition's hammerlock on political power ever since 1958, ventured forth with Radio Riposte in 1979. It attacked government policies directly and quickly was jammed. At one point the police blockaded a building from which Socialist leaders were broadcasting. That leadership stood trial for its illegal act in August 1979. The party leader, François Mitterand, said, "We wanted a political trial, and now we have one." One observer was cynical that any of this would have a lasting effect; she stated, "When the dust has settled, it appears sure that the old arrangement will remain unchanged, the state monopoly secure and the Socialists in quest of another issue."[51] In two years' time, Mitterand had won the presidency. For the first time in over 40 years, there would be a private alternative from within France.

The Socialist Reform (1981–1986)

For all of their campaign rhetoric about the need to liberate broadcasting from close government control, to make it more objective, to decentralize it, it took the victorious Socialists a while to change the law, and some of the political moves that accompanied the process were reminiscent of the "good old days." In his second month in office, Mitterand appointed a study commission (the Moinot Commission) to develop proposals for a new system. The report came out in September. Several months passed before the government—

chiefly the prime minister and the newly created post of minister for communications, supposedly symbolic of the new administration's intent to reform all communications enterprises—had a proposal ready for Parliament. In the meantime, reports began to surface that the new minister and other government officials were calling on news and current affairs staff in particular to pressure certain colleagues to resign. The administration, which had pledged that there would be no witch hunts to cleanse broadcasting of some of its allegedly anti-Socialist staff, nonetheless sought the resignations of the directors of the three TV companies. Prime Minister Pierre Mauroy stated in a June 1981 press conference, "We haven't asked anyone to go. But it is true that we are not asking anyone to stay."[52]

When Parliament finally received the government's proposals in April 1982, there were some interesting changes between what the Moinot Commission had recommended and what the proposals contained. The commission had recommended several specific steps to be taken in distancing the government from broadcasting, allowing the latter to act more independently. It also recommended the rapid development of local radio. It particularly wanted to see the budget for broadcasting disbursed through a new body, the Haute Autorité (High Authority), which also would license all new broadcast operations that were not part of the national system. The HA, as it came to be known, would be a nine-member body, with three members appointed by the president and three by the chief French legal/constitutional bodies; those six in turn would choose three members from a list prepared by the National Audiovisual Council. That, the commission felt, would help to minimize direct political influence over the HA, which also would hear complaints regarding objectivity.

The government's proposals said little about the development of local radio, nor would the HA have any control over broadcasting's finances. Georges Fillioud, the minister for communication, stated during the National Assembly debate on the bill that "as public funds are at stake, there can be no question that the state [government and Parliament] could delegate this responsibility to the Haute Autorité." Furthermore, the HA itself would have nine members, but three would be appointed by the president, and three each by the speakers of the Senate and the Assembly. Thus, politicians would be in charge of all appointments, and the ruling party or coalition probably would be able to control the majority of them. The president also would choose the HA's president. The structure that had been in place since 1974 largely would remain intact, although regional TV stations were to have more independence from the national system and greater financial support.[53]

There was little in those actions to cause most people to expect radical changes in the broadcast system, but changes were taking place even before the bill passed later that spring. Political figures who hadn't been seen or heard over French broadcasting for years began to reappear; some were appointed to administrative positions in broadcasting. Those appointed generally were Socialists or favorable to Socialist policies, and it seemed to some audience members and critics that the Socialists were getting more than their fair share of broadcast time. Also, some TV entertainment shows were dropped from the prime-time schedule in favor of educational programs, discussions and other fare designed to enlighten viewers, rather than simply distract them. Angry viewers began to express their sentiments—one report noted that half the mail received by Mitterand consisted of complaints about programs influenced by the government[54]—but they also began to listen more and more to the hundreds of pirate radio stations springing up across the land.

The pirates had existed since the mid-1970s, and the government had managed to shut most of them down in short order. But because the Socialists had used pirate radio to strike back at the government in the late 1970s, and because they had promised a more liberal policy with respect to independent radio, it was difficult for them to silence such stations now that they held power. At first they didn't even try, but so many stations came on the air in Paris that it was evident that there would have to be a modicum of regulation applied to them. They certainly represented a variety of opinions and styles. Some were run by minor political parties, others by homosexuals, still others by émigré communities such as North African Arabs. A number of them were strongly antigovernment; I once heard one in Rouen do a satirical skit on the government's proposed tax increase, which suggested that listeners should liken paying taxes to having an orgasm: the more, the better. The station followed this with a reading of a letter allegedly received from a French paratrooper temporarily on duty in the former French African colony of Chad, helping the government there to suppress a "rebel" opposition force. Most of the "letter" was a thinly veiled indictment of the Socialist government's Chad policy.

The government announced late in 1982 that it would grant licenses to radio stations, subject to two major conditions: that the stations operate on low power (500 watts) and that they not finance themselves by selling advertising time. Also, there would be limited frequency space for the stations, so it was suggested that those located in the same community consider making joint applications. Many hundreds applied. In some of the larger cities, there were far more applicants than the frequency spectrum (FM only) could hold, so the Haute Autorité, which granted the licenses, issued some with the condition that the frequency be shared by two or more stations. Some stations were willing to go along with the decision, but others refused and continued to broadcast illegally. Many of the stations began almost immediately to violate the no advertising rule, simply because they could not make ends meet otherwise, and in April 1984 President Mitterand announced that the stations could carry ads, after all. A number of stations sought to increase their audience size by transmitting at more than 500 watts. One of them, Radio NRJ (Paris), was banned from broadcasting for 30 days because it transmitted at 30,000 watts, interfering with emergency services. The station owner refused to abide by the decision, and thousands of protesters turned out in Paris to denounce the action.[55]

The Mitterand government's authorization of private radio was the first major sign that broadcast policy under the Socialists was going to be substantially different from what it was under the Conservative coalitions. It's difficult to say whether the Socialists' own use of pirate radio while in the opposition virtually forced them to open up radio to private operators, but it probably hastened the process, at the least. That step soon was followed by others: The government announced in mid-1983 that there would be a new over-the-air pay-TV service, chiefly featuring movies but with provision for program sponsorship by advertisers, as well. There was no open competition for a license; the government, and not the HA, simply granted it.[56] This new service, Canal Plus, required a special decoder (to descramble the signal) and aerial, and thus was costly enough that few but wealthy households were expected to subscribe to it—hardly the sort of enterprise supported by traditional Socialists! And cable TV, which had been the subject of experiments in a few French cities in the 1970s, but which never had really amounted to anything,[57] now received strong support from the government in its highly publicized 1982 "Plan Cable," which envisaged 1.4 million homes served by fiber-optic cable by the middle of the decade (a figure not yet reached even a decade later). Direct broadcast satellite service was to begin by 1986.[58]

Whereas the satellite service clearly was to be national, the Mitterand government touted its cable plan as another move to strengthen local government, since local authorities were to have a major voice in how cable services would be set up in each community. As it turned out, they didn't. The national government required that all communities licensing cable companies also name a local council member as president of the company, and a "prefect" (local government representative of the national government) as a member of the company's board of directors. The Haute Autorité was given considerable regulatory power over the local companies. When some of the communities tried to establish cable companies, several were told that they couldn't proceed as they intended because their approaches didn't fit in with national planning.[59] Furthermore, there were conflicts between the national government's Direction Générale de Télécommunications (DGT) and the local cable interests. The DGT was interested in the installation of the hardware, and charged a high price for it; the cable interests were interested in the software (programs), and wanted to keep the price low.[60]

The driving force behind the Socialists' radical shift in communications policy was economic. The major manufacturers of communications and space technology were government-owned, and the Socialist government didn't care for the prospect of losing out to other European and North American nations, not to mention Japan, in the race to secure markets. The government also was willing to throw a few roadblocks in the way of those competitors, as it did early in 1983, when it began to require that all Japanese videocassette recorders pass through customs inspection. The inspection added to the cost of the recorders and delayed their progress to retail stores. Inspections ended just a few months later when the Japanese reached an agreement with a French electronics firm to allow the latter to manufacture up to a million Japanese VCRs per year.

Then in January 1985, Mitterand announced the authorization of private, commercial television. Ironically, he did so in the course of a televised speech in which he praised the public broadcast service as a "guarantor of quality"; just after that remark, his image faded from the screen, thanks to a technical disruption. As one French critic remarked, "The breakdowns have come to symbolize the badly run, overstaffed, and under-efficient ... state-controlled French television channels."[61] The president claimed that there was room for 80 to 85 local television stations. Actually, some were on the air already, operating illegally: Télé Alphonse Jouy, for example, served a number of Paris city council apartment blocks for the poor with community programming delivered by cable. Several cities and towns across the country were at work on private projects, some of which were supported by opposition political parties. Again, Mitterand appeared to be bowing to the inevitable, perhaps hoping to win a bit of public favor by supporting diversity in broadcasting. Some of his aides reportedly opposed his proposal, partly because they feared that the political opposition would be able to take advantage of the new outlets, partly because they thought that investors would be drawn away from the cable and satellite systems being pushed by the government.[62] There were well over 300 applications for new licenses in the first four months following Mitterand's announcement.

Certainly the government continued to use its own political influence on broadcasting, although not in as obvious a manner as had its predecessors. Ever since the founding of the Haute Autorité in 1982, it had been rumored widely that, even though the HA was to choose the directors general of the program services, nominees had to meet with Mitterand's approval first, usually through personal interview.[63] Gradually, all of the program services came under directors general who were aligned with the government; Mitterand's appointment of a noted Socialist, Jean-Claude Heberlé, as head of Antenne 2 (TV) in October 1984 seemed to some observers to show clearly how little say the HA had in the appointment process.[64] The first director of Canal Plus, André Rousselet, had been the director of Mitterand's personal cabinet. Still, the Autorité received praise from some normally critical sources for having prepared a number of excellent reports on needed changes in broadcasting, and for not having become the servant of the Ministry of Communication.[65]

In 1985, the government commissioned a report on possible future directions for audiovisual communications media. The Brédin Report, as it became known, urged the expanded development of privately financed television, but within a complementary system: Public broadcasting would continue to play a major role, and private broadcasting would have certain public service obligations, such as 60 percent European program content for private TV. Media reaction generally was favorable, but some critics wanted full-blown competition between the public and private systems, in part because that would create more jobs in TV. Government officials were generally positive, with Mitterand advocating that obligations be placed on private operators through the licensing process.[66]

In November 1985 the government signed an agreement with a private consortium to permit the latter to place a private network, La Cinq (Channel 5) on the air, probably by late February 1986. Here, too, politics likely played a role. Sixty percent of the shares in the new company were to be owned by a group headed by a "wealthy industrialist with left-wing sympathies," but the remainder were to be held by Italian commercial television magnate Silvio Berlusconi. Furthermore, La Cinq would begin its broadcasts a few weeks before the next national election, which presumably would help to remind voters of how respectful the Socialists were of their wishes.[67] (Surveys indicated that many viewers felt that commercial TV would improve their range of program choice significantly.)

The March 1986 election resulted in a moderate loss of seats in the National Assembly for the Socialists—just enough to allow a Conservative coalition to take over the reins of government (although Mitterand remained president) and to overturn many of the major changes that the Socialist government had brought about in media policy. A few weeks after the election, Conservative government officials announced that they would abolish the Haute Autorité and replace it with a national commission on audiovisual communication that would have broader powers than the Autorité. Those officials also announced their intentions to revoke the license of La Cinq, to break the previous government's agreement with the European Consortium regarding operation of a communications satellite, and to convert one and possibly two of the three public TV services to private networks. While French broadcasting clearly had become far more diverse and objective during the five years of Socialist rule, the Conservative victory served as a fresh reminder of the ephemeral character of French broadcast regulation. Diversity was to increase under the new government in the sense that there probably would be more TV stations authorized, but how objective they'd be was anyone's guess, and past experience under the Conservatives wasn't very reassuring.

The "New Conservative" Era (1986–1988)

The broadcast law that finally passed in September 1986 in some ways was a matter of old wine in new bottles. The Haute Autorité would be abolished, but the National Commission for Communications and Liberties (CNCL) that would replace it bore a marked resemblance to it. The CNCL would have 13 members, six of them appointed in much the same political fashion as had been all appointees to the HA, three more to be appointed by and to come from the judiciary, one member of the prestigious Academie Française (chosen by the Academie), and three members representing audiovisual creation, telecommunication and the print media (chosen by the 10 other committee members). Members would have nine-year terms, which would be neither renewable nor revocable, and they would elect their own chair.

The CNCL's duties went beyond those of the Autorité. They included the licensing of private broadcasting and cable networks, appointment of senior personnel in public broadcasting, monitoring of advertising and of children's programs, and the safeguarding of public interests in the form of election broadcasts, anticompetitive practices, and equal treatment of users of telecommunication services. They also would advise on numerous aspects of telecommunications policy.[68]

Whether the CNCL could play a truly independent role remained to be seen. On the one hand, it had more power at its disposal than had the HA. On the other hand, it was subject to political appointment, for the most part, and the new Conservative government could prove just as loathe to give up power as had earlier Conservative governments. A test case soon arose: The new government had announced its intention to sell off one of the three public TV services, TF1 (Télévision Française 1). That announcement itself provoked a May 1986 strike by some public broadcasting staff and many discussions in Parliament and in public forums, such as letters to newspapers, as to whether this was a good idea and whether it was legal for a government to sell something that had "belonged" to the public. The public itself didn't seem too pleased at the prospect of "losing" TF1 to private hands: There were protest demonstrations, petitions and surveys which suggested as much.[69] But the legality of the sale was confirmed, and the CNCL had the duty of examining bids, taking testimony on the merits of the proposals, and then selecting the winner.

The process ended in April 1987. In the meantime, several bids had appeared, some were withdrawn or were merged with other bids, and finally there were two combatants left to battle for a prize that would cost the victor Fr 3 billion ($500 million) for 50 percent ownership. One was a consortium headed by the Hachette publishing firm, which already operated a TV production house, had part ownership in the French-language commercial station Europe No. One, and enjoyed close ties with Conservative politicians. The other consortium was headed by Bouygues, France's largest construction firm, with Robert Maxwell, an English "media baron," as a 10 percent investor. Betting was on Hachette, with its Conservative connections, and the chair of the CNCL, Gabriel de Broglie, had even given Hachette some advice regarding ways of making the application stronger.[70] But when the vote came, a majority favored the Bouygues application. One reason appeared to be that Bouygues indicated more of a commitment to domestic program production than did Hachette, and another that awarding TF1 to Hachette would give it an even more dominant position in the mass media, but commission members also may have been put off by Hachette's seeming assumption that it obviously was the stronger candidate and enjoyed support in politically influential quarters. In other words, the commission didn't consider itself a rubber stamp and showed it as clearly as possible.[71]

The privatization of TF1 was part of a larger pre-election promise made by the Conservatives. They were furious that Mitterand and the Socialists had authorized private television shortly before the general election of 1986 and thus had been able to award licenses for the two services to their own "deserving" friends. The Conservatives almost immediately promised that they would withdraw those license grants, but they soon discovered that the licensing terms included a provision that would force the government to pay a considerable sum in compensation to the two groups that held the licenses if they were withdrawn. When the CNCL considered the relicensing issue in February 1987, it awarded the license for La Cinq to a group made up of Conservative publisher Robert Hersant (who really had wanted TF1, but who withdrew from that race) and Berlusconi-Seydoux, the majority owners of the old La Cinq. That settled that compensation issue. Le Six was less of a problem, since there was a much smaller investment in it, and it was re-awarded to the Companie Luxembourgeoise de Télédiffusion and to Lyonnaise des Eaux, a major utilities group, which also was involved with cable. (The company's chairman, Jérome Monod, was a close personal friend of Conservative Prime Minister Jacques Chirac.) In both awards, there also were smaller shareholders, primarily banks.[72]

The political independence of CNCL was called into question when the French press revealed in November 1987 that its relicensing of FM stations in the Paris region seemed to have been influenced by political and economic factors, for example, licensing a new Arabic-language station (France Maghreb Media) because one of its backers was "close to" the office of the mayor of Paris. Several stations lost their licenses in the process, but the CNCL gave no specific reasons for its decisions. Some of the losers brought a court case against one member of the CNCL; he was indicted for "passive corruption" (taking a bribe) in 1988,[73] and in 1989 de Broglie resigned as chair of the CNCL, in disgrace and named in a lawsuit.[74]

The new government announced late in 1986 that it was reconsidering policy on cable and satellite development, and that it was not prepared to subsidize the development of either or both to the extent that the Socialist government had been. Cable could develop freely, but the government would not insist upon widespread installation of two-way cable, which the Socialist government had supported. Satellites could go ahead, but the financial risks clearly would have to be those of the potential users. Both moves were consonant with a free enterprise philosophy, but both also removed France from the ranks of those nations seeking to develop fiber-optic cable and satellites to result in foreign sales of technology and thus a boost for the domestic economy.[75]

The major media reform of the Conservative government—the privatization of TF1—was working out beautifully as an example of free enterprise. The network dominated the commercial TV scene, while La Cinq and Le Six (M6) lagged far behind in commercial revenue and were proving to be champion money-losers. La Cinq in particular had suffered from its ambition: the huge salaries it paid to attract prominent talent from TF1 had drained its resources, and most of the new hires had left La Cinq within the year. The channel's losses were roughly Fr 850 million (c. $170 million) in 1987 and Fr 840 million (c. $168 million) in 1988. It began to devote more and more time to inexpensive game shows and U.S. series.

M6 followed along much the same path. It had been licensed as a music channel catering largely to the youth market. When it was reassigned to new owners in 1987, its new charter called for a schedule of 40 percent music and 60 percent general programming. That forced it to compete more directly with TF1, La Cinq and A2. It, too, turned more heavily to U.S. series as a solution.

At that point, the CNCL intervened. It had been heavily criticized for its apparent political bias, but also for its relative inaction in enforcing government-decreed quotas on amounts of French and European programming to be carried by TV stations. In spring 1988, the CNCL reviewed the quota issue in its examination of the schedules of all three commercial TV services. For the quota of 50 percent French programming, TF1 had 34 percent, the other two roughly 25 percent each; for the quota of 60 percent European (including French) programming, TF1 had 39 percent, the other two roughly 35 percent each. All three were ordered to comply with the rules starting in 1989, or face fines ranging from Fr 20,000 to Fr 60,000 (slightly under $4,000 to c. $11,500) per hour of program time needed to reach the quota. TF1 was particularly criticized for "getting around the law by showing 80 percent of its French and European programs at [late] night, when viewing is practically nil."[76] TF1's obvious hope was to make plenty of money by broadcasting lots of inexpensive but popular U.S. programs during prime-time hours, whatever that might say about the drawing power of French-made fare. La Cinq tried to get around the quota by claiming that an American-made movie which had not been shown in France was really a "telefilm," and didn't count as a movie. The CNCL ruled against La Cinq, and the Conseil d'Etat, to which the private broadcasters then took their cases, upheld the regulatory agency.[77]

That was to be the last major act of the CNCL. The French presidential election took place in 1988, with the Conservatives sensing victory over François Mitterand. During the campaign Mitterand suggested that the body responsible for broadcast regulation (currently the CNCL) be strengthened by constitutionally guaranteeing its existence.[78] He had managed to retain some degree of influence over broadcasting even during the previous two years, when the Conservatives held a clear majority in Parliament, and rumors about that influence circulated during the presidential election campaign. One of the more unusual claims (probably true), made by the newspaper *Quotidien de Paris,* was that, during the campaign, A2's station identification symbol bore the faint but distinguishable image of Mitterand![79] He was reelected; then the Socialist Party won a plurality in the parliamentary election of 1989, formed a coalition with the Communist Party, and soon thereafter France had its third broadcast regulatory commission in seven years.

The Return of the Socialists (1989–1993)

The new commission took on a new name—Conseil Supérieure de l'Audiovisuel—but structurally resembled the old HA and CNCL. The CSA quickly picked up on an initiative that had Socialist roots: devolution of political power to local authorities. However, this particular form of local power owed its existence to the CNCL, which had decided in the late 1980s to license private local TV stations in as many as three dozen communities throughout France. That decision fit in nicely with the Socialist creation of local private radio in the early 1980s, and the CSA wasted little time in licensing three such stations, in Lyon, Mount Blanc and Toulouse. They were to earn most of their income through advertising—a source of income more often associated with Conservative governments, but the Socialists had already shown that it was perfectly acceptable to them, as well. There was skepticism about the practicality of local advertising as the chief source of revenue, since most private local radio stations had found it difficult to interest local businesses in spending their francs on radio advertising, but the stations found ways to cut corners: they took the bulk of their programming from Télé Monte Carlo or other syndication sources, and thus held down costs. Even so, all three stations, plus two more (in Nimes and in the Périgord region, just outside Sarlat-la-Caneda), lost quite heavily, although the Toulouse and Lyon stations showed signs of beginning to turn the financial corner by the mid-1990s.[80]

Local television also was becoming available to certain communities that had cable TV. The first full coaxial cable service was introduced in Biarritz in 1981. By the end of 1989, there were some 70 such services around the country—a very slow rate of growth. Furthermore, subscribership also was low: Few of the cable companies had more than a few thousand subscribers. Because the companies were so unprofitable, the CSA decided not to require them to provide locally originated programming, although the law allowed it to do so.[81] As of the late 1990s, there may be no more than two dozen (out of several hundred) local cable companies which furnish local programming.[82]

The Socialist government of the early to mid-1980s had placed considerable emphasis on the development of communication satellites. The Conservative government that succeeded the Socialists de-emphasized that development, at least to the extent of spending large sums of governmental funds on it, but it did get off the ground, so to speak. The TéléDiffusion Française (TDF) project was to support itself largely through user fees, and there were hopes that the technology would be so superior that it would become a moneymaker on the international market. No such luck. The TDF-1 and TDF-2 satellites made it off the launch pad, but four of the 12 transponders on the two satellites malfunctioned. Since the annual rental price per transponder was set at $12.5 million, that represented a potential loss of $50 million; worse yet, it made potential users, not to mention potential purchasers of the technology, more than a little wary. There also were hopes that the satellite system would spur the development of DBS services, but that didn't occur, either.[83]

What the satellites did affect was the development of local radio. By the end of the 1980s, there were approximately 1,500 local radio stations scattered around France. Many of them had started life as very modest operations, closely tied to various interest groups—political, cultural, religious, etc.—in their communities. The groups had a great deal of energy at first, but little financial support for the long term, and even after advertising was allowed on the stations, many of them found that advertisers were few in number. The one great exception was the pop music services—NRJ, Radio Nostalgie, FUN Radio, etc.—originating in Paris and spreading to other large cities. Using satellites, the services set up full national networks at low cost, and many local groups were happy to recoup some of their losses when NRJ and others came around with buy-out offers. The stations promptly lost their localness, except for occasional local advertising inserts (most of the advertising was national) and station IDs that linked the names of the old stations and the new owners.[84]

The CSA proved to be a tougher regulator than had its two predecessors. It was particularly tough on broadcasters who violated the already-established quotas on French content. Its staff was too small to keep track of radio stations all over the country, but it could check on the activities of the major radio networks. Its efforts to enforce a 30 percent French music quota probably helped to stimulate the French popular music industry, although much of the output bore heavy marks of American and British influence. Its real impact came with television, which was much easier to track, since there were relatively few networks and very few local TV operations. The two remaining public TV networks, A2 and FR3, had little difficulty meeting the 50 percent French content rule, but the commercial services—La Cinq, M6 and even TF1—found the task much more difficult. That was chiefly because of the large sums they spent in attracting and retaining top-quality performers, who were in short supply. The reluctance of French advertisers to shift more of their advertising budgets in the direction of television didn't help, either.

French independent television producers soon attempted to band together in order to fight the strict quota requirements, but also CSA restrictions on commercial breaks in dramas (only one break within a drama, which led private services to broadcast more game shows and less drama, since the game shows could be interrupted more often). But their specific interests proved to be far enough apart that the group, Television for Tomorrow, was relatively ineffective. Some group members predicted economic disaster for French electronic media operations if the quotas weren't relaxed, arguing that private services couldn't afford to purchase large amounts of French-produced material, which is considerably more expensive per hour than is programming purchased from abroad.[85]

The CSA pressed on, and the prediction of disaster soon came true. La Cinq was in poor financial shape by the early 1990s, and sought relief from the CSA quota requirements. Instead, the CSA threatened to take away its license because of its inability to meet its financial obligations. La Cinq declared bankruptcy in 1992, and, after several potential buyers (Canal Plus and Berlusconi included) bowed out, the service went off the air in April 1992 with a broadcast "wake," still owing tens of millions of dollars to various production companies.[86] Its vacant channels around the country then were made available to a new French-German noncommercial TV service, Arte. La Cinq's disappearance also helped M6 and TF1, since they now had one less commercial competitor, albeit one with low ratings. Whether the CSA's persistence in enforcing the quota scared M6 and TF1 into complying more closely with that quota is another question; TF1 in particular continues to receive fines from time to time for quota violations, but the profitability of the imported programming apparently offsets the fines, and any negative publicity surrounding them doesn't seem to matter.

The great success story of the 1980s was Canal Plus, the over-the-air (and now on satellite and cable) pay-TV service. By the early 1990s, roughly 15 percent of all French households subscribed to it, and it had created partnerships in Germany, Spain and Belgium. It had no problem with quotas, since well over 50 percent of its airtime was and is devoted to French-produced material, mostly feature-length movies which are repeated frequently. It even created its own film production studio, and made numerous coproductions with other European production houses.[87]

Involvement in coproductions outside France was slow in coming, thanks to the CSA's insistence that they display overwhelmingly French involvement—scripts written in French, largely French-speaking casts, etc.—in order to qualify as French content. The European Community had begun in 1991 to encourage just such coproductions through its MEDIA Fund, and several French studios, including two of the largest (Studio Canal Plus and Hamster Production), were entering into more and more of them. But the struggle between the more internationally minded media operations and the "French TV for French audiences" quota supporters seemed very much in line with the overall development of French broadcasting over the decades.

Being French in the 1990s

If politics is a spectator sport, the French must have gotten their money's worth in the period running from 1981 to 1998. No government managed to stay in power for more than five years at a time, and most lasted less than that. In 1993, the Socialists lost their slim parliamentary margin and were replaced by the Conservatives. President Mitterand then announced that he would not run for a third term (he had cancer, and died in 1995). Conservative leader and then-Prime Minister Jacques Chirac ran for the presidency in 1995 and was elected.

Before and during the 1993 parliamentary election campaign, some of the Conservative candidates and their supporters had raised the possibility of getting rid of the CSA and installing something more like the old CNCL.[88] TF1 was closely connected with several Conservative politicians, and the many fines that the CSA had levied against the private TV service had angered its chief executives. To TF1's surprise, the Conservative victory brought no such change. According to former CSA staff member Guillaume Sainteny, the Conservative leaders decided that scrapping the CSA and creating what would be the fourth electronic media regulatory agency in 11 years would sharply reduce public confidence in whatever the new agency might do; it would be seen as too obviously political, even for a nation well accustomed to such moves.[89] As a result, the CSA functioned under the Conservative government much as it had functioned under the Socialists, and appears to have gained a reputation for being relatively free from political pressure and relatively strict in enforcing its own regulations.

The battle over quotas continued, with the private operations—radio, TV and cable (DBS operations were insignificant at the time)—complaining about the difficulty of making a profit in such tightly regulated circumstances. The CSA eased the qualifications for coproductions somewhat, but basic content regulations for TV—50 percent French production, 60 percent European (including French)—remained in place. The French music quota for radio stations actually became tougher—40 percent, starting in 1996, replacing the former level of 30 percent. Stations complained that average time spent listening to the radio was declining, largely, they felt, because there wasn't enough good French pop music that suited the tastes of younger listeners.[90]

The competitive playing field also appeared to level off a bit during the mid-1990s. TF1 dominated the market in terms of shares of audience until 1992; France 2 then began to recover some of its lost ground, primarily at the expense of TF1, and sometimes came out ahead of the latter with certain specific shows and on certain evenings. However, there was some concern among critics and viewers as to whether France 2's recovery had come at the expense of quality and diversity. Most of the channel's successful shows were mysteries ("Maigret"), reality-based programs ("La Nuit des Héroes") and game and quiz shows ("Fort Boyard"). The basic strategy had been set late in 1991, when A2 chairman Herve Bourges announced that he would cut low-rated programs such as the news by nearly $10 million, and put an additional $17 million into sports and original programming.[91] France 3 also gained a bit of ground, perhaps because of an increase in airtime for regional programming, which proved very popular if only because viewers had had so little of it up to that time.

Canal Plus continued its expansion, and had four million subscribers by the mid-1990s: roughly a third of all French TV households. Its satellite service, Canal Satellite, was founded in 1993, and had over 500,000 subscribers by 1997. Canal Plus already had moved into a number of other European markets, and by 1996 was involved in joint television ventures in Spain, Belgium, Germany and the Netherlands. It also invested in a number of cinema coproductions in other countries, not least of all the United States. Cable and satellite subscriptions continued to grow slowly—a situation certainly not helped by France's continuing high unemployment rate (roughly 12 percent as of late 1997), although satellite households showed some promising growth starting in the mid-1990s, climbing to 1.5 million by 1997. Local television, both terrestrial and cable, remained modest, with virtually no growth in locally originated services during the mid-1990s. Videocassette recorders were in two out of every three households by the beginning of 1997.[92]

The Conservative government also began to prepare a new broadcast law that would deal more specifically with satellite services, now that they were acquiring sizeable numbers of subscribers. They were unregulated for the time being. The Conservatives already pass a bill (the 1994 loi Carignon) that allowed a single (including single corporation) shareholder to hold as much as

49 percent ownership in a media company, and had also given the TF1/M 6 satellite service, TPS (Télévision par Satellite), the *exclusive* right to France 2 and 3. That provided TPS with considerable advantage over Canal Satellite, and following its launch in December 1996, the new service gradually moved ahead of Canal Satellite in numbers of subscribers. The latter launched a new digital TV satellite-delivered service, Canal Satellite Numérique, in the same month, and subscribers have been quick to sign up: nearly 700,000 by the beginning of 1998. A third satellite service, AB Sat, had a trial period in 1996, and began to market itself in earnest by the end of the year, but lagged far behind its two competitors. In short, the Conservatives took very good care of private industry.

It was not good enough, however, to keep them in power. A Socialist coalition replaced the Conservatives in mid-1997 and promised new media legislation; the prime minister, Lionel Jospin, had made a point in his campaign speeches of berating the Conservatives for favoring the private sector and neglecting the public services, especially France 2 and 3. (A report commissioned by the new government and released in November 1997 noted that the two services were poorly administered, inefficient, and suffered from low morale and neglect by the government.)[93] The new government expected to introduce the legislation in Parliament by spring 1998. That didn't come to pass, for a variety of reasons, of which two stand out. First, Jospin's advisors appeared to lack a full understanding of the rapidly-changing media landscape, and the bill that they drafted largely failed to take into account the need to harmonize French audiovisual policy with evolving pan-European policy; second, the new minister of culture and communication, Catherine Trautmann, was highly intelligent but lacked a full understanding of the complexities of moving a bill through Parliament.

She also did something very unusual in French political life: she actually sought to consult *in advance of* submitting the bill to Parliament with the various parties who would be affected by the proposed legislation—public and private broadcasters (even the small community radio stations), new media service providers, etc. The draft bill, dubbed la loi de l'audiovisuel, limited individual investors in the electronic media to 25 percent ownership, pushed the CSA to move away from its overall policy of near-automatic renewal of licenses and toward a closer examination of licensees, and sought to open up competition in satellite services. Predictably, private industry blasted away at the bill because it "stifled competition," the PSBs felt that it offered very little promise of helping them to retain their viability, and a number of the Socialist Party's more important figures saw it as far too easy on private industry. The print media admired Trautmann's intelligence, sincerity, and energy (she met with dozens of groups, many of them visibly hostile), but questioned her political acumen. After two redrafts (one of them containing the provision that the government, and not the CSA, should appoint the heads of the major PSB companies—a pre-1981 practice that the Socialists got rid of as soon as they came to power in 1981), Prime Minister Jospin announced on December 1, 1998, that the bill would be withdrawn and resubmitted in the spring of

1999. As the year closed, few were prepared to say what might eventually become of the loi de l'audiovisuel. [94]

The Threads of History

Looking across the history of French electronic media, a number of threads emerge: continuous *political* influence, especially from the party or coalition in power; a conviction that the media should be French in *cultural* content first and foremost, but insufficient *financial* support to make that commitment more meaningful; and widespread indifference on the part of the general public toward political manipulation of the media. Some of those same threads emerge in the media histories of other industrialized nations, but the particular forms in which they've manifested themselves in France seem to have made the general public, and certainly the intellectual elite, more cynical about the electronic media than it is elsewhere. *Economics,* linked with politics, is playing an increasingly important role, but *technological* development lags although satellite TV is beginning to take hold.

FINANCING

The public service system in France (Radio France, France 2, France 3, La Cinquieme, Le Sept and Arte) derives its financial support mainly from license fees and, for all but La Cinquieme, from advertising. It also earns modest revenues through sale of its programs abroad, mainly to other French-speaking nations. (Many programs, however, are free of charge to former French colonies in the Third World, since the French government feels that those programs help to maintain the French cultural presence abroad.) The joint French-German TV service, Arte, as well as La Cinquieme, are also supported by annual government appropriations. Also, the government may make special assistance grants to the public stations, as it did in 1994, when France 2 and France 3 asked it for one billion francs in order to balance their budgets (they received 640 million). The private sector, radio and TV alike, relies almost entirely upon advertising to generate its income, although the handful of local television stations also has received operating subsidies from city and department (regional) governments. Canal Plus, the DBS satellite services and the cable companies depend upon subscriber fees. As of 1997, Canal Plus charged subscribers Fr 175 (about $30) per month, and the satellite services such as AB charged as little as Fr 45 (about $8.20),[95] and Canal Satellite Numérique (CSN) Fr 120 ($20) per month for basic service (eight channels on AB; 27 on CSN). Some of the cable companies and Canal Plus earn modest revenues from the sale of advertising time. Noncommercial community radio stations receive on average $50,000 per year in the form of subsidies from the national government.

License fees are set by Parliament, although broadcast administrators may suggest increases whenever they choose. Increases come about, on the average, every four years. As we've already seen, Parliament is quite willing to use license fee revenue as a club to hold over the heads of public broadcasters. As of 1998, owners of black-and-white TV sets pay Fr 471 ($85) a year, while color set owners pay Fr 735 ($130) a year. There's a value-added tax (VAT) on the license fee, as well. Over a third of all households with black-and-white sets only are exempt from paying the fee on grounds of war injuries, old age, etc. There are no exemptions for color TV set households, on the grounds that anyone owning a color set can't be all that economically disadvantaged. There are no license fees for radio sets. Between 20 and 25 percent of all French households pay no license fees; that, coupled with a fee that's low by European standards, virtually guarantees that the public TV channels badly need another source of income—in this case, advertising.

There have been ads on French public TV since 1968—20 minutes per day per channel at first, rising slightly to the present 24 minutes per day. But they were a major source of income for the two national channels, TF1 and A2, partly because there was no real competition until early 1986. In fact, while the quality-points system described earlier was in force, those two channels paid little attention to it, because the amount of money they would receive for putting on high-quality shows paled in comparison with what they could make by putting on highly popular shows.[96] One reason the Mitterand government dropped the quality-points system in the early 1980s was that it seemed to make so little difference in program quality, especially in view of all the effort that went into making the quality assessments.

Because airtime for ads was so limited before 1986, the two most popular TV channels, TF1 and Antenne 2, often weren't able to accept all demands for ad time; a 1982 estimate for Antenne 2 indicated that the channels had to turn away 70 percent of all requests.[97] What made ad time especially attractive before private television came was that it was sold mostly for the early to middle evening time block (6:30 to 8:30 p.m.), when the largest audiences would be present. Also, the price per second was the same whether the ad ended up next to "Dallas" or next to a low-rated show. (Ads cannot interrupt shows on public stations; they're clustered in short blocks between programs.)

The first two private TV stations to be licensed didn't affect that situation materially, because the stations started out modestly, covering only Paris and its environs. La Cinq grew faster than did Le Six (it was better-financed), but by early 1988 still reached only about half of the nation's TV households. However, the privatization of TF1 brought profound changes to television advertising practices. The TF1 service already had full national coverage, and now it had to rely wholly on advertising, with no license fee to offset expenses. That gave advertisers access to more airtime, but also gave TF1 the incentive to get as much of their business as possible. The growth in coverage area of La Cinq and of Métropole TV (the new title for Le Six, usually shortened to M6) helped to increase their ad revenues, but TF1's national coverage virtually guaranteed it 40 to 50 percent of the viewership from the moment that it was reborn as a commercial operation, and made it the overwhelming choice of most advertisers. And when La Cinq folded, that helped TF1 all the more.

When TF1 was privatized, the government cut the annual license fee, so that A2 and FR3 received only what they had received before privatization. (However, the fee began to increase by the early 1990s.) TF1's obvious advantage in terms of sales of ad time led A2 and, to a lesser degree, FR3 to request greater freedom to advertise: more time, fewer product restrictions and so on. The commercial TV services strongly and successfully opposed such an adjustment, and the two public TV services had to manage on smaller budgets, because the increased competition for viewers left them with smaller shares of audience, making them less attractive to advertisers. The PSBs continue to deal with tight budgets. Their government appropriation for 1996 contained an increase of roughly 3 percent; the increase for 1997 was just under 2 percent[98]—not enough to keep up with inflation. That encouraged the 1997 administrative merger of La Sept/Arte and La Cinquieme.

Certain products may not be advertised: alcoholic beverages (including beer), tobacco products, tourism, jewelry, retail stores, building societies, publishing and computers. Most of those restrictions are designed to protect print media ad revenues. Also, toys and pharmaceutical products require special authorization. Sponsored programming hasn't been allowed on the public channels, but Canal Plus can and does accept it (the channel also has a noontime talk show program which is advertiser-supported and which is not "scrambled," so that anyone can watch it), the private stations certainly want it, and the remaining public channels probably will wish to follow suit. That has had some effect on programming, with increased need for cheaper programs that please a larger audience. There also are "télé-achat" (teleshopping) programs, such as TF1's morning teleshopping show, two cable and satellite shopping channels (Club du Téléachat and Télé Achat), and a classified ad service, Canal Plus-owned Rapido Annonces. None of those cable and satellite services comes into more than a fourth of the approximately 10 percent of French households subscribing to cable.[99]

The introduction of TV advertising on the regional service, FR3, came in January 1983 to a few of its 12 regional public TV stations, and expanded to include most of them by the end of the 1980s. It was highly controversial. The regional press, most of which is much weaker financially than its Parisian counterpart, worried that this would bite deeply into its already none-too-substantial revenues, and some critics claimed that the Socialists would profit from a weakened regional press because so many of the papers were anti-Socialist—the same argument that was applied against the Conservatives when TV advertising was introduced in 1968! But so far there has been no great exodus of advertising money to regional TV, where the ads are very simply produced and where regional and local advertisers still seem to have a low regard for broadcast advertising. After all, they've had little previous experience with it. Local private radio and TV stations carry ads for a wide variety of local and regional products and services, usually for very low rates. The local TV stations complain particularly about not being allowed by the CSA to carry ads for nationally-marketed products and services—a measure that is in place to help protect local newspapers. Private station staff have told me that business is slow because local advertisers are conservative, and so far the regional and local press don't appear to have lost much business to radio.

The HA and the CNCL had the legal right to monitor broadcast advertising, but didn't exercise the right very often. The CSA had the same right, until the Bureau de Validisation de la Publicité (BVP) was given the task in the mid-1990s, and was slightly more zealous in exercising it. With some 1,500 local radio stations around the country and 200 staff members, frequent monitoring was out of the question, and isn't any more likely under the BVP.

GOVERNANCE AND ADMINISTRATION—INTERNAL

In sharp contrast to most of the other systems covered in this book, the internal governance and administration of French broadcasting is quite simple to describe. Each of the companies within the national public broadcasting organization (the old ORTF), excepting France 2 and France 3 (A2 and FR3 were renamed France 2 and France 3 in late 1992), is headed by a president appointed by the government. One president heads France 2 and 3—supposedly a cost-saving measure,[100] although there are suspicions that this was done to make it easier for the government to influence public TV. All but one of the companies has an administrative council of five to 10 members, chosen variously by the National Assembly, the Senate and the chief executive (president of the republic). Most of the top administrative positions in the companies also pass under government review, but the broadcast regulatory agency (at present, the CSA) ultimately approves them. Administrators acquired more freedom to make decisions following the 1982 Socialist reforms, but government officials of whatever political party still feel freer to intervene in broadcast decision-making in France than they do in any other west European country. Nor do they intervene solely in the case of news and informational programs. In 1982, Regis Debray, cultural advisor to President Mitterand, told a press conference that he felt that a highly sophisticated (and very popular, often drawing 5 million viewers)[101] book review show, "Apostrophes," was being run too dictatorially by its host. Debray stated, "We have some plans to relieve that program of its monopoly on the choice of titles and authors."[102] As it turned out, President Mitterand was a devoted fan of the show, and nothing happened to it, but Debray was operating on the basis of a long-standing assumption that it was perfectly normal for government officials and advisors to tell broadcasters what to do.

Up until 1981, almost all decision-making power resided at the national level, but the new Socialist government had featured decentralization as one of its campaign pledges, and that applied to broadcasting as well as to many other enterprises. The considerable increases in amounts of airtime for regional TV productions, plus the creation of several new "local" (really subregional) public radio stations, expanded the possibilities for local decision-making. Station managers were appointed by broadcast administrators in

Paris and usually came from the ranks of those who had had experience in the national public system, but they might well come from the regions or cities served by the stations, and they would have to be prepared to make decisions without referring them back to Paris. My visits to regional and local stations in 1983, 1984, 1986, 1989 and 1995 revealed that local station managers were reasonably autonomous, although they were unlikely to program material that challenged the establishment point of view.[103] Broadcasts by avid Breton nationalists, for example, would be a rarity over Radio Bretagne Ouest, although there could be news items about some of their activities, and they might appear on discussion programs.[103a]

Where production of programs is concerned, French public broadcast administrators have other problems. The first is lack of money, or at least lack of money to spend on production. Most government commissions on broadcasting have noted that the system is top-heavy with management, and commissions reporting on the 1974 reform soon found that the division into separate companies added to economic inefficiency. Each company could produce a fair share of its own programs, so long as they were done in the small studios and with the modest technical facilities available. News programs, interviews, talk shows and so on, all fell into that category. Larger productions had to be put up for bids, and the "official" TV production company, SFP, was long expected to be chosen often enough that it at least would spend its own budget—this despite allegations that the productions of the official company often cost two to three times what an independent production company would charge for the same product.[104] That situation led to a second administrative problem: lack of control over program costs. There was little that an administrator could do to spend production money wisely when so much of it was outside her or his control. In short, it was not an administrative system where staff found much scope for the exercise of traditional administrative talents.

Commercial competition brought some changes, particularly in the direction of creating a need for more French electronic media production houses. SFP slipped badly in this highly competitive new world, and began to run up losses in the tens of millions of dollars. That same competition forced A2 to cut back sharply on its production budget, and it had been SFP's largest client. SFP cut roughly a third of its staff in 1991, and began to solicit coproduction work outside of France.[105] While its financial situation has improved slightly since then, it still isn't a sound or very efficient operation. The newer, smaller production houses have a decided edge in flexibility. However, the economic recession of the early 1990s, coupled with the demise of La Cinq and the large losses of revenue by A2 and FR3, depressed the production market for virtually everyone. As of mid-1992, France's top 20 production houses had an estimated turnover of $40 million or less, with very low profitability rates for about 70 percent of those houses, and losses for the others.[106]

In theory, the administrative councils associated with the public services (they aren't required for private stations) could act as a force for improvement, but in practice most council members haven't seen themselves in the role of whistle-blower or efficiency expert. Most are in political sympathy with the company president, and in personal sympathy with the services from the standpoint of acknowledging the lack of money and/or power to change things in any fundamental way. There have been changes, to be sure, and council members and presidents have helped to bring about some of them, but the scope for change is decidedly limited.

There's also a small measure of self-regulation in the form of establishing self-regulatory guidelines. In 1994, TF1's editorial board developed a set of 18 "ethical principles," such as respecting privacy, restricting scenes of violence, etc. However, those principles affect only the newsroom's output, and have no effect on other programs broadcast by TF1, including reality-based shows and news magazines not prepared by the newsrooms.[107]

GOVERNANCE AND ADMINISTRATION—EXTERNAL

Governmental

The National Government

As should be amply evident by now, the French government, and the executive branch in particular, has a great deal to say about the way in which electronic media operate. There are direct appointment powers, held by the president, the National Assembly and the Senate. There is also the unofficial power of approval of still other appointments, which is exercised chiefly by the president and/or the prime minister—the former if the president and the parliamentary majority are from the same party, the latter if they are not. Thus, there is a virtual guarantee that any individual who occupies a high-level position within French public broadcasting will be at least mildly favorable to the majority party of the moment. The 1982 Broadcast Law contained provisions designed to help make certain appointments somewhat less political—members of the Haute Autorité were chosen for nine-year, nonrenewable terms and could not be removed from office for other than serious crimes—and the 1986 Broadcast Law took the same approach. Still, the Socialists lost little time in replacing broadcast administrators sympathetic to the Giscard administration with administrators who would be more in tune with the Socialist philosophy, and the Conservatives returned the favor shortly after they resumed power. When the Socialists succeeded the Conservatives in 1989, their coalition government lacked the political strength necessary to carry out any major changes, besides which the growth in electronic media outlets made public broadcasting services less important as instruments for shaping public opinion. Nor did the Conservatives return to power in 1993 bring the sort of major housecleaning that had occurred in earlier decades.

The National Assembly continues to exercise considerable control over public broadcasting through the budget. It approves the annual license fee and also approves the annual budget for the public service broadcasting system. The Ministry of Finance also is involved in approval of the annual budget. The days of line-by-line approval of specific expenditures are long since gone, but it's a rare year that lacks prolonged hearings on that budget. Furthermore, both the Assembly and the Senate appoint special committees to examine in detail one or another aspect of broadcasting, and financial issues have been frequent targets. Unfortunately for the public broadcasters, those examinations often turn up evidence of carelessness, wastefulness and even improper handling of finances. Given such a legacy, it's difficult for public broadcasters to reassure government officials that they deserve still greater fiscal freedom. The National Assembly and the Senate also have the power to approve or disapprove laws relating to the electronic media, but the ruling party, if it so wishes, is able to push through laws that it desires and to remove "unfriendly" amendments to those laws. It also can proclaim decrees that have the force of law, and that often have much more influence on the workings of the media system than do the laws themselves. Those decrees can be discussed by the Assembly and the Senate but cannot be modified or repealed by them.

The Courts

In theory, the judicial system plays a role in broadcast regulation, in that it's possible for individuals to bring right of reply cases to the courts for possible redress, if the special right of reply commission hasn't produced a satisfactory (to the plaintiff) decision. Before 1982, they had to do so as individuals, not as members of larger groups, and the "offensive" broadcasts had to have been directed against them personally. Given those conditions, it wasn't surprising that few cases were brought to the courts. The 1982 law granted right of reply to "legal persons" as well, so that groups, organizations and corporations could be covered. So far, there have been few instances of requests for right of reply, which also has been incorporated in subsequent laws.[108]

There have been several court cases involving rights of transmission and rights of compensation. Before La Cinq came on the air, its owners got authorization from the national government (in this case, from the president) to use the Eiffel Tower as a transmitting tower. That enraged many people, including then-Mayor of Paris (and later, Prime Minister; after that, President) Jacques Chirac. The city of Paris took the case to the Constitutional Court, where it argued that the city had sovereign rights over the use of the Tower, which belongs to Paris. The Constitutional Court ruled in December 1985 that the national government's action was unconstitutional, mainly on the grounds that the basis for the action did not sufficiently protect the rights of owners of other tall structures. In less than two months, La Cinq gained access to the Tower, although only with the help of police, and even then it took several weeks more to clear away the remaining legal obstacles.[109] In a compensation case, the Council of State ruled in February 1987 that the former owners of La Cinq and Le Six were entitled to recompense for at least part of their investment; the national government had argued that the owners had been awarded the license illegally, and that no compensation was due.[110]

Cases involving programming arise far less often, but plagiarism was grounds for a $10 million award in 1993 by a French court of appeals (Versailles), which found that TF1 had copied one of A2's highly rated reality-based shows, "La Nuit des Héroes."[111]

Regulatory Agencies

There is no exact equivalent of the U.S. FCC, although the Haute Autorité, the CNCL and the CSA all bear some resemblance to it.[112] The HA was the first quasi-independent French regulatory agency for broadcasting, and its powers were quite broad, at least on paper: licensing of all private stations, appointment of top-level public broadcasting administrators, monitoring of "fairness" in broadcasting, conditions for allocation of airtime to politicians, promotion of regional languages and culture through broadcasting and so on.[113] The nine-member council (all full time, and paid quite well) was hampered in carrying out that sweeping mandate by three factors: a small support staff; a limited budget for travel; and the political process that appointed them in the first place, raising questions of independence from political control.

The first president of the HA, Michele Cotta, had excellent credentials as a broadcast journalist (France Inter, Luxembourg) and good connections with a wide assortment of politicians, and several other council members had media experience, but accusations of political bias quickly arose: When the council announced decisions on the first round of licensing for private radio stations in 1983, there were some complaints that the Autorité had been pressured by politicians not to award licenses to some of the fringe political groups seeking them. (However, there also were examples of such groups receiving licenses.) Furthermore, President Mitterand in effect told the council to approve his nomination for president of A2 in 1984, and the council complied. On the credit side, the council warned TF1's director general in 1985 to assure that the prime minister's monthly program be matched by time for the opposition. The French Council of State upheld the HA's action.[114]

The CNCL took up its duties late in 1986, with a mandate very similar to the HA's. Its initial action—the appointment of new administrative heads for the public broadcasting services—was not promising: Political "payoffs" seemed to govern the choices, which even the minister of culture and communications criticized for their low quality.[115] There was a greater show of independence in the awarding of TF1 to the Bouygues-Maxwell consortium, although that award, as well as the licenses for La Cinq and Le Six, went to known supporters of the Conservative coalition.

The CNCL also paid no more attention to private radio licensee performance than did the HA. Stations were required to provide service as community voices, but many that I observed did little but play recorded music. News was a rare commodity on most local private stations, and truly local news even rarer. When the CNCL relicensed stations in Paris in 1987, many of the more innovative special interest stations suddenly found themselves either off the air or forced to share a frequency with one or more groups. *Journal An-*

tennes Broadcast, one of the very few French broadcast periodicals (and, along with *Médias Pouvoirs,* the only critical periodical), referred to the relicensing as "The Battle of Paris," and criticized the CNCL for its unwillingness to disclose why it had taken away certain licenses and awarded others.[116] Some of the evicted stations simply became "pirate" operations, while stations dissatisfied with their frequency allocation or power limitations—and there were quite a few—ignored either or both. (I recall driving in and around Paris on two separate occasions in the late 1980s and finding several frequencies on the car radio where two or three stations were overlapping each other's signals.)

Given the lawsuits and other negative publicity concerning some CNCL commissioners, it was almost a foregone conclusion that, when the Socialists returned to power in 1989, they would abolish the CNCL and set up what would be the third electronic media regulatory agency in seven years. The "new" CSA resembled both of its predecessors in strengths and in limitations. It could penalize electronic media operations for technical and programmatic violations. It could regulate advertising (a function it lost in the mid-1990s to the Bureau de Vérification de la Publicité).[117] And it appoints the chairs of the public broadcasting operations, both at the national and regional levels. However, it also has differed in certain respects. It's been zealous in enforcing "French content" quotas, both under Socialist and Conservative governments. It also has regulated programs "unsuitable" for young viewers much more tightly: in 1989, it published a directive on juvenile protection that penalized media outlets which carried depictions of violence or eroticism between 6 a.m. and 10:30 p.m. Several broadcasters, but particularly TF1, La Cinq and M6, have been warned and occasionally fined for not observing the directive.[118] There's also a specific decree requiring TV outlets to warn viewers of the level of restriction (not for children under 12, not for children under 16) attached to films made for cinema distribution, but later shown over TV.[119]

Political influence on its decisions does occur from time to time. In fact, one of its first major appointments, of Philippe Guilhaume as head of the newly combined A2 and FR3 in 1989, upset the Socialist government to the point where its minister of communications made it clear that the government would make life very difficult for him, and it did: he resigned halfway through his term of office. As Jean-Claude Sergeant observes, " ... after this original political gaffe the CSA has toed the line by appointing unfailingly to the head of the various state-run broadcasting companies people who were known to be sympathetic to the left."[120] And when a Conservative government came to power in 1993, it soon pushed the CSA to replace many of the perfectly competent (but "left-wing") managers of France 3's regional stations with ("right-wing") managers.[121] However, its record with respect to political influence seems a bit better on the whole than the records of its predecessors.

The CSA has nine council members who actually make the rulings. Three are appointed by the president of the republic; three by the president of the National Assembly; and three by the president of the Senate. Each is supposed to have some background in the electronic media, and most do. Most are politically active, and well-connected with one or another party. They hold office for six years, and three seats come up for replacement (members may not be reappointed) every two years. The roughly 200 staff members are civil service employees, most with no fixed term of employment. The CSA has a range of powers: it issues licenses to all but the public stations, and can issue temporary licenses for stations to operate during local or regional fairs, cultural events, etc. It can issue warnings, which are published in the French government's official gazette. It can levy fines, and can suspend licenses for varying periods of time, during which the station may not broadcast. It can take licenses away, as well, but that's rare, and usually involves stations which already had stopped broadcasting on their own. It conducts or commissions research studies on the impact of the electronic media on society, and can request the Council of State to issue what amounts to a cease and desist order against a media outlet that isn't responding to the CSA's demands for action. And it continually prods the media to use "correct" French, although I've never known of a penalty levied for failure to do so.

As Marcel Machill indicates, the CSA has a particularly difficult task in regulating radio stations. It's nearly impossible to verify that the vast majority of stations specializing in music are following the quota (currently 40 percent French music), and indications are that the vast majority do not (each station proposes its quota at the time it applies for its license or renewal; once that is set, the station is required to abide by it). The CSA issues warnings, and often levies fines, but they tend to be modest: a few hundred to a few thousand dollars. If there are serious violations of the law (which rarely would involve music), the CSA may suspend a station's right to broadcast for a certain period of time, as it did with the national commercial station Skyrock in 1995. A news presenter on the station had repeatedly referred to the death of a policeman as "good news," and the Tribunal de Paris (law court) ordered the presenter to pay 25,000 francs (just under $4,000) to the family of the deceased. The CSA imposed a 24-hour broadcast ban on Skyrock, but the station then declared that it would use its facilities as an "open channel" for the day, and encouraged listeners to phone in comments and discussion. Machill feels that the CSA is caught between the proverbial rock and hard place: Governmental demands for French-language and content programming on the one hand; and the demands of a heavily commercial radio industry (the commercial stations account for nearly 80 percent of the radio audience), some of its members quite influential in political circles, for "loose" regulation on the other.[122]

The CSA also helps to protect licensed media outlets in one interesting way. The initial license is for a 10-year period. Under a 1994 law, the CSA is expected to renew the license without inviting any contesting applications for two additional five-year periods. It may set aside automatic renewal only when there's evidence of serious misconduct on the part of the licensee, or when the licensee has failed to "maintain pluralism" (meaning in practical terms that the licensee was strongly biased in presenting information and opinion). Licensees pay nothing for their licenses, although they must pay TDF for the costs of transmitting programs, since TDF operates their transmitters. Hearings for licenses are public. The CSA may set conditions for types of programming, but not for amounts of each type—and even the broader conditions seem to be no more than expectations. If there are competing applications for a given frequency, "pluralism" and a readiness to abide by restrictions on material unsuitable for children, etc., are supposed to guide the CSA's decisions.[123]

What it cannot do, aside from no longer regulating advertising, is to guarantee that the electronic media be free from political bias. No regulatory agency in the world can, but the CSA actually has the legal power to do so in one specific respect: there's a "three-thirds" rule requiring that any political material relating directly to the various parties and their activities be divided equally among the government (president and ministers), the parliamentary majority and the opposition (meaning *all* opposition parties with representation in Parliament). The CSA monitors programs and quantifies appearances by political parties, but admits that there are plenty of ways for the majority party to be the focus of bona fide news events, thus escaping the formal designation of "political material."[124] Hoffmann-Riem claims that the CSA itself regards the three-thirds rule as a failure, and Serge Régourd contends that the principle of pluralism supposedly represented in the rule clearly has not worked.[125]

Finally, although the CSA is supposed to function as a protector of the interests of the citizenry, individuals have no legal standing before the agency, and thus cannot bring cases on their own. They can seek right of reply, but must do so by sending a registered letter to the chairperson of the relevant media outlet, and, if that doesn't produce the desired result, can carry the case into the courts;[126] the CSA has nothing to do with it. However, a 1994 law does allow for complaints to be brought before the CSA through either "professional or trade organizations representing the broadcasting sector" or by "family associations."[127] The CSA has monitoring committees based around the country; they review license applications in their regions and make recommendations on the candidates to the home office in Paris. They also report on possible violations of license conditions.[128] Since the committees operate regionally, they should in theory be more accessible to family associations and the citizenry in general, but my own inquiries about their work seem to indicate that they do little or nothing to bring themselves to the attention of audience members, and most of their monitoring seems to involve technical violations (for example, broadcasting above the authorized power limits) and "French music content" quota violations, particularly by local radio stations.

Nongovernmental

The Public

Citizens' groups concerned with one or another aspect of broadcasting have been active in France since the 1930s, but they have limited legal standing and most of them suffer from a lack of continuity, funds, members, or all three. When parliament has considered media bills or appointed special commissions to examine broadcasting, group members have appeared to give testimony, but most of the groups appear to be active only at such times, and it's doubtful that they've made any lasting public impression. A French scholar conducting research on such groups told me in 1972 that many of them were temporary in nature, and some didn't even have members![129]

At moments of crisis—usually when the government and a particular staff group (e.g., journalists, producers, etc.) are in conflict—statements opposing the government's action will appear in some of the leading newspapers, signed not only by the staff group, but by some of the leading French intellectuals. So far, no one group has managed to attract the ongoing support of enough intellectuals to give itself the aura that might make it truly effective. Perhaps the problem is that most intellectuals don't have a particularly high opinion of broadcasting. They come to its defense when there's a specific freedom of speech issue but take little interest in pushing for any fundamental reform to the system. It also may be that they, or any other citizens who criticize the media, doubt their ability to influence any fundamental reform. It seems clear enough that the impetus for reform can and has come from both the legislative and executive branches of government, but the executive branch almost always has ended up dictating the specific nature of reform. If it's that difficult for citizens to influence governmental decisions, why bother trying?

Still, the 1990s have seen some fresh efforts, stimulated in part by an August 1989 conference of citizens concerned about TV. The conference stemmed from a series of debates held in eight cities, and sponsored by the Catholic magazine *La Vie* and the League for Instruction.[130] Much of the focus was on the negative effects of television on young people, as well as on the lack of positive programming for and about that group. The conference may have had some effect, because both the public and private sectors soon began to hold conferences, step up the reviewing of possibly objectionable programming, etc. Leading the way was Média, Télévision et Téléspectateurs (MTT), which has hosted annual conferences since 1990, confers awards for outstanding productions, publishes a monthly newsletter and works to improve media education.[131] Another group, Carton Jaune TV, is made up of an unusual coalition—lawyers and TV producers. Its most memorable feat was to bring a lawsuit against Patrick Poivre d'Arvor in 1993 for the TV newsman's faked "interview" with Fidel Castro.[132]

There also have been some prominent individual efforts to "reform" TV, such as a French mother's 1993 lawsuit against France 2 for having broadcast an episode from the U.S. TV series "MacGyver," in which the hero manufactured a homemade bomb. The mother claimed that her 17-year-old son and his friend had imitated MacGyver, and were killed in the explosion that followed. She saw the lawsuit as part of a campaign against TV violence, and various politicians, psychologists and others pledged support. The lawsuit failed, but there's been more debate about violence on TV, especially during the daytime. Canal Plus, responding to a viewer's letter of concern about violence, said, "We avoid broadcasting violent films during the hours when children are watching television," and reminded parents that they could block any Canal Plus program by using their decoders.[133]

Still, there was enough concern about the issue that the CSA and the TV networks agreed upon a five-level system of program classification, mainly to "protect" young viewers. It was designed to help parents and educators influence and supervise the viewing habits of that audience, but the CSA made it clear that it would be watching to see whether the networks and producers did their part in reducing levels of violence in the prime-time hours.[134] It entered into effect in mid-November 1997.

As noted earlier, it's possible for citizens and groups who feel that they have been treated unfairly in broadcasts to take their cases to the courts. For example, a law passed in 1984 makes it illegal for the media to present images deemed to be degrading to women: images that constitute "incitement to discrimination, hatred, violence, insult or defamation." A person or institution found guilty of violating the law could face a prison term of up to a year and fines of up to several thousand francs. So far, no such cases have been heard in court, perhaps because of the difficulty of proving that a specific image contained in a given media outlet actually incited a given act. Family associations also may use the courts to appeal instances of deception by the electronic media. (French law requires that the media be "truthful," but doesn't provide a usable definition of "truth" or its absence.)

That doesn't mean that French audiences are all that satisfied with the media. A 1994 eight-nation study (the French portion was conducted by the IPSOS Institute) showed the French to be the most critical population in terms of media performance: 46 percent deplored both "failure to respect privacy" and the "invasion of advertising." Nearly 40 percent criticized "love of sensationalism," and 43 percent disliked "media hype." A 1994 SOFRES survey indicated that 65 percent of those responding thought that journalists didn't stand up to political pressures, and 61 percent thought that journalists couldn't resist the lure of money.[135]

Unions

In the past, unions played a major role in French life, but their influence appears to have diminished greatly over the past two decades. Administrators certainly haven't gone out of their way to be favorable to unions; as George Ross notes of the French mass media in general, "The media originally tried to ignore unions. When unions, for whatever reason, became strong enough to achieve certain of their objectives, the media tended to portray them as one major cause of French difficulties. When unions plunged to the depths of weakness and ineffectiveness, as they seemed to with cyclical regularity, the media played up the 'crisis of unionism.'"[136]

Still, the French media industry—the public sector in particular—remains highly unionized, and strikes are frequent, although they've been far less so since the 1982 Socialist reforms. Still, there was a 24-hour strike by journalists and technicians in November 1982, and the first broadcast of the new breakfast-time TV service in 1985 didn't go on air because of a technician's strike in which the demands were for extra staff and more pay. There also was the May 1986 protest strike over the sale of TF1. The merger of A2 and FR3 in 1991 was marked by a 24-hour strike on the part of FR3 personnel (FR3 took a far greater share of cuts in the merger).[137] As many management staff are chosen by the government in one way or another, the adversarial relationship between labor and management—present in most systems—is likely to be even more hostile, and especially in those cases where administrators seem to know little and care less about broadcasting. The Mitterand administration exercised some care that the HA would appoint administrators who had had backgrounds in broadcasting and who seemed to take a genuine interest in what they did, but there also were individuals who received their appointments as rewards for faithful service to the party. That continues to be the case.

That's far less true of the private TV stations, although, as politics continue to play a role in the licensing process, it certainly could influence administrative appointments. The unions have found it much more difficult to negotiate with the private TV stations than with their public counterparts, since the former are far more cost-conscious than the latter, and more anti-union, as well.

Religious Organizations

There are many countries where religious organizations operate electronic media outlets on their own (Latin America, Scandinavia, the Netherlands, the United States), or where it's a legal requirement that media time be made available to them (several European nations); France has made no such provision. Perhaps that's because Catholicism is so deeply embedded in French life. By that token, the Catholic Church hasn't had to insist upon, or even request, airtime; it simply is available. More importantly, the Catholic Church itself approaches the electronic media with the assumption that they, too, are deeply imbedded in French life. In that light, the most important mission of the church is not to be concerned so much with airtime for itself[138] as it is with ensuring that the church influences how others use airtime. When the RTF was founded just after World War II, the Catholic Church named a Dominican priest, Father Pichard, to be ecclesiastical advisor to the service. That wasn't seriously questioned, since the church long had been influential in print media activities, where it was (and still is) an active publisher of newspapers and magazines.[139]

The specific nature of church influence has varied over time, but material with sexual connotations generally has been high on the list. Long before the famous (or infamous) "Dr. Ruth" made her appearance on U.S. television, dispensing sexual advice to the audience, France had a famous radio equivalent, "Dr. Sex." But the program wasn't broadcast within France; it came to France from Radio Luxembourg. French radio wouldn't have carried such a program, chiefly because the Catholic Church wouldn't have permitted it. The program may well have gained more notoriety (and publicity) because it came from Luxembourg, but at least French radio maintained its purity!

Finally, most of those citizen groups with any claim to longevity or influence, as well as most of the magazines that have attempted to remind French electronic media operations of their obligations to society, have been organized or published by the Catholic Church. One of the largest-circulation weekly electronic media guides in France, *Télérama,* is a Catholic publication; it also is just about the only large circulation guide to urge the media and their audiences to demand "quality" programming.

PROGRAMMING

Philosophies

Early in the history of French broadcasting, there were individuals who felt that broadcasting had a certain role to play in French society. Some looked upon it as guardian of language standards, and as already noted, many of the decrees passed in the 1920s required that stations avoid the use of slang and dialect. That concern has carried through to the present day; part of the CSA's mission is to ensure the usage of "proper" French in broadcasts. Similarly, most French ministers of culture have spoken of the need for French broadcasting to give a prominent place to the display of French culture, past and present. To that end, French broadcasters traditionally set self-imposed limitations on the use of foreign programs. That didn't keep shows such as "Dallas" from appearing in prime time and outdrawing most other programs on French TV ("Dallas" reruns continued to appear in prime time as of 1997, and continued to do well in the ratings, occasionally appearing in the top 10 shows of the week), and it hasn't kept U.S.-made movies from appearing two or three times a week on public stations (more often on Canal Plus and the private stations) in prime time, either; but it's meant that there has been money available for the production of some quite lavish entertainment series, for example, "Chateauvallon."

Some of the concern over the issues of safeguarding the language and promoting French culture probably stems from the fact that France exports many of its programs to its former colonies and protectorates, especially in Africa. Since the citizens of those countries don't enjoy the benefits of total immersion in French life, it's especially important to the government that whatever they receive from France be the best possible representation of that life.

As for informational broadcasts, again it's quite clear that the government has taken a great interest in such programs from the first decade of radio's existence to the present. During the initial period of coexistence for public and private broadcasting, it was harder for the government to achieve total compliance with its wishes, but by the end of the 1930s its control was essentially total. Creation of a broadcast monopoly made the task of supervision easier, and as we've seen, the pattern of direct ministerial involvement in shaping the contents of daily newscasts began at least as early as 1948. In 1981, the Socialist government removed the direct ministerial controls over newscast content, but not the indirect controls; just as its political predecessors had done, it took special pains to see that the "right" (but not in political terms!) people were appointed to head the news departments.

The authorization of local private radio stations in 1982 broke the monopoly, and the authorization of private television in 1985 completed the break. However, the radio stations initially lacked a network structure that might allow them to develop informational programs that would be competitive with the public system on a nationwide basis. By 1986, a few of the largest stations in Paris (NRJ, RFM) had begun to use satellites for distributing their music programs to local stations throughout France, and news services sometimes were part of the package, but the local stations seldom supplied news to the "network." By 1984, an all-news station (Radio Express) had emerged, but it failed through lack of interest, and the only all-news radio station currently active is France Info, a highly successful part of the public service company Radio France.[140]

The two initial private television stations were almost completely entertainment-oriented at first, but the relicensing of February 1987 brought promises from the new owners that news operations would be developed, and La Cinq quickly established a news production facility. Still, entertainment remains far and away the major function of M6, although it provides news "flashes" at 8, 9 and 11:50 a.m., and at 8:54 p.m. Starting in 1995, M6 encouraged some of its larger local outlets around the country to prepare and insert their own local newscasts, which has had a positive effect on the channel's local ratings and image. The CNCL also made the domestic production of entertainment a condition of licensing for both stations—within three years, 50 percent of the programming was to be French-made and only 40 percent could be non-European[141]—but the temptation to make lots of inexpensive programs, such as quiz and talk shows, and to schedule many of the non-European programs in prime time, proved too strong.

The peripheral stations all carried newscasts, but they too were subject to government pressure during the 1960s and 1970s. The prevailing tendency over the decades for any French government in a crisis situation was to place tight controls on newscasts, peripheral or domestic. A Senate committee sent the then-three public TV networks a questionnaire early in 1987 in which the networks were asked to furnish information on which crew members covered the student demonstrations in Paris of November 1986, what their journalistic briefs were, which freelancers (including some working for peripheral stations) contributed to reporting the riots, and so on.[142] And Hachette, which purchased the controlling block of stock in Europe No. One early in 1986, fired one of the station's commentators a few months later, allegedly because he was a co-sponsor of an "antiprivatization" (of TF1) petition.[143] Francis Bouygues, president of TF1, sacked Michel Polac, producer/host of TF1's

"Droit de Réponse" ("Right of Reply") in September 1987 because Polac criticized the CNCL for a licensing decision and a week later criticized Bouygues for asking him to apologize for the attack on the CNCL.[144]

By the end of the 1980s, direct interventions seemed to subside, perhaps because there were few crises that would have provoked them. But it also may be that the sheer variety of electronic media outlets available, at least to those who could afford cable or satellite subscriptions, made it that much harder for a government to intervene effectively. In October 1995, the Conservative prime minister, Alain Juppé, became the subject of a public "scandal" involving what amounted to virtually free (and luxurious) housing. He defended himself, and was defended by President Chirac. But the various news programs, public service and private, gave plenty of coverage to the criticism—something that almost certainly wouldn't have happened 10 years earlier, and most certainly not in the pre-1981 period.[145]

Radio

The French public radio system, Radio France, features four major national services and four specialized services, as well as 39 local stations. The major services resemble those of many large European countries. France Info, as noted earlier, is a 24-hour all-news service, with many feature program slots on economics, legal matters, cinema reviews, etc. France Inter also is a 24-hour service, with brief and longer newscasts hourly (and sometimes on the half-hour, as well), several interview shows, some cultural features and some music, most of it popular (including a fair amount of jazz). The tone for the most part is light and chatty, there are few talk shows that permit audience interaction, some of the disc jockeys run on in lengthy and at times nearly incomprehensible soliloquies. France Inter outstripped the other French public and private stations in numbers of listeners as of the late 1980s, but a decade later RTL (Luxembourg), NRJ and Europe No. One were drawing as many or more listeners daily, and France Inter was the only Radio France service to make the Top Ten in the Médiametrie national surveys for the overall period September 1994-June 1995.[146] France Musique also is on the air for 24 hours a day, carries five 5- to 10-minute newscasts, but devotes most of the remaining time to classical music, although there are presentations of jazz once or twice daily as well, and occasional cultural features (European cities, famous artists other than musicians). France Culture broadcasts from 7 a.m. to midnight, with six newscasts, daily radio dramas, discussions of books, the arts, the sciences, and four to five hours of music, mostly classical but again with some jazz. France Culture emphasizes French culture almost exclusively: reviews of French books, presentations by French scientists, performances of French music (with some works from other countries) played by French musicians.

The specialized services are Radio Bleue, a 24-hour daily service consisting of news, music, interviews, commentary and advice programs, and intended particularly for older listeners (retirees or those near retirement); Le

Mouv' (initiated in 1998), a youth-oriented service featuring music by such performers as Radiohead, but also programs dealing with AIDS, the Palestinian situation, and the extreme right political movements; Sorbonne Radio France, with five hours a day of lectures from the Sorbonne in Paris; and France Inter Regions (FIP), serving Paris and eight other large cities (e.g., Lyon) 24 hours a day with brief newscasts, lots of popular music and frequent traffic reports. FIP was one of the few experiments with specialized radio initiated during the Conservative government's pre-1981 period of control; it started in 1970. (There had been a brief experiment with a youth-oriented radio service in the 1960s, and there were radio services for summer vacationers in certain resort cities, e.g., Biarritz and Cannes, starting in 1960.)[147]

The first of nearly 40 Radio France local stations began to operate at the end of the 1970s, some claim as a belated bid by the Giscard government to show that it was interested in decentralizing broadcasting. Only three such stations were in existence by the 1981 election; the Socialist Party, making good on its announced intention to decentralize broadcasting, increased their number to 15 by 1983 and proclaimed that there would be over 90 by 1988, but there aren't even half that many as of 1998. Most have several journalists, and well-equipped studios, although few are in buildings designed originally as radio stations: warehouses, floors of apartment buildings and other structures have been converted for the purpose. Each is on the air for 12 to 18 hours a day, starting around 6 a.m. and signing off anywhere from 6 p.m. to midnight. There are local disc jockeys for the many popular music programs, but most of that music can be heard over most other stations broadcasting to or within France, although occasionally a local rock group, municipal band, or school or civic choral group will perform. But the news has a decidedly local flavor: Radio Périgord concentrates heavily on agricultural activities, Radio Bretagne Ouest on fishing, and so on, because those activities are the lifeblood of the area. Some programs, both news and interviews, may be done in the regional or local language or dialect. Radio Bretagne Ouest carries one to two hours per day of programming in Breton, and Radio Périgord features 10 to 20 minutes a day in Occitan, although few listeners speak it with much fluency. Many programs encourage phone-ins, and to judge from my own listening experience, a wide variety of listeners take advantage of the opportunity. A majority of station staff come from the regions to which they broadcast, and both ratings figures and personal messages from listeners indicate that the stations have fairly large (for radio) and devoted audiences.

The officially licensed local private stations numbered over 1,200 as of 1997, a considerable drop from over 1,800 as of 1991. However, it's difficult to get a precise count because some go off the air temporarily or permanently and don't always notify the authorities. They exist even in towns of several hundred people, and there may be as many as 100 in the Paris region alone. By law, they are not to exceed 500 watts, but many go beyond that limit, and few are punished for doing so because, unless someone complains, the authorities don't investigate, and routine patrols by signal detection trucks are few in number and generally limited to major cities. Cross-channel interference among stations in the major cities, especially Paris, often is incredibly bad, but the authorities rarely interfere—the more so as some of the stations are run by politically influential people. Some groups share frequencies with one or more other groups. Most are on the air 10 to 12 hours a day, but those affiliated with the nine satellite-based music networks (e.g., FUN, NRJ, Nostalgie) operate 24-hour services. Starting in 1996, the affiliates could break away from the networks for brief periods of time, do a bit of local programming, and earn some extra income by selling ad time locally. Most commercial private stations feature lots of popular music (a few began to specialize in "100 percent" French music in the mid-1980s, most of it from the 1950s), much of it by request, because that is the least expensive program format.

Slightly over five hundred of the local stations are community-based nonprofit operations, and rely heavily upon volunteers and on individuals willing to work for next to nothing. Sometimes the amateurism shows, as I have witnessed in listening to broadcasts where it took a staff member five minutes to get on the right microphone. They may carry numerous programs in minority languages (the four Basque stations do); they may devote themselves to religious music, news and services (there are Islamic, Jewish, Catholic and a few Protestant stations, most of them in Paris and the larger cities); they may be university campus-based stations (seven of them operate under the title Radio Campus). There are several "nationality" stations, e.g., Radio Armenie. And there are a few stations outside Paris which attempt to serve local migrant communities; one of them, Radio Agora (Montpellier), broadcast illegally but openly for over 10 years before the CSA closed it down in 1995, but protests from angry listeners and their supporters brought it back on air.[148]

There were many more community stations in the early to mid-1980s, but the growth of the commercial networks and the difficulties of raising money at the local level and finding fresh supplies of volunteers drove their numbers down, to the point where some critics doubted that more than a handful would survive into the 1990s.[149] However, they have, and may even be gaining back a bit of ground, despite the fact that roughly half of them function on annual budgets of less than Fr 400,000 (c. $75,000).[149a]

The community stations do their utmost to elicit telephone calls, because this is about the only tangible evidence of listenership that most of them can present to would-be advertisers, but often their efforts go unrewarded despite the offers of small cash or other prizes for giving the correct response to quiz questions: I once listened to Radio Loriént, a small station in Lorient (south coast of Brittany) and nearly 20 minutes elapsed before anyone bothered to call the station to answer a simple question about a film star. Some of the stations have provided unusual, provocative material, particularly the now-defunct gay-run station (Fréquence Gaie) in Paris, Radio Pays in Paris (seven French minority languages such as Basque, Breton and Provençal), and the politically oriented stations (one or more in all of the large cities) of the sort already described in Rouen. There probably are a few hundred illegal local private stations in France, most of which sound like most of their licensed counterparts. Those outside the large cities generally go unmolested, but those in the cities often must dodge the authorities, moving their equipment from place to place, usually on the warnings of neighbors that the detection team is in the neighborhood. Despite the proliferation of radio outlets in France over the past several years, the overall amount of time that the average listener spends with radio remains quite constant: roughly two and a half hours per day as of 1995.[150]

While national radio services retain some measure of importance, particularly to the small audiences for classical music, drama and jazz, and to the larger audiences of motorists who can listen to traffic reports frequently and just about anywhere in the country, it seems clear from my discussions with officials at the national, regional and local levels that most people think of local radio as the most significant and worthwhile use of the medium. Most of the local public stations seem bent on involving the listening public as much as possible with the broadcasts, albeit rarely to the extent of setting up community advisory boards: Professionals by and large still feel that they know what's best. Local private radio is another matter. Unless stations can solve their financial problems—and there's a modest government grant program to which noncommercial stations may apply—there seems little prospect for them to develop much truly local programming.

Television

The two national public services of French public television really are one national service (France 2) and one service divided between national and regional programming (France 3). France 2 and the privatized former national service, TF1, clearly are the ratings leaders, and are often very similar in their program formats, although traditionally there's been some attempt to provide viewers with a genuine choice at any given hour. However, there are periods of head-to-head competition, such as the hour just before noon until just before 1 p.m., when each channel carries two half-hour game shows. Each starts its major evening newscast a minute or two before 8 p.m. All three services followed the usual European practice of broadcasting little or nothing during the weekday morning hours up until the late 1980s, although A2 (as it then was) also began to carry breakfast-time television in January 1985 (6:45 to 8:30 a.m.). Initially it had a hard time establishing itself in the daily lives of the French because they weren't used to sitting down to a leisurely breakfast, and because the TV set usually stayed in the living room. TF1 added its own breakfast show shortly after privatization, and the two channels now compete directly during much of the 6:30-8:30 period.

The afternoon hours on TF1 and France 2 are filled with a mixture of short (15- to 30-minute) and long (45- to 50-minute) episodes of drama series, talk shows, documentaries, and, at the end of the afternoon, cartoon shows and minidocumentaries for children. Game and quiz shows were relatively rare on French public TV before TF1 was privatized, although France 2 has a daily series, "Des Chiffres et des Lettres" ("Numbers and Letters," 4:45-5:15 p.m.), that goes back more than two decades, but seems to retain its popularity. Game shows are plentiful during the late morning to late afternoon hours, and many of them are either French productions of U.S. shows ("Wheel of Fortune") or approximate imitations.[151]

One which is not was France 2's "Fort Boyard," set in a real seaside castle. Two teams of young, athletic men and women compete, and the challenges they face can include slithering through a plastic tunnel infested with rats, or retrieving a box containing a clue (to the next challenge) from a chest filled with tarantulas and scorpions. The final challenge usually involves finding the prize before something terrible happens to two of the female team members; one episode I watched had them chained to pillars, with "wild" and supposedly hungry tigers ready to be unleashed by a pair of dwarves if the time to complete the challenge ran out—which of course it didn't.

The evening period (prime time[152] in France starts around 8-8:30 p.m., due to the late dinner hour, and lasts until 10:30-11 p.m.) once contained lavishly produced variety shows, documentaries, nature programs, dramatizations of novels (usually by French authors), feature films (often French, and if not, sometimes dubbed) and, although rarely, a sports event (sports are more apt to be carried on weekends; soccer, rugby and cycling lead the list). Privatization of TF1, and the resultant competition between it and A2/France 2, have made many of the more expensive productions (variety shows, original documentaries, novels and plays adapted for TV) relatively rare; talk and magazine shows, crime and detective shows, and feature-length films (usually French or American, and made originally for cinema), as well as sports events, have predominated during the 1990s. There are brief newscasts shortly before or after midnight or 1 a.m. on TF1 and France 2, usually followed by repeats of daytime shows, feature films and other dispensable material.

France 3 and La Cinquieme/Arte follow a rather different schedule. France 3 comes on at 6 a.m. with Euronews, and follows it with a mixture of travelogues, series ("Miss Marple," a British detective series), cooking shows, game shows, talk shows and book reviews. Some of France 3's 13 regional TV stations come on the air as early as noon with a regional newscast, and all have their own regional breakouts during France 3's prime-time news show, "Le 19-20 de l'Information." The evening hours are devoted to magazine shows, each of which usually centers around a given theme (travel, science), but may be a miscellaneous collection consisting of subjects as diverse as Burmese pagodas and the workers who paint the Eiffel Tower. Some evenings will feature a classic of French cinema. There's a regional TV program once a week, at 11:10 p.m.; it often displays coproductions by the 13 regional stations. The broadcast day closes at 2 or 2:30 a.m., usually with a short classical music selection. Weekends on France 3 often are somewhat lighter, with sports represented more heavily on Saturdays, and children's programs on Sunday mornings.

La Cinquieme/Arte split the broadcast day; the former signs on at 6:45 a.m. and off just before 7 p.m.; the latter opens at 7 and runs until 2:30-3 p.m. Both display a mixture of documentaries, cinema classics, talk shows, and, on

La Cinquieme, plenty of educational programming (foreign languages, math, science, sociology); much of the sort of educational programming that once was on TF1 and A2 in the pre-privatization period has migrated to La Cinquieme.[153] While those schedules bear some generic resemblance to what TF1, France 2 and France 3 carry, the specific subjects included in the programs are often for more specialized tastes, and much of Arte's programming highlights French and German productions, in line with Arte's two co-supporters. Some of those programs delve into sensitive subjects, such as neo-Naziism, French collaboration with the Nazis during World War II and the treatment of ethnic minorities in each country. The overall program balance of both channels is decidedly in favor of factual programming, and Arte has a 10-minute news program each evening.

The private television stations initially were quite different in their programming lineups: La Cinq broadcast little but imported drama and situation comedy (chiefly old U.S. series), plus quiz shows, while Le Six broadcast little but music videos. Both began to diversify slightly toward the end of 1986, putting on some "blockbuster" feature films such as "Les Charlots Contre Dracula," probably in hopes of improving their chances for renewal of their franchises. Neither service produced news or sports; they operated on a financial shoestring, and although they were supposed to produce original shows as a condition of their franchise, that obligation remained largely unfulfilled.

When their licenses were re-awarded, but with stricter programming obligations (increased amounts of French-produced material), they had to contend with a recently privatized TF1. Both continued to rely heavily upon imported material, although La Cinq developed its own news program. La Cinq's owners also began to spend quite freely to strengthen the station: A "talent raid" in April 1987 brought two of the most prominent TF1 light entertainment stars (Stephane Collaro, whose mildly satirical, "Muppet Show"-like "Cocoricocoboy" usually was in the weekly top 10, and Patrick Sebatier, host of the popular variety show "Grand Public") and TF1's head of light entertainment, who had brought a French version of the U.S. game show "Wheel of Fortune" to TF1 only three months before. But TF1's owners were ready to spend at least as much to retain the channel's large lead over La Cinq, and they did. One result was that roughly one-fourth of TF1's news reporters quit during summer and fall of 1987, most of them because of what they saw as the network's reduced commitment to the news operation.[154]

The (unequal, given TF1's vast resources) battle between the two channels left La Cinq very little better off in terms of ratings—it still hovered around 5 percent of the audience, as compared with TF1's 40 percent or more—and far worse off in terms of capital. It changed its program lineup frequently over the next few years, but never found a winning formula, and, as we've seen, finally went off the air.

Le Six changed its name to M(étropolitain)6 (and later to Métropol 6), but continued its heavy emphasis on video clips, which helped to hold down its budget. It shifted away from that emphasis as La Cinq began its slow death, and soon featured a lineup that still had several hours of video (particularly between 7 and 9 a.m. and 3:15 to 5:30 p.m. on weekdays, and late at night on all seven days), but included many old U.S. series ("Little House on the Prairie," "Bewitched"), feature films from France and elsewhere, brief (5-10 minute) news "flashes" six times a day, and occasionally, some original drama ("Santa Claus Is a Shit," about a young couple who work for a "help for distressed people" telephone service.)[155] Its introduction of breakout periods for its local outlets in several French cities in the early 1990s appears to have been a bid to increase the overall ratings of the channel. It did result in some extra publicity, but the initial journalistic efforts were quite modest. In the same vein, M6 developed a few prime-time news magazines in the mid-1990s. And, as its profitability began to increase, it invested more heavily in new production.[156]

Canal Plus, the private scrambled-signal channel, carried little besides entertainment over its first several years, most of it in the form of feature films, but also a few old U.S. series (e.g., "Batman"), a bit of sports (including U.S. professional football), and a handful of talk, game and variety shows, plus three or four brief news flashes a day. Its license required (and still does) that some of its daytime offerings be descrambled; as of the mid-1990s, about four hours a day of Canal Plus' 21-hour schedule (6 a.m. to 3 a.m.) is descrambled.

Canal Plus added more variety to its schedule by the early 1990s, and now offers a mixed lineup, with more airtime devoted to movies than anything else (and more recent—Canal Plus may show French films 12 months after their theatrical release, whereas other TV channels must wait two to three years to do so), but with a number of short programs that are quite different from anything it had carried in its earlier years. "The Guignols" is another "Muppet Show"-like satire, with perhaps a sharper political edge than "Cocoricocoboy." Canal Plus has been happy enough with the show's ratings—it's on during "descrambled" periods from 6:55 to 7:30 p.m. Mondays through Thursdays, with a weekly "best of the Guignols" on Sundays—that it's produced a similar show for Spain. It also presents a six-day-per-week employment journal, with job openings and tips about making oneself employable. It initiated a weekday seven-minute program, "Cyberflash," with news about CD-ROM, the Net, etc., as well as a monthly magazine program ("Cyberculture") on the same subject. It introduced a weekly interactive program, "L'Hébdo," in late 1995, with the idea of bringing viewers directly into the program through Internet, fax, Minitel and other interactive devices. Almost simultaneously, it introduced a five-minute weekly (Sunday) program, "Pas si vite" ("Not so Fast!") in which some more or less philosophical questions ("What is self-image?") were put to well-known personalities, who would then spend the remaining time answering them. It has increased its production of documentaries, as well, sometimes in coproduction with other broadcasters such as the BBC. And, although its policy of running large numbers of French films (some produced by its own studios) has been of real benefit to the French cinema industry, fully a third of its roughly 45 movies in any given month may be U.S.-made, and another third from other parts of Europe, but also Africa, Asia and the Middle East. It also carries the "CBS Evening News" six mornings a week.

Until the late 1990s, there were five local terrestrial channels, in Toulouse, Lyon, Nimes and the Périgord and Mt. Blanc regions. They broadcast a mixture of inexpensive locally produced material (news, community calendars, talk shows, spotlights on the arts, employment, panels and debates with viewer participation through the Internet, Minitel, etc.) and material from outside sources, particularly Télévision Monte Carlo.[157] Locally produced programs in minority languages such as Provençal (in Nimes) and Occitan (in Périgord) also appeared on the schedule, although the more recently arrived minority groups and languages, such as North African Arabs/Arabic, or Turks/Turkish rarely received attention over these stations. By 1998, only the Toulouse, Lyon and Mt. Blanc stations were left. Fiscal problems had elimitated Nimes and Périgord, and threatened to do the same for Mt. Blanc. The three remaining stations all are on very thight budgets, which has reduced program quality and quantity.[158] The roughly 20 local channels in the cable TV systems follow much the same programming practices as did the local TV stations in better days. Some have imported bits of Arabic-language programming from Morocco or Egypt to fill out the schedule and make a symbolic gesture to minority groups.[158a] None seems to carry a locally originated program for such minorities.

A foreign viewer watching French television entertainment over terrestrial, cable or satellite outlets over an extended period would become aware of three things: first, that there are many repeats of programs; second, that there are many feature films in prime time; and third, that there are few original (French-written, French-produced) prime-time dramas by modern writers, whether written for TV or not. (Traditional writers such as de Maupassant and Hugo fare only slightly better.) Lack of money, or, to be more specific, lack of money for original productions, seems to be the root cause, but it also may be that, unlike the situations prevailing in Great Britain, Germany and Japan (for NHK, at least), serious creative artists don't find it particularly rewarding to express themselves through television. There are exceptions. In their day, the satires of Jean-Christophe Averty were very creative, and Canal Plus' puppet satire "Les Guignols de l'Information" has some nice satirical touches, such as a President Chirac figure (a bird) complaining about back pains; he can't see that they're caused by the knives, axes and hatchets of his Conservative political rivals.[159] Some of the documentaries show considerable inventiveness. However, the usual entertainment program is no more than competent. The often meager production budgets don't help, nor does the long-established reputation of television as "servant of the government," but there's also the long-standing rejection of television by intellectuals that has little to do with budgets or with government interference. It may be that intellectuals simply cannot conceive of an instrument of mass communication as a suitable vehicle for the transmission of what they accept as material of artistic merit.

When the occasional original drama of merit does come on the schedule, it often reaps critical acclaim and solid ratings. Such was the case in late 1995, when France 2 broadcast a nine-part, nearly two-hour-per-episode original TV drama by Josee Dayan, "La Riviere Esperance." Based on a historical incident involving a mid-19th century peasant's revolt in the Dordogne region (east of Bordeaux), the series had the usual melodramatic touches of historical drama—clashes and romances between rich and poor, divided families, characters swiftly rising to and falling from power—but the level of acting, the quality of the scripting, the on-location shooting, the care taken with historical detail, all combined to produce a riveting production. The result was a several point improvement in France 3's usual ratings for the time period, and one episode actually drew better ratings than TF1's broadcast of "Indiana Jones and the Last Crusade."[160]

While most of the standard program formats are represented on French TV, a few formats were rare until the 1990s. Soap operas and sitcoms were almost totally absent from the TV screen until a few years after the privatization of TF1, although there were occasional U.S. and Australian[161] imports, and the rarer purchase of a U.S. program concept such as Norman Lear's "Maude," which became "Maguy" in France. (It did relatively well in the ratings, but spawned few imitations.) By the early 1990s, soap operas and sitcoms, along with game shows, became considerably more plentiful. What they added by way of originality is another question. Reading the general story outlines of Jean-Luc Azoulay's sitcoms, they could be transposed to U.S. television with little difficulty.

> "Helene and the Boys" (1993): "Helene has left her family to live on campus. She begins a new life with her new friends. Through their enthusiasm and youthful outlook on life, they recreate the world and they also learn to become adults."
>
> "The Girls Next Door" (1994): "Tired of men and hazardous married life, three friends move together with kids and luggage in[to] a big apartment next to two incorrigible seducers who are slowly going to disturb their resolutions about men."[162]

Azoulay is among the most successful of French producers of commercially successful programming, especially of the multi-episode ("First Kisses," about teenagers in love, ran for 318 episodes—a short run by U.S. standards, but long by French), rapid-production, low-cost variety. He claims to "have the same tastes as the public."[163] He probably is right: French tastes where TV is concerned *do* appear to have changed, particularly in terms of acceptance of recycled formulas. Comic sketches rework the same themes season after season: Stephane Collaro's various comic series (e.g., "Cocoricocoboy") are sure to contain intellectual-but-sexy females whose bodies will be subjected to pinches and pats by various lecherous males. The game shows are more challenging than their U.S. counterparts, but not by much (the 30-year-old "Des Chiffres et des Lettres" on France 2 is a notable exception), although they're generally free of screaming and jumping contestants, flashing lights and obtrusive hosts and hostesses.[164] Veteran performers such as Patrick Sébastien strike some critics as trying harder and harder, but falling deeper and deeper into the "télé-poubelle" (TV garbage can). In his 1995 series "Osons" ("Let's Dare"), he introduced a takeoff on Jean-Marie Le Pen, leader of the ultranationalist political party Front Nationale (FN), singing "Break the Blacks" (Africans living in France) with a supporting cast of actors playing skinheads and "FN Girls." There was an inquest as to whether Sébastien was inciting racial hatred, which he disclaimed.[165]

The many reality-based shows that came on French TV in the early to mid 1990s—12 of them were introduced between September 1992 and September 1994—struck some critics as a watershed event in the evolution (or devolution) of French TV, in that the shows seemed to give up any claims of quality, or even "Frenchness." Some featured psychoanalysis (of couples with marital problems), some traced missing persons, some probed the supernatural, some showed daring rescues made by emergency services. Most bore considerable resemblance to U.S. models. Bernard Pivot, the long-time host of the book-discussion program "Apostrophes," remarked of them that, "The more I learn that my neighbors are up shit creek, the more I see them undressing, arguing, being shouted at, crying or calling for help, the more I'm content with my own lot in life: Hell is other people."[166]

As for the evolution of news coverage, newscasts were a part of French television almost from the beginning, but early TV newscasts were brief and uninteresting, and the de Gaulle era saw the credibility of TV news greatly diminished. Several French magazines published articles during the 1960s and 1970s comparing French TV news with what other European systems provided,[167] and the French product always suffered by comparison: It was less free, less interesting visually and the presenters were boring. The presentation of news improved considerably during the early to middle 1980s, although lack of an equivalent to the satirical weekly newspaper *Le Canard Enchainée* probably meant that few intellectuals found it all that rewarding. The biggest improvement was in the relatively greater freedom to cover stories unfavorable to the government, although French mass media scholar Claude-Jean Bértrand observed that investigative reporting was not a strong suit for any of the French media, TV included, and that reporters generally lacked much sense of professionalism.[168] There also was the creation of teams of news presenters who seemed at one and the same time to be knowledgeable and attractive. This was particularly true of the A2 team of Patrick Poivre d'Arvor and Christine Ockrent, which in late December 1982 raised A2's ratings for the 8 p.m. "Journal" (newscast) above those of the TF1 "Journal" for the first time in French TV history. Although theirs was not the "happy news" approach followed by so many U.S. stations, they did emerge as distinctive and attractive personalities.

A decade later, Poivre d'Arvor was considerably less attractive, as his fake interview with Fidel Castro came to light. That was followed by the revelation that he had accepted gifts (free travel to the Caribbean; all-expenses-paid weekend at the Cannes Film Festival) given by a Lyon businessman, Pierre

Botton; Botton apparently hoped that his association with Poivre d'Arvor would help him develop contacts needed to put together a business deal. Although he was indicted, Poivre d'Arvor wasn't convicted, and his employer, TF1, kept him on air[169] throughout the "scandal." His former co-anchor, Christine Ockrent, remained with A2, but was heavily criticized (and provoked a strike at A2) when it was revealed in 1988 that she was being paid nearly $250,000 a year.[170] Some newscasters were noted for their many mistakes in delivering the news; Jacqueline Alexandre, anchor for FR3's newscast "Le Soir," earned a certain notoriety for the number and "quality" of her errors.[171] Legal challenges to the "star" system and a poorly-handled TV debate featuring President Chirac in 1997 may have cost France 2's "Journal Télévisé" dearly in its "race" with TF1 news.[171a] Nor did anchorpersons benefit from the revelation in 1997 that some of them at FR3 had been "moonlighting" by making fake news programs for use by private corporations in their sales meetings. What made this worse was that the anchors used FR3 news studios, complete with FR3 logos. One anchor was suspended, and FR3 executives denounced the activity, but in fact FR3 did rent out its studios to corporations on occasion, as an extra source of income.[172]

Documentaries still manage a certain degree of critical bite, whether they're about foreign situations—inhuman acts taking place in Bosnia—or about France. One particularly interesting monthly documentary series, "Etat d'Urgence" ("State of Emergency") takes a hard look at such sensitive subjects as whether the already stiff regulations discouraging drinking and driving need to be applied more rigorously. Arte has produced special reports on Algerian "terrorist" activities in Paris. Canal Plus has broadcast frank and even brutal documentary feature films about such subjects as the criminal justice courts and those who appear before them. But documentaries or extended interviews that probe very deeply into the activities of politicians and political life are rare.

THE AUDIENCE

France's public system didn't emphasize audience research until the 1960s, and even then seemed more interested in the regular analysis of listener and viewer mail than it did in the collection of data through more rigorous, scientifically respectable methods. Some of the mail was elicited through panel members appointed by ORTF, and it indicated not only who viewed or listened, but also of what they thought of the program, as expressed through a 10-point scale (awful to excellent) and through narrative comment (sometimes terse: One disgusted viewer described a J. C. Avérty program on Salvador Dali as "a loony depicted by a loony"). But panel sizes often were small for a given program, and selection of panel members not random, yielding inconclusive results.

Interest in more systematic audience research picked up during the 1970s, as TF1, A2 and FR3 all appointed directors of audience research. Not all were of top-quality, but TF1's Michel Souchon came to the job in 1984 with an excellent academic reputation. Antenne 2 developed a simulation system to aid in scheduling programs to maximize audience size and began to use some research data to help sell advertising time.

Because of some of the obvious deficiencies in RTF and ORTF audience research, and because most of the data weren't available publicly, other groups began to enter the field in the 1950s. Chief among them was the Centre d'Études des Supports de Publicité (CESP), founded in 1956 and still very active. It's a nonprofit organization supervised by an administrative council made up largely of its various mass media users. The Centre usually designs studies but has them carried out by other organizations such as IFOP (Institut Français d'Opinion Publique). Its questionnaires once were lengthy, which probably explains a refusal rate that averaged about 20 percent. Also, up until the mid-1970s, stations knew well in advance when CESP would conduct another survey, and would flood the market during those times with billboards, bumper stickers and other self-promotions, such as, "Never alone with RTL." CESP then began to keep the dates of the survey periods secret.

Another major organization involved in audience research is the Centre d'Études d'Opinion (CEO), formed at the time of the breakup of ORTF in 1974. Originally, its research was intended chiefly to serve the public service broadcast organizations, but within a few years Europe No. One and RTL both subscribed to it. The CEO developed a national random sample-based panel system with a 1,400-member panel; panel members were to fill in questionnaires on their daily listening and viewing and mail the questionnaires back to CEO at the middle and end of their particular sample week, and there were new panels each week. But mounting problems with survey techniques and faulty data-collection equipment finally brought the three heads of the public networks to threaten a cutoff of funding for CEO unless things changed.[173] They did. The CEO became a new operation, Médiamétrie, in 1985. It was dissociated from the prime minister's office and set up as a private corporation. It had installed about 1,000 well-constructed black boxes by January 1986 and now was able to provide reliable overnight ratings. It set up a nationwide telephone polling service, yielding data on program preferences and reactions to commercials for 185 TV viewers daily.

Other major public opinion survey organizations are Nelson-Taylor Sofrés, Ipsos, and CSA-TMO. But consolidation seems to be the order of the day, and these and other organizations are likely to enter into new mergers.

The privatization of French broadcasting has had its effects on the ratings system. Ratings rivalries now are more intense, and so are criticisms of methods used to determine ratings. New firms have sprung up. One of them, Sofrés-Nielsen (the U.S. ratings service), began to install peoplemeters in 1988. The service was particularly attractive to the independent TV companies because it wasn't financed by the major networks; its early audience figures (based on a very small sample) in fact showed larger audiences for M6 than had ever appeared through Médiamétrie's surveys.[174] Médiamétrie introduced its own peoplemeter service, Médiamat, soon after.

The ratings services indicate that French viewers favor most of the same program genres that dominate the monthly top 10 in other countries. The September 1997 composite monthly list includes four French comedy and drama series, two French magazine shows, two U.S. movies ("In the Line of Fire" and "Romancing the Stone"), a European Cup football (soccer) match and a special broadcast of Lady Diana Spencer's funeral from Great Britain. Most of those programs were broadcast over TF1, which attempts to be as "generalist" as possible.[175]

Figures on relative credibility of the media show what one might expect in a nation with such highly politicized media outlets: surveys conducted by Sofrés in 1989 and 1993 showed radio, TV and the press all losing points with the public, but with TV losing most of all. The 1989 percentages were 34 for radio, 33 for TV and 16 for the press; the comparable 1993 figures were 23, 0 and -4.[176]

MINORITIES AND THE MEDIA

France's émigré and guest worker communities first came to the country in any number in the mid-to-late 1950s. By the mid-1990s, those communities accounted for close to 10 percent of the total population, and thanks to larger than average birthrates, that percentage is bound to increase in years to come. The advent of local private radio gave some of them a voice of their own, at least in the largest cities, but there's almost no foreign-language programming for such groups on the large national commercial stations or on Radio France. However, satellite channels for radio have become inexpensive enough that some of the Paris-based Arab-language stations have been able to relay their signals to other parts of the country where there's a fair-sized North African population, but not quite enough to support a station of their own. Such a situation exists in Toulouse, where there's a low-power FM station that relays broadcasts from Radio Beur in Paris;[177] as of late 1996, six French cities were carrying the service.[178] The association Radios Muselmanes de France SA, with 99 percent investment by a Lebanese group owned by Lebanese Prime Minister Hariri, provides another satellite-relayed service for Arab listeners, Radio Orient.[179]

The portrayal of minorities on television, public or private, is almost nil: it's a rare drama or even newscast item that shows them to the rest of France. The average French viewer finds them more and more a part of urban life, without receiving much help from the electronic media about the sorts of lives they lead. There are exceptions, including documentaries such as "B3—the pure pleasure of dance," broadcast by Arte in October 1995: it portrayed a French dance troupe composed of blacks, whites ("blancs") and "beur" (North African Arabs), which performed rap, break dancing, etc. The documentary was made by a German group. Arte's French production company, La Sept, has made documentaries about North African Arab artists, such as the filmmaker Youssef Chahine. France 2 has broadcast telefilms such as the

1995 production "Le Mouton Noir" ("The Black Sheep"), about a French and a Tunisian couple who swap houses in their respective countries: the Tunisians are delighted with their end of the bargain; the French wife is horrified at the differences she encounters in Tunisia, but she eventually learns to adjust and even to enjoy her very different cultural experience.

There was a brief period in the late 1980s to early 1990s when one could see a greater number of dramas and documentaries in which North Africans living in France, most as French citizens, played major roles. The private channels did very little along those lines. The public TV channels, A2 and FR3, took the lead in broadcasting those programs, most of which lasted for periods of one to three years. While immigrants (and not only North Africans) themselves were the primary intended audience, some of the producers hoped that they would reach a broader audience, and thus act as bridges between cultures. Perhaps the most ambitious was "Rencontres" ("Encounters"), made by an Arab-run production house. It ran on FR3 from 1989 to late 1991 as a weekly show, and sought to reach second-generation viewers, as well as some of the more recent and neglected minorities from Asia and the Middle East. It was fast-moving, and combined news, features, opinion, comedy, a portrait of some successful individual or group, cultural features, legal advice, etc. It underwent a schedule shift (for the worse) and a time reduction (from 90 minutes to one hour), and finally was taken off the air by the minister for Social Affairs and Integration, for no specified reason. Such time shifts, sudden cancellations and poor time slots (7 a.m., for example), characterized the period.[180]

The politics of such actions are somewhat puzzling, since that period of activity coincided with the Socialist government's term in office (1989-93)—meaning that Socialists apparently helped to get such programs on the air, but also supported them poorly and removed them quickly. That may have been because of the increasing success of Jean Marie Le Pen and his followers, with their strongly anti-immigrant rhetoric. The Socialist margin of power was slim even with the coalition, so it may have seemed expedient to not appear to be too favorable to immigrants.

While those minority groups found fewer and fewer chances to portray themselves, some of them found a substitute of sorts: satellite-delivered services from Algeria, Tunisia, Morocco, Turkey, Egypt, Portugal, Greece, Italy and Poland. The roughly 2.3 million satellite dishes in France as of 1998 probably include a substantial number of households of émigrés and French citizens of Arabic or Turkish descent, and the programs those viewers receive do nothing to help them integrate with mainstream French culture; nor do they help mainstream French viewers to understand the natures and problems of those groups.[181] That may suit the mainstream French quite well—you stick to your lifestyles, and we'll stick to ours—but it doesn't suit the younger generations who have grown up in France and who wish to both take from and give to French culture, and perhaps help to develop a more tolerant and worldly outlook on the part of the mainstream French and their own elders.[182]

As for France's "mainstream domestic" minorities, recall that the Socialist government had made regionalization and localization among its top priorities starting in the early 1980s. France has some particularly rich and old regional cultures, with bodies of literature that could, and sometimes do, make good broadcast material. The Breton, Provençal, Basque and Alsatian regions are particularly well-endowed in that respect. But bringing such material to the screen, and encouraging modern regional writers to think of broadcasting as a natural outlet for their talents, takes money, and little of it has flowed to the regional and local levels (although certainly more than did in the past). And how far should the central government go in encouraging regionalization, when there have been rather strong and sometimes violent separatist movements in Corsica and Brittany? Those factors seemed to have discouraged government support for Corsican, Basque, etc., electronic media outlets. Still, the Basques, Alsatians, Provençaux, Bretons, Corsicans and Occitan speakers found that the opening of radio to private interests in the early 1980s sparked considerable interest in using the medium to broadcast their own cultures and languages.

The small FM stations that sprang up also helped to push Radio France's regional stations to increase their efforts along those lines; stations such as Radio France Alsace, which had offered perhaps a half-hour per day of programming in Alsatian as of the early 1980s, had expanded to several hours a day in the language by the 1990s. France 3 now offers roughly two hours a day of news and informational programming for Alsace, with programs in Alsatian occupying an average of 30 minutes a day. Whether that coincided with, or instead helped to promote, greater use of Alsatian by more of the population would be hard to say—probably a combination of the two. But I spoke with a number of people, and especially young people, who took obvious pride in hearing their language on the air and in speaking it themselves.[183]

There also has been some media activity on the part of an almost-invisible minority: ex-convicts. One of them, Louis Ferigo, started an association named "Dédans-déhors" (In and Out) in 1995, and worked with other ex-prisoners to develop a weekly radio program ("Ici l'ombre," or "Here Are Shadows") which is relayed by satellite from Radio Soleil in Lyon to several other French radio stations. The programs deal with the problems a parent faces while in prison, how to warn young people away from criminal activities, and the difficulty of reintegrating oneself in society.[184]

France's record of support for minority-run or -directed electronic media of any sort has been meager, on the whole. That could be attributed to a strong feeling on the part of many French citizens that immigrants and their descendants should and even must seek to become as much like the "mainstream" French as possible. France's steadily high unemployment rate throughout most of the 1990s—between 12 and 13 percent—has pushed some to claim that such groups must either assimilate completely or leave the country. The mainstream French minorities may be a different case, in that some of them—for example the Basques and Bretons—go back farther in historical time than do the mainstream French themselves. But they, too, receive little support from the government, and some suspicion: the community-run

Basque radio stations have found themselves the target of police raids and investigations from time to time, on the grounds (unsubstantiated) that they may be fostering "terrorist" activities.[185] The future may offer no better prospects.

PROBLEM AREAS

It may be stating the obvious to say that political bias is a major problem area in France, but it is worth noting again nonetheless, because the five initial years of Socialist government lessened but certainly did not eliminate it. That government itself, as we've seen, acted at times as if it had learned little from its predecessors, although on balance the electronic media are far more open to the portrayal of divergent points of view than they had been before 1981. President Mitterand drew heavy criticism and opposition party complaints to the Haute Autorité for having been interviewed on TF1 in March 1986, during the three-week campaign period when there is supposed to be no political advertising (political ads appear in the press, but not on the electronic media). The Haute Autorité seemed uneasy in deciding that this was neither an advertisement nor a "communication of the government" (which would have opened it to right of reply), but it did take the unusual step of requiring the network to broadcast opposing politicians' reactions to the interview. Criticisms of bias in broadcasts sometimes have emerged when there seem to have been no real grounds for them, but that may be in part a reflex action based upon the conditioning that took place in the '50s, '60s and '70s, which the Haute Autorité acknowledged in deciding on the 1986 Mitterand case.[186] All of that is part of the larger issue of public confidence in the integrity of broadcast journalism—certainly an artifact of the long period of Gaullist influence (1958-81), but the scandals involving Patrick Poivre d'Arvor in the 1990s didn't do much for public confidence, either.

A second problem—the foreign cultural invasion of French television—may be more in the minds of certain TV critics, intellectuals and the Socialist-era minister of communications and culture, Jack Lang, than in the minds of the public. The public stations don't carry all that many foreign television programs, although imported feature movies (especially U.S.) are very common. The private stations do use far more imported material. Even before the expansion of TV in the mid-to-late 1980s, certain of the foreign TV programs, especially "Dallas," were very popular—despite (or because of?) the almost universally negative comments of the critics. Since then, the European Community (now Union) quota restrictions on the amount of foreign material that can be shown on television have come into force, and the French government has supported them strongly. At the same time, creation of the new commercial TV services and privatization of TF1 have created an even greater market than ever for foreign—especially U.S.—material. Figures on the amounts of TV drama broadcast over the three public channels for the period 1980-84 showed that French productions outstripped foreign productions by fairly wide margins up until 1984, when the imported programs showed a slight lead. The quotas eventually put French programs in the lead again, but under circumstances that hardly represented a victory: the prime-time hours are dominated by U.S. programs and French productions of U.S. concepts, especially quiz shows and reality-based shows.[187] Kuhn saw the situation in more pessimistic terms even before the introduction of private TV, predicting a marked increase in imports and noting a growing tendency to imitate the U.S. product, especially such things as "the horrendous American practice of breakfast television."[188]

A third problem is the employment and portrayal of women. With few exceptions (notably Jacqueline Baudrier), women played relatively minor roles in broadcasting until the early 1980s, but now they're quite prominent: One of the leading TV news anchors starting in the early 1980s was Christine Ockrent, while Jacqueline Baudrier was head of radio news for France Inter in the late 1960s, head of TV news for the second TV channel (later to become A2), and president of the first TV channel (later to become TF1) in the early 1970s. Furthermore, one can find women in a number of midlevel decision-making positions. Marie-France Briére was credited with revitalizing light entertainment on TF1 in the mid-l980s. Pascale Breugnot, director of production at A2 in the mid-1980s, popularized such potentially difficult subject matter as economics (in the series "Vive la Crise");[189] by the end of the 1980s, she was director of fiction and documentary magazines for TF1, where she helped to develop an interactive serial program for teenagers, "Salut les Homards": Viewers were urged at the end of each episode to call in their comments on where the plot should go from there. She also helped to create TV magazines such as "Ushuaia" and "Chocs," which dealt with social questions such as prostitution, child abuse and drugs, but most of those shows came on late at night.[190] Jeanine Langlois-Glandier managed FR3 and the INA in the 1980s, then in the early 1990s became director of television for the venerable production company, Pathé.[191] Michele Cotta was the first president of the Haute Autorité, Catherine Tasca served as deputy minister for communications from 1988 to 1991, and Catherine Trautmann became minister of culture and communication in 1997. Whether any of this has affected the portrayal of women is another matter. The ads and many programs reinforce long-standing stereotypes of woman as mother, housekeeper and sex object, but women's liberation groups either aren't as active in France as they are in Germany, Great Britain and the United States, or they're less concerned about their portrayal.

There was a short-lived women's radio station in the 1980s. Les Nanas Radioteuses, a 1981 union of two women's pirate radio stations, obtained a license in 1982, and later joined forces with a "grassroots" station, Radio Canaille FM, which furnished the studio in which Les Nanas produced and broadcast a weekly six-hour program with feminist themes. Unfortunately, Canaille FM decided to sell airtime starting in 1984 (when that became legal), and dropped Les Nanas. It then drifted from station to station, and went off the air in 1985.[192]

FOREIGN INFLUENCES ON PROGRAMMING

Most French are well aware of the foreign influences on their broadcast services, television in particular. Sitcoms, quiz shows and reality-based programs, particularly on the commerical services, owe a great deal to U.S. models. Increasing numbers of coproductions with European partners,[193] such as Italy's public service RAI,[194] have presented French viewers with some non-French ways of looking at things and probably have caused French producers to rethink some of their concepts. News producers and presenters are familiar with how newscasts are done in other European countries, Great Britain's BBC and IBA being cited as particularly good models. And private media outlets rely heavily on imported material.

Granted, some of the French electronic media industry still appears to be a law unto itself. There is a combination of formalism (in settings and in acting/performing) and slowness of pace in many of the PSB programs that seems typically French, and outside any foreign influence. The themes of the crime shows and domestic dramas are little different from those same genres elsewhere, but they often seem easygoing compared with British, German, Japanese or U.S. productions. France 2's "Télématin," a breakfast TV show (6:30-8:30 a.m.), is even more casual than are its U.S. and British counterparts.

It may be that the French policy of maintaining the "Frenchness" of its former colonies, through television as well as through other means, has led the PSBs to develop and maintain a unique style—one that's easily and immediately identifiable as French. It would be fascinating to study the domestic television production styles of former French and former British colonies, to see whether they reflected identifiable colonial origins. And certainly the French government spends a great deal of money both to export French broadcasts and to bring broadcasters, particularly from former French colonies, to France for further training.

RELATIONS WITH OTHER MEDIA

During the 1920s and 1930s, there was a close relationship between the press and private radio, since newspapers frequently were part or full owners of such stations. That relationship ended early in World War II, and numerous attempts on the part of several French newspapers to reinstate private broadcasting after the war and on up through the 1970s were unsuccessful. With the re-establishment of private radio in the early 1980s, some newspapers did choose to invest in the medium. However, less than 10 percent of all private radio stations feature any degree of press ownership.

Television has been a much more attractive proposition. As soon as the Socialist government announced its proposal to license private television, several press and publishing interests announced their intention to be among the investors. Two of the major figures were the press baron Robert Hersant (owner of the French pro-Conservative daily *Le Figaro*) and the Hachette publishing firm[195] (which once had been a major shareholder in the Companie Luxembourgeoise de Télédiffusion), while Les Éditions Mondiales also expressed its interest. All of those groups already employed individuals who had worked in French television, several of whom had been top-level executives with TF1. The largest private ad agency in France, Publicis, also announced its intention to seek a license in cooperation with Europe No. One, which long had wanted to obtain a license and which already was involved in producing and distributing TV programs. The first TV license went to the Berlusconi-Seydoux group, but Publicis, Gaumont and commercial radio station NRJ obtained the license for Le Six shortly thereafter.[196] In the 1987 relicensing, Publicis, NRJ and Gaumont failed to retain their shares in Le Six, but Hersant acquired a large block of La Cinq, and a financial newspaper also acquired minor share blocks in it.

Aside from press and publisher ownership of broadcast stations and cable operations, the press has played a role in the development of French broadcasting by acting as a gadfly. Over the years, the general tone of French press comment on broadcasting issues has been highly critical. Even newspapers such as Le Figaro which were known to be favorable to the centrist coalition led in turn by de Gaulle, Pompidou and Giscard d'Estaing often criticized the government for its various abuses of broadcasting. Newspaper critics writing about individual shows were very likely to take a condescending attitude toward them, treating them as second-class entertainment or information. Although some newspapers have acquired ownership in commercial TV stations, that doesn't seem to have had much effect on the adversarial relationship (a one-sided relationship, since the press does most of the criticizing), and TV critics often look down their noses at much that appears on "le tube."

The French press began to see public television in a particularly negative light once the government had authorized the sale of ad time on TV in 1968. Television news may not have been much of a competitor for print journalism, but advertising certainly was a competitive arena. Eventually, TV began to eat into the newspapers' share of the advertising pie, but particularly once commercial TV services such as TF1 and M6 had become established: annual advertising income for the press in 1989 was 26.2 billion francs, and for TV, 11.4 billion; by the end of 1993, the figures were 22.4 billion for the press, 15 billion for TV.[197] Another sign of change: as of 1970, the total daily publishing output for the 94 French dailies was over 11 million copies; by the mid-1990s, it was below 10 million, for just over 70 dailies.[198]

French newspaper investment in local radio has been quite modest. Kuhn notes that some of the leading regional newspaper groups, such as Sud-Ouest (Bordeaux), set up their own radio stations in the 1980s. A few still are involved, but for many it turned out to be a poor investment, at least from the standpoint of commercial success.[199] A number of press-owned stations eventually were sold to owners who then affiliated themselves with one of the commercial music networks.

Ad agencies and broadcasting also have had an interesting relationship over time. Agence Havas, one of the world's largest ad agencies, was involved in broadcasting before World War II and continued its involvement after the war, albeit in different forms. It became a major investor in the commercial peripheral service, RTL. When advertising was authorized for French TV, Havas claimed a considerable share of the business. And when the Socialist government decided to allow advertising on FR3 as well, Havas and Publicis divided the business between them. Though not officially an agency of the French government, Havas was closely connected with it until 1987, and the Havas president held that position only with the blessing of the French president.

Relations with the film industry were uneven for many years. The industry received some legal protection from television through a legal requirement that French television not show movies (unless made specifically for TV) until three years after their debuts in cinemas. Canal Plus received its license in 1984 on the understanding that it base its schedule on feature films. It could only survive financially if it offered its potential subscribers something more than what they could receive on "free" TV. Therefore, it needed a smaller interval between cinema release and release on Canal Plus. Initially it negotiated for a nine-month interval, but eventually it settled for 12 months. Another part of that negotiation with the film industry involved determining the numbers of movies to be shown on Canal Plus—it wanted 375 films a year, while the industry proposed 250—and the price, with the industry pushing for a minimum price per film and Canal Plus offering a collective price for all films produced each year.[200] Eventually they compromised: there would be 320 features a year (raised to 364 in 1985, partly because Canal Plus was not attracting as many subscribers as it had projected).

All in all, the film industry received something of a financial shot in the arm through this transaction, but its concessions represent a recognition that TV is a more important customer than are cinemas—a recognition that seems to have taken longer in France than in most western nations, despite the clear evidence of declining cinema attendance. (The growth of VCRs in France also has opened an important market.) However, those concessions also led the Berlusconi-Seydoux group to demand concessions for La Cinq, and it negotiated a two-year wait, rather than the three-year wait that public television had to observe.[201] Actually, "negotiated" is too weak: The government simply conceded the point during contract negotiations, and the film industry was powerless to do anything about it.

The FR3 service was allowed from its debut to enter into coproduction agreements with movie producers (TF1 and A2 received such permission in 1980), and it quickly won critical acclaim for those productions. (French critics are far more kindly disposed toward film, which they treat as an art form, than toward TV.) Many were exported, especially to French-speaking nations, and children's shows have become quite important in the export market. Much of the production was done in 16 millimeter, and conceived in terms of TV, and not the movie screen.[202]

As the film industry has recovered some degree of prosperity through the support of television, it has become increasingly vocal about what it feels are abuses by almost all of the television services, public and private alike, of various agreements to hold down the broadcasting of theatrical films so that cinema houses can continue to attract audiences, too. The industry wants reductions both in the numbers of movies broadcast overall and in the number of movies broadcast in prime time. The increased competition brought on by the privatization of TF1 and the licensing of Canal Plus and M6 has made films an especially attractive and inexpensive programming element that hurts cinema attendance. However, commercial broadcasting is so well-established by now that the film industry is unlikely to recover its lost ground.[203] Still, there are a few ways in which the movie industry receives favorable treatment vis-a-vis TV: Wednesdays remain largely movie-free on all of the terrestrial TV services except for Canal Plus, because that's the day of the week when the French cinemas change their feature films.[204]

But there still are allegations of unfavorable treatment. In 1996, the CSA and TF1 concluded an agreement which notably reduced (to 15 percent) the amount of independent television and film material TF1 would be required to broadcast. Furthermore, it was allowed to increase its advertising revenue earned through broadcasting those programs by 50 percent, making room for the additional ads by cutting program material. The Trade Union for Audiovisual Production's president threatened to stir up political pressure,[205] but with little eventual effect.

INTERNATIONAL COOPERATION

France is a very active exporter of radio and television programming to its former colonies and protectorates, as well as to other French-speaking European nations and to Canada. Most of that export trade is in the form of entertainment programming and is on videotape, but in 1984 France linked up with Switzerland and Belgium, and later with Canada, to develop a jointly programmed service for distribution to cable TV outlets via satellite. The service, TV5, contains a mixture of information and entertainment from the four nations, but France supplies over three-fourths of the material. Because TV5 is intended for more than just French-speaking audiences, the French Foreign Ministry pays for the majority of its operating costs. Whether it's worth the investment is another question: figures from the late 1980s showed tiny audience figures for Europe. That also led to questions about its long-term viability, and its structure was changed in the early 1990s. It began to advertise itself as "a European service in French."[206] But the predominance of material made in France for French audiences continues to give TV5 a decidedly French flavor.

One aspect of French TV program distribution that used to limit the size of the export market was the small amount of programming available in other languages besides French, but in 1979 the Ministry of Foreign Affairs created a special department to increase the dubbing of programs into English, which has facilitated sales abroad. That move is indicative of the view of past and present French governments that French television can serve as a useful form of cultural propaganda; in that light, it's perfectly proper for the government to be involved. Private firms become involved, as well: The government also helped to subsidize an ill-fated attempt to supply French TV programming to the U.S. cable market, through TeleFrance USA. There were hopes that the organization could distribute to many of the larger cable operations on a daily basis, but TeleFrance USA never made it past New York and Boston for more than a few days each week.[207] TeleFrance folded in 1982.

France has entered into coproduction arrangements with most of the other major European broadcasting organizations and several of the smaller ones at one time or another. "Chateauvallon" was a notably ambitious example, but each year there are numerous documentaries, cultural programs and children's programs done as coproductions. Belgium and Switzerland are natural partners because they are in part French-speaking, but Germany, Italy,[208] and Great Britain also have been frequent collaborators. Still, the coproduction business is far from robust: during the period 1993-95, coproduction numbers and income-generated dropped, the latter by about a fourth.[209]

In addition to those more or less standard forms of international activity, the French government established an organization that either controlled or strongly influenced several foreign broadcast stations, three of them just outside the borders of France and with French audiences as their primary targets. SOFIRAD eventually acquired the informal title of "the octopus," for reasons that will be evident. Its predecessor came into being in 1942 through a cooperative arrangement between the German government and the government of Vichy France, and controlled the newly created (by the Germans) Radio Monte Carlo. It became SOFIRAD in 1945; the French government took over full responsibility for its financial support and appointed its administrative council. It acquired partial or total ownership of Sud Radio (Andorra-based, directed to Southwestern France), Radio Monte Carlo (Monaco-based, but with its transmitter on French soil and directed largely to France), Europe No. One (transmitter based in the West German state of Saar, studios in Paris and directed to France), and several overseas operations: Radio Monte Carlo Middle East (Cyprus-based, directed to the Middle East), Afrique No. Une (Gabon-based, and directed largely to central and west Africa), Radio Mediterranée Internationale (Morocco-based, and directed largely to North Africa), and Radio Caribée Internationale (Dominica- and Saint Lucia-based, and directed to the Caribbean). It also had been financially involved in Télé-Liban (a television station in Lebanon), Télé Monte Carlo and Télé-France Internationale (a supplier of prerecorded French programs for overseas distribution; TeleFrance USA was a part of it).

Clearly SOFIRAD was an operation of major proportions. Whether it exercised control over the programming of its many "tentacles" was more difficult to discern, and whether that control was the result of pressures from the government still more difficult. Interviews with SOFIRAD officials elicited strong denials that the company had anything at all to do with program content; they claimed that their role was strictly financial.[210] However, certain crises within France led to specific acts of censorship of broadcasts and punishment of broadcasters that clearly were inspired by government displeasure at material carried by the peripheral stations with which SOFIRAD was connected. Notable examples were the firing of several of Europe No. One's broadcast journalists following the 1968 disturbances and the sacking of Maurice Siegel, Europe No. One's director general, in 1974, on the public grounds that he'd been there too long, but with the accompanying statement by Denis Baudouin (SOFIRAD's then-director) that he (Baudouin) was tired of the station's "bantering tone" toward the government.[211]

On the whole, the two other peripheral stations under SOFIRAD's influence, Sud Radio and Radio Monte Carlo, caused fewer problems for the government than did Europe No. One, and found themselves rewarded on occasion for their "good behavior." When Sud Radio lost its access to its transmitter in Andorra in 1980, the French government allowed it to use a French transmitter until access was regained in 1983, although the station could not carry commercials during the time if broadcast from within France. And when Radio Monte Carlo wanted to increase the range of its transmissions in 1974, which could be done only by finding a more suitable transmitter-antenna site, the French government arranged for the lease of land within France itself—a move that angered officials at Radio France tremendously, since they had been struggling to keep the peripheral stations from taking away even more of their audience.[212]

When the Socialists came to power in 1981, they indicated that the peripheral stations, too, would see changes. The licensing of local private radio hurt the peripherals at first, but they soon exploited the opportunity to buy up some local radio stations and acquire licenses for others, and RTL, RMC and Europe No. One were able to establish nationwide networks, which put them in an even better competitive situation than they'd enjoyed earlier. In early 1986, the French government began to sell off parts of SOFIRAD. The first major element to go was Europe No. One; the giant publishing company Hachette acquired controlling interest. Sud Radio, one of its weakest revenue producers, was sold to RTL in 1987. Even so, SOFIRAD remains an active investor in private radio, both in France and elsewhere.

THE NEW MEDIA

As of 1998, close to 10 percent of all households subscribe to cable; likewise for satellite TV. If France had been able to capitalize on the implementation of several domestic technological developments during the 1970s—videotext, fiber optics, multichannel cable TV—by now it could have had a commanding lead over other west European nations in exploitation of the new media. However, the economic problems that beset most of French industry during the middle-to-late 1970s[213] also hit the French telecommunications industry, and the experiments remained few in number and were exploited to only a fraction of their potential. The government also seemed reluctant to encourage the development of cable: Kuhn suggests that President Valéry Giscard d'Estaing (a Conservative), was reluctant to offend the Gaullists, who wanted to retain centralized control over broadcasting. One important basis for that fear was that Socialists and Communists, who were quite prominent in local governments around the country, could use locally based cable to their political advantage.[214]

By the end of the 1970s, the French government had decided that it was time to intervene in the languishing telecommunications industry, which then began to receive some government assistance. If that industry could be stimulated, so the reasoning went, France might have a strong entry in the export market, especially in western Europe where various trade agreements gave west European products an edge over those produced in North America and in Japan, the two major telecommunications exporters. The Mitterand government continued that stimulation policy, and also erected further trade barriers of the sort described earlier for Japanese-made VCRs, but the Chirac government dropped the barriers in 1987.

Fiber-optic cable was one of the first beneficiaries of the stimulation policy, and in mid-1985 the government approved a plan that called for cable service to some 450 cities, serving over 15 million people, by the end of the decade. The Biarritz experiment in fiber-optic cable had begun in 1981; by 1985 it had 600 subscribers, and by the end of that year a little over a thousand. It was evident that French industry was not geared to mass production of fiber optics. Subscribers had a limited choice of programming fare by North American standards: 10 TV channels, including various French and other European services, with a local channel by late 1985. Subscribers paid Fr 55 (about $10) a month, with various additional services (videotext, videophone) carrying supplementary charges.[215] The service has long since been discontinued.

The Conservative government's announcement in January 1987 that it would drop the Socialist project of wiring the nation with fiber-optic cable, but would encourage French investors to wire individual communities with coaxial cable, could have stimulated the more rapid development of cable service, since coaxial is so much cheaper than fiber-optic.[216] Various private cable companies wanted to be able to set up their own systems and develop their own marketing strategies, but the government-owned telecommunications company, France Telecomm, was given a mandate to "cable the nation" (a process that continues to go slowly, thanks in part to France's often low population density). The private companies and local authorities sometimes fought against France Telecomm, and particularly against its high cabling costs per household, but came to an understanding of sorts by 1990.[217] Since then, cable rates have dropped, and more communities—small communities in particular—have found it possible to introduce cable on a cost-effective basis.

Potentially the biggest stimulus to the further development of cable TV in France was Paris Cable, owned in part by Lyonnaise des Eaux, which also had invested heavily in M6. Two hundred homes signed up for Paris Cable in December 1986, with company predictions that there would be 1.3 million homes hooked up by 1992. Yet, by 1996, the count stood at perhaps a 10th of that figure. While cable certainly has grown more rapidly since then (roughly 2.5 million by mid-1998), it's far from being a successful industry. Its subscribership ratio, though increasing, is the lowest of all of the northern European countries. Joint investment from abroad (the U.S. cable giant TCI, for example) has been modest.

I've heard several explanations for that state of affairs, ranging from, "Most French are satisfied with the choice they have among the terrestrial stations" to, "The monthly subscriber fee (usually 100 francs [$17] for basic service) is too high for most households." But it may be a matter of channel choice: outside of the largest cities, 12 to 20 channel systems still predominate. Most cable service currently available in France is through coaxial cable. There also is master antenna service to apartments, and roughly 30 percent of all French households have it, but with few exceptions it carries only the usual terrestrial services, and households using it aren't counted in the totals for cable. As Canal Plus and the commercial networks established nationwide distribution, that also appeared to reduce interest in cable. A steady increase in VCR ownership—nearly two-thirds of all French households had one or more by 1997—also makes movie-oriented cable TV services less attractive.

Those systems which have been more successful at attracting subscribers seem to have done so at least in part on the basis of their own local and subregional programming. For example, the Alsatian city of Epinal [pop. roughly 12,000] and its surrounding communities began to operate a local channel (Images Plus) on their cable system in 1990. It set the ambitious target of 18 hours a day, which at first featured lots of repeats and "filler," but which later contained local news, sports, talk shows, amateur films and videos, programs from schools, etc. By the mid-1990s, over half of the households in the service area had subscribed—one of the highest rates in the country.[218]

Direct broadcasts from satellite-to-home receivers had been one of the great fascinations of the Socialist government during the early 1980s, and in 1984 the French and Luxembourg governments signed an agreement to finance and jointly program a DBS operation. President Mitterand almost immediately called for the creation of a license-fee-funded cultural channel, which started life as a production company, but which was eventually to function as a DBS service (La Sept). The return to power of the Conservatives in the 1986 elections threw the DBS picture into further confusion. Conservative spokespersons for communications policy announced in early April that they were annulling the existing DBS agreement (largely because they disagreed with the Socialist government's choices of participants) and would reopen the bidding process (which probably would favor RTL).[219] Launch of the first French DBS satellite was scheduled for November 1986, but the launch problems that had plagued so many nations in the mid-1980s also hit France, delaying launch of the satellite, TDF-1, until late 1988. Further communication satellites have been launched since that time, but now they're joint European ventures, and not exclusively French. Four were delivering French-language services as of 1992, confusing potential subscribers as to which, if any, to subscribe to. In short, French policy toward the newer electronic media has been as politicized as has policy toward conventional broadcasting.

The channels available for both cable and satellite are much the same, with the exception of TPS' exclusive rights to carry France 2 and 3: a children's service (Canal J), a "teens and 20s" channel (Canal Jimmy), Eurosport France, three cinema channels, Télé Monte Carlo, a music video service (MCM), Paris Première (popular and "high" culture, fashions, etc., all Paris-based), TV5 (French-language "international" service, with programs from France—many already seen on French terrestrial channels—Switzerland, Belgium and Quebec), Planète (documentaries), Disney, a weather channel (with information on health and beauty, as well!), and two all-news services, "La Chaîne Info" (LCM, which is 100 percent owned by TF1), and Eronews. LCM has won considerable praise from critics for its ability to pack a lot of information into its compressed news format, and to present it in a lively, but not "dumbed-down," way. Many of the cable companies offer still other services brought in from around Europe (Switzerland, Great Britain, Germany and Italy in particular). Whether such services are particularly attractive is another question, since the French appear to be even less interested in watching programs in foreign languages than do their European neighbors. But the relatively slow growth of cable and satellite subscribership has discouraged French investment in further program services, which almost certainly discourages potential subscribers.

As for Internet services, France lags far behind Germany: Mid-1997 figures showed roughly one million French Net users, and more than three times that number of German users. That was one of the major concerns voiced in the course of a two-day "Internet Fair" held in late March 1998 by the Institut Français pour l'Internet (IFI), which advocated a goal of 8 million by the year 2000, as well as one Internet terminal for every three French schoolchildren. But the IFI wondered whether the government was willing to deregulate, subsidize and reduce user fees to the point where such growth could take place. The French government has often criticized the Internet because not enough of its content is French. However, as IFI has pointed out, the situation certainly will not improve unless the French become more heavily involved; if they do not, the technological world will simply move on, leaving France in the dust.[220] There have been some modest experiments with interactivity, as well: Subscribers to Télévision par Satellite (TPS) could use their remote control devices to open a virtual catalog when an advertisement for Renault's multipurpose vehicle "Kangoo" appeared as a regular commercial on TF1 or M6. The catalog allowed them to "open" and "shut" doors, view from an assortment of angles and in various colors, see a finance plan, etc.[221]

Even though Internet development has lagged, France has mounted what so far is the most comprehensive study of the possible impact of the Internet on society—French society only, to be sure, but the study clearly has implications for other industrialized nations. French Prime Minister Lionel Jospin

(Socialist Party) gave the Conseil d'Etat the responsibility for carrying it out, and it reported back in July 1998. The major concerns were predictable: protection of individual privacy; safeguarding copyright of intellectual property; developing a secure system of encryption; making electronic commerce less risky, especially for individual Internet users (in French, "Internauts"); protecting children from pornography; and discouraging racist material.[221a]

However, one of the most interesting facets of the report is the Conseil's attempt to describe a regulatory body that could help to deal with those concerns. It recognizes the difficulty of doing so on a strictly national basis: the Internet is too international in nature to make that feasible. Rather, it argues that the European nations must continue to work on a common approach, as the EU and Council of Europe already have begun to do, but with "space" (freedom) provided for national variations that would fit within the overall approach, yet allow for the inclusion of national approaches and sensitivities. It rejects governmental regulatory agencies, and proposes (pp. 214-215) a *private* structure: a "general interest" association that would have dues-paying members with interests—personal, professional, corporate—in the Internet, acting through a general assembly. The day-to-day work of ensuring that Internet usage be socially responsible would be in the hands of an administrative council of 15 members, six of them appointed by the government, nine by the general assembly. Proposals made by this body could be enacted as laws or decrees by the government.

If this doesn't sound much like self-regulation, that shouldn't be surprising: the French have very little experience with self-regulation, and the Conseil report notes (pp. 208-210) many failed attempts at it where the Internet is concerned. And the proportion of representation accorded to the government in the administrative council shouldn't be surprising, either, given the historical nature of French government involvement in regulation of the electronic media. Still, the Conseil's attempt to articulate the issues and to consider how to achieve the "best" (in moral terms, at least) approaches to regulating the Internet without stifling it, or without creating something that would be impractical or useless, are worth consideration as other industrialized nations try to decide how to—in some cases, *whether* to—regulate this most individual, supranational, polymorphic of the electronic media.

CONCLUSION

French broadcasting has been dominated by *political* pressures throughout most of its history, to a degree remarkable among European nations. The electoral victory of the Conservative coalition in 1986 and the ensuing "media reforms" showed once again how difficult it is for any long-range planning to be accomplished where broadcasting is concerned, since a new government is almost certain to undo much of the work of its predecessor. Still, the opening up of broadcasting to more licensees, and the greater degree of freedom of expression enjoyed by broadcasters, are likely to remain as legacies of the Socialist government; the Conservatives are not about to attempt to restore the monopolistic system or the tight controls over broadcast content of the pre-1981 era.

France also has emphasized its own *culture* in its electronic media output, sometimes to the point of seeming overly chauvinistic, especially by comparison with other European systems. The licensing of commercial radio and TV stations in the early to middle 1980s brought with it larger amounts of foreign program material, and some of it seems to have been quite popular, but government officials remain wary of foreign incursions, and French talent unions have lobbied for tighter controls on imports. The 1994 "loi Toubon" is only the latest legal manifestation of that policy, which also explains why the French government has placed so much emphasis on exporting its culture through the electronic media.[222] The intellectuals have expressed alarm over the prospect of a cultural invasion through TV. French officials are aware that the new technologies make it almost impossible to restrict the flow of foreign programs into France in any major way, but they do seem determined to support French production so that at least French programs will be able to compete on a reasonably even footing. Even so, imports and imitations of foreign programming have made notable inroads on "homegrown" material.

Economic considerations, too, are becoming more important in shaping French electronic media. The development of cable (especially fiber-optic cable) and satellite technology was a high-priority item for Conservatives and for Socialists alike in the early to middle '80s. Even as the government subsidized work in those fields, however, it expressed concern over the rising costs of production, the need for increases in the annual license fees, and possible inefficiency in the administration of the public broadcasting services. Those concerns have been present over the past few decades, but they became more serious by the end of the 1980s. It wasn't surprising that the newly elected Conservative coalition announced in April 1986 that there might be privatization of one or two of the public TV services, and that in fact no public broadcasting service was sacred. Nor was it surprising to learn that some government officials were considering the removal of advertising from public television so as to provide more revenue for private TV.[223] It may have been more surprising to see the Conservatives back off from the subsidization of fiber-optic cable and DBS, given their earlier support for both, but that action was consistent with the new economic conservatism of the middle-to-late 1980s, which was finding expression in many parts of Europe. By the 1990s, the economically driven commercial radio and TV sector was easily outstripping the public broadcasting sector in terms of ratings success, although France 2 was mounting something of a challenge to TF1's supremacy.

Whether France can maintain a high level of domestic cultural TV production in a large and economically driven media system is another question, as is the question of political control or influence over such a system. The French public system generally was amenable to the influence of the government of the day, Conservative or Socialist, when it came to emphasizing the portrayal of French culture. Reconciling political, cultural and economic considerations in the more complex dual (public-private) system that developed in the 1980s has proven far more difficult. The regulatory system, whether HA, CNCL or CSA, has had the continuing responsibility of imposing and enforcing French content quotas, but hasn't been able to do much about quality, or about the influence of foreign (especially U.S.) models. Given the (slowly) continuous expansion of French electronic media activity, the job won't become easier in the future.

Thiérry Védel and Jérome Bourdon see a decline in the importance of political influence over the electronic media in France.[224] Jean-Claude Sergeant has a very different viewpoint: " ... the reluctance of successive governments to renounce their ingrained hands-on approach to broadcasting seems to be a national feature inherited from centuries of Jacobin rule."[225] I think that Sergeant is correct, although I also feel that political influence now can be seen far more often in economic terms, e.g., who is awarded the moneymaking commercial licenses, than it is in immediately apparent political terms. Still, neither form of influence has brought credit to the French electronic media.

3 The Netherlands

Plurality in an Era of Competition

The electronic media system in the Netherlands often has been acclaimed as a model of how those media can be structured to serve society (as opposed to serving government, advertisers, media managers, the "power elite," etc.). While that structure is very different from any other in the world, there are doubts on the part of many Dutch observers that it can adjust to changes in society and in technology, yet retain its individuality. A combination of physical and societal conditions has helped to shape the Dutch system, but recent changes in some of those conditions have weakened its foundations.[1]

BASIC FACTORS

Geographic

It's difficult to imagine a geographical situation more conducive to the growth of terrestrial broadcasting. The Netherlands is almost as flat as the proverbial pancake and is the most densely populated nation in Europe (423 inhabitants per square kilometer). It is approximately 150 miles long and 120 miles wide at its broadest points, and its major population centers all lie within a 30-mile-wide, east-west band running through the middle of the country. It has two other nations on its land borders: Germany to its east and southeast, Belgium to its south. England lies some 50 to 150 miles across the English Channel and North Sea. While the nation isn't really circular in shape, it's possible to broadcast from a central point and cover all of it with a 75-mile radius signal, and with little spillover into the neighboring nations.

Neighbors also play a role in shaping Dutch broadcasting. The northern half of Belgium, which borders the southern Netherlands, is Flemish-(Dutch) speaking. Broadcasts from Belgium may be heard throughout the Netherlands and seen in much of the country. The same is true for Germany, and many Dutch citizens can understand German quite well, although those with memories of the Nazi occupation during World War II often prefer not to speak it. English radio stations also can be received throughout the country, and British TV comes in along some parts of the Dutch coast. Since most Dutch citizens have studied English in school for several years, they can follow British broadcasts with relative ease. The spread of cable TV in the Netherlands also has helped to bring television from each of these countries, and others, to Dutch viewers. Broadcasts from the Netherlands can be heard in parts of all three countries, as well, but only in northern Belgium is there likely to be much of an audience for them, since few Germans or English are fluent in Dutch.

Demographic

Not only is the Netherlands densely populated, but its people are remarkably homogeneous. Most of the 15 million Dutch were born and raised there, and their family trees go back for centuries. This has led some observers to claim that the Dutch are overly class-conscious,[2] but it also enables broadcasters to assume certain shared national traditions. When broadcasting began in the early 1920s, that homogeneity was almost total. Broadcasters cared little about serving the few non-Dutch speakers (aside from Frisian, linguistically related to Dutch and spoken by perhaps 250,000 people living in the north) residing in the country. Regional dialects are spoken in the home and among friends, and appear on regional and local media services, but rarely over national services.

However, the past few decades have seen some marked changes in the nation's homogeneity. Although precise figures are hard to come by, there may be some 40,000 Moluccans, 230,000 Surinamese, 75,000 Antilleans, and over 400,000 "guest workers" from southern Europe, Turkey and Morocco living in the Netherlands. Some estimates place the total émigré population at nearly 10 percent of the overall total. The Moluccans are there because their island home, once part of the Dutch East Indies, was incorporated into Indonesia in 1950; many did not welcome the change and left. The Surinamese came from former Dutch Guiana and the Antilleans from the Netherlands Antilles, just off the northern coast of South America. Their major reason for coming was to escape the poverty of their native lands. The guest workers came during the economic expansion of the 1960s, when there were too few Dutch citizens willing to take or to continue on in some of the really grimy, physically exhausting jobs that opened up during that period. First-generation members of those groups keep largely to themselves, and few speak or understand Dutch all that well. Subsequent generations are more fluent in the language. Most émigrés live in the larger cities, but it isn't unusual to see Surinamese and Moluccans living in smaller towns.

Economic

The Netherlands is a prosperous nation, although the Europe-wide recession that began in the late 1980s had a dampening effect on the Dutch economy for a few years. However, the country has recovered more quickly than have most of its European neighbors. Certainly the country has a high enough per capita income to be able to support with relative ease what is, as you'll see, an expensive media system. Unemployment was running about 6-7 percent as of the late 1990s—an excellent figure by overall European standards. Cooperation between labor and management also appears to have been better than in most European nations.[3] Almost every Dutch household has a number of radio sets and one or more TV sets. Most Dutch citizens are urban dwellers, working in businesses, the professions, government and manufacturing. Roughly 5 percent of the population is employed in fishing and agriculture. Radio pays special attention to the latter two through detailed marine weather forecasts and early morning programs on agricultural development.

Political

The Netherlands is a constitutional monarchy, in which the sovereign (currently Queen Beatrix) has little to do with the governance of the nation. Fourteen political parties are represented in the Dutch Parliament as of 1998; most are involved in coalitions in order to gain more voting strength. In 1964, a coalition government even fell from power because of its inability to present to Parliament a suitable proposal for an additional television service—probably the only time in history, Dutch or anyone else's, where a policy issue involving television has caused the downfall of a government. Major political parties also are involved with some of the country's major broadcasting organizations, and all political parties represented in Parliament receive free airtime for party political broadcasts.

Cultural

The Dutch are able to draw upon a rich cultural tradition going back to the Middle Ages and including such figures as Rembrandt and Escher. Thanks to the presence of a universal and high-quality system of education, literacy is very high, and many works of Dutch novelists and playwrights who are unknown outside the country are widely known and appreciated within it. Some of those works have become popular favorites when adapted for television. But there also is a considerable following for foreign culture, ranging from avant-garde theater and painting to hip hop (rap) and U.S. TV series such as "Law and Order."

Religion plays an especially important part in Dutch culture, although surveys indicate that nearly one-third of all Dutch citizens don't think of themselves as members of any organized religion, and church attendance is dwindling. A 1987 survey showed that nearly half of the population considered itself unaffiliated with any organized religion.[4] Still, the largest groups—Roman Catholics, Calvinists—continue to exercise considerable influence in Dutch society. They operate their own school systems from kindergarten through university and have their own newspapers, political parties and broadcasting organizations, in addition to sports clubs, youth groups and even, for Catholic farmers, a goat-breeders association. This pervasive involvement by organized religion, along with political parties, in the life of the nation often has been called the "pillar" concept, with each organization seen as one of the chief pillars supporting the national structure. Where broadcasting is concerned, three main religious organizations (Roman Catholic, Calvinist, Liberal Protestant) became involved in the middle-to-late 1920s, along with a sociopolitical organization, the Socialists.

But Dutch culture is very supportive of the expression of minority opinion, and dozens of artistic and social reform groups bring their viewpoints and works before the public. Associations and foundations for sexual reform, moral rearmament, freethinkers, Freemasons, Christian Scientists, Humanitarians and many others flourish in the Netherlands, and many receive continuing allocations of airtime to present themselves over Dutch radio and television. It isn't unusual to hear a Dutch citizen complain about the "kooks" and "oddballs" one sees and hears, especially in the larger cities, but the same person may well observe with pride that tolerance and even encouragement of such activity is what makes Dutch society different (meaning "better"). That affects the media as well: During the 1960s and 1970s, the most radical of the broadcasting organizations, VPRO (Liberal Protestant), found that its dues-paying membership often came dangerously close to dropping below the minimum number specified by the Media Act for the lowest category of organization entitled to major blocks of airtime. When that happened, VPRO regularly received membership dues from people who stated that they didn't agree with its programming but respected and encouraged its right to continue.

A BRIEF HISTORY

Some Dutch historians have claimed that the world's first regularly and continuously scheduled radio broadcasts for the public came about in the Netherlands in November 1919.[5] An engineer, H.H.S. a S. Idzerda, began to broadcast from the Hague laboratory of his company, the Netherlands Radio Industry. His broadcasts were financed out of his own pocket, and on occasion, by listeners from as far away as England responding to his appeals for funds. The next few years saw several manufacturers of radio equipment initiate their own broadcast services, presumably in hopes of stimulating the sale of radio sets and parts. By 1923, the minister of public works attempted to bring a greater sense of order to the situation by calling for formal applications for franchises to broadcast, but there were too many to accommodate, so, much as had been the case in Great Britain, the minister called upon applicants to submit a joint application. Only one company, the Netherlands Transmitter Industry, followed through. (Idzerda's company was nearly bankrupt by then.) The company was allowed to lease airtime to interested organizations, and by 1928 there were five of them, broadcasting on two transmitters. They were:

NCRV	(Netherlands Christian Radio Association), 1924
VARA	(Workers Radio Amateurs Association), 1925
KRO	(Catholic Radio Broadcasting Foundation), 1925
VPRO	(Liberal Protestant Radio Broadcasting Association), 1926
AVRO	(General Radio Broadcasting Association, originally made up of people who had constructed their own sets and wanted to promote their hobby by making broadcasts), 1928

From the beginning, then, the government made two important decisions: first, that it would ensure some degree of order and stability in broadcasting, and second, that it would not operate broadcast services itself. However, no single organization would be permitted to claim exclusive rights to operate such services, either. Organizations that did claim airtime were required from 1923 on to provide a reasonably complete range of programming, not only for their own particular supporters, but also for the Dutch citizenry in general. This concept of broadcasting might be called "pluralism within a monopoly," since the government decided who was entitled to broadcast and what the general shape of the program schedule would be, but permitted several quite diverse groups to exercise that right.

The process of deciding which groups would be entitled to do what and for how many hours brought to the fore some deep divisions between those groups. John Hiemstra's detailed account of the negotiations and politicking that went on in the mid-to-late 1920s reveals often bitter conflicts. For example, when AVRO was to receive a reduction in airtime and VARA an increase, an NCRV spokesperson opposed the plan, claiming that, "The members of the NCRV consider the principles of the socialistic VARA a disaster for our country and we have the duty to do everything possible to oppose those principles." Certainly there was cooperation and respect, but plenty of disrespect and antagonism, as well.[6]

Under the terms of a 1928 ministerial order, the groups also had to agree to share the two transmitters. In 1927, KRO and NCRV had cofinanced the construction of the second transmitter, which they then reserved for themselves. AVRO claimed near-exclusive rights to the first transmitter, leaving little time for VARA and VPRO. All this now changed: The four largest groups were given equal amounts of airtime on the two transmitters, while the smaller VPRO received a lesser amount. Size of membership thus became a criterion for amount of airtime; for the pillar organizations, it remains so to this day. It's difficult to determine just why those particular organizations received airtime, although their size, and their prominence in Dutch political, social and cultural life, certainly were factors. There was only moderate support at that time for a national system of broadcasting along the lines of the BBC, and little for a government-run service.[7]

The various broadcasting organizations were responsible for raising their own finances. Voluntary contributions from listeners, as well as support from the parent organizations (e.g., the Roman Catholic Church), formed the not always reliable mainstays of that support. After the first few years, no advertising was allowed for Dutch audiences, although a few English firms sponsored popular music programs in order to reach British listeners (the BBC didn't broadcast ads), and a few Dutch firms furnished gifts to be given away on programs so long as the brand name of the gift was mentioned.[8] Advertising stopped altogether in 1935. There was no listener license fee, either, even though that practice already was widespread in Europe.

During the first decade or so of Dutch broadcasting, the government did not concern itself overmuch with specific broadcast content. The need for each broadcasting organization to present a balanced service never was governed by set percentages of program categories or standards for program content; however, general regulations concerning public order and other related matters were issued in 1930, and smaller organizations (e.g., the Radio People's University) were authorized small amounts of airtime. But in the early 1930s, the government showed that it was quite ready to express concern over content, even without specific standards. In 1933, the Socialist broadcasting organization, VARA, observed a minute of silence after the execution of van der Lubbe, the man the Nazis had accused of setting fire to the Reichstag building in Berlin. The government felt that this was prejudicial to its policy of political neutrality and withdrew one hour of broadcasting time from VARA as "punishment." As a gesture of solidarity, the other broadcasting organizations mutually agreed not to use that time themselves, so the hour went unfilled.[9] In 1934, with the depression causing high unemployment and with Naziism growing in Europe, the Dutch Communist Party, Dutch Nazi Party, and several other parties became involved in various disturbances; at one point, the Communists declared a "Red front" and made illegal broadcasts over a transmitter in "the heart of Red Amsterdam,"[10] but they soon went off the air.

When the Netherlands was occupied by Nazi Germany in 1940, all of the broadcasting facilities came under Nazi control. The various broadcasting organizations ceased to function, although many of their staff members continued to work for the German occupation government. Also, the occupation government instituted a license fee for listeners; the Dutch government had drafted legislation approving a fee in 1939 but hadn't passed it by the time of the occupation.[11]

When the occupation ended in 1945, the broadcasting organizations were anxious to get back in business and immediately sought to move into their former buildings. However, the Dutch government did not turn control of the facilities back to them immediately. It wanted to discuss the matter of whether the prewar system should resume, or whether it should be replaced by a national system of some sort. There was some criticism of the prewar system on the grounds that it wasn't very open to the expression of minority viewpoints from within the various organizations. The Labor Party adopted resolutions calling for a more truly national system. But leaders of the Catholic and Calvinist "pillars" pushed for a return of the old system, the Socialists gave it grudging support for fear of being left out, and back it came.[12]

The license fee that had been passed by the occupation government was continued by the postwar government, and its proceeds were divided among the various organizations according to their transmission time (still equal for the four largest organizations, with a much smaller amount for VPRO), with a sum set aside for fee collection and for transmission. Even with this additional revenue, the organizations could see the wisdom of pooling their resources, particularly for studio utilization, news coverage, broadcasts of large musical groups and so on. All five of them agreed in 1947 to form the Netherlands Radio Union (NRU). The organizations retained their autonomy but worked cooperatively through the NRU board. The minister of education, arts and sciences approved the creation of NRU, stated his ministry's jurisdiction over broadcasting and appointed a commissioner to serve as liaison between the ministry and NRU. While the commissioner could pass along to the minister any and all board decisions for review and possible annulment, the latter never occurred. The minister also decreed that airtime be allotted to the various churches, reflecting a traditional Dutch concern for freedom of religious expression. Mainline religions had been broadcasting for some time but now were joined by smaller groups with brief periods of airtime.

This cooperative atmosphere also brought renewed attention to educational broadcasts, which had begun in 1926 with broadcasts by the Educational Foundation of Inland Navigation to children of families living on barges that plied the country's many waterways. Broadcasts for Protestant and for Catholic schools began in 1947 and 1948 through NCRV and KRO, and in 1951 AVRO, VARA and VPRO combined their resources to begin broadcasts for nondenominational schools. The Radio People's University had been broadcasting adult education programs since 1931; in 1946 it began to receive a small share of the license fee.

The Growth of Television

Experimental broadcasts with television took place in the late 1930s. There seemed to be little enthusiasm on the part of the pillars for actually putting a TV service on the air; the high costs of doing so, coupled with a lot of mutual suspicion among them as to who would benefit most, made them reluctant to become involved (Jan Wieten cites a number of instances in the minutes from executive board meetings of the pillars which indicate that the suspicions had some foundation. In a 1938 meeting of the KRO [Catholic] executive committee, the group discusses subsidizing Catholics who are ready to conduct experiments with TV transmissions, which would help KRO when TV actually starts up, but notes that this would "have to be done covertly, so that it is not obvious that the movement is led by Catholics." See Wieten, 12; endnote 13 has full source citation). Even the possibility that the Philips Company (electronics) might convince the government to let it set up television broadcasting on its own didn't bring them together, although it did make them worry that, if Philips succeeded, the pillars might never get the chance to start their own TV service. But the rising costs of experiments with TV and declining support for Philips slowed things down, and the Nazi occupation of the Netherlands in 1940 put an end to them.[13]

Experiments began again in 1948, with Philips again conducting them. The radio broadcasting organizations feared the high costs of television, but pressure from Philips helped to lead in 1951 to the establishment of the Netherlands Television Foundation—this despite a government report that had concluded the country could not afford TV yet. The radio organizations agreed that they would have to cooperate to an even greater degree than they already were doing through the NRU. They also agreed to finance television out of their existing revenues for a further two-year experimental period. The Philips Company furnished most of the technical gear, some of the staff, and the transmitter, while the post office (PTT) covered transmitter operating costs. Parliament debated the future of TV in 1953 and decided to make the service permanent, although it wasn't until 1956 that it approved a separate license fee for TV set owners that would help meet the added costs of the new service. The Ministry of Education and Culture was made responsible for television, drew up regulations for it and created a Television Advisory Council to assist in keeping track of how it performed.

While the 1950s saw a continuation of cooperation among the organizations, there were incidents that revealed just how far apart they remained in some respects. The most striking example was a pastoral letter from the Roman Catholic bishops in 1954: It forbade Catholics membership in the Socialist trade union movement, attacked the Socialist Party and warned Catholics against "frequent tuning in to Socialist broadcasts." It's doubtful that many Catholics took it seriously, but it did cause the near rupture of the Labor-Catholic coalition. (A 1965 press release from the bishops reaffirmed most of those bans, including one on broadcast listening and viewing.)[14]

A 1956 incident revealed something of the government's attitude toward the mass media. Stories were appearing in the British and German press about Queen Juliana's use of a faith healer to treat her daughter. The Dutch prime minister called a meeting of the chief editors of newspapers and radio services. No TV editor was invited, TV apparently being considered too insignificant (its news service *was* minuscule at that time). The editors were asked not to print or broadcast anything on the story in view of "possible constitutional consequences," and they complied, despite the fact that there was considerable public knowledge of it. Broadcast journalists in the Netherlands had little experience with independence of expression, thanks to the "pillars," and the government wasn't about to encourage them to acquire it.

As Dutch society moved into the 1960s, there began to appear evidence of a more liberal spirit, often in ways that shocked many Dutch citizens. Amsterdam became known as the "hippie capital of the world," and traffic in drugs was common. The Beatles gained many Dutch fans, partly thanks to the broadcasts of the Dutch and British pirate radio stations operating in the English Channel, and several Dutch Beatles-like groups sprang up. The Dutch television service, unable to afford the heavy costs of broadcasting only Dutch material, carried large amounts of foreign programming (particularly British and American), and some of it presented new ways of looking at society. The marriage of Princess Beatrix to a German commoner who had done military service in World War II, and the revolutionary pronouncements of Pope John XXIII, added to the sense of turmoil, excitement and change.

The pirate radio stations carried little but popular music, and music of a sort (the Beatles, the Who) unlikely to be played often over the rather staid Dutch system. They soon acquired large audiences. The stations also broadcast ads, but most listeners didn't seem to mind them, and some said that they even enjoyed them. In 1964, a pirate TV station, TV Noordzee, began broadcasting from an offshore platform. It provided a heavy diet of imported light entertainment; again, there were ads, and again, viewers seemed not to mind them. The government, after considerable debate, sent in a military force by helicopter in December 1964 to put the station off the air.[15]

All of that illegal activity helped to spark a major debate in Parliament over the future of broadcasting. Various proposals came up, including a national system (no pillars), an advertiser-supported system, a renewal of the existing system, and modifications in the system to allow a wider range of organizations more ready access to airtime. A second TV service started in 1964, programmed jointly by the five pillar broadcasting organizations, but the costs involved in operating it highlighted the need for additional revenues. Raising the license fee was not a popular option for Parliament, which would have to approve any such increase.

To add to the complexity of the situation, the International Telecommunications Union authorized a third television frequency for the Netherlands, and some Dutch commercial interests applied to the government for permission to operate and finance such a service through sale of ad time. (Ad-supported TV had been considered as early as 1953, and it was one of the earlier applicants for such a service, REM, that had set up TV Noordzee after having had its application turned down.) The Dutch government already had presented proposals to Parliament in 1961 and 1963 that would have authorized Dutch firms to establish a second television service that would be ad-supported. Parliament had turned down both proposals, partly because of strong opposition from the existing broadcast organizations—themselves linked with various political factions.[16] In 1964, the coalition government again presented a proposal for an ad-supported television service, this time along the lines of Great Britain's Independent Television Authority (ITA), but again Parliament refused to accept it. The coalition resigned, a new coalition was formed and a new broadcast law was its first major order of business.

The New Broadcasting Act and Its Effects (1964–1970)

As legislation was being drafted for the new act, various political factions and other interest groups reached agreement on the introduction of advertising into Dutch broadcasting. They created an organization known as STER (Stichting Ether Reklame, or Broadcast Advertising Foundation), which would preview all ads for acceptability of content (the foundation was to develop content regulations), set rates and place limits on allowable amounts of advertising time (95 minutes a week for TV starting in January 1967, 26 minutes a day for radio starting in 1968; both have been increased since then). The broadcasting organizations would have no direct connections with advertising, which in theory meant that their programs wouldn't be influenced by it, but they would receive proceeds from the sale of ad time in rough proportion to their overall airtime. In order to protect newspapers that might be harmed by losses in advertising revenue, 40 percent of the proceeds was set aside in a special fund to aid them. (This was reduced in 1970 and replaced in 1974 by the Trade Fund for the Press; however, part of the money for that fund came from a 5 percent increase in STER's advertising rates.)

Meanwhile, new proposals for broadcasting indicated that Parliament seemed ready to allow other sorts of groups besides the "pillars" to apply for major blocks of airtime. That concept became known as the open door, and Parliament approved its inclusion in the Broadcasting Act in 1967, amidst sharp debate. Although the act wasn't slated to come into effect until 1969, one new broadcasting organization and several small groups were authorized to begin operations immediately. The organization, Televisie Radio Omroep Stichting (TROS), had been formed chiefly by supporters of TV Noordzee, and in no sense was it a "pillar" of Dutch society.

The Broadcasting Act of 1967 didn't do away with the "pillar" system, since the five original broadcasting organizations remained on the air, but the act did make it awfully difficult to determine whether the character of a would-be broadcasting organization could be taken into account in deciding whether to allow it to broadcast. The act contained a provision that organizations "must aim at satisfying cultural, religious or spiritual needs felt among the population, to such an extent that their transmissions may on that account be deemed as serving the public weal" (Chapter 2, Section 13.2), but those were very loose criteria. The existing organizations lobbied hard to obtain postponement of the act but were unsuccessful. One of their worries—and a worry of many observers of Dutch broadcasting—was that still more organizations without any special character and with little but light entertainment to offer would join the Dutch system, taking up precious airtime (precious to those who already had it, certainly!).

Furthermore, because the act did specify numerical (membership) criteria for four categories of broadcasting organizations, because airtime increased as one moved up in the categorical list, and because ad revenues and proceeds from license fees also were apportioned on that basis, an organization that could appeal to mass audiences would realize several financial benefits if it succeeded. As the "new kid on the block," TROS stood as a primary example of what the older organizations feared. Without waiting very long to see whether their fears were justified, three of the older organizations began to "popularize" their programming, a process Dutch critics called "trossification." Two pillars, VARA and VPRO, resisted the temptation to a greater degree; each had set ideas as to how broadcasting could serve its members and society in general. Also, VPRO was too small to hope for huge numbers (although it did begin to recruit "culturally progressive" members), and VARA felt that its members were particularly loyal.

The early 1970s saw the creation of two more broadcasting organizations. The EO, or Evangelical Organization, was more or less in the tradition of "pillars," although there was some concern that its broadcasts were too narrowly devoted to the interests of its members—and there is that requirement in the act that speaks to serving the public weal, meaning the broader public. But the second organization, Veronica Omroep Organisatie (VOO), posed more problems. Much like TROS, it had been formed by the followers of an outlawed pirate station, in this case Radio Veronica. The act had set specific criteria of size for broadcasting organizations but also had created a *candidate* status, which would allow aspiring broadcast organizations to come on the air for three hours a week on radio and/or one hour a week on television. Such status would last two years; during that period, the organization had to increase its dues-paying membership from the 40,000 required for candidate status to the 100,000 that was then the minimum for a Class C (smallest) regular broadcasting organization.

A list of 40,000 VOO members was presented in 1974, but VOO also indicated that it would rely almost entirely on popular music. The minister of culture (the government minister responsible for broadcasting at that time) decided that VOO didn't show enough variety in its programming to warrant candidate status. That ruling was contested by VOO; the Council of State (the highest court of appeal under the terms of the act) reversed the decision. The organization went on radio in December 1975 and on TV in April 1976. In June 1976, it submitted lists with names of 100,000 members, but irregularities (more than half of those listed had not paid their dues yet, and the act counts only dues-paying members) delayed VOO's acceptance into Category C until late 1978. Clearly, size of membership had become increasingly important as a criterion for who was to broadcast, and just as clearly programming that catered to mass tastes would have advantages in increasing that size.

One other very important result of the 1967 act was the strengthening of the centralized program-making bodies. The NRU and the Netherlands Television Foundation (NTS) had been formed by the broadcasting organizations themselves. Because of the heavy expenses of television, the foundation had been responsible for a good deal of centralized program-making, and even though it was the creation of the organizations, it had acquired something of a life of its own. The NRU had done the same, to a smaller degree. The act created a new body, the Netherlands Broadcasting Foundation (NOS), that would combine the functions of the old NRU and NTS. It would receive a guaranteed share of airtime (minimum of 15 percent of total radio time and 25 percent of total TV time, maximum of 40 percent for each medium), a share of license fees and ad revenues, and would be governed and advised by various boards and committees whose membership would come from government appointees and from the other broadcasting organizations. In other words, the NOS now would become a competitor for money and for airtime, and no longer would it be so much under the control of the broadcasting organizations. The NOS also assumed the task of coordinating the overall broadcast schedule and of administering TV and radio studios (the latter only when organizations lacked their own).

The NOS was to function under a broad mandate. The act stated that it was charged with "looking after affairs which are of interest to radio and television as a whole" (Section 39, Part 2a), and NOS consolidated its hold on such categories as newscasts, actualities and sports—the latter highly popular among Dutch viewers—but also broadcast children's cartoons, jazz, original drama and other entertainment, as well as documentaries. It did not compete with the other organizations in providing serialized entertainment or "mass appeal" feature films, however.

Thus, while the 1967 act didn't represent an attempt to create a new broadcasting system, it did weaken the "pillarized" concept in several ways: by encouraging the establishment of nondenominational, nonpolitical broadcasting organizations (whether that was the intent of Parliament is another question, but that was the net effect); by strengthening the centralized portion of the system (NOS); and by giving the other broadcasting organizations less control over NOS, even though they were its original creators. However, it didn't appear to be a case of the government wanting more control over broadcasting.

As the act was debated, passed and put into effect, the broadcasting organizations themselves were reacting to a growing climate among the Dutch of questioning and challenging long-held beliefs. The Catholic KRO aired interviews with Catholic leaders in which interviewers sometimes were skeptical or even caustic; VARA did a program on abortion at a time (the mid-1960s) when that topic was considered off-limits for public discussion; VPRO frequently broadcast speeches of and interviews with members of radical political movements. The government generally kept its hands off such programs, although there sometimes was plenty of opposition to them within the organizations themselves, and several instances of self-censorship. However, in 1963 the government warned KRO that it was prepared to take the picture off the air if KRO broadcast an interview with Georges Bidault, head of an illegal (in France) French "terrorist" opposition group known as the Organisation de l'Armeé Sécrete (OAS), and KRO backed down. Both VPRO and VARA were "deplored" by the government on several occasions in the late 1960s and early 1970s for "tasteless" programs, among them an impersonation of the queen and a composite image of the pope standing among some attractive women in an item about a literary ball.[17] Still, in no instance could the government take effective action against the broadcasters because the only legal grounds were "danger to the security of the state, public order and morality" (Paragraph 4, Section 10.2). "Morality" is almost impossible to define, and application of the other grounds in the KRO case resulted in the passage of a motion of censorship against the government by the Parliament—in a televised debate.

After the 1967 Act (1970–1988)

In the 1970s, the broadcasting organizations began to face more competition from broadcasters outside the country. Some Dutch viewers already could receive Belgian, West German and British television stations, depending upon the part of the Netherlands in which they lived. As cable TV spread throughout the country (to improve reception in cities, to broaden program choice, to eliminate unsightly rooftop antennas), all of those stations became more widely available and diverted some viewers away from Dutch TV. In 1979, an Amsterdam cable TV firm, Kabeltelevisie Amsterdam (KTA), became the unconscious carrier of yet another form of programming when illegal operators began beaming signals carrying illegally acquired tapes of first-run movies, some of them pornographic, at the KTA master antenna; the antenna then automatically passed the signal along to its viewers over a channel that had signed off for the evening. The illegal operators sold ad time at bargain rates, and as the ads went only to the local area (legal Dutch TV ads went nationwide only at that time), meat markets, furniture stores and other places of business found the new service very attractive. Such operations sprouted up in other Dutch cities, and some became very specialized: One offered a 20-part course in black magic![18]

Feature-film distributors and exhibitors claimed to be hard-hit by these pirate activities (one TV guide for the illegal services even called itself De Piraat), and in late 1981 the Motion Picture Association of America (MPAA) won a suit in a Dutch court banning pirates from exhibiting MPAA films. The Amsterdam Court of Justice decided that cable transmission was a new form of publication for which copyrights were due and required that the cable companies themselves close down a channel as soon as a pirate transmission broke into it. Also, those who advertised over pirate transmissions could be prosecuted. The net effect of all of those measures was to sharply reduce pirate TV activity.[19]

Land-based radio pirates, which had been around in small numbers in the more sparsely populated northern and eastern parts of the country during the 1950s and 1960s, also became very active in and near major urban centers during the late 1970s. Most were low-power, had highly irregular broadcast hours and were run as hobbies. However, a few became more powerful and regular, which made them more attractive to local advertisers but also more of a threat to other forms of radio communication that had the legal right, as the pirates did not, to operate on certain frequencies. As of the late 1990s, there may be hundreds of these stations—far too many for the small force of detection crews to locate and to remove from the airwaves, besides which the Radio Controle Dienst (the government detection service) has no investigative authority but may act only on the basis of complaints. The radio pirates have their own monthly magazine, *Free Radio,* which has been around since 1973.

In the early 1980s, some of the Dutch cable systems began to receive broadcasts from satellites (Optical Technology Satellite, ECS-1, Soviet). The ECS-1 service (Sky Channel, a Rupert Murdoch venture), an ad-supported British venture that carried mostly U.S. and British TV entertainment for several hours a day for cable operations in various parts of Europe, seemed to some Dutch critics a harbinger of worse things to come. Direct broadcasts from satellites (DBS) to home receivers had been under discussion in western Europe for several years, and finally in 1981 the western European nations agreed on an allocation plan for DBS frequencies.

Luxembourg seemed likely to initiate such a service along the lines of Radio Luxembourg: mostly light entertainment interspersed with ads placed by firms in countries such as the Netherlands, where various restrictions discouraged them from advertising over their own systems. Radio Lux had had a Dutch service since the 1930s, and critics wondered whether a similar TV service would add further impetus to the process of "trossification." (Eventually, it did.) Then there was a major review (1979-82) of the future of Dutch broadcasting undertaken by the Scientific Council for Government Policies (an advisory body to the Dutch government).[20] Unlike the British system of broadcasting, there is no provision for periodic review in the Netherlands, so reviews usually arise in response to actual or anticipated problems. There were several reasons for conducting the review: the advent of the new technologies, controversy over just how open the system should be to what sorts of organizations (including pirates), and cost-effectiveness of the present system (widely held to be inefficient and even wasteful).

Already the "trossification" of Dutch broadcasting had resulted in an amendment to the Broadcasting Act that would make it more difficult for new organizations to be admitted to the system. The amendment came into force in 1980 and set higher membership standards for size of organization, ranging from 450,000 or more (Category A) to 150,000-300,000 (Category C). Aspirant groups had to show a membership of at least 60,000; they would have up to three years to reach Category C, but would have to show that they offered programs that "differ from those already available." Several new organizations applied (e.g., an Islamic group, a Hindustani group), but none was granted aspirant status.

The council's report dealt with "trossification" from a different angle. It advocated a high (elite) culture service for TV, to be run by a new organization. If the old organizations insisted upon continuing their pursuit of high ratings through mass appeal programming, at least there would be one reliable source of high culture. But airtime for the new service would have to come from the existing two-channel service, as the council rejected suggestions for a third channel on the grounds that it almost certainly would have to be supported by advertising. Yet it argued that more airtime should be devoted to commercials, both to help offset the rising costs of TV and to further encourage Dutch companies not to advertise over foreign stations viewable in the Netherlands. The council also called for an opening up of cable TV so as to allow local cable franchises to offer a wider range of services (e.g., subscription TV) and perhaps to interconnect as networks. The press would be allowed to invest in cable, as would existing broadcast organizations. Local cable could carry commercials but couldn't claim any portion of the annual license fee.

The government responded by issuing a white paper in August 1983. By that time, the governing coalition was Christian Democrat-Conservative and favorable toward private enterprise (deregulation, reductions in public sector spending). The white paper went far beyond the council report in proposing revisions. It advocated allowing subscription TV, but not allowing the broadcasting organizations to operate it. It advocated cabletext and cable newspapers (including ads), but only the press was to operate them. It also advocated breaking up the NOS: There was to be a facilities department (studios, etc.), which was to become an independent company whose shares were to be held by the state (a majority) and the broadcasting organizations (a minority); there would be a program service for "centralized" programs (news, sports, etc.), which also would be an independent company, governed by a board on which the broadcasting organizations would be in the majority but with government representation as well. The coordination and planning of the overall broadcast schedule, an NOS function, was not covered in the white paper. The NOS itself would cease to exist.

One of the government's intentions seems to have been to reduce the cost to the public of what admittedly was an expensive system. Even before the white paper, it had proposed both budget cuts and a cancellation of projected increases in the annual license fee. It also favored a limitation on the proposed expansion of broadcast advertising time, so as to minimize harm to the press—a medium even more closely tied to political parties than was broadcasting. The various new services (teletext, etc.) would have to be paid for by individual users, and not by the general public through increased fees.

But deregulation would have its limits. The white paper stated that the four radio services were not distinctive enough in their programming, and raised the possibility that the government would do something about it if the broadcasting organizations could not. Also, the organizations were given a program formula for the first time in Dutch broadcasting history: 20 percent culture, 25 percent information, 25 percent entertainment and 5 percent education (various categories make up the remainder). The categories weren't tightly defined, largely because they couldn't be. The minister of culture was to enforce them.

The NOS reacted with dismay, of course, but the other organizations weren't very happy, either, since they had hoped to be allowed to compete in providing the new cable services; nor were they particularly pleased about the plan for fiscal austerity. The white paper was debated in Parliament in 1984, and passed largely intact. In July 1984, a steering committee and seven working groups were established to carry out the paper's proposals. They reported at the end of 1984, recommending that NOS be divided into a limited company for the provision of production facilities and a foundation for producing limited amounts of broadcast programming. Its other functions were to be handled by a Media Authority (Commissaraiat voor de Media). There also was to be a new Media Council to replace the existing broadcasting, press and (in part) advertising councils.

The fact that the pillars were unable to influence a majority of Parliament to change many aspects of the government proposal that they disliked showed that the pillar system had lost some of its power. In fact, the history of Dutch broadcasting could be described as a fairly rapid rise of "pillar power," followed by its gradual decline, although certainly not disappearance. The changing character of Dutch society, where religious and political organizations clearly had become less important in people's everyday lives, undoubtedly played a role here (ironically, broadcasting itself probably had a lot to do with that change, since it had increased people's access to a wider range of information and entertainment, which at least had the potential effect of broadening people's viewpoints). But so did the coming of cable, teletext and other new media. And so did the recession of the late 1970s and early 1980s, coupled with the replacement of the Socialist-dominated coalition government by a Christian Democrat-Conservative coalition. Even at that, the Cabinet of the new governing coalition declared that it intended to protect the national culture, and issued a memorandum on satellite and cable services that set a requirement of at least 5 percent national material in their transmissions, rising to 20 percent over a five-year period.[21]

Some of the proposed reforms never occurred, for a reason that's quite common in European political life: There was a national election in May 1986, and since the parties backing the proposed broadcast reform hadn't been in any particular hurry to pass a new media act, they were overtaken by the election. The governing coalition was returned to power, but the Liberal Party lost some of its strength. Since it had been the coalition partner that had pushed the hardest for greater commercialization of television, its hopes for a new, fully commercial third TV service vanished. The government soon announced that there would be a new third service (recall that a third channel had been available for about 20 years by now), but that it wouldn't be commercial. Instead, it would accommodate NOS services and most of the very small broadcast organizations, such as the Humanists, SOCUTERA (social-cultural welfare) and so on.

That proposal itself showed that NOS would not be totally abolished, but simply segregated. Nederland 1 and 2 would accommodate the eight "pillars": The "entertainment" companies (AVRO, TROS, VOO) would go on Nederland 1, while the three larger "ideological" companies (VARA, KRO and NCRV) would go on Nederland 2. The smaller ideological companies (VPRO, EO) would have small amounts of time on each of the two channels. The redivision of channels was scheduled to occur in the fall of 1987 but later was put off until the spring of 1988. The companies almost immediately began to wonder where they would find the money to fill the increased airtime that most of them would have. Amounts of advertising time could be increased, but the press objected to that strategy, and the press still represented a powerful lobbying force. Nevertheless, Parliament decided to increase the allowable amounts of ad time, but also required the broadcasters to share their extra revenue with the press.

As for the other white paper proposals, some appeared in modified form, while others failed to appear in the 1987 Media Act. The NOS shed its production facilities, which now would be handled by an independent, limited liability company, the Netherlands Production Broadcasting Company (NOB). However, the various broadcast organizations, including the NOS program departments, were required to use NOB for 75 percent of their TV production requirements and 100 percent of their radio for the next few years. The NOS Research Department might or might not be privatized. (In the long run, it wasn't.) The NOS itself would continue to coordinate the overall schedule and would act as collective representative of Dutch broadcasters in international forums such as the ITU and EBU. The new Media Authority (Commissariaat voor de Media, sometimes translated as Media Commission) would take over most of the broadcast supervisory functions of the Ministry of Culture. The new act came into effect in January 1988. Yet, even with all of those changes, the act represented a compromise rather than a wholesale revamping of the broadcast structure.

The 1987 Act and Its Consequences (1988–1998)

Several months after the radical (by Dutch standards) restructuring of the system, an unexpected challenge arose. Over the years, a few of the pillars had threatened to leave the system and set up their own fully commercial stations, but legal and monetary constraints prevented them from doing so. Now, satellite-delivered cable TV services from outside the country offered a way to make good on that threat—but not until the case for full commercial operations had gone to the Dutch Supreme Court and one of the pillars very nearly was removed from the broadcast schedule for several weeks.

The first attempt came in the form of Cable One (chiefly an audio service with visual supplementation), which originated in Great Britain but had Dutch shareholders and Dutch-made programs. The newly created Media Authority had ruled that it was a foreign station, which meant that Dutch cable systems could legally carry it. In March 1989, the NOS filed a suit on behalf of the pillars with the Supreme Court. It charged that Cable One's foreign identity was largely a fiction. The court agreed, and the service ceased operation late in 1989.[22]

Several months earlier, two very similar satellite-to-cable services had announced their intent to begin transmissions before the end of 1989. The NOS quickly sought an injunction to deny them access to Dutch cable systems, on the same grounds: their foreign identity was a sham. The Media Authority had already ruled that one of them, TV 10 SA, was essentially Dutch and shouldn't receive access to Dutch cable, but that the other, RTL-Veronique, had substantial financial support from RTL, and thus should be considered as foreign. That led to a series of complex legal maneuvers, but in October 1989 the Dutch Supreme Court ruled in favor of the Media Authority's action (actually, RTL-Veronique had commenced broadcasting two days before the Supreme Court decision, probably because it was confident of political support from the ruling Conservative coalition). The Dutch minister of culture labeled the ruling "historic," since fully commercial broadcasting (almost all of it delivered through cable, as it is today) now was legal, so long as it came from a "foreign" source.

But *how* foreign? RTL-Veronique, as its name implied, featured considerable investment in money, programming and management from VOO. It soon dropped "Veronique" from its title, and replaced it with the number 4, implying that it was the fourth Dutch TV channel. Stories concerning VOO's financial support began to appear in the newspapers. The Media Authority then proposed that VOO be fined, and also lose its broadcast rights for a period of time, because it had misused public funds (its share of the annual license fee). VOO countered by claiming that the money it had invested in RTL-4 came from sales of the VOO program guide, and not from the license fee.[23] The Authority voted in July 1990 to impose the fine and the suspension; the latter would begin in January 1991, and would last for seven weeks on both radio and TV. Three months later, the Supreme Court issued an injunction halting both actions; eventually VOO paid the fine, and the suspension was dropped.

RTL-4 had marketed itself from the beginning as an alternative to the pillars, and in several respects it certainly was: It could broadcast for 24 hours a day, and eventually did, whereas the pillars had to squeeze all of their programs into the 3:30 p.m.-to-midnight period. It carried many "erotic" films and a risqué talk show, which none of the pillars would have dared to do. And its programming consisted of little but general entertainment (quiz and game shows predominated), while the pillars had to provide a wide mix of genres. Within a few months, it was clearly ahead of Netherlands 3 (NOS and various small organizations) in the ratings, and in a few more months it was on a par with Netherlands 1 and 2, which it soon left behind.[24]

Interestingly, its success came largely as a result of its Dutch-produced programs, and not its English and U.S. imports. Its quiz and game shows had U.S. formats, by and large, but Dutch hosts and audiences. Its most popular program, the five-night-per-week soap opera "Good Times, Bad Times," came from a concept developed and rewritten by an Australian production company, Grundy, but featured Dutch casts, situations and settings. Better yet for RTL-4's profitability, those program formats were amazingly cheap: $35,000 per 25-minute episode for "Good Times, ... "[25]

The pillar organizations clearly were concerned by the threat posed by RTL-4. They had commissioned the management consultants McKinsey and Company to assess their future prospects, and met at the end of 1990 to discuss the McKinsey report.[26] The report projected that RTL-4's share of the audience was almost certain to grow still further unless the pillars undertook a radical reform of their program schedule and cut production costs:

> The public broadcasters have enjoyed a rich past, but unless drastic cuts are made, the future will be bleak. ... The advance of commercial TV is now impossible to stop. There will be a drop of advertising income allocated to the public sector. ... Unless urgent action is taken now, further erosion of programme quality will be inevitable.[27]

McKinsey saw the problems as centering around the extremely high cost of production brought about by the multilayered administrative structures of the pillars and the poorly planned scheduling of programs. High cost had been a perennial problem, but its resolution could be delayed as long as there was no alternative approach. But now RTL-4 had shown that it was possible to produce a low-cost show that would have plenty of audience appeal. As for scheduling, there were too many time periods in which roughly similar shows were on two or three of the channels. McKinsey recommended that, for any time period, there should be two channels carrying shows of general appeal, and one channel with more specialized material. Highly specialized material that would attract audiences of less than 2 percent should be moved out of prime-time slots, and should be "livelier." Informational programming should be a high priority, since the pillars would probably devote more time and support to it than would the fully commercial services, but it should be presented in ways that would "get people talking."[28]

McKinsey also recommended that the pillars produce more Dutch drama. RTL-4 had shown that the public liked it, and in fact a March 1991 survey showed that only five of the top 20 shows were produced abroad; Dutch quiz shows, drama and satire all did well.[29] The pillars also hoped to receive the government's permission to broadcast for 18 hours a day starting in 1992 or 1993, but they also calculated that they would have to program a number of repeats in order to fill such a schedule.

While the pillars could acknowledge that they faced a crisis, actually doing something about it was another matter. It's one thing to agree that too much money is spent on administration, but quite a different thing when it comes to getting rid of some of the administrative "fat." And program producers, too, had long been accustomed to relatively fat production budgets, with little outside competition to show how productions could be "leaner and meaner" and still have great appeal for viewers. The 1988 reform which saw the creation of a separate production center had not yet led to cost reductions; in fact, a combination of administrative problems, protection for trade unions and a guarantee to provide 75 percent of the production facilities needed by the pillars actually led to financial losses,[30] even as competition from newly created and more cost-effective independent Dutch production companies was growing.

Although radio didn't face the same sort of competition, the 1987 law had made it possible for independent local, noncommercial (and later, commercial) radio stations transmitting through cable to broadcast at low power over the airwaves, and many began to do so. However, none of them enjoyed anything comparable to RTL-4's budget, and, aside from two youth-oriented pop music services and some of the local noncommercial stations, they've remained a minor part of the average Dutch listener's diet. The regional radio structure authorized in the 1987 law has done somewhat better, and all 13 Dutch provinces now have their own stations, with the more populous provinces subdivided into as many as four service areas. There were early fears that the provincial governments might seek to influence programming, since the regional stations received their financial support from the additional annual license fee of up to ten guilders ($5) that provincial governments could levy. So far there have been few indications of interference. Another fear was that the revenue from license fees wouldn't be sufficient to allow for more than a few hours of programming per day, but stations in the more heavily populated areas (Radio Rijnmond in Rotterdam) soon moved to 12 hour days, and most of the other regional stations followed;[31] some now broadcast for as many as 18 hours a day.

Radio's major problem is at the national level, where listenership has been falling even as it has risen for local, regional and some foreign stations (especially those with "nonstop pop" formats, such as the U.K.-based Sky Radio). The satellite-delivered foreign stations seemed to derive much of their popularity from the "less talk, more music" approach taken by their disc jockeys. Also, the growing numbers of émigrés in the Netherlands have been able to gain access to satellite-delivered radio services from their homelands, such as Turkey and the Netherlands Antilles. Surveys taken in the late 1980s and early 1990s showed that younger individuals were less and less drawn to radio, although the children of émigrés seemed to prefer Dutch radio services over programming that featured material about their émigré cultures.[32]

By the mid-1990s, there was clear evidence that the pillar system was crumbling, most visibly through VOO's decision to leave the system completely in September 1995, and thus to give up any claim to license fee support or the right to use any of the three pillar TV channels. It would join with the largest Dutch commercial TV production company, Endemol, which had been created through the merger of two Dutch production companies in late 1993, and which was earning hundreds of millions of florins per year by 1996 in its production of TV entertainment programs for the Netherlands, Germany and other European nations.[33] It hoped to move into the news production business in 1997, by producing a light news/infotainment program, "Bild-TV," for Germany's largest-circulation daily newspaper, *Bild Zeitung;* however, as of 1998, nothing had materialized.[34] As for RTL-4, its success was so great that it led to the creation of RTL-5 in October 1993. Where RTL-4 had women and less well-educated viewers as its prime target audience, RTL-5 aimed to reach young people, men and more highly educated viewers.

NOS, acting on behalf of the pillar organizations, had engaged in discussions with Endemol in 1994-95, and it appeared that an agreement had been reached whereby the pillars would guarantee Endemol a fixed percentage of their program production needs, and NOS would share sports rights with Endemol. The Media Authority stated that the deal wouldn't be illegal, but that it might be against the intent of Dutch media law, which supported the concept of a strong *public service* broadcasting system; the deal between the pillars and Endemol might compromise the pillars' ability to furnish the wide range of choice in programming that many hold to be the chief characteristic of such a system.

Before the deal could be completed, however, Endemol called it off, and it and VOO, now calling itself Veronica, announced the creation of a new cooperative venture, the Holland Media Group (HMG), which would unite Veronica, Endemol and RTL-4/RTL-5. NOS and most of the pillar organizations were furious over what struck them as negotiating in bad faith. They also were concerned about HMG's power: the shares of audience commanded by Veronica and RTL-4 and RTL-5 often came to over 40 percent. A modification of the Media Act in 1994 gave the pillars more TV airtime, by extending the time available in afternoons and late at night, and another modification had extended the amount of time available for commercials. However, Veronica, RTL-4 and RTL-5 each could broadcast for 24 hours a day, if they wished, had larger amounts of time for commercials, and, working through Endemol, could probably hold their average production costs to lower levels than could the pillars. That combination almost certainly would give HMG a competitive advantage.[35]

Much as they had done in the past, the pillars decided in 1995 to reshuffle the cards and come up with a new cast of characters for each of the three channels. The result:

Netherlands 1: AVRO, KRO, NCRV and smaller religious broadcasters
Netherlands 2: EO, TROS and two educational broadcasters
Netherlands 3: VARA, VPRO, NPS and one educational broadcaster
NOS provides news and informational programming, plus sports, through all three channels.

Whether this will help to preserve the pillar system is another question. There's nothing in the reconfiguration that would necessarily make it easier for viewers to identify with one or another channel. Nor are the channel lineups the result of natural partnerships. For example, if Netherlands 1 were to be the "religious pillar" channel, then EO should be in the lineup. Instead, it's coupled with TROS, which is the most general, secular, nonpolitical of all the pillars. Still, the collective shares of audience for Netherlands 1, 2 and 3 have improved to the point where they may outdraw the Holland Media Group by as much as 10 to 15 percent, although they sometimes trail HMG by similar margins.

The European Union's European Commission helped the pillars when it ruled in 1996 that the Holland Media Group would have to convert RTL-5 into an all-news operation, because HMG controlled too much of the market.[36]

That would create more diversity in the HMG lineup, and thus better serve the public interest (although that wasn't a specified reason for the decision); it also would almost certainly reduce RTL-5's share of audience. The "new" RTL-5 began to broadcast the all-news lineup in 1997; its share of audience dropped from roughly 5-7 percent to perhaps half that level.

Further competition arose as still other satellite-delivered (almost always to cable—only 5 percent of all Dutch households use DBS) services came on the scene in the early to mid-1990s. Sport 7, MTV, the Cartoon Network, CNN, Discovery and the NBC Super Channel had been available through cable for several years, but aside from Sport 7 (which ceased operation in late 1997), they drew only a few percent of the audience. The introduction of the Scandinavian Broadcasting System (SBS 6—the self-proclaimed sixth Dutch TV channel) in 1995 represented a more formidable challenge, since SBS 6 brought a wide range of light entertainment (much of it U.S. and British imports, and often old ones, at that—"Happy Days," "Webster"), but it also presented "Hart van Nederland," which provided only news about the Netherlands,[37] plus weather reports, a horoscope, talk shows, home improvement and cooking programs, a Dutch soap opera and even regional inserts for the national newscast. While it's rare for SBS 6 to place any of its programs in the Dutch top 20, its daily overall shares of audience range between 5-10 percent.

A government-appointed committee, the Ververs Committee, set to work early in 1996 to determine how the pillar organizations should prepare for the more competitive future. It came out with its report in June.[38] Not surprisingly, it called for cost reductions, most of them to come from a slimmed-down administrative structure. The pillars sought to respond, but the sacrifices seemed too great for many of them. A several-day session in the town of Kortrijk, held in September 1996, appeared to be headed in the direction of a breakup of the existing system, with some of its members going fully commercial and others unsure of their direction. Then the head of EO fashioned a compromise, reminding his colleagues that, if they didn't hang (remain) together, they'd probably hang (die) separately. Partly because of EO's religious character, and partly because the breakup of the pillar system had seemed imminent, the agreement soon was dubbed "the miracle of Kortrijk." Its chief feature was a streamlined administrative structure with an administrative office and a general council ("superboard") overseeing the three TV channels, each of which would have a single manager; the pillars would give up considerable authority in this arrangement, although the members of the general council and the councils for each channel would be drawn from the pillars. The entire structure would eventually result in a projected savings of Fl 250 million (roughly $135 million) over the period 1997–2000. The minister of culture, Ad Nuis, was hopeful that this would sharply reduce the power of the individual pillar groups.[39] The reaction of Parliament was mixed, but mildly skeptical,[40] and of course most of the savings would come late in the period, so it would be some time before anyone would know whether the new structure was any more economical than the old one.

Still, despite all of the changes that the pillar structure underwent during the decade 1987–97, the system managed to maintain a considerable degree of diversity, with satires, original drama, some highly unusual children's shows (including a newscast specifically for children), and various ethnic and cultural minority programs, some of them furnished by newly licensed (1993) Hindustani and Muslim groups. And commercial television began to specialize, with sports channels, a weather channel and a news channel joining the general entertainment services such as VOO, RTL-4 and RTL-5, and SBS 6. The Fl 30 ($15) monthly fee paid by most Dutch households with cable brought them far more choice than they had had at the beginning of the decade, although some of that additional choice was made up of imported programs that looked alike because they *were* alike.

As of the late 1990s, the Dutch electronic media lineup looks like this:

National

Public Service	*Commercial*
5 radio channels (Hilversum 1-5)	10 Dutch radio services, most music; 6 imported services
3 TV channels (Netherlands 1-3)	Holland Media Group (3 TV services) SBS 6; Filmnet (pay-TV), roughly 25 imported channels (U.S., U.K., etc.)

Regional

Public Service	*Commercial*
13 radio services	6 radio services
5 fully public TV services	Nieuws TV (5 provinces)
6 public-private TV services	4 individual TV services in 4 provinces

Local

356 radio services; 109 TV services

The Threads of History

Throughout much of the history of Dutch electronic media, changes were relatively slow to develop. When they did take place, they usually came about through the initiative of the pillar organizations, which also managed to block or slow down changes on several occasions. The 1960s brought a reshaping of the concept of pillars, largely due to the challenges of pirate radio and TV and the positive reception that much of the public (younger people in particular) and a number of members of Parliament (often reacting to the public) gave to the pirate's largely light entertainment-oriented programming. Some of the existing pillars began to copy the pirates in placing more emphasis on light entertainment, and began to resemble one another more and more. Other pillars resisted for a while, but gradually moved more in the same direction, driven partly by ratings, partly by the numbers and sentiments of their dues-paying members.

Commercial television and radio came along in the 1990s, and began to challenge the pillars. Their advent was due to several factors, and furnishes an excellent example of how the various basic factors noted in Chapter One can converge to influence a major electronic media development. *Geography* and *demography* favored the growth of cable because the Netherlands is flat, compact and densely populated; the Dutch *economic* situation was healthy, which meant that most Dutch households could afford to subscribe to cable; Dutch *culture* featured openness to other cultures and knowledge of their languages, which meant that foreign TV channels would be both acceptable and "user-friendly;" the nation's *political* majority throughout most of the 1980s and 1990s supported private enterprise, as did the policies of the European Union; and developments in satellite and cable *technology* in the late 1980s to early 1990s made it more and more economical to establish services outside the country—the Holland Media Group, SBS 6, Sport 7—and make them available to virtually all Dutch households. Public demand for commercial services was negligible before they arrived, but RTL-4 in particular captured so much of the audience in so short a period of time that it became impossible for the government to continue to oppose them.

The development of Dutch broadcasting has been neatly summarized by media scholar Denis McQuail, who observed that, "Despite changes, which are still occurring (more under the pressure of circumstance than by choice), the Netherlands retains the core elements of a system that to a reasonable degree gives reality to the principles of broad access and cultural, social, and political diversity. The scope and ambitions of the public service [pillar] system have been reduced, but there remains guaranteed space for cultural quality and authenticity, for uncommercial sources of programming, and for minority points of view."[41] But it remains an expensive and, in some ways, inefficient system, and it's an open question as to whether the younger generations of Dutch viewers and listeners will continue to support those inefficiencies as more and more electronic media alternatives become available.

FINANCING

Dutch broadcasting organizations receive their financial support from several sources. The annual license fee assessed on all households with TV sets (Fl 184, or about $100, as of 1998) is divided among the organizations according to their airtime; as of 1998, all seven pillars receive equal amounts, since all have enough members to qualify for Category A status. Some of the fee money also supports transmission operations, and a small share goes to the post office for costs of license fee collection. The process of division is not by rigid formula—the organizations submit their annual budgets to the minister in charge of broadcasting and to Parliament—but there is no indication that minister or Parliament manipulate the budget in order to reward or punish organizations. The advertising revenues collected through STER are added to the license fee money and divided together with it.

The Dutch are quite diligent in paying the annual license fee. Year in, year out, less than 15 percent of all households fail to do so—a very good record by European standards. Still, there are some who criticize it on the grounds that a) they never watch or listen to any of the PSB services, so why should they pay to support them; and b) the PSBs should stop relying on this "public subsidy" and start competing for audiences, perhaps by charging on a monthly rate basis for each PSB service used in each household, which would be easy to collect from cable viewers, but somewhat more difficult for the 10 percent of the households that aren't on cable. The Media Council (an advisory body only) stated in a 1995 report that the annual fee was outmoded, because cable now supplied so many channels that viewers weren't so dependent on the public services. A one-time member of the Media Council, Walter Etty, has proposed having the public TV services available only through scrambled signals, which would allow viewers to decide whether they wanted to pay for the services, but would also intensify the link between the services and their publics, and would make it possible for the services to market various materials for sale to the public, thus reducing dependency on advertising.[42] Etty's viewpoint seems to have attracted little support, and the license fee seems safe for the time being.

The broadcasting organizations also earn money through the assessment of membership fees, which must be a minimum of 10 florins ($5) for basic membership and 30 florins ($15) if there also is a subscription to the organization's weekly program guide. The membership of most of the pillar organizations is predominantly at the Fl 30 level, but VPRO has a slight predominance of Fl 10 members, and EO a heavy predominance of them, mainly because many Dutch wish to show their support for the most distinctly alternative pillars, even if they seldom watch their programs. Most pillars charge more than Fl 30. VARA, for example, sets its full membership fee at Fl 66.20 ($30+). No one is compelled to belong to an organization, but until the early 1990s only they were allowed to publish detailed guides. Endemol now publishes similar guides, and makes a tidy profit, but many members of organizations have developed a sense of loyalty to "their" particular guides over the years. Each organization may highlight its own programs but must list all programs on the air. Up until 1982, newspapers carried only brief daily listings, but then a Dutch newspaper began to print more detailed listings, claiming that it was reprinting them from Belgian guides that listed Dutch programs. The lower court accepted that defense, and several other Dutch newspapers began the same practice. The higher court ruled in 1983 that the practice was illegal because it went beyond using the program information supplied by the NOS on behalf of all Dutch broadcasters to the NDP (Netherlands Daily Press, the umbrella organization for Dutch newspapers). NOS then agreed to supply NDP with somewhat more detailed program information for the use of its members.

Not only do the guides generate revenue by attracting members; they also provide space for sale to advertisers, and ads placed in the largest-circulation guides (e.g., AVRO's Televizier, the largest weekly magazine in the Netherlands) bring in tens of millions of florins each year. Some of the organizations have attempted to make their guides as much like general-purpose magazines as possible, despite a ministerial order that limits nonbroadcasting editorial matter to a maximum of five pages, and there are occasional ministerial reminders that one or another organization is exceeding the limits. By the same token, organizations may spend a few minutes of airtime each month promoting themselves and soliciting new members; this too occasionally becomes excessive and results in warnings.

All broadcast advertising on the pillars is handled by STER, which has the power to accept and to reject ads and even to take them off the air if it feels that an ad has been on long enough, or if the advertising standards set by the Dutch Advertising Code Foundation are violated, in STER's opinion. (Advertisers may challenge STER's rulings in court.) STER once had a much higher rejection rate for ads, but commercial competition and a government-expressed desire for a "gentler" regulatory climate starting in the early 1990s prompted STER to relax its standards, and as of the late 1990s, no more than 1 or 2 percent of all ads submitted were turned back, usually on the grounds of exaggerated, deceptive or unsubstantiated claims.[43] Ad time for the pillars is limited to an average of 6.5 percent of broadcast time per day for radio and TV; limits for commercial radio and TV are 15 percent. Those limits have been established by the European Union for all EU broadcast organizations. Top advertisers include the usual: banks, soft drinks (Coca-Cola is a top 10 advertiser), laundry soaps and beer, but total ad income is shrinking,[44] despite (or perhaps because of) steady growth in the numbers of TV channels available through cable. The public service broadcasters in particular have seen drops of as much as 25 percent of their yearly income from advertising in recent years; since just over a third of their overall financial support comes from the sale of ad time that loss is significant.[45]

Ads on the pillar broadcasts must appear in blocks and not within programs, as in the German public broadcasting system; there are no similar restrictions for the commercial broadcasters. Television ads on pillar broadcasts once had occurred only during the early to middle evening hours, just before and after the newscasts, but that period was increased when the 1987 Media Act came into effect. Advertising wasn't permitted on Sundays (another influence of religion) until the early 1990s. Ads for tobacco products aren't permitted, ads for pharmaceuticals have to be approved by an expert panel, and ads for candy must be displayed with the superimposed outline of a toothbrush! Many restrictions are designed to protect the newspaper industry's advertising income. The most detailed regulations—eight pages of them in the 56-page Dutch Advertising Code (1996 edition)—apply to alcoholic drinks, and seek to protect minors and pregnant women (neither can appear in an ad for alcoholic beverages), guard against claims that consuming alcoholic drinks improves one's health or stamina, etc. [46]

The money earned through advertising on the pillars is used to pay the costs of operating STER, but the Media Act of 1987 permits the minister of culture to use the balance for any/all of 12 different purposes, among which are: to help to subsidize "failing" newspapers; to help offset NOB's operating costs; to fund a consultative committee for local radio and TV; to share in the Netherlands' costs of contributing to a European television program (Euronews); and to be shared among the pillars. One other purpose is to support the Dutch Cultural Broadcasting Productions Promotion Fund, which encourages productions of "a specifically Dutch cultural nature"; the act directs the minister to make available a minimum of one-sixteenth of STER's annual revenue for this purpose. That amounts to many millions of dollars per year, and enables the pillars and noncommercial organizations to produce some very ambitious Dutch cultural programs.

Sponsorship of programming began to appear with some regularity in the late 1980s, but few of the pillars now use it, although most of them experimented with it in the late 1980s to early 1990s. VARA dropped it completely because it felt that the sponsors were becoming more and more interested in influencing program content.[47] The 1987 Media Act was amended in 1994 to include specified limitations on the use of sponsorship by Dutch public broadcasters: it would be allowed only for sports and cultural programs. Furthermore, sponsor identity can be indicated only through a five-second oral (and, on TV, visual) announcement, with no display of trademarks or logos.[48] The Dutch commercial stations have much greater latitude to use sponsorship, and even have carried government-sponsored "infomercials" on occasion.[49]

The financing system does lack flexibility where the pillar organizations are concerned. Aside from increasing memberships and selling more ad space in the guides, or charging more for them, they have no power of their own to increase revenues. The government sets license fees and amounts of ad time, and STER sets advertising rates. And the system *is* expensive. The existence of a full complement of administrative staff for each organization drives up the cost, as does the seeking of new members, work on program guides, and other matters not directly related to program production. As one observer put it, "Instead of all this money filtering out and providing a breeding ground for programme makers, directors, writers and actors, it has been sucked in by a swollen bureaucracy. Far too much of television's resources are eaten up in fat salaries and office furniture."[50]

The "closed shop" situation of Dutch broadcasting also has been a factor: Up until the end of the 1980s, few productions could be made by anyone outside the existing pillar system, so there was no particular pressure to economize in order to meet competition. Also, the Dutch trade unions made it very difficult to discharge nonproductive staff or to hold down the numbers of people needed for studio or remote productions. Various government reforms have been aimed at cutting costs, but a number of the cost factors simply aren't very amenable to reduction—and Dutch-language productions featuring Dutch society and culture aren't likely to find much of an export market, so they don't offset those costs.

Cable television is available in roughly 90 percent of all Dutch households (5.7 million households out of a total of 6.4 million subscribed as of 1996), and the nation's high population density helps to hold down costs of installation. Just as in the United States, cable started as a highly localized, small business venture, but large corporations such as KPN (the privatized Dutch Post, Telephone and Telegraph service) have formed cable conglomerates. The KPN cable company, CASEMA, has well over a million of the nation's 5.6 million subscribers,[51] but Mediakabel has 2.2 million.[52] Charges vary slightly throughout the Netherlands, but average around $20 per household per month for a 25-30 channel service. Add-on (pay-cable) services, such as the movie channel Filmnet, charge about $10 per month. After a slow start, Filmnet's subscribership has risen to about 400,000 as of 1997. The operation hasn't been very profitable, but France's highly successful Canal Plus bought its parent company, Nethold, in 1996, which may improve its financial prospects.[53] Only 6 percent (350,000) of all Dutch households had DBS as of 1997, chiefly because cable has been so well-entrenched for so long, and because there are very few areas in the Netherlands where cable isn't available. There's no pay-TV service on DBS yet, primarily because of the high cost—Fl 2,000 (roughly $1,000)—of boxes, dishes and installation for digital reception.[54]

Sales of Dutch programs in foreign markets are few, with Endemol beginning to enjoy success in Germany and central and eastern Europe, but such income as the PSBs receive from those sales (Fl 12 million or so a year) goes to support a Co-Production Fund (for) Domestic Broadcasting, to encourage original productions of the performing arts and involving filmmakers, theatrical groups, etc.[55]

GOVERNANCE AND ADMINISTRATION—INTERNAL

The Decision-Making Structure

Until 1997, Dutch pillar broadcasting had featured two sorts of overall decision-making bodies: the NOS and its various committees, and the individual broadcasting organizations, plus other groups that are allotted smaller amounts of airtime (Muslims, Humanitarians, Freemasons, etc.). As the NOS was responsible for a larger portion of the broadcast schedule than was any other single organization, and as its administrators decided (in consultation with administrators of the other organizations) what it would broadcast and when, much of the schedule was built around NOS programming. There were NOS program boards and program coordination committees for radio and for television; all eight broadcasting organizations (seven after VOO dropped out in 1995) were on the two boards. The boards and committees reported to the NOS executive board, a body that once had 30 members—hardly conducive to speedy decision-making! The 1987 Media Act cut the number to 13 members, eight chosen by the organizations, four by the minister of culture from various sociocultural organizations, and a chair appointed by the government of the day through the queen or king. The executive met every month to make final decisions on broadcast policy; its meetings were open to the public and often were very lively, although it sometimes was accused of hamstringing the NOS by not approving potentially positive NOS proposals, yet being unwilling to see to it that one of the other broadcasting organizations would undertake them. A seven-member board of management, composed in like fashion, was responsible for policy preparation and reports to the executive. The eight "pillar" organizations became a majority on the various NOS boards, although the chair still was appointed by the government.

Some of that structure remains in place, but with some important changes. A Board of Management remains in place, for three members instead of seven, and all three are appointed by the Ministry of Culture. The Board has day-to-day responsibility for supervision of NOS, which includes planning the overall program schedule for the pillars and NOS. The General Board is now called the Supervisory Board, and, although its structure remains similar (10 representatives from the pillars, five government appointees) to that of the old General Board, it has less direct involvement in day-to-day decision-making than it did. There is a ten-year license for the public broadcasters (NOS and pillars), with an independent committee appointed by the government every five years to determine whether the system is meeting public needs and expectations. These changes attempt to streamline decision-making, to reduce some of the delays and inefficiencies caused by an excess of bureaucracy, and to make sure that the public's money (the annual license fee) is being well-spent. There's always the danger that the public sector now is open to more governmental interference, but there's a long history of noninterference, and any major attempt by any political party or coalition to exercise power would almost certainly result in negative publicity.[56]

Program coordination is a sensitive subject. Many of the pillar organizations want to place a large number of popular programs in the prime-time periods, but pressures from the Media Authority, the Board of Management and the government, still are in the direction of a more even mix of mass and specialized programming. Coordination does work reasonably well for scheduling between channels: A listener or viewer generally can count on having a genuine choice between what's on each of the five radio services and three TV services—for example, a popular music show opposite a documentary or religious talk. If two organizations appear to be duplicating, the arbitration committee is to resolve conflicts (which are rare).[56a]

The individual organizations each have their own decision-making structures: a board of directors and a full-time administrative staff. Annual dues-payers, *not* including the 10 florin members, also may become directly involved in decision-making, usually at annual meetings. For certain of the more ideologically oriented organizations, such as VARA, VPRO, NCRV and EO, decisions will be taken with an eye to satisfying the perceived programming needs that fit in with the world outlook of the members, for example, pro-Socialist programming for VARA. For the more mass-audience-oriented organizations, such as TROS and AVRO, decisions often are aimed at increasing membership as much as possible. KRO seems to be striving to reach both sorts of audiences. Increasing competitive pressures are forcing two of the larger ideological organizations, VARA and NCRV, to become less overtly ideological and more popular; VARA announced in 1987 that it no longer considered itself obliged to serve as the "Socialist megaphone."[57] VPRO began to de-emphasize political "radicalism" and to favor cultural "radicalism" in the late 1980s, partly in order to help attract a larger audience.[58]

While all of the pillar organizations aside from NOS have dues-paying members, that doesn't guarantee that members have any influence on program decision-making, although VPRO encourages members to write, telephone or visit its offices in Hilversum (where all of the organizations are located, and which is no more than a few hours' drive or train ride from any part of the country). Many VPRO members used to pay such visits. A few still do, and they may have very specific suggestions to offer, but the spirit of member activism seems to have all but vanished, perhaps because so many have gotten used to television as it is, VPRO included, and don't think of attempting to change it.[59]

At VARA's local, regional and national conferences members discuss program policies, pass along comments to VARA's board of directors and elect delegates to the annual meeting of the organization. At that meeting, members propose resolutions and speak up freely about their likes and dislikes. If a majority of the members approve a resolution, the board must attempt to carry it out. More often, the board presents resolutions to the members, which usually pass with little discussion. That wasn't always the case: back in 1972, the board proposed banning boxing from the VARA schedule on the grounds that a Socialist organization shouldn't be promoting violence. The members rejected the proposal, apparently because they felt that boxing at least had rules to govern its violence![60] But today's membership appears quite indifferent to programming policy issues, and the lively debates of yesteryear are little but a memory now.[61]

The other organizations do little to promote member involvement, aside from printing occasional surveys in the programming guides, asking members to send them in, then publishing the results in a subsequent issue. There is no requirement in the act that an organization maintain contact with its members, nor that it pay attention to their comments. Members may protest the actions of broadcast staff, including top administrators, but that won't necessarily lead to actions favored by the members. In 1994, KRO's board of directors gathered to consider a report that KRO had broadcast concerning the possible involvement of a prominent Christian Democratic politician in a tax fraud case. The board met because some of KRO's membership were unhappy with KRO (more than 1,000 had canceled their memberships) for possibly ruining the politician's chances for victory in the parliamentary election. In other words, KRO shouldn't have carried the report, whether it was true or false. The chair of KRO defended his decision to carry the broadcast, and was supported by the board, although the vice chairman disagreed and resigned.[62]

Keeping members content certainly is important to an organization, since membership has so many financial implications, but those organizations are general enough in character that their members ordinarily don't expect or desire involvement in program decision-making. The EO does appear to go out of its way to maintain the organization's original emphasis on family-oriented programming, but that comes from the convictions of the top administrators, with the strong support of the membership.[63]

GOVERNANCE AND ADMINISTRATION—EXTERNAL

The National Government

There are two major sources of government involvement in broadcasting: the minister responsible for broadcasting (usually, but not always, the minister for culture, welfare and recreation) and the Lower House of the Parliament. The minister may propose amendments to the Broadcasting Act, but they must be approved by Parliament. She or he also may take specific actions with respect to broadcasting, but these may be challenged by the broadcasters through Parliament or in the court system. The minister is advised by a Media Council of 17 members, appointed by the minister of culture with parliamentary approval. The council meets 15 to 20 times a year, publishes an annual report, responds to ministerial and parliamentary requests for advice on media policy, and may disagree openly with the minister's recommendations and actions, but it has no power other than moral ("Why did you appoint us if you won't take us seriously?") to stimulate action. The minister also is sometimes advised by the Media Authority, although the Authority is independent of any ministry; thus, it resembles the U.S. FCC and Canadian CRTC.

Parliament may discuss and vote upon broadcasting issues whenever it wishes. Broadcasting falls under the purview of the standing committee on welfare and culture, but any member of Parliament may raise questions concerning it. Parliament also votes upon ministerial recommendations and approves the annual budget for broadcasting derived from license fees and STER revenues. Neither Parliament nor the minister seem willing to use the budget to pressure broadcasters, although the minister did delay approval of VOO as a Category C organization for a few years in the 1970s, which certainly had an effect on VOO's budget.

The minister also functions as one member of the Dutch cabinet, and is subject to the influences of other ministers, her or his political party and the ruling coalition. As coalitions occasionally change composition, and as governments move in and out of office with some frequency, there's a tendency not to let party and coalition politics play a large role in broadcast regulation; an incoming coalition or party might use an outgoing coalition's or party's actions to the latter's disadvantage.

By long tradition, the minister isn't supposed to be very active or particularly public in regulating broadcasting, but in 1985 Minister Elco Brinkman was both. Under the general terms of the Broadcasting Act of 1982 (amended), he imposed heavy fines on several of the organizations for spending too much airtime promoting themselves so as to increase their memberships and for carrying "hidden" ads (e.g., performer or host mention of some product or service during a show). Parliament rescinded some of his decisions and cut back the amounts of the fines, but the organizations still were shocked that he would even take such a step.[64]

The Media Authority was created (1988) chiefly because the minister of culture had to spend too much time dealing with broadcasting.[65] Its three members (the Media Act permits three *or* five members, but so far the Authority has always had three) represent each of the three major political parties, and work an average of three days a week. Once appointed (for five-year terms, renewable once), a minister cannot dismiss them on the grounds that she/he disagrees with their decisions, which provides them with some measure of independence. The Authority recommends to the minister the issuing of broadcast, cable and pay-TV licenses, but the minister has the final decision. It also is supposed to encourage cooperation and coordination among the various broadcasting organizations—a function the NOS also performs. But it is the Authority that actually allocates airtime to the national organizations, and to regional and local organizations, as well.

The Authority's most visible functions stem from its power to determine whether the organizations are complying with the terms of the Media Act. It may warn them, it may fine them as much as Fl 200,000 (about $110,000) per violation, and it may withdraw or reduce airtime for the pillar organizations. When VOO was found to be illegally assisting the start-up of RTL-4 in the early 1990s, the Authority imposed a penalty of Fl 15 million ($7.5 million), which was the profit that VOO had made by doing so. Ironically, RTL-4 itself cannot be penalized by the Authority, since it functions under the laws of Luxembourg, its base of operation. The Authority has warned broadcasters on a number of occasions not to broadcast films unsuitable for minors before either 8 p.m. (for films unsuitable for minors under 12) or 9 p.m. (minors under 16).[66] And it has fined the commercial broadcasters many times for including hidden advertising or unacknowledged sponsorship in their programs. Its decisions may be reversed by higher courts, or by Royal Decree at the recommendation of the minister.[67]

There's also a supranational organization that can influence Dutch media policy. The European Union has approved a number of "open market" policies which are designed to promote the greatest possible flow of electronic media programming and investment throughout Europe, and the Netherlands has felt the EU's regulatory pressure on several occasions, a few of which were noted earlier. Since those EU policies have fit in nicely with the pro-private enterprise stance of Dutch governments throughout most of the 1980s and 1990s, the country rarely has been at odds with the Union. A more nationalistically protective Dutch government could seek exceptions to EU regulations, but most of them are so well-founded by now that it would be difficult to turn the clock back.

Regional and Local Government

Even in such a small country as the Netherlands, there are regional and local differences.[68] However, it was only after World War II that there was any broadcasting at the regional level. But local broadcasting took much longer. Local radio supplied by pirate stations began to appear in the 1960s; a few officially approved local radio services appeared as experiments in the mid-1970s, and came on local cable beginning in 1983. The first local cable TV service appeared briefly in 1971; local demand for it in a small community in Limburg Province, plus some support from the Philips Company and from a large Dutch publishing firm, brought it about. However, the minister of culture claimed that it was illegal: Communities could grant franchises for cable but didn't have the right to initiate their own services. Only the minister had the power to allow the latter. In 1975 and 1976, six communities set up two-year experimental TV services through cable, with the permission and financial assistance of the minister. In no case did the minister attempt to dictate broadcast policy or program content, and the six services differed widely in what they offered, but they had only three hours a week apiece in which to do it.

In the late 1970s, the minister of culture stated that she would no longer request that government money be used to support such broadcasting. By then, six regional services had formed an association and lobbied for the expansion of regional broadcasting to all provinces. However, they wanted a continuation of national government support, which they felt would minimize regional government interference. The minister felt that the regions themselves should provide the money—an argument that ministers have continued to make to this day. The stations weren't allowed to broadcast commercials and couldn't solicit memberships, although they could accept donations.

Local and regional radio and TV both received specific authorization in the 1987 Media Act, and regional (but not local) governments then acquired the power to assess licensed households an additional Fl 10 for its support. As a result, it has flourished, and all 13 provinces have radio, while most have television, as well. In theory, the regional governments were to have no additional control over regional stations through the surtax, but some regional broadcasters with whom I spoke in October 1986 thought that some individuals within regional governments might find the prospect of such control (or at least influence) tempting, and the Limburg Provincial Council already had applied pressure on Radio Limburg on two occasions.[69] However, few such incidents have arisen during the first 10 years (1987-97) under the new financial system. Local radio stations were quite well-established by the late 1980s, almost all of them transmitting exclusively through cable. They also formed an association—OLON is its Dutch acronym—to coordinate activities and to lobby on behalf of local broadcasting. Some of them, plus some newcomers, began to apply for low-power terrestrial frequencies then, and in 1988 the government began to issue such licenses. There are over 350 such stations now in existence, almost all of them run by a few low-paid staff members and dozens or even hundreds of volunteers. They may carry limited amounts of advertising, but are expected to negotiate agreements with the local press that will help to compensate the press for loss of advertising revenue.[70]

Regional and local commercial broadcasting began in the early 1990s, even though there were strong doubts about the ability of such stations to survive economically. Both radio and TV stations transmit through cable, although an increasing number also are using limited power AM (mediumwave) or FM (ultra shortwave) frequencies, as well. There are several commercial local radio stations in each province, and commercial local TV is beginning to appear in a few. The appearance of the latter has caused noncommercial regional and local TV to call for more financial support, so that they can compete with the newcomers. The Fl 10 surcharge is too little in all but the most populous provinces to finance adequate TV production, both in quantity and in quality.[71] Some members of Parliament and some of the regional stations would like to see NOS provide two-hour "windows" for the use of the regional TV stations, with NOS footing the bill for both production and transmission costs. NOS is reluctant to open such windows if it doesn't get additional budgetary support (one member of Parliament accused the NOS Council of being more than "reluctant"; he called it "arrogant and shortsighted" in its failure to recognize the popularity of regional TV. See "Nuis botst het kamer," Algemeen Dagblad, 5 September 1996). The minister of culture was pushing Parliament as of late 1996 to approve yet another Fl 10 surcharge that each province could assess for the support of regional broadcasting.[72] There was insufficient support for the measure, so the minister came up with Fl 40 million ($20 million) from broadcasting funds to help support such ventures.[73]

Nongovernmental

Because so many organizations and groups have access to broadcasting, it isn't surprising to find that very few citizen involvement groups exist in the Netherlands. Most people find that the system is more or less open to them. The minister receives proposals for airtime from groups wishing access; if a group wants that access on a continuing, scheduled basis it must present evidence that its programming will be important to a reasonable number of people (no number specified) and that such programming is not already provided. Groups may be dropped from the authorized list if they turn their time over to others, as one group did in the mid-1970s, or if they fail to make ongoing use of the time they are allotted, or if they become too small to seem to require a broadcast outlet. It isn't particularly difficult to obtain airtime on a one-time basis, and not even all that difficult to gain continuing access. The relative ease with which small, land-based pirate stations once operated also answered the apparent needs of some who were dissatisfied with the official system, although in November 1987 the government announced a higher level of penalties for those operating and those advertising over such stations, discouraging many of them.

It is relatively easy for groups to secure airtime for themselves or to be interviewed, but it's also a fairly simple matter for those who feel that their interests have been harmed through a broadcast to seek airtime for a correction or rebuttal—in other words, right of response. The 1982 Broadcasting Act stated that "every institution having obtained transmission time may be obliged, in the event it has transmitted any factual data which is incorrect or misleading through incompleteness, to transmit a rectification upon the demand of someone directly concerned in such communication, if the latter has a sufficient interest in such rectification" (Section 38). The president of the District Court of Amsterdam set the manner and time of reply on the advice of the minister's commissioner for broadcasting (regulation of right of response has been handled under the Dutch Civil Code since 1997). Few such cases have arisen in a given year; most have been objections by cultural and religious groups, or by manufacturers, concerning the ways they were portrayed in consumer-protection programs such as VARA's "De Ombudsman" and in newscasts, documentaries, minidocumentaries such as the NOS "Journaal" and TROS "Aktua TV." The broadcasters usually have been able to settle them before they reached the court.

Some programs are quite likely to elicit strong emotions or even calls for help or advice. One of the most notable was an October 1994 television documentary by IKON (a religious organization) about an assisted suicide, showing the actual moment of death.[74] Many of the broadcasters transmitting potentially disturbing programs use a service paid for by NOS and the Department of Health, "Korrelatie," whose telephone number is displayed during the program and/or in the title credits. People are available at phone banks to give advice, provide information, make referrals or sometimes simply listen.[75]

Unions aren't particularly prominent as shapers of programming policy in the Netherlands, although the Netherlands Union of Journalists (NVJ, in Dutch) is a vigilant defender of the rights of journalists to pursue stories free from pressure on the part of broadcast management. A new union was formed in 1996: the Netherlands Union of Broadcast Workers (NVO, in Dutch).[76] The NVO is made up of administrative, programming and operations personnel, and has attempted to unite with the NVJ, which would create a potentially more powerful lobbying organization.

PROGRAMMING

Philosophies

The history of Dutch broadcasting reveals above all an attempt to create and maintain a system that offers access to a variety of organizations and groups. That was part of the broadcast regulation of 1928, and it has been part of the Dutch pillar system ever since. There also has been the continuing requirement that organizations provide programming for their own members but also for the larger public, and that the programming be a mixture of information and entertainment. A few of the organizations, particularly TROS and VOO, have tried to blend the mixture with as much entertainment as possible, including informational programs that tend to be light features about personalities, but most pillar organizations do make an effort to attain some balance. The more recent commercial services emphasize general appeal programming, but most of them have produced a fair amount of Dutch programming to complement or even equal the amounts of imported material. They might well have done so on their own, but it didn't hurt that the European Union has required the television operations of all EU member states to broadcast at least 50 percent European-produced material. Neither the Dutch PSBs nor the commercial stations are obligated by law to provide airtime for minority groups; the former provide a fair amount, the latter almost none.

Whether the pillar organizations truly have philosophies of their own is another question. The chairman of TROS was once reported to have said, "The essence is to give the people the programmes they want to see. ... The viewer is the boss."[77] That *is* a philosophy, but it comes close to avoiding responsibility: Any "bad" program can be excused by saying, "But just look at the size of the audience!" In the battle for members, some of the older organizations moved in TROS's direction. Still, most of them do wish to reach certain sorts of audiences with specific programs some of the time. The religious organizations broadcast not only church services and discussions of religious issues, but also claim to select their entertainment programming with some regard for what will contribute to (or at least not work against) the moral development of the audience. For example, NCRV has stated that "when acquiring foreign productions, the NCRV fully applies the standards of quality and ethics it is committed to by the 'C'[hristian] in its name."[78] That may be good business: Why risk offending members? But programs transmitted by those organizations sometimes do offend, anger or upset, and usually that is deliberate. Most often VARA and VPRO do this, but so has KRO, notably in broadcasts made by a Monsignor Bekkers, who called among other things for a more open attitude toward birth control.[79]

Because its mandate is quite different, and because it doesn't have members in the usual sense, NOS (and its 1995 "offspring," NPS) might be expected to have a different philosophy than do the other organizations. In a way, it does: It presents current affairs programs on touchy topics, features spokespersons with very strong viewpoints, and, through NPS, specializes in presenting minorities. But it does all of this within an overall framework of balancing program genres with the output of the pillar organizations.

Radio

As has happened over much of the world, radio has become increasingly dominated by music in the Netherlands. That already was occurring in the early 1960s, as TV claimed a larger and larger share of the budget, but it received further encouragement through the "nonstop pop" provided by the offshore pirate radio stations. The broadcasting organizations proposed a third radio service, which would be largely pop music with appropriately informal disc jockeys. The service would be legal, of course, and Dutch artists and recording companies would receive performance fees, which pirate stations rarely paid. In other words, the situation was much like that in Great Britain at the same time, and the solution was similar. The third service came on the air in October 1965, became a 24-hour service in 1973, and was cut back to 17 hours a day in 1979. But classical music fans were unhappy with the prominence this gave to pop music and lobbied vigorously for a "serious" radio service along the lines of the Third Programme services in Great Britain and West Germany. They were successful: In December 1975, Hilversum 4 came on the air.

Almost predictably, complaints began to appear about the programming on Hilversum 1 and 2. According to some listeners, they seemed to have little distinctive character, so the organizations (with some ministerial pressure) made Hilversum 1 a family-oriented service and Hilversum 2 an informational service starting in 1979. Hilversum 5, a target-group station (for ethnic, linguistic and cultural minorities) began service in 1984 for about one hour per day. It had grown to nearly 14 hours a day by 1987, and has remained at that level, but most of that expansion was in Dutch-language programs, health programs, children's programs and so on. There's a daily 2- to 4-hour block divided among four linguistic groups: Turkish, Moroccan Arabic, Berber and Chinese. There are Saturday afternoon program blocks for Moluccans (30 minutes), Surinamese (60 minutes) and Antilleans (30 minutes), and a 60-minute broadcast of a church service for Surinamese on Sundays.

All five radio services provide news and music (least of all on Hilversum 5), and Hilversum 1 (mainly news and sports) and 2 (light entertainment of various sorts) have several discussion programs, many of them presented by NOS and featuring in particular the viewpoints of "nonmainstream" individuals and groups. Hilversum 3 is the popular music service; its usual share of audience—12 to 15 percent—easily tops the shares of the other four services. The NOS also plays the role of promoter of the arts as do the BBC, ARD, NHK and French radio: It supports various orchestras and choruses, commissions new musical works and radio plays, prepares documentaries and so on. Most of that material appears on Hilversum 4, the classical music/"high-culture" service. A few of the other organizations do so, too, but more rarely. The NOS also broadcasts daily summaries of parliamentary activity, and occasionally parliamentary debates. A little over three hours each week goes for educational (in-school) radio broadcasts, about a third of them prepared by NCRV, KRO, VARA and AVRO, and about two-thirds by NOS. Adult educational broadcast services such as TELEAC also present a number of radio programs each week. Much popular and classical music, as well as some newscast material, comes from abroad; other productions generally are Dutch.

Younger listeners sometimes criticize the formality that characterizes so many PSB-produced radio programs, even presentations of pop music (where, to be sure, there's some informality, but not the sort that one gets from the land-based pirates or the newer pop music services delivered by satellite).

And because so many broadcasting organizations and groups have to be accommodated, the schedule for each of the five services looks, on paper, like a patchwork quilt, although they don't sound that chopped-up most of the time, as most broadcasters follow similar presentational styles. Hilversum 1 and 3 are 24-hour services; Hilversum 2 and 4, 18 hours; and Hilversum 5, 17 hours.

Most commercial competition for the five services comes from two sources: satellite-delivered pop music channels from abroad (Radio 10 Gold, Sky Radio, New Dance Radio, Kink-FM) or from domestic satellite-delivered music services, many of which began life as cable radio services (Classic FM, Hitradio Veronica, Concertradio, Concertzender, Jazzradio, Radio 121, Noordzee Nationaal, Radio 538). Most are on air for 24 hours a day. None of them offer anything substantial by way of news, and none operate their own newsrooms. The most commercial popular service, Sky Radio, pulls average daily ratings of well over 10 percent, which is nearly as much as the most popular noncommercial service, Hilversum 3 (12-15 percent). Furthermore, the major commercial services are gaining ground on the five Hilversum services.[80] The regional commercial services have low ratings, but noncommercial regional radio has an average daily audience share of roughly 15 percent.

Most of the regional noncommercial radio services broadcast from anywhere between 7-9 a.m. until 6-7 p.m., although Radio West (The Hague) runs for 24 hours. All of them emphasize news, sports and culture of regional interest; and interviews fill a great deal of airtime, as do music shows. A few of the stations, Radio Rijnmond (Rotterdam) in particular, offer some distinctly alternative programming; Rijnmond carries a locally produced version of the old U.S. radio and TV classic, "King/Queen For a Day," in which the winning (most moving hard-luck story) contestant gets her or his wish (so long as it doesn't cost much—this *is* local radio!). Radio Fryslan broadcasts heavily in Frisian, and stations in more rural areas, such as Radio Drenthe, feature local dialects quite often. Radio Gelderland (Arnhem) seems more typical of the regional stations, however, with its lineup of local news, talk shows and music, and its heavy orientation toward older (mid-30s and up) listeners.[81] Most of the remaining local pirate stations feature popular music, with very informal and even amateurish announcers and appeals to the audience for mail and phone calls, which shows just how much they fear detection by Dutch authorities.

Specialized cable radio services are most numerous in Amsterdam and Rotterdam, where one can find programs for homosexuals (M/V Media), the "counterculture" (Radio X), Hindustanis, Turks, Antilleans and other linguistic minorities; most of the language services come via satellite from India, Turkey, etc. None is supposed to carry ads, but most have various tradeoffs that they've arranged with travel agencies, music stores and other appropriate clients, in exchange for subtle and not-so-subtle mentions of their support and services. Cable radio sometimes has relatively large audiences, especially for services such as U.S. hard rock music, children's programs and specific types of jazz such as Dixieland. Over 70 percent of cable TV households also are hooked up to cable radio,[82] but it's useless in households where most or all of the radios are portable.

Many of the local stations have acquired limited-power terrestrial transmitters starting in the late 1980s, which has broadened their potential audience. However, most of those stations continue to live a very hand-to-mouth financial existence, since there's no Fl 10 surcharge to help pay for local radio, and local governments generally haven't been all that supportive. As a result, and much like community radio stations all over the world, few staff members are paid, and those who are work for very little. Still, many such stations manage a quite diverse array of programming, and often try to reach ethnic minority groups living in their service areas. Stadsomroep Arnhem even carries a weekly program, "Babylon," which features the activities, problems and hopes of Surinamese, Turks and other minorities living in and around Arnhem; its volunteer staff won a national prize in 1994 for the program's high production quality and content.[83]

Television

There's been a radical change in Netherlands 1, 2 and 3 during the 1990s, due largely to commercial competition. Up until 1993, there was only in-school educational television in the morning and early afternoon hours, aside from a five-minute subtitled newscast at 1 p.m. for the hard of hearing, and there were large gaps between many of the programs. In 1993, the three channels began to offer programs starting at 7 a.m. (Netherlands 1 and 3) or 9 a.m. (Netherlands 2), and didn't stop until midnight (Netherlands 2 and 3) or 1:30 a.m. (Netherlands 1). Much of the material is repeated from other days and times, although teletext fills the 7 a.m. to noon slot on Netherlands 3. There is no equivalent to the highly informal news-weather-sports-features morning programs such as ABC's (U.S.) "Good Morning America" or Great Britain's "The Breakfast Show" (BBC) on either public or commercial channels. Cartoons and teen-oriented soap operas (the Australian "Heartbreak High") predominate in the late afternoon hours, although Netherlands 2 offers a news-sports-weather block at that time. One of the more unusual late afternoon programs is the NOS-produced "Jeugdjournaal": news for children in the 10-12-year range; Netherlands 3 carries it five days a week at 6:30-7 p.m. The commercial stations have had an unusual daytime lineup, in that RTL-5 didn't come on air before 4:35 p.m. weekdays until it was converted into an all-news and information service in 1997; SBS 6 doesn't come on air until 3:15 p.m. weekdays; Veronica carries "Call TV" (see below) from 7 a.m. until 4 p.m.; and only RTL-4 offers a mix of programs (brief newscasts, cartoon shows, Oprah Winfrey, "Santa Barbara," "As the World Turns" and other similar fare).

Evenings bring a mix of entertainment and informational programming. Dutch-produced newscasts, quiz programs, sitcoms, musical and variety shows, talk shows, sports and documentaries, as well as occasional sports, miniseries and single-episode dramas, account for about two-thirds of the prime-time schedules for the pillars. That ratio is reversed on two of the three HMG (RTL-5, Veronica) and SBS 6, while RTL-4 manages 50 percent or more Dutch material each evening. The Dutch-produced material on the commercial services takes the form of newscasts (RTL-4 and SBS 6 only), talk shows, game and quiz shows, soap operas, sitcoms and police/detective shows, with a few documentaries (usually about personal health) and two reality-based shows: SBS 6's "Helden van 06-11" ("Heroes of 06-11" [the Dutch equivalent to 911]) and RTL-5's "Elke seconde telt" ("Every Second Counts"). Two or three of the Dutch commercial stations offer feature films (usually from the United States) each night, along with imported sitcoms ("Murphy Brown"), talk shows ("Ricky Lake," "Jerry Springer") and action/adventure shows ("Tropical Heat," "The Commish").

Tight budgets are most evident in quiz and game shows, such as the VARA-VPRO-NPS-produced "Lingo," a slow-moving, amiable "guess the _____ letter word" program featuring an electronic bingo board and lots of chat. Talk and "human interest" programs show the same austerity: SBS 6's "Blond, Blond en Blond" has three blond female interviewers (sometimes singly, sometimes together) interviewing (and attempting to help) people with emotional problems. Interviewing is on-site with portable cameras; visualization is limited, and talk predominates. The highly popular evening soap opera "Goede Tijden, Slechte Tijden" (RTL-4, weekdays, 8-8:30) often shows the effects of its $35,000-per-episode budget in its relatively simple sets, slow pace and talky nature. The newer RTL-5 soap, "Onderweg naar Morgen" ("On the Way to Tomorrow," weekdays, 7:25-8) is closer to U.S. soap operas in its faster pace, more rapid scene shifts and more elaborate sets; so is its interplay of dramatic devices, such as contrasting "good" and "bad" pregnancies. But perhaps the most cost-efficient show of all is Veronica's "Call TV" (weekdays, 7 a.m. to 4 p.m.): a number of largely young, male "talk jockeys" run telephone contests, play old music videos, interview guests (many of them amateur and semiprofessional performers—the shows seem to play a "talent scout" role), all from tiny and very bare-bones sets. (Veronica has received a subsidy of a few million florins yearly from the European Union because the series has experimented with a wide-screen format—this despite the absence of sets that would profit from such a format! [Discussion with Kees van der Haak, Hilversum, October 1996.])

Miniseries once were more common on the PSB schedule. When they appear nowadays, they often are quite bold in subject matter and experimental in production style. Very rarely are they produced by any of the Dutch commercial services. One of the more notable and widely discussed of recent miniseries, the late-1996 "Zwarte Sneeuw" ("Black Snow"), was produced by NCRV and broadcast in hour-long episodes on 12 successive Tuesdays, with repeats on Sundays. Many critics compared the series to the U.S. "Twin Peaks" (produced by David Lynch), since the plot (centered around a young woman in search of the truth about her dead/dying parents) was disjointed, the pace varied from slow to fast, many of the scenes were quite surrealistic, and flashbacks (shot on location in various parts of Europe, making the production cost soar) frequent. Viewers seemed to love or hate it, critics likewise. NCRV provided an Internet address for those computer users who wanted more background on the actors, locations and plot trivia, and a 900 number (roughly $0.33 per minute) for others.[84] It did fairly well in terms of share of audience, with some episodes achieving 15 percent or more, but Veronica's broadcasts of feature films such as "The French Lieutenant's Woman" drew shares two to three times as large.

Children's programming also used to be more prevalent on the PSB schedule, and still is available in some of the late afternoon hours (but surprisingly not on Saturday mornings) on all three channels. Certain programs are imported (the U.K.'s "The Wild Wood," the U.S.'s "Sesame Street"), but some are produced by the pillars themselves, such as NCRV's "Children of the World" and VPRO's "Villa Achterwerk." The latter must be seen to be believed, because it contains a number of serialized mini-dramas featuring children (usually ages 9-13) in various adult-like situations, facing adult-like problems such as how to care for a baby: a 10- or 11-year-old boy is temporarily in charge of one, but he and his 10- or 11-year-old "girlfriend" decide to set up housekeeping in an abandoned apartment, where the work involved in obtaining blankets, food, etc. (some of which they steal) proves too much, and the experiment ends within a few hours. Challenging authority and convention is a frequent theme of "Villa Achterwerk." One late October 1996 episode showed a second or third grade teacher (male) being so overwhelmed by his students' birthday presents for him that he decides on the spot to take them on an unauthorized field trip, which requires them to sneak out of the school under his guidance. As they pass one classroom, the (older male) teacher loses control of the class, runs out into the hallway in frustration, pulls out a flask of brandy and takes a slug. Once the class has arrived at a city park, they bring out their lunches, and the teacher has provided himself with a bottle of beer, which he opens and drinks as they eat!

Children's programming on the commercial channels is far more conventional, and for RTL-4's Saturday morning (7 a.m.-noon) "Telekids," highly popular: it typically draws shares of 40. "Telekids" uses large amounts of foreign cartoons, but also has several of its own continuing features, including quizzes, "funny face" contests, etc. RTL-4 also carries a Sunday afternoon "kid's talent show," in which children imitate their favorite performers. RTL-5 carries "Power Time" on Mondays through Fridays (4:50-5:35 p.m.); "Battletech," "Power Rangers," "Masked Rider" and other hyperactive imported cartoon series fill most of its airtime.

There also are a number of educational programs available through the pillar channels, generally in the morning or late at night. Some are for in-school use, where they are supplementary to the curriculum; some are for adult learners. There's a Dutch Open School which simply serves to broaden people's knowledge and does not grant degrees, for which TV is used;[85] there's also a Dutch Open University, founded in 1984, which does grant degrees, and is modeled on the British Open University. Television plays an important role in delivering course-related programming, but printed material is more important, and one's self-study habits must be quite well-developed in order to pursue a degree program successfully. (A Dutch broadcaster with whom I spoke in 1996 was nearing completion of her Open University requirements, but was working through the British Open University, which she found much superior to the Dutch version in terms of its variety and quality of coursework, as well as administrative efficiency.) The commercial channels carry no equivalent programming.

The newscasts on both public and commercial TV tend to be a bit stodgy, although they do provide quite broad coverage of world events. The principal public broadcast source for international news, NOS, couldn't afford worldwide coverage on its own, but has been helped enormously by the European Broadcasting Union's Eurovision News Exchange. The Exchange also provided something of a model to Dutch broadcast journalists for coverage techniques in the early days of TV journalism. Only RTL-4 presents a national/international newscast that matches the scope of NOS's 25 minute "Journaal"; it draws most of its international material from syndicated sources abroad. Newscasts are very straightforward, and investigative reporting is rare. The latter may be hampered because Dutch courts generally don't recognize the right of a reporter to refuse to disclose sources of stories.[86]

Documentaries produced by the pillars vary in quality, but can be exceptionally rigorous. An October 1996 NCRV documentary, "Eindpunt Hoogvliet," dealt with a run-down district in Rotterdam, and provided a grim picture of everyday life there, with homelessness, drug dealing, prostitution and physical abuse shown vividly. In the latter part of 1996, AVRO ran a series on children in Dutch society. "Einde kind" was a dramatized documentary series, and showed the sorts of problems and pressures children from families of various income levels face as they grow up, including the ease of obtaining drugs (even in "nice" neighborhoods), pressures for sexual relations among early teenagers, and lack of communication with parents, as well as indications of parental frustration in trying to raise their children.

All political parties represented in Parliament have guaranteed access to radio and TV, but amount of time available is limited: one 10-minute period per week on TV and six 10-minute periods per week on radio, to be used in rotation by each of the 15 or so parties while Parliament is in session. Total amount of airtime increases in the three-month period just before national elections. The prime minister is interviewed on TV every Friday, except for public holidays. There's also a nightly summary of parliamentary activity during those periods when Parliament is in session. The NOS carries up to eight one-minute spot announcements on TV each week for government public service messages. The government may request (or demand, if necessary) airtime whenever it wishes, but it rarely exercises the privilege. If it does, the broadcaster may announce that airtime has been made available at the government's request, thus distancing itself from the government.

Politicians also receive coverage in a form that might not always be quite so welcome: satire. There usually are three or four satire programs on the schedule, some by the pillars, some by commercial services. Politicians aren't the only targets; arts and entertainment (including television) also are subject to ridicule. The EO-produced "Van Henegouwen VPP" (Saturdays, 9:24-9:57 p.m.), is especially fond of mocking news analyses, commercials and other often cliché-ridden forms of programming.

The scheduling patterns for public and commercial TV are quite different. Because so many organizations and groups must be fit into so few hours on the public channels, most programs are no more than 30 minutes long. The U.S. concept of block scheduling (e.g., a full evening of situation comedy) simply does not work on Dutch "pillar" television, where a typical prime-time period will be programmed by a mixture of "pillar" organizations and smaller groups. The NOS presents one newscast per channel each evening (25, five and 15 minutes); sports and weather are in separate programs. Some of those programs will come on air at very regular, predictable times (e.g., 8:30-9 p.m.), while others will end three minutes before the hour, begin eight minutes after, etc., and run for odd time lengths. The Dutch commercial TV services feature very regular break times and lengths, although a few may be in blocks as short as five minutes. This may make the Netherlands a channel-hopper's paradise!

Much like other European systems, the Dutch 1987 Media Act had a stipulation (Sections 53, 71g and 72.2) that "adult" films or parts of films should not be presented until 8 p.m., if unsuitable for children under 12, and 9 p.m. (amended to 10 p.m. in June 1997)[87] for those under 16. The Media Authority frequently penalizes stations (usually commercial services) for putting adult-oriented material on air too early. After 9 p.m., some of the channels (usually the Dutch commercial services) carry "erotic" movies and talk shows, but they are far outnumbered by travelogues, U.S. and British sitcoms and dramas, etc.

Finally, unlike some of the public broadcasting systems in other industrialized nations, most notably Great Britain, Japan and France, the Dutch pillars haven't been given the task of upholding a specific standard of correct speech in their broadcasts. Those organizations do have standards of pronunciation and usage, and regularly receive advice on those standards, but presentational styles appear to vary from one pillar to another. Some observers even claim that they can tell which pillar is involved almost as soon as a broadcast comes on air.[88]

THE AUDIENCE

In the days before advertising, Dutch broadcasting organizations had little need for continuous audience research on the size, composition and program preferences of the audience. Membership payments, as well as letters, telephone calls and personal visits, seemed sufficient measures. Even the advent of commercials did not increase the need for audience research that much; the more popular a program, the higher the ad rate for that time period, but ad revenues were divided among the organizations according to their total amount of airtime per organization and not on the basis of audience size for a given program.

In the mid-1960s, the broadcasting organizations pooled their resources in order to conduct continuous audience research, and with the creation of NOS, audience research became part of that organization. The other organizations retained small research offices in order to maintain liaison with NOS's audience research department, to interpret research results to staff colleagues, and in a few cases to conduct projects of their own.

The NOS has several methods of gathering data: telephone calls, electronic measurement of set usage, and, more rarely, face-to-face interviewing, laboratory viewing and content analysis. Diaries were used until 1987; viewers from age 3 on up had their own diaries (parents assisted young children) in which they indicated programs watched and an "appreciation" score of 110 (a marking system used in Dutch schools) for each. The diary was replaced in 1987 by a "peoplemeter" type of electronic interactive measurement device, with overnight data on viewership and appreciation scores (the average TV program scores just under 7), and results appearing on teletext the following day.[89]

Sitcoms and sports events, usually football (soccer), generally predominate in each week's top 10, but comedy programs such as "Oppassen" and "The Andre van Duin Show" also do well, and the nightly NOS news program, "Journaal," usually draws audience shares around 30. Certain highly specialized programs do very well: RTL-4's home and garden show, "Eigen Huis & Tuin" (Saturdays, 6:15-7 p.m.) draws audience shares around 40 and ratings around 10. (Few people rival the Dutch in their devotion to their homes, lawns and flowers!)

For more specific qualitative data, the research department conducts 26 sets of telephone interviews in the October-April period; sample size is 700 viewers aged 12 or older. One problem here is that only about two-thirds of all Dutch households have their own telephones; the more transient and those lower in the economic scale tend to be underrepresented. There is a similar set of telephone interviews for radio listening, carried out yearly from January through April. Topics covered generally concern size of audience and enumeration of preferred programs. As with audience research departments almost everywhere, the NOS department doesn't have a particularly easy time of it convincing producers, directors and administrators that they should treat results of studies seriously: they feel perfectly justified in ignoring what they don't like or understand.

The rapid growth of commercial television led to the creation of still other audience research companies, the largest of which is Intomart, which uses a large TV panel for continuous surveys, and employs over 250 different variables in order to supply its commercial clients with just about every bit of demographic data they might want.[90] Several of the departments of sociology and political science in Dutch universities also conduct research projects on listener and viewer reactions. Most are conducted at the university's expense, as there is little tradition of governmental or private foundation support for such activities.

Research studies conducted by NOS over the years have revealed fairly high audience satisfaction with Dutch broadcasting. Some of the more specialized programs and services, especially Hilversum 4 ("serious" programs) and Hilversum 5 (minorities), show a very predictable profile: small audiences, high degrees of satisfaction. Programs attracting large numbers of viewers often receive appreciation scores in the 6-8 range. Quiz shows bring both large audiences and high scores, as do sports events and as does the VARA-produced situation comedy, "Oppassen." Pop music programs do especially well among younger viewers. When asked what they would like more of, many viewers say feature films, sports and nature documentaries. They also would like to see more Dutch-produced drama, but seem to realize that the high cost (and lack of prospects for overseas sales) of such drama makes it difficult to produce more. Radio and television newscasts produced by NOS have high credibility, as witness a 1994 NOS survey (N = 1,500): When answering the question, "Which medium brings the most reliable news and information?" 18 percent said radio, 18 percent newspapers, 2 percent other and 49 percent television—a six-point gain for TV compared to results from a similar survey in 1983.[91]

The impact of broadcasting on Dutch society is more difficult to assess. There have been several NOS and university studies that have revealed that certain programs intended to reduce people's negative feelings toward immigrant groups in the Netherlands, or negative feelings about traveling to parts of neighboring countries not usually visited by tourists, actually have heightened those negative feelings. Violence on television was not as much of an issue as it had been in Great Britain, the United States or Germany until the 1990s, when Dutch commercial TV services brought a number of imported (usually from the United States, the U.K. and Germany) police and detective shows onto their schedules, and began to produce some of their own. It's difficult to say whether public criticism was responsible or not, but the commercial channels cut back quite sharply on the number of such programs that they carried. Even so, critics still raise questions regarding the more excessive amounts of gratuitous violence they claim to see on commercial TV police/detective shows.[92]

Certainly viewing and listening are popular activities: Figures for 1995 showed that the average person listened to radio for nearly three hours per day and watched TV for 145 minutes per day. Viewing figures were up somewhat from 1985 (124 minutes), but the most notable change over time was in numbers of channels viewed: 1982 figures showed an average of 6.3, while 1995 figures were 20.6.[93]

MINORITIES AND THE MEDIA

It is no exaggeration to state that the Netherlands has the world's best record of providing electronic media access for minorities.[94] The airtime available over national radio service Hilversum 5 is just one aspect of its performance. There's much more activity at the local level, particularly in Amsterdam, which is home to the largest and most diverse minority population in the country. But even in smaller cities around the country, many of the local stations carry at least a few programs for (and often by) minorities. Harderwijk's local station carries a weekly "Iran Hour"; Lelystad has an Islamic program; Hengelo's 30-minute weekly India program is produced by three men ranging in ages from 64 to 75. Such programming isn't required by law, but local radio staff often feel a strong commitment to mirror and to serve more than just the mainstream community.[95]

Those initiatives also are helped by the presence of a government-funded organization—the Stichting Omroep Alloctonen (STOA)—whose specific charge is to push the broadcasters, and public broadcasters in particular, to provide fair, balanced and continuing coverage of minorities, both in informational and entertainment programs. STOA also has lobbied the Dutch Parliament regularly for funding for training programs and other forms of assistance for minorities wishing to present themselves through the electronic media. And it has served as a clearinghouse for minority individuals interested in media work and media operations looking for qualified media personnel.

Those tasks were not easy to carry out. Members of ethnic minority groups, the Moluccans in particular, had pressed for the creation of special broadcast services in their own languages for many years, but there were none on TV until 1976 (radio had carried very limited services from 1966), and then in very small amounts. There was an expansion of such services in the early 1980s, in some cases only after settling out dissension within the groups as to whose voices should be heard. That was a particular problem within the Moluccan community, which really was several more or less warring factions. Then the economic recession of the late 1980s and early 1990s, coupled with a predominantly Conservative Parliament, saw many government-funded programs coming under threat of reduction or extinction. But STOA, through vigorous lobbying, managed to maintain and even increase funding for its sphere of activity. (One NOS official who often dealt with STOA in the early 1990s told me that the organization often "made a pest of itself" in its persistence. However, the official saw that as absolutely necessary if time-honored prejudices, as well as neglect often borne of ignorance, were to be overcome. [Discussion with Kees van der Haak, Nijmegen, October 1995.])

It also was the case (and sometimes still is) that most of the pillar organizations, as well as the NOS, didn't take kindly to being told that they sometimes were unfair in their portrayals of minorities, sometimes ignored them, or were unwilling to work with them to address their concerns. STOA's persistence over time won over some broadcasters and wore down others, and the increasing presence of minorities within the broadcast organizations meant that pressure could be applied from the inside as well as from the outside.

The presence of cable throughout the country also helped minority groups to gain some experience with the electronic media. The first major effort came in the form of "Migranttelevisie" ("Migrant TV"), which first appeared in 1983 on an Amsterdam cable channel, with relays to four other Dutch cities. Professional broadcasters worked with Surinamese, Moroccans, Turks, Italians, Portuguese, Spaniards and Latin Americans. A three-year training and production cycle gave groups the ability to make their own programs; however, few got the opportunity to show their work on cable TV more than once a month. Some trainees entered further training programs with pillar organizations.[96] "Migrant TV" gradually increased its production capacity, mainly by shooting on-location with portable cameras (its studios are tiny), and was broadcasting about 100 hours a year as of 1995, 60 hours of which were its own productions. The programs themselves are magazine shows, with a mix of news and current affairs, culture and information (on health, legal advice, welfare problems, etc.). Its chief target audiences are Moroccans, Turks, Surinamese, Antillians and Spanish speakers living in and around Amsterdam. When the programs are broadcast in those languages (which is the case more often than not), they're subtitled in Dutch. "Migrant TV" functions on an annual budget of about Fl 1.3 million ($600,000), half of which comes from the city of Amsterdam.[97]

Gradually, more outlets developed, both in radio and in television, at national, regional and local levels. One of the most significant where migrants were concerned was SALTO (Stichting Amsterdamse Lokale Televisie/Radio Omroep), founded in 1985 to supervise and develop programming for Amsterdam's Open Kanaal (Open Channel) system, which now includes five radio channels and one television channel. Although migrants are only one category of SALTO activity, they're sufficiently numerous, important and active to fill one 24-hour radio channel, use substantial portions of airtime on another, and bits of airtime on two more, as well as reports and inserts for the television service. SALTO receives its funding from a mixture of sources: the city of Amsterdam, Kabeltelevisie Amsterdam, charges for studio use (for those organizations which can afford to pay), and sponsorship. It subsidizes the activities of a large number of the nearly 100 organizations which broadcast. It commissioned Intomart to conduct two surveys in 1994, one of which dealt with perceptions and usage of Open Channel programs by Dutch (N=1,554), Turkish (N=158) and Moroccan (N=154) listeners: it showed that, while few in the Dutch population made use of those programs for local news or information, the figures were somewhat higher for Turks (15 percent for news, 7 percent for information), and considerably higher for Moroccans (39 percent for news, 33 percent for information). For Open Channel TV, the figures were Turks 50 percent and 36 percent, Moroccans 36 percent and 31 percent.[98]

Increasing numbers of ethnic minorities are taking their places in the major Dutch broadcasting outlets. The NVJ has established a working group,

"Émigrés and Media," to recruit more minority journalists, and that group has developed a set of guidelines and suggestions for reporting on émigrés and their activities.[99] Several minority group members have become familiar figures on public and commercial TV: Rocky Tuhuteru (anchorman on KRO's "Ontbijt-tv"); Griselda Visser (reporter on "RTL Sport"); and Humberto Tan (reporter on NOS's "Studio Sport"). Several drama series have featured and even centered around émigrés, such as "Domburg" (produced by the small religious public broadcasting organization IKON), which dealt with the lives of Surinamese in the Netherlands. On the whole, however, drama series and comedies remain basically "white." A 1993 study of émigrés in Dutch TV dramas by Soerba Ramkalup showed that the highly popular VARA comedy series "Oppassen" had no continuing parts for minorities, although they occasionally appeared in guest roles. Another comedy series, "Ha de Pa," had no minorities at all, and "Good Times, Bad Times" had 25 white Dutch characters, one minority character. Some series had a better record: "Medical Center West" had 24 continuing roles, four of which were played by minorities; the comedy series "Lady Birds" had 15 continuing roles played by white Dutch actors, and five roles played by minorities; and the drama series "The Old North" had figures of 20 and five. "Lady Birds" struck the researcher as remarkably free of stereotypes, and "The Old North" seemed particularly good at presenting a great deal of background information on the home lives of its minority characters.[100]

The Internet, too, has received some attention from minority groups. Mellouki Cadat, vice chair of the antiracist organization "Nederland bekent kleur," and others have formed a watchdog group to identify and combat racist material on the Net, and the National Bureau Against Racism (Landelijk Bureau Racismebestrijding) has set up a website and message exchange center.[101]

The electronic media situation of minorities in the Netherlands may be far better than it is in other industrially developed nations, but it's far from perfect. There are very few minorities (or women) in high-level decision-making positions. The PSB regional stations provide very little by way of programming for or about minorities, the Dutch commercial TV services likewise. Among the pillars, KRO, VARA, EO and VPRO appear to be more active in presenting minorities and a broader range of minority situations and problems than do NCRV, TROS and AVRO. And finally, the very thing that has opened up more possibilities for minority involvement in the electronic media—the tremendous expansion of media outlets—carries with it the potential danger that, unless their efforts are more widely publicized, viewers and listeners simply won't be aware of them.

The Board of Management took special notice of minorities when it released its recommendations on future directions for public broadcasting in its May 1998 policy paper, "Public Service in the Future." It stated that, since the Netherlands now had a more or less permanent and sizeable population of "resident immigrants," the PSBs should take them more into consideration when buying feature films from aborad, creating entertainment, or producing information programs. Whether this will translate into more money for productions more closely tailored to emigre tastes is yet to be seen.[101a]

PROBLEM AREAS

One of the more sensitive issues on the Dutch electronic media scene is protection of children from "harmful" broadcasts and other electronic material. The Netherlands has yet to experience anything as sweeping as some of the German attempts to block access to various Internet services. However, the rapid growth of Dutch commercial TV has led to accusations that the commercial services continually test the readiness of the Media Authority to invoke the "not before 9 p.m. (for children under 16)" rule noted earlier. Despite frequent fines, there continue to be occasional instances in which the commercial channels will broadcast "erotic" programs starting at 8:30 (as SBS 6 did on October 31, 1996 [Thursday], with its presentation of the "erotic thriller" "Indecent Behavior II"), and more than occasional instances of similar scheduling for relatively violent U.S. crime series or movies ("New York Undercover," "Victim of Beauty"). Whether sexual content is of great concern to Dutch parents is another question. An NOS Audience Research Department study carried out in 1989 revealed that, in contrast with an earlier U.S. study,[102] Dutch parents tended to place one item common to both studies, "Television increases children's interest in sex," in the column of Positive Effects factors; the U.S. sample (admittedly a narrow subset: parents who also were media scholars) recorded this as an Antisocial Effect. The Dutch authors explain this by stating that, " ... policy on the broadcasting of sexual images is much more liberal in the Netherlands than in the United States. The vast majority of the Dutch population accepts the transmission of erotic images which leave little to the imagination."[103]

The issue of children as targets of commercial advertising is somewhat more contentious. Several European consumer's organizations, including some in the Netherlands, have campaigned during much of the 1990s for tighter regulations on advertising directed at children, and the European Commission of the EU has begun to consider whether certain restrictions should be imposed on all EU member states.[104] The Commission set up a pilot project in the Netherlands in 1996 to educate children (and their parents) so that they could appraise ads of all sorts more critically; the early stages have consisted of informational booklets. But the Dutch Consumer Federation head, Erik van Rijn, foresees the possibility that various European consumer federations will demand a total ban on advertising for children, as several of them have done already.[105] European Union policy doesn't allow member states to block the dissemination of television advertising from media services in other countries, although Sweden is battling to maintain its ban on all advertising directed at children under 12 years of age.[106] The Dutch Consumer Federation has argued for more limited bans, on -06 (pay-per-minute) telephone calls, advertorials and marketing in schools.[107]

There remain complaints from women's organizations that women hold few decision-making positions in broadcasting, and that the portrayal of women in drama programs and in ads is stereotyped and even demeaning. The pillar organizations appointed an "emancipation worker" in 1980 to help identify and rectify problems encountered by women working in broadcasting, but also to sensitize programmers to the need to improve their portrayal of women.[108] Minority women have had even more complaints, particularly in terms of what they see as a lack of distinction in TV's portrayal of first-generation and second-generation minority women.[109] In 1991, the NOS Portrayal Department was established as part of the NOS Audience Research Department, largely because of pressures applied by an NOS working group, "Vrouw in Beeld" (Women in the Picture). It has commissioned outside studies, and has conducted several studies on its own, ranging from fairly simple to highly complex content analysis, usually of dramas (including sitcoms). Their findings probably won't surprise anyone familiar with similar studies in Great Britain and the United States, but do support the overall contention that women are portrayed about equally in leading roles, but far less often in supporting roles; that women are shown predominantly (a ratio of 84-to-16 of scenes) in and around the home, whereas the proportion is far more even for men (53 in and around home, 47 in public locales); that male characters speak for about 25 percent longer than do women; that female colleagues speak far less often with one another than do male colleagues; and that women talk with each other about personal relationships far more often than do men, whereas men speak far more often with one another about business matters (money, work). The Portrayal Department also analyzed the drama series "Het Pleidooi" ("The Appeal"), about a Dutch co-op law firm of two women and three men, one of them an Egyptian. Their analysis revealed that almost all of the stereotypes detected in other series were absent in this one, proving that it could be done in a way that still would result in a popular program. The Board of Management's May 1998 "Public Service in the Future" policy paper noted the need for balance in the representation of men and women, but did not disclose the steps (and the financing) that might be needed to achieve this.[110]

There were several attempts made by women's collectives during the 1980s to broadcast in their own right. Many of them ran into an assortment of problems: disagreements within the collectives as to approaches, lack of time for program preparation, lack of financial support. Birgitte Yallov documents the experiences of several such groups in the university city of Nijmegen, where none was able to sustain the effort for very long.[111] A few women hold high administrative positions in the electronic media: Vera Keur chairs VARA; the TV production house TV-Dits has a female manager; and two of the three members of Sol Film Producties' managing board are women.[112]

Blue-collar workers sometimes complain that the general public sees very little of what a worker's life is really like, although VARA in particular has attempted to involve the workers themselves in producing programs that come closer to real life. Throughout the 1970s the VARA series "Van Onderen"

("From Those Below") showed viewers the lives of the workers themselves: Producers talked with workers, shot material segment by segment, then showed each segment to the workers and elicited suggestions as to how the portrayal could be made more accurate. It was a slow and costly process, but it won the praise of workers and of many VARA members for its authenticity.

More surprising, given its target audience, was the decision of NCRV, AVRO and KRO in 1996 to include a weekly (Friday) segment in their jointly produced late afternoon children's program "Alles Kits" that featured two railway station toilet cleaners. Some of the situations resemble the rough and ready comedy of vaudeville, but others delve into how such workers feel about the way they're treated by others, their feelings for each other, and the sorts of lives they live when not at work.[113]

FOREIGN INFLUENCES ON PROGRAMMING

The large proportion of imported programs in the prime-time TV schedules of the Dutch commercial services, coupled with the ready availability of broadcasts from neighboring countries, means that Dutch listeners and viewers have plenty of exposure to foreign broadcasting. Foreign popular music places prominently in the Dutch top 10, foreign TV dramas once did the same (but rarely do nowadays), foreign news (often supplied through foreign wire and telefilm services, as well as Eurovision) takes up a large portion of the main evening newscasts. Quiz shows often are prepared according to U.S. formulas. Does such a seemingly heavy dependence upon foreign sources concern Dutch viewers and listeners?

There's no absolute answer to that question, as audiences differ in their tastes and tolerances, but in general it doesn't appear to be a matter of great concern. Dutch audiences are accustomed to a heavy diet of imported programs. Also, the broadcasting organizations, commercial and public alike, do manage to produce a number of TV dramas each week, some of them one-time shows, some of them miniseries. A number of them have been produced at great expense, for example, the aforementioned "Zwarte Sneeuw." Some have probed sensitive areas in Dutch society, such as personal relations between Dutch and Surinamese (IKON's "Domburg").

Still, many dramas are based upon plots that would be recognizable to any viewer of U.S. or British prime-time soap operas, sitcoms and crime dramas, not to mention game and quiz shows, and raise the question of whether foreign influence has penetrated Dutch productions themselves. But Dutch viewers are likely to be thankful enough that more and more Dutch actors and actresses are performing in Dutch settings and speaking Dutch (almost all imported programs are subtitled), and don't appear all that concerned over possible foreign influences. During prime-time hours, there usually are at least three or four channels broadcasting Dutch productions at any given hour, while two or three (or more) do so during off-peak hours. Furthermore, many of the dramatic elements in Dutch and foreign TV programs are common to western civilization: jealousy, greed, loyalty, expressions of love, all have been staples in western literary traditions long before TV. Aside from a few Dutch newspaper critics, religious figures and politicians, there seems little public fear that Dutch culture might be "lost" because of foreign domination of broadcast programming. To better ensure balance between domestic and imported programming, the 1987 Media Act requires that there be at least 50 percent domestic production in all program categories.

There's a pragmatic factor at work here: Many of the Dutch with whom I have spoken seem aware of the high cost of producing original drama, unless artistic standards were to be lowered. They seem to prefer having a smaller number of well-produced productions—and some of those productions almost always place in the Dutch top 10. Also, they realize that their country is small, and doesn't have the breadth of artistic resources to turn out vast amounts of TV entertainment. And they have found entertainment value in Archie Bunker, Fred Sanford and J. R. Ewing,[114] who didn't really seem all that foreign to them. As citizens of a small country, the Dutch are used to interacting with many foreign cultures; broadcasting is only the most recent mode of interaction.

RELATIONS WITH OTHER MEDIA

The relationship between broadcasting and the press in the Netherlands is colored by the "pillar" system, since broadcasting organizations and newspapers often find themselves in the same "pillar." In some cases, that has meant that newspapers will not criticize their "fellow" broadcasting organizations too severely, although they feel quite free to criticize other organizations and the NOS. Most newspapers of any size have regular columns of broadcast criticism and also cover parliamentary debates and government proposals on broadcasting.

Newspapers regard the electronic media as rivals for advertising revenue, which is why STER originally set aside a portion of broadcast ad revenues: It would help to cushion the blow by making available a source of financial support for the newspapers, particularly failing ones. That same protectionist spirit can be found in the 1987 Media Act, with its provision for sharing of increased ad revenues. Still, the press remains sensitive on that point, the more so because money from STER has been an "on again, off again" proposition. When the broadcasting organizations made a plea for fairly sizable increases in ad time in the late 1970s and early 1980s, intensive lobbying by the press led to a reduction in the amount of that increase.

Although newspaper circulation has dropped over the last two decades, the electronic media aren't blamed for that situation as often as they are in many other industrialized nations. Newscasts on radio and TV are brief (the longest is 30 minutes, on RTL-4), RTL-5 and Veronica don't carry newscasts at all, and regional and local news receives relatively little coverage, although it's increasing as SBS 6 and the regional and local services establish themselves as important players in the contest for viewers and listeners. It's more likely that slumping circulation stems from declines in some types of ad revenue (e.g., job announcements), increasing distribution costs and reader indifference to heavy concentration on party politics, although that's changing as some newspapers drop their party affiliations. And, as is the case in other industrialized societies, young people seem less and less interested in reading newspapers on a daily basis. Annual figures for the period 1975-90 show a decline from the already low figure of 13 percent to a still lower 11 percent.[115]

A few of the newspapers have become important investors in electronic media. One of the larger dailies, *De Telegraaf*, is part owner of two of the commercial services: it holds 30 percent of the stock in SBS 6, and held 5 percent in the now-defunct Sport 7. The Wegener publishing enterprise bought the Arcade Media Group, an owner of commercial radio stations, in 1996; Wegener also is the largest operator of cable-delivered newspapers. The VNU has a nearly 40 percent share in RTL-4, some ownership of regional TV (Noord Brabant and Limburg), and some ownership in the British-Dutch production house Chrysallis/ID-TV.[116]

The Dutch film industry is tiny and if anything has benefited from the existence of television. Television documentaries in particular often are shot by or with film companies, and there are many on the air each year. In the 1980s, Dutch broadcasting organizations and film companies agreed on a method of having TV contribute to the financing of feature films (usually 10-20 percent of the cost) in return for being permitted to show them on TV at some date acceptable to the film producer. In 1986 the government appealed to the broadcasting organizations for further help in strengthening the Dutch film industry. The VPRO responded by agreeing to employ a few directors and scriptwriters each year, leaving them free to produce feature-length films, helping to secure financing for the films, and then arranging that the films be shown first in cinemas.[117]

There also is a coproduction agreement between Dutch ballet companies and some of the broadcasting organizations; it calls for at least three coproductions a year. Dutch broadcasters have been working on something similar with Dutch theater; there once were some 40 TV productions done from theaters each year, but that number dropped to around 10 by the early 1980s, as more and more productions took place in TV studios.[118] And there's a newly created (1997) funding organization, Telefilm, which will support production of six made-for-TV films during a six-month pilot project. The pillar organizations select scenarios, and contribute roughly one-fourth of the Fl 1.7 million ($800,000) cost of each production.[119]

INTERNATIONAL COOPERATION

While coproductions are increasingly common in Europe, the Dutch broadcasting system is less able to profit from that method of sharing production costs than are the larger systems. Part of the problem is a lack of money to invest in such productions. Cost savings arise because a coproduction usually falls into the "spectacular" category, which no one broadcaster could fund; and with little enough to spend on its own domestic productions, Dutch broadcasters would find it hard to justify investing in elaborate coproductions. But there have been several cooperative ventures with Belgian Radio and Television (BRT). Here, the common cultural heritage and common language make coproduction easier.

Eurovision provides an important avenue for cooperation, and the NOS takes full advantage of it. As is usually the case with the small to medium-sized European nations, the Netherlands is far more a taker than a giver where Eurovision's daily news exchange is concerned. It isn't at the center of European activity in the sense that Switzerland and Belgium are; it isn't a major financial center, it isn't home to NATO or to the European Union, and its cultural productions, aside from certain classical music ensembles and the Royal Dutch Ballet, are not in high demand in other parts of Europe. Its position in those respects is much like that of Scandinavian countries, which nonetheless exchange a fair amount of material among themselves.

THE NEW MEDIA

The Netherlands was one of the first countries in Europe to adopt cable television on a widespread basis. The 1982 report of the Scientific Advisory Council devoted more than a fourth of its space to consideration of future uses of cable, including viewdata (already available experimentally), cable newspapers, interactive services and pay-cable.[120] In 1986, the government began a scaled-back $21-million five-year pilot project for interactive cable in 20,000 homes in Limburg Province. Two-thirds of the money came from the national government and one-third from the provincial government. However, the government made it clear from the beginning that it would do little to subsidize the upgrading of cable.[121] Even without such support, the Netherlands quickly grew to become one of the most heavily cabled nations in the world.

There are many private companies that handle videoconferencing, high-speed data communication and video telephony services, but those are small-scale operations, for the most part. Cable TV remained a passive service until the late 1980s, when interactive technologies began to appear. However, it took several years before cable companies were willing to undertake a major test project with a fully interactive "Electronic Shopping Mall" project. The then-second largest cable operator in the Netherlands, CASEMA, teamed up with ABN Amro and IBM to initiate such a project with a limited number of cable subscribers in Veenendaal, who would receive a modem free of charge, and who would enjoy the security of the Secure Electronic Transaction protocol.[122] Nozema and the Media Institute teamed up in 1996 to offer courses of study in various subjects through land-based digital interactive systems; the initial experiment involved 35 students, to be followed by one involving a thousand.[123]

Some of the pillars have begun to experiment with Internet applications, as well. As of early 1998, nearly 40 percent of all Dutch households had PCs, and over 20 percent of PC users had Internet access, so there's a fair-sized potential audience.[123a] In addition to AVRO's use of Internet in connection with "Zwarte Sneeuw" (mentioned above), EO's "Reality" came on air in September 1996, advertising itself as "EO Internet in the digital Netherlands." It was produced as a 12 part on-air series, and had its own website, but also included a double CD-ROM, a magazine and a book. It featured a Dutch "Internet guru," and promised access to a wide range of EO material.[124] VPRO provided coverage of several "music tents" at the Lowlands pop music festival in 1996, and invited Internet users to select the tents they wished to "visit." The Dutch commercial services have been active, as well: SBS 6 not only offers a homepage with details on upcoming programs, but also provides a dating service. So does Veronica, which also displays "Baywatch" photos through the Net.[125] However, NOB Interactive announced in early 1997 that it was ceasing work on interactive applications, and wouldn't recommence until there was enough cable capacity to make video-on-demand viable.[126]

Videocassette players have sold moderately well in the Netherlands: as of 1997 over 60 percent of all Dutch households had them. One striking indication of their popularity is the growth in sales of videocassettes (mostly of Disney productions): 1990 sales figures were Fl 50 million ($22 million) for 1.6 million cassettes; 1995 figures were Fl 238 million ($115 million) for 8.2 million.[127] The most popular items are feature films (chiefly rentals) and children's movies and programs (chiefly purchase); sports and soft-porn material lag far behind. Popular titles include many U.S. movies ("Jurassic Park," "Free Willy") and virtually every Disney movie of the past 15 years ("The Lion King" is the clear leader, with "Snow White" and "The Jungle Book" as runners-up). Dutch and other European productions rarely appear in the leaders' list. Video rentals haven't had the same success: Fl 174 million ($82 million) for 33 million rentals in 1990, Fl 173 million ($80 million) for 27.6 million rentals in 1995.[128]

Pay-cable services were a disappointment, at least to their investors, until the mid-1990s. The government began to license them in 1985, and 10 applicants received authorizations to begin service later that year. Three actually did so. As of 1997, only Filmnet remained: purchase of its parent company, Nethold, by France's Canal Plus may increase its subscribership. It offers little besides feature films, and the market for that product appears to have been covered by VCRs. The Media Act of 1987 permits anyone to start such a service without governmental authorization, although notification to the Media Authority is required.[129] The now-defunct Sport 7 began operations in the mid-1990s, offering sports events via pay-cable, but problems with the decoder system plagued it from the start. Then Philips and US West developed a joint venture called A2000, which began to offer cable households in Amsterdam and Rotterdam a "Pluspakket" which included Sport 7, a science fiction channel, a soft-porn channel, Super Channel and a Chinese channel, for Fl 20 ($10) a month. Several more Dutch urban areas, including The Hague and Hilversum, have been added to the service area. A2000 is an analogue system, but operates over fiber-optic cable in some areas. In the first half of 1996, A2000 had gross profits of roughly Fl 750 million ($375 million) from the Hilversum and Amsterdam markets alone.[130]

DBS isn't likely to become an attractive alternative source of television, either. Most of the country is so densely populated that conventional over-the-air TV brings a wide range of choice to such rural areas as there are, and the larger cities all have cable TV. Satellites have been used to bring signals to cable TV operations for several years now: A number of the Dutch cable firms began to bring in the signal from a Soviet TV satellite in the early 1980s, until the Dutch government objected on the grounds that the Soviet satellite was not a broadcast satellite. There was a brief experiment with the European Orbital Test Satellite (OTS) in 1982 in which several European countries prepared special programs for reception throughout Europe, presumably through satellite-to-cable, since very few Europeans had satellite reception equipment at the time. The Dutch were leaders in that experiment, as they were in its successor, the Europa project, which started in 1985 but went off the air late in 1986. I watched it shortly before its demise, and if my viewing during a several-day period gave me a representative sample, it probably died because a large share of its material consisted of reruns, including Dutch reruns. Increasing financial conservatism within the five to six nations that participated in it probably hurt, too: Its founders had hoped to sell ad time on it but had few takers. The Dutch government's ban on advertising in Dutch to Dutch audiences over satellite-delivered cable services certainly didn't help matters. (That ban was successfully challenged by advertisers in a case decided by the European Court of Justice in April 1988.) But the growth of direct-to-home (DTH) satellite service in the 1990s has been very modest: only 350,000 Dutch households—about 6 percent of the total—had DTH service as of 1996, with prospects for the future uncertain. They might be helped by the Holland Media Group's 1996 decision to convert to digital signals (SBS 6 and Sports 7 already were digital), but most of those households would have to purchase a new decoder to receive those signals, at about $1,000 per unit.

CONCLUSION

Even with the many changes that have taken place on the Dutch electronic media scene, certain elements that have been around from the early days seem destined to remain in place for some time to come. The "pillar" organizations are still there, although they aren't quite so identifiable as separate organizations now, and they've been joined by other organizations that are not at all pillarlike. Smaller groups continue to have access to the air, and no one has suggested seriously that they should not. In fact, the increase in media outlets and airtime at the national, regional and local levels means that they now have even more airtime. However, it's easier for viewers to ignore them now that there are so many channels available. Still, the commitment to provide minority services does seem to be quite firmly established.

Under the new Media Act of 1987, the government retained its traditional freedom to involve itself in the regulation of broadcasting, but it usually restricts itself to warnings and shows only occasional disposition to intervene in programming matters. The Media Authority appears to have established itself as a buffer between government and broadcasters, even if such a role isn't as necessary (and, for that same reason, isn't as difficult to secure) as it has been in France. Yet the sorts of checks and balances that are built into the Dutch system of government—the many political parties, the shifting coalitions, the presence of the "pillars"—haven't acted as a brake on major changes in the electronic media system. Technology, geography, demography and political changes at the national and supranational level (through the European Union) have pushed the Dutch to create what is in effect a dual system: a long-established but now somewhat weakened public sector, and a growing commercial sector.

Despite that, the public sector continues to draw support both from the public and from the government, and the complex arrangement of annual license fees, limited advertising and membership dues that have kept the pillars largely in place looks as if it will hold together for the next few decades or even beyond. The Board of Management clearly regards its chief mission as getting the public sector to differentiate itself even more from the commerical sector, and to make more efficient use of license fee money, and NOS has been busy publicizing the gains in fiscal responsibility that the PSBs are making. However, a number of Dutch public broadcasters with whom I've spoken in the mid-1990s regard it as quite likely that there will be only two public TV channels by the first decade of the next millennium, with TROS and possibly AVRO opting out as pillars. Perhaps Arend Lijphart's description of the Netherlands as "the politics of accommodation" applies equally to the electronic media. And if the pillar system finally collapses, it won't have been the Samson of Dutch commercial television that will have caused its downfall; it will be a combination of the lack of political courage on the part of members of Parliament (and lack of public pressure on them) to support a costly but still highly diverse public system, as well as of bickering among the pillars regarding ways to lower costs on that costly system. Fortunately for the future of public broadcasting in the country, the politicians and the pillars seem to be working toward the same end: a more cost-efficient approach which at the same time doesn't starve the system of the resources needed to present what is a remarkably diverse array of original programming for such a small nation.

4 Germany

States' Rights, National Goals and Unification

More than is the case with any other major system, German electronic media have undergone frequent and substantial restructuring since the early days of radio. There have been six points in time when the system was altered in a fundamental way. Certain domestic developments, most of them political, have had a lot to do with this, but so have influences from beyond the country's borders. And, although the German electronic media system has won praise for the generally high quality of much of its programming, cultural material in particular, its record on political broadcasting has given rise to some concern. While it existed, the Communist-operated East German system stood in strong contrast to its western neighbor; taken together, the two systems presented a vivid portrait of the fundamental differences between broadcasting in communist-socialist and capitalist-socialist societies. Since unification of the two Germanies in 1990, cable, direct-to-home satellite services, VCRs, Internet, and commercial radio and TV have grown to the point where the once-dominant public broadcasting services now are just one pair of players among several—but still important players.[1]

BASIC FACTORS

Geographic

Germany presented many geographical difficulties at the moment of the birth of broadcasting there in 1923. The country wasn't even fully contiguous, since East Prussia was separated from other German states ("Laender"). Despite the loss of about an eighth of its territory following its defeat in World War I, Germany still was the largest nation in Europe, and over 700 miles separated northern East Prussia from the southern Black Forest. Mountains were not a major problem since, aside from the Harz range, they lay at the country's edges. But population distribution was terribly uneven, with heavy concentrations in the Ruhr industrial area and in a few other major cities scattered around the country, and relatively light concentrations elsewhere. The geographic situation certainly didn't favor the development of a highly centralized broadcast system, and at the same time made it virtually certain that, unless there was some measure of central political pressure, some parts of the country would be poorly served or served not at all.

Germany had plenty of neighbors, as well: 10 as of 1923. They ranged in size from Lithuania and Luxembourg to France and Poland. A few already were active in broadcasting, and their incoming signals had helped to stimulate German appetites for a broadcast service of their own. In several others, German was spoken by some of the population (Switzerland, Austria, Czechoslovakia, Poland), and the spillover of German signals had various influences, positive and negative, on their systems.

The division of Germany following World War II considerably altered the geographic situation. Population distribution in West Germany was affected by the millions of German refugees who arrived from East Germany and the eastern territories (now part of Poland and the Russian Republic), but there remain many thinly populated areas. East Germany's population changed very little; in fact, the country occasionally recorded negative annual figures for population growth. There were fewer neighbors for each of the two Germanies, although there was considerable spillover of radio and TV signals between them and from West Germany into Denmark, the Netherlands, Luxembourg, France, Switzerland, Austria and Czechoslovakia, as well as from East Germany into Czechoslovakia and Poland. Signals from West Berlin, an enclave in the middle of East Germany, reached western Poland quite easily.

Demographic

For a large country, Germany was and is very homogeneous. Its post-World War I losses deprived it of most of its non-German-speaking minorities: Poles, Danes, French, Belgians and Czechs. (There are some thousands of Danish-speaking German citizens living in an area just south of the German-Danish border; they receive some broadcasts in Danish from German stations.) From that standpoint, broadcasting had an easier time getting established, since the system didn't have to take into account the need for a multilingual service. But in the 1960s, "guest workers" and their families were brought to West Germany from Turkey, Greece, Italy, Spain, Portugal and elsewhere to help supply factories with laborers during the economic boom. Many of them stayed on, and were joined by still other émigrés, so that Germany now has an émigré population of over 6 million today, or roughly 8 percent of the total population. Nevertheless, Germany is a German-speaking country. Granted, there are many dialects, and a Frisian fisherman and a Swabian farmer who attempted to converse with one another in their respective patois would not get very far. But neither of them would have much trouble speaking a standard form of German that is taught in all the schools and used in broadcasting. The one "native" linguistic minority is the 50,000 Sorbs, who speak a Slavic tongue.

Since the "guest workers" weren't expected to stay in West Germany on a long-term basis, little was done at first to integrate them into West German society, and that included broadcasting. Brief broadcast services in their languages began to appear in the early 1960s and have been expanded somewhat since but still remain confined largely to radio. Some of the guest workers have learned to speak German more or less well, but many have not, even though their descendants often speak it fluently. Most live in the poorer districts of the larger industrial centers. West Germany's economic slump in the early 1980s made their lives far more difficult, yet their homelands presented even worse prospects, so they attempted to stay. The Sorbs of East Germany didn't present the same sort of problem, since they continue to live in their age-old district in the southeast corner of the country. They still receive schooling in German but are allowed and even encouraged to maintain their own language, in which there are daily radio broadcasts and modest numbers of television programs.

Economic

Germany became a major industrial nation in the late 19th century. At the time of Germany's emergence as a unified nation in 1871, some two-thirds of the population were rural dwellers; less than 50 years later, some two-thirds lived in cities. World War I crippled German industry, and war reparations to the Allied governments also played havoc with the German economy, but by the mid-1920s the nation was regaining some measure of prosperity. The Great Depression proved a temporary setback, as the ascent to power of the National Socialist Party (Nazis) in 1933 was followed by increasing industrialization. Throughout the entire period of industrialization, agriculture lagged: Farming methods were not very progressive, and much of the soil was of poor quality.

The division of Germany after World War II exacerbated some of those conditions. The western part of Germany always had been more industrialized than the eastern part, which now had the additional burden of fulfilling some very stiff reparations claims by the Soviet Union. Thus, East Germany had to create an industrialized economy out of almost nothing, despite which the country eventually became one of the world's larger industrial powers and was recognized as having the highest standards of production within the Soviet-created eastern Europe economic community (COMECON). West Germany, thanks in part to economic help from the United States through the Marshall Plan, rebuilt its industries and soon became a major industrial power, not only in Europe, but around the world. The unification of Germany in 1990 proved to be extremely expensive, since the East German level of industrial development was so far inferior to the level in the west. Unemployment soon soared to over 10 percent, much of it made up of laid-off or prematurely retired East German workers, and has remained at that level in the late 1990s.

Agriculture was somewhat inefficient in both Germanies, at least when compared with some of the other nations of Europe and North America. Only some 3 percent of the population were and are engaged in it. They receive small amounts of radio programming about their particular concerns and interests. Mining, fishing and forestry engage even smaller percentages of the population. Most Germans, West/East and now unified, live in cities and work in government, industry, businesses and the professions. West and East Germans enjoyed high per capita incomes compared with their western and eastern neighbors, and both were major exporters of manufactured goods; it was not until after unification that the differences in quality and economic efficiency became apparent. Electronics was a major industry in both Germanies, and has continued to be important in post-1990 Germany.

Political

Following the dissolution of the monarchy at the end of World War I, Germany embarked upon an experiment in parliamentary democracy. Many of the years of the Weimar Republic (1918-33) were marked by strife, but a democratic system of sorts seemed to have taken root by the mid-1920s. The coming of the Great Depression at the end of the 1920s and the resultant high unemployment helped to weaken the fragile democracy to the point where Hitler and the Nazis, who had come to power more or less within the democratic framework, soon were able to subvert the system to their own autocratic ends; radio played an important role in their consolidation of power.

By the end of World War II, there was little semblance of government in Germany, and the Allied powers set about rebuilding a democratic system that would govern all of the country. It soon became apparent that the Soviet Union and the three major western powers (France, Great Britain, the United States) had widely differing ideas of what constituted a democracy, and the two segments of Germany moved farther and farther apart. The western powers moved toward a system with multiparty participation, a division of power between state ("Land") and federal ("Bund") government, a strong Parliament and so on, while the Soviet Union shaped a system with one dominant political party (Socialist Unity Party [SED], which was Communist), concentration of power in the national government (the "laender" eventually were abolished in favor of smaller districts, or "Bezirke"), and a rather weak Parliament. Both Germanies could claim to be democracies in some respects, with universal suffrage, various constitutionally protected freedoms and so on. The exercise of those freedoms and that suffrage was another matter, and in most respects West German citizens had much greater freedom than did their East German counterparts, who faced a visible reminder of one lack of freedom—to travel—in the presence of the Berlin Wall and the Iron Curtain of watchtowers, mined land and electric fences that ran along the border separating the two Germanies. By the 1980s, East Germans had acquired the relative freedom to watch and listen to West German broadcasting undisturbed.

Certainly the various political parties in West Germany—two major ones, several smaller ones—sought to use broadcasting to bring their views to the public, but they also complained from time to time about the broadcasts of their political opponents, and there were periods when West German broadcasting took on the appearance of a political battleground. East German political broadcasting presented no such problems: Although there were several political parties, the SED predominated, and the others supported it rather than challenged it.

After unification, the political scene has been dominated by the three leading West German parties—Christian Democrats (CDU), Free Democrats (FDP) and Social Democrats (SPD). The first two have served as the ruling coalition over the past few decades; the CDU is the larger and more conservative of the two. The SPD is socialist, but has gradually moved toward a more centrist position. The Green (ecology) Party joined the SPD as a governing coalition partner following the 1998 national election.

Cultural

The Germans have one of the greatest cultural traditions in Europe, stretching back to the early Middle Ages and embracing painting, poetry, music, drama and other arts. Philosophers such as Hegel, Buber and Kant; composers such as Bach, Beethoven and Brahms; novelists, poets and dramatists such as Schiller, Goethe and Thomas Mann; and painters such as Durer, Menzel and Kollwitz were and for the most part still are major influences in European and even world culture. Electronic media have played a part in the dissemination of that culture, but also have brought foreign cultures to Germany in sometimes new forms, and "Baywatch" and other U.S. (and occasionally British) TV series have many devoted viewers. U.S.-style fast-food restaurants have spread around the country, and blue jeans were even common in *both* Germanies.

Religion doesn't appear to be a major influence in contemporary German culture, for various reasons. Although over half of all Germans profess to follow one faith or another, the churches have little influence over the educational system, in marked contrast to the Netherlands. Nor is there a state church. Churches were allowed to exist in East Germany, but they weren't encouraged.

The Germans themselves are voracious consumers of culture, at least according to certain indices. Their annual level of book reading is among the highest in Europe, they are frequent visitors to art galleries, they attend many concerts, and they seem willing to support state subsidization of the arts. They sometimes are accused of being quite conservative in their artistic tastes, and even intolerant of avant-garde movements or figures, yet Germany (and Berlin in particular) was home to some of the most active avant-garde movements and figures during the 1920s, and West Berlin regained something of that reputation over a period stretching from 1948 (the Berlin Blockade) to 1991 (unification and the end of the Berlin Wall). Broadcasting was the vehicle for some of that avant-garde expression: The playwright Bertolt Brecht was active in radio during the 1920s, and the composer Karlheinz Stockhausen has written many works specifically for transmission over radio starting in the 1960s. East and West Germany alike encouraged their best writers to write for radio and television and gave them considerable creative latitude.

The public, too, appears to regard broadcasting as an important medium for cultural expression, although audiences for high-culture broadcasts often are small. At the same time, German and other critics have pointed out that there is a considerable following for kitsch and low comedy in Germany, and one could discover many examples of each in the two German broadcast systems, as well as following unification.

Technological

While the current level of technological development is high in Germany, it took a bit longer for some of the new media to establish themselves there than was the case in the United States, Canada, Belgium and the Netherlands (for cable), and Great Britain (for direct-to-home satellites). The chief reason seems to have been the exercise of states' rights by the various "laender" on the one hand, and the "gold-plated standard" approach to the installation of cable by the country's PTT—at present, Deutsche Telekomm, or DT—system, on the other. The states couldn't agree with one another on whether or how to license cable, often because of political disagreements; the PTT charged such high fees for doing so once a few experimental cable services were operating that few households could afford them. Once an interstate agreement was reached, and once DT decided to lower its fees, cable took off quite rapidly. For satellites, the Germans were early leaders in developing the technology, but had a string of bad luck with launches and with postlaunch "glitches." The Germans are very active in the European satellite consortium; there now are several communication satellites serving Europe, and over a third of all German households subscribe to satellite services.

A BRIEF HISTORY

It's hard to imagine more difficult conditions for the creation of a broadcast system than those that existed in Germany in the early 1920s.[2] The country was emerging from World War I with its economy shattered, its monarchy gone and its territory and population reduced. The war reparations obligations placed upon it by the Allied governments were nearly impossible to fulfill and helped to lead to rampant inflation and to a devaluation of currency that must be unparalleled in economic history: The Reichsmark, which had stood at about nine to the U.S. dollar just after the war, fell to over 4 billion to the dollar by November 1923! Yet all during this period various German businesses, government departments and individuals were busy experimenting with wireless transmission (Germany had made considerable progress on this before and during the war). There were experimental broadcasts of concerts and operas starting in December 1920, all carried out over the German Post Office (Reichspost) transmitter at Konigs-Wusterhausen near Berlin, and radio amateurs all over Germany and beyond received them and commented on reception conditions. An Economic System Broadcasting Service was set up in 1920 but at first used telegraphy to convey economic data (stock market reports, etc.) to its customers and did not utilize wireless telephony until 1922. Even at that, the public could not (or wasn't supposed to) listen to the service; it was to be received over licensed sets only, and the sets themselves were tuned to one frequency.

When broadcasting to the general public finally did begin in October 1923, those who invested funds to establish the stations hoped for some financial return from them, perhaps through sale of airtime to advertisers, perhaps through increased sales of phonograph records (the Vox record company's headquarters in Berlin was the site of the first broadcast), perhaps through rising public demand for radio receivers (some of the investors were connected with radio dealerships). In fact, they received very little return at first: The government placed high annual taxes on radio receivers, which discouraged people from buying them (although it did lead to sharply increased, and illegal, home construction of receivers). The tax was reduced in March 1924, and just as had happened in Great Britain, following such a move the number of licensed sets increased enormously: Fewer than 10,000 registered and taxed sets as of April 1924, nearly 550,000 by the end of the year. The tax revenues themselves made the individual stations considerably stronger economically, and ad revenues increased as the economy improved.[3]

As radio grew in strength, the stations set up a cooperative association, partly in order to be able to protect themselves from the encroachment of the post office. That association lasted only a few months and was succeeded by the German Radio Society (Reichs Rundfunk Gesellschaft) in 1925. The society concept had been suggested by the German Ministry of the Interior, which remained quite distrustful of the idea of such a powerful medium of communication resting in private hands. The charter for the society granted controlling power to the post office—the private businesses saw little reason not to, since the post office supplied them with the major share of their revenue through the taxes it collected—but also made the society itself responsible for a wide range of functions, including regulation of program exchange among the stations. This meant that, indirectly at least, a government ministry would have some degree of influence over programming decisions.

That wasn't all. The radio stations now were required to accept the supervision of "cultural committees" which would be appointed by the respective state ("land") governments; those committees would examine the program output of each station to see that it was serving the cultural interests of society. In addition, there were to be supervisory committees at each station, one member appointed by the national government and two by the state government; those committees would attempt to keep radio from being used for partisan political purposes. The founders of the stations had not expected them to function as important sources of information, and the newscasts had been supplied through a governmentally supported wire service (DRADAG—Drahtlose Dienst A.G.), so the new restrictions weren't all that bothersome. However, they did frustrate some of the more extreme political parties, the National Socialists (Nazis) in particular, and made the Nazis all the more determined to shape radio to their own purposes when and if they came to power.

For the remainder of the 1920s, radio served as a considerable cultural force by broadcasting German and foreign drama, some in transcription and some originally written for radio, talks on cultural subjects, and music, popular and classical. News broadcasts were brief, political discussion programs were rare, commentaries were nonexistent. And when in 1932 the government passed radio reform legislation, which further centralized control of the medium by creating the post of radio commissioner in the Ministry of the Interior to supervise informational broadcasting, the move brought some public criticism (especially from the radio periodicals) but little else. Even the states raised little protest, probably because by this time their status in the German political system was much weaker. It's doubtful that most of the public noticed the difference. Newscasts already were bland and supercautious; now they became more so. Those portions of the legislation that pertained to entertainment broadcasting were so general in tone, but so contradictory, that one writer for a radio periodical said, "How many questions of conscience must a [station] manager submit to himself and inwardly answer today, before he can label a program 'good,' if he does not want to be entangled in the mantraps of these definitions?"[4] The chief outcome of the reform was a notable increase in last-minute cancellations and substitutions of entertainment programs. Germany was rapidly descending into chaos, thanks to the Depression and to the increasingly violent activities of some of the political parties, and the government of the period, such as it was, wanted to guarantee the neutrality of radio in every way possible, wanted to avoid giving offense. Centralization made this easier to do. It also made things much easier for the Nazis when they finally came to power. Unfortunately, neutrality was the last thing they had in mind.

The Thousand-Year Reich (1933–1945)

The first head of radio in the Hitler era, Eugen Hadamovsky, made his (and the Nazis') excitement at finally getting control over radio very obvious when he stated, "While in the opposition, we wrote the word 'radio' with three exclamation points. We still do it today, as well, for we are possessed by the magic strength of electric sparks which open the heart and set the spirit in motion, a strength which does not stop at city limits and is not turned back from closed doors, which knows no boundaries and is able to draw the people into the spell of one mighty spirit."[5] That fascination with radio's "magic strength" was shared by many Nazi leaders, German Chancellor Adolf Hitler and his propaganda chief Joseph Goebbels in particular. They soon set in motion plans shaped many years earlier to make radio serve as the instrument by which "the entire nation will be drenched through and through with our philosophy."[6] The 1932 reforms had simplified their task, but due in part to economic conditions, radio was not yet as all-pervasive as the Nazis wished. Therefore, they soon implemented several steps that would bring the medium to virtually every German citizen, and several more steps that would ensure its "proper" use.

Since many people could not afford to purchase radio sets, there already existed in Germany many informal clubs and associations where one set served a group of people. The Radio Participants' League was the largest and most national of those associations, and the Nazis had begun to infiltrate league groups even before 1933. Now such groups were encouraged even further, because they had the added benefit of bringing people together under conditions where trusted Nazi party members could get the groups to discuss what they'd just heard; hopefully, that would ensure that the Nazi message was properly understood, but also that "deviants" in the groups could be spotted, singled out and persuaded to change their thinking.

But people also wanted to be able to listen on their own, and for this, too, the Nazis had a solution: an inexpensive radio receiver. The People's Radio Receiver ("Volksempfaenger") was inexpensive because it was simple—so simple that it would receive only one or two frequencies, which of course were those of the German broadcast service. In that way, "alien" broadcasts from other parts of Europe (some of them in German, especially from the Nazis' sworn enemies in the Soviet Union) wouldn't reach the ears of at least some of the people. By the outbreak of World War II, it became a crime punishable by a prison term or even death to pass on to others what one had heard on those alien broadcasts. The People's Receivers were a huge success, and by the late 1930s, Germany had the largest number of radio sets per country in all of Europe.

Although the existing broadcast system featured transmitters and studios all over the country, transmitter power was weak enough in some cases that not everyone could hear broadcasts clearly, so the Nazis strengthened transmitter power to the point where that no longer was a problem. (Such a move was especially important because the People's Receivers weren't particularly sensitive, and a weak signal, even if on the correct frequency, would be almost inaudible.) And finally, even though the annual license fee for having a radio set in the household was quite low (24 marks [$6] a year—which it remained until 1969), the Nazis allowed many exemptions to it, especially among war veterans, old people and the physically handicapped.

It was just as important to ensure that listeners received politically and culturally correct information, so the Nazis also remodeled the administrative structure of German radio. The advisory and supervisory councils were abolished. Radio stations throughout the country were placed under managers who would have total power over program content. Those managers were trusted Nazi Party members. Political and cultural elements deemed undesirable by the Nazis—meaning Jews and Communists in particular, but also those whose approach to the arts, journalism and so on was "decadent" or "negative"—had no place on the radio, although it took a few years to remove them altogether. That was made all the easier because one person, Joseph Goebbels, headed all three of the agencies that were most important to the functioning of radio: the Propaganda Ministry, the Nazi Party Office of Broadcasting, and the Reich Chamber of Culture (a "union" of producers, writers, etc.).

The Nazis also created new studios and transmitters in German cities which had never had them, but they also gradually squeezed out regional programming by claiming more and more time for the national service from Berlin, which once again served as the German capital.[7] All of the important public speeches of Hitler were broadcast, of course, but so were those of other party leaders, including Goebbels himself. There were plenty of talks and other features about National Socialism, too, some intended for the general public, others for specific groups, such as housewives, factory workers and so on. Music broadcasts increasingly took on a German character, with less and less time for foreign works. In October 1935, jazz disappeared from the broadcast schedule; it was considered to be too decadent for the new Germany.

One of the most striking demonstrations of the power of radio, at least as the Nazis wielded it, came in late 1934 to early 1935. The Saar, a small but industrially significant territory on the French-German border, had been placed under French supervision by the League of Nations just after World War I. The League decided to hold a plebiscite to determine whether the Saarlanders wished to remain under French jurisdiction, return to Germany, or opt for independence. The Nazis saturated Germany and the Saar with broadcasts urging a return to Germany: There were approximately a thousand separate broadcasts on the subject within a two- to three-month period. The persuasion was almost entirely positive, emphasizing the many benefits to be had through union with the new Germany. The vote, too, was overwhelmingly positive, and the Nazis credited radio for their success. In a way, the Saar campaign was a tune-up for the propaganda barrage the Nazis directed to Austria in 1937-38 and Czechoslovakia in 1938,[8] except that, in those cases, threats definitely were mixed in with promises. Both campaigns were successful.

The Nazis also were interested in television. Several German scientists had been working with the medium since the 1920s, and in 1935 the Nazis proclaimed the first "regular" TV service in the world—regular because it was on the air three days a week and on a fixed schedule. Most of the receivers were set up in public places, and none were available for general public purchase. The initial standard was crude (180 lines), but by 1937 there was a 441-line system, and shortly thereafter a few receivers were placed on sale at very high prices (650 reichsmarks, or $160). The outbreak of World War II halted the production of sets; there were only 600 of them in households by then, so very few would have been inconvenienced (aside from military personnel in hospitals in and around Berlin, who had access to sets), but the transmission of a regular service continued until 1944.[9]

The outbreak of war in 1939 brought other changes to broadcasting. Listening to foreign broadcasts became illegal. More and more airtime was taken up with patriotic music and with announcements of victories, which themselves were handled very cleverly: The national service would receive reports of military triumphs at various times during the day, but rarely announced them immediately; instead, it broadcast "special announcements," complete with trumpet fanfares, that indicated the coming of major declarations. The hope was that people's curiosity would grow and word would spread, so that the audience would become as large and as attentive as possible. By 1943, defeats had become more frequent than victories, but even these sometimes served the same purpose, since they could be described as "strategic retreats designed to lure the enemy into a trap." Goebbels disclosed his increasing pessimism about the outcome of the war in his diaries,[10] but went on to note some of the new propaganda twists he was devising to keep the German people as optimistic as possible.

As the war continued, some listeners became disenchanted with the service provided by the national radio station. Regional services were on during the morning hours only, and in any case were no real alternative. There were enough listener protests over the almost incessant German marches and waltzes that the stations eventually cut them back to something more closely resembling balance in presentation. The accuracy of the newscasts was something else again; no one dared to protest openly in that case, but a fair number of Germans found ways of obtaining or modifying existing receivers (even the People's Receivers) so as to be able to receive broadcasts from outside the country. That was risky, of course, and German jamming (electronic interference with incoming broadcast signals) made it difficult to listen, anyway. However, German morale remained remarkably high in the closing period of the war, and Nazi radio probably can claim some of the credit for that.

During the early and middle periods of the war, the Allied forces were successful in bombing a few of the German transmitters, but auxiliary transmitters usually got stations back on the air within minutes, so technical services were maintained throughout the conflict. Late in the war, as the Allies pushed into Germany itself, the German military frequently blew up their own transmitters in order to keep the Allies from using them. The Soviet advance from the east was so rapid, however, that the Red Army was able to enter Berlin, capture the national station intact, retrain the existing staff, and begin to broadcast from it in less than two weeks. The remnants of the German government fled to northern Germany and attempted to continue a national broadcast service from there, but the war was over within a few weeks. The Thousand-Year Reich had lasted barely 12 years, and for all its effectiveness as a propaganda instrument, the German radio service could do little to prolong its life. Its ultimate masters, Adolf Hitler and Joseph Goebbels, had committed suicide together in an underground bunker in Berlin, even as German radio exhorted the people to fight on.

Broadcasting under the Occupation (1945–1949)

Germany's defeat at the hands of the Allies was followed by several developments that neither it nor they could have foreseen. Although Germany and its capital, Berlin, were divided into four zones (in Berlin, sectors) of occupation, that was to be a temporary measure, and the country and the capital would be treated as one entity, the four occupying powers coordinating their activities with one another. That was the plan. It didn't work in practice, and the three western zones and sectors, under the French, the British and the Americans, pulled closer and closer together and farther and farther apart from the Soviet zone and sector. The country's veins and arteries—its postal system, telephone lines, road, rail and canal networks, and its broadcast service—all were subdivided sooner or later.

Attempts to coordinate policy took place over many months and in many meetings, but their net result usually was the same. The Soviet Union seemed interested chiefly in extracting as much in reparations from Germany as possible, while the three western Allies worked toward the economic reconstruction of the country. Broadcasting proved to be an especially difficult matter: Many of the regional stations in the western part of the country had been destroyed or severely damaged in the closing months of the war and in any case never were designed to be heard throughout the country, whereas the Soviet army had captured the national station intact. It mattered not at all that the station was located in what turned out to be the British sector of occupation in Berlin; the Soviet Union was able to treat it as an enclave and had full rights of entry and exit—rights maintained until the early 1950s, when a new broadcasting center was built in East Berlin.

It seemed logical, at least to the western Allies, that the Berlin station should be used by all of them to broadcast to all of Germany. The Soviets agreed in principle. It wasn't so easy to gain agreement in practice. At one point, as the western Allies pressed their claim for airtime, the Soviets offered one hour per day. When the western Allies stated that they did not think that an hour apiece was very much, they were told that they had obviously misunderstood: It was one hour to be subdivided among themselves as they saw fit! At that point, the western Allies decided that their own efforts to re-establish broadcast services would have to go ahead without any assumption that they eventually might form part of a broad national service.

Already there were stations in several of the larger cities of western Germany: Munich, Frankfurt, Hamburg and Stuttgart all had been placed in service again, although with staffs made up largely of print journalists and others inexperienced in broadcasting. Most of the experienced broadcasters were or were assumed to be Nazis or Nazi sympathizers and were on trial or in jail. German-speaking Americans, British and French not only ran the stations but did some of the on-air work at first; soon, German staff took over all but the top management positions, and in the U.S. and French zones, those too went to Germans within a year or two. The Soviet Army had brought along with it a number of Germans who had worked for Radio Moscow's German service during the war; they now formed an important part of the Soviet zone broadcast management structure.

The occupation zones led to some peculiar results simply because of their peculiar geography. Some observers commented that the British got heavy industry (the Ruhr), the Americans got scenery (the Bavarian Alps) and the French got wines (the Rheingau, plus Baden-Wuerttemburg). There were more profound underlying reasons for the choice of zones, but the division created a need for broadcast facilities in places where there had been few or none up until then. For example, the French chose as their administrative center the spa and casino town of Baden-Baden, which never had had a station of its own. Now it had one. The United States needed an enclave in the British zone in order to handle shipping, since the main U.S. zone in southern Germany was completely landlocked; it got Bremen and Bremerhaven, and soon put in operation a station in Bremen, which had had no more than a small studio before that time. The Soviet Union had the main station in Berlin, but also one in Leipzig, and it soon added others in order to provide a small amount of localized broadcasting. In fact, until 1952 there were two networks in the eastern region, a North German Network based in Berlin, and a Central German Network based in Leipzig, although the greater share of the program material originated in Berlin.[11] The merger of the two networks into one centralized service coincided with the abolition of states in East Germany and was part of an overall move toward centralization.

The military occupation governments were determined that another Hitler should not rise again, but West and East went about the task of preventing that in very different ways. The Soviet zone was to feature a strong national government with little power in the hands of the states (which eventually were abolished), but with a considerable amount of oversight by the Soviet Union itself. The western zones were brought together gradually (and not without some disagreement among the western Allies) into a federal structure, with certain rights guaranteed to the states and others to the federal government; there would be decreasing oversight by the Allied occupation governments. Broadcasting was reserved for the states, with the hope that that would keep any demagogue from making effective use of the medium nationwide. Broadcasting was separated from the post office in all four zones; in the western zones, that move appears to have been taken because Germans were fearful that the national government could use the post office to influence broadcast policy, as it had done starting in the mid-1920s.

Some Germans agreed with the states' rights policy, while others saw it as wasteful, inefficient and possibly unworkable. The issue of freedom from interference by the government, federal or state, was something else: as Michael Hofmann observes, "American-style ideas on freedom of broadcasting without government interference could hardly be found in any [German bureaucrats]. As a matter of fact, they were hard to comprehend for any lawyer who had been raised in the tradition of German public law."[12] But the western Allies had agreed upon it, and although the provisional legislatures in the various West German states had to draft broadcast laws themselves, those laws had to win occupation authority approval. Therefore, all of them ended up bearing considerable resemblance to one another. And when a constitution was drafted for the federal government, it recognized states' rights in this and other domains. Thus, the western part of Germany ended up with a broadcast system that bore very little resemblance to anything the country had ever had before: one in which there would be no nationally administered service.

Unfortunately, the states themselves had not been designed with broadcasting in mind. Some were quite small, others were large, and two of them—Hamburg and Bremen—were tiny city-states. Also, the occupation authorities had followed some of their own national tendencies in setting up broadcast systems within their respective zones of occupation. The British and French each developed a single major broadcast center (the British in Hamburg, the French in Baden-Baden), as was characteristic of their own national broadcast services. There were smaller stations elsewhere in their zones, but they were decidedly secondary. The Americans were less centrist: Each large city in the U.S. zone had a station, which meant that Munich, Stuttgart, Frankfurt and Bremen all became broadcast centers, with some degree of cooperation among them but also a fair measure of independence.

When all of this came together in the new federal republic in 1949, it was not exactly a seamless robe. Barely 60 miles separated Hamburg and Bremen, yet each had a broadcast center. The states of Baden and Wuerttemburg were joined together, giving the combined state two broadcast centers, in Baden-Baden and in Stuttgart, also about 60 miles apart. (The two centers were merged in 1997.) The station in Hamburg was to provide service to the city-state of Hamburg and to three other north German states, although in 1954 a subsidiary station in Cologne became a broadcast center in its own right and served its particular area; it eventually became the largest public broadcaster in West Germany. The Saar once again was under French administration, and by the time it rejoined Germany in 1957, once again through a plebiscite but without an intensive radio propaganda campaign as accompaniment, it already had a station of its own even though it was one of the smallest of the states. In other words, the system that evolved lacked geographical logic. It also turned out to lack economic logic, as soon would become very evident.

One of the features common to all broadcast laws in the western zones also was one of the most revolutionary. The Allied authorities wanted guarantees that the German people would become involved in the administration of broadcasting—again, in the hope that that would help prevent another Hitler from taking over radio. Few countries ever had tried to institutionalize citizen involvement, although one of the U.S. networks, NBC, had had an advisory council made up of leading figures in society, Great Britain had had more broadly based advisory councils for the BBC since 1935, and France had had citizen councils that actually wielded some power for a few years in the mid-1930s.

The modus operandi was quite interesting: divide society into interest groups (educators, labor, religious groups, business and manufacturing, politicians, cultural organizations, etc.), then draw up a council that would represent those interests without particular reference to their numerical strength. Each state broadcast law had to contain provision for such a council, although variations were permitted, as a result of which some councils were and are larger than others, have certain interests represented that others do not and so on. The councils were to have real power in the administration of their respective stations—hiring and firing the station manager, examining the yearly budget and sometimes even having limited veto power over expenditures—and the groups themselves would get to choose their own representatives; they would not be selected by the broadcasters or by the state governments (except for those council members who represented state governments). The councils were to be as independent as possible.

None of those features characterized broadcasting in the Soviet zone. Organization was at the national level, and there were no broadcast councils. There was no need for the latter, in theory: Communism followed the Lincolnesque precepts of government of, by and for the people. Therefore, broadcasters (and the government that controlled broadcasting) were of the people and naturally would work in the people's interests. There was one respect in which broadcasting in the four occupation zones was very similar, however: Stations everywhere gave prominence to programs detailing Nazi misdeeds, called upon listeners to recognize their own roles in allowing and even encouraging that to happen, and urged them to be vigilant in the future so as to prevent any recurrence. That was a necessary part of the rehabilitation process that would lead Germany back to democracy and full sovereignty. By the time that finally occurred, it was clear that there would be two very different Germanies.

The names taken by the two new Germanies portrayed very clearly one of the most fundamental differences between them: The western portion called itself the Federal Republic of Germany, thus emphasizing a division of power between the federal and state governments; the eastern portion called itself the German Democratic Republic (GDR), thus emphasizing an approach to governance that the other, not "truly" democratic Germany perhaps could not claim for itself. The broadcast systems displayed the same fundamental difference. However, while the East German system remained essentially unchanged in its structure from 1949 until unification in 1991, the West German system underwent several changes, some by mutual agreement among the stations, some as a reaction to state and federal government pressure, and some as a reaction to changes in external situations.

The Republics Establish Themselves (1949–1961)

In 1951, the federal government, then led by Chancellor Konrad Adenauer and the Christian Democratic (Conservative) Party, or CDU, made the first of several attempts to establish a national broadcast system alongside the state system. It was unsuccessful; but undaunted, Adenauer mounted further efforts, seemingly driven by the conviction that some stations in the existing system were "Red" (Socialist-influenced).[13] The German "father of broadcasting," Hans Bredow, remained faithful to his conviction that a unified, centralized system was a better guarantor of national strength, which supported Adenauer's philosophy, if not his approach.[14] In 1959, the CDU-led government proposed an omnibus broadcasting bill that would establish a second TV service (the state system had begun to add television to radio in 1952), which was to be set up along the lines of the British ITA.[15] The bill also called for the federal government to take over the tiny international broadcast service (Deutsche Welle), which was being operated as a joint venture by the state systems, and to establish a new German-language radio service (Deutschlandfunk) ostensibly intended for German-speaking listeners outside the Federal Republic (East Germany, Switzerland, Austria and various pockets of German speakers elsewhere). It soon became evident that the TV portion of the bill would not pass, so the two radio stations were made the subject of a separate bill, which did pass. Then Adenauer and a few of his close political associates worked with a group of businessmen to establish a second TV service that would come into being without federal legislation. A company was established during 1960 and was scheduled to go on the air in February 1961.

The states reacted predictably to the proposed TV service, took the case to the West German Supreme Court, and in 1961 received a favorable verdict, at least in part: The court declared that the federal government had no right to establish a domestic broadcast service, as the federal basic law (constitution) reserved that power for the states.[16] But the court also ruled that the federal government should have jurisdiction over the telecommunications services, which would turn out to be important when cable began to establish itself.[17] Still, the decision represented the first clear victory for the constitutional principle of states' rights where broadcasting as programming service was concerned, and it represented a stinging defeat for Adenauer and the CDU. The widespread discussion of a second television service did arouse public interest, and it emerged in 1963, albeit in a rather bizarre organizational form, about which more later.

The state stations already had taken steps to strengthen themselves, beginning with the creation of the Arbeitsgemeinschaft der Oeffentlichrechtlichen Rundfunkanstalten Deutschlands (Working Group of German Public Service Broadcasting Organizations, hereafter referred to as ARD) in 1950. The stations had exchanged ideas and programs with one another during the occupation period but felt the need for a more permanent organization through which to carry out such activities. Also, it was evident that furnishing a full range of broadcast programs would be difficult for any one of the largest stations, and almost impossible for the smallest ones. The stations soon established an ongoing program exchange service that not only took into account the financial ability of individual stations to contribute to a program pool but also recognized certain "spheres of influence"—specific kinds of programs that would come from certain stations because of their already-established expertise in that area. The stations also agreed to establish a news production center in Munich (later shifted to Hamburg) in order to serve all parts of the country with a more comprehensive national and international news service than any one of them could furnish. (All continued to cover regional and a limited amount of local news.)

The stations themselves financed the ARD, but they also worked through the organization to rectify some of the financial imbalances in the broadcast system. Since each station received license fee money from listeners in its particular state, some stations had far larger revenues than did others. Hamburg's NWDR received revenues from an area with a population of over 25 million, while Radio Bremen's area had perhaps 1 million, and SR (the Saar) not much more. Therefore, the stations worked out a revenue-sharing scheme that had the larger stations subsidizing the smaller ones—a scheme that continues to function to this day. The stations also agreed on some general limits for amounts of advertising to be carried (the Americans had introduced radio advertising on stations in their zone in 1948, mainly to help encourage growth in the economy). A few stations such as NWDR that could afford such a policy declined to carry any at all. The ARD also allowed the stations to negotiate from a position of collective strength—important in dealing with unions and with state legislatures, since any increase in broadcast license fees must be approved by all of the legislatures. Even with the ARD acting as coordinator, it's a clumsy, tedious, time-consuming process.

Television presented another set of problems for the stations. Following a series of tests, the first regularly scheduled TV service by an ARD station came on the air in December 1952; by 1954, several other ARD stations had TV services, and they again pooled their programming resources. For TV, that was far more crucial than it had been for radio, since the costs were so much higher, and the stations devised a fixed exchange system that would see stations contributing specific programs and series on a regularly scheduled basis. Most of the ARD prime-time schedule was and still is put together in that manner. Again, the stations developed a central news organization—actually an expansion of duties for the existing operation in Munich. While all stations contributed to the total program pool, obviously some were far better situated to do so than others, but all stations were and still are required to contribute a minimum of 3 percent of the program material for the collective program. (Individual ARD stations also produce and purchase programs for non-prime-time hours, including local and regional news.)

During the first decade or so of its existence, the new West German broadcast system earned high marks for the quality of its productions, although some critics observed that the amount of programming about the Nazi past seemed to have decreased once the occupation period ended. Politics was a frequent program topic, and the system appeared able to defend itself against attempts at political influence. However, when NWDR was divided into two stations in 1954 (NDR in Hamburg, WDR in Cologne), politicians took advantage of the opportunity by changing the manner in which members of the broadcast councils were chosen; the new radio laws for the two stations specified that the state legislatures would appoint the members, and unlike the other state broadcast councils, there was no specific indication of which societal groups should be represented. Some critics have seen this as the first move in an increasing politicization of German broadcasting. Since appointments were based on political party affiliation, and council seats were divided roughly along the lines of political party representation, there certainly was the potential for greater political influence from the councils. The move also had its effect on the appointment of broadcast administrators: Increasingly during the late 1950s the councils—and not only those of the NDR and WDR—took the concept of "Proporz," or proportional balance of political parties, into account when considering staff appointments. "Proporz" is now an accepted part of German broadcasting, however much it may represent a departure from what the Allied occupation authorities had in mind.[18]

Finally, some of the larger state broadcasting stations began to offer second and even third program services over radio during the 1950s, so as to provide some listening alternatives. While the first and second services usually were quite similar, the third services, where they existed, were far more specialized and closely resembled the BBC's Third Programme for that same period: lots of "high" culture, such as plays in their original languages, avant-garde musical works, and presentations of highly specialized cultural and scientific topics. The state stations saw themselves as patrons of the arts, and several of them created folk, jazz, chamber and symphonic groups to play standard and specially commissioned music; they also commissioned some of Germany's best writers to write radio and television plays, and Heinrich Boell, Gunter Grass and others willingly did so because they saw that broadcasting was treated as a serious artistic medium.

The East German broadcast system remained monolithic throughout the 1950s, although a television service came on the air in 1952 and four more radio services were added during the decade. All services were under the control of the state Committee for Broadcasting, whose chairperson held cabinet rank and was a relatively senior SED party official. More regional stations came on the air in the 1950s, but they had only a few hours each day on their own and otherwise served as relays for the programs coming from Berlin. East German broadcasting, too, took upon itself the patron of the arts role, creating orchestras and commissioning music and plays, but both often had a strongly ideological flavor: Plays often were about the sacrifices that "good" citizens made on behalf of the nation and about the evil designs of West Germany and its U.S. supporters on East German society. Music often consisted of well-known works from the past, but commentary on them often would emphasize the difficult social conditions facing composers such as Beethoven or Mozart. There also were "popular" songs composed especially for presentation over radio or TV and with the lyrics, melody and chords printed in the weekly radio-TV guide; they included such subjects as why bad drivers are a menace to society, why collective farms are good for society and so on.[19] And in 1960, East German television introduced a program that was still on the air (although it was temporarily off during the mid-1960s) at the time of unification: "The Black Channel" consisted of excerpts from West German television, analyzed and placed in "correct" political perspective by East German commentator Karl Edouard von Schnitzler. East Germany was becoming more and more aware of the influence of West German broadcasting on its own listeners and viewers and was fighting back not only with "The Black Channel," but also with improved programming (especially variety shows) of its own.

From the Wall to the Treaty (1961–1972)

The erection of the Berlin Wall in August 1961 did more than symbolize the division between the two parts of Berlin; it also cut off West Germany from continuing and easy access to East Berlin, making it that much more difficult for broadcasters, among others, to learn just what was taking place in East Germany, what East Germans thought about the issues of the day and so on. Before August, it had been relatively easy for East Germans to visit West Berlin and to use it as a means to leave East Germany for good; some East Germans even worked in West Berlin, coming and going on a daily basis. East Germans also had fair access to information about the West, although radio broadcasts intended specifically for East Germans were jammed (RIAS Berlin, a U.S.-supported station, was the primary target of the jamming),[20] and the watching of West German television was discouraged by various means, including the use of "goon squads" that occasionally climbed up on roofs and twisted or tore down antennas that were oriented to receive western TV. At the same time, the East German broadcast system redoubled its efforts to present its viewers with interesting, high-quality programming.

The West German Supreme Court's 1961 decision upholding states' rights in broadcasting gave the states a renewed sense of their own strength but also thrust upon them further responsibilities. The West German public clearly wanted more broadcast services (especially TV) than the present system was providing. If the federal government was not allowed to provide service, then either the state broadcasting systems themselves or other systems licensed by the states would have to do so. There were several interested parties who wanted to set up private, commercial TV stations; most of them were publishers, who could see the opportunity both for profit and for protection of their publishing interests. But the states generally were opposed to considering commercial broadcasting of that sort. At the same time, setting up a second TV network through ARD seemed far too costly; license fees would have to be increased tremendously, and state legislatures didn't care to consider that option. However, the state stations did patch together a second television service as a stopgap measure while a more permanent solution was being devised.

The second television service that finally emerged in 1963—called, not too imaginatively, Second German Television (ZDF)—was a strange compromise, and highlighted the difficulty of changing the electronic media system when every state had to be involved in the process. All West German states were co-signers of the legal agreement creating ZDF, so that, technically (and legally) speaking, the new service *was* a state function. However, ZDF was a centralized organization, with its administrative headquarters and main production facilities in the neighboring cities of Mainz and Wiesbaden, and with very small studio facilities (enough for interviews, panels, etc.) in many cities throughout the country. Its program output certainly didn't represent the collective efforts of individual state stations.

The legislation for ZDF embraced the concept of a broadcast council, but on a much larger (and national) scale: The ZDF council had 66 members (the largest ARD station had 49, and the average was a bit over 30) representing various groups in society, selected by those groups on a national, rather than state, basis. It also included representatives of the various state governments. The ZDF would receive a share of the license fee money, and the license fee itself, which had remained at two marks ($0.50) per month from the mid-1920s until 1959, was increased to take into account the higher operating costs of television. The ZDF also could advertise, but under the same restrictions as ARD had devised for its members: brief blocks of ads for nationally advertised products and services only, interspersed with other program material in the late afternoon to early evening hours, and with virtually no sponsorship of programs. Nevertheless, ZDF was an attractive buy for advertisers, because they had one station rather than several to deal with. The program mix was much the same as on the state television service, and the two services were required to coordinate their broadcast schedules for maximum service to the public, avoiding the simultaneous scheduling of similar programs and providing plenty of fare for "minority" tastes (operas, original plays on controversial topics, etc.).

The largest state stations were able to consider adding their own second television services starting in 1964, and several of them did so: NDR, WDR, Bayerischer Rundfunk (BR) in Munich, Sudwestfunk (SWF) in Baden-Baden. Eventually they were joined by the other ARD stations in regional groupings. For example, SWF, Suddeutscher Rundfunk (SDR) in Stuttgart and Saarlandisches Rundfunk (SR) in the Saar banded together, as did NDR, Radio Bremen and Sender Freies Berlin. Hessicher Rundfunk (HR) in Frankfurt, WDR and BR each provided their own second TV services. In each case, these services, collectively labeled the third service, featured more specialized fare: educational material, foreign films in their original languages, discussion programs involving specialized topics.

During the 1960s there were numerous political controversies. One of the largest involved East-West relations. While the Christian Democratic Party remained in power (from 1949 to 1969, although in a coalition with the Socialist Party, or SPD, for the three final years), there was little disposition to make overtures to the East, and especially to the Soviet Union, Poland and East Germany. The West German media commonly referred to East Germany as "the so-called German Democratic Republic," and West German maps continued to show the former Reich territory east of the Oder and Neisse rivers as "under Polish administration," even though Poland and its eastern European associates considered it as an integral part of Poland. However, in some of the states there were Social Democratic Party governments, and there one sometimes could hear and see commentaries, documentaries and reports advocating changes in West German policy toward the East, discussing the Nazi past in frank terms. One NDR commentator, Gert von Paczensky, did not have his contract renewed in 1963 because the NDR broadcast council and some NDR administrators, along with Conservative politicians working through them, thought that he was going too far in airing such material.[21]

But when the Social Democrats came to power at the federal level in 1969, and former West Berlin Mayor Willi Brandt became chancellor, there was a new era of "Ost-Politik" (eastern-oriented political policy). Derogatory references to East Germany didn't cease immediately, but there were more and more programs about steps that could be and were being taken to bridge the East-West gap. Brandt visited Poland and declared that the western part of that country was an integral part of it, and not "under Polish administration." Discussion with East German authorities finally led to an interstate treaty in 1972, which among other things provided greater visiting rights for West Germans wishing to see relatives in East Germany and granting media personnel in both Germanies freer access to people and events in each.

The gradual thaw in inter-German relations and the signing of the treaty brought to an end the activities of two unusual East German radio stations. The Soldatensender had begun its broadcasts in 1960 and was intended for troops serving in the West German army. The Freiheitssender 904 (Freedom Station 904—the number for its frequency) was the "unofficial" station of the West German Communist Party and had begun operation in 1956, just one day after the West German Communist Party was declared illegal. Both stations strongly denounced western political, economic and military policy, criticized West German political leaders, and called attention to the Nazi-era activities of some of them. They would have been "undiplomatic" in this era of greater cooperation, and besides, the West German Communist Party became legal again in 1971; immediately after that, Freiheitssender 904 went off the air, and Soldatensender followed in 1972. The two major stations broadcasting from West Germany, RIAS Berlin and Deutschlandfunk, continued on the air. Apparently they were not considered to be as baldly critical of East German policy as the two East German stations were of West German policy, and besides, they functioned openly, rather than as stations pretending to broadcast from within West Germany, as Soldatensender and Freiheitssender did.[22]

One East German broadcast activity for listeners in West Germany continued unabated. West Germany had experienced a large influx of guest workers from southern Europe and Turkey during the 1960s, and many of the state stations had begun to provide limited broadcast services in Turkish, Greek, Italian and other languages. The East Germans also began to provide services in some of those languages, but of course the content of their programs was considerably different, emphasizing the exploitation of workers by employers and the hostility of West Germans toward guest workers.[23]

Politics, the Economy and the New Media (1972–1987)

"Proporz" first emerged as an issue in the late 1950s. During the 1960s, it grew in importance, and several German critics began to lament the disappearance of the "nonpolitical" broadcast system that the Allies and Germans had crafted so carefully in the pre-1949 days. Social Democrats often complained that commentaries on ZDF were biased in favor of CDU policies and personalities; CDU members often said the same thing about stations in states with SPD governments. The Young Socialists, considered more radical than the mainstream of their party, complained that their views didn't get aired at all, and in the 1970s began attempts to place their members in stations, preferably as journalists. Political discussions, long a prominent and popular feature of West German radio and television, seemed to some observers to be getting sharper, more contentious, and with moderators sometimes appearing to play favorites.

A related phenomenon was "Mitbestimmung," which began around 1969 but became a major issue in the early 1970s. It involved attempts on the part of broadcast journalists to have more of a say in whether and how their stories would be used by their stations. It was a demand for codetermination of editorial decision-making and extended beyond the newsroom to include representation on the broadcast councils. Not all stations were equally involved with this movement, which continues in weaker form to the present, but most changed their procedures to some extent as a result of it. It is unlikely that it would have arisen with the strength it did if "Proporz" itself had not become so much a part of West German broadcasting.[24]

The West German economy boomed during the 1960s and into the 1970s, bringing with it increased purchase of color TV sets (color TV was introduced in 1967). The demand for more and more productions in color placed a considerable strain on the state stations and the ZDF. However, there was no license fee surcharge on owners of color TV sets that could help to meet the increased costs of programming in color. The state legislatures were reluctant to raise the basic license fee but eventually had to do so, in 1974, 1979 and 1983, always by less than the stations said was needed. The would-be private commercial broadcasters continued to press their case, offering the argument that they could supply further television services without (direct) cost to the public, and certainly there were plenty of advertisers who were eager to advertise but for whom there was insufficient time on the two existing TV services. The states continued to control the licensing of broadcasting, but now a few of them were considering the possibility of licensing private services, in addition to maintaining the existing ones.

The Bavarian government gave such a proposal serious consideration in the early 1970s. That government was in the hands of the CSU (the Christian Democratic Party in Bavaria calls itself the Christian Socialist Party), and the CSU's powerful leader, Franz-Josef Strauss, felt that a private commercial service would be both good business and a useful counterweight to the state service (BR), which he and some other CSU members considered too liberal. Attempts to gain the approval of the Bavarian Parliament for such a service eventually failed, as did the CSU's attempts to radically restructure the BR broadcast council (although it was enlarged and in the process made more political).[25]

The next major move in that direction came in the late 1970s. The states of Lower Saxony and Schleswig-Holstein had been partners with the city-state of Hamburg in NDR. Gains in CDU strength in the two states, and increased tensions with SPD-governed Hamburg, led to calls for the withdrawal of the states from the NDR, together with the licensing of new broadcast stations in each. A 1980 agreement managed to hold the NDR structure together for the time being, but Lower Saxony and Schleswig-Holstein announced their intention to license new television and radio stations. That agreement also brought about a reorganization of the NDR broadcast council, making it conform much more closely with the model followed by the majority of states. Now a third of the council's members would be appointed by the state legislatures, instead of all, and nine seats on the council would be open to applications by groups that considered themselves representative of significant public opinion in any of the three states.[26]

Although Lower Saxony and Schleswig-Holstein now had legal authority to set up new stations, they didn't exercise that option immediately. Instead, both expanded the NDR facilities within their own states and also claimed more airtime for those expanded services. Then the German Supreme Court, in the 1981 FRAG decision, sanctioned the creation of private, commercially funded electronic media, although they would be held to a relatively high (but not as high as the PSB) standard of public service.[27] Two other states eventually became the first to license private broadcasting, and in each case it represented an outgrowth of cable radio services set up in 1985. Early in 1986, both Bavaria and Rhineland-Palatinate licensed private, commercial radio stations. Schleswig-Holstein followed in mid-1986 and Lower Saxony in early 1987.

There also was the matter of cable television. Many West German households had received their signals through cable for years, but over master antenna systems in apartment houses; these simply retransmitted existing signals, improving technical quality but adding no new program services. The ruling Socialists (SPD) were opposed to any real growth in cable. When the 1983 elections resulted in a strong CDU majority, the possibility of having "real," multiple channel cable systems, increased. The CDU was favorable to private industry, and the new minister for posts and telecommunications, Christian Schwarz-Schilling, was a strong supporter of commercial broadcasting. He quickly increased the Bundespost's (the German PTT) budget for the laying of cable, and threatened to suspend laying cable in those SPD-governed states which hadn't yet authorized the licensing of commercial television.[28] (The jurisdictional question of whether the states were responsible for licensing cable had been resolved in their favor in the early 1980s.) In 1985 Bavaria licensed West Germany's first full-fledged cable system, complete with access cable and cable radio. Similar systems soon began operating in Munich, Berlin, Ludwigshafen/Mannheim, Dortmund and some smaller towns, but they had relatively few customers because there wasn't all that much available by way of additional programming material. Cable connection costs initially were very high: DM 675 (about $325 as of the late 1980s) per individual household, with a decreasing scale of fees for apartment dwellers, further discouraging potential subscribers. The cabling of the nation (or most of it, at any rate) began in a major way in 1985 and within three years passed about 40 percent of the nation's households, although subscribership was at about 15 percent.[29]

Satellite TV also became a public topic in the late 1970s, and in the early 1980s discussion of it increased because of Luxembourg's proposal to use its satellite channel to beam German, French and possibly other commercial TV services into Germany and France. The French and German governments strongly protested, but there was nothing that either could do about it. It would be several years before Luxembourg went ahead with its plan, but the large German publishing firm of Bertelsmann worked out an agreement in 1982–83 for a ground-based "satellite" operation to beam commercially supported TV from Luxembourg into nearby areas of West Germany. That service, RTL Plus (shortened to RTL in the mid-1990s), had to be received through a special dish antenna and decoder or through one of the four cable systems available at the time, and the signal was sent through microwave. But the reception technology was much like what would be required for satellite reception, and it served as a sort of trial balloon.[30] In 1985, a consortium of West German publishers developed a satellite-to-cable service, SAT1. Its initial purpose was to feed more programming into the Ludwigsburg cable project, but it quickly expanded into other markets.

By 1987, the pieces were in place for a true dual system (public and private broadcasting sectors as more or less equal forces). The German Supreme Court had ruled in 1986 and again in 1987 that private broadcasting was entitled to full rights of existence alongside public broadcasting, and need not be held to the same obligations for providing a full range of balanced programming, but that the PSBs should continue to receive the necessary financial and other means to remain fully competitive with the private sector.[31] This confirmed the rights of states to issue "private" licenses, even to investors from the press (although it did issue warnings about media concentration) but only if licensing conditions included the same sorts of restrictions as pertained to public stations, among them the establishment of broadcast councils.[32] The ministers-president of the state governments agreed to an Interstate Broadcasting Treaty in 1987 that would help the separate state regulatory agencies for private and public to coordinate their work. The expansion of cable and satellite into a significant force on the German electronic media scene would take several years more, but a far more remarkable development was to take place first.

The Final Years of East German Broadcasting (1988–1990)

East German authorities had worried about pressures and temptations from the West for many years, but their attempts to block the reception of West German television had grown more and more feeble, and most East German households could view its programs at will by the mid-1980s. When Poland, and then Czechoslovakia, began to show signs of breaking away from Soviet control, and even from communism itself, that was far more worrisome to the authorities, because those two nations were East Germany's eastern and southern neighbors, and had formed a sort of Communist-governed security belt around the country flanks. To the west was West Germany, but the East Germans and Soviets had developed a literal Iron Curtain along that border, complete with barbed wire, watchtowers and watchdogs, and land thick with mines. Very few escaped across it.

When Czechoslovakia and Hungary began to show signs of independence, East German citizens were quick to recognize the existence of a much less risky escape route from East Germany. Growing numbers did so during summer and fall of 1989, driving across the Hungarian or Czech-East German border, and then out through Austria. The exodus, modest at first, received very little coverage from the East German media, but a great deal from West Germany. That helped to inspire protest demonstrations in East Germany, mostly by groups wanting greater freedom of speech and movement, but not pressing for the dissolution of the East German state. Those demonstrations did attract East German media attention, which at first was negative and emphasized the small size of the groups and their disorderly behavior. Some of the reporters for the East German media began to discover that they could get away with more balanced reporting, which seemed to be a sign of uncertainty and even weakness in the East German government.

Those reporters and others began to report more and more freely on the demands of the groups. A clear sign of public interest in the reports was the ratings for Deutsche Funk und Fernsehen's (DFF—the East German broadcast system) evening television newscast, "Aktuelle Kamera." It had audience ratings of 10 percent on October 1, 1989; by October 31, the ratings were 40 percent,[33] simply because the news was worth watching.

There also were changes in other programs. Some of the old style hardline Communist programs were dropped, including that hardy perennial "Schwarze Kanal," which appeared for what turned out to be the last time on October 29, 1989. The host, Edouard von Schnitzler, bowed out by saying that he had "no regrets. The bare truth can be difficult to handle but it is satisfying. Goodbye."[34] Also, the authorities began to modify the long-standing policy of originating almost all programming in East Berlin. The generally minuscule regional stations were to originate more of their own material, but also to acquire some genuine freedom of choice in what they chose to originate. The change started with Antenne Brandenburg in Potsdam, in May

1990.[35] Two months later, the East German minister for the media announced that East Germany's system would be reorganized along West German lines, with each state having its own station. Those reforms were to take place within the next few months.[36]

The Effects of Unification (1990–1992)

Events quickly outstripped plans. With the overwhelming approval of East German voters, the country ceased to exist on October 3, 1990. The West German broadcast services had been preparing to enter into cooperative agreements with the recently announced East German state stations. In August 1990, Sender Freies Berlin had invited the newly formed Antenne Brandenburg (AB) to merge with it, but AB's director turned down the invitation.[37] Following the vote on unification, the West German stations moved ahead. The two PSBs, ARD and ZDF, gained the support of the West and East German majority CDU in their bids for the broadcast frequencies used by DFF. Rudolf Muehlfenzl, a journalist with close ties to the CDU, was given responsibility for handling media affairs in the unification process. He stated in November 1990 that he would see to it that ARD and ZDF would be firmly established in the former East Germany before any commercial stations received frequencies there.[38]

That declaration was implemented by the end of November, but without parliamentary debate or even review: the CDU leadership simply decided the matter, much to the anger of the opposition parties and some independent observers, who pointed out that West Germany's constitution guaranteed the right to establish their own broadcast systems to *all* of the states. Brandenburg's prime minister, Manfred Stolpe (the only non-CDU prime minister in the five new states), said that the CDU action was reminiscent of the conduct of the SED when it was in power in East Germany.[39]

The closing down of the various DFF services might have been a logical next step, but things didn't work out that way. East Germany's international radio station, Radio Berlin International, was folded into West Germany's Deutsche Welle; it marked its final moments on air by playing "The End," performed by the Doors. However, some of the domestic service staff were retained, aside from certain top-level administrators who were regarded as Communist functionaries, and not as broadcasters. Many journalists were retained, and they continued to present news programs on both radio and TV. Still other East German programs, including the popular (in both Germanies) children's show, "The Little Sandman," "ELF 99" (a teenager-oriented show with music videos), and an assortment of discussion programs and cultural programs, moved over to ARD's national schedule.

It might seem surprising that many of the same voices and faces which had presented the ideological messages of the East German government remained on hand after East Germany's disappearance. Who could possibly believe them? But they seemed to arouse very little resentment or suspicion on the part of former East German audience members, who may have not held them responsible for what they had to report, and who may have been impressed by the way in which many of those journalists were quick to take advantage of the increasing freedom to report on sensitive issues in the final months of East Germany's existence.

At least as surprising was the fact (shown by surveys) that the "Ossies" (former East Germans) actually seemed to *prefer* to watch and listen to the information programs presented by those familiar figures from the past. West German media researchers felt that such a preference might be connected with the disillusionment experienced by East Germans following unification. The process had been carried out with very little consultation by West German officials with their East German counterparts, or with the public. Unification also had led to massive unemployment and higher prices for most goods in East Germany. The "Ossies" appeared to want symbols that were truly their own as reminders of their separate identities, and the former DFF reporters and other staff helped to serve that function.[40]

In mid-1991, there was a reorganization of broadcasting in the five new states. The broadcast services in three of them agreed to band together, largely as an economy move, as a cooperative association: the Mitteldeutscher Rundfunk, headquartered in Leipzig. One of the remaining two new state services, for Mecklenburg/Vorpommern, weighed the possibility of joining with the fifth new state service, in Brandenburg, or with the NDR in Hamburg, and finally opted for the latter, leaving Brandenburg's Ostdeutscher Rundfunk as the only new service still operating on its own. The Mecklenburg situation probably was influenced by political considerations: members of Germany's third party, the Free Democrats (FDP), campaigned to get the state service to join with Hamburg, where the city-state is Socialist (SPD), in order to embarrass Mecklenburg's prime minister, a Christian Democrat (CDU), who wanted to see the service merge with Brandenburg[41]—a tangled but not atypical example of German media politics!

Competition and Expansion (1992–Present)

Commercial broadcasting had little impact at first in the former East Germany, although a group of West German investors quickly obtained a license to establish a radio station in Halle. In the rest of Germany, it took off rapidly in the late 1980s, and by the end of 1991 there were well over 200 new private radio stations, some of them statewide services, others purely local. While popular music was the dominant format, many of the stations had at least brief newscasts, and some devoted a number of hours each week to informational programs.[42]

Private commercial television developed along other lines. The two major services from the mid-1980s, RTL Plus and SAT1, expanded as cable grew. They moderated by the end of the 1980s, and by the early 1990s were beginning to receive authorization from the individual states to broadcast over terrestrial transmitters. By early 1991, SAT1 matched or surpassed ARD and ZDF in the average 7-8 p.m. time slot in the roughly 20 percent of all German households then subscribing to cable.[43] By the end of 1992, the public and commercial stations were about even in the ratings race in all households, and commercial services were ahead in cabled households,[44] meaning that Germany now had a true dual system. The commercial services, including also the newer and weaker PRO7 and Tele5, were producing more of their own shows, and not relying so heavily on U.S. imports. The success that RTL Plus and SAT1 enjoyed with their news programs—more animated, somewhat "warmer," and with shorter items than was typical of ARD and ZDF—had made them realize that they could mount effective challenges to the public service system. They began to produce children's programs, game and quiz shows, sports, police/detective shows and sitcoms, often following U.S. "models" and even purchasing rights to make their own versions of such programs as the U.S. "Wheel of Fortune."

The growth of direct-to-home satellite reception also had helped the commercial TV services to reach more viewers. German experiences with satellites in the late 1980s wouldn't have given anyone much confidence that DBS would be much of a factor in the country's electronic media mix. Aborted launches and malfunctions spoiled every attempt. Finally, late in 1989, two satellites began to carry both PSB (ARD's Eins Plus and ZDF's 3SAT)[45] and commercial services, and in 1990 RTL Plus and SAT1 began to lease time on a Luxembourg satellite. Since then, satellite growth has been extraordinary, and over 30 percent of all German households have direct-to-home service. Even TV viewers in households without satellite or cable can pick up seven or eight services, depending upon where they live.

The expansion of cable and satellite also helped to fuel the growth of smaller, niche services such as tm-3 (a women's channel, originating in Munich), Premiere (a movie channel), a home shopping channel,[46] Nickelodeon Germany and ARD's Kinderkanal[47] (children), Deutsches SportFernsehen (DSF), VIVA (music videos), and n-tv (all news and information). The German and French governments also agreed to jointly finance a noncommercial cultural TV service, Arte, which came on air in 1992,[48] but which attracts little viewership. By 1997, there were over a dozen German private national services, plus many more channels brought in from other countries. Cable radio also began to tap the growing market in Europe of satellite-delivered radio services. Nearly 80 of them were receivable through satellite by 1996, roughly a fourth originating in Germany; cable offered a number of them, plus a few cable-only stations: KLASSIK Radio (pop classics) and Radio MELODIE (easy listening). Truly devoted (and wealthy) music fans with digital radio receivers and satellites could subscribe to DMX (Digital Music Express), which offers some 60 channels of music in various styles, for a subscription price of just under DM 20 ($12) a month. The growth of terrestrial private and community radio and private local television also continued—rapidly for the first, slowly for the second and third.

A few stations marked for extinction, such as East Germany's Deutschlandsender and RIAS radio in West Berlin, sometimes managed to survive in new guises. Those two Cold War operations merged with another such station, the West German Deutschlandfunk, to emerge as a paired service: the first two as DeutschlandRadio Berlin, the second and third as DeutschlandRadio/DLF Cologne. Whether the unified nation really needs two such services is another matter—many German radio stations regard DeutschlandRadio as a "Frequenzfresser" (broadcast frequency "hog") because of its boundless appetite for more good frequencies and its ability to take them from other stations[49]—and hard-core radio listeners certainly have a great deal of choice already, although DeutschlandRadio is one of the few *national* German radio services available (and the only such service available to motorists).

The Threads of History

If there's one basic factor that has been chiefly responsible for shaping the development of German broadcasting over time, that factor surely is *political.* Whether during the years of the Weimar Republic, the Nazi era, the post-World War II occupation period, under Socialist or Conservative or Communist rule, whether commercial or public broadcasting, cable or satellite, the nation (*two* nations for the period 1949-90) has had frequent reminders that politicians are interested in the electronic media, and have the power to shape them. *Technology* also has played an important role, particularly in the form of cable and satellite, which enabled commercial television to become competitive with the PSBs within five years, but one has the strong impression that the CDU was so determined during the 1980s to favor the development of the commercial sector that it would have found other ways to accomplish the task if cable and satellite hadn't been available. The federal courts, and especially the German Supreme Court, have forced governments (CDU governments in particular) to back down in their challenges to states' rights where broadcasting is concerned. As newer delivery systems which are better-suited to larger territories come along, there are likely to be more court challenges. The eventual compromise among the states over the licensing of cable weakened some of the logic undergirding those rights, and they may or may not stand the test of time. The present system is quite awkward and somewhat wasteful financially; removal of states' rights to license most electronic media would save money and increase efficiency, both important values to Germans. What such a removal would mean to diversity of programming in general and of expressions of opinion is another question.

The *economic* factor is gaining in importance, as the private companies secure more dominant positions in the market. Cross-ownership/investment in media operations is perfectly legal in Germany, and there's a great deal of it. The "Big Four" of German electronic media—Bauer, Bertelsmann, Kirch and Springer (Kirch is a major investor in Springer and, as will be seen later, is not at all hesitant to use his influence on items in Springer publications with which he disagrees)—each have substantial investments in television services, TV production companies, multimedia firms, radio stations and publishing firms (magazines and newspapers). They dominate the private sector in electronic media, and it's doubtful that any other substantial challenger is likely to emerge. Their leaders are well-connected with the Christian Democratic Party; even if they were not, they are by now too firmly in control of things to suffer because of a change in political leadership.

The CDU's pro-private industry stance has another economic dimension which surfaces from time to time: attacks on the relative (to private industry) economic inefficiency of the ARD and ZDF. Those attacks are not without substance: the two services have close to 25,000 staff members and income from license fees and advertising of over five billion U.S. dollars a year, but claim financial hardship. ARD in particular provides a range of services at the regional and local level that no single private broadcaster begins to match. But criticisms of what do seem to be excessive administrative costs find their way into the print media, as do questions raised by CDU (and sometimes Free Democrat, the CDU's usual coalition partner) spokespersons regarding the need for ARD and ZDF satellite TV channels. A CDU parliamentary media committee went so far as to pass a resolution in 1992 calling on ARD and ZDF to stop their new joint breakfast show (an "unnecessary investment"), which certainly would have made RTL Plus happy, since it would have remained as the only national breakfast show provider in the country. Those attacks will continue, on and off, whether the CDU is the ruling party or not. The chief question is how public opinion responds to them; the answer so far seems to be "without much interest," but a continuation of high unemployment rates could change that state of affairs.[50]

FINANCING

There are three major sources of financing for German electronic media: license fees paid by households, advertising/sponsorship and subscription fees for cable and satellite users. Sales of programs abroad are growing in importance,[51] but still account for just 1-2 percent of annual revenues; aside from sports, German programs generally are not all that attractive to most non-German-speaking countries (the Netherlands is a minor exception), and Austria and Switzerland cannot afford to pay all that much for what they use from their northern neighbor. Unlike Great Britain and the Netherlands, German broadcasters do not sell radio-TV guides. Ironically, some of those firms that do, notably the Axel Springer publishing firm, also were among the strongest advocates of private commercial broadcasting, and the Springer firm is an important investor in SAT1, DSF and 12 radio stations. (Springer publishes three guides, including the market leader, Hoerzu.)

License fees for the public service broadcasters, ARD and ZDF, are collected by the GEZ, an organization created by the state stations and ZDF in 1976. (Before that time, the post office collected the fees and received a small percentage of them for its services.) There are separate radio and TV fees (very rare in Europe), in a roughly 1-to-2 ratio (as of 1998, DM 9.45 [$5.65] per month for radio, 18.80 [$11.30] for TV), although most households have both media and pay a lump-sum fee. Roughly 6-8 percent of all German households (retirees, war veterans, etc.) are excused from paying the fee. The fee money is credited to the station serving the state in which a given household is located. It doesn't matter whether listeners and viewers in that household may receive better technical service from transmitters located in another state, or that they may spend little or no time viewing or listening to the station located in their own state. Each such area precisely represents one or more states, except for Baden-Wurttemburg, which is divided into two broadcast service areas, for SWF and SDR. Radio Bremen, Saarlaendischer Rundfunk and Sender Freies Berlin (SFB), all serving geographically tiny areas, derive little income from fees (each has less than a million households in its area) and must be subsidized from the license fee revenue of the remaining states.[52] The SFB also used to receive extra money because it had the additional mission of transmitting into East Germany. Because it's a national service, DeutschlandRadio receives a small share of the radio portion of the fee. The ZDF, also a national service, receives 30 percent of the fee money earmarked for television. The joint German-French TV service Arte has a subsidy of slightly over DM 200 million ($120 million).[53]

While there are no guarantees that the license fee system will continue, or that it will rise with any overall inflationary increases, the German Supreme Court rendered a decision in 1994 that at least set a legal benchmark. It indicated that the public broadcasting sector should continue to be supported by a license fee, and that the license fee should be sufficient to support that sector at a level sufficient to enable it to fulfill its obligations to provide an independent public service. While there was no way for it to legally compel the states to provide support at a fixed level, the court's decision certainly underlined the principle of continued support for public broadcasting.[54] No other industrialized nation has gone so far to guarantee the survival of public broadcasting, although the Netherlands has come fairly close.

In earlier periods, there sometimes were questions regarding the amount collected through fees in relation to how much the broadcast services actually spent to operate. Hofmann points out that the Allied occupation authorities and state government officials argued over how the fees were to be used: the state governments regarded them as "culture taxes," and any excess revenue they produced should be turned over to the state for financing other cultural activities (including, for Bavaria, covering part of the budget of the Ministry of Culture), while the Allies saw them as meant only for broadcasting.[55] The issue never really was resolved.

The GEZ tries to track down households where the fee hasn't been paid (about 10-12 percent annually), and there are stiff fines for evading payment, but so many Germans live in multistory apartment houses that electronic detection methods aren't of much use. On the whole, Germans seem to feel that they get good value for the money, but as noted, state legislatures are reluctant to raise fees very often, and the procedure for doing so is time-consuming. That becomes evident when examining the list of fee increases. A separate fee for TV was added in 1953. The next increase was in 1970. There have been seven increases since then, the most recent on January 1, 1997. The pace of increases picked up sharply after the signing of the Interstate Broadcasting Treaty in 1987, when the states agreed in principle to raise the fee every two years. That worked until 1993: the next fee increase didn't come until 1997. One reason for the gap probably was the higher-than-expected cost of German unification, which made increasing the license fee even more unpopular than usual, at least for politicians. But the CDU-led states also wanted to reduce the cost of public broadcasting. Their pressure led to development of a new regulatory agency, the Kommission zur Ermittlung des Finanzbedarfs der Rundfunkanstalten, or KEF, which assesses the "necessary financial provisions" for public broadcasting and recommends license fee increases. It could be considered a fiscal watchdog, one more layer of bureaucracy or one more example of political interference.

Advertising had become more and more important as a source of revenue for West German broadcasting (East German broadcasting carried very little of it) even before the commercial services came along. Between 1963 and 1967 alone, ZDF saw its advertising income increase from just under $10 million a year to nearly $40 million a year. The ARD stations received about 20 percent and ZDF about 40 percent of their annual incomes from advertising during most of the 1980s, but ARD experienced a steep decline in ad revenue over the period 1988–1992, to the point where it covered only about 14 percent of annual income. ZDF managed somewhat better, declining to about 36 percent.[56] Since then, the decline has continued, and ZDF saw its ad income drop by 50 percent from 1992 to 1993. RTL Plus had its first "billion deutsche mark" year of ad revenue in 1991; SAT1 followed suit in 1992; and Pro 7 joined that club in 1994.[57] As of 1997, RTL alone has annual ad revenue more than three times larger than ARD-TV and ZDF put together.

Airtime for TV advertising on ARD and ZDF has increased very little over time. It went from eight minutes a day in the late 1950s to 20 minutes a day at present, and remains limited to the 6 to 8 p.m. period for the ARD state TV stations and for ZDF. The ARD third (TV) services are not allowed to carry advertising at all. There are varying periods of time for public (ARD) radio, with some stations devoting as much as 18 percent of their broadcast time to advertising blocks, varying portions of which carry ads, on certain of their services. The commercial radio and television stations all carry advertising, and must follow European Union limits on its amount: no more than 20 percent (12 minutes) per hour. Before the advent of commercial broadcasting, the PSBs were not permitted to advertise on Sundays or national holidays; they now may do so after 8 p.m. on those days. The state broadcasting and media councils enforce regulations on advertising. For both the PSBs and the private stations, there is no political advertising, no advertising of tobacco products, and numerous other restrictions abound, especially for advertising directed to children. Alcoholic beverages may be advertised, and even ads for strong beverages such as "doppelkorn" (somewhat like refined moonshine whiskey!) appear in later evening hours, with people drinking and seemingly enjoying them—something that never appears on U.S. TV screens. Each state station has its own advertising code (although the codes closely resemble one another); all advertising is handled by a separate organization located within the corporate structure of the station, which underlines the idea that, while ad revenues can be (and are) taxed, the rest of the station's revenues should not be. Everything possible is done to separate advertising from other program content, and even the blocks of ads are broken up by short features, brief cartoons and other devices designed to set them apart.

The commercial stations also are required to maintain divisions between advertising and other programming, and they, too, usually cluster the ads in blocks. Advertising is not supposed to interrupt news programs, but as recently as 1996 I have seen private stations carry ads for various products as running superimpositions, scrolling across the bottom of the screen, during TV newscasts. Presumably that isn't a "true" interruption. The stations do tend to push the restrictions on advertising to the limit when dealing with the state media councils. Schulz offers an illustrative example: ads for products which also play roles in children's programs (Smurfs, Power Rangers) are not to be shown just before or after *any* of the children's programs. But, as he observes, "In fact, the children's programmes carried on private television are saturated with advertising which encourages children—directly or indirectly—to buy products, often products which are the subjects of children's programmes."[58] He and other media scholars feel that the media councils generally lack the will to enforce restrictions on advertisers, who, in any case, are more adept at exploiting legal loopholes than the councils are at plugging them. As Schulz puts it, "Long before a legal grey matter is clarified by the latter (councils), the former (marketing experts) will have found new ways of overcoming potential restrictions."[59] Furthermore, some of the ground has been cut from under the councils by such actions as the signing of an Interstate Broadcasting Treaty in 1987, in which the states agreed to ease regulations, including those dealing with advertising, for the private stations.[60]

Because there was little time available for advertising on the public stations in the days before commercial broadcasting (the limit of 20 minutes per day for TV was absolute), and because the West German economy was relatively healthy, demand for ad time was very heavy, and there were waiting lists for most ad-time blocks. In fact, ad time could be purchased only once a year, in the fall. That "seller's market" allowed the stations to set high rates, but advertisers were willing to pay the price. But that situation also made advertisers anxious to see the development of private commercial services, and they were a powerful lobbying force in support of CDU's "pro-private industry" media policy. That was especially true for regional and local advertisers, who weren't allowed to advertise on ARD or ZDF (it might harm the local newspapers). They quickly became customers of the local and regional commercial stations, as well as of cable TV.

In reaction to private competition, ARD and ZDF began to request increased amounts of TV advertising time[61]. While a few restrictions were lifted, total advertising time per evening remained at 20 minutes, and is likely to stay fixed at that level for some time to come. The private stations have a powerful persuasive argument when they claim that a) the ARD stations and

ZDF are supported by one of the higher license fees in Europe; and b) the inefficient ARD organizational setup itself wastes money. Therefore, why should they receive even more money through advertising, when that would cut into the sole means of financial support for the private sector? Furthermore, the long-ruling CDU supports a strong private sector, and doesn't care to raise license fees (but neither does the SPD).

Most ads run for 15 to 30 seconds and use techniques and formats that sometimes seem dated by U.S. standards: lots of singing commercials on radio, some relatively unadorned settings on TV. Food, cosmetics and cleaning products predominate, and there often appears to be a stronger tone of sexism to ads than in the United States. Housewives are shown as ready to bend over backward to please their grumpy husbands, male and female children take "appropriate" male and female roles when imitating grown-ups and so on. There has been a small but growing amount of protest over such ad content on the part of feminist organizations.[62] Every now and then, an ad will feature a husband at the stove or changing a diaper, but usually that's done to show how simple it is to use the product. Identifiable ethnic minorities almost never appear in ads. There is a growing number of ads for other radio and TV stations, as well—certainly a reaction to the rapid expansion of the private sector and the perceived need to make one's own station stand out from the crowd. Sponsorship is allowed, but it must be clearly identified. Sponsored programs carry the title "Werbesendung" (advertising broadcast) in the lower left corner of the screen throughout the program.

The style of many ads is a bit old-fashioned, but there are a number of exceptions. As one example, an ad I saw for Bounty (a candy bar something like the U.S. Mounds bar) on SAT1 in October 1996 showed a woman in a museum, seated before an abstract painting of a rectangle within a rectangle within a rectangle, each rectangle a different shade of blue. As she unwraps a Bounty bar (an act that would get her tossed out of most German art museums!), the painting morphs into a coconut breaking in half and spilling its milk, then into a famous Van Gogh, Gauguin, Henri Rousseau, etc., then back to the original painting and the woman, who has finished the bar. The morphing was highly skillful, the message ambiguous, although there probably was a connection between warm colors and places and the sensations that eating a Bounty bar would give. (I *did* wonder about its exact contents!)

Because of the manner in which it's organized, the state PSB sector is bound to be expensive. Each station has a sizable administrative staff, whether the station's service area is large or small. The requirement that even the smallest stations contribute 3 percent of the total collective (evening) TV program schedule increases program diversity but is not very cost-effective. Broadcast union demands also have increased production costs, particularly in the area of broadcast journalism, where crews of three or four individuals may be sent out to record a very simple interview. Technical standards are among the highest, and most costly, in the world. Few Germans seem ready to dismantle that system, but if license fees had to be increased sharply to offset that lack of cost-effectiveness, they might wonder whether perhaps a better way could be found. The private TV stations seem to operate without too much public objection to the amount of advertising they carry, which isn't a great deal more per hour than what ARD TV stations and ZDF carry during the 6-8 p.m. period. Since the private stations don't enjoy license fee support, German viewers sometimes wonder why the ARD stations would need longer periods of advertising. They also may wonder why ARD needs as much license fee money as it claims, but so far that hasn't been a major public concern, even if it's a major CDU concern.

East Germany

While East Germany existed, the state Committees for Radio and Television made annual budget requests, which were considered by the East German Parliament but which weren't subjected to rigorous examination. The money itself came as an annual appropriation from the national budget and not from license fees, although license fees of up to OM (East marks, which were officially at par with West German marks) 10.50 ($6.30) a month were assessed and then absorbed into the national budget. It was up to the government to determine how much it could afford to put into broadcasting, and to the broadcasters to live within those means. There was a small amount of TV advertising, usually 10 minutes or less each day between 5:30 and 6:30 p.m., but any money earned went into the national budget, as well.

GOVERNANCE AND ADMINISTRATION—INTERNAL

The Decision-Making Structure

The state stations (ARD) and ZDF are quite similar in terms of their decision-making structures, which isn't surprising given their origins: Both were created (with a lot of help from the Allied occupation authorities in the case of the state stations) by the states. Each has a manager ("Intendant") responsible for day-to-day administration of the station; each has a *broadcast council* ("Rundfunkrat") responsible for some degree of supervision and/or advice on overall programming and administrative policy, and an *administrative council* ("Verwaltungsrat") drawn largely from the "Rundfunkrat" and responsible for specific budgetary and administrative issues;[63] and each has a full complement of program, administrative and technical departments whose heads usually are selected by the manager in consultation with one or both councils. All of the broadcast councils have representatives from various groups (listed in the broadcast law of each state). A few require a minimum number of women.

I have included the broadcast and media councils under Internal even though the stations have nothing to do with their structures, procedures or appointment of members. But they are integral to station operations to a degree unequaled by other, roughly similar councils. Wolfgang Hoffmann-Riem, one of the leading German media scholars, refers to them as "internal control bodies" in his 1996 book *Regulating Media.* The state stations also work through the ARD, but there is no legal stipulation that they do so, and any station may opt out of a program feed coming through the ARD network if it chooses, as some have. (The Bayerische Rundfunk at times has found TV programs coming from other state stations politically or socially offensive—Bavaria is quite conservative—and has replaced them with locally available material.)

How the manager, councils and departments work together is another matter. Each station follows its own practices, and those may change over time. As the councils usually meet four to six times a year, and for one day each time, there are limits to their influence, although some council members visit their stations more frequently, and most councils have a few "movers and shakers" ("Koenigsmacher") who wield a great deal of power. Also, the concept of "proporz" extends to the councils, and, as Hoffmann-Riem indicates, council members usually "form coalitions along party lines, meeting in so-called cliques ("Freundeskreis") to agree upon joint conduct."[64] The broadcast councils generally hire, renew and discharge the manager, although the administrative council performs that function at WDR. No manager ever has been discharged by a council, although a few either were not renewed or were given short-term renewals while the council searched for a permanent replacement. Other officials have been, however. In 1995, the NDR broadcast council voted unanimously to remove the deputy manager of NDR, in part because of nepotism.[65] One of the two councils, and in a few cases both, approves the annual budget, accounts and report. The broadcast council also deals with program content, but it isn't always clear whether that's done on an advisory (to the manager) basis or whether the council has the right to require airing or cancellation of a program or series. It generally seems to be accepted by councils and managers that the role is advisory, but occasionally council members have felt that a manager's decision to drop a program was the result of their expressions of dissatisfaction, and that those expressions went beyond being advice.

The administrative councils, which usually contain a majority of members appointed by the broadcast council and a minority chosen by station staff, control the station's conduct of business and audit the annual budget, accounts and report. In most cases, their power does not extend to rejection of specific items in the budget, although the NDR council once was able to exercise such power if it involved free-lance work done for the station and if it were in excess of a certain sum. It used that power on one occasion in 1972 to attempt to block the making of a program that was judged by some of its members (and by politicians working through those members) to be politically sensitive—a program called "Bauern, Bonzen und Bomben" (Farmers, Politicos and Bombs) involving a violent uprising by Schleswig-Holstein farmers in 1930, but with some implications in terms of West German urban violence in the early 1970s. The money finally became available and the program was made, but the NDR administrative council had shown its willingness to overrule the manager.[66]

The influence of the councils is reduced further by two factors: size and composition. Some of the broadcast councils are quite small (16 to 25 members) and can conduct a good deal of business in a one-day meeting, but others are large (35 to 58 members, and for ZDF, 77), often causing decision-making to be a lengthy and inconclusive process. Furthermore, the very diversity of council membership, ranging from educational groups to religious bodies to women's groups to business, labor and political parties, is almost guaranteed to produce a certain amount of posturing for the public record. Most councils release abstracts of their meetings to the media, which may or may not publish or broadcast them; often the council's particular station doesn't even broadcast them. In short, many councils are quite inefficient, and a clever manager can have them tied in knots, or get them to tie themselves in knots, without much difficulty, especially if she or he has a few close allies on the council. The council members themselves often form internal coalitions along political lines, which might help them to exercise power more effectively at times, but which does little for their independence of judgment.

Political considerations are never far from council deliberations, and now and again break into the open. In 1994, the chair of the media council in the state of Hesse resigned, on the grounds that the state's governing coalition (SPD and Federation 90/Green Party) had pulled the council increasingly to the "left," had meddled in its administrative work, and probably wasn't serious about developing a viable "dual system" (public-private) of electronic media (meaning that it didn't want private media to become strong). The state government had just renewed the law dealing with the media council, and had abolished the designated council seats for the universities, manual laborers and industry/business; since the chair occupied the last-named seat, he would have been out of office by the end of the year, anyway, so he was in an excellent position to resign in a highly public way.[67]

There is also the question of just who or what council members represent. Most organizations that are "represented" on the councils do not elect those representatives, and many of them don't even bother to inform their members that there is a representative on such a council. The representative has no legal obligation to report back to her or his organization, and even if an attempt is made to do so, there may or may not be adequate channels of communication between the organization and its members to get the message across. Furthermore, council members are encouraged to think of themselves to some extent as representing the general viewing and listening public, which may come in conflict with group loyalty. As representatives may be reappointed (the usual term of appointment is three years, and renewals likewise), there is a natural tendency for a person who enjoys this particular sort of activity to keep the interests of the organization foremost when making decisions.

Remember, too, that most of the councils were created back in the late

1940s, well before the guest workers were a prominent feature in German life, and before some of the more militant women's organizations had become active. In other words, the councils tend to be frozen in time. Even when the respective state legislatures agreed to merge SDR (Stuttgart) and SWF (Baden-Baden) into a unified organization—Suedwestrundfunk (SWR)—in mid-1997, the "new" 74 member council looked very much like a merged version of the two old councils, with a few additional places created for groups such as "auslaendische Mitbuerger" (foreign residents) and "Landesnaturschutzverband" (protection of nature).[67a] A state legislature may modify the composition of the council by amending the broadcast act, but that isn't easy: Legislators generally recognize that the councils often are too large already and don't wish to add members or create new categories by abolishing old ones. Even if those problems didn't exist, there is the risk that, by adding a new group to the approved list, there would be many more groups that would insist upon being added.

The 1986 Supreme Court decision required that state governments write new laws to deal with private cable, satellite and terrestrial radio and television. Those new laws established *state media councils* ("Landesmedienanstalten"),[68] some of which have taken into account changes in society in a given state; but there is a strong likelihood those new councils also will appear frozen in time within a few years, although a few of them already have seen certain categories of representation removed and added by their state governments. They are smaller than the broadcast councils, ranging from 11 to 50 members.

The media councils operate in very much the same manner as the broadcast councils, although in the past there was one exception: since they licensed the satellite-delivered nationwide commercial services such as SAT1, those services could bargain with individual councils by saying, in effect, "You want to place this restriction on us. Well, the council in ______ didn't do that. Is it really justified?" Now such services must win the approval of only one state media council in order to be able to broadcast throughout Germany,[69] although individual states can attach specific conditions to service for their regions, most often in the form of requiring the service to provide regional "windows" for programs for that particular state. For example, when the media council for Lower Saxony considered RTL Plus' (now simply RTL) application for a license to operate there, the Green (environmental) Party coalition made it a condition of licensing that the service carry a separately licensed "window" for a regularly scheduled documentary program produced by a local TV documentary filmmaker, Alexander Kluge. The program loses audience for RTL in Lower Saxony, but there's nothing that the service can do about it![70] (It helped the council that Lower Saxony is a wealthy, populous state, and therefore RTL was eager to serve it.)

In view of all of the weaknesses that broadcast and media councils have exhibited, it isn't surprising that there have been calls for the abolition of the system. The larger councils are quite expensive—North Rhine-Westphalia's broadcast council had an operating budget of DM 27 million ($18 million) in

1995—and there are real doubts in some people's minds as to whether the councils can possibly ride herd on electronic media services of so many different types and with so many capable lawyers to advise them.[71]

Still, councils of both types do have some impact upon station decision-making. Managers often have found that council members can supply useful insight on the wisdom of adding a new program or abolishing an existing one. Program directors often have found that councils are useful sources of reaction to embryonic program ideas. Station staff sometimes have found the councils a useful way of getting points across to otherwise unreachable senior administrators. Councils serve as a potential safeguard for fiscal responsibility. In each of those cases, the presence of a council, where there is the possibility of public disclosure of what goes on inside broadcasting and where the collective membership will raise a range of issues and opinions, gives the station something that it would not get from its own internal discussions and reliance on a few trusted advisors. Both councils also have one important limitation: they cannot prevent a program from being broadcast, but must confine themselves to dealing with programs that already have been on air.[72]

Unions can have a relatively large impact upon broadcasting, but their power has faded over the past decade. The Radio, Television and Film Workers' Union (RFFU) has some 20,000 members in broadcasting and represents a solid majority of those involved in production. (The RFFU is part of a 200,000-member media union, IG Medien, which includes print and other media, and may by now have become part of a still larger "service workers" union which would have well over 1.2 million members. "HBV, DPG und IG streben Verbund an," *Handelsblatt,* 29 October 1996, p. 1) Union demands regarding size of production crews for broadcasts or taping outside the studio have resulted in high production costs and, some claim, cutbacks in outside productions, to the detriment of the program schedule.[73] The union also has worked hard for better benefits and more permanent employment for freelance broadcasters and managed to convince the courts in the late 1970s that such broadcasters were entitled to both. This again has led to claims that the move only succeeded in causing the stations to cut back on their use of freelancers, who often had brought fresh approaches to program-making.[74] There also is an association of German journalists, the Bundeskorrespondent; it operates in Bonn, the federal capital, and seeks to ensure equal access by media correspondents to politicians and government officials.

As the privately financed and operated electronic media gain a foothold in Germany, the unions are finding it more and more difficult to function effectively. German private enterprise is not well-disposed toward unions and has a powerful ally in the ruling Christian Democratic Party, which doesn't favor them, either. Production staff members with whom I've spoken during my visits to Germany in the 1980s and 1990s seem by and large less interested in unions than they were in the 1960s and 1970s. This is especially true of younger staff members, which is not a good sign for the future health of unions. Their feeling seems to be that they belong to unions (which not all do—membership isn't compulsory) largely because they believe in the idea of unions, but they don't see them as particularly useful. A few even consider unions as unnecessarily obstructionist in the adoption of modern technology. (For example, electronic news gathering was quite controversial in the early 1980s, as unions saw it reducing crew size.)

Interestingly, German unions by and large haven't seemed all that interested in presenting themselves through the electronic media, although there were some radio programs in which they became involved during the Weimar period, as well as some consideration of setting up their own radio station. Once the Nazis came to power, any hopes along those lines were ended.[75]

The ZDF and the collective television service (Deutsches Fernsehen, or German Television) of the state ARD stations must by law coordinate their program schedules, the only nation in the world where that is a legal requirement. The two bodies conclude coordination agreements for two- to three-year periods, and a coordination committee with equal numbers of representatives from each body meets every six months to consider possible changes in the overall agreement. Also, representatives from each body meet every month to discuss specific program details before press releases announce the schedules.

The administrative structures of the newer private stations for the most part run along the same lines as are followed in the public stations. In part that's a consequence of the public service tradition in West Germany: Much like Great Britain, where the Independent Television Authority was expected to follow the path of the BBC in many respects (advisory councils, audience research department, etc.), German private broadcasting has councils and internal administrative structures similar to those found in public stations. The private stations generally function with fewer production staff than do their public counterparts, which in part may be because the unions do not seem to play as much of a role in their operations. Small or nonexistent newsrooms and substantial amounts of programming produced by outside firms also reduce the need for staff.

GOVERNANCE AND ADMINISTRATION—EXTERNAL

The National Government

Compared with systems in other parts of the world, electronic media in Germany are relatively free from formal control (although certainly not from political influence) at the federal (national) level. There is a measure of technical control in the form of PTT (currently Deutsche Telekom, which should be more or less fully privatized by sometime in 1998) operation of television transmitters for most public and private broadcasters (the ARD first service is an exception), and control over the laying and servicing of cable lines. The PTT also allocates frequencies, and at one time could keep a proposed service from coming on the air if there were no suitable frequency available. Some of the private stations claimed in the late 1980s that the PTT was slow in processing their frequency requests, allegedly because the post office felt that handling the requests made more work and risked cluttering the spectrum, all for services that didn't seem particularly worthwhile, in their opinion.[76] In fact, more spectrum space already was available, thanks in part to a 1985 agreement among European broadcasters to use more of the UHF spectrum for radio broadcasting and in part to a willingness to consider licensing low-power (50-100 watt) stations for localized service. Now the PTT informs the media councils of frequencies available, and the councils decide who gets to use them.

The federal government's Cartel Office also sometimes plays a role in media regulation, and Porter and Hasselbach feel that the role has strongly political-economic implications. They cite several cases in which they allege an anti-public service broadcaster bias on the part of the Cartel Office: the banning of a four year ARD/ZDF contract with the German Sports Federation; the banning of WDR from participation in a service (Radio NRW) set up by the North Rhine-Westphalia broadcast regulatory agency; and the toleration of "anti-competitive practices in private broadcasting, whilst attempting to limit the financial strength of the public broadcasters."[77]

The federal government may appoint commissions to study aspects of broadcasting and make recommendations for possible changes, and it has done so on several occasions. The second Michel Commission, for instance, studied (1968-70) the possible duplication of services caused by having two stations (SWF and SDR) serving the same geographical area and made recommendations as to possible solutions to the problem. But it was up to the stations and to their respective state legislatures to decide whether to act upon any of the recommendations. They agreed to coordinate more closely, however, and to jointly provide a morning service on radio. And in mid-1997, the legislatures agreed to merge them. The federal government is not even involved in license fee collection, so it can't withhold or threaten to withhold license fee money, as can (and as have) so many other national governments.

Certainly politicians at the federal level are interested in broadcasting, and every year they make plenty of comments about it, in Parliament, in press conferences, in interviews and so on. Chancellor Konrad Adenauer, as we've seen, took a very keen interest in creating a second TV service. Chancellor Helmut Schmidt made numerous public statements about television, often criticizing it for its allegedly negative influence on young people, on the more traditional cultural activities (e.g., book reading), and on family life; he even proposed that there be a television-free day each week, but he had no power to create one.[78] The chancellor from 1983 to 1998, Helmut Kohl, reflected his CDU background in pressing for the development of alternative sources of television (cable and satellites), and wanted to see them in the hands of private industry, but it wasn't up to the federal government to decide whether they should be authorized. That was the responsibility of the states. However, the national leadership is in a strong position to influence policy decisions in the states, and especially in those states where the government is in the hands of the same political party. Kohl was well aware of that, and often spoke publicly, particularly on what he saw as the need for a major structural reform of public broadcasting—one that would likely place the private broadcasters in an even more favorable position to dominate the audience ratings. Neither was he terribly fond of license fee increases.[79]

State Government

Nowhere else in the world do states possess the power (in theory) to regulate electronic media that they enjoy in Germany. The state legislatures pass and amend the laws establishing their respective broadcast stations, as well as the newer laws regulating cable. They have the power to amend those laws or even abolish them altogether and start over with a new system. They also enjoy a measure of financial power, since it is up to them, acting collectively, to decide when and by how much to increase license fees. Aside from the matter of fees, however, that power generally goes unused. For reasons already mentioned, legislatures have been reluctant to modify the membership structures of the broadcast councils, although the structure of Radio Bremen's administrative council was modified in the early 1970s to permit the addition of two broadcast staff as council members with full voting rights—part of the controversy over editorial codetermination—and Bremen also passed a new broadcast law in 1979 that enlarged the broadcast council from 25 to 36 members, then later increased it to 37 to permit representation of the Green (environmentalist) Party.[80]

In general, state legislators seem satisfied with the broadcast laws, which go into considerable detail on matters of administration and supervision, but which confine themselves to general, if lofty, statements on program policy matters. Laws passed to cover the newer private stations closely resemble the laws for public stations, although, as noted earlier, the councils for such stations (and for cable) are likely to include some of the newer public interest groups, such as guest workers. The private stations do react more often to what they see as an unnecessarily complex legal system, although some media scholars contend that private television faces fewer restrictions than does its public counterpart.[81] Individual legislators often speak out on broadcasting, but seldom do they call for changes in the law itself.

The biggest problem facing the states is coordination of overall policy. When Adenauer made his bid to create a second national service, the prime ministers of the states met and developed a counterproposal. But political lines were not so firmly drawn then as they are now, which made it very difficult for the states to reach an agreement on an overall policy regarding cable and satellite TV services. They finally did so early in 1987 (the Interstate Broadcasting Treaty), in part because they feared that the federal government, possibly supported by some degree of viewer agitation for the new services, would find a way to circumvent the law and authorize the establishment of such services itself.[82] In a way, that weakened the power of states' rights, because it was very clear that each state could not in fact act as a fully independent entity, but ultimately had to go along with whatever the majority decided.

East Germany

Since the East German government included a designated place for states only at the beginning and the very end of the GDR's existence, state control over broadcasting would have been impossible, but even while states existed there, the national government had control over all important functions—and that certainly included broadcasting. The fact that the state committee members also were members of the SED (Communist Party) took care of many potential problems. First, it minimized the possibility that the broadcast services would air anything likely to embarrass the party or the government, since the party members serving on the committees would know the latest interpretations of party and government policy, or, if they didn't, would ensure that broadcasting refrain from setting forth any interpretation of events until one became clear. Second, it ensured that broadcasting wouldn't become a political football, with arguments over whether one party or another received more favorable treatment. Third, it meant that the broadcast system would have access to the highest levels of decision-making should it have points that it wished to call to their attention; broadcasting was considered by the SED and the government—for all practical purposes one and the same—to be extremely important in the development of society, and proposals for modification and expansion to better serve society were likely to be considered seriously. East German broadcasting never included provision for broadcast councils, nor did the government ever encourage the creation of interest groups which might have worked to reform programming practice. In a Communist state whose official philosophy was that power rested ultimately with "the people," those holding power were reluctant to let the people speak in their own right, aside from carrying some "the audience speaks" programs, where listener and viewer letters could be preselected.

Local Government

There is no provision for local government involvement in German electronic media policy-making—not in post-1990 Germany, nor in the Federal and Democratic Republics that preceded unification. Local governments watched the development of cable television experiments in their communities (West Berlin, Munich, Ludwigshafen/Mannheim, Dortmund) in the 1980s, but they really had little or no influence on policy-making. Local private radio stations also began to appear in the late 1980s, but they too were subject to the jurisdiction of the state governments, as were the private regional radio stations. City governments sometimes subsidize various cable program-making ventures, but they make up only a small percentage of the total number of operations. City-states (Hamburg, Bremen, and, in some ways, Berlin) are an exception to that rule, since they enjoy the full authority of states.

Nongovernmental

The broadcast and media councils are a form of institutionalized representation in decision-making, but there are many societal groups without representation (e.g., guest workers) and others which believe the organizations that might in theory represent them don't do so in practice. Women's organizations, for example, often tend to be represented on the councils by the more traditional, less militant Deutsche Frauenbund, although several of the councils, e.g., WDR's (Cologne), now require minimum numbers of women on their broadcast and administrative councils. There also are political parties (e.g., the Green Party, identified with ecology, a nuclear-weapon-free world, etc.) and splinter groups within political parties (e.g., the Young Socialists) which don't believe that their views and interests are reflected in the councils. One call for reform of council structures in the late 1970s advocated that "a group's chances for gaining access to the broadcasting council should be inversely proportional to its chances for gaining access to public communication."[83] Only Bremen and Hamburg followed the spirit of that recommendation, the former by making provision in its 1979 broadcast law for the appointment of five representatives from "schwer organisierbare" (difficult to organize) groups, the latter by opening nine council seats to applications from any group in its 1980 broadcast law.

Some interest groups have developed media interest sections and have made public statements of their views on broadcast policy. Often, those statements have appeared only in the group's own media outlets (magazines and newsletters), but occasionally the groups have commissioned studies that have been reported by some of the more "mass" media. One group particularly effective in raising issues involving ethics, freedom of speech and so on is the Evangelical (Lutheran) Church, which operates its own press service and through it publishes a periodical, Kirche und Rundfunk (Church and Broadcasting) (now called epd medien). Its leaders often have spoken out on matters of broadcast policy and often have received media coverage of those statements. As in many other countries, German newspapers take some pleasure in calling the public's attention to problems in the electronic media sector.

Most groups have a relatively narrow focus for their broadcast-related activities, but Aktion Funk und Fernsehen (Radio-TV Action Group) takes on a much broader range of issues, particularly morality in television programming and the defense of Conservative causes. In those respects, it is similar to Mary Whitehouse's VALA in Great Britain and to Accuracy in Media in the United States, although not as well organized or with as many members. Advertising that depicts women in highly traditional, subservient roles has been a frequent object of protest since the early 1970s, but so far the groups opposing it haven't been able to muster enough support for their cause to achieve more than minimal change.

The Weizsaecker Commission[84] noted in its 1994 report on television that there should be an independent, professional institution at the national level which would function as a consumer (audience member) advisory service on program content. A Media Consumer Assocation had already been founded in 1992, and has taken on the role of advisory service, particularly on films and publications it considers "dangerous." One potential problem here is the risk of exaggerating the sensational; as Barbara Eschenauer put it, "Without wishing to dismiss such dedicated groups and associations, it must be pointed out that they devote too much of their attention to themes which have significant publicity value, such as violence, horror and pornography in the media, and that this often results in them becoming the mouthpiece of a youth protection movement which in an all too populist manner makes the media the scapegoat for all that is bad in this world."[85] But such groups feel quite strongly about what they regard as a large increase in the number of violent TV programs as a result of the development of a private, and highly competitive, television sector. When a 1992 content analysis[86] disclosed that the four leading commercial channels were "littering the screen with bodies" (roughly 4,000 bodies a week for those four channels, ARD's first channel and ZDF), the chairman of North Rhine-Westphalia's Landesanstalt fuer Rundfunk called for "radical changes in TV programming,"[87] and received some favorable press coverage for that stance.

PROGRAMMING—WEST GERMANY AND UNIFIED GERMANY

Philosophies

The post-World War II history of West German broadcasting was characterized by an unusually strong devotion to the principle of fairness. That didn't mean freedom of access to the airwaves for any person or group wishing to express opinions or beliefs; rather, fairness in the West German system involved protecting individuals and groups from harm. Given the nation's experience during the Nazi period, it's hardly surprising that there should be a desire to protect individuals and groups from attack or exclusion. Each state broadcast law still contains provisions guaranteeing this: Article 2.4.i of the law governing SDR (Baden-Wuerttemburg) states that "no broadcast shall be permitted that might cause prejudice or discrimination against individuals or groups because of race, religion or color." Article 2.4.h, after guaranteeing the right of "democratically minded commentators and speakers" to criticize wrongs, goes on to state that those criticized also have the right to defend themselves. The federal constitution (Basic Law) goes even further; Article 5 states that "anyone has the right to freely express his opinion through the spoken word, in writing or through pictures. ... There will be no censorship."

That same devotion characterizes unified Germany, by and large. Limitations on broadcast frequencies, airtime and money mean that not every voice will be heard, or at least not as often as some individuals and groups would like, but the electronic media do have an obligation to promote diversity of opinion, although that obligation is clearer for the public broadcasters than for the private sector. As a result, informational programs, and discussions in particular, often are very freewheeling affairs in which one may see and hear a wide range of views on topics of the day. It isn't terribly difficult for an individual or group with an extreme point of view to receive airtime for its expression, although it may be broadcast over one of the less popular radio services and at an "off" time of day. However, there is no institutionalized access along the lines of the Dutch system, nor is there anything quite like the former U.S. fairness doctrine. There are only a handful of radio stations that resemble community radio services in other countries, and, while the "Open Channel" radio and TV outlets are used by individuals and groups, some states don't have them yet. And there is no broad legal guarantee of right to reply to broadcasts, aside from whatever each state may choose to include in legislation establishing the broadcast and media councils, although it's possible to seek damages in cases of defamation of character, libel or slander.

Starting a few weeks before election day, political parties usually are entitled to airtime in proportion to their strength in the state and federal parliaments (although the two major parties receive equal amounts). Parties campaigning in *all* of the states, even if they are unrepresented in the state and/or federal parliaments, also may receive airtime. The time itself is used by the parties as they see fit, usually in brief blocks (two to three minutes), and always in prime time and at the same time on the first and second public TV channels.[88] Radio has roughly similar arrangements.

Certainly the current German electronic media don't suffer from the apolitical blandness of German radio during the Weimar Republic. News broadcasts on the PSBs generally are comprehensive and objective; most of the private media operations feature briefer news programs, if they provide them at all. (RTL is the major exception; its evening newscast "RTL Aktuell" is gaining ground in the ratings battle with ARD and ZDF newscasts.) But political features, commentaries and discussions abound, particularly on public stations, and some of them can be quite partisan: ZDF's "Frontal" often appears to express the viewpoint of the more conservative wing of the CDU. That may rankle viewers who oppose those views, but it's perfectly legal so long as there is no evidence that ZDF allows only that point of view on its programs.

Whereas the PSBs are expected to present overall balance in their presentations, the private stations may or may not face that obligation. If there are three or more competing private services in a given reception area, there is usually no such requirement;[89] that rests on the dubious assumption that a certain number of stations will guarantee diversity of viewpoints, but the assumption still hasn't been successfully challenged in court. The one condition under which a private station *may* be urged to show diversity is if a station obtains an overall share of audience higher than 30 percent, it must either work to reduce its market share, establish an advisory council for programming, or allocate transmission time to independent third parties.[90]

The philosophy underlying cultural programs is harder to discern. The concept of fairness to individuals and groups has some influence on it, especially where the PSBs are concerned, but that influence sometimes is lacking in situations where one would expect to see it. For example, despite the regional structure of the first and third ARD television services, there's little evidence that the system is employed to promote regional cultures. Such cultures do exist; they're more prominent in some parts of the country than in others and exhibit varying degrees of difference, so one might imagine that it would be part of public, if not private, television's (and radio's, which does offer some programming along those lines) cultural mission to display them. Yet there is no legal requirement to do so. The provision that all state stations contribute at least something to the collective service (Deutsches Fernsehen) of the first program (ARD) doesn't ensure that any part of what a station contributes will be unique to its region, and usually it is not; in fact, it's quite difficult to discern the place of origin for most of the programming on ARD.

The Interstate Broadcasting Treaty contains a set of provisions, derived from the federal government's Criminal Code, that forbid public and private broadcasters from transmitting any program that glorifies war or violence, incites racism, threatens human dignity, is pornographic, or seriously endangers a young person's sense of morality. Material that could impair the mental (including psychological) or physical well-being of young people falls under time restrictions: it may not be shown before 8 p.m., 10 p.m., etc.[91] When there were so few TV services available nationwide, that sort of expectation was easy to fulfill. The private broadcasters are more willing to bend that rule, and very rarely receive a reprimand, much less a fine (which can be as much as DM 500,000 [$300,000] per offense) from a media council for violating it. But another expectation—that broadcasting serve as vehicle for the display of a wide range of German culture—is harder to fulfill, simply because it costs more money to produce one's own programs than to purchase them, especially when those production costs cannot be offset by large-scale sales to other countries. The German-speaking market is a limited one.

The private stations on the whole rely quite heavily on entertainment rather than information. Private TV services carry a large share of light entertainment, much of which comes from abroad (imports account for about 5 to 10 percent of the total on public television), and the private radio stations spend almost three-fourths of their program time on light music (pop and rock), about half of it German.[92] Clearly their predominant concern is to attract audiences that will be attractive to advertisers, although a number of their programs do deal with problems and concerns of individuals and groups (but rarely ethnic minorities), locally, regionally and nationally.

Radio

German radio has undergone much the same sort of transition as has radio elsewhere in Europe and North America. The rise of TV in the late 1950s diverted more and more audience and financial support from radio and led to the decline and eventual disappearance of such mass entertainment fare as quiz shows and popular serial dramas that had dominated radio schedules from the late 1940s to the late 1950s. That did not mean that all such shows were dropped, however. Radio plays continue to be presented by German public stations, and some offer them once a week. All public stations also provide broadcasts for schools, political talks and discussions. There are serialized readings of novels, gymnastics exercises, religious thoughts for the day, roundups of world press opinion, and of course news, weather, traffic and sports reports.

And there is music, more and more of it, to the point where it sometimes can be difficult to distinguish public radio services from private ones—not the best endorsement for the "unique role" of public broadcasting, but it helps to hold down costs, and it's popular. There are many musical request programs. German music and/or performers (most of the public stations have one or more orchestras, small or large, popular, classical or folk) make up a fair share of the total for most music programs, but there also are many selections from other parts of Europe and from North America, and occasional presentations of Latin American music. Music of émigré groups (Turkish, Italian, Greek, Portuguese, Arabic) receives little airtime on the more popular public radio services, but a bit more on the specialized ones. Two late night/early morning music services, one middle-of-the-road and the other classical, are offered through the ARD network, and the state stations take turns producing them.

Germany takes great pride in the technical quality of its music broadcasts. Germans are fond of music, but another factor is the country's early development of FM broadcasting. Because West Germany was still something of an outcast when the European nations met in Copenhagen in 1948 to reallocate radio frequencies, it received very few on AM. But FM wasn't affected, both because its signals didn't carry as far and weren't influenced by time of day, and because few other European nations had much interest in utilizing it at that time. So West Germany moved quickly to develop and manufacture the necessary transmitters, receivers and so on, and as a result soon had a heavily FM-based transmission system, with all of its advantages for static-free, high-fidelity reception.

All of the state public radio stations broadcast at least four separate services, and a few provide five. Two of the services may resemble one another at times and may include periods of simulcasting, especially in early morning hours. There also is an increasing amount of program sharing between two or three stations. One of the services usually specializes in material for smaller segments of the audience: experimental music and radio plays, talks on unusual subjects and so on. Five of the stations offer an early evening program block for émigrés, with programs in Turkish, Italian, Greek, Serbo-Croatian and/or other languages spoken by sizable numbers of émigrés in the station's coverage area. WDR offers a 12-hour daily service for emigrés in various languages (see below). There also are many breakout periods for broadcasts by branch studio services of the central stations. A few state stations, such as NDR and WDR, now offer "youth radio" channels, in a bid to try to win back some of that audience from the private stations.

During the first few years of their existence, the private radio stations displayed some interesting differences among themselves. Radio 4, the service for Rhineland-Palatinate, included four different (separately owned) operations, the two smallest of which had one hour each per day, the largest just over 17. Disc-jockey-hosted pop music shows took most of the airtime on all four operations, but the smallest ones, Linksrheinische Rundfunkunion (LR) and Radio 85, often devoted from a fourth to a third of their airtime in a given hour to interviews with people from the region, for example, the head of a woman's institute talking about a new leadership program for women. On the other hand, Radio Schleswig-Holstein in Kiel broadcast little but popular music from the very beginning, with brief newscasts and few interviews with the public.[93] The Radio Schleswig-Holstein model has prevailed, and most private stations now depend on music for well over 80 percent of their airtime. However, specialized format stations also have appeared: all-jazz, all-oldies, etc.

Both German public and private radio have become much more prominent locally over the past decade. The major PSB broadcast centers always have had branch studios within their coverage areas, but those were limited to supplying material (usually interviews) that would be broadcast throughout the region. They certainly didn't function as local stations. However, beginning in 1975, the centers gave some of those studio operations small blocks of airtime, usually 20 to 30 minutes early in the day, and perhaps also in the afternoon, and the use of transmitters serving their particular areas. As one example, a branch of SDR Stuttgart, Kurpfalz Radio (in Heidelberg, and later, Mannheim), was offering three program blocks per day, for three hours, by the early 1980s. Much of the material was news and interviews, especially with local figures and occasionally in dialect, but there was music by listener request, and vignettes on the history of towns and villages. Station staff sometimes found that local government officials weren't very radio-conscious, in the sense that those officials rarely if ever had been interviewed by the state stations and sometimes didn't know quite how to handle requests for information from the local stations.[94] But most learned quickly enough.

Local radio is a recent enough phenomenon that its staff members and its listeners both are still discovering what it can most appropriately provide. When various incidents of racism, usually directed against Vietnamese, Turks and other visibly "different" peoples, broke out in Germany in the early to mid 1990s, a number of local stations in North Rhine-Westphalia took it upon themselves to alert their communities to what was going on, why it was so evil, and how it might be combated. A content-based study by Ralph Weiss reveals that the four stations he examined were persistent in their antiracist campaigns, and that they broadcast a variety of messages touching upon different dimensions of the problem.[95]

Community and "alternative" radio stations still are rarities in Germany. The best known of the lot, Radio Dreyeckland (Freiburg), was a pirate stations for years (often broadcasting from France) before it received a "real" license in 1988. Its program lineup consists largely of "alternative" music, discussion programs, etc., produced by homosexual and lesbian groups, ethnic minorities and others. Their sometimes loose observance of program content and technical regulations brings them reprimands and fines.[96] Nuremburg's Radio Z and a handful of others follow in Dreyeckland's footsteps, but it was difficult for them to raise enough money to pay the few salaried staff members, repair broken equipment, etc. That changed in 1995, when the states agreed to include independent noncommercial radio stations in the division of the license fee receipts. Each state media council receives 2 percent of the license fee, and decides how much of that to use for the noncommercial stations, which must be able to show that they're truly needy.[97]

There also are alternative radio services available through some of the cable outlets, as *Offener Kanaele,* or open channels (see below).

In contrast with the Dutch and British situations, German radio had little experience with pirate radio stations. Land-based pirates have come along every now and then, usually in connection with Green Party activities, for example, a 1979 demonstration against the construction of a nuclear power plant at Gorleben, when Radio Regenbogen (Rainbow) broadcast the demonstration. In most cases, the diligent German authorities usually have tracked them down and put them off the air in short order.[98]

Public radio still often sees itself as guardian of high standards of language usage, and its broadcasts tend to be quite formal, correct and dignified, with some relaxation of standards for youth services. That's particularly noticeable when listening to the disc jockeys on the private stations, who are less formal than their public radio counterparts. Slang rarely is used on the public stations, except for the "youth" radio services, where its influence may be quite profound.[99] Broadcasts in regional dialects are rare, except over subregional and local stations, where brief remarks by dialect speakers on such subjects as the coming of fall will be used to provide a bit of local color. There's a rich tradition of radio plays in dialect running from the 1920s through the 1960s, but most of that has vanished by now.[100]

Television

German public television used to follow a typical west European weekday schedule, in that the earlier morning hours (6 to 10 a.m.) either were devoid of programs or contained educational material, some of it for adult education (the Telekolleg—mainly foreign languages, history and various social sciences), some for primary and secondary schools (largely those same subjects, but with a differing lineup from one state to another—not all states had or have educational TV). Finally, commercial competition drove ARD and ZDF to create a morning news program in 1992, along the lines of those on the U.S. networks, the BBC and IBA, and France's TF1. Also, starting in 1985, ZDF and ARD began to present a block of repeat programs from their evening schedules of the previous day or week. The block lasted from 10 a.m. until just after 1 p.m. The third program services limited themselves to occasional educational programs until 5 p.m. Early afternoon hours generally were without programming, as well. Both ARD and ZDF offered videotext materials from

1:15 until 1:30, more as an advertisement for this service than anything else, and repeated it at 3:40 p.m. At 4 p.m., the state stations and ZDF provided a mixture of feature films, imported TV shows, children's cartoons and brief newscasts, all scheduled so as not to duplicate one another. The third service offered educational material such as "Sesame Street," and shows for niche audiences, such as teenagers, or on unusual topics (one October 1984 program dealt with the role of garlic in promoting one's health).

All of that changed radically with the advent of competition from commercial TV. Now the schedules of ARD (first service), ZDF and several German private TV stations run for 24 hours, although ZDF's 2:40-5 a.m. block is teletext. Repeats are common in the late night, morning and early afternoon hours. ARD and ZDF continue to offer their joint breakfast show, "ARD/ZDF Morgenmagazin" (5:30-9); SAT1 matches it with "Deutschland Heute Morgen." The other channels have either children's shows, usually American ("Bugs Bunny," "The Waltons," "The Wonder Years"), or more adult-oriented fare such as the U.S. detective series "Cannon" or the U.S. sitcom "Roseanne." The late morning-early afternoon period sees a mixture of old sitcoms, dramas and occasional feature films; those on ARD, ZDF and RTL are predominantly German, those on the other channels American. Later afternoon programming is heavy with family, adventure and children's shows, with similar divisions in program origination. There are a few German talk shows and quiz shows in the afternoon hours on RTL, SAT1 and Pro 7, and a lengthy procession of children's shows, some of them German ("Vampy," best described as a wimpy vampire with a great curiosity about how things work), many American, on RTL-2. The eight ARD third services come on air anywhere between 6 and 8 a.m. and sign off a bit before or after midnight, often present educational programs during the morning hours, offer lots of old German entertainment shows at various times of day, but also in many cases provide regional news and culture: ORB in eastern Germany has occasional documentaries and plays about the ethnic minority Sorbs who live in that area.

In certain respects, the prime-time schedule repeats the daytime patterns, in that ZDF, ARD, RTL and SAT1 are 100 percent German during most evening hours, Pro 7 manages 90 minutes or so of German material, RTL-2 perhaps 45 minutes, Vox and Super RTL almost nothing German. Most of the public and private services offer newscasts, ranging from 15 to 30 minutes. They are quite comprehensive, and present a good selection of national and international news, leaving the German regional news to the ARD third services and, to a lesser extent, RTL's regional breakout newscasts. Both ARD and ZDF carry interview and discussion shows on political issues and with politicians, although they were much more frequent in prime time 10 years ago. Documentaries about "serious" subjects such as the Nazi period tend to be scheduled late in the evening, and are rare on the private channels. ARD and ZDF carry a number of specialized magazine shows on economic issues ("WISO"), traffic and transportation ("Verkehrsgericht"), research and technical developments ("Globus"), or contemporary social and political issues ("Frontal"). Some of the private services carry magazine shows, as well, but they tend to be more like U.S. "infotainment," although RTL's "Nachtshow," a 45-minute Monday through Friday talk show, sometimes deals with more serious issues, and Pro 7's "Die Redaktion," a weekly show featuring reporters, does so quite often.[101]

As for entertainment, the "Big Five" (ARD, ZDF, RTL, RTL-2, SAT1) are the only channels to present original situation comedy and drama. There aren't that many of the former, although sitcoms are growing slightly in the late 1990s. They're often reminiscent of U.S. sitcoms, or even based directly on them, as with "Hilfe, Meine Familie Spinnt" ("Married With Children") and "Wer Ist Hier Der Boss?" ("Who's The Boss?"), or built around already-famous comedians.[102] There's considerably more drama, ranging from animal ("Ein Heim fuer Tiere," about a veterinarian) to hospital ("Hallo, Onkel Doc," featuring a pediatrician) to family ("Der Klan der Anna Voss," a complex set of intra- and interfamily business and personal relationships) to crime. It's a rare evening that doesn't have two or more "krimis" on the schedule, and there are some interesting differences in them: those presented by ARD and ZDF ("Die Kommissarin," "Tatort," "Die Partner") usually feature detectives and police officers who use reason, rather than strength, to catch a criminal. The leading roles often are taken by women. The pace is quite leisurely. The RTL Plus and SAT1 "krimis" ("Eine Frau wird gejagt," "Doppelter Einsatz," "Schwarz greift ein") favor the more action-oriented approach of U.S. police and detective shows, and women are more often victims than police officers. The private services have been criticized for presenting too much violence and excessive force (particularly by law enforcement personnel) in their "krimis," and appear to have toned down those programs by the late 1990s. ARD has received similar criticism for some episodes of its "Tatort" and "Polizeiruf" series, and the criticism came not only from viewers and some TV critics (one characterized a 1994 "Polizeiruf" episode entitled "Run, Anna, Run" as "a mixture of obscenity and brute force"), but also from the NDR Director of Television.[103]

One unusual crime show is ZDF's "Aktenzeichen: XY ... ungeloest" ("Case XY Unsolved"). On the air since 1967, and hosted throughout by Eduard Zimermann, this hour-long monthly program presents the facts of unsolved crimes, with as much visual depiction (including re-creation of some elements) as possible of what's already known, together with interviews of people who can shed some light on the crime. Viewers are urged to call law enforcement authorities if they think they can add to the sum of information, and both the program and the TV guide entries for it furnish telephone numbers for the purpose. The program is presented with a good deal of drama. Some feel there is too much drama—that it encourages amateurs to transform their own possibly doubtful pieces of information into "hard facts," sometimes bringing suspicion on innocent individuals. However, viewer information has led to numerous convictions (but one viewer failed to identify the swindler he'd invited into his apartment at the very time "Aktenzeichen" was on, and its "star" criminal was the very same swindler!), and the show is enormously popular, usually placing in the top 10 for its week.

Variety, musical and "star" shows have disappeared from the TV schedules of many industrialized nations, but Germans have their choice of several each week, and most of them feature top entertainers: singers, dancers, stand-up comics and others. Furthermore, the staging usually is quite spectacular. The shows usually are presented before "live" audiences; and some of them travel from one city to another, sometimes include local talent, and may feature a brief segment about the city itself. Quite aside from their entertainment value, they make for excellent public relations.

Nearly as popular are nature, travel and wildlife shows. The ARD third services and WDR (Cologne) carry a considerable number of them in prime time, and there's even a weekly quiz show built entirely around questions about animals. The private stations and ZDF schedule far fewer of them, perhaps for demographic reasons: they tend to attract older (50+) and young (under 12) viewers, and advertisers in Germany, as in most industrialized nations, are not particularly interested in those segments of the audience (however, it's my impression that German advertisers aren't as driven by demographics as are their U.S. counterparts).

"Erotic" programs aren't all that heavily watched, but the commercial channels offer a number of them, usually movies and usually after 11 p.m. One exception in both of those respects is PRO 7's "liebe suende" ("Love Sins"), a "sexuality journal" broadcast from 10:15 to 11 on Wednesday evenings. It features discussions of aspects of sexuality. It's somewhat less sensational than Vox's "Wa(h)re Liebe" (a play on words: "Wares of Love" without the h, "True Love" with it), Thursday evenings at 11:15, and with a transvestite host(ess), "Lilo Wanders" (aka Ernie Reinhart). The latter's depictions of sexuality include scenes showing how couples have outfitted their bedrooms with various devices to excite themselves. And there's also "Peep," with Veronica Feldbusch, on RTL-2. Cable programmers in particular want to see the 1968 law on pornography liberalized, so that cable can "be a part of the new media landscape."[104]

Surprisingly for a nation with such a robust commercial TV sector, Germany isn't home to very many game and quiz shows. "Gluecksrad" ("Wheel of Fortune") is a popular Monday through Friday prime-time feature of SAT1's schedule, and the channel carries two other daily quiz shows, at 5 p.m. and at 6 p.m. RTL Plus carries "Jeopardy" and "Family Feud" from 5:35 to 6:35 in the morning (!), "Der Preis ist heiss" ("The Price is Right") and a repeat of "Family Feud" from 11 to 12 a.m., and "Jeopardy" again at 5 p.m. Pro 7, RTL-2, Vox and Kabel 1 don't carry any at all. The public stations have a few weekly game and quiz shows, such as ARD's "Die Goldene 1—ARD-Fernsehlotterie," but they usually have more the appearance of a variety show (singing, dancing, comedy sketches) within which there are game show segments. ZDF's "Wetten, dass ..." ("I'll Bet that ...") is closer in style to commercial TV game shows, and sometimes is the highest-rated German TV program. Some of the third service stations also produce weekly quiz shows.

"Reality" shows also are fewer in number than might be expected, given the number of German commercial TV services. In fact, they were more common in the early 1990s, when "Eyewitness Video," "Of Life and Death," and "Distress Call" all were available on RTL Plus alone. Much like their U.S. counterparts, the shows featured bloody crimes and life-threatening situations, many of them re-enacted, but some actually taped on the scene: a 1993 ZDF documentary actually showed footage of a firefighter battling a blaze, his camcorder running! A CDU spokesperson actually called for a ban on the genre in 1993.[105] RTL dropped its reality shows by the mid-1990s, and there are few to be found on any of the channels as of the late 1990s.

There's a rich tradition in Germany of satire, but television does very little with it; it usually appears in the form of segments within variety shows, or as part of the routine of a stand-up comedian or program host. Some of the humor featured in sitcoms centering around bigots—"One Heart, One Soul"'s Alfred Tetzlaff in the 1970s, "Motzki" in the 1990s—could be called satirical, although, much like the U.S. sitcom "All in the Family"'s Archie Bunker, there probably are a fair number of viewers who are pleased that at last television is showing someone who "tells it like it is." As one example, in the first episode of "Motzki," the lead character (Motzki, a highly conservative, 60-ish male), shows his Turkish friend Gulusan around his apartment, and says, "Now you can see how a German apartment looks from the inside. We hang our coats on these hooks. Everything in order. Coats and jackets, with their buttons facing to the right."[106]

ARD and ZDF broadcast relatively few programs about the Nazi past[107] until 1979, when a showing of the U.S. series "Holocaust" in West Germany prompted renewed viewer interest in the Nazi era. The series was particularly controversial because ARD and ZDF turned it down at first, partly on the grounds that it lacked sufficient authenticity; then ARD agreed to show it, but only over the third TV service, which promptly got its highest ratings ever: Some episodes scored in the 30 percent range. Since then, there have been a number of TV programs and series about the subject, including some made abroad, e.g., "Shoah" and a 1992 CBS "60 Minutes" episode about neo-Nazism, which included some edited-in (by Germans) footage of the Los Angeles riots, accompanied with the German announcer's voice-over stating, "These are the people who are criticizing us."[108]

The ARD regional stations (third service) offer prime-time productions that often are more spartan, but generally are well-produced and provide a clear alternative for devotees of chess, gardening, jazz, regional history and other "off the beaten path" subjects (for most TV systems) to indulge their tastes. Some of the third services also provide an unusual form of educational television, usually during the morning. The "Telekolleg," started in 1966, allows people who dropped out before completing their secondary education to finish the necessary coursework through a combination of television and correspondence. The course offerings aren't as comprehensive as those offered through Japan's NHK Correspondence High School but do include physics, chemistry, foreign languages, history, geography and a few other subject areas.

There are a few local and regional terrestrial and cable TV stations around the country, such as Fernsehen aus Berlin (also on cable), TV-Muenchen and TVBerlin (successor to IA Berlin and Brandenburg). On occasion, they come up with some highly interesting programs, such as a September 1995 IA documentary on how teenagers feel about having sexual relations—produced with openness and sensitivity. However, IA's "morning show" ("Bilderbogen") was three hours (6-9 a.m.) of what a camera mounted on the dashboard of a car "saw" as the car drove through the Berlin-Brandenburg area, with no explanation of anything, and no music.[109]

There are no quotas on how much foreign TV programming can be carried, aside from the overall European Union "restriction" (EU members are urged to try to enforce it) of no more than 50 percent non-European material. The "Big Four" manage to meet or exceed that quota, Pro 7 misses it by a fairly wide margin, and the other private stations don't even come close to matching Pro 7's performance. Local TV station Kabel Berlin and regional station IA Berlin and Brandenburg do nearly as well as the Big Four in terms of amount of German production.

Scheduling practices of the public and private television services are very much alike, with programs of uniform lengths (10, 30, 50, 55 and 60 minutes are most common) and a general tendency to break on the hour and half-hour during other than the prime-time period (7 to 10:30 or 11 p.m.), when five and 15 minutes after the hour become prevalent. Most series are produced in limited numbers of episodes—six, eight, sometimes more—and long-running entertainment series (year after year) are the exception rather than the rule. However, commercial TV stations seem increasingly interested in 15- or 20-episode series with good prospects for renewal from season to season.

Overall, there are quite clear distinctions between the program profiles of the public stations and the private stations, although both RTL Plus and SAT1 have added more German programs to their schedules, and have carried more and more "serious" drama and reportage, over the past few years. The remaining national commercial channels are heavily dependent on U.S. productions, and are the leading reason why Germany is the leading customer for U.S. television. The local and regional commercial TV services show some promise of originality, but there are too few of them as yet to make predictions as to how they will fare in the future.

Whether the public stations have lowered their qualitative standards in order to recapture viewers from the private sector is an open question. Certainly many of the Germans with whom I've raised that question have little doubt that standards are lower. They point to the decreased number of public affairs programs on ARD and ZDF. They claim that the newscasts no longer sound quite so authoritative. They bemoan the decline in numbers of operas, original drama by leading authors, symphony orchestra concerts, plays televised from theaters. On the whole, their criticism seems to rest more on cultural broadcasts than it does on informational programming. The one empirical study I've seen that deals with this issue—conducted annually for the past several years by Udo Michael Krueger of the Cologne Institute for Empirical

Media Research[110]—is based chiefly on program categories, and deals with content only to clarify or refine the categories. It indicates that the PSBs continue to provide a good balance of information and entertainment in prime time, and that they have a markedly different programming profile from that of the private broadcasters.

Since his is a continuing (annual) study, Krueger can discern trends, and one of the more interesting is the move by RTL Plus and SAT1 in the early 1990s to provide increasing amounts of informational programming in the prime-time period, at the expense of fictional entertainment. However, he regards much of the former as "infotainment," and thus somewhat more like the latter than it might seem at first glance. His future studies are quite likely to reveal that some of the infotainment has become more informational, and deals more often with "serious" subjects in a more professional way. They also are likely to show RTL Plus' and SAT1's evening news programs challenging ARD's "Tagesschau" (still the clear leader) and ZDF's "Heute" in terms of ratings and in terms of quality.[111] And if he were to analyze the content of TV drama, he might find a slight increase in sensationalism on ZDF and ARD, a slight decrease on SAT1 and RTL Plus. In short, it may be that the two pairs of services are influencing one another. But I have little doubt that he would deplore the preponderance of U.S. programming (much of it in non-prime-time hours) on most of the other German private stations, as well as the generally tasteless German programming they do provide—which may account for the generally low ratings most of them receive, aside from Pro 7.

PROGRAMMING—EAST GERMANY

Philosophies

The overriding purpose of East German broadcasting was to improve society through all types of programming: entertainment, education, information. Radio and TV were to provide examples of socially acceptable and socially unacceptable behavior, through items on newscasts, musical lyrics, actors in dramas, contestants on quiz shows, competitors in sports events and so on. Socially acceptable behavior consisted of such things as helping others in society, both in East Germany and abroad; working on behalf of society and not of oneself; and fighting injustice (however that might be defined).

It wasn't easy to realize such lofty goals when West German radio and TV programming were readily available to the vast majority of East German listeners and viewers. In order to keep them from consuming even more western programming than they already did, East German programs couldn't be too heavy-handed with their social messages too much of the time. Not every song that was broadcast could be in praise of socialism or against U.S. actions in Central America when East German teenagers were almost certain to be attracted to the latest hits from the West and when they could listen to them so easily. Therefore, many of the songs presented on East German radio or television (there were music videos, after a fashion) often were about love and its problems for teenagers, social alienation and so on. Television variety shows offered both "Communist" and "non-Communist" music. And there were TV programs imported from the West, although often they showed some undesirable aspect of western society, such as greed or lust. (Whether East German viewers even noticed those aspects or found them undesirable is another question.)

Radio

There were four national radio services in East Germany: DDR 1 and 2, Berliner Rundfunk and Stimme der DDR (a 1971 merger of Deutschlandsender and Berliner Welle). Stimme der DDR and Berliner Rundfunk were on 24 hours a day, DDR 1 for nearly 21 hours and DDR 2 for 14 hours a day. All four carried music for half or more or each broadcast day; DDR 2 offered more classical music than did the others, but all carried both classical and popular music. There was nothing resembling a nonstop pop service, nor even a service such as the Soviet Union's Mayak, with music and short newscasts throughout the day and night. Program blocks featuring one particular kind of music seldom lasted more than two hours and more often ran for an hour or less; furthermore, they were quite likely to be intermixed with programs for children, programs about politics and so on.

The DDR 2 service was more "serious" than the other three, carrying school broadcasts two or three times a day, readings from novels, talks on culture, and programs on the nature and history of socialism. Several radio plays were presented each week, usually original works by East German writers (often on the theme of individuals helping others) or adaptations of novels and stage plays (often by other east European writers). A quiz show of some sort usually was available each day, and often more educational than entertaining. News came on the hour over most services, and on the half-hour as well during the 4 (East Germans were expected to rise early!) to 7:00 a.m. period on DDR 1 and Stimme der DDR. The newscasts came from a central newsroom; there was no variety between the four services in that respect, although one or two services did carry newscasts at times when the others didn't. The usual news lineup started with items about governmental and political activities in East Germany, then dealt with other east European countries, and ended with a few items about West Germany and other nations around the world. Almost without variation, news about the "socialist world" (East Germany, the U.S.S.R. and other east European countries, plus perhaps Mongolia, Cuba, Vietnam, North Korea, Kampuchea and possibly Nicaragua) was positive. Crimes and disasters taking place there rarely were reported. News about the West was quite the opposite: strikes, disasters (particularly industrial) and crimes made up the bulk of the coverage. Tone of voice and choice of language, however, generally were neutral throughout the newscasts, giving them a somewhat disembodied sound. The Soviet policy of glasnost had little effect on East German broadcast journalism until the last months before unification.

Aside from specific program content, the overall schedule differed from that of West German radio in offering a great deal of programming for and by children, from preschoolers to teenagers. A number of the broadcasts featured popular music, but there also were interviews conducted by teenagers, fairy tales, music performed by children and teenagers, radio plays for children (again, usually featuring individuals or small groups working to help others, or stories of inspirational figures, such as cosmonauts) and features about things to make and do around the home. Clearly East German broadcasters believed that radio continued to be relevant for younger listeners and wasn't just a source of music. One sign of the importance to the East German government of attracting young listeners was its willingness to tolerate one "young listener's station" that often carried "decadent" western jazz, rock, heavy metal, etc. The station, DT 64, was one of the very few East German broadcast services to survive unification, although that was only after protest demonstrations by its devoted fans.[112] It now broadcasts as part of the Mitteldeutscher Rundfunk (Leipzig), over the ASTRA satellite.

The regional stations in East Germany—there were 11 of them, distributed quite evenly across the country—had morning and late afternoon periods when they broke away from the national service and carried local and regional news. The station in Cottbus broadcast for 30 to 60 minutes a day in Sorbisch to serve the 50,000 or so Sorbs living in that area, and the station in Rostock, on the Baltic coast, had a special holiday service for vacationers during the summer months, with information in German, Czech, Slovak and Polish about what to see and do in the area. There also was a special international fair service in Leipzig for the weeks in the spring and in the fall when the Leipzig Trade Fair was on. The larger stations had their own broadcast orchestras and also sometimes produced radio plays. Regional stations also had stringers reporting from the smaller cities and towns in their areas. During the 1950s, those stringers also were expected to report on any "politically suspicious" behavior they observed, but that simply made people unwilling to cooperate with them in developing news items, so the observation task was dropped.[113]

Television

While the variety of programming on the two East German television services didn't begin to match that of West German TV, it was far greater than what was available to other east European viewers at the time (aside from the U.S.S.R. and those Hungarian viewers who had cable), and it was very well-produced, on the whole. High production quality was in part a response to West German programming and was supposed to help attract both East German and possibly West German viewers. The broadcast day on both channels began shortly before 9 a.m. and ended around midnight, often with one to three hours blank in the early to middle afternoon on weekdays. Much of the morning program block consisted of repeats from the previous day or week, as on West German TV, and for much the same audience: shift workers and viewers in the other Germany. There also was educational programming for primary and secondary schools.

The first service carried more light entertainment than did the second, but both carried a few to several hours of educational broadcasting each day—for schoolchildren on the second service (chemistry, biology, geography, civics, music) and for adults on the first (English, Russian), as well as some repeats of second service educational material. Feature films, not all that common on West German public TV in the period before commercial TV, were available almost every day of the week on East German TV and ranged from the Eisenstein classic "The Battleship Potemkin" to "The Coast of Love" (French), with films from east European nations predominating. East German TV also had access to a huge stock of German films from before 1945 and showed them often; they were great favorites among older West German viewers, since few of them were available over West German TV. Newscasts were on five times a day over the first service, twice a day on the second, and were much like radio news in content, with the addition of visual material from Intervision, Eurovision and the Fernsehen DDR crews. There were few East German broadcast correspondents stationed outside the country—the cost in precious hard currencies was too great—so foreign items usually were handled through voice-overs in the studio.

There was a wide variety of material for hobbyists: gardening, pet care, photography and other hobbies all received frequent coverage, sometimes in weekly series. Quiz shows were few, but variety shows, often with lavish costumes and sets, were common. There were several travel programs as well, some to highlight various cities and nature areas of East Germany, others to present foreign lands. Because few East Germans enjoyed the freedom to travel widely, travelogues were a substitute, but they also might have reminded viewers that there was a lot that they couldn't see for themselves.[114] Television plays, original and adapted, classical and contemporary, were on almost nightly. Commemorative ceremonies, such as the opening of the rebuilt German Playhouse in East Berlin in 1984, received heavy coverage, perhaps because they gave the government a chance to tout its support for culture.

As with radio, TV had a great deal of material for children, especially toward the end of the afternoon.[115] Most of the programs were full of suggestions for hobbies (pet care and gardening seem to lead the way) and for good behavior. Perhaps the most subtle of the behavior programs was the nightly "Sandmaennchen" ("Little Sandman"), a 10-minute show that combined puppet and toy figures with brief film clips showing such things as model families (e.g., a father who has educated himself and who has a responsible job in a factory, but who helps his family members and neighbors, too) and model acts (e.g., obeying traffic signals, keeping the dog on a leash). They were charmingly done, and not at all heavy-handed. Many West German viewers who lived within range of East German TV seemed to watch them quite regularly. The "Sandman" was one of the very few programs from East German television that survived unification, and it remains on the air.

East German coverage of sports was plentiful, if one-dimensional. The country's athletes did well in international competition, and their triumphs probably added to the average East German's sense of self-worth. Televising the events also allowed for interviews with the athletes, who often were encouraged to tell viewers how much they (the athletes) owed to East German society for having made possible all of the training, including workouts with neighbors and co-workers, that led to victory. But occasionally athletes in some of the more demanding sports would admit on camera that their neighbors and co-workers often lost interest in working out with them!

During the 1970s, East German television took on a much more relaxed character. There were fewer and fewer instances of variety show hosts, performers, characters in dramas (I cannot recall ever seeing an East German situation comedy) and other entertainers reminding viewers of East German economic progress, the advantages of living in a socialist rather than a capitalist Germany and so on. Also, there were fewer dramas stressing such themes as individuals working on behalf of society, the dangers of ideological contamination from the West, and the need to work together to achieve progress, and when those themes did appear, they were presented more subtly. Spy dramas still tended to present U.S. and West German agents in very broad, stereotypical ways, but the same could be said for most U.S. TV dramas with spies from "the other side." And there were far fewer newsreel-type shows featuring developments in the other east European countries, whereas these had been on several times a week in the 1960s. Still, those in charge of television in particular remained sensitive to anything that might upset the Soviet Union: an East German producer who included an anti-Stalin statement voiced openly by Marcus Wolf (the "master spy" of East Germany) in a 1988 documentary tribute to Wolf's father (the author Friedrich Wolf) saw the statement disappear from the initial broadcast. It reappeared in repeat broadcasts in 1989, by which time it seemed clear that the Soviet Union no longer was so menacing.[116]

Certainly the major commemorative events, such as the 35th anniversary of the founding of the German Democratic Republic, included many references to what had been achieved over that time, and there were many short, "person-in-the-street" interviews in which people were asked what the event meant to them (their replies often sounded bored and formal, as if they were scripted—which in some cases they may have been). But all in all the use of television as an ideological transmission belt was far less obvious and rather less frequent than it had been before the conclusion of the interstate treaty in 1972 and the widespread diplomatic recognition of East Germany by western nations at about the same time. West German TV certainly had some influence, but a greater sense of self-confidence and security within East Germany had its effect, too.

THE AUDIENCE

The German broadcast system's interest in audience research dates back to the mid-1920s, when mail questionnaires, usually distributed by and through magazines for fans of radio, were used to learn more about audience reactions to programming. That interest continued during the 1930s, although surveys became less and less frequent as World War II approached, and the practice pretty well ceased during the war. During the occupation period, many surveys were conducted, and starting in the early 1950s West German broadcasters and academics became more involved in the practice than ever. Each state station conducted or commissioned others to conduct surveys, usually by mail or in person at first, but more and more by telephone as well, as telephones became more common. The stations recognized the wisdom of working through a national organization in order to obtain audience reactions from all around West Germany. It wasn't all that essential to have the data for advertising purposes, since commercial time was limited (ads didn't appear on TV until 1956) and since advertising had no direct connection with individual programs, anyway. But programmers did want some indication of how many of what kinds of people watched and listened to which shows, and how much they appeared to like them. Therefore, both demographic and program quality data were gathered, the latter by asking people to rate the shows they watched and listened to on a 10-point scale.

Infratest of Munich won the first national research contract in 1961. When ZDF came along in 1963, it joined in with the state stations on the arrangement. Infratest held the contract until 1974, when it lost out to teleskopie. Teleskopie conducts specialized surveys of TV viewing, but also uses meters (TeleMetron) attached to sets, much in the manner of the Nielsen peoplemeter, for continuous measurement of viewing in some 1,400 randomly selected households (4,200 individuals) throughout Germany. The peoplemeter system has been in use in Germany since the late 1970s.[117] GfK Fernsehforschung has since become the leading national broadcast research organization, although it faced a bit of a challenge from the U.S.-based Nielsen corporation in the mid-1990s, as Nielsen contracted with the pay TV service Premiere to sample 300 Premiere households with meters, with the intent of providing detailed socioeconomic data on their viewing.[118]

German broadcasters and advertisers use survey research methods of all standard types: diaries, in-person interviews, telephone surveys, mail questionnaires and mechanical devices. In addition to the continuous data gathered on TV viewing by GfK, there are many individual projects conducted by ZDF (which has a sizable research department), the state stations (all of which have research departments), the various "Landesmedienanstaelte," a number of institutes (e.g., the Institute for Research on Children, in Munich), and certain of the universities (e.g., the Hans Bredow Institut at the University of Hamburg); there also are several independent organizations that conduct advertising research, such as the Broadcast Advertising Association.

According to data gathered just prior to and five years after unification, West Germans are interested but not addicted radio listeners and TV viewers; (former) East Germans are heavier consumers of both media. For 1990, West Germans averaged 135 minutes a day watching TV, 170 minutes listening to radio, while figures for East Germans were 171 for TV, 182 for radio. The figures for 1995 were West Germans 150 minutes for TV, 152 for radio, and East Germans 191 for TV, 200 for radio.[119] Figures for 1996 were computed on a different basis: no longer were guests in the household counted as viewers. West German teenagers (13+) and adults viewed an average of 190 minutes a day, while East Germans in that category viewed 216 minutes a day.[120]

A 1996 survey indicated that the most popular shows were quiz programs such as "Wetten, dass ..." ("I'll Bet that ..." on ZDF, with 18 million households viewing on the best nights), followed by variety shows (e.g., "Mainz, wie es singt und lacht," on ZDF—nearly 12 million households on top nights), then crime series along the lines of "Tatort" (ARD—over 11 million households for best nights). "Action" series such as "Alarm fuer Cobra 11," on RTL Plus drew a maximum of 10 million viewers. Best showing for news programs was ARD's "Tagesschau," with an *average* figure of nearly 8.5 million viewers—twice the average for the most heavily-viewed private newscast, RTL's "RTL Aktuell," which averaged 4.25 million, but which also was gaining nicely over previous years.[121]

Several of the university and private institutes and research organizations have conducted research on the influence of television on its audiences. In relative terms, there's as much research on the influence of TV on children in Germany as there is in the United States, and just as much contradiction in the results: Some studies show that certain kinds of TV viewing seem to encourage criminal behavior, lead to poor performance in school and so on, while other studies show that there are very few measurable effects.[122] Studies of bias in television news were quite numerous in the 1970s and 1980s, but also contradictory, although results in general showed relatively little measurable bias for either ARD or ZDF.[123] The research agenda changed somewhat in the 1990s, according to Wolfgang Hoffman-Riem: he detects a greater emphasis by researchers on such issues as media convergence (the increasing similarity of public and private programming practices, for example)[124] and "videomalaise."[125] Some of the research falls in the "I didn't need research to tell me that" category: a 1994 Hans Bredow Institut study of television viewing habits concluded that television no longer was a "family medium," since so many households had two or more sets, and since viewing preferences within families varied so much—a situation that had existed since the beginning of the 1990s.[126]

Research appears to be regarded as a necessary evil by many broadcast staff members, especially producers and program planners. A strong audience appreciation (10-point scale) figure for a show with a small percentage of viewers can help to save it from cancellation on a PSB service, and occasionally the GfK data will be used to help rearrange the PSB program schedule, but there is little evidence that survey or laboratory research will have much influence on the content of specific programs or will lead to their cancellation, if that research were to show possibly harmful effects on viewers. Nor will critical praise for a series, especially on commercial TV, save it from cancellation if audience numbers are judged too low. Pro 7's "Der Gletscherclan" (a family drama) was nominated for the highly prestigious Grimme Prize in 1995. That was Pro 7's first such nomination, but it canceled the series after six of its 10 episodes had been run because of "weak" viewing figures. Hopes were for 1.5-2 million viewers, but the average per episode was a million.[127]

Aside from audience research, there are other feedback mechanisms that allow for assessment of audience likes and dislikes. Although German broadcasters don't specifically encourage letter writing and telephone calls (aside from musical requests, quiz show entries and information on upcoming events), listeners and viewers write tens of thousands of letters every year and call stations by the hundreds every day with reactions to everything from technical problems to "offensive" programs. Also, special interest groups (morality in media, women's rights, political factions) have sought to influence programming by developing protest campaigns of various sorts, but broadcasters usually disregard their efforts, reasoning that they represent only a tiny fraction of the total audience.

The PSB television schedules at times include programs designed to educate the audience as to what goes on in television: how programs are made, what sorts of problems arise and so on. The aim appears to be to make the viewers become more discerning consumers of television. ZDF's long-running 1980s series "Glashaus" ("Greenhouse") allowed members of a studio audience to criticize various aspects of television programming. Such programs now have become rare.

East Germany

There were sporadic and rudimentary attempts at audience research in East Germany during the 1950s and early 1960s, but anything more permanent or better developed was hindered by the "of the people, by the people, for the people" stance of the SED, which claimed that there was no need for audience research in a society where government, audience and broadcaster were so closely linked.[128] Also, Communist leaders often branded survey research as a capitalist tool for the exploitation of the masses. However, Hungary and Poland began to make regular use of it by the early 1960s. East Germany established a television research department in 1964, and in 1968 it began to carry out surveys every two weeks, using questionnaires with a set of standard questions and a set of questions especially drawn up for each survey period (e.g., What constitutes a "hero" in a TV drama, and which figures do you find "heroic"?). Radio had started the same practice in 1966. In both cases, surveys were nationwide and respondents were selected randomly: 1,000 for TV surveys, 1,500 for radio.[129]

Weekly surveys of TV viewing of East German programs conducted between 1987 and 1990 showed low viewership for specifically political programs until late in 1989, when viewership doubled and even tripled. It was evident that, due to the uncertainty of political developments in that period, it became more worthwhile to watch those programs. In contrast, programs that provided advice of various sorts and entertainment programs saw a decline in viewership starting in late 1989—probably the result of viewers wanting to spend only so much time with East German TV, and choosing to spend more of it on political programming.[130]

Survey results rarely were made public. Variety shows and travelogues appeared to be the most popular TV program genres, with foreign films close behind. Survey results didn't indicate the extent of viewing of West German television, but reports of West Germans who visited relatives in East Germany indicated that it was viewed much more heavily than was East German TV, and that its news and other informational programs were particularly popular. However, those same reports also indicated that at least some of the West German news reinforced some of the more negative images of life in a capitalist society: it's a competitive jungle, employers are heartless, the country is an armed camp and so on.

Data on radio listening showed that the popular music programs attract the largest audiences, and that brief newscasts were more attractive than longer ones for the majority of the listeners. As something like three-fourths of all East German teenagers had their own radio sets, the radio services were forced to consider how to retain the young audience, since broadcasts from West Germany were easily receivable in East Germany and were very popular there—especially the American Forces Network station in Berlin, RIAS Berlin, the British Forces Berlin station and a few of the West German state stations that played large amounts of the latest hits.

East Germany didn't encourage letter writing to the same extent as did the Soviet Union, but there were occasional programs on radio and television where audience reactions were read and replied to, and quite a few programs where audience requests for music were honored. Also, East German broadcast personnel were expected to get out and meet with the public, at factories, in schools, in old people's homes, and even in jails. They also were expected to return to their stations and share with their colleagues the information gathered in those meetings, although how much effect that had on program decision-making is impossible to discern.

MINORITIES AND THE MEDIA

German broadcasters were almost totally uninvolved with broadcasting for minority groups until the 1960s, and even then their involvement was extremely modest.[131] "Guest workers" from various southern European countries, Turkey and North Africa had begun to arrive in Germany by the late 1950s, but they were few in number at first, and confined largely to industrial centers. Some of the state radio stations began to provide bits of airtime in their languages by the early 1960s—perhaps weekly, perhaps less often.

Those language services eventually coalesced into a language block, produced by WDR (Cologne), and were broadcast through most ARD state stations in the Monday through Friday early evening hours. Then, in 1998, WRD initiated an émigré service called "Funkhaus Europa" (*http://www.wdr.de/radio/radio5/funkhauseuropa*). It is on air daily for c. 12 hours, and broadcasts mainly in émigré homeland languages (most of them European, but also Turkish and Arabic, and once a week in Kurdish). Most program blocks include light entertainment and news/public affairs. Many programs deal with émigré experiences in Germany; some provide information on specific sources of assistance. Few ARD stations other than WDR contribute programing to this service.

The first real breakthrough in television came in 1963, when ZDF initiated what turned out to be a very long-running program, "Nachbarn in Europa" ("European Neighbors") (ZDF's original charter [1963] contains under Program Guidelines the provision that it is to "provide an objective, overall view of multicultural life ..."). Some at ZDF had hopes that it could help to combat prejudice, and to that end decided to subtitle in German any of its program material that was in a foreign language. And, because they also hoped that the program would help to ease homesickness, much of the material was in Italian, Spanish, and later on, Serbian/Croatian, Turkish, Greek and Portuguese. The program started out on a biweekly basis, but went weekly in 1979; it became more structured, offering news segments about events "back home" (reported and written by largely nonminority ZDF staff) and events in Germany, along with some entertainment and reporting furnished by stations in the "home" country. It went off the air in October 1995, after a 32-year run, allegedly because too few of the minority groups it sought to reach wanted to watch bits of programming from back home, or (for younger viewers) even really cared that much about keeping up with events in the homeland.[132] ZDF also had created another series, "Nachbarn," in 1992. It is in German and focuses on the problems faced by émigrés and Germans living together, as well as prospects for success in such situations. It has remained on air.

Another type of program came along as Germany began to change its immigration policy starting in 1975. "Wir bitten um ihre Aufmerksamkeit" ("We Request Your Attention") contained material gathered and written by ZDF journalists, but translated and presented by journalists competent in foreign languages. The material dealt directly with the things an émigré would need to know: obtaining work and residence permits, getting a driver's license, etc.

ARD's first television program for émigrés, "Ihre Heimat—Unsere Heimat" ("Your Homeland—Our Homeland"), came on air in 1965. It used ARD foreign correspondents to report to émigrés on events in their homelands. It lasted until 1993, when it was replaced by "Babylon," which presented some material from émigré homelands, but placed more emphasis on the situations of émigrés in Germany and how they might best integrate with (or perhaps be integrated by) German society. ARD's "Die Sendung mit der Maus," a highly popular (usually the highest-rated children's TV show) twice-weekly series that dates back to 1976, contains quizzes, games, cartoons and other vehicles that present images of other cultures; furthermore, they're presented in foreign languages. However, the program is intended to increase children's knowledge of other cultures, and not ordinarily to help them understand the specific situations of émigrés in Germany. ZDF's "Karfunkel" (1991-95) also was a children's series, but here the focus clearly was on émigrés, because they wrote the scripts, which were 30-minute stories with different feature characters, but three continuous roles. Some stories were comic, some dramatic; a plot line might involve the grandchildren of a Russian and a German who had been World War II enemies.

"Lindenstrasse," an ARD family series that ran from 1985 to 1994, appears to have been the first fictional serial program that featured émigrés as regular cast members, although they didn't show up in any number, or in roles that helped viewers to understand their situations, until the early 1990s. Turks, who constitute far and away the largest of all émigré groups, didn't appear at all.

There have been many other individual films and TV plays that have dealt with minority issues. Some of them have been written and/or produced by minorities. However, the continuing programs generally have been produced and written largely or entirely by Germans, with the exception of "Karfunkel." Émigré producers and directors working for the mainstream public or private radio and TV stations are few. They are far more evident in various "Offener Kanaele" (open channels, for both radio and TV) services on cable, particularly those in Hamburg and Berlin, where there are large numbers of émigrés. The "Offener Kanaele" (OK) are financed by a surtax (the "Kabelgroschen") on the monthly fees paid by cable TV households, whose members occasionally call OK staff to complain that they should have to pay anything to support programs "that we Germans can't even understand." The surtax pays for the buildings, equipment and training, so OK program-makers use the service free of charge. There were 62 OKs as of mid-1998; four of the states had none at all.[132a] Groups wishing to establish OKs don't necessarily receive money from the surtax: My visit in October 1995 to what is surely one of the smallest OKs in the country, OK Tudorf (a service area of perhaps 1000 households) revealed a homegrown operation with its studio in the converted second floor of a medium-sized ranch home. Community members gathered news of local events (year-end school ceremonies, festivals, etc.) and presented a quite professional-looking 60-minute news and features hour twice a month. Despite their obvious commitment, they were unable to convince the state authorities to provide surtax support.

The OK don't operate for the exclusive use of émigrés, who in fact usually are outnumbered by members of the majority white German population, although those individuals and groups usually represent minority interests: gay and lesbian, motorcycle clubs, etc. However, the OKs do attract many minority groups, and they tend to be among the more faithful or persistent users of the services in terms of their longevity.[133] They seem especially attractive to younger émigrés, who may see themselves as culturally different from both their parents' generation and the majority culture, yet often blending what they see as the best elements of the two. Naturally, younger émigrés grow older, and if they continue to broadcast, that may prevent the next batch of younger émigrés from gaining access to airtime. Usually the OK administrative staff can work with both parties to reach an accommodation on sharing airtime, but not always, and there's rarely enough airtime to go around, at least at the more desirable transmission hours. In any event, most user groups are limited to 15- or 30-minute time slots, once or twice a week, which means that the audiences they seek to reach—sometimes émigrés like themselves, sometimes the broader émigré community, sometimes the majority culture, and sometimes all three—have very limited opportunities to see or hear their work.

Émigré programming on the OKs usually includes a mixture of cultural and political material, the former as guest appearances of poets, dancers, singers, etc., and the latter as news from the ethnic homeland and news about activities of the émigré community in Germany. Religious and political proselytization isn't unknown, but it does seem rare, although that can be difficult for administrative staff to judge if the broadcast is done in the émigré group language; administrators usually rely on reports from unhappy listeners and viewers in the émigré community to report such activity, which is in fact allowable so long as the presenter doesn't attack other groups.

It is very difficult to determine the extent to which programs over the OK reach their intended audiences, or whether the audiences really appreciate and profit from what they hear and see. Very few OKs have conducted surveys, and the one survey I've seen (Berlin, 1994)[134] shows very low overall listening to and quite modest viewing of them. However, that was a random sample of the Berlin population and didn't distinguish respondents on the basis of "identity," so that, if audience numbers were higher among émigré populations, that wouldn't have been reflected in the results. Nor do we have anything other than anecdotal evidence that émigrés who gain experience through the OKs are then able to secure employment in mainstream electronic media.

A recent major initiative in multicultural broadcasting is SFB creation in 1994 of SFB4, the MultiKulti Programm. Available only over a weak FM transmitter than doesn't quite reach the full Berlin metropolitan area (one of the world's largest) and over cable radio, the service has an unusual schedule: most weekday morning (starting at 7 a.m.) through mid-afternoon programs are in German, but prepared and delivered by ethnic minorities who speak it well; broadcasts from 4 p.m. until 10:20 p.m. mainly are in 16 foreign languages; and at 10:30 on Monday, Wednesday and Friday nights, there are lessons in German for foreign speakers. Weekends feature more emphasis on music, with some foreign-language programs mixed in, and a 2–7 p.m. multicultural youth program, with many young ethnic minority announcers. SFB itself furnishes the major share of financial support, but the German Federal Ministry of Labor and Social Affairs covers about 40 percent of the cost. A number of the music programs appear to have attracted many mainstream

German listeners, although it's less certain whether they listen in any number to the morning-to-mid-afternoon news, commentary and discussion programs in German.[135]

Certainly there are actors and actresses, news and sports presenters, and other on-screen personalities who clearly are of non-German origin (and who usually speak excellent German, although I have overheard more than one "native" German question their pronunciation, word usage, etc.). Some examples: Yvette Ablanvi Dankou, part African, and moderator of Kabel 1's interactive game show "Hugo"; Arabella Kiesbauer, Pro 7's part-African hostess of "Arabella Night," a "soft" (e.g., a behind-the-scenes look at the fashion industry) feature series; Minh-Khai Phan-Thi, a Vietnamese moderator for "Hugo"; Cherno Jobatey, Asian, and a commentator for ZDF; Miro Nemec, a Croat who had a lead role as a police commissioner in ARD's "Tatort"; Charles Muhamed Huber, an Afro-German, part of the criminal police team in some of the 1995 episodes of ZDF's police drama "Der Alte"; and a Black African lead character in a late 1995 series, "Mein Unbekannter Mann" ("My Unknown Husband"), who wanted to remain in Germany, and to do so convinced his white German girlfriend to marry him. Media critic Volker Lilienthal feels that it helps a great deal if such minorities are young, attractive women (often of ethnically mixed origin), which the first three clearly are; he also sees many shows, documentaries in particular, that play up the exotic side of minorities, and a number of family dramas, including the popular "Lindenstrasse" and "Marienhof," where the minorities are the victims of mindless hatred or the (perhaps unconscious) violators of "mainstream German" customs.[136]

Media scholar Christof Butterwegge expresses another sort of concern. In his 1996 study of connections between the mass media and racism in Germany, he concludes that racist attitudes in Germany may not be fueled by mass media portrayals of ethnic minorities, but they aren't dispelled, either. That, he feels, is because of the often abstract, impersonal manner in which the media portray émigrés, and the general lack of opportunity for the public to hear and see the experiences and points of view of émigrés themselves.[137]

There are signs that some German electronic media services are becoming more sensitive to words, phrases and depictions that may offend émigrés and may reinforce negative stereotypes. The most concerted effort along those lines seems to be SDR's (Stuttgart) Auslaenderredaktion, created in 1989 in order to help break down internal ("native German") staff resistance to accepting émigré colleagues, being more careful in their word choice, seeking out stories that could help to break down stereotypes, etc. The department's task hasn't been easy, and its work also has brought it threatening calls (including death threats) and notes from the outside, but SDR's central administration has persevered in its support of their work, and has backed that support with disciplinary action against SDR staff who don't go along.[138]

All in all, the various efforts just described are a considerable step forward from what was available for, by and about minorities over German radio and TV, cable and satellite, until the end of the 1980s. They still don't provide most "native Germans" or émigrés with much continuing, easily accessible exposure to émigré cultures or the experiences of what it's like to be an émigré in Germany. When there are hate crimes such as the burning of a house sheltering émigré residents in Solingen, there's a great deal of news coverage of the event, and radio and TV talk shows feature it, as well. Happily, there are few such dreadful events. But the sort of petty hatred that arises in daily life doesn't receive much attention from the electronic media, just as it does not in most nations. And Germany's largest minority, the more than two million (some estimates run to three million) Turks, receives little notice at all, save for one highly popular (among Turks) source.

Because Turks have been in Germany for roughly four decades, because they are numerous, and because many have done quite well financially, many Turkish households subscribe to either cable or satellite services. A 1993 Germany-wide study (N=1,380 Turkish households) showed that, of those households with TV sets (most of them), all but 14 percent subscribed to cable, satellite or both.[139] There are 10 or so Turkish channels available to those subscribers; most are beamed from Turkey via satellite, while a few have offices in Germany and produce a modest amount of programming on their own. A study reported by Josef Eckhardt in 1996 indicated that the Turks strongly preferred viewing programs from Turkey to watching German-made programs.[140] That raises a concern that Turkish émigrés may be opting out electronically from German society. It also could lead to an attitude on the part of German electronic media operations that, if the Turks (or any other ethnic minority group) wish to behave that way, why should the German media bother to pay attention to them? That in turn could deepen the gulf that already exists between a number of minorities in Germany and the mainstream German population.

One further minority has entered the German electronic media scene: handicapped persons. The Arbeitsgemeinschaft Behinderte in den Medien e. V., based in Munich, has managed to secure channel time over several cable outlets, including RTL's regional "window" for Bavaria. It presents a modest number of programs ranging from newscasts featuring items by, for and about the handicapped to mini-documentaries, televised sports contests for the handicapped, and even occasional dramas concerning them. The association holds video workshops, and has a video library of captioned feature films (including some made for TV), to serve those with severe hearing loss.[141]

PROBLEM AREAS

Most aspects of German broadcast programming arouse little controversy. There is some expression of concern over the possible harmful influences of TV on young viewers. Germany has highly protective laws regarding audio and video material that may not be shown to children at all, under a certain age, etc., contained in federal laws, and in the *Strafgesetzbuch* (StGB—the penal code) under provisions o 131 StGB (on the portrayal of force) and o 184 StGB (on pornography). The German Society for the Protection of Young People works with the editorial staff of the bimonthly *Jugend Medien Schutz—*Report (Report on Media and the Protection of Youth) to inform electronic media operations (and many others) of classifications of movies, videos, video games, audio recordings (mostly music), computer software programs, CD-ROMs, books, brochures, magazines, laser- and videodiscs and comics.

Increasing criticism in the early 1990s of violent programming on TV, most of it on the private stations, led the private industry in 1994 to increase its voluntary self-regulation (through the Freiwillige Selbstkontrolle Fernsehen, or FSF) of material that might violate the legal regulations on the protection of young people by examining such material prior to broadcast. That didn't stop the state media and broadcast councils from amending the Interstate Treaty on Broadcasting to include broader rules with more specific details on that protection,[142] although there is little sign that the action has led to many more fines for violation of the rules. Still, it's quite possible that the very existence of strengthened rules has "persuaded" the broadcasters to reduce the level of violence displayed.

Concerns about violence on TV, particularly in terms of its potential effects on young viewers, seemed to have lessened by the mid-1990s. However, competition between the private broadcasters is fierce, and it's always possible that one or another of the operations will try to gain audience by slipping more violent material into the earlier evening hours—not so much to reach young viewers, but to win their parents away from other channels. That could produce some interesting court cases, pitting "economic necessity" (we *have* to do this if we're to survive in such a competitive situation) against "protection of minors." And any service that doesn't transmit terrestrially might argue that the parents have made a conscious decision to subscribe to cable or satellite, so it's up to them to regulate their children's viewing. (Much the same argument has already been made where "erotic" material is concerned.)

Women's groups have protested the sexist portrayal of women in the electronic media, especially in advertising; they also have protested what they regard as discriminatory employment practices, especially the lack of women in major decision-making positions in the media industry. Broadcasts for and by women have a long tradition in German broadcasting. There were many regularly scheduled women's programs during the 1920s and during the Nazi era. However, they tended to reinforce the image of "Kinder, Kirche und Kueche" (children, church and kitchen) as the "proper" domain of women. As Kate Lacey points out, some programs during the Nazi period sought to give the impression that women had actively sought to establish their superiority in those respects, and for that reason should be considered full and active partners in a National-Socialist-run Germany.[143] Things didn't change much during the Allied occupation, although a number of women were employed at the occupation authority-administered radio stations, and a few of them, notably Ilse Weitsch at Radio Muenchen (Munich, in the U.S. zone), were able to introduce program material intended to break down some of the old stereotypes. Others followed their example: Lore Walb succeeded Weitsch at what by then had become the Bayerische Rundfunk (Bavarian Radio, or BR, in Munich). Up until the late 1960s, she and her colleagues dealt on occasion with topics such as sex education (highly controversial in staunchly Catholic Bavaria) and the "self-sacrificial mother" role. On the whole, however, they were careful not to "rock the boat," or to appear "too well-read" in the eyes of their supervisors.

After 1968, claims Walb, there were major changes. Inspired by U.S. author Betty Friedan's book *The Feminine Mystique,* and encouraged by a program reorganization at BR that gave the Frauenfunk a five-day-per-week schedule (up from two per week), the staff began to include programming that pushed for the acceptance of equal partnership and shared responsibility for men and women. It also paid much more attention to problems faced by underprivileged people. Bavarian Premier Franz Josef Strauss observed in 1971 that the Frauenfunk (and the Jugendfunk, or Youth Radio program) had been "injected ... with a little drop of Red [here meaning Communist] poison."[144]

In 1975, the first detailed report on the portrayal of women and treatment of women's issues on TV appeared. That inspired a number of meetings, and those same topics arose again and again, but there was little concrete action, although the Fall Assembly of Women in Media (first held in 1978, and annually thereafter) came out with a "Saure Gurke" (sour pickle) award for the most anti-woman television show of the year. Other studies followed. A 1981 study by Kotelmann and Mikos showed that over a third of all portrayals of women through TV advertising were of the "housewife and mother" variety, just under 4 percent were in occupational roles, and with women rarely presenting anything with "real content."[145]

Female news presenters and editors increased their presence at ZDF and the ARD in the 1980s. When one ZDF in-studio editor, Ruth von Wutenow, turned 50, she was taken off the set. Public outrage was great enough to get her returned to it. But women were still rare as guest experts or as high-level administrators of broadcast operations. Anne Rose Katz observed that TV news staff claimed to be looking for women as "important" guests: *"Really!* But they find none. Just as few as they can find for high administrative posts."[146] Some women took matters into their own hands: three female editors at ZDF developed a pilot project in late 1989 for ZDF's 3SAT satellite TV service on their own time, with the aim of presenting information in a way that seemed sensible to them. Each episode of the series, "NOVA," was to center around a topic or situation important to women, and the first episode presented four perspectives on women at work.[147]

More opportunities for female producers, directors and administrators arose starting in 1995, when a satellite-to-cable service, tm-3, was developed in Munich. This was the first "Frauenkanal," or woman's channel, in Europe. At first, it shared channel time with other services. Its program lineup sometimes was reminiscent of its approximate U.S. equivalent, "Lifetime," in that it appeared to be aimed at chiefly mainstream culture women. Émigrés, the urban poor, lesbians, were not ordinarily part of the picture. "Kinderella," an interview program produced by women, centered around babies, youngsters and adolescent children in one's life. An October 1996 episode contained an interview with a midwife, who noted the satisfaction she got from her work; interviews with mothers, children and teachers (fathers were seen but not heard) stressing the importance of preparing one's child for the first day of school; contrasting approaches to raising children, with some mothers pampering their teenaged and older children and not wanting to see them leave home, while others had jobs (one drives a small earthmover for a landscaping firm) and expected their children to be independent; an interview with the author of a book, "Nicht ohne meine Mutter" ("Not Without My Mother"), as she explained why mothers react in such different ways; and a final section in which a male pediatrician discussed child care, and how some couples are driven apart by their different attitudes on child-raising, or having children at all. "Kinderella" was followed by "Nathalie's Society," which was much like the U.S. "Lifestyles of the Rich and Famous," and in the episode I saw, the interviewer, Nathalie, visited a wealthy French clothing and fabrics manufacturer, a French flask-maker, and the Lalique family (famous crystal), with considerable emphasis in each case on expensive decorative objects. After that came a set of reviews of new movies, conducted by female journalists.

By 1997, tm-3 had become a full-time commercial channel, and was receivable in some but not all states, with an audience "reach" of a bit over 50 percent as of late 1997. However, low ratings and consequently low income had forced it to turn more and more to imported programming thought to be suitable for women (although it dropped its original title, "Fernsehen fuer Frauen") in the mainstream culture. While its original programming hasn't completely vanished from the screen, there's far less of it—especially information programs for women—than was the case earlier, and far more game shows and foreign movies.[148]

Women also are quite active in the OK system: many of the OK radio services, and several of the TV services, carry programs made by and for women, and here the range is wider, with lesbians, women of color and other minorities presented and presenting themselves alongside more mainstream culture women.

Opportunities for women in the electronic media have improved considerably in the 1990s, but top-level decision-makers continue to be very rare, just as they are in most industrialized nations. Those gaining administrative experience through tm-3 may be recruited for similar positions in other electronic media organizations, but the cultivation of any sizable number of female administrators is apt to take some time. Newsrooms are showing more signs of change; as in the United States, it no longer is all that rare to see women as editors-in-chief, although they've been scarce at the news departments of the "Big Four."

The subject of politics and TV amounts to a national preoccupation, at least on the part of politicians, the media, media scholars and various public-interest groups. Few of them seem satisfied with the present state of affairs, and most of them claim that the problems have been increasing almost from the start of the Federal Republic. Some of the specific instances that they cite have been mentioned already: Adenauer's attempts to set up a national TV service; the change in the manner of selecting members for the broadcast councils of NDR and WDR; the von Paczensky and "Bauern, Bonzen und Bomben" incidents at NDR; the CSU attempt to set up commercial TV and to "pack" the broadcast council at Bayerischer Rundfunk; the threatened breakup of the three-state agreement that governs NDR. There are many more; the following are a brief but reasonably representative sample:

1. The WDR license fee case: When it considered the proposed license fee increase in 1973, the state Parliament of North Rhine-Westphalia engaged in a sharp debate over it, and political lines were firmly drawn. The fee increase finally passed, but a number of the more conservative members of the Parliament pressed for greater control over the liberal WDR, particularly financial control. In 1974, the Parliament passed an amendment to the broadcast law that gave the state Rechnungshof (audit bureau) review power over WDR's annual expenditures, thus treating the station as though it were a state agency.[149]
2. The 1973 election of NDR's manager: The NDR broadcast law specifies the date for the election of the station's manager and deputy manager (the two must be chosen at the same time). In late 1973, the date came and went without such an election because the SPD and CDU could not agree on a suitable candidate, and the NDR administrative council, which was politically appointed, reflected that stalemate. Since the broadcast law makes no provision for an interim manager, a solution had to be improvised, and during that period (which lasted 15 weeks), the three states directly involved with NDR agreed upon a statement in which they claimed the right to "take further supervisory measures if an election has not been held by December 31, 1973, *and the functioning of the station makes this seem imperative*" (italics mine). Since the station continued to function normally, there was no state intervention; what form it might have taken is unknown, but the case is a graphic illustration of just how powerful political influence could become.[150]
3. The 1977 "Save freedom of broadcasting" movement in WDR: The television news staff of WDR long had had a reputation for (alleged) left-wing sympathies. In 1977, the television controller, Werner Hofer, retired; he was replaced by a CDU member, Theo Loch, and very soon complaints began to arise within the editorial staff that Loch was seeking to interfere with their work. Within a few weeks, trade unionists, some politicians (generally associated with the left) and a mixture of intellectuals had organized a citizen's initiative group called "Save freedom of broadcasting in the WDR" to prepare for the passage of

protective legislation if the situation did not improve. There were some informal concessions by Loch, the group did not have all that much staying power, and the controversy continued to simmer, but at a sufficiently low level that no legal action was taken.[151]

4. The Hammerschmidt-SWF case (1977): Helmut Hammerschmidt, the manager of SWF (Baden-Baden), was deeply disturbed by what he regarded as overly liberal reporting by broadcast journalists, especially in the northern Germany stations. He proposed a set of guidelines for ARD journalistic practices, and his chief argument was that there should be severe restraints on expression of political comment. Other ARD managers by and large opposed his proposal, chiefly on the grounds that broadcast journalism shouldn't be reduced to "purely factual" reporting, even if such a thing were possible. That would militate against the role of journalism in a democracy. Their opposition was strong enough to have the effect of strengthening the hand of the journalists.[152]
5. The mid-1980s cable access cases: As cable experiments were set up in various states, and as smaller cities and towns began to acquire "passive" cable, which would allow them to bring in outside services from satellites, politics once again played a role. The Bavarian government, dominated by the Christian Socialist Union (Conservative), forbade the reception of the ARD satellite service, Eins Plus, on the grounds that it was "too liberal." The state of Hesse, dominated by the SPD (liberal), forbade reception of SAT1 on the grounds that it was "too commercial," by which the government seemed to mean "too mindless, too anti-social activism." Both states had dropped those restrictions by 1987, when all of the states concluded their agreement on the licensing of the new media, but their initial actions were symptomatic of a deep philosophical division between the CDU/CSU and the SPD, one seeing every good economic reason for introducing more broadcast services, the other being wary of such a move on the grounds that additional services could harm society, perhaps by making it more dependent on the products of foreign cultures, perhaps by making people too self-satisfied or self-indulgent.[153]
6. The Leo Kirch-NDR case (1995): Not long after Leo Kirch had acquired a 35 percent share in the Springer group, he was invited to become a member of its board of directors. In August 1995, the German Supreme Court ruled that Bavaria (Kirch's home state) would have to forbid the display of crucifixes in public schools—a bitter pill to swallow for such a staunchly Catholic state. An editorial writer for *Die Welt,* the most prestigious newspaper in the Springer group, praised the decision. When Kirch learned of that, he called upon Springer to dismiss the writer. Springer did not, but the attempt itself drew a great deal of criticism from mass media around the country, who saw the action as an indication of how a powerful "media baron" such as Kirch might try to exercise editorial control. Interestingly, ARD was set to

carry a commentary criticizing Kirch, but substituted another subject, allegedly the decision of a Bavarian who supervised the broadcast ("ARD Aktuell") in which the commentary was to appear.[154]

How much effect the increased politicization of the electronic media has had on actual program content is difficult to tell. There are frequent accusations that a given station treats politician or political party X favorably or unfavorably, but those accusations themselves often come from partisan quarters, as they generally did when the ARD broadcast a tape of Prime Minister Kohl's 1986 New Year's Day address to the nation on New Year's Day 1987; the mix-up appeared to be an honest mistake, but a number of CDU officials and journalists favorable to the party saw it as an act of political sabotage. There does seem to be general agreement that ZDF is more favorable toward the CDU than toward the SPD. Since ZDF is a single national service, and since the prime-time schedule of the state stations represents all of them, there is a more natural tendency toward diversity in political viewpoint on the latter. There's general agreement that the private stations favor the CDU, although the Bertelsmann group seems to be regarded as more balanced than its competitors. There also seems to be general agreement that there has been a greater tendency for TV commentators to be more cautious over the past 20 or so years than they were earlier, although that could be the result of a keener recognition of TV's power. Where entertainment is concerned, some of the state stations certainly haven't hesitated to opt out of the prime-time schedule when they felt that a program contained morally offensive material. The fact that that has occurred most often in states where the CDU was in power may or may not indicate that the decision was politically motivated.

There also is the issue of media concentration. Several industrialized nations besides Germany feature a high degree of press ownership of broadcast media: the commercial services in Japan and Australia have been that way for decades, and Great Britain, France and several others have begun to open the broadcast media to press investment. If radio and television were media for entertainment only (which most were, or very nearly so, in radio services during the 1920s), it isn't likely that there would be much objection to cross-ownership. However, radio became prominent as an informational medium in the 1930s, and television in the 1960s (with some earlier exceptions), and survey after survey in the industrialized nations reveals that television is both the most popular and the most trusted medium for news of current events. Therefore, having both the press and broadcasting under the same editorial roof, so to speak (and that isn't inevitable), could lessen the diversity of viewpoints available to the media public.

As noted earlier, the large press concerns in Germany—Springer, Bertelsmann, Bauer and several smaller operations—began to agitate for the opportunity to establish commercial broadcast media back in the 1950s. Most of the states, including not only those governed by the SPD, but also a few of those led by the CDU, wanted to preserve their monopoly. The resumption of

CDU leadership at the federal (national) level in 1983 coincided with a general move throughout most of the industrialized world in the direction of more private ownership of broadcasting in those nations where it was minimal or didn't exist at all. It also coincided with overall economic prosperity and the fuller development of cable and satellite transmission systems. Leading figures at the major publishing houses were well-connected with leaders in the CDU; furthermore, those firms already had experience with media operations, and were perhaps better-prepared than most other potential investors would have been to risk investing in the electronic media. They also had been knocking at the licensing door for so long that they weren't about to give up their efforts. The states themselves, through their media committees, generally were ready to allow publisher ownership, although there are differing degrees of such ownership in the various states, and there's nothing in the Interstate Treaty on Broadcasting that requires the states to coordinate their policies in that respect,[155] although there are regularly scheduled joint meetings of the heads of the media committees.

By the early 1990s, it was evident that the publishers and Germany's major movie distributor, Dr. (he once was a professor) Leo Kirch, had locked up most of the national commercial television services,[156] while individual publishers and groups of publishers essentially controlled much of private radio. The latter was of less concern to media critics than the former: Private radio seemed unlikely to become important as a major informational medium, but television was a different case. Also, accusations began to surface that at least one of the private TV services, SAT1 (43 percent ownership by Leo Kirch), had provided highly favorable television exposure for Chancellor (Prime Minister) Helmut Kohl—a close friend of Kirch—through a series of gentle and positive interviews just prior to the 1994 national elections, and under the title "Zur Sache, Kanzler" ("Get to the Point, Chancellor").[157]

Kirch himself is a remarkable figure—quite publicity-shy and very secretive, but highly ambitious and exceptionally rich and powerful.[158] He and his son Thomas have assembled a media group that has investments, many of them controlling, in SAT1, Pro 7, Kabel 1, DSF, DF1, HOT and Premiere. The group also controls more than a dozen film and TV production firms, and is a major supplier of programming to ZDF, RTL Plus and numerous other terrestrial, satellite and cable operations. It has over a third of the shares in the Axel Springer publishing firm, which also has major holdings in the electronic media industry. Kirch and Springer also control Germany's major acquisitions firm for the rights to broadcast international sports events. And Kirch is attempting to establish a supranational firm in Milan, Italy, that would include Silvia Berlusconi, Rupert Murdoch, France's TF1 and Pearson (U.K.)—all "heavy hitters" with a capacity for real influence, politically and culturally.[158a]

Aside from his apparent business acumen, one reason for the dominance of Kirch and the other German "media moguls" (Bertelsmann, Springer and Bauer, whose shareholding profiles look much like those of Kirch)[159] is that the regulatory system rests in the hands of the states, through the "Landesmedienanstalten." As noted earlier, private broadcasters have been able to use a "divide and conquer" approach to gain much of their strength, and also that the CDU has worked to favor their development. Also, as Hoffmann-Riem indicates, the sheer complexities of electronic media regulation in Germany tend to discourage outside investors,[160] which leaves the field that much more open to German companies, and especially to those companies which already have a great deal of experience with the system. The Federal Cartel Office, according to Porter and Hasselbach, also has tolerated anticompetitive practices in private broadcasting.[161] And finally, the media councils are made up largely of amateurs whose chief "expertise" is supposed to be directed at program content: they can react as viewers might react. The media concerns operate chiefly on an economic basis, and employ legal experts to help them to expand. The councils often discover after the fact that a media concern has expanded once again.[162]

Whether the concentration of power in the hands of so few media concerns is a problem for the viewing and listening public is another question. Over two-thirds of all German households subscribe to cable and/or satellite services, and as a result enjoy a considerable range of channel choice, even if many of the private operations offer roughly similar programming. Although those operations haven't made extraordinary efforts to employ and to portray women and minorities in other than stereotypical positions and roles, their performances in that respect aren't all that much different from most of what ARD and ZDF have done. The public broadcasters can point with some pride to programs such as "Nachbarn in Europa," "Karfunkel," and services such as WDR's "Furkhaus Europa" and SFB 4's "Multi-Kulti," but that doesn't constitute a major commitment. But perhaps the majority of mainstream, and even minority, audience members doesn't really want more programming along those lines, and doesn't care that the private concerns haven't come up with similar programs. News and informational programming might be a more sensitive aspect with respect to concentration of power, and the interference of Leo Kirch with *Die Welt*'s editorial policy shows that the media concerns are willing to use their power. That was a prominent case because other media were willing to discuss it, and it's worth recalling that ARD pulled back from broadcasting a commentary critical of Kirch. The news lineups of the major evening news programs for the "Big Four" at times can be quite similar, so the public may be unaware of such nuances as there are in coverage of the same event. (In my viewing experience, there's been a greater tendency to sensationalize or trivialize the news on the commercial newscasts, although that doesn't reach the heights [depths?] of some U.S. local commercial TV newscasts.) In other words, if media concentration is to be regarded by the broader public as a problem, media scholars and critics will have to find more compelling ways to persuade the public that it is.

One further instance of concentration of power didn't involve a private firm, but a public one: Deutsche Telekom. It operated until 1998 as a monopoly, and provided various communication services, chiefly telephone and telephone-related, until 1998, when it was privatized. DT had and still has a cable network (facilities only—no programming) that serves more than a third of all households (17.5 million as of mid-1998) receiving TV. The European Commission (of the European Union) had seen that as a possibly undue concentration of economic power, and pressured DT to separate its cable network from its telephone service.[163] Following privatization, DT set up the network as a subsidiary.

FOREIGN INFLUENCES ON PROGRAMMING

Although German public television uses relatively little imported material in prime-time hours, aside from feature films (two or three per week for ARD's first service and ZDF combined, one or two per night for the ARD third services), it uses somewhat more in the daytime and late-night periods, largely U.S., British and Australian ("The Flying Doctor") series. The private channels rely much more heavily on imports at all times, although RTL Plus, SAT1, and, to an increasing extent, Pro 7,[164] carry a predominance of German material during prime time. Detective shows ("Murder, She Wrote"), children's programs ("The Flintstones"), comedy (the U.K.'s "Benny Hill," the old U.S. series about a prisoner-of-war camp in Germany, "Hogan's Heroes") and adventure series suitable for family viewing (including such ancient fare as "The Waltons") are the leading genres. Most of them are dubbed,[165] rather than subtitled, as surveys have revealed that Germans are not particularly fond of subtitles. Some items on the nightly newscasts will come from Eurovision's news exchange, and sports events, too, often originate elsewhere and come to German viewers through Eurovision, although Kirch's sports channel, DSF, holds the rights to increasing numbers of sports events.

Large numbers of foreign channels are available to cable and satellite households, but none commands more than a tiny share of the audience; it's a rare weekly top seven or 10 that includes a single imported show. Germans display a strong preference for their own material. The week of September 16-22, 1997, was typical: for the five major program categories—Newscasts, Light Entertainment, Feature Films, Political-Current Affairs and "Krimis"—listed in the leading TV guide, *Hoer Zu,* four of the top seven films, "Robin Hood" among them, were imported, but nothing else was, although two of the light entertainment programs were based on U.S. funniest video shows.[166]

Radio plays a large number of U.S. and British pop music selections, U.S. jazz and a great deal of classical music from other European nations. Disc jockeys sound livelier and more informal now than they did 30 years ago, which could have its roots in the influence of American Forces Network stations, but is just as likely to be part of the rise of private radio, whose owners often studied U.S. radio styles and have consciously imitated them.

Certain crime shows bear some resemblance to their British and U.S. counterparts. Those on the PSBs are more likely to take after the British model—less violence, more deliberation. The private channel versions are more likely to show U.S. influence, with auto chases, considerable violence, women as victims and pawns. Hospital dramas such as RTL Plus' "OP ruft Dr.

Bruckner" bear a strong resemblance to their up-tempo, conflict-ridden U.S. counterparts such as "ER." The PSB hospital dramas, such as popular "Fuer alle Falle Stephanie," are much warmer, with kindly and ever-attentive doctors and nurses—and those who aren't soon are reformed. Most of the quiz shows carried by the private stations feature much the same sort of bubbly, extroverted male host and attractive female assistant as do quiz shows in other parts of western Europe and North America, and many of them are directly based on (and carry the names of) U.S. quiz shows, with use-of-formula rights paid to the U.S. producers. The PSB quiz shows feature a considerably slower pace and higher intellectual level of questions than do those in the U.S. The talk shows on private stations, e.g., RTL's (formerly on SAT1) "Schreinemakers live," have much the same combination of sensationalism and sentimentality as do their U.S. cousins. Newscasters by and large still don't exhibit the informal, almost conversational approach that characterizes their U.S. colleagues;[167] in fact, the tone is even more formal and sober than it is on British television.

The plots of the more popular prime-time German TV dramas often seem to exhibit more or less stereotypical German characteristics such as the need for thrift or great pride in one's family "line," although the themes may be familiar enough: divorced or divorcing parents having problems with each other and/or with their children, people frustrated in their ambitions to rise higher in society or at work, family members not understanding one another. The few satire programs sometimes contain elements that are cruel, although anyone who has watched such shows as the U.S. "Saturday Night Live" or Japan's "Go Ahead and Laugh" should realize that cruelty certainly shouldn't qualify as an exclusively German stereotype. Nevertheless, ARD's "Schmidt-einander" will show a doctor stubbing out his cigarette on a patient's bloody leg stump. SAT1's "Benissimo" contains skits showing "Doctor Ben" (wearing a pink-red, flowing wig and green gloves, with eyes heavily blackened [in good German cabaret tradition]) demonstrating how to cook, but placing his hands on hot grills, cutting himself, etc.; or, with a policeman as accomplice, setting up a street checkpoint and hauling over young drivers and passengers, accusing them of being "druggies" (with no evidence—just intimidation), knocking them around and stuffing them in the trunks of their cars, while a voice-over describes in solemn, "reportorial" tones what's happening and why society should applaud such diligence.[168]

East Germany

East German broadcasting had to contend with the very powerful influence of West German programming almost from the beginning, which seems to have helped to make East German TV, if not radio, the most professional in quality of production of any of the east European television services. Aside from that influence, there were also the influences of those other east European services. Items furnished through Intervision appeared nightly on TV newscasts, but generally reinforced the tendency in East German broadcast journalism to rely heavily on politically "safe" items such as receptions, arrivals and departures of distinguished visitors and ceremonies marking major events and their anniversaries.

Feature films, too, often came from the other east European nations. Hungarian films often were lively in theme, style of acting and editing, but there was little sign that they influenced East German producers. Instead, East German feature films shown on television bore more resemblance to those made in Czechoslovakia, Bulgaria and Romania: quite somber and plodding, in acting, plot and editing. There were exceptions, such as the popular (in East Germany) Czech series "Hospital at the Edge of Town," which showed two doctors with very different personalities, both of them very human. On the whole, however, the thematic influence of imported shows was more likely to be along the lines of "working on behalf of society," or, in the rare case of imported material from the West, "the decadence of capitalism." In the 1980s, there was a greater tendency for East German TV drama to show characters with more doubts, and in greater conflict with themselves and with others, than had been the case. It's quite likely that both western (especially West German) and eastern (especially Hungarian and Polish) TV drama were partially responsible for the change, although it also may have been one more reflection of a more confident society.

RELATIONS WITH OTHER MEDIA

Newspapers and magazines in Germany furnish considerable coverage of broadcasting. All major papers, and many smaller ones, have broadcast critics who write daily columns. Controversies within stations, which are frequent and which often have, or are alleged to have, political origins, sometimes receive front-page treatment. Condensed broadcast schedules appear in most newspapers, and there are several major and very competitive TV guides, all published by private concerns (some of which have major investments in the electronic media); they carry far more detail on programs than do the papers but rarely provide critical commentary on programs, station politics or any other broadcast-related issues. Instead, their features deal with the lives of stars, how certain programs were made and so on—all "safe" and entertaining topics.

Newspapers long had an abiding fear of broadcasting, and TV in particular, as a source of competition for advertising revenue. Even though broadcast advertising on the public services was restricted to national products and services only, the newspapers feared that this might change, largely for two reasons: Public radio and TV were quite attractive to advertisers, and the stations were in frequent financial difficulty thanks to the high costs of their operation. Fears of competition for advertising revenue were strong enough just after the creation of ZDF that they became the subject of investigation by a federal commission, the first Michel Commission, which reported in 1967. The Michel Commission found those fears to be exaggerated, and strongly recommended against one of the solutions the press had proposed: to be allowed to invest financially in broadcasting.

With the coming of private radio in 1985, the press finally had its opportunity, and most private radio stations feature very heavy investment by the press. RTL Plus and SAT1 are chiefly press investments. Whether this has meant that those services are controlled editorially by the press is another question. Initially, some of the programs on SAT1 reflected those press interests; for instance, a program on fashions was backed by Burda, West Germany's largest fashion magazine publisher. Most of those "publisher's programs" had vanished from SAT1 by mid-1986 because they failed to draw and hold viewers, but some publishers would like to see them reappear, if not on SAT1, then on another satellite service. Some have, but they tend to be programs by opinion magazines such as *Der Spiegel* (Spiegel TV) and *Stern* (Stern TV).

At first, most of the private TV services showed little inclination to produce daily newscasts of any real magnitude; even by mid-1987 the longest on any of them was less than 10 minutes, and there were never more than two per day. Since that time, RTL and SAT1 have developed newscasts that truly compete with ARD and ZDF, and their magazine programs have become somewhat more serious. Pro 7 also is making efforts to establish a better journalistic reputation, but so far its heavy financial investments have brought it little success.

The German film industry has achieved a reputation for provocative, well-produced films in recent years, thanks to the efforts of Wim Wenders, Rainer Fassbinder and Werner Herzog. Those films represent a small percentage of the total output, and in any case are not the sort of fare one expects to see on television. Their themes and styles generally have appeal for select audiences. However, Fassbinder's "Berlin Alexanderplatz" is an outstanding example of a film made for television but clearly just as viable for cinema, which is where it was shown in the United States.

Before private television came along, there was little TV free-lance work available on a scale and with a continuity that would have appealed to most film producers, and there weren't many feature films on public TV. Nevertheless, ARD and ZDF have signed a series of five-year agreements with the Filmforderunganstalt (FFA), starting in 1974, and with pledges in the tens of millions of deutsche marks for coproductions, plus further sums for FFA's own projects.[169] Those agreements are voluntary, but the film industry long has been protected under the terms of the Cinema Promotion Act where cinema owners are concerned: A levy on ticket sales brings in tens of millions of deutsche marks a year. In the mid-1980s, the industry began to lobby to have the act applied to the new private television ventures and to distributors of videocassettes. That eventually led to proposals for a new law requiring such financial support, but it hadn't passed by late 1997, and both the PSBs and the commercial services opposed it.[170] However, some private stations do have contracts with film production companies and make contributions to film funds (particularly in Berlin-Brandenburg, North Rhine-Westphalia and

Bavaria, according to Jochen Zimmer, who furnished me with this information in November 1997).

One respect in which the film and television industries do not appear to agree is on the place of film critic's shows in the television schedule. Up until the early 1980s, there were several film-related shows on ARD and ZDF, such as ARD's "Kennen Sie Kino" (a quiz show about movies) and ZDF's "Neues von Film" ("What's New in Movies"). Most of those shows were dropped, and in late 1987 ARD canceled "Treffpunkt Kino" ("Rendezvous at the Movies") and ZDF announced plans to shorten and change the viewing day of "ZDF Kino-hit-Parade." As the movie industry had seen a considerable decline in production of theatrical films, it became concerned that the chief force in that decline—television—also was cutting back on a type of program that probably attracted a fair share of the movie audience. As Klaus Dahm, head of publicity for Warner Brothers in West Germany, put it, "If the general public is to be kept informed about theatrical films it is one of the networks' *duties* [italics mine] to help in doing that."[171]

The German movie industry began to recover some of its past glory in the early 1990s, helped by the unification of the country. (East German cinemas almost never showed West German films, and vice versa.) By 1993, it was experiencing billion deutsche mark years in receipts, and it's continued to grow, taking in over DM 600 ($400) million in the first half of 1996. Interestingly, the greatest hit of 1996 (and the strongest opening weeks of any film in the history of German cinema) seemed to have been modeled in many ways on the lead characters in the TV shows "Ein Herz, Eine Seele" and "Motzki." "Werner," a cartoon feature-length film, stars a rough-talking, highly opinionated, "haesslicher Trottel" (repulsive idiot). "Werner" soon made his way to television: Pro 7 displayed the film in March 1997, and it was the top-rated animation program for the week, for all but 3–9-year-olds. He may or may not get to star in his own series.[172]

The two industries are linked in another interesting way: The Radio and Television Union and the German Union of Film Workers merged in 1968. One issue taken up by the combined union, now called the Radio-Television-Film Workers' Union, has been better social security for free-lance workers in the broadcast and film media.

INTERNATIONAL COOPERATION

The larger German state stations and ZDF have been able to enter into coproduction agreements with almost every other television service in Europe, although most often with British, French and Italian television; they are more apt to have the money necessary to carry out the large-scale projects that typify coproduction. There also have been several smaller-scale coproductions with the Swiss and Austrian systems, where the very similar cultural heritages and the presence of a common language make such cooperation desirable, natural and fairly easy. The private stations have been far less active in that regard, and even rely to some extent on production houses in smaller nations, e.g., Endemol in the Netherlands, to produce original programs for them.

German public TV services are frequent donors, as well as recipients, in Eurovision's news exchange. The state stations (working through ARD) and ZDF both have correspondents in many foreign countries, and the news budgets are large enough to afford satellite reports from them. As Germany is a major political and economic force in Europe, domestic coverage of events often is in demand by other European TV systems. In 1996, the German PSBs sent over 600 items to the news exchange. German television is also heavily involved in the exchange of sports news through Eurovision.

The ARD and the ZDF services cooperate with the federal government through an agency called TRANSTEL, a nonprofit corporation founded in 1965, to place West German TV programs with foreign systems. Those systems pay fees according to the economic strength of the nation, so Third World countries get TRANSTEL-distributed programs for next to nothing. Roughly a hundred nations receive programs, which range from documentaries about Beethoven to a series of five-minute tips on soccer playing.

THE NEW MEDIA

The city-state of Bremen was set in 1974 to become the first place in Germany to have cable service roughly equivalent to what already was available in North America, Belgium and the Netherlands. In 1974, the mayor of Bremen proposed a three-month cable experiment, largely in one of Bremen's newer housing areas. It would relay existing TV services, but would add a local newscast that would not be available over Radio Bremen. The other state stations were alarmed over this proposal, since it came without warning and presented them with a challenge to their usual ways of thinking about broadcasting. The mayor dropped the plan after speaking with the West German postal minister.[173]

The federal government already had appointed an inquest commission on new media (Commission for the Construction of a Technical Communications System, or KtK) in November 1973, simply because cable and satellite were becoming common topics of discussion all over Europe, and West Germany had a vested interest through its electronics industry in seeing what might develop and be developed. Also, there was the question of jurisdiction: Were cable and satellite broadcast media, in which case the states would regulate them, or were they properly part of the postal service, which was a federal government function? The KtK reported at the end of 1975 and recommended that a few experimental projects be set up in various parts of the country but also made it quite clear where authority over the new media should lie: "Objectively speaking, it is indispensable that the states, which have particular legal responsibilities in the area of broadcasting, come to a decision forthwith on the ... question of supplying programming [for cable]. The construction of the [cable] network depends upon this decision."[174] The federal government, seeing an opportunity to become involved in broadcasting, claimed that the post office should establish and license cable TV, no matter what the KtK report recommended. The states quite naturally contested that claim, but it took 14 years to work out a compromise that would lead to a state cable policy. Once that occurred, cable and satellite services developed rapidly, and, as already noted, Germany has become the largest market in Europe where those media are concerned.

The digitalization of television has come along more slowly than many had expected. There's a shortage of frequency space for TV services, and digital compression is one way around the problem. In summer 1996, the Kirch-financed DF1 digital transmission satellite service began to operate. It might have begun a year earlier, except for the disagreements among its then-likely financial backers, Bertelsmann, Kirch, and, somewhat later, Rupert Murdoch. Bertelsmann, Kirch and Canal Plus already had the analog pay TV Premiere service, but could see the wisdom of going digital. However, Kirch and Bertelsmann had differing ideas on what sort of decoder should be developed, and mistrust between the two (particularly on the part of Bertelsmann) kept an alliance from developing.

When DF1 began service, the Kirch group predicted that it would have 200,000 subscribers by the end of the year. It had only 20,000. Then Murdoch decided in March 1997 not to exercise his option to purchase 49 percent of DF1's shares. Talks between Kirch and U.S. satellite service DirecTV, and with NBC's parent company, General Electric, got nowhere. In July 1997, Kirch and Bertelsmann announced that they had agreed to cooperate in the development of a joint service. Deutsche Telekom, which was in the process of becoming a private company, said that it would agree to providing the new operation with access to the 17 million cabled homes that it served. With the right pricing structure, and presuming that the alliance holds together, the venture may yet succeed.[175] And, once again, there will be alarms raised over yet another example of media concentration.

Videocassette recorders have become common household items in Germany: 62.5 percent of all households had one by the end of 1997. They are used most often to play videocassettes of movies and other prerecorded entertainment and instruction, rather than to record TV programs for later playback. Comedies and action films easily lead other rental categories: they account for over 50 percent of all rentals. Sales of videocassettes moved ahead of rental sales starting in 1993, and have continued to broaden their lead.[176] Concern over the ease with which young people could obtain videocassettes of pornographic and violent material led the federal government in 1985 to pass legislation making it more difficult for young people to rent cassettes. Still, younger viewers are far heavier users of videocassettes than are their elders: a 1996 survey showed that just under 20 percent of those in the 13–19-year-old groups, and just over 13 percent of those aged 20–29, reported viewing videocassettes several times a week, while all other age categories were below—and mostly well below—10 percent. The same survey showed all age groups reporting a rising, and then declining, estimated time budget for minutes spent each day on watching videocassettes over the years 1987-96.[177]

The growth of Internet services in Germany has been hampered by overall lack of interest in personal computers: as of 1996, over 70 percent of all German household didn't have one, and another 24.6 percent didn't have modems. Less than 4 percent subscribed to online services.[178] The latter figure increased considerably by mid-1998, when roughly 3.5 million Germans (over 10 percent of all German households) were subscribers to one or another of four major online services, and 6.6 million Germans 14 and older claimed to use online services at work and/or at home.[178a]

All of the major TV services have web sites with program information, and there have been several ventures into interactive programming, including Kabel 1's interactive game program, "The Hugo Grameshow." NDR (Hamburg) began to place filmed sections of its news programs "Tagesschau" and "Tagesthemen" on the net in August 1996. ZDF's "WISO," a weekly program about the economy, broadcast a virtual reality episode in April 1995, and WDR (Cologne) has experimented with electronic backdrops on its "Computerclub" program. A number of media staff and administrators remain skeptical that the cost of interactivity or virtual reality is justified in terms of what audiences receive that they couldn't obtain by using the telephone, or that really adds to what they get from watching the program without such devices.[178b]

But the experiments continue, and they have a strong orientation toward young Internet users. Hessiche Rundfunk's (Frankfurt) HR3, pop music service, went on line in August 1996, and racked up over 230,000 hits for the month. Other public and private radio stations have gone in the same direction, attracted by prospects for advertising revenue. As commercial Radio RPR's (Ludwigshafen) Program Director Uwe Frigge phrased it, the "medium is absolute hip with advertisers," and a number of his colleagues at other stations see radio and Internet as a natural partnership, while still others add television to the mix. Over 50 broadcasters have websites on the Internet. Whether any of them will draw substantial ad revenue is yet to be seen, but they may help to attract new viewers and listeners.[179]

By 1998, all of the ARD stations and ZDF had their own websites, many of them with RealAudio, all of them with program schedules and details on programming. However, interactive services were still a relative rarity: four of the ARD stations had chat rooms, and two had interactive serial programs, both of them comedies. The 1998 Federal Elections saw ARD and ZDF offering a host of online information services: the latest poll results; direct comparisons of candidate statements on key issues; and information on election campaigns of the past. "Jugendradio Fritz," a service of ORB (Potsdam) for younger listeners, engaged some of them in online discussions of the campaign as it progressed.

Realizing that younger audience members are particularly interested in the Internet, and that they are the potential PBS audience of the future, several of the PBS operations have developed interactive services for them, including discussions of movies, presentations of their own artwork, collective production of radio plays, etc. The most ambitious effort so far is SWR's "Das

Ding" ("The Thing"), a daily program featuring newscasts, a "topic of the week," and pop music. "Das Ding" uses RealAudio, Internet text and conventional TV in different mixtures, and experiments with new ways to combine them most effectively.[180]

Germany gained a sort of Internet-related fame when state and federal prosecutors began to clamp down on individuals and corporations for either providing access or for not doing enough to prevent access to pornography, Nazi-oriented material or material which encourages or appears to encourage terrorist activity, e.g., how to make bombs or derail trains. Perhaps the most famous case so far involved the German head of Compuserve Germany, who was indicted in 1997 for aiding in the distribution of child pornography. The charge was that the company failed to do enough to block Germans from gaining access to such material, as well as pro-Nazi material, coming from U.S.-based servers. A mid-1997 Berlin court judgment dismissed charges against a student for having used her Internet homepage to provide a link to a "forbidden" magazine, *Radikal,* which appeared to advocate terrorist activities. In fact, the magazine was easily obtainable, despite efforts of the German Federal Criminal Office to require all Internet users in the country to block access to its site, because the magazine's supporters then simply copied it onto more than 50 "mirror" sites around the world. Despite the apparent failure of the blockade, state and federal authorities seem determined to continue their efforts.[181]

East Germany

There was no true intermedia competition in East Germany. Film, press, radio and television were regarded as complementary, and they didn't compete for advertising money or for funds from the national budget. The degree of artistic freedom was higher for film than it was for television, and the print media enjoyed slightly more journalistic freedom than did their electronic cousins, but the differences weren't great. The official East German wire service, Allgemeine Deutscher Nachrichten (General German News) supplied both newspapers and broadcasting, and there was great similarity of style and content in press, radio and television presentation of the major news items of the day. East German feature films appeared often on television, and some were quite recent, even though that probably had a negative effect on cinema attendance. The East German film industry was paid for the use of films on TV, but both were government operations, so there was no question of profit.

CONCLUSION

Even though the occupation following World War II resulted in the creation of two very different German nations, one thing seems quite clear: Radio and television served to maintain or establish at least some traditions common to the two. The popularity of a series such as "Schwarzwaldklinik" (a hospital in the countryside, with kind but authoritative doctors) in West Germany and "Hospital at the Edge of Town" in East Germany seemed to have stemmed from a shared taste for sentimentality, goodness and paternalism. There were West and East German "Sandmen" to dispense moral lessons to young viewers. Variety shows often featured comedy routines and songs familiar to German audiences on both sides of the wall. Old German movies appeared regularly on the East German TV schedule (West Germany had fewer of them), and drew many older viewers in the West.

Now that the two Germanies are one, and now that there's a full-fledged dual system in place, the sorts of questions that arise about the future shape of the system are quite different. The West German state-based system was an excellent way of preventing a central government from accumulating and exercising power over the electronic media, but it was and is not economically efficient at the national level. It also took nearly 10 years for the states to agree among themselves on an overall cable-satellite policy, and even then there were the "rear guard battles" fought by Hessen and Bavaria that showed that politics would play a major role with the new media just as politics had played one with the old. At the federal level, the CDU has weighed in heavily on the side of private electronic media services, and in certain respects has been rewarded by them.

The states are divided: those with CDU/CSU leadership take a rather open-market position and (for some of those states) advocate abolishing the ARD's national service—the usual prime-time ratings leader—leaving it with a strengthened Third TV service; those with Socialist (SPD) leadership push for stronger support for public broadcasting, tighter regulation of media concentration and a single, powerful licensing body for commercial broadcasting.[182]

Perhaps it's time for a new approach to regulation—one that takes into account both the new realities of cable, satellite and Internet, and the past realities of a dictatorial central government that brought misery and disaster to so many.

The newer electronic media and the rise of commercial broadcasting also have raised the issue of the level and manner of financing for public broadcasting. The 1994 Supreme Court decision helped to reinforce previous decisions regarding the necessity of maintaining not just the license fee, but a license fee set at high enough levels to permit the state services to carry out their public service functions. The state prime ministers agreed in October 1995 to a "guarantee of existence" for ARD and ZDF over at least the next five years, but required that they increase efforts to "rationalize" their operations.[183] But if the public services were to seek to rationalize by imitating the approaches to programming taken by the commercial services, including the purchase of more foreign programming and the production of less expensive but more formulaic programming, to what extent would the public continue to regard them as *public* services? "Public" often is taken by Germans to mean programming that one can't receive for "free" (which of course it isn't) from private stations. So far, any imitation seems to have run in the other direction, with some of the private services seeking to increase the quality of their news and information programming, as well as drama. Whatever the Supreme Court decides, it will ultimately be public sentiment that either supports the license fee and increases in it, or allows it to languish or disappear. One thing seems certain: the PSBs are likely to have to work even harder in the future to differentiate themselves from private services. More programming for, by and about minorities and women would be one way to ensure distinction, since the private stations aren't likely to do much along those lines. And yet the PSBs can't go too far in that direction, or they're likely to antagonize mainstream viewers. It will be an interesting challenge for the public sector.

Finally, there is media concentration. It may or may not be regarded as a potential danger by the German public in the future; up until now, it hasn't appeared to be all that threatening. A new "watchdog" agency, the Kommission zur Ermittlung der Konzentration im Medienbereich (KEK) began in 1997 to examine cases where there were concerns about media concentration. While it's too early to tell how effective it will be, there have been a few early signs that it might be inclined to favor private industry.[183a]

But if a "media baron" with more subtlety than Leo Kirch and wealth to match were to emerge,[184] the potential for public influence would be tremendous, since the present media conglomerates seem to be drawing closer and closer together—driven in part by the simple fact that most of the private TV services continue to lose money (only RTL Plus and Pro 7 had begun to show positive balances by the end of 1996, and the worst-off service, DSF [sports], had aggregate losses of DM 750 million ($470 million) since its debut as Tele 5).[185] The media councils may be out of their depth in attempting to regulate the private sector. They could play something of a watchdog role in alerting the public to any media baron interference, as may the print media (if *they* can retain their editorial independence), but viewers and listeners will have to judge for themselves. It will be an interesting challenge for the public.

5 The Soviet Union and Russia

From Communism to Capitalism?

Despite exceptionally difficult economic, geographic and linguistic conditions, the U.S.S.R. and Russia have managed to bring radio and television to the great majority of their citizens.[1] What that population saw and heard during Soviet times often differed sharply from what western European and North American audiences received from their electronic media, because the Soviet government saw those media as important instruments in creating a Communist society. Yet the Soviet system wasn't unchanging or unresponsive to public opinion, nor were its broadcasts an unending stream of praise for the Communist way of life. Much of the programming was far less ideological than that. Pressures that led to programming changes came from a variety of sources, some internal, some external. The basic structural form didn't change from the early 1930s to the early 1990s, but it did possess a certain measure of dynamism.

When the U.S.S.R. began to break apart in the early 1990s, the electronic media played important roles, both as mirrors of change and as pawns in various power struggles. Once the breakup was complete, the Russian Federation inherited most of the old Soviet structure, and its leaders began to reshape it. They opened the electronic media to competition, but it wasn't competition in the sense that most westerners use the term. Certain Soviet traits remained, including a readiness to tell media supervisors what the government wanted them to carry and what it didn't. Still, the competition has been sufficient to provide Russians, or at least those living in and near the larger cities, a degree of program choice that they had never had in the Soviet era, and sometimes a wider range of political viewpoints, as well. Whether audiences are happy with what they hear and see is another question.

BASIC FACTORS

Geographic

The vastness of the Soviet Union was difficult to grasp. To say that it occupied a sixth of the world's land area still sounds quite abstract. To make it more concrete, think in terms of time zones: There were 11 across the U.S.S.R., which meant that it would be early afternoon in Moscow when it was very early morning of the next day in Vladivostok. That is true of the Russian Republic, as well, even though it's roughly 30 percent smaller than the U.S.S.R. Large as it was, the U.S.S.R. had a population perhaps 13 percent greater than that of the continental United States, which is little more than one-third the size of the former Soviet Union. Anyone who has traveled through the western part of the United States knows that there are long stretches of land with very few people. A traveler in Siberia experiences much the same sensation, magnified three times! Furthermore, the climate often is hostile: The land mass lies farther north than does the United States, and large portions of the country are in the grip of winter for almost half of each year.

Those conditions have led to a very uneven distribution of population. Roughly three-quarters of all Soviet citizens lived in the western ("European") U.S.S.R., which made up about one-fifth of the total land area. There also was a sharp increase in urbanization: Roughly three-fourths of the people lived in rural areas in the early 1920s, whereas less than a third were rural dwellers as of the late 1980s. The U.S.S.R. attempted to control population distribution by limiting the issuance of work permits for positions in the more popular cities such as Moscow, Kiev and Leningrad, and by offering inducements such as higher salaries and better housing in the less desirable areas, especially Siberia, but many individuals found ways to live in the more popular areas, anyway. The situation for the Russian Republic is almost identical, and large cities are experiencing increasing amounts of pressure on already overcrowded housing.

For such a large country, the Soviet Union had relatively few neighbors, in part because the Arctic Ocean forms most of the long northern border, the northern Pacific Ocean much of the eastern border, and the People's Republic of China a large part of the southern border. The Russian Federation has more neighbors, largely because the other Soviet republics now are independent. Most of the larger cities are some distance from the borders, so there is limited spillover of broadcast signals that any substantial number of Russian citizens could receive. (International broadcasts and Internet services from more distant nations are a different matter.) Yet another factor that reduces the effect of any spillover of signals is the uniqueness of the Russian language itself: There is limited similarity with Czech, Bulgarian and Polish, and almost none with any other language used in a neighboring country, although the former Soviet republics continue to provide some broadcasts in Russian.

Demographic

In the years before the breakup of the Soviet Union, a visitor to Moscow on May Day or on the anniversary of the October Revolution could receive a graphic demonstration of the demographic diversity of the U.S.S.R. Not only did the flags of the various Soviet republics fly all around Red Square, but also Moscow's streets were crowded with people from all over the country, many of them brought to the capital as honored guests for outstanding service performed on behalf of society. There were reindeer herders from the far north, Uzbeks from central Asia, Ukrainians and many others, all of whom could speak Russian more or less well (it was the chief language of instruction for the entire Soviet educational system) but many of whom might have been more comfortable speaking Tadzik, Uighur or any of the 110 languages other than Russian that were in use somewhere or other in the country. Because Russian was spoken throughout the country, and because the languages other than Russian usually were spoken only within a particular region, broadcasting faced a difficult but not insuperable task. Russian could be used for broadcasts throughout the country, with the other languages employed within particular geographical regions. In that way, the many peoples of the U.S.S.R. could maintain their sense of cultural identity and at the same time be part of the entire nation.

Quite apart from its role in helping to build a sense of national unity out of what was a highly diverse mixture of cultures and nations, the universal employment of Russian in education and in broadcasting had another purpose: It permitted the national government to send "greater Russians" (the usual term for citizens of the Russian Soviet Federated Socialist Republic [RSFSR], largest by far of all of the 15 Soviet republics and, since 1991, the Russian Federation) to work in government, education and other fields in the other republics. That further encouraged the use of Russian throughout the country, although some have claimed that it also indicated greater Russian insecurity and/or arrogance—an unwillingness to trust those who weren't greater Russians to perform the really important tasks of society. There were Ukrainians, Georgians, Byelorussians and other "nongreater Russian" national groups represented in positions of high national responsibility, but the central Asian national groups, which were the fastest growing of all in terms of population, were far less evident at that level.

There was some disagreement over just how unified the Soviet Union ever was. There were many manifestations of cultural diversity in folk music, literature and other art forms, much of which came to the entire nation over radio and television, so that most Soviet citizens were well aware of the great variety of cultures in their country. The political histories of the various regional groups, especially those with some tradition of national independence (e.g., Latvia, the Ukraine), generally weren't that well-known outside or even within the region itself. Broadcasting rarely portrayed political diversity. Soviet authorities probably saw political diversity, even within the overall framework of communism, as less compatible with national unity than was cultural diversity.

The Russian Republic may not be as diversified as was the U.S.S.R., but it isn't far behind. However, the remaining ethnic minorities are far smaller population groups than were the Uzbeks, Kirghiz, Ukrainians and others identified with the former republics. Most of them also were under czarist Russian rule for centuries, and some built up deep and abiding resentment of their Russian rulers during that time. Current problems in Chechnya, Ingushetsia and other Russian hot spots in the 1990s have deep historical roots.

Economic

The Soviet Union had a fairly high percentage of its population employed on the land: About one-fourth worked in agriculture, forestry and fishing. Farms were state-operated collectives, but increasing numbers of farmers tended private plots in their spare time and often sold their excess produce to supplement their incomes. Business and industry, too, were state-operated, but people in certain lines of work, especially anything having to do with machine repairs, sometimes found ways of moonlighting in order to supplement their incomes and often expected payment in material goods rather than in money. Private enterprise wasn't an official part of the economy, but it served an important function for consumers.

Because of a rather poor transportation infrastructure and frequent harsh or uncertain climatic conditions, the Soviet economy often turned in uneven performances, and manufactured and agricultural goods often had to be imported. Nevertheless, government propaganda steadily urged Soviet citizens to work to overcome those difficulties, even though rewards in the form of direct benefits to their lives weren't all that apparent. When there were improvements, perhaps in the increased construction of housing units, broadcasting and the other media were sure to highlight them. The media might or might not mention economic setbacks, but there would be an accompanying explanation of the circumstances, and an indication that things were almost certain to improve, especially if people redoubled their efforts.

The Soviet Union went farther than did most nations in linking broadcasting and the major occupations. Many of the collective farms had their own radio operations, as did a fair number of the larger factories. There were special programs on the larger stations at the national and republic levels for teachers. News and light entertainment programs regularly featured people who were engaged in some form of work and usually provided numerous details on the nature of that work, its value to the nation and so on, often in boring detail. Broadcasting also informed citizens of the country's overall economic progress, often related in highly detailed figures and, in the case of television, with pictures of tractors in the fields, sheets of steel rolling through factories, fish hauled in by the netful, a new rail line coursing through Siberia. (But the footage sometimes looked suspiciously similar to earlier footage of sheets of steel, tractors in fields, etc.)

The economy of the Russian Federation presents a radical departure from Soviet practices. Private enterprise may not dominate every sector of the economy, but it's well-established in many of them. Outside investment, particularly from the Soviet Union's former capitalist adversaries, is welcome, at least officially; the maze of laws and requirements regulating economic activities, and the involvement of the Russian Mafia in various investment schemes and protection rackets, have discouraged many such would-be investors. Rampant inflation has hurt the country, as well, although the ruble began to stabilize as of the late 1990s. Even without the other former Soviet republics, the Russian Federation has considerable mineral wealth and technological expertise, and is a potential major industrial power. However, high unemployment and a desire for some of the stability, if not prosperity, of Soviet times, has contributed to the unstable atmosphere that pervades national life.

Cultural

As already mentioned, the cultural diversity of the Soviet Union was great, and broadcasting played a major role in displaying and promoting it. The traditions behind that diversity were religious, feudal and many other things that were discouraged or even forbidden by the Soviet government, but the songs, dances, folktales, costumes and other cultural manifestations often continued with the government's blessing and even encouragement. Often they were placed in a "correct" Soviet context: Viewers of a TV program featuring old Kirghiz songs and dances were quite likely to be told of the economic oppression, the male chauvinism, the blind devotion to religious leaders that characterized the society of those songs and dances. They also were told how much better things were in the present-day Kirghiz Republic. But the songs and dances occupied center stage, because they so vividly displayed the U.S.S.R.'s rich cultural tradition and the concern of the government that the tradition be preserved. Furthermore, they were a lot more enjoyable to hear and see than was a boring talk about how communism promoted cultural diversity.

There were certain aspects of Soviet cultural life that were common in other countries but rare in the U.S.S.R. The Soviet Union was an atheist nation, so of course there was no state church. That didn't mean that people had no freedom to worship, and there were churches, synagogues and mosques throughout the country, with fair numbers of believers present on days of worship. But those religious institutions couldn't operate their own schools or recruit members, and couldn't convey any messages that could be considered as even remotely anti-Communist. Furthermore, people willing to identify themselves as believers often found it difficult to rise to positions of major responsibility in government, industry or education, all of which were government-run. Attacks upon religion through the media became less frequent over time, but it wasn't that uncommon even in the late 1980s to see a television play in which a character held notably "backward" religious views.

Certain kinds of foreign music were discouraged by the Soviet government until the 1960s. Jazz and rock music in particular were rare to nonexistent on the Soviet airwaves until the late 1960s, when Soviet rock and jazz groups, which had been playing for years in nightclubs in some of the large cities, began to appear live and in recordings over Soviet radio and TV. Even the western groups which served as models for the Soviet groups now appeared occasionally on music request programs. Jazz and rock had been regarded earlier as symbols of western decadence, but international broadcasters such as the Voice of America (VOA) and the BBC found plenty of listeners, younger ones in particular, ready to hear the "decadent" messages of the Beatles, Elvis Presley and the Rolling Stones. Some of the more modern forms of classical music, especially that of the twelve-tone school (Arnold Schoenberg, Anton Webern) and of Igor Stravinsky and the neoclassicists, were discouraged for the same basic reason. The fact that Stravinsky had been born and raised in Russia (czarist Russia, to be sure) and that some of the objectionable works were by Soviet composers (Prokofiev, Shostakovich), mattered not at all. That, too, changed in the 1960s, in part as a result of the relaxation in cultural vigilance that followed Soviet Premier Josef Stalin's death in 1953.

Russia itself has a very rich literary and musical tradition, and broadcasting was used from the earliest days to bring books, drama, poetry, opera, orchestral concerts and vocal and chamber music recitals to a wider public. Some works were by Soviet writers and composers; others came from czarist Russian artists. The national broadcast services placed heavy emphasis on works written in Russian, although works by Georgians, Kirghiz and other nationalities also appeared in translation. The republic services frequently featured the works of native writers, and national and republic broadcast services offered many dramatizations of novels studied in secondary schools. Even the cultural broadcasts for the general public were quite apt to contain a fair amount of explanation of a major literary or musical work; the process of education didn't stop with the end of formal schooling, and broadcasting was one of the most efficient ways in which to continue it. There were plenty of foreign musical and literary works, too, although sometimes they were selected for their ideological content, such as the protest novels and poetry of U.S. black writers.

Education was a universal right, and school attendance was compulsory to age 17, in theory (full secondary education facilities were lacking in some rural areas). Adult education was strongly encouraged; factories, collective farms and large businesses often made special provision for their employees to continue their formal education during their working hours. Radio and TV played major roles in both types of education, and primary and secondary schools, farms and factories made considerable use of them. Many Soviet citizens also pursued self-education at home, and here, too, television and radio were important. Broadcasting of university-level courses was much less common.

Most of that emphasis on culture and education through the electronic media disappeared with the collapse of the Soviet Union. The aggressive commercialism that dominates the airwaves of the Russian Federation leaves little room for material that isn't likely to attract sizable audiences. Furthermore, the chief emphasis in Russian-produced entertainment programming is on life in Russia's largest cities; life in the rural areas is largely ignored, even in the programming of stations in small cities.

Political

The Soviet Union did not feature a multiparty system of government. There was only one party—the Communist Party of the Soviet Union (CPSU)—and voters had the choice of voting for its candidates or leaving their ballots blank. There was little distinction between government and party. A given individual could speak as a government official or as a party member; the message might be the same, but remarks coming from someone claiming to represent the party, or perceived as doing so, usually carried more weight than remarks made by someone speaking as a government official. There was a perception of greater collective weight behind party statements, which often were thrashed out in high-level meetings before they were released to the public. Government officials might speak off-the-cuff (and off-the-record), but that would have been rare behavior for a party official speaking as a member of the party. But caution was the hallmark of all officials, and it could take hours or even days for government or party to decide how it wished to respond to a situation. Until there was an official response, the mass media remained silent, even though broadcasts coming from outside the country were covering the event in considerable detail.

Government functioned at several levels in the Soviet Union: national, republic, district and local. Its basic organization at any one level was the same throughout the country, even though the various parts of the country had featured many different approaches to government before they all were consolidated in the Soviet Union. Any responsible position in government was almost certain to be filled by a member of the CPSU (only about 5 percent of the population belonged to the party). The same was true of industry, the collective farms and the mass media. That unity of party and government with the economy and the media ensured rapid and widespread dissemination of party decisions, although it couldn't ensure that it would lead to the desired actions. People with complaints about the way in which things were working, all the way from the difficulty of purchasing the right kinds of light bulbs to accusations of graft or fraud on the part of a manager of a large factory, were supposed to present them to local officials, who would decide whether they should be passed on to higher authorities or not. Again, catching the attention of a party member generally got faster results than did working through government officials, who probably would check with the party before acting, anyway. Many Soviet citizens resorted to the media to voice their complaints, through letters to the editor and radio and TV call-in shows, although most complaints surfacing through those channels tended to be minor ones, and they might or might not get action. (It often helped if the newspaper printing the letter was an official organ of the Communist Party.)

Both government and party officials made heavy use of the broadcast media to communicate with the general public, although, as in most nations, the communication flowed overwhelmingly in one direction: from the top down. Probably there was more of such communication in the Soviet Union than in most other nations: Very few days went by without several official statements carried by radio and television, most of them originally written for publication in the print media and too long, detailed and formal to be effective when read on air. Many nongovernmental groups that worked closely with government—trade unions, teacher's associations, young people's organizations such as the Young Pioneers—also used broadcasting quite regularly to communicate with their members and to inform nonmembers of what they were doing to aid the progress of Soviet society. Broadcasting definitely was seen by officials as an important part of the apparatus of governance. Whether the governed saw it in a similar light was another matter.

The political complexion of the Russian Federation has been very different in many respects, but quite similar in others. Russia is a multiparty parliamentary democracy, with a host of political parties ranging from tiny to large and from extreme nationalist to radical socialist. Most of them have at least a few former Communists in their ranks, and the Communist Party of the Russian Republic bears a strong ideological resemblance to the old CPSU. The Russian Parliament, or Duma, has considerably more power than did the Supreme Soviet, but the Russian presidency has considerably more power than does the Duma. The electronic media are supposed to furnish free airtime to all political parties represented in Parliament, in rough proportion to their strength, but the Yeltsin administration generally is able to obtain airtime when it wishes and, aside from election periods, often can block other parties from using the airwaves. In that respect, the tactics of Yeltsin and his followers seem somewhat reminiscent of Soviet days, when the Communists had total control over the media. But now the Communists find themselves on the outside looking in.

Technological

The Soviet Union inherited a czarist Russian economy that was beginning to industrialize, but that had not moved ahead very rapidly in terms of communications technology. As you'll see, Soviet leader Vladimir Lenin invested heavily in the rapid development of radio broadcasting. Several decades later, the Soviet Union stunned the world by launching the first communications satellite (Sputnik, 1957), although its only signal was a simple beep. By the mid-1960s, the nation had developed satellite services which brought the major population centers from east to west into instant electronic contact. (I recall watching the major evening news program, "Vremya," in my 1970 visit to Moscow and asking an academic colleague at Moscow State University why a seemingly meaningless news item from Vladivostok—an admiral discussing preparations for a naval maneuver of the Far Eastern Fleet—was included in the newscast. "Because it reminds us how marvelous it is that we can see things in real time from one end of the country to the other" was his somewhat facetious reply.) But the U.S.S.R. was slow to pick up on the newer media services such as cable, videocassettes, fax and computer networks, which some authorities on the Soviet media (Ganley, Mickiewicz, Shane) feel influenced the demise of the Soviet Union in 1991.

Russia has been somewhat more receptive to technological development, and that has included opening the telecommunications system to modest outside (largely European and North American) investment. It also has involved disentangling (or attempting to do so) the rather confusing combinations of ministerial controls over space technology, licensing and other facets of a telecommunications system that grew in somewhat haphazard ways during the Soviet era. Still, the Yeltsin administration has been careful to retain a high level of government control over the technological sector of the economy, and has retained a number of the same administrative units, such as Minsviazi (the Ministry of Communications).[2]

The Soviet Union

A BRIEF HISTORY

In the period before the Russian Revolution of 1917, there was considerable experimentation with wireless transmission in Russia, and in fact the Soviet Union claims that a Russian, Alexander Popov, was the first individual to demonstrate wireless transmission of a signal (code, not voice). Popov did conduct a number of impressive experiments as early as 1895, but like the other father of radio, Marconi, he was not interested in developing anything resembling radio broadcasting for the general public. By the time of the First World War, Russia had wireless transmission stations and receiving stations for the army and navy.

When Lenin returned to Russia to lead what eventually would be called the Bolshevik Revolution, he already had had experience in working with newspapers. As he learned more about wireless transmission, he became excited about the prospects for a "newspaper without paper and without boundaries." He saw radio as a way to communicate with Russia's masses, many of them illiterate and unorganized. Radio could bypass illiteracy and could help to unite a nation that was made up of so many disparate parts.[3] He encouraged transmission experiments that already were underway at a laboratory in Nizhni-Novgorod (about 150 miles east of Moscow). During the revolution itself, he used radio to communicate the Bolshevik call to revolution to military personnel and to foreign countries, although it's probable that the message was carried in Morse code. He even devoted a portion of the country's scarce gold reserve to those experiments. Concerts, talks and readings were broadcast starting in August 1922, over a 12-kilowatt transmitter (the largest in the world at the time) that had just been installed in Moscow; Lenin had high hopes that it would reach most of the country. He also was anxious to overcome the negative influence of non-Communist teachers by using radio to present the instruction of the few Communist teachers available.[4]

Interestingly, Lenin did not establish radio broadcasting as a department of the government or as a function of the Communist Party. He seemed content to let it develop along its own lines, provided that they were compatible with the overall Communist philosophy. Radio amateurs were active in the Soviet Union at the time—already there were hundreds of them—and they were encouraged by the government because their experiments and their reactions to the broadcasts coming from the Nizhni-Novgorod transmitter were invaluable for the development of broadcast technology. Some of those amateurs set up their own stations. So did trade unions, collective farms and other elements of Soviet society. The official station founded in 1924 was to be supported and administered through a joint-stock operation, with teachers and trade unions subscribing the stock. There were at least two other stations in Moscow as of the mid-1920s. The party took considerable interest in them, but didn't dictate their contents at first, although a series of orders and decrees from the Central Committee between 1925 and 1927 made it clear that the party wanted close coordination and supervision of agitation and propaganda broadcasting.[5] However, stations around the country remained responsible for their own programming—there was as yet no network—and the carrying out of those decrees and orders probably differed from station to station.

Lenin and the staff at the Nizhni-Novgorod laboratory realized that the manufacture of individual radio receivers would be slow to develop, partly because of the country's tight economic situation, partly because so few households were electrified. Loudspeakers placed in public squares and public buildings were one answer, and Lenin called for their manufacture and installation. A few were placed in service for special events as early as 1921. Wired radio, roughly similar to cable TV, seemed to offer a solution, too, and again Lenin took great interest in that development. The first wired radio installation was made in Moscow in 1925; within three years there were over a hundred such installations, most of them in cities in the European part of the U.S.S.R. Usually they relayed the signals of broadcast stations, but occasionally they originated their own material—a practice that grew as the years passed. By 1928 there were between 25 and 65 of them (Soviet sources disagree on the exact number). Again, most of the stations were in the European part of the country and in larger cities; the rural areas and most of the Asian U.S.S.R. were very poorly served by radio.

If Lenin had lived longer (he died in 1924), it's entirely possible that radio would have developed at a faster rate. He had great hopes for it and frequently saw to it that those who were developing it received special treatment in food, money and supplies (particularly fuel, very scarce in the Soviet Union in those days). But after his death the radio technicians appeared to fall from favor, as Lenin's successor, Josef Stalin, and his closest associates seemed far less interested in the medium than Lenin had been. The radio amateurs continued to promote it, and the newspapers gave it considerable publicity. It was used by many different groups to communicate news of their activities to their own members, and in 1926 the Central Committee of the Communist Party ordered stations to broadcast workers' news once a day and farmers' news three or four times a week. Some stations went further: Leningrad carried news programs for children, students, soldiers, Young Pioneer and Komsomol members. Some of these groups even developed their own radio reporters. Such practices led to a fractionalization of the broadcast day but caused more people to become more involved with radio.

In addition to the many news programs, radio also provided a great deal of music, ranging from folk and popular to classical. Lenin, Trotsky and other Soviet leaders felt that it was necessary to bring culture to "the masses," and more than one musician or actor spent a lot of time in the early 1920s giving performances in factories and farms, sometimes in unheated buildings in the dead of winter! Radio made it much easier to reach the masses, and phonograph records as well as live performances formed a major part of the broadcast schedule. Russian works predominated, although gradually the Ukraines, Georgians and others began to hear their own music, drama and poetry. Other forms of entertainment were in short supply or nonexistent. Radio wasn't considered an entertainment medium; it was for the enlightenment of its listeners, and often for their instruction in the rights and obligations of members of a Communist society. That was radio's *agitation* function, in the Soviet use of the term: broad cultivation of the correct ways of thinking among the masses.

Radio had another function, which the Soviets called *propaganda*. Propaganda was more sophisticated than agitation and was aimed at narrower segments of the public, especially party workers, who were expected to take propaganda messages and adapt them in ways that would make them more palatable and more understandable to the masses. Certain broadcasts were intended for that specific purpose; although other listeners could tune in, it is doubtful that most of them would have found the subject matter very interesting, and the programs often were quite long.[6]

In 1928, the post office took over the operation of the Moscow radio station, and, through a Central Radio Committee, supervised other radio stations in the country. The Central Radio Committee was closely linked with the Central Committee of the Communist Party, and in 1933 the radio system was removed from the post office and placed under the direct supervision of the Council of People's Commissars, or cabinet. Day-to-day direction of operations was carried out by the All-Union Radio Committee, whose chair became a cabinet member, although of relatively low rank. The tightening of control over radio during the period 1925-33 was no surprise to anyone familiar with Stalin's tactics. While he paid lip service to the idea of semi-independent republics within the Soviet Union and semi-independent people's councils, or soviets, he was far more comfortable with centralization and moved to achieve it as rapidly as possible. Lenin might have done the same, although he appeared to be somewhat more tolerant and even encouraging of diversity than was Stalin, who saw the press, and by extension broadcasting, as a way of ensuring that "the thread from the party, through the newspaper, extends to all worker and peasant districts without exception, so that the interaction of the party and state, on the one hand, and industrial and peasant districts, on the other, is complete." His "interaction" was a one-way street, and he did not want to see the press used to disseminate alternate viewpoints arising within the party, lest that damage the party's "iron discipline."[7]

Despite centralization, radio was carrying more and more entertainment, such as sports (the first test broadcast of a soccer match came in 1929) and programs that mixed music, weather reports, responses to listener's questions and brief news bulletins. But there was a centralization of news, through the creation in 1932 of a central editorial bureau; no longer would there be a host of largely uncoordinated news broadcasts for different segments of the audience. And now that there was a fair-sized body of Communist literature, music and other cultural material, in 1932 the Central Committee created an Artist's Union of Workers for Cultural Broadcasting, to ensure the use of radio for the promulgation of "socialist realism" (the dignity of labor, the rejection of individualism, etc.). Radio also began in 1928 to provide educational broadcasts for the masses, under the broad title of "the radio university," although the "courses" offered didn't carry academic credit.

Radio reception remained a problem. There were fewer than 1.5 million sets in the country by 1932, and all but about 100,000 of them were wired radio receivers, which were limited to picking up whatever the 4,800 wired radio central exchanges provided (which usually was the Moscow station or a major republic station, but not both at the same time, since the service was limited to one channel in those days). Most of the exchanges and receivers were located in the European part of the country, and villages, where the bulk of the population still lived, had just under 26 percent of the receivers as of 1932. There were various calls in the five-year plans starting in 1929 for the increased construction of transmitters, studio equipment and receivers, but progress was slow: By 1937 there were some 3.75 million receivers and over 9,000 wired radio exchanges, but only 321,000 radio sets capable of receiving a variety of signals. Such sets were especially needed in Siberia, where there were few stations or exchanges, but few Siberians had them. And the villages were slipping in terms of the percentage of receivers located there, from 26 percent in 1932 to 23 percent in 1937. In part that may have been a reflection of increasing urbanization in the Soviet Union, but many thousands of villages in the country remained without radio service.

Throughout the 1930s, broadcasting was dominated by the Moscow service, which steadily assumed the function of the central station in a network. Most of the republics had their own stations by that time—Byelorussia, the Ukraine, Azerbaijan and Kazakhstan all had them by 1927—and those stations all broadcast in the major languages of the republic, as well as Russian. But the Russian services were relays of Moscow, and the All-Union Radio Committee, working through radio committees at the republic level, ensured that the medium would be used properly. Most of the wired relay exchanges originated very little of their own material, and some originated nothing at all. Still, control was not completely effective, and many radio officials were criticized for their lack of emphasis on "pointed Bolshevik material" and overemphasis on "objective" or "trivial" news items.[8] A few officials were removed from stations in the Ukraine, Byelorussia and elsewhere on charges of "nationalism" (meaning, for instance, that they overemphasized Ukrainian or Byelorussian nationalism).[9] The wired radio exchanges, too, sometimes decided for themselves whether they wanted to carry some of the material coming from Moscow, and the All-Union Radio Committee in 1935 issued a decree that had the effect of limiting the freedom of the exchanges to select programs. In fact, the majority of the exchanges were forbidden the privilege of originating any programs whatsoever.[10] And in 1939, the Radio Committee publication Radiofront called for "a more unified direction of radio broadcasting,"[11] which indicates that some still felt the system to be too tolerant of differences.

World War II

At the outbreak of World War II in 1939, the Soviet Union still could afford to relax, since the country was not involved in the war. Some predicted that it surely would become involved sooner or later, but almost nothing was done to prepare for that possibility. Where radio was concerned, that proved to be a costly mistake. The country continued to rely heavily upon wired exchanges, which had the decided advantage of keeping enemy messages from the ears of the people; no relay exchange operator was likely to pick up and relay broadcasts from the Nazis, British or any other foreign service without explicit permission to do so. (It had been illegal since 1924 for a listener to record and disseminate foreign broadcasts, but it wasn't yet illegal to listen to them.)[12] Since wired receivers outnumbered standard radio sets by more than five to one as of 1940, there were few people around the country who had any real choice in what they listened to. But wired receivers became a liability when Germany declared war on the U.S.S.R. in June 1941 and moved rapidly across Byelorussia, the Ukraine and much of the European part of the Russian Republic, gaining control of the wired exchanges as they did so. People in many villages had not a single standard set among them, so they were cut off from the rest of the country, and the Germans, when they wished, used the exchanges to disseminate their own messages. The Moscow station almost immediately added broadcasts in Ukraine, Byelorussian and other languages to its schedule, but few people were in a position to hear them.

The Soviet government decided early in the war that it would be better not to take any chances that people in the unoccupied parts of the country listen to foreign broadcasts, so it confiscated all standard radio sets in private hands. Possession of a private set and, worse yet, listening to foreign broadcasts, were crimes punishable by special wartime laws. Soviet citizens listened through wired exchanges or in public places, where extra loudspeakers were installed. After the war, sets were returned to their owners.

Wartime programming continued in the same vein as before the war, but with certain added features, such as messages from and to front-line military personnel, instructions and morale boosters for guerrilla fighters active in the Nazi-occupied areas, dramas and documentaries on the acts of individual heroes, and a good deal of specially composed patriotic music. But many of the standard orchestral works continued to be broadcast, most of them Russian or Soviet, and music took up about a third of total airtime. Much of the music was provided by live ensembles; the Moscow station, as well as many of the republic stations, had their own folk, popular and classical orchestras and choruses and also commissioned many original works. A BBC Monitoring Service Report on the Moscow Municipal Network, a wired radio service, vividly describes the nature and purposes of that service:

> With the exception of some music there is nothing which has not a direct bearing on the war. Clearly the intention is to impress upon listeners the fact that this war is a total war rather than to make them forget the horrors of the struggle and to provide relaxation. Considerable time is devoted to reports of military operations, descriptions of acts of bravery occupying a prominent place. Partisan activity has come increasingly to the foreground during the recent months, and the heroic spirit of the Soviet people in the present struggle is illustrated by numerous examples.[13]

One might question how much effect radio had on public morale during the war, simply because not many individuals had access to it under conditions where they could concentrate on its messages. Public listening areas weren't conducive to concentration, and wired exchanges were not universal. Furthermore, a number of them were out of service in the early war years because of lack of spare parts. The larger cities were better off in that respect, and there radio may have had some impact, especially in Leningrad, which remained under siege for over 900 days, yet was able to keep its radio station in operation throughout and used it to sustain morale by passing along messages of support from the rest of the country and the free world.

From Stalin to Khruschev

At the end of the war, the Soviet Union was economically devastated but probably more psychologically unified than it ever had been. The war seemed to have pulled the diverse population together in a way that no previous action by the government—collectivization of farms, purges of "dissident" elements—ever had done. Radio service was restored quickly to the villages and cities of the western U.S.S.R., some parts of which had been under German occupation from 1941 to 1944. The radio industry had begun to produce more equipment for the wired exchanges by the end of 1942, and in the next three years 1,800 new exchanges were established, but few standard radio sets were manufactured during the war. By 1945, the industry was able to gear up for peacetime production, and the manufacture of both wired and wireless receivers was a high priority. The government continued to place great emphasis on the former, since wired receivers were so inexpensive and since many villages still did not have exchanges, but it was clear that standard receiving sets were in high demand, too. For those with standard sets, the choice of domestic services still was very limited: the national service from Moscow and one or two republic services, in most cases.

Nor did the programming change radically following the war. The special wartime programs were dropped, of course, but examples of heroism and sacrifice were not: Listeners were reminded daily of how much the country had suffered during the war, of how much they owed to those who defended the motherland, and of the need for eternal vigilance and readiness to detect and oppose any future military threat. It was implied, and sometimes stated outright, that the country faced further sacrifices in the form of continued high expenditures for military purposes, with fewer consumer goods than people might feel entitled to now that the war was over. Programs about the war remained a major and constant feature of Soviet broadcasting, although the message about the need for continued sacrifice in the form of better standards of living gradually began to be handled more subtly or even dropped completely.

Stalin's preoccupation with maintaining the "iron discipline" of the party seemed to have increased after the war, and some of his close associates rode herd on the mass media to ensure their purity. A. A. Zhdanov, a high-ranking party member, attacked several Soviet composers in 1948 for writing music that was too formal, academic and tuneless for the people, and radio stations not only had to rid their record libraries of "offensive" works, but also try to anticipate whether any new work might upset some high party official. But the increased manufacture of standard sets—there were just under 500,000 of these at the end of the war, but over 3.6 million by 1950—made it easier for people to listen to broadcasts from foreign countries, which no longer was illegal.

Some of those sets could receive shortwave broadcasts, since the Moscow station used shortwave as well as long- and mediumwave transmitters, and Great Britain, the United States and a few other countries were broadcasting to the Soviet Union in Russian by the late 1940s. Those stations often carried a wider range of music than did the Soviet domestic services and began to add more and more popular music that Soviet radio would not carry because it was too "decadent" and "capitalistic." They also carried a great deal of news that was not available to Soviet listeners, either, and began to attract the attention of the Soviet government in two forms: increased arrests of people who allegedly passed along to others what they had heard over the BBC, VOA or some other unfriendly station, and jamming (electronic interference) of the signals of those stations. At the same time, people were warned of the dangers of listening to such stations, sometimes in highly colorful terms: "Many rusty nationalist hooks with rotting maggots have been thrown into the ether by our bitter enemies in the hope that maybe some fool will bite. And unfortunately there are those who then go and talk, and repeat all manner of lies."[14]

As the "cold war" between the western and Communist worlds set in, foreign stations increased in number and in amount of broadcast hours in Russian, and a few began to add broadcasts in Ukraine, Byelorussian and other major languages of the Soviet Union. Radio Liberty, a U.S. government-supported (Central Intelligence Agency) station based in Munich, carried as many as 17 Soviet languages, including a 24-hour-a-day service in Russian. During most of the 1950s, the Soviet Union stepped up its attempts to block listening to the stations through increased arrests, warnings and jamming. However, toward the end of the decade certain officials, including Premier Nikita Khruschev, issued calls, usually through the Communist Party, for Soviet broadcasting to fight back by offering a better product—more complete and up-to-date newscasts, more interesting announcers, a wider range of music. But reforms were slow to appear, and the party continued its criticism, as in this commentary in the party's leading theoretical journal, Kommunist: "There is often little information, insufficient commentary in our newspapers and on radio to help understand current policies. In our time, when radio receivers are in almost every home, to ignore this or that event, to fail in pointing it out from the standpoint of socialist ideology means to give 'freedom of action' to the falsifications of bourgeois propagandists. ... One must admit that bourgeois information agencies have achieved great efficiency, reacting quickly to everything occurring in the world, while we sometimes are late."[15]

The Soviet radio system had increased listener choice to some degree in 1946, when it added a second national service during the late afternoon and evening hours. It added a third service in 1947 (evening hours only), but it wasn't available to the entire country. Those changes added little that was new, since the second and third services simply increased the amount of "serious" material available: operas, concerts, plays, educational broadcasts. The content of the news did not change at all, and there was little growth in light programming.

Finally, in 1964, the Soviet listener got a real alternative. Mayak, or "beacon," came on the air with a 24-hour-a-day schedule made up largely of brief newscasts and music, presented in a somewhat more relaxed fashion than characterized the existing program service. Some of the transmissions were on frequencies used by foreign stations broadcasting to the U.S.S.R., and the late night programming furnished better competition for the foreign broadcasters, who before then had been able to take advantage of the fact that Soviet radio generally signed off at midnight.

Television had made its debut in the Soviet Union just before the war but was suspended during the conflict. It came back on the air a month or so after the end of the war in Europe, but it was many years before any substantial number of viewers had their own sets; by 1950 there were roughly 12,000 of them. The main stations were in Moscow and Leningrad, but amateurs were constructing stations in Kharkov, Odessa and Dniepepetrovsk, much as radio amateurs had done in expanding radio in the early to mid 1920s.[16] By 1960 there were just under 5 million, with television stations in most of the large cities, but they broadcast for only a few hours each day, and the republic stations took the bulk of their material from Moscow, translating it into the appropriate republic languages.[17]

In the early 1960s, Soviet Prime Minister Khruschev and his associates began to see television as one of the chief symbols of a more consumer-oriented policy, and encouraged its manufacture and sale, chiefly by making it possible for people to buy TV sets on the installment plan—then a rarity in the country. By 1964, the year when Khruschev was deposed by the party leaders, there were nearly 13 million sets in Soviet households. Development of a second service in Moscow and other large cities, and third and fourth services in Moscow later on, continuation of installment plan purchase, the introduction of programming in color in 1967, and expansion of broadcast hours and relay transmitters, helped to bring about a doubling of that figure within the next four years.

Structurally speaking, there had been an administrative change of sorts in 1953, when the All-Union Radio Committee came under the direction of the Ministry of Culture, but that did not mark any fundamental alteration in the programming of radio and television. In 1957, the All-Union Radio Committee became the State Committee for Radio and Television Broadcasting (more commonly known as Gosteleradio) and was made a department of the Council of Ministers (cabinet) itself. There were some minor name changes later on, but the basic organizational structure remained intact until the collapse of the U.S.S.R. itself.

Handling Competition and Diversity (1965–1985)

The Soviet Union long had faced the problem of serving its rural areas. Many villages still had no electricity as of the 1950s and thus had no wired radio service. (It's possible to establish a wired radio service with a power generator, but that itself costs a good deal, and there must be a continuously available source of fuel and spare parts—both often in short supply in the more remote areas of the country.) Radio sets were becoming more and more common, and some villagers could afford them, but broadcast signals often were weak because there was no nearby relay transmitter. As for television, most villagers had heard of it by the early 1960s, but few of them had sets in their own homes, and if they had them, few were close enough to a TV relay (which has a much smaller radius than do long-, medium- and shortwave radio transmitters) to pick up a signal.

Construction of more standard radio receivers, especially low-priced, battery-powered transistor models, increased markedly in the 1960s. By the mid-1960s, the numbers of standard sets finally exceeded the numbers of wired radio receivers, and by 1970 there were nearly 50 million standard sets in the U.S.S.R. However, there still was a good deal of emphasis on developing the wired exchanges, since they afforded villages the opportunity to insert material of particular local interest. The Party Central Committee even passed a resolution in 1967 calling for the accelerated development of wired radio exchanges, especially in connection with the government's attempts to encourage settlement in Siberia, where in some areas only one out of every 10 villages had exchanges.[18]

Television was a far more difficult matter, but Soviet technology found a solution in the development of an elliptical orbit satellite—one that would stay close to the ground over the Soviet Union, then go far out into space in a cigar-shaped orbit. The first test of such a satellite, dubbed the "Molniya" (lightning) series, was in 1965, and by 1967 there were seven of them in orbit, with ground receiving and relay stations at some 20 locations across the country. Many areas now began to receive television for the first time. The expansion continued in the 1970s, and in late 1975 the first geostationary orbital TV satellite, "Raduga" (rainbow) was launched.

That expansion encouraged a real boom in the purchase of sets; by 1970 there were nearly 35 million of them in the country, and by 1974 over 50 million. But it also was becoming evident that many of those sets weren't in use, not because of dissatisfaction with the programming (although that wasn't absent), but because the sets broke down so often. There were estimates that one in every three sets was nonfunctional at any one time. Part of the reason was poor quality standards, but part of it was also lack of competent repair personnel. Letters to newspapers began to recite tales of how set owners had to take sets to the shop (house calls almost always required a bribe of some sort, usually vodka or food) three or more times to get the same problem fixed. Some newspaper reporters even conducted their own investigations of the situation by removing a tube from a TV set in their home, taking it to a shop, and being told that the problem was very severe, would cost a lot to solve, and would take a lot of time, but perhaps not quite so much if the customer could help the process along with a small "contribution." Despite the complaints and articles, standards of production and repair remained a problem.

Broadcasts from outside the country continued to concern party leaders and government officials, who issued frequent calls for "brighter" programs, more up-to-date news and better standards of production. A 1967 article in *Komsomolskaya Pravda* contended that educational television was watched by very few students and had failed to identify who it should serve and how.[19] A survey conducted in Leningrad in that same year revealed that news broadcasts were among the lowest rated of all TV programs.[20] A survey in Sverdlovsk around 1970 yielded similar results. A Kazahkstan TV official offered some self-criticism in 1970: "We still have much work to do to deliver the air from dull, stereotyped broadcasts which offer little to the mind and heart, to get away from sketchiness, an illustrative nature, and a dry, informative nature, and to overcome relapses into superficiality, pomposity and declamatoriness."[21] (His oral prose style—typical of what viewers heard on most informational programs—was itself a good illustration of the problem.)[22]

Improvements were slow in coming, but by the middle-to-late 1970s there were visible changes in the style of presentation of television news. In 1978, Soviet television added a twice-nightly news program, "Today in the World," where the style of delivery was far less formal than on other news broadcasts, where a rotating staff of commentators had more than the usual freedom to comment on current events, and where there were live reports from overseas correspondents. The program may have been a response to remarks made by Soviet President Brezhnev to the November 1978 plenary session of the Central Committee of the Communist Party: "It is high time to make reporting on international affairs prompt, more understandable and more concrete ... not a repetition of the accepted truths but an in-depth and well-argued analysis of the facts of international life."[23]

The construction of a new television building in the late 1960s finally had made it possible for producers to mount ambitious productions in TV studios, but for the most part they were slow to take advantage of their state-of-the-art technology. Dramas, unless they were shot on location, often were stiff, featured artificial-looking settings, and were shot unimaginatively. The best writers saw little to interest them in television, preferring instead to write for film or the stage. Party and government criticisms rarely mentioned drama, and changes came more slowly, but dramatic production, too, finally began to improve to the point where more prominent dramatists were quite eager to write for TV.[24]

Still, choice remained limited. Muscovites had access to four or five TV channels (a UHF service began in 1984); other big-city dwellers had two or, for Leningrad, three TV channels; and rural areas might be within range of one TV signal. Anyone with a reasonably good radio set could pick up several radio stations within the country and more from outside it, especially if, as was often the case, the set can receive shortwave broadcasts. Up until 1970, most rural dwellers on collective farms relied on the wired exchanges, which seldom carried more than one radio service. That situation changed during the period 1970-89, as more and more rural households acquired wireless sets.[25] It was a major accomplishment to supply that much broadcast service to such a huge and linguistically diversified country. Yet listeners and viewers, the latter in particular, almost certainly would have appreciated a greater choice. Videocassette recorders, which began to make their appearance in the early 1980s as more privileged Soviet citizens brought them back from their travels abroad, might have offered a solution, but their domestic manufacture, which started in 1985, wasn't a high-priority item. However, video rental and sales shops spread quite rapidly in the largest cities. Cable TV was limited largely to master antenna installations to improve reception for apartments; access cable was unheard of. Television's rapid development during the 1960s and 1970s was in part a response to public demand for more and better service, but the government appeared to see no real need, and some possible harm, in letting the medium expand to the multichannel dimensions that characterized much of western Europe and North America.

Mikhail Gorbachev became prime minister of the U.S.S.R. in early 1985. Within a few months, he began to challenge some of the practices of the Soviet media, for most of the same reasons voiced by his predecessors: dull, slow treatment of events. Unlike those predecessors, he used himself as a role model, encouraging television camera crews to cover his often informal, spontaneous behavior, and using radio and television to tell Soviet citizens that all of them had the duty to improve production methods, even if that meant challenging their supervisors. He conveyed that message in vivid terms, often visiting factories and farms and engaging workers and farmhands in discussions concerning what sorts of improvements were needed. Encouraged by his example, reporters and editors tested the waters of glasnost (openness) by introducing stories on alleged corruption by plant managers, bribe-taking in the apartment-leasing business, etc. They generally found little or no official opposition, some unofficial encouragement and considerable public support.

Glasnost Comes and (Partially) Goes (1985–1991)

Habits of self-censorship that had been built up over decades do not disappear overnight, and much about Soviet broadcasting remained unchanged for the first few years of the Gorbachev era, while some of it never changed at all. The Chernobyl nuclear plant explosion in 1986 was a classic example of government suppression of a "bad news" event: it was nearly three days after the disaster that Soviet media mentioned it, and even then the coverage was brief. It appeared to take Gorbachev considerable time before he began to use the initially slow and meager coverage as a pressure point to develop reforms in both media practices and the behavior of party members.[26] Stevenson and others conducted a comparative study in early 1987 of the leading daily newspaper, *Pravda*, and Soviet TV's chief national newscast, "Vremya" ("Time"). They found that the latter was "more internationally minded and more oriented toward glasnost-inspired reporting" but also that both sources were "slow, plodding and frequently professionally inept," as well as "predictable."[27]

"Vremya" had always been the mainstay of informational programming on Soviet television, so the relative lack of change in its approach shouldn't have been surprising. If substantial change were to occur, it probably would begin at the margins, rather than in the center. And it did, notably with the weekly discussion program "Vzglyad" ("Glance" or "View").[28] It came on air in October 1987, and rather quietly at first. As time passed, it took up more sensitive and sensational subjects: political dissidents, "punk" and "rocker" gangs in Moscow, etc.[29] Finally, on April 21, 1989, a theater director who was a guest on the show mentioned that perhaps it was time to treat Lenin like any other mortal, and remove his embalmed body from its tomb in Red Square and bury it in the ground. Within less than a month, the head of Gosteleradio, Aleksandr Aksenov, was discharged from his position "in connection with his retirement," but unofficially because of laxity in controlling program content.[30] As a late April meeting of the Central Committee of the Communist Party had dealt with the "Lenin's tomb" incident, Aksenov's removal wasn't all that surprising. During the meeting, Georgi Zhukhov asked, "Why is our television—state television, party television—tolerating such statements?" Vladimir Melnikov inquired, "Where's the patriotism, the civic attitude?"[31]

But "Vzglyad" remained on air, and was joined by other controversial programs such as "Seven Days," which entered the schedule in November

1989, in a choice prime-time slot: Sunday evenings. It featured investigative reporting on such touchy subjects as a tribute to dissident Andre Sakharov and strikes in the Soviet Union.[32] "Fifth Wheel," a weekly program from Leningrad TV that had come on air in 1988, was the target of frequent criticism from party conservatives for its revelations of past wrongs, such as recollections by victims of Stalin's purges, and present problems, such as a potentially dangerous nuclear power plant near Leningrad.[33]

Foreign radio broadcasts also became more accessible to Soviet listeners, as jamming of various Russian-language services ceased during 1988, including the unexpected halt to jamming of Radio Liberty in late November—unexpected because Soviet Foreign Ministry spokesperson Gennadi Gerasimov had condemned Radio Free Europe and Radio Liberty less than a month earlier, calling them "subversive stations, staffed primarily by turncoats and traitors," and adding, "they deserve to be jammed."[34]

Soviet broadcast journalists continued to expand their use of "on the street" interviews and live transmissions of public meetings. Sessions of the Congress of People's Deputies and of the "working" Parliament, the Supreme Soviet, once boring and predictable but now quite often lively and even contentious, were broadcast live for as much as six hours at a time. Occasionally the sessions became unruly, and even attempts by Gorbachev himself to impose limits on the rebroadcast of such debates on the evening news failed.[35] Perhaps the most memorable broadcast was of a May 1989 speech by a former Olympic weight lifter, Yuri Vlasov, newly elected to the Congress. He criticized "Vremya" for downplaying or eliminating remarks by "radical" speakers in the Congress, and for giving full coverage to speakers loyal to the government. But his most biting comments were reserved for the dreaded KGB (the Soviet security agency), calling it an "underground empire," accusing it of responsibility for the deaths of millions of people, pointing out its self-indulgences, such as its own "enormous ultramodern" hospital next door to a "rundown" tuberculosis hospital, and calling for it to leave the Lubyanka (its headquarters in Moscow) as a sign that it was renouncing its past behavior.[36]

A six-city random sample telephone survey on the day of Vlasov's speech indicated that from 69 percent to 93 percent of the respondents claimed to watch the broadcasts of the Congress "constantly" or "more or less constantly." Clearly people were fascinated by what they were seeing, although it's likely that a number of viewers were made uncomfortable by the disorder, uncertainty and challenge to authority that those broadcasts represented. A majority of the Supreme Soviet apparently felt the same way, because live broadcasts of its sessions were replaced by edited excerpts not long after Vlasov's speech.[37]

Outbreaks of violence between Armenians and Azerbaijanis in 1988-89 revealed that there were still some limits placed on freedom to report on sensitive issues, and that the government still made heavy use of broadcasting to support its version of events.[38] However, amateur-made videotapes of disorder in that region, and, more sensationally, of harsh Soviet military suppression of April 1989 demonstrations in Tbilisi, Georgia, made their way to western television and occasionally onto Soviet TV; some were even shown to the Soviet Parliament.[39]

Lithuania's declaration of independence from the U.S.S.R. in March 1990 was covered by Soviet media as an illegal act that disregarded the rights of Russian and Polish minorities living there.[40] Such coverage continued throughout the year, although Lithuanian media, and occasionally Leningrad TV, presented the pro-independence viewpoint. In January 1991, a Soviet armored detachment came into the Lithuanian capital, Vilnius, to "restore order," which included taking over the broadcast facilities. The station in nearby Kaunas remained under the control of the pro-independence forces, and criticized the Soviet takeover. "Vremya" covered the situation solely from the Soviet government side, and Aleksandr Nevzorov, host of Leningrad TV's popular and often controversial information program "600 Seconds," praised the Soviet troops as heroes.[41]

The tightening of government control over Soviet broadcasting appears to have started in late 1990. Ironically, it came only months after the Soviet Parliament had passed a new Press Law[42] and President Gorbachev had signed a presidential order on broadcasting. The Press Law emphasized the right of Soviet citizens to obtain information and to establish their own media outlets. The latter provision was controversial, and several party members attempted to block it.[43] The presidential order contained a roughly similar provision for broadcast outlets to be run "independently of political and social organizations" and to provide "impartial and thorough" coverage of events. However, the order also stated that local or republic takeovers of Gosteleradio services would have to be coordinated through the central government; otherwise, they would be "invalid."[44]

Some republics—the three Baltic states, plus Georgia—had already assumed such control, and Armenia and Azerbaijan had used Gosteleradio stations to broadcast their respective positions in their conflict. In mid-1990, the Russian Republic (RSFSR) under Boris Yeltsin's leadership also assumed control, although a new Russian Republic TV service didn't come on air until the following May. Since the central government had never formally approved any of those assumptions of control, it could have declared them invalid, and retaken them. Its overall failure to do so, aside from the temporary occupation of the Vilnius station, is one of the more fascinating mysteries of the central government's decline in power, because it would have been relatively easy, given the limited number of stations, to reimpose control. I suspect that it did not for several reasons: because Gorbachev was courting world opinion as a "liberal" Communist and didn't want to be seen as reverting to "traditional" Communist behavior; because the central government thought that it could control the overall flow of negative (in its eyes) information by canceling individual programs, thus discouraging others from continuing or initiating similar programs; because that government failed to realize the changes in the electronic media situation, including the increased diversity of means of dissemination (audio- and videocassettes, fax, satellite-to-telephone links, computers, etc.); and because it felt that the vast majority of the public still was essentially passive, and might tolerate slightly more control as long as some vestiges of freedom of expression remained, but might be less forgiving of a total takeover.

Gorbachev had advocated the development of "genuine political pluralism"[45] but didn't indicate how that was to be achieved. Since control over most broadcast facilities remained in the hands of the Communist Party/Soviet government, it was fairly simple to refuse transmission time to anyone requesting it, or to cut off transmission of "disruptive" material. There was a vivid example of the latter in TV coverage of the 1990 May Day parade in Moscow, where Gorbachev and other leading officials were greeted with critical banners and posters by some "unofficial" paraders in Red Square. Soviet TV showed all of the official part of the parade, but cut off the unofficial part after 15 minutes or so.[46]

The apparent uncertainty over broadcast policy, with major differences of opinion between leading party members,[47] seemed to have been resolved in November 1990, when Gorbachev appointed Leonid Kravchenko as head of Gosteleradio. Over the next few months, several of the more popular[48] and controversial programs such as "Vzglyad," "TSN," and "Author's Television" either were dropped, placed under tighter supervision, or shifted onto less widely available channels. ("Vzglyad," one of the most outspoken of the programs, was taken off the air at the end of 1990, but continued to produce programs in the same critical vein, and to give copies of them to the more independent TV operations in the Baltic republics, Georgia and Armenia, as well as TV Kamchatka and even some of the local cable services. See Gladys Ganley, "Unglued Empire" [Norwood, N.J.: Ablex, 1996], 117.) In January 1991, Gorbachev asked the Soviet Parliament to approve a temporary ban on some of the new freedoms allowed under the Press Law of 1990. His proposal was rejected,[49] but he continued to criticize some of the bolder programs.

Controlling Gosteleradio was simpler, since it already was highly centralized. It became even more so after February 8, 1991, when Gorbachev signed a presidential decree which placed the organization directly under presidential control, and removed most of Parliament's power to affect its operations. The decree did appear to give individual republic stations somewhat more freedom than they had had under the former system, although it soon became apparent that Central Television in Moscow would interfere with programming it disliked. Ukrainian TV was told not to broadcast an episode of its informational program "Hart," apparently because it contained an item critical of Soviet policy toward Lithuania.[50] Gorbachev placed the increasingly independent-acting Leningrad TV service under Kravchenko's direct control in late June 1991.[51] Yet a few independent stations such as TVK in Kamchatka and Radio Roks appeared within months of the decree, joining some already active quasi-legal stations such as Youth Radio M-1 in Vilnius and TV-Siberia.[52]

"Vremya" continued to support the Soviet government's policy toward Lithuania, emphasizing the statements of pro-Soviet officials and justifying the need for armed intervention.[53] And when Gorbachev campaigned for a positive vote on a nationwide referendum on preservation of the union of Soviet republics, he received ample airtime on "Vremya," whereas his chief opponent, Russian Republic head Boris Yeltsin, secured airtime only on Radio Rossiya[54] and over Leningrad television.[55]

Gosteleradio head Leonid Kravchenko and his deputy, Piotr Reshetov, appeared on television in February 1991 to justify Gosteleradio's increasingly conservative programming policies. Reshetov stated that surveys showed that "80 percent of the citizens wanted depiction of normal life."[56] (In other words, they supposedly wanted less controversy.) However, the leading U.S. scholar of Soviet electronic media, Ellen Mickiewicz, cited survey data showing that Soviet viewers were very fond of "Vzglyad," and that 62 percent of Communist Party members responding to that survey named it as their favorite show.[57]

Still, some Soviet journalists who had enthusiastically embraced the opportunity to report more critically now wondered whether they might have gone too far. Arytom Borovik, a journalist for the liberal weekly magazine *Ogonyok* observed that, "We really felt like a team headed by [*Ogonyok* editor Vitaly] Korotich to blow up all those old Empire State Buildings of our mentality. ... In the process, many people came to think of freedom as synonymous with bad news—ethnic conflict, food shortages, political discord. If you ask people now whether they want bread and order or freedom and democracy, they will say we want bread and order." He then said (glumly, according to correspondent Bill Keller), "The nation is ready for strong rule."[58]

The tensions displayed in Soviet broadcasts throughout this period were in some respects akin to earlier expressions of unhappiness with TV's criticism of Soviet society. Certainly the issue of greater or lesser degrees of independence for republic stations has its precedent in the already-noted crackdown on republic radio in the 1930s. Even after the tightening of control in 1990-91, there were some quite unexpected signs of liberalization, such as the amazing (for an officially atheistic nation) decision to permit broadcast of the Russian Orthodox Easter service in 1991. Almost as startling was the publishing on January 24, 1991, of an open letter in *Komsomolskaya Pravda*, a newspaper directly associated with the Communist Party. The letter was signed by over 60 leading actors, playwrights and producers, who stated that they would not work for Gosteleradio until the "garrote of censorship" was removed.[59] Many individuals, broadcasters and members of the general public, had decided that they liked at least some of what Soviet broadcasters could now do, and were willing to support the "new look." There were real limits to how much of that look the Soviet government could erase. Very soon, there would be no Soviet government to erase anything.

The Demise of the Soviet Union (1991)

The beginning of the end of the Soviet Union came on August 19, 1991, although that wasn't apparent at the time. Soviet President Gorbachev appeared to be losing his grip on power, although he was a highly popular visitor to western nations. He went on vacation to the Black Sea; a few days later, rumors of an attempted coup d'etat began to circulate. I remember vividly hearing a report on those rumors over National Public Radio, and tuning to Radio Moscow's World Service (English) to learn what might be happening. There were roughly 20 minutes of innocuous music, and then an announcer came on. She stated that she was reading an announcement "at the direction of" (a phrase she emphasized) the State Committee for the State of Emergency. The committee stated that Gorbachev was ill, and that it was taking power. It was clear that it had already done so where the national broadcast services were concerned.

But ultimately the coup attempt was unsuccessful, for several reasons. The coup leaders hadn't been able to secure the loyalty of enough military commanders, they hadn't coordinated their strategies very carefully, and they failed to consolidate their control over mass media outlets, especially the many foreign correspondents stationed in Moscow, who were able to file written and oral reports on what was happening in the Soviet capital.[60] Media personnel at the White House, including "Fifth Wheel" producer Bella Kurkova, set up a loudspeaker system over which several leaders in the Russian government could address the Moscow citizens surrounding the White House to defend it from the coup leaders.[61] A new (1990) independent radio station, Moscow Echo, was able to report freely during several brief intervals as the coup attempt was in progress, although station head Sergei Korzoun was certain at times that the station's calls for resistance to the coup would mean sooner or later that the coup leaders would order a tank crew to demolish the station. Nevertheless, station staff stuck to their work, convinced that they were making a stand for something literally worth dying for, and perhaps for freedom to report and receive information most of all.[62]

When the coup attempt ended on August 22, Gorbachev resumed power, and attempted in a number of appearances on television to show the public that he really was in control. But he was not. Soviet TV had replaced "Vremya" with "TV Inform," whose co-anchors had been fired five weeks earlier for their "liberal" ways, and Gorbachev had appointed a new head for Tass.[63] No one was mislead into equating those actions with real power. Boris Yeltsin appeared as the true "savior" of the nation, thanks to his leadership of the anti-coup forces from the Russian Republic's governmental offices in the White House (so named for its color, and not because of any likeness to its U.S. namesake). He already had proven to be a colorful media figure, and would continue to be one. He and his followers also were convinced that the Soviet Union itself was no longer viable, and on December 25, 1991, Mikhail Gorbachev resigned as president of the Soviet Union, which itself was officially dissolved, although there would be attempts in the years ahead to revive a union of at least some of the republics. Boris Yeltsin took control of the Ostankino facilities in the name of the Russian Federation, and a new electronic media era (with some very distinct traces of the former system) was under way.

The Threads of History

During the time that the Soviet Union existed, *politics* was far and away the most significant force shaping the nation's broadcasting system. But *culture* and *demography* also were important elements, since the strongly multicultural—therefore potentially fragile—nature of the U.S.S.R. virtually demanded the creation of a national, centralized system that would deliver a monolithic message to the nation as a whole so as to maintain its unity, while at the same time acknowledging its cultural diversity through regional and local outlets. *Economics* and *geography* were important factors insofar as supporting such a vast broadcasting network was concerned, and the amounts of money the Soviet government was willing to spend on setting up a national radio service in the early 1920s and a communication satellite-delivered service in the 1960s are clear indications of just how important broadcasting was to the nation's political leaders. *Technology* also played a role in making it possible to establish nationwide radio and television services, but cable TV and computer-driven services, as well as videocassettes, were slow to develop, probably because the government saw them as potential threats to the monopolistic control it had been able to maintain over previous electronic media services.

FINANCING

Soviet broadcasting featured a very simple mode of financing: The money was provided by the government. The State Committee (Gosteleradio) prepared and proposed an annual budget, and the government decided how much it received. Those figures weren't made public, so Soviet viewers and listeners had no real sense of how much of their annual taxes went to support broadcasting. There was a more direct form of contact between audience and broadcaster in the past. When Soviet broadcasting officially began in 1922, listeners were required to register their radio sets and pay a license fee on them; while the fee money went to the government, there was a general understanding that it helped to offset the expenses connected with broadcasting. Interestingly, not everyone paid the same fee: soldiers, sailors, those handicapped with war or work injuries and students living on a fixed stipend all paid one ruble; workers, employees, military officers and students not living on a fixed stipend paid three rubles; and other citizens paid 10. Clearly the government wanted to encourage listening by people with low incomes. In 1926 the government changed the fee structure to one based on type of set, although clubs, societies, groups and periodical rooms in rural areas paid a reduced fee.[64]

When television became available to the general public just after World War II, the government assessed a separate license fee on owners of TV sets. That lasted until January 1, 1962, when license fees were abolished. At that time, license fees for radio were about $3 per year and for TV $12. The fees didn't begin to cover the costs of the services, especially television, and they were very difficult to collect in the thinly populated areas of the country. There also was some evasion of payment. The leading Soviet newspapers heralded the dropping of the fee as a "Gift to Ten Million," but some viewers wrote in to say that, given the poor quality of TV programming, it would be more accurate to describe the fee as a "Gift from Ten Million," since viewers were forced to give money to the government and got little in return.[65] The fees were replaced by an excise tax levied on each set at the time of purchase—much easier to collect, difficult to evade. Again, the government received the money and applied it toward the costs of providing broadcast services; Gosteleradio had no absolute rights to it. The excise tax has remained in effect even after the demise of the U.S.S.R. (1991), but produces uneven amounts of annual revenue, since there is fluctuation in numbers and types of sets sold each year, as well as a number of black market sets which bring in absolutely no tax revenue.

Advertising was a part of early Soviet broadcasting, although apparently very few ads were carried. In 1935 the practice was forbidden and did not resume until 1947 (apparently it was considered too capitalistic). After that, both Soviet radio and television carried advertising, but not in any great quantity. Radio ads ran between 7 and 9 a.m. and 5 and 8 p.m.; television ads appeared in the morning on Channel One and in the evening on Channel Two, and were clustered to minimize interruption of the programs. There was no sponsorship. Most ads were short and to the point, emphasizing clear and simple delineation of the product's qualities; psychological appeals of the "be more popular" or "stand out from the crowd" sort were rare,[66] in keeping with communism's discouragement of "individualistic" behavior. Many ads were for food, drink and clothing, and often appeared when an overstock of an item had developed. For example, if a factory making winter coats ran into production or shipping delays (quite frequent in the U.S.S.R.), it and/or the stores selling the coats could place ads calling people's attention to their "unexpected availability." (They probably sold quite well, since the tendency of most Soviet shoppers was to pick up an item they might eventually need, or that someone they know might need, because there might not be another chance for a while.)[67] The money generated by advertising might go to help offset the costs of broadcasting but certainly wasn't considered to be profit. Other sources of financial support were insignificant. Program sales abroad were rare; program exchanges were far more frequent.

GOVERNANCE AND ADMINISTRATION—INTERNAL

Soviet broadcasting had a simple approach to internal governance and administration. Gosteleradio was in charge of governance and administration for the overall system; the head station in each republic had a republic committee; and there were similar committees for other stations. Ultimate power (internal) was in the hands of Gosteleradio, which didn't concern itself overmuch with the operational details of the other stations. Its chairperson and other members were appointed by the Soviet cabinet; they often had no experience with broadcasting, but they almost always were party members of some standing. The republic committees were appointed in a similar manner by the republic cabinets and had similar backgrounds.

The Decision-Making Structure

Under Gosteleradio and the republic committees was an organizational structure that divided activity into four main spheres—radio, TV, foreign broadcasting and material/technical—and subdivided programming into its general categories: news, children's, drama and so on. Each sphere had a head who was a vice chairman of the committee and almost certainly a member of the Communist Party. (The head of material/technical often was an exception, since that sphere didn't involve program content.) Heads of program divisions generally were party members. There were frequent meetings within each program division to discuss program strategy and content, and heads of the divisions as well as others within them might meet with the state or republic committee from time to time, but there was a fair amount of autonomy in day-to-day decision-making. Because top decision-making positions all were in the hands of the "nomenklatura," or list of important positions to be filled by the party, those decisions remained in "safe" hands.

The basic rules were clearly understood. Decision-making autonomy rarely included sensitive issues such as corruption by party officials, major natural disasters and human-made accidents, although Gorbachev's policy of glasnost enabled reporters and editors to be at least slightly quicker to cover and broadcast such issues. Slow Soviet media coverage of the nuclear plant explosion at Chernobyl in 1986 brought considerable criticism from high-ranking party and government officials for giving Soviet citizens one more excuse to listen to western radio stations in order to be fully informed. That in turn caused Soviet media to treat the Chernobyl situation far more fully and frankly once they began to cover it (nearly three days after the explosion) than ordinarily was true for such events, where the tendency was to mention them briefly, if at all.[68] Certainly glasnost led television to cover events that it would have ignored earlier, such as the large and sometimes violent demonstrations in Armenia in late February 1988. However, as James Oberg has pointed out, it was rare for the Soviet media to cover problems which seemed to have no immediate solutions.[69]

The news departments were the most politically sensitive programming units, but here, too, there was some autonomy—more in the Gorbachev years because of glasnost and increased emphasis on timeliness of news. There were daily editorial meetings, and disagreements surfaced regarding which stories should be carried and what they should contain. The official Soviet news agency, Tass, provided the bulk of the material for newscasts, but its items could be and were sometimes rewritten, and any station of any size had its own reporters who gathered additional items. Stations in the smaller republic and rural areas also relied to some extent on "citizen reporters" for some of their items. Since there were several newscasts each day on radio and on television in the larger cities, editors often couldn't wait for guidance from above and made their own decisions on the spur of the moment. Often those decisions were cautious—better to eliminate an item or to include the official version word-for-word than risk being wrong—but editors took risks on occasion and sometimes incurred the wrath of local party officials, especially when a story called attention to foul-ups or corruption in management and the manager in question was a party member of some standing. Still, editors rarely attempted to challenge the basic system of censorship that sat above the broadcast services themselves.

Although *unions* (e.g., of writers or journalists) existed within Soviet broadcasting, they didn't constitute a separate and potentially opposing element in its operation, as they did in many western broadcast systems. They didn't go out on strike; instead, they generally assumed a cooperative role, looking for new and better ways to accomplish the goals of the system and "socializing" new union members in the ways of the organization. The Union of Journalists was particularly important. According to Reino Paasilinna, it "assisted the party in the socialization of journalists." It also was part of a self-sealed system: only employees in editorial offices could be Union members, and the editorial offices employed only journalists who were approved by the Party Central Committee.[70] However, journalists organized their own independent union in 1990, and in 1991 published a weekly bulletin, *Golos*, which exposed the "lies and disinformation" coming from the Soviet government-controlled media, especially Gosteleradio.[71]

GOVERNANCE AND ADMINISTRATION—EXTERNAL

Government and Party

The major source of external influence over the governance and administration of Soviet broadcasting was the Communist Party. Actually, since most of the middle- and high-level administrators of the broadcast system were party members, it's difficult to separate "internal" and "external." But there were times when the party clearly assumed an external role, particularly when its leaders criticized broadcasting. Occasionally the Party Central Committee or republic committee met with media editors to discuss overall priorities, strategies and approaches. And finally, since party was virtually synonymous with government, any directive coming through the latter had the blessing of the former.

There were specific governmental departments that had a more day-to-day relationship with broadcasting. The most important was Glavlit, or the Chief Administration for the Protection of State Secrets in the Press. Such an agency had existed in czarist times and was revived by the Soviet government in 1922. During a period running from the 1930s to the 1950s, it exercised considerable direct power over broadcasting, in that it could and did judge the "acceptability" (to the government, and therefore the party) of an enormously wide range of subjects: Military, political, economic and cultural information all fell under its purview. Its chief duty was to see to it that no information potentially damaging to the country[72] appeared in print or over radio (it published annual lists of forbidden topics), and its stamp of approval was required for most spoken and written material (which meant, of course, that spoken material had to be delivered from written texts, depriving radio broadcasts of spontaneity). It sought to exercise authority over material that would be potentially damaging to personal morals as well.

Glavlit wasn't always a model of efficiency, despite the fact that it worked closely with the security police. Archives providing details on Glavlit's work were found by the German army when it captured Smolensk in World War II.[73] They reveal an agency that sometimes was understaffed, had too few trained personnel and lacked solid criteria for making judgments. It appears to have become better organized and more strict during the war and on up to the death of Stalin. Khruschev's 1956 criticism of some of the excesses of the Stalin years seemed to encourage newspaper and broadcast editors to be a bit more bold, especially after Khruschev and other party leaders had criticized the media in the late 1950s and early 1960s for being too slow, incomplete and dull. During the Gorbachev era, the government's and party's desire for more media spontaneity made Glavlit less relevant for broadcasting; although there still were Glavlit personnel on duty at broadcast stations, their role in clearing acceptable material seems to have become more limited.[74] Also, broadcast personnel themselves probably internalized the ground rules laid down by Glavlit over the decades, so self-censorship would have done much of Glavlit's job for it.[75]

During the last few years of the Soviet Union's existence, there were several revelations of Glavlit's procedures and shortcomings, some voiced by Glavlit personnel. Vladimir Vatchenko, the chief censor for Glavlit in the department of Novosibirsk, stated in a 1989 interview with a newspaper editor that Glavlit wasn't responsible for protecting *real* state secrets: "The most absurd and comic part of our work is that Glavlit staff couldn't recognize real state secrets." The head of Glavlit in the Latvian SSR stated in a 1990 interview that, "In 1985, when I began my censorship work, I was absolutely certain that I was effectively protecting state secrets. But now, I rather think that we protected parochial interests which, for some unknown reason, were associated with state interests." The Novosibirsk censor also claimed that Glavlit's staff actually grew even as its workload diminished.[76] Herman Ermolaev contends that, during this period, Glavlit paid far more attention to the mass media than it did to literature, but it also lost considerable power in terms of the scope of material that it was responsible for reviewing.[77]

Glavlit was transformed into the Chief Administration for the Protection of State Secrets in the Press and Other News Media (GUOT) in 1990, following passage of the Press Law of 1990. However, the resolution effecting it called for continuity in Glavlit's function, and the new head of GUOT was the old head of Glavlit, and other staff followed him. And, since the list of information not to be published was secret, media organizations wishing to avoid trouble with the government or party ended up paying for their services as "consultants," since the Press Law had abolished censorship![78]

The Communist Party had an organization similar to Glavlit. It was called AgitProp when it was developed in 1920, but in the mid-1960s it acquired the less colorful title Department of Propaganda.[79] It functioned within the Party Central Committee and at the republic and larger local party levels. It was subdivided into sectors responsible for the different media of communication. It often played the reverse role to Glavlit: its time more often was spent in trying to get certain messages placed in the media than in trying to keep them out. As broadcast programmers had to accommodate differing tastes and many demands with limited amounts of money, talent and airtime, staff members of a department of propaganda couldn't just say, "The party insists on it." For example, they might attempt to get the television service of one of the Asian republics to carry more dramas, documentaries and other programs about "modern" and "feudal" views of women in society (some of the Asian republics were and still are quite feudal in that respect).

Given the nature of media censorship, it's difficult to find precise documentation on it in Communist nations, but in late 1977 a Polish censor defected to Sweden, bringing with him several hundred pages of official documents on censorship. Many of the prohibitions were predictable, such as "no information written in an approving, tolerant, understanding tone about hippies in Poland may be published." Some others were amazing, such as "banned is all information about food poisoning and epidemics affecting larger groups of people."[80] The overall thrust of the prohibitions seemed to be to keep any potentially negative (that is, contradictory to the continued improvement of standards in a Communist nation) information from the general public. By that token, plane crashes, train collisions and ferry boat sinkings ordinarily wouldn't be reported, and generally speaking they weren't, although glasnost began to change some of those practices. The Polish system probably didn't differ very much from the Soviet system; certainly there was a close resemblance between the categories of material *not* released to general audiences in the two countries. From what we know about the master list of categorical descriptions (known within the U.S.S.R. as "the Talmud") of what was not to be published or broadcast, the systems in fact were very similar.[81]

The Ministry of Communications was responsible for allocating broadcast frequencies. Military services had top call on frequencies, but broadcasting came in a strong second, and denials of requests were rare. Legislative bodies at the various levels of government could and sometimes did debate aspects of broadcasting, and in theory could punish radio or television by cutting or threatening to cut a portion of the annual budget request, but the budget was an area in which the cabinet made the real decisions.

The Soviet legal system became involved with broadcasting in several ways, but rarely in direct connection with the official broadcast system. There was no fairness doctrine in Soviet broadcast law. Although any Soviet citizen could protest unfair broadcast treatment, no right of reply guaranteed airtime for responses. There were laws on libel and slander, but it wasn't easy to invoke them against government-operated media. Most laws applied to listeners (it was illegal to pass on to others any information of an "anti-state nature") and to amateur radio operators (who were licensed, and who could not transmit "pornography").[82]

The Press Law of 1990 was in effect for too short a period of time to have had much impact on the governance of broadcasting; in any case, the government had taken a far more conservative approach to program content by early 1991. That did not stop media outlets such as the RSFSR's six-hour program block on Channel Two or the recently formed Moscow independent radio station Moscow Echo from carrying material critical of the government, but the vast majority of electronic media content came under tighter supervision. As Vladimir Molchanov put it in a 1991 roundtable discussion, "When I first started to work for 'Vremya' ... we had no problems as to what news went on the air. Fifteen minutes before airtime, Ligachev phoned to give his instructions; ten minutes before airtime another high official phoned to give his own instructions. Then that stopped. Now the practice is coming back."[83]

Nongovernmental

There were no formal structures permitting public involvement with broadcasting in the U.S.S.R.—no broadcast councils, and no public organizations dealing specifically with broadcasting. Trade unions, youth groups and other organizations might have "interest sections" that concerned themselves with broadcasting, and they could bring pressure to bear on broadcasters to modify program content. But for the general public, the main avenues for expression of dissatisfaction were through party officials, government officials and letters to newspapers and to stations. From time to time, stations encouraged letter writing, and many stations offered regularly scheduled programs on which letters were read and reacted to. There were accusations that some of the letters were fabricated by stations so as to be able to appear responsive to public complaints, but the writing of letters of complaint to the mass media was a long-standing practice in the U.S.S.R., and the vast majority almost certainly were genuine. Most seemed to be of the, "Why can't we have more (or less) of ... ?" or, "Why was (program or individual) dropped?" There were between 1 and 2 million letters each year; only a very small number were read on the air, and the majority were requests for musical dedications, information or announcements on behalf of some group or other. However, when there was a major event, such as the drafting of a new Soviet constitution in 1977, the party pressed the media to urge the public to write or telephone their reactions, and many letters were read on the air.

PROGRAMMING

Philosophies

Various statements on the purpose of Soviet broadcasting indicate that it was to improve the condition of society by making citizens aware of their obligations to others; the need to remember the sacrifices of those who built and defended the Soviet Union; the country's "diversity within unity"; the blessings of communism; the equal status of all humankind (the classless society); and the inevitable triumph of communism and just as inevitable decline of capitalism. It was to inform, enlighten, persuade, inspire, and to guide proper behavior. The list didn't include the need for entertainment after a hard day's work (in fact, Soviet sociologists found it very difficult to accept the concept of entertainment as a mass media function and often tried to describe it as something else, such as "relaxation"); the provision of information that might help someone cut through bureaucratic red tape; or the satisfying of people's desires to see and hear about "morbid" events (disasters and crimes).

But entertainment, consumer-oriented information and "sensational" material was a part of the broadcast schedule, too, and not all of it could be justified in the name of the Soviet broadcasting philosophy, for one simple reason. Soviet broadcasting had to respond to two realities: the availability of money and talent, and the ability of the audience to choose to listen and watch or not. In the early days of the system, much of the programming was of the "purposeful" variety and was intended to carry out the lofty ideals just stated. But few would have been willing to listen to talks all day long, and developing more subtle means (dramas, comic skits, etc.) to express those ideals took both time and talent, not to mention money, so music became an early staple of the daily schedule. It was cheap, it was available, listeners liked it, and it could even help to illustrate the cultural diversity of the U.S.S.R., although listeners probably didn't want to be lectured on that between every selection. In the late 1930s, broadcasters decided to use the attractive value of music within a program that had news and features intermixed with it; thus, listeners lured by the promise of music might stick around to hear the talks and news. Increases in broadcasts to the U.S.S.R. from outside the country, and seemingly popular broadcasts at that, caused Soviet broadcasters to respond with Mayak in 1964; it offered more music and less talk than Soviet listeners usually got, and it became quite popular.

In short, what Soviet leaders said they wanted the broadcast media to do and what the media actually did were somewhat different, at least in terms of emphasis. Programs that illustrated one or more of the basic purposes were available every day, and even every hour, but they shared airtime with material that contained few if any "purposeful" elements and seemed intended for relaxation, enjoyment and satisfaction of curiosity. And it was the latter, so audience research data revealed, that attracted audiences, while the "purposeful" broadcasts often drew small numbers and were criticized by the audience, the press and the party for their dullness.

Radio

Soviet radio operated at national, republic, district and local levels, but was coordinated by Gosteleradio, which approved the schedules of all stations.[84] The task was made easier because stations below the national level took a share of their programming from Moscow Central. Some was broadcast in its original language, Russian, because it was the national language and because many individuals throughout the country used it as their first language. Some was translated into local languages.

The situation in Taganrog, an industrial city in the southern part of the Russian Republic (RSFSR) with a population of somewhat over 250,000, was fairly typical of the choice available to a listener in a larger population center. If she or he had a good radio set, it would have been possible to pick up three national services from Moscow, a service from the major regional ("oblast") station in Rostov, and a city radio station in Taganrog itself. Other stations might be receivable but probably would have been less clear. If the listener happened to work in one of the 10 local factories that had in-plant radio services, that added to the choice. On the other hand, if the listener was on the wired radio exchange, there was only one channel: the First Service from Moscow from 6 a.m. to midnight, with a two-hour-a-day block for the Rostov station and roughly two hours a week for the Taganrog station. Even the listener with a standard set would have less choice than it might seem, since the city station usually was on the air for just an hour a day at 5 p.m., and the factory stations could be heard only within the factories themselves. Those stations, too, broadcast for an hour a day, at noon.[85]

As for the three national services from Moscow, Moscow 1 began its broadcast day at 5 a.m. with a short newscast, press roundup (Soviet dailies) and calisthenics, then some light music. As the day progressed, there were further newscasts and press roundups, as well as a great deal of music—folk, popular, classical. Special reports on activities of various groups (Young Pioneers, Komsomol) also were part of the schedule, as were educational programs for primary and secondary schools. Toward the end of the afternoon, there usually was a children's radio drama or after-school educational program, perhaps on the life of a famous writer such as Turgenev. Classical music took up the supper hour and often was followed by a radio play, sometimes original, sometimes an adaptation of a classic (Lermontov, Jack London). Sports events sometimes were covered in the evening, and if there was a major chess match, there would be brief reports on its progress. Live transmission of theatrical productions and concerts also was fairly common in the evening. Sign-off came shortly after 1 a.m.

Moscow 2 (Mayak) was a 24-hour service of music, news and brief programs for and about certain groups (young people, soldiers, etc.), with popular music predominating. Moscow 3 carried mostly classical music, educational programs for adults and plays in its 7 a.m. to midnight schedule. Moscow 4 was available only to listeners in the Moscow area; it specialized in classical music and ran from 4 p.m. until midnight. Both Moscow 3 and Moscow 4 broadcast blocks of airtime in stereo.

The regional ("oblast") and republic capital stations concentrated much more heavily on informational broadcasts; only about 20 to 25 percent of the broadcast day (from 10 to 20 hours, depending upon the size of the city and region) consisted of music and other entertainment, and the music often had a particular local or regional character. Much of the informational programming dealt with agriculture and industry in the region and frequently included radio portraits (a combination of interview and documentary) of model workers and citizens who exceeded production quotas, helped out in old people's homes and contributed in other ways to the betterment of society. (The model citizens usually weren't very comfortable in front of the microphone, and often sounded as if they were reading prepared responses to questions. That began to change as glasnost took hold, and reporters tried to get more spontaneous expression of viewpoints.)

City and factory or collective farm radio stations broadcast little but information, although occasionally a local musical or other cultural group appeared. Announcements of activities; orders; readings from the city, factory or collective farm newspapers filled the hour or less of airtime that such stations usually had. Portable equipment and trained personnel often weren't available at this level,[86] and on many stations, material was written out before being put on the air, then often monotonously read. That lack of spontaneity drew the criticism of party and government officials and the listeners themselves but was the result not only of lack of equipment and trained personnel, but the need to check material over carefully and perhaps pass it by censors before it was broadcast.

Readings of material from newspapers probably were more common over Soviet radio than over any other radio system in the industrialized world. Lenin clearly saw this as one of radio's chief tasks in the early 1920s, when well over half of the population was illiterate and when newsprint was scarce. As both literacy and newsprint increased, it might not have been so essential, but it did provide listeners with the highlights of editorial opinion, which was the main thing many of them wanted from the papers: some indication of how to interpret the day's events. It also provided radio personnel with ready-made and approved broadcast copy.

Soviet radio made a considerable effort to act as a patron of the arts, and not only had its own orchestras and choruses at the national level, in the republic stations and in some of the larger city stations, such as Leningrad, but also commissioned original musical works and radio plays. Stations frequently broadcast young people's, factory's and collective farm orchestras and choruses, and hosted music festivals centering around folk, jazz and classical music. Young people also were directly involved in producing material for certain shows, such as the daily "Yunost" ("Youth") program. And poetry, a major element in the country's culture, often appeared on stations services at all levels.

Finally, radio stations were expected to broadcast programs about (and sometimes from) the other "people's democracies" (the eastern European countries plus Vietnam, Mongolia, North Korea and Cuba), Third World nations, some of the other European nations and other parts of the U.S.S.R. Music was the most common feature of such programs, but sometimes they covered the history of the country or people, talked about its landscape, or even provided weekly summaries of recent events.

Because music forms such a major element in the various radio schedules, it wasn't surprising that music broadcasts drew a large share of the criticism that the stations received.[87] Listeners might object to jazz (it was discouraged during Stalin's rule, and Khruschev claimed that it gave him "gas on the stomach," but it became more common by the 1970s) as too "jarring" or "decadent," but they also might complain about the large quantity of classical music, certainly far more prevalent over Soviet radio than over radio services in western Europe or North America. They also sometimes disliked the endless repetition of the same tunes in the many listener request shows; one Soviet sociologist explained the apparent reason: "As a rule the same works are presented over and over again in such concerts. This happens because over many years precisely these compositions become known to the broad circle of listeners, and naturally it is they that appear above all in listener's letters. The radio editorial board has the illusion in reading mail from listeners that they are able thus to determine listener's interests and requirements, although in reality they learn only from such letters which works they are actually playing most often in musical request programs, including in concerts composed of listener requests."[88]

There was a fair amount of variety on Soviet radio, but listener letters revealed a desire for considerably more, and surveys revealed a considerable amount of tuning to foreign stations—the BBC, VOA, Deutsche Welle and Radio Liberty—for news, those same stations and a number of the Polish, Hungarian and Czech stations for greater variety in music, especially popular music. Some listeners even took matters into their own hands and created their own "stations." While amateur radio was legal in the Soviet Union, it had to be licensed, and amateur operations weren't allowed to function as broadcast stations. Yet there sometimes were a few hundred illegal amateur stations on the air, broadcasting material ranging from jazz to "samizdat" (self-published writings, usually critical of the Soviet government, and also illegal) to pornographic material. Soviet law provided for fines and possibly jail terms for illegal broadcasters, which some received after show trials designed to hold them up as bad examples, but it didn't seem to discourage them. They usually operated on shortwave and over a limited radius and didn't follow predictable schedules. They gave themselves colorful titles, such as Lion, Dragon or King, and usually were one-person operations. They presented a sharp contrast to what was available over Soviet radio, especially in their informal style of presentation.[89]

Television

Television faces far more severe technical limitations than does radio. There is no way to transmit television signals over short- or longwave and thus compensate for the huge distances and sparse populations that characterize nations such as Canada and the Soviet Union. The advent of broadcast satellites in the mid-1960s helped, but the satellite transmissions still had to be received by earth stations and then retransmitted. Canada invested heavily in small-scale earth stations, but the U.S.S.R. did not; even to the present day, there are large areas of the country that receive no television at all, and other areas that are served by "passive" relays, with no programming specific to their regions. The cost of television, too, meant that many Soviet cities and towns with their own radio services weren't licensed by Gosteleradio to set up their own TV stations.

As a result, television programming generally was far less local in character than was radio. There were several dozen television studio complexes in the Soviet Union as of 1991, all of them in republic capitals or, with few exceptions, in cities with more than 100,000 people. Most originated their own programs for no more than a few hours a day, and many for an hour or less. Their main source of supply for the remainder of the schedule was Moscow. Several cities with populations in excess of 250,000 had no TV studios of their own. Moscow residents were "television-rich" compared with most other Soviet cities, and even major centers such as Leningrad and Kiev had far less TV airtime: Most large cities had no more than two channels, but Leningrad had three. Moscow had four, although a fair share of broadcast time was in the form of repeats at different times and days.

Channel One began its broadcast day at 7 a.m. with a relatively informal, somewhat "Today"-like breakfast show containing news, interviews, weather and some "soft" feature material, delivered quite informally from a living-room-like set. It came on the air early in 1987, probably as part of the glasnost spirit; there never had been anything quite like it on Soviet TV. Much of the morning period was taken up with repeats, usually sports, films and documentaries and a pause at about 11:15 a.m. after a brief newscast. Transmission resumed at 2:30 with a newscast, followed by a film or documentary, TV dramas (one-shot and serial), a newscast at 6:45 ("Today in the World"), concerts, ballets, operas, plays (many of them televised live or recorded at the theater or concert hall), documentaries and TV dramas, "Vremya" at 9 p.m., more concerts, drama or sports, and "Today in the World" at 10:55, with sign-off around midnight. On a few days of the week there were quiz and variety shows, the latter often featuring "People's Artists" who were honored for their performing skills, whether music, acting, juggling or some other form of artistry. Aside from feature films (some of them appearing on TV even as they were making their debuts in the cinema houses), few programs ran as long as an hour, and many were 30 to 40 minutes. There also were series on science and technology, ideology and other specialized subjects, usually presented during the daytime and/or on weekends, when Channel One's schedule ran straight through from morning to night. Sign-off ordinarily didn't come until nearly midnight on Saturday, since Sunday was a day of leisure. Sports were available on most nights, whether live transmissions of hockey, soccer or some minor sport, or excerpts from sports events held earlier that day, e.g., reports from championships in gymnastics being held in another country.

Channel Two's schedule bore a close resemblance to that of Channel One, with two major differences: the daytime break in the schedule didn't come until 3:30 p.m., with broadcasts resuming at 6 with the news, and there was heavy emphasis on educational and instructional material, starting with gymnastics at 8 a.m. and continuing with material for adults and schoolchildren during the morning and early afternoon. Geography, government, foreign languages, Russian, botany and many other subjects filled the screen, usually in 30-minute blocks. Channel Three was for the Moscow area only, ran from 7 p.m. to 11:15 p.m., and featured news, sports and information about local organizations and activities, plus occasional films and concerts. Channel 4, on the air from 4 p.m. until between 8 and 9 p.m., carried repeats of some of the educational programs, occasional feature films and features about scientists, military leaders, cosmonauts and so on, as well as model workers, farmers, schoolchildren and others whose good examples should be an inspiration to all. The UHF channel (33) did little but repeat programming carried on the other channels.

The schedule was arranged so that viewers generally would have a fair range of choice, although "Vremya" was simulcast over the first three channels. Soviet TV had often been criticized for stacking the schedule in such a way that viewers had little choice among types of programs, but by the mid-1980s there was far more diversity at any one time: a documentary on one channel, a championship sports contest on another, an educational program on a third, a pop music concert on a fourth. Feature movies appeared on one or more of the channels each afternoon and/or evening and ranged all the way from silent film classics to the latest releases. Soviet cinema attendance dropped sharply as TV viewing became more widespread, and managers of cinemas sometimes protested that they couldn't be expected to show strong attendance figures when television made some of the latest movies available to their viewers. Apparently the government felt that the attractive value of the movies (which could be preceded or followed, or sometimes interrupted, by political, economic or social material) outweighed concerns about cinema attendance. Well over half of the movies shown were Soviet-made, but many came from the eastern European countries, some from Third World nations and a few from the west. Many were heavy on "pro-social" content—the sacrifices made by peasants, factory workers, military personnel and so on to help build socialism and to oppose its enemies, but some were relatively deep studies of human nature, not all with happy endings.

The regular schedule often was interrupted by telecasts of special events—major political addresses, the visits of important foreign dignitaries and above all anniversaries of everything from the 1917 Revolution to the births and deaths of distinguished leaders, but perhaps more than anything else the important events of World War II. The mass media in general, and television in particular, commemorated those events not only because the Great Patriotic War, as it was called in the U.S.S.R., was such a unifying experience for the nation, but also because it reinforced the message of the need for eternal vigilance and the sacrifices it required of the people. It appeared in feature films, newscast items, commentaries, special interviews, quiz shows, children's programs and just about every other program genre. A very popular program called "With All My Heart," which resembled U.S. shows of the "This Is Your Life" variety, sometimes had reunions of World War II comrades who were separated in battle, lost track of each other and may even have believed each other dead. Russians are very sentimental people, and such episodes could move them on purely human grounds but also serve to highlight such values as loyalty to and sacrifice for others.

Still, while those values and others might be highlighted in most program genres, there were many hours of entertainment on Soviet television. Quiz shows, some of them featuring audience participation, contained a number of simple (and simple-minded) questions, just as quiz shows do all over the world. Satires often poked fun at bureaucratic red tape. Variety shows featured some of the best entertainers available, and singers were more apt to offer such time-honored favorites as "Moscow Nights" than they were songs of praise to Lenin, Marx or (in a show at the time of a mid-1970s Communist Party Congress) "My [Communist] Party Card!" Shows about nature and geography usually avoided heavy social and political issues and were very well-produced.[90] And some of the messages were woven into programs very subtly, as in the long-lived series "Let's Go, Girls!" which featured weekly competitions among women engaged in specific occupations, such as hairdressers. The participants displayed their skills in a variety of ways but also talked about why they chose their line of work and what they liked (and perhaps disliked) about it. That reinforced the value of the dignity of labor and the importance of everyone's contribution to society, but the message usually came out quite naturally and took up little airtime. Most sports shows were light on the political angle, too, although interviews with athletes sometimes included questions designed to get them to say how much they owed to Soviet society for allowing them to excel.

Using humor to convey certain pro-social messages wasn't all that common on Soviet TV, but in the glasnost era the Drama Department came up with a few shows that did. One, "Apartment for Rent," portrayed everyday life in a Moscow apartment block (most Muscovites live in apartments), with plenty of emphasis on the need for mutual consideration (Soviet teenagers like their music as loud as do their counterparts elsewhere, and older people frequently complain about the racket), for the restraint of pets, and for cooperation in keeping the building clean. There also were jabs at the governmental bureaucracy for being slow to repair leaking roofs and dripping faucets and for being frequently unresponsive to people's complaints. The series proved effective enough to cause the bureaucracy to protest to the Drama Department that it added to officials' workloads.[91]

Certain material rarely if ever appeared on Soviet television. Criticism of communism itself was out of the question, as was the party as an institution. If party officials made serious mistakes or committed crimes, that might be covered, and the guilty parties might even confess their crimes and make their apologies on television, although such appearances were far more apt to feature political dissidents.[92] Major officials almost certainly wouldn't be placed on "TV trial"; instead, if they were demoted or dropped from the party, they simply disappeared from view, became "nonpersons" and spent the rest of their days in obscurity. That changed with glasnost: starting in 1987 some of them, such as Bukharin and Khruschev, began to be mentioned. The dramatized portrayal of Khruschev in the 1987 TV drama "Risk" generally was favorable in showing him as a "man of action" during the 1962 Cuban missile crisis.

Disasters, especially those caused (or even possibly caused) by human error, generally were reported only when they were so prominent that it would be almost impossible to hide them, as was the case with the crash of a Soviet plane at the Paris Air Show in 1973. Stories of more routine disasters—auto accidents, fires and so on—that are so prominent on U.S. television simply didn't show up on Soviet TV, and reports of criminal acts were almost as rare. When the latter did appear, generally they were presented as stories with beginnings, middles and ends: Viewers learned of how the criminal got started down the wrong road, what she or he did and how the trial came out; thus, they saw how well the Soviet criminal justice system worked. Only in rare instances of really dangerous criminals would unsolved crimes be reported, as was the case in the Moscow area in the mid-1980s when a rapist-murderer was at large and panic was rising.

Occasionally there were televised criminal trials,[93] but for their educational value, and not to cater to any public taste for sensationalism. A few surveys revealed that viewers would like to see more reporting of "sensational" events, and it was doubtful that they wanted this for educational purposes, but it remained a rarity. Sexual display rarely went beyond slightly low-cut gowns, unless it was essential to a drama—a rare exception. Violence also was limited to what was dramatically essential, although it could appear, often as excerpts from western news broadcasts, in news and other information programs to show antigovernment demonstrations in the capitalist world.

Quality of production in Soviet television improved considerably during the 1980s. Before then, most of the camera work was unimaginative and the staging rather flat. In the early days of TV, most of the dramas, operas, ballets and other spectacles were shot in theaters, and with relatively little use of close-up shots. When they were produced in TV studios, they sometimes featured a proscenium arch, in order to create the impression of being in a real theater. By the mid-1970s, the shooting had become far more typical of what viewers in other industrialized nations were used to. Lighter material, such as quiz shows and satire or comedy (but nothing resembling U.S. situation comedy), featured a more leisurely pace of editing than was customary in western Europe, North America and Japan. Newsreaders, too, became more relaxed, although none emulated the chatty approach taken by many U.S. newscasters. Also, partly thanks to satellites, film clips and on-the-scene reports became far more common. Up until the Gorbachev era, interviews usually were very sober affairs, especially when a high government official was being interviewed.

As Gorbachev assumed leadership, Soviet viewers began to see a very different sort of political leader on TV—one who displayed and even encouraged spontaneity. (As I sat in the office of Gosteleradio vice chairman Henrikus Yushkiavitshus in September 1985 and watched the relay of a transmission from Siberia showing Gorbachev making spontaneous comments, mixing with the crowd, encouraging others to be frank and open, the vice chairman told me, "I think your Mr. Reagan has met his match!") Not all high-ranking Soviet officials followed Gorbachev's lead, but clearly he hoped that more would, and he frequently appeared in newscast items as the questioner, the challenger, seeking more direct involvement by officials and the broader population alike.

Visitors from western industrialized nations who watched Soviet television found Soviet TV newscasts very different from what they usually saw. Material about the Soviet Union took up about two-thirds of each edition of "Vremya" and about half of "Today in the World." That material almost always featured the activities and statements of Soviet leaders, included at least one item about increases in factory or collective farm production, and was filled out with other positive items about the nation. There often was an item or two about some model citizen. There also may have been one or two items on such social problems as industrial pollution, alcoholism or drug abuse (the two latter issues were brought to the fore in the Gorbachev era), but quite often the problem was presented so as to show that someone either had a solution to it or was working on one. Soviet TV rarely left its viewers in suspense, at least regarding events and situations within the country. The foreign news items generally included positive stories about the country's allies and about the Third World nations, and almost always featured problems in the capitalist world: strikes, inflation, unemployment, crime waves, racial prejudice,[94] although that decreased during the glasnost era.

Whether items were fresh or a few days old didn't seem to matter, so long as they illustrated some important point. Items might even be held back for a few days so that their disclosure would coincide with the occurrence of a predictable event, e.g., the release of an item on a defector from the North Atlantic Treaty Organization (NATO) on the day NATO began its annual conference in 1980. Soviet journalism operated under very different standards than did western journalism, by and large—standards that stressed the ideological value of information as illustrations of Marxist tenets such as the progressive nature of socialism/communism and the decline of capitalism. Not that western journalism isn't ideologically based, but Soviet journalism entailed a more conscious process of displaying ideology.

That extended to some entertainment programs, as well: In the course of my September 1985 visit to Moscow I saw a delightfully produced animated program (paper cutouts) for children which illustrated a poem by Marshak entitled "Mr. Twister." A rich American turns away a hungry black man, then, for whatever reason, travels with his family (wife, daughter, daughter's pet monkey) and his car (the "Twistermobile") to Leningrad. He checks into an elegant hotel, only to discover that there is a black guest, which causes him to depart immediately. But the hotel clerk telephones other clerks and tells them about this prejudiced American who probably will come to their hotels, with the result that all of the hotels in Leningrad sprout "no vacancy" signs and the Twister family spends the night on park benches, then leaves the country the next day. The one thing that the program does not point out is that Marshak's poem was written in the late 1920s, yet much of the production gave the impression that this was a slice of contemporary America.

Regional capital and other large-city television stations took far more from Moscow than they sent to it. Many of them received two services, via land line or satellite, as a mixture of programming from the various Moscow channels, with the exception of Channel Three. There were to be two services for the entire nation by the early 1990s, but the U.S.S.R. didn't reach that goal before its dissolution. Stations outside Moscow did contribute to the central operation, and several productions each week came from Kiev, Leningrad, Tashkent, Alma-Ata and other centers, which also provided items for "Vremya" and "Today in the World." There were weekly series on Soviet TV that featured life in different parts of the country, such as "Atlas of the Soviet Peoples." A Soviet sociologist conducting an ethnosociological study in Moldavia in the late 1970s estimated that about 5 percent of Moldavian TV's First Program was devoted to such programs.[95]

Regional TV also was used to instill more "modern" values in "traditional" societies. That was seen as particularly important in the predominantly Moslem republics of central Asia, where religious customs, holidays and practices still played important roles in many people's daily lives, despite the government's attempts to discourage religious practices. Television and the other mass media were used to replace (or to attempt to replace) religious holidays and observances with secular ones, such as Shepherd's Day.[96] In republics with a strong Russian Orthodox tradition, TV sometimes was even used to show viewers how such events as weddings should be treated. The problem here was that weddings handled by the local government (the only "proper" Communist way) were so cheerless, bureaucratic and even rude that many people, believers and unbelievers alike, wanted the dignity and splendor of a church wedding. By watching "proper" weddings on TV, bureaucrats might understand that they could do considerably more to give weddings meaning and beauty, and viewers in general might be more inclined to use such services.[97]

There was scattered evidence to indicate that audiences couldn't find much that was truly local or regional in local and regional broadcasts.[98] A few of the regional TV services took special pains to produce high-quality programming because they had some outside competition. Parts of the Ukrainian Republic and Byelorussia adjoined Poland, much of Estonia was within reach of Finnish television, and Moldavia bordered Rumania. In every case, some (and for Estonia nearly all) viewers could understand the other languages, and especially in the case of Estonia-Finland during the Soviet era, they could see television fare that differed from much of Soviet TV. Producers in those republics tried to present material in a livelier style and to emphasize regional events and culture in ways that avoided the sometimes stereotypical approach of the national services. Estonian TV even developed a monthly program in the late 1960s in which government officials were confronted with questions called in by viewers, some of them very direct.[99] Polish TV had a similar program in the 1970s, but nothing like it appeared on national television in the U.S.S.R. until a year of so after Gorbachev's rise to power.

THE AUDIENCE

For the past several decades, most western broadcast systems have utilized survey research to assess the size, composition and preferences of the audience. Soviet assessments developed along somewhat different lines. For one thing, the "of the people, by the people, for the people" aspect of communism seemed to retard the development of survey-based audience research, not only in broadcasting, but in most other fields; there was little need to assess audiences, since those in charge of broadcasting naturally would have the best interests of the public in mind (and often thought themselves to be in a better position to judge what those interests should be than was the public itself). For another, Stalin and his closest followers had little love for sociological research, perhaps because they found it too heavily influenced by bourgeois (meaning western) thought and practices, perhaps because they were so autocratic that they saw little value in asking the public's opinion on anything. At any rate, after some promising beginnings on the development of Marxist-Leninist-based sociological research methods in the 1920s, such research came to an almost total halt by the early 1930s and didn't resurface until the late 1950s, following Khruschev's 1956 denunciation of many of Stalin's more brutal and restrictive practices.[100]

Soviet broadcasters did encourage audience members to write letters, which were regarded as an important element in assessing audience reactions. There was nothing very systematic about that encouragement, however, and therefore no way for broadcasters to conduct analyses of trends in viewing or listening. Also, there was no way for broadcasters to determine how representative such letters and their writers were of the more general public. As a result, although the 1 to 2 million letters sent to Soviet radio and TV stations each year were subjected to more careful analysis than they would have been in most western countries, they did leave large gaps in the overall picture.[101]

By the late 1950s, it was clear to Soviet broadcasters that they needed to know more about their audiences, yet even then broadcasters seemed reluctant to establish units to conduct the necessary research. It was obvious that western broadcasters were reaching a fair share of the audience (precisely how much was unknown, due to the lack of survey research), and anecdotal evidence indicated that Radio Liberty, the BBC and the VOA were enjoying some credibility. Yet the first survey-based studies of the broadcast audience didn't come along until 1962,[102] and even then radio and television were a small part of a larger area of inquiry. Those "time budget" surveys (How do people spend their leisure time?)[103] almost always looked at the pursuits of urban dwellers, either en masse or as some specific occupational category and almost never looked at the satisfaction or dissatisfaction the audience might express about programming in general or in particular. The first few surveys showed people spending far more time with radio than with television—not surprising, since there were not as yet all that many TV sets in the country—but surveys taken in the late 1960s showed TV pulling ahead of radio by a substantial margin and in fact outstripping all other leisure-time activities.

Most surveys in the 1960s were conducted by sociologists from the major Soviet universities (Moscow State, Leningrad, Kiev); Soviet broadcasters took some interest in the results but rarely conducted their own survey research. However, Gosteleradio carried out a major survey in 1968, with a sample size of over 5,000 and at 30 locations, urban and rural, throughout the country. Furthermore, the major object of inquiry appears to have been degrees of satisfaction with various media presentations of various types of material. Newspapers were favored for foreign news, followed by radio and then TV, but there was widespread dissatisfaction with the amount of foreign news on radio and television (although collective farmers by and large felt there was enough). Broadcast media interpretation and comment on international affairs also got fairly low marks for amount and for credibility (collective farmers, Communist Party members and government workers gave the broadcast media higher marks than did other occupational and social groups).[104]

But the most sensational survey from the 1960s was a detailed study of audience preferences for TV programs in Leningrad, conducted by University of Leningrad sociologist Boris Firsov in 1967.[105] Sample size was nearly 2,000, all of those surveyed lived and worked in Leningrad, there were roughly equal numbers of each sex, and there was representation of different educational levels. About 85 percent of them had TV sets (unusually high for the Soviet Union at that time, but Leningrad viewers already had access to three TV channels, and the city was prosperous by Soviet standards). Nearly 40 percent of those who had sets said that TV lived up to their expectations, but nearly 40 percent said that they felt "some disillusionment" with the medium, while slightly over 20 percent found it "hard to say" how they felt.

Educational programs and broadcasts on sociopolitical themes got "hard to judge-rarely watch" responses from over half of those surveyed, and serious music and opera just half in that category. Twenty-five percent of those sampled said that they did not like serious music and opera broadcasts. Only one program type turned out to have a higher dissatisfaction figure, but it was an extremely important category: news and current affairs, where 27 percent said they did not like such broadcasts. In another section of the survey, Firsov asked viewers what it was that they found most inadequate in television information broadcasts. Roughly a third of the respondents said that they had no specific complaints, a fourth of them answered that they rarely watched such broadcasts (Firsov did not ask why), and just under a fifth criticized them for lack of candor and for poor on-the-spot reporting of events. A smaller-scale survey done in Sverdlovsk in 1971 showed much the same results, as did a study of rural viewers undertaken at about the same time, although the latter showed even less interest in watching informational broadcasts. They appeared to regard TV almost exclusively as an entertainment medium.[106]

In 1969, Soviet sociologist L. Kogan summarized various studies of television audiences and concluded that people tended to look to the medium for general information and for entertainment. He intimated that those in charge of TV shouldn't expect to use the medium as a transmission belt for heavy, detailed propaganda.[107] When I visited Moscow State University's Faculty of Journalism in 1970, one researcher told me that broadcasters and government officials alike were quite concerned over the various indications of public disinterest in or dissatisfaction with TV news but seemed at a loss to know what to do about it. His proposal for a study of psychological characteristics of audiences in terms of their preferences for different types of news and modes of presentation met with little response, probably because it was considered too "radical."

Further studies undertaken during the 1970s tended to reinforce those earlier conclusions, but also showed that party workers and government officials had high levels of interest in the news and its interpretation.[108] A 1979 Firsov study in Leningrad (N=800) sought to discover whether people thought that newspapers, radio and TV should be more active in "expressing public opinion," "informing people on work done by governmental bodies" and so on. Depending upon the specific question, between 35 percent and 53 percent of the sample thought that newspapers and radio should become more active, but the figures for TV ranged between 12 and 18 percent.[109] That seems to confirm Kogan's earlier suspicion that most viewers didn't look to TV as a major source of detailed information, although it was impossible to tell from the survey data whether that was because they got plenty of it from other media, whether TV did a poor job of presenting detailed information, whether people craved relaxation so much that they resented anything that took time away from it, or some combination of those elements.

Despite the negative findings, Soviet citizens clearly liked a lot of what they saw on television. Set sales and amounts of viewing time continued to increase, although some of the studies revealed that better-educated individuals spent considerably less time (as much as a third less) watching than did others.[110] Older people tended to watch more, and men spent more time with TV than did women. That probably was in part a function of the dual role of so many Soviet women, who very often had full-time jobs *and* were expected to "keep house." However, one survey report (date probably the late 1980s; method not indicated) was interpreted by its author as showing that " ... women prefer reading books and magazines, while men prefer consumption of information."[111] Why such preferences existed went unexplored.

Survey results, especially those resulting from studies undertaken by the broadcasters themselves, rarely were made public. University studies became quite numerous by the late 1970s, and some were reported in Soviet journals, though not always in enough detail to answer important methodological questions. But most of the studies were very general, very "safe" or both. Time-budget surveys in particular had the virtue of being as politically nonsensitive as anything could be in the Soviet Union. There were few qualitative studies of audience interests, desires and opinion; they generally indicated quite widespread dissatisfaction with a lot of the informational programming on Soviet TV, and Soviet broadcasters seemed to accept their results as valid. Yet there were almost no research projects employing in-depth interviews to get at more specific causes of dissatisfaction or indifference, and almost none that tested the effects of varying styles of presentation on comprehension of programs, audience satisfaction and other subjective factors.

Such studies wouldn't have been out of order in Soviet society, and people probably would have responded to penetrating and critical questions quite honestly, although Soviet citizens were far less accustomed to being asked such questions by survey researchers than are Americans. But there was something of a "we know best" attitude among many Soviet broadcasters, as there was and is the world over, and when that attitude was coupled with the overall "from the top down" pattern of decision-making in Soviet society in general, that didn't produce an optimal climate for meaningful and influential survey research.

The glasnost spirit did produce a few changes in that climate; in fact there were attempts to learn more about audiences desires shortly before Gorbachev came to power.[112] Gosteleradio established a full-fledged research department for broadcasting in 1984, and the head of the department, V. P. Volkov, told me in a 1985 interview in Moscow that the department's real breakthrough in establishing respectability came when the producers of a series called "Youth and the World" realized through survey data that their program drew very few viewers within its target audience: teenagers. At first the producers refused to accept the data as valid but eventually asked the research department to try to discover why the program wasn't popular. The department's in-depth research showed that teenagers didn't like the "canned" interviews: The Soviet and foreign interviewees seemed to be responding to formulaic questions with formulaic answers, most of them heavy on ideology. They didn't sound like "normal" people. Teenagers wanted to know more about the everyday lives of the interviewees and wanted to see them speak in "natural" language and in "natural" settings. The producers made such changes and soon saw their target-group ratings double and even triple. Other producers realized the value of carefully conducted surveys, and the department's workload increased to the point where it had to schedule some surveys a year or more in the future. According to Volkov, it helped a great deal that Gosteleradio itself took the department's work seriously and made it clear that it expected producers to do so as well.[113]

Soviet sociologists also began to ask more pointed questions about media use. A survey by Oleg Manaev (N=2,000 for one data set, N=800 for another) conducted between 1984-88 asked younger (ages 18-30) people in the Byelorussian Republic what they thought of media output intended for them in particular. There appeared to be a growing distrust of the media among that group, and it was the older (21-30) members who were more dominant in the "distrustful" segment of the sample. Manaev also asked whether his respondents listened to western radio stations. The first sample set, collected in 1985, had 63 percent who claimed to do so more or less regularly, while the second sample set (1987) had 83 percent who made the same claim. His correlation of those distrusting Soviet mass media and trusting western radio showed that the latter was trusted by a seven-to-one margin over the former. He even included in his published article on the survey the bold (for a Soviet citizen) conclusion that " ... glasnost has considerably expanded people's possibilities for satisfying their needs for information yet has left the possibility of free expression of their own opinion unchanged." He then discussed the growth of community newspapers in Byelorussia, where people *could* express themselves more freely, and concluded by saying, "The model of a truly democratic system of mass communications may be conceived as a forum accessible to all, in which everyone can speak his mind, a kind of information market where the social exchange of knowledge, values and norms takes place."[114] The Soviet system was hardly such a market, even with glasnost and an increasing awareness among party officials of the value of sociological research in understanding attitudes and behavior.[115]

MINORITIES AND THE MEDIA

Official policy in the Soviet Union was color-blind and status-blind; all citizens were equal.[116] That meant ethnic minorities, as well, and the country had many such groups, from Inuit in the far north to Kazakhs and other central Asians to small enclaves of "Volga" Germans, Chechnyans, Ossetians and Sami. A number of them received broadcast services (mostly on radio, and for limited amounts of time per day or week) in their own languages. Most of the programs tended to be somewhat folkloric (music, dance, crafts, folk tales), although there often were the themes of opposition to religious practices and of criticism of the economic "backwardness" that had characterized many ethnic regions before the Bolshevik Revolution.

National television (Channels One and Two) featured a few programs each week about various minority groups. Here, the emphasis was on how well each group had managed to balance its own language, customs, etc., with its more broadly Soviet character, thus underlining the message that the U.S.S.R. was a nation founded on the principle of "one out of many," where the many could both remain Chechnyans, etc., and take their places of duty, mutual respect and honor within the Soviet Union. The regional and republic broadcast services often carried several hours a day of programming in "minority" languages (that is, non-Russian, although most groups thus served wouldn't have regarded themselves as minorities in their own republics). Some of that programming allegedly consisted of programs produced in Moscow but dubbed into other languages, although Henry Norr points out that it was difficult to determine whether the dubbing actually took place.[117]

A "newsmaker" (one who is interviewed, quoted, discussed or mentioned in TV news items) study conducted by Mickiewicz and Jamison between 1987 and 1989 revealed that central Asians were heavily underrepresented, Transcaucasians (Georgia, Armenia, Azerbaijan) quite underrepresented if one removed items about Soviet Foreign Minister Eduard Shevernadze (a Georgian), and people from the Baltic republics (Latvia, Lithuania and Estonia) slightly underrepresented. People from rural areas rarely appeared as newsmakers, whether they were minorities or not.[118]

Old animosities between minorities almost never were mentioned in broadcasts, and absolutely never when the animosity was between the minority and "greater Russia." Even before the collapse of the Soviet Union, the conflict between Armenians and Azerbaijanis showed that old grievances were far from dead; the fierce and devastating war between Chechnya and Russia in 1995-96 underlined that message.

PROBLEM AREAS

So much about Soviet broadcasting was not made public that it was difficult to discern problem areas. In line with the overall Soviet philosophy of concentrating attention on positive aspects of Soviet society, broadcasting was not subjected to continuing critical evaluation. However, party and government officials made critical comments from time to time, newspaper reporters occasionally wrote articles about the shortcomings of broadcasting, and newspapers as well as radio and TV carried extracts from audience letters, some of which featured very sharp criticism.

Technical problems appeared to head the list. Television sets broke down too easily, and repairs were hard to arrange and often were unsatisfactory. Following that would be the issue of *program choice,* although viewers in Moscow and Leningrad had less to complain about on that score than did the tens of millions of people living in rural areas and small towns (or even some fairly large cities), where there was still only one TV channel available. Even where there were two or more channels, viewers sometimes complained that there was no real choice between them, because both often carried the same sort of program at the same time. By the mid-1980s, program schedules seemed more often to be arranged so as to give more real choices during the same time period.

Dissatisfaction with program content may have been common enough, but there was less direct evidence of it. Audience letters on the subject appeared in newspapers and on the air, and occasional surveys referred to it as well. Certainly the sorts of surveys that asked people to express their program preferences showed that a fair share of informational programs, which took up a large portion of airtime, didn't attract many viewers. But those surveys didn't indicate why that was so; what we know along those lines came out of some of the letters and also was reflected in party and governmental criticism of the broadcast media. From those comments, we learn that informational broadcasting often was seen as slow, incomplete, predictable and dull.

One particularly prominent example of what viewers didn't like was the "model person," whether factory worker, soldier, teacher, farmer, student or whatever else. Such figures appeared over radio and television daily, most often in news items, but also in documentaries, features, interview shows and even contest shows, as in "Let's Go, Girls!" They also cropped up in feature films. Part of what made them boring was the very predictability of those appearances. I sometimes heard Soviet viewers say, when watching a newscast, "It's about time for another hero to appear," and usually they were right. The "model," or hero, hardly was a Soviet invention—Russian Empress Catherine the Great issued a directive outlining a "positive hero's traits" more than two centuries ago and advocated that writers include them in their works[119]—but they were seen by Soviet authorities as especially important in reinforcing the concept of "the new Soviet man." Often, however, they were simply too good, smart and strong to be true to life;[120] often, too, when actual Soviet citizens were the "heroes," they sounded as if they were reading lines for the interviewer, which probably was true on some occasions.[121]

Yet another example of predictable, boring material was the tendency of news and other informational broadcasts to illustrate the progressive nature of socialism by showing activity on a collective farm or factory while reciting highly detailed figures on the latest reported increase in industrial or agricultural output. Viewers sometimes pointed out that TV used stock footage for some of the farm and factory scenes, even when they claimed to be presenting a specific factory's or farm's output, and viewers and listeners alike found it difficult to grasp the significance of the specific percentages and other numbers that came pouring out of the loudspeaker. The predictability of the appearance of such items on newscasts matched that of items on heroes: Viewers and listeners knew just about when to expect them and what they would say and show. Viewers also compared the conditions under which some model worker fulfilled her or his quota with their own working conditions, as did a worker interviewed for a *Pravda* article in 1982: "Often when taping a program about 'model' workers the producer doesn't show that production is the hard work of many different workers. When you watch the film you hear the announcer telling about records, percentage of growth, but on the screen the workers are smiling and doing something easy. In that way we get an incorrect idea of the price of a record and the work that goes into it. When talking about socialist competition one has to look at work conditions, is there enough equipment."[122]

Soviet broadcasting continued to feature "hero" and "progress" items, despite any indications of audience lack of interest, because they were so basic to Communist philosophy. What was surprising about this is that there was so little apparent attempt to make the items fresher, livelier and less predictable. Perhaps those in the highest level of authority didn't really understand such a need, while those lower in command understood it but didn't dare to take corrective measures until encouraged to do so under glasnost. Even then, much did not change.

Certain departments, the Youth Department in particular, did make some breaks with that tradition even as glasnost was being proclaimed; the Youth Department series "Twelfth Floor" (the department's location), a live studio show that encouraged young people to pose tough questions to administrators and others in power, was quite bold by the standards of Soviet TV—too bold, perhaps, because it was dropped from the schedule in 1988 after having been watered down.[123] Maintaining the interest of younger viewers was a top priority—there were concerns that they would be indifferent to the medium because they might not see it as terribly relevant to their own lives—so a limited degree of experimentation may have been more acceptable in that area.[124]

Basic comprehension of broadcasts also seems to have been a problem. Soviet reporters and writers, much like their counterparts in most broadcast systems, had a tendency to write and speak in terms that they themselves understood. When there's a long-standing tradition of discouraging the rewriting of political statements (most of which sounded very formal), some audience members may have wondered just what the message was. Soviet surveys reported by Mickiewicz seem to indicate as much:

> In the Taganrog survey, respondents were asked to define fifty words commonly used in newspaper articles in foreign affairs. About a quarter of the respondents had absolutely no understanding of the word "colonialism" and about two fifths had no understanding of "dictatorship." Almost half were unable to say what "imperialism" meant. ... In a survey on television programs, 93 percent of the rural Russians with up to a fourth grade education could not understand programs on socio-political topics. ... Nonetheless, even though lack of audience comprehension was more widespread than had been expected, Soviet theorists still widely held that this differentiation, attributable to lack of formal education, would not be permanent.[125]

Soviet television portrayed women in much the same stereotyped way that most electronic media systems have done: usually as housewives, rarely as newsmakers or as experts. However, it did pay some attention to their roles in working on collective farms, in factories and in hospitals (the majority of Soviet doctors were women). Accusations of stereotyping often were directed at TV's failure to show viewers how the Soviet boast of full equality for women was almost never true within the home, where men generally expected women to do virtually all of the work. Sociologist N. Kirillova could just as well have been speaking of television when she observed of the press that, "An increased role for men in these matters [raising children, household work] is not simply desirable: it is necessary for the normal development of the family and of children, and for raising the prestige of fathers. ... The press can do a lot more. It would be useful to expand publications about the distinctive features of women's work and daily life ..."[126]

During the glasnost period, some women did attain positions of greater responsibility and visibility in television. Perhaps the most notable example was Bella Kurkova, producer on Leningrad TV's "Fifth Wheel," one of the more outspoken public affairs programs to appear on Soviet television.

Neglect of rural areas probably wouldn't have been considered a problem by Soviet viewers living in or near the nation's largest cities. In fact, those living in smaller cities and in rural areas might not have perceived it as a problem either, since Soviet national broadcast services always had neglected them. Furthermore, there were wired radio services, many of them with studios, in a number of the collective farms. However, L.N. Denisova makes it quite clear that there *was* a feeling of being ignored and forgotten among rural residents,[127] who felt some resentment toward the Moscow-dominated character of so much TV programming from the national services. Furthermore, rural areas often were underserved in terms of numbers of TV sets. That led the government to furnish rural and smaller urban sites with TV sets installed in cultural and social clubs, but even as late as the early 1980s, many clubs still didn't have them. The government also began to equip mobile video units in the late 1980s. They traveled from one rural location to another, providing small numbers of people—the self-contained trailer-like units could hold only 15 at a time—with at least a bit of occasional exposure to television.[128] But there never were many of them, and one wonders whether rural audiences appreciated such token service.

FOREIGN INFLUENCES ON PROGRAMMING

Aside from recorded music, Soviet radio used very little imported program material. Soviet television, on the other hand, made quite heavy use of broadcasts originating in other countries, especially the socialist nations of eastern Europe. Some of the programs were prepared especially for Soviet TV by East German, Hungarian and other broadcast systems, but more were news items and sports coverage exchanged through the Intervision system. It was a rare night without at least one such news item on "Vremya" or "Today in the World," and a rare week when there weren't two or three sports events (usually highlights, but sometimes complete coverage) from East Berlin, Warsaw, Sofia or elsewhere in eastern Europe, usually received through the eastern European Intervision TV Exchange system. Feature films from those same nations often appeared on Soviet TV, as well. Such material helped to reinforce the message of "socialist solidarity."

Broadcast systems in the Third World (developing nations) occasionally placed material with Soviet television—usually feature films. When news items originated in such countries, usually they were produced by Soviet reporters or were picked up from news services such as Visnews or UPITN, then given voice-overs in the studio.

Entertainment programs from western broadcasters rarely appeared on Soviet screens before glasnost, although BBC's television adaptation of John Galsworthy's *The Forsythe Saga* was carried in the early 1970s and seemed to be quite popular. (The description of it in the Soviet TV guide highlighted the class-based structure of British society portrayed in the series and stated that present-day British society still showed many of those same features.) Documentaries appeared somewhat more often, but most of them were critical of some aspect of capitalist society. Feature films from western nations were shown on Soviet TV every now and again; they, too, were apt to portray the negative aspects of life in those nations.

Intervision and Eurovision regularly exchanged material, and the Soviet Union received news items and sports coverage from western Europe (and occasionally the United States) through this channel. In fact, Soviet TV officials were fond of pointing out that they received from the west far more than the west took from them. The figures seemed to bear them out: The average yearly ratio was between 4- and 5-to-1, and the lion's share of imports from the east were sports programs, not news items.[129] A Polish TV news director mentioned to me during my 1978 visit to the Polish broadcasting facilities that Polish TV itself rarely took news items offered by Soviet TV through Intervision "because they were so boring." But that, too, appeared to change as a result of glasnost, and the more conservative Czechs and East Germans sometimes refused items from Soviet TV because they were too "radical."

Whether any of the imported programming had any effect on Soviet TV production and programming practices is questionable. Most of it was chosen for ideological reasons, and not for whatever entertainment value it might have had. But some of it may have had an unintended effect on viewers: Even shows featuring crime, police brutality, greed and so forth may portray fascinating or attractive settings. The fashions, house furnishings, automobiles and many other things that western viewers would have taken for granted often caught the attention of Soviet viewers. Whether they believed what they saw is another matter, and if they did believe it, they may have felt that the price to be paid for it—slums, crime, unemployment, which usually were prominent in such programming—wasn't worth it.

RELATIONS WITH OTHER MEDIA

The Soviet press regularly carried information on broadcast schedules, but few newspapers featured a daily column of criticism and evaluation of broadcasting, as do many western European newspapers. Party and government comments about broadcasting were published, and often those comments were highly critical. Yet the press didn't often take it upon itself to rake television or radio over the coals. When it did, the criticism probably was inspired by comments made by a party or government official. For example, a 1982 article in *Pravda* favorably reviewed changes in the presentation of radio news, but not for coverage of economic news: "The economy is invariably the focus of public attention, but analysis of it on radio programs often suffers from dryness and narrowness of theme. 'Fulfilled,' 'overfulfilled,' 'competing to fulfill,' 'brought into operation,' 'commissioned'—phrases like those and figures are constantly heard in bulletins and often provide no impression of the scale of successes or the way they were achieved. Of course, it is not easy to do without weighty figures. But all the same, the impact on the listener is more effective when a vivid comparison is made or a story about people and their destinies is told."[130]

The Soviet central news agency, Tass, supplied a daily service to all Soviet broadcast stations, but its style was more suitable for newspapers than for broadcasting, since it was full of just the sort of precise figures and other details mentioned in the *Pravda* article. Even so, Tass output was regarded as the backbone of newscasts, and much of its copy was read on the air verbatim, making many newscasts sound very much like "oral newspapers," which was one of Lenin's original purposes for radio.

There was considerable cooperation between broadcasting and the Soviet film monopoly (Goskino). Soviet television made some of its own short films, but most feature films came from the Goskino studios. Many were made for distribution through both cinema and television and often were released through the two outlets almost simultaneously. Television paid for any films it commissioned, but as both media were operated by the state, there was no profit involved. Soviet cinema operators often complained about the negative effect that TV had on cinema attendance, especially because of the policy of showing brand-new films on television, but the complaints fell on deaf ears: The public had become far too accustomed to seeing new films on television to tolerate their disappearance.

Shortly before the breakup of the Soviet Union, there was another example of a liberalizing trend in the media, although it had little effect on TV. The first independent film studio, Fora-Film, appeared in 1989, and by 1991 there were roughly 140 such studios, working through the Independent Film Association. The independent producers had little success in placing their work on TV, which remained faithful to its Goskino partners, but somewhat better luck with videocassettes.[131]

INTERNATIONAL COOPERATION

In addition to its exchange of materials through Intervision and Eurovision, Soviet television sometimes became involved in coproductions with TV systems in other countries, such as "Toilers of the Sea" (a Victor Hugo novel) with French Pathé. "Peter the Great," a four-part 1986 miniseries on the 17th century Russian czar, involved the joint efforts of the U.S. NBC network and the Soviet Gorki Film Studios, plus several other European television systems.[132] The scale of activity picked up in the glasnost years, particularly for film production.[133]

The U.S.S.R. also held an annual TV program convention starting in the mid-1960s, mainly for the purpose of encouraging program sales to nations that weren't members of Intervision. Intervision members got to display their work to interested buyers from two to four dozen other countries, usually including several from western Europe and many from the Third World, such as Iran and Argentina. Entertainment programs attracted the most attention, especially children's programs (a category in which many of the eastern European nations and the U.S.S.R. excelled—they were imaginatively produced and carried well-nigh universal messages such as "be kind to others," "respect your parents," etc.) and TV productions of classical drama such as Chekov's "The Sea Gull." Documentaries on cultural subjects and on nature also drew some business.[134]

THE NEW MEDIA

The Soviet Union developed a very ambitious system of communication satellites far earlier than most other industrialized nations, but in most other respects it lagged far behind in working with the new media. There were several million TV sets in large cities that were served through master antenna systems, but none had the capacity for program origination. Aside from that, there was no cable television, although many Soviet citizens knew about it. Soviet authorities announced early in 1987 that fiber-optic cable would be laid throughout Moscow over the next two years, in order to improve reception: Most Soviet citizens, and those in Moscow in particular, lived in medium- to high-rise concrete and steel apartment houses, and reception sometimes was poor.[135] That turned out to be largely just another unfulfilled promise.

Audiocassette recorders fulfilled a larger media function than was typical in industrialized nations. They were used to record and play back programs from Radio Liberty, the Voice of America, the BBC and other western broadcasters targeting the Soviet Union. They also served as transmission belts for "magnetozdat": materials taped by Soviet citizens with dissenting points of view to express. They might be poetry or prose, spoken or sung, poorly or well-recorded; they might be duplicated in the hundreds or in a few copies only. A 1980s song by Alexander Galich honored their creators:

> There is no orchestra, no loge or tier
> No claque with its hullaballoo
> A "Yauza" tape recorder's here,
> That's all, but it will do.[136]

Direct broadcasting through satellites (DBS) would have been feasible in the U.S.S.R., since Soviet satellite technology was sufficiently advanced. Furthermore, it would have helped to extend service to the most remote corners of the nation, especially in Siberia. Many small Siberian villages received little if any TV, and authorities were aware that its availability might help to induce people to remain in remote areas.[137] But it never became a high-priority area, and one high-ranking State Committee official with whom I spoke in 1985 thought that it might be a decade or more before it was. A Soviet telecommunications official stated in mid-1986 that the first scheduled launch of a DBS-capable satellite was to take place "before the end of the decade" but said nothing about whether individual households would be equipped to receive it.[138] Gladys Ganley claims that some Soviet citizens constructed their own satellite dishes to receive television programs from abroad,[139] but given the zeal with which Soviet authorities searched out illegal electronic equipment, it's doubtful that many people did so. And, as Ellen Mickiewicz indicates, homebuilt dishes aren't very efficient.[140]

Videotape recorders were available before glasnost, but they were expensive (roughly $2,500) and there was little prerecorded material for them. Videocassette recorders also were available in special stores that accepted only "hard" currencies (dollars, Swiss francs, etc., but not rubles), at $3,500-$4,500 for Japanese-made machines, and there was a black market in used western machines, which cost slightly less. Soviet citizens fortunate enough to travel abroad often brought back recorders, which could be converted quite easily to fit Soviet standards (SECAM). There was little prerecorded material on cassette, but again the black market provided some western cassettes, and in 1982 the government announced new laws that required customs officials to check any cassettes brought into the country and to confiscate any that "could harm the country's political or economic interests, state security, public order or the population's health or morals." Even so, there were black market rings and illegal clubs where enthusiasts could view and purchase movies from the west. There also were growing numbers of home video makers, who produced and exchanged cassettes among themselves.[141]

In 1984, the Soviet Union began to produce its own VCRs, basing them on Japanese technology, but a 1984 article in *Literaturnaya Gazeta* (Literary Gazette) indicated that the software (prerecorded programs) simply wasn't available; the Soviet broadcasting and film industries hadn't recorded cassettes of the most popular Soviet TV shows and films, much less made any special productions for distribution through VCR.[142] Within a year, such cassettes did begin to appear, in part because of the black market in western cassettes, especially feature films. A few video rental shops were in business by the end of 1985, and they continued to grow; most of what they distributed was Soviet-made material. Much of it was excellent, with top-level performers (Bolshoi Ballet and Opera, for example), and a range of "how-to" (remodel an apartment, swim, train your dog) cassettes,[143] but TV administrators and performers didn't address some of the more difficult issues, such as performers' rights to extra compensation.[144]

Videocassette recorders played an important role during the August 1991 coup attempt. Although the coup plotters took over Gosteleradio, various individuals (foreign visitors and Soviet citizens) possessing videocameras were able to tape some of the coup activities, including resistance to the attempt; a number of those tapes quickly appeared on western television and even may have been shown on some cable television stations around the country.[145]

There seem to have been two major reasons for the slow development of the new media in the Soviet Union. One was the tendency of many Soviet officials to identify many of those media with the "decadent" west and with "mindless entertainment." The other was the complex structure of COMECON, the economic community set up to coordinate the production of the U.S.S.R. and the socialist states of eastern Europe. By mutual agreement, the various members of COMECON were supposed to determine who got to produce what. Some tentative decisions were reached regarding production of the new media, but no single COMECON member appeared ready to move ahead in a major way. That may have been part of an overall reluctance to set in motion a type of activity that would give the public a much freer and greater choice in what they received, and that might even have encouraged a measure of decentralization in business and industry. According to Rex Malik,[146] "Far from the Soviet Bloc catching up, the consensus seems to be that it is falling further behind. The snag with a philosophy of copying our [the west's] successes is that by the time they have been copied we have already moved on." While Malik's remarks dealt mainly with computers and the transfer of data, they also were relevant for the new media in the U.S.S.R. Computer education in the grade and high schools began in the mid-1980s and spread slowly through the education system, but it was far ahead of the development of VCRs or interactive cable.

CONCLUSION

Clearly Soviet broadcasting wasn't immune to change. Stalin would not have recognized much of what he would have seen or heard on Soviet TV or radio in the late 1980s, and he probably wouldn't have approved of much of it, either. Even Leonid Brezhnev, who died in 1983, would have been astonished to see such programs as "Twelfth Floor" or unrehearsed, unstaged press conferences, or coverage of the war in Afghanistan in which Soviet citizens could actually see their nation's soldiers wounded and dead. Until late in 1984, the war was presented very abstractly, but at that time the newspapers, followed later by broadcasting (a typical pattern—the latter usually waited for the former to take the first step), began to single out heroes who had died in combat and began to show actual combat footage.[147] Gorbachev's support for glasnost, plus his own enthusiastic television personality,[148] touched off a minor revolution in broadcasting, where presentational styles and topics sometimes became warmer and more self-critical than they had ever been in the past.

Prime Minister Khruschev also pushed the mass media to become more personal, more self-critical, speedier in reporting events, but some of those changes disappeared when he was deposed. Yet some of them remained (especially Mayak), just as some of the changes encouraged by Gorbachev remained after the collapse of the Soviet Union. But broadcasts from outside the country remained quite popular even when the glasnost spirit was at its peak. That was especially true when rumors spread and people wanted to check up on them (on Afghanistan, for instance, where a 1985 Radio Liberty survey of Soviet citizens' sources of information on the war there showed foreign radio and Soviet radio named almost equally, while both were several percentage points ahead of Soviet television).[149] Decades of distrust weren't about to vanish within a few years.

Despite certain geographical and technological circumstances that enabled the country to shut out unwanted messages from abroad with reasonable success for some period of time, the broadcast system had to try to adjust in order to hold its audiences, especially young people. There was genuine concern among Gosteleradio staff with whom I spoke in 1985 as to whether the present young generation could really understand the sacrifices of World War II, whether they would be ready to make the same sacrifices themselves, and whether TV could find ways to keep that sacrificial spirit alive in them.

In early 1986 Gorbachev stated that "only ideologically motivated literature could educate people to shoulder the burden of their time."[150] But it was not so easy to humanize that literature, whether radio news or TV drama, so that listeners and viewers would welcome it. In an increasingly diversified media environment, viewers and listeners in the largest cities did have other choices, and it wasn't easy to eliminate them. Whether Soviet officials liked the idea or not, their media world increasingly was driven by one powerful market force: competition. Not every viewer or listener necessarily welcomed change. Media accounts of corruption by officials, poor hospital care and so on, caused some citizens to write letters containing observations such as "even an avowed enemy of the U.S.S.R. would think twice before saying this about our motherland."[151] There was no single audience in the Soviet Union, any more than there was or is a single audience anywhere else. But those in charge of the electronic media often seemed unable to discern the differences between audiences; as a consequence, they often seemed unable to adapt their messages accordingly when it was obviously much easier to think in terms of "one audience, one message."

The Russian Federation

A BRIEF HISTORY

Boris Yeltsin and his followers had managed to lay the foundation stones of the Russian Federation's electronic media system even before the Soviet Union disappeared. Clearly they intended it to be different from the old Soviet model, but not terribly different: Much of the media-related legislation passed by the Soviet Parliament or decreed by Gorbachev in 1990-91 was included in the new Media Law adopted by the Russian Parliament at the end of 1991. It was supposed to go into effect on January 1, 1992, but didn't. A number of deputies wanted to include further restrictions on the media, including one that required journalists to disclose their confidential sources to courts and to investigative officers. Speaker of Parliament Ruslan Khasbulatov was particularly insistent on having tighter control over the media, and strongly disagreed with media criticism of Parliament. Yeltsin eventually signed the bill, and also issued a few restrictive decrees on his own, including a presidential edict in January 1992 ordering officials to use existing (Soviet) documents to guide themselves when looking into the publication of state secrets. And he also created a successor to Glavlit/GUOT: the State Inspectorate for the Defense of the Freedom of the Press and Mass Information, which, despite its title, was a censorship bureau, although it was to censor material only after its publication or broadcast.[152]

The government also would have a great deal to say about what the central broadcast service carried, and other services would be licensed only so long as they didn't stray too far from the government viewpoint. Those other services all were supposed to be under private ownership, and to support themselves through sales of ad time. But by mid-1992, it already was clear that radical adjustments to the nation's economy, moving from a Communist system to a capitalist one, were creating problems. Some of the state-supported industries were slow and highly reluctant to convert to profit-driven operations; some were so inefficient that they went out of business; and the new private businesses often were slow to take off, thanks to a combination of licensing problems, a hopelessly tangled regulatory bureaucracy and galloping inflation. The government also was proving reluctant to allow any stations to be owned wholly by private companies; instead, it preferred to maintain or obtain a share of the stations, and thus some degree of direct control.

One hope of the Russian government had been that media-related businesses would attract large numbers of investors, which would hold down influence from any one of them. But because the economy was so weak, and because the little strength it showed was in the hands of a small number of influential investors—banks and energy and construction companies in particular—they would come to dominate investment in the newly licensed electronic media services. Unlike private radio station Moscow Echo, most of whose backers and staff were experienced broadcasters, those new investors cared little for the public service side of broadcasting. They aimed for maximum profit, and there was little in any of the media laws to induce, much less require, them to invest in high-quality Russian-produced programming. North and South American fare, some of it already familiar and popular in the last few years of the Soviet Union, became even more familiar.[153] Sensationalism and pornography, rarely or never seen in Soviet days, became quite common. Even the broadcasts of Radio Liberty (RL), the last western station beamed at Soviet audiences to still be jammed, began to be heard over new private stations in Russia and some of the other republics, as those stations sold airtime to RL for solid U.S. dollars.

As of December 1992, all of the TV channels in Moscow still were either under government management or featured major investment by the government. It had taken over the Soviet Union's Ostankino Channel One service, which covered the Russian Federation and all of the other former Soviet republics; it had founded (1990) RTR, the television service of the Russian Republic, operated it over the old Channel Two, and still owned it; in 1992, it expanded St. Petersburg (formerly Leningrad) Channel Five into a national service, made it a joint-stock company, and owned 70 percent of its shares; the old Moscow Third Channel became a collective, owned by a group including the Moscow City Council and the Russian government; and the old Fourth Channel (educational) was split between Ostankino and Rossiya.

It wasn't until January 1993 that a 100 percent privately owned TV service, TV-6, came along, with investment in part by Turner Broadcasting Corporation (TBC), which later withdrew. It took a portion of the airtime on Channel Four. A few months later, another private company, NTV, was authorized to operate on Channel Three. The new private companies were outnumbered by the government channels, and the latter had had a year or more, depending upon the channel, to establish themselves.[154] The Russian government was taking very few chances of losing control of television, the more so (or so it must have seemed at the time) because the two major figures for heading the two private channels, Eduard Sagalayev and Igor Malashenko, both had worked for Gosteleradio.

In fact, it was very difficult during the first few years of the Russian Federation to find administrators of radio and TV stations, government or private, who had *not* had such experience. Where else could anyone in Russia have received it? That didn't necessarily mean that the private stations would be under government influence, as well, but it did increase the possibility that the degree to which their programming could reflect a truly independent approach would be more limited.

The practice of importing foreign programming grew rapidly even as the economy worsened. That probably was the dual result of an escapist tendency—life is so bad that it's at least some comfort to look at a glamorous life far away—and the very practical consideration of the low price of most imported programs. But the worsening economy also provoked instincts that hadn't been far below the surface in the Soviet Union, and occasionally surfaced even then. Anti-semitism was one of the more vicious forms, which was somewhat ironic, in that several of the leading figures in the media world were Jewish. Brian McNair notes the distribution in Red Square and elsewhere in the summer of 1993 of an article by Mikhayev which made the argument that the Russian state TV service was run by "a clique of 'non-Russian' co-conspirators with pro-Zionist sympathies who are undermining Russia's national pride."[155]

That emphasis on "Russianness" took still other forms. When Yeltsin assumed control over Ostankino, it could have been for any number of reasons, ranging from "because it was there" to "because we didn't want it used against us" to "we can use it to maintain Russian hegemony over the other republics." Since it could reach the entire area covered by the old Soviet Union, the Russian Federation enjoyed an advantage possessed by no other republic. Furthermore, Russians were used to ruling many of the countries around them, and the Soviet government had attempted to strengthen the union by emphasizing the teaching of Russian throughout all of the republics. And even though some of the transmitters used by Ostankino were being taken over by the former Soviet republics, many remained available to carry the old Channel One national service. Igor Malashenko wrote in an April 1993 issue of *Nezavisimaya Gazeta* (Independent Gazette) that, "Knowing that the same programs were being watched in Georgia, the Baltics and Central Asia helped many people to feel that they belonged to a historical community, even one which had been deprived of its name."[156] Oleg Slabynko, who succeeded Malashenko as Director of Television at Ostankino, stated that "the role of Ostankino as a unifying broadcaster is very important," noted that high percentages of the non-Russian populations in some of the former Soviet republics watched it, and felt that "Ostankino may be the station which can keep all these different peoples together, and help resolve ethnic problems."[157]

There was some consideration of setting up a truly inter-republic TV company, but the idea never really took off, due to quarreling of factions within the Russian Parliament and the unpopularity of a company that lay outside Russian control.[158] Even if it had been formed, one wonders whether it could have lasted for very long: the former republics often weren't on good terms with one another, most were suspicious of Russian motives in general, and the temptation of some of the really autocratic republic governments, Belarus in particular, to use such a service for obviously self-serving propaganda would almost certainly have angered some and bored many, destroying both faith and interest in its programs. The one company that attempted to provide any substantial form of interstate programming, Mir, received very little airtime for the purpose and soon went off air.

Yeltsin appeared to become more and more interested in using television to boost his own sometimes fading political stock. Starting in late 1992, he dismissed a number of top administrative Ostankino staff, replacing them with people who generally lacked experience with television, but whom he regarded as politically loyal. And they were. Vyacheslav Bragin, appointed as Director of TV in 1993, saw to it that airtime was readily available for the president and his trusted followers, even when it meant interrupting popular programs, although Yeltsin's political opponents were told that the schedule couldn't be altered. News items favored Yeltsin both in number and "slant": during the lead-up period to a national referendum in April 1993, he often was shown and heard in excerpts, whereas the Speaker of Parliament Ruslan Khasbulatov would be shown with a voice-over summary of his arguments.[159] (There were four points to the referendum; all of them related to support for Yeltsin, including one point calling for an early presidential election, which

Yeltsin and his supporters opposed. That turned out to be the closest thing to a vote against Yeltsin: 50 percent of the voters favored such an election.)

According to Mickiewicz, TV coverage of the referendum campaign exhibited "the traditions of Soviet television: excessive concentration on the capital city, with only cursory attention to the rest of the huge and highly differentiated country."[160] It is a common tendency of television services in industrialized nations to concentrate heavily on major urban areas, not only in their informational programming, but also in their factual and fictional entertainment. But in a nation exhibiting the degree of social, economic and political instability of Russia, knitting the nation together would seem to be a logical top priority for the government, and reaching out to the usually neglected cities (some of them with several hundred thousand people) and the almost totally neglected towns and countryside probably would have been as welcome as it was unprecedented. Perhaps Russian television was unable to manage the task for the simple reason that so few individuals in positions of control would have had any comprehension of how to reach those long-neglected viewers with messages that acknowledge the country beyond Moscow/St. Petersburg.

The referendum itself also revealed yet another aspect of reliance on the United States where TV was concerned. In this case, it was campaign advertising. Advisors from a California ad agency came to Moscow, met with Yeltsin's campaign manager, sketched out ideas, sent them back to California for semifinal production, got script for the production translated into Russian and sent it to a playwright for reworking into "culturally correct" form, then faxed the finished script to California for final editing. Getting Russians to see themselves as casting meaningful votes on something that would have a real impact on their lives was part of the objective; showing that Yeltsin's team could do what the Russian Duma (Parliament) could not was the other part. The vote went in Yeltsin's favor, but there were numerous allegations following the vote that not only had U.S. advisors worked on his behalf, but also their work was paid for in part from U.S. funds.[161] That was reinforcement for the point constantly made by anti-Yeltsin forces: Russia was giving up its birthright to American influence, and one had only to look at Russian television to see proof of it.

Television had two more important roles to play in what turned out to be a highly eventful 1993. The Russian parliamentary election in December saw something of a repeat performance in terms of the ways in which the Yeltsin forces used TV to support the party they favored ("Russia's Choice") and to thwart the opposition. It was Russia's first multiparty election (13 parties were on the ballot), but it also included a referendum on a new constitution that would give the president much greater power, and that was where Yeltsin concentrated his energies. He had disbanded the Parliament in September, and was free to develop and sign presidential decrees, one of which governed televised campaigning. It was actually quite evenhanded, in the sense that equal amounts of free airtime were available to each party registered for the election. The decree covered only Channels One and Two, both under government control, and state-administered radio; it did not include private stations.

There was an election commission to help assure fairness in media coverage of the campaign, and it ruled against the Yeltsin forces on more than one occasion, notably in its attempt to get the commission to forbid criticism of the draft constitution. However, it failed to do so in the case of Channel One's election eve showing of a film entitled "Hawk," which portrayed the most popular opposition figure, the ultranationalist Vladimir Zhirinovsky, through footage assembled from various rallies and other appearances by him.[162] Campaign rules forbade campaigning just before election day, yet "Hawk" had every appearance of being a campaign broadcast. The Yeltsin government also revoked the limitation on paid political advertising: it stood at 30 minutes per party at the start of the campaign, but vanished when the Yeltsin forces became concerned over Zhirinovsky's rise in popularity and attempted to outspend him. That brought welcome financial relief to the stations, but sent campaign costs soaring. Even with all of those special favors, Zhirinovsky's party (the Liberal Democrats, although they were neither liberal nor democratic) received the most votes—23 percent, eight points ahead of Russia's Choice.[163] Voters approved the proposed constitution by a slim margin.

Television's other major role in 1993 saw the medium become a very literal target for the opposition. The October 1993 anti-government revolt ended even more swiftly than had the 1991 coup attempt, but this time television became directly involved. President Yeltsin had suspended the Congress of People's Deputies (the larger Parliament) by decree on September 21. That also in effect cut off deputies' (members of Parliament) access to the airwaves, although it didn't stop broadcasters from criticizing the position of anti-Yeltsin members of Parliament and referring to "so-called deputies." Much of Parliament remained in the White House, now serving as Parliament's home, ordered Yeltsin to be removed from office, and named his vice president and rival Aleksandr Rutskoy as acting president. The Interior Ministry encircled the building with barbed wire, posted troops around its perimeter, and the nation waited to see whether the "rebels" would respond to government demands that they surrender and leave the building by October 4.

They didn't wait that long. On October 2, demonstrators confronted the troops as the rebels encouraged them to break through the cordon. Very soon, the cordon was gone and Rutskoy, Speaker of Parliament Khasbulatov and others moved to capture the nearby office building housing the offices of the mayor of Moscow and of the two private TV stations. They then set off for Ostankino's two buildings (studios and administration), where security forces were light. The rebels rammed a truck through the entrance to the studio building, and later fired a grenade launcher at the entrance; the security forces fired in response. Some Molotov cocktails (homemade incendiary bombs) were tossed into ground-floor rooms. The Head of Ostankino, Vyacheslav Bragin, could see what was happening from across the street, and issued an order that Channel One should shut down. An announcer came on in the midst of a televised football (soccer) match to tell viewers that the building was under attack and would go off the air. The announcement was so brief that viewers almost certainly were confused, but for the moment there appeared to be no other source of information available to enlighten them, and only a placard on the screen stating that, "BROADCASTS ON CHANNEL ONE AND FOUR HAVE BEEN CUT BY AN ARMED CROWD THAT HAS BURST INTO THE BUILDING"—something of an exaggeration, since few were inside the building yet, and Bragin himself had made the decision to cut the broadcast.[164]

Fortunately for the government, there had long been a system for allowing Channel Two (also under government control, but located elsewhere in Moscow) to switch over to Channel One frequencies (the Channel One network was the more extensive of the two), and it did. The government was able to keep the population informed as to what was happening, and the revolt turned out to be less extensive than it at first appeared to be. While the rebels did penetrate the ground floor of the Ostankino studio building, that's as far as they got. Meanwhile, Yeltsin had ordered the military to shell the White House, which was quite severely damaged. (One wonders how he himself felt about shelling the very place from which he had directed resistance to the coup attempt in 1991.) Large numbers of famous people from the arts, the trade unions, Parliament (the "non-rebels") and other walks of life came to Channel Two's studios despite sounds of gunfire, and proclaimed their support for the government and for law and order, some in heartfelt and passionate terms. First Deputy Prime Minister Yegor Gaidar called upon the citizens of Moscow to turn out and show their support for the government, and some did: David Remnick speaks of "thousands, maybe fifteen or twenty thousand."[165] Yeltsin decreed a state of emergency, complete with censorship powers over the media, and they were exercised against a number of "fascist" and "communist" newspapers. When the dust had settled, many government officials, Yeltsin included, publicly thanked Channel Two for its role in bringing a quick end to a situation that, in their opinions, could easily have led to civil war.[166]

As of 1994, the electronic media still were covered under the 1991 Mass Media Law passed by the Soviet Parliament. The Yeltsin government had regulated the media largely by issuing decrees on specific activities, for example the decree guaranteeing citizens' rights to information, issued in January 1994. The newly elected Parliament, fragile as it was—its predecessor had been suspended only a few months earlier—set to work on several proposed pieces of legislation regulating the media, including a comprehensive statute on broadcasting that would build on the 1991 Mass Media Law. In the summer of 1994, another piece of draft legislation was introduced that would affect one of the most fundamental aspects of media control: financing. It took a quite different approach to state (government) financial support for media enterprises, and called for creation of a National Fund for Media Development, which would manage funds and control stock in privatized mass media operations. The head of the government's Committee on the Press (which controlled government subsidies to the press) attacked it on the grounds that it was just another scheme to shift control, and therefore influence, over media operations into another set of hands, presumably the Parliament's.[167]

The Yeltsin government generally was successful in blocking those parliamentary initiatives, but the economic situation was worsening, making it more and more difficult to fund state-operated broadcast stations. It provided Russian Television (RTR) with roughly 18 percent of the funding it needed in order to operate, and Ostankino with 25 percent of its budgetary needs. It's little wonder that the government attempted through various means to discourage the independent program companies which had been buying time on the state TV services; if the state services had more advertising time to sell, they would be better equipped to make financial ends meet.[168] Even that was not enough to bail out the services, which were falling farther and farther behind in paying the Ministry of Communications for the use of satellites, local transmitter sites for their electricity bills and broadcast staff members themselves, many of whom hadn't been paid in months; that drove some of them to go out on strike in February 1994, and many of the TV screens in Russia went dark.[169]

The privatization of Ostankino was the next step. It occurred in November 1994, as Yeltsin signed a decree providing for 51 percent of the company's stock to be held by the State Committee for the Management of State Property (thus assuring a continuation of state control), and the remaining 49 percent to be held by a dozen or so carefully selected private investors.[170] Ostankino staff weren't enthusiastic about the change in status, but it probably struck them as better than being merged with Channel Two, which some government officials had proposed. As for the investors, few stepped forward to risk their cash, and within a year of the sale of stock there were only four of them: two banks, the government's own natural gas monopoly and Logovaz, an industrial conglomerate headed by Boris Berezovsky.

Clearly Russian electronic media were moving away from the public service broadcasting model and toward a commercial model. The increase in dependency on advertising was quite amazing for a system which had been so staunchly anti-capitalist up until 1991. A 1994 *Izvestia* article indicated that Channel One increased its advertising time from an average of 36 minutes daily in February 1993 to 59 minutes for weekdays and 73 minutes for weekends in November 1993.[171] While the November figure wouldn't seem excessive to U.S. viewers, it must have struck Russian viewers as astounding, since there were so very few ads only years before. What's more, a number of the ads were for foreign products, which added more fuel to the fire of those who denounced the "Americanization" or "westernization" of Russia through mass media content.

One small television company had been battling that "westward drift." Moskovia came on air in 1994 as a service for the greater Moscow region; the government of the region furnishes most of its financial support. At first, it shared Channel Three with two other services, MTK and 2 x 2, which themselves were absorbed in the new Moscow city government service, TV-Centre, in 1997. Its chief driving force, Alexander Krutov, had earned a reputation as a persistent investigative reporter for one of the first informational programs to be guided by the glasnost spirit. (The program, "Prozhektor Perestroiki" ["Perestroika Spotlight"], came on air in August 1987 and soon earned a reputation as a champion of the average citizen, as it went to various parts of the U.S.S.R. looking for stories about people with serious complaints against the government [usually local], factory bosses, etc. See Mickiewicz, "Changing Channels," 76-78, for a description of it.) But Krutov also was and is an ardent Russian nationalist, and programs on Moskovia tend to focus on smaller towns and rural areas, rather than big-city life, with emphasis on the essential goodness, common sense and deep religious beliefs of "the people." He has his own program, "Russky Dom" ("Russian Home"), and in it often attacks what he sees as "signs of Satan" (credit cards, sex education).[172] Moskovia is on air for only two hours a day, broken into three segments which are scattered across the program schedule, and Channel Three transmits only to the greater Moscow region, so there are decided limits to its influence. Still, it may represent broader viewer discontent, and it will be interesting to see whether it expands on the national level, or inspires imitators in other parts of the country.

Major crises involving television seem to come along every other year, and the crisis for 1995 was bloody, in more ways than one. The small region of Chechnya was Russian in the sense that it lay within the boundaries of the Federation, Russian was its main language and ethnic Russians made up about 75 percent of the population of its capital, Grozny. But various ethnic Chechen factions had begun moves toward independence in the early 1990s, and finally, in mid-December 1994, the Russian military was sent in to put an end to such rebellion. President Yeltsin had ordered the attacks, but television coverage of them appeared to disturb enough of the public to cause him to appear on television on December 27, 1994, with a national address in which he ordered a halt to the bombing of Grozny. The bombing continued, so he again ordered a halt to it, on January 4. Yet on January 5, bombs and rockets destroyed the presidential palace in Grozny. Meanwhile, the official media sources were proclaiming that Russian soldiers were in full control of Grozny.

In the old days, that would have been the only version of events that Russians would have seen, heard or read. But now there was an independent TV channel that emphasized informational programming, and did its best to tell and show its viewers that official statements and actual events were at odds. NTV's evening news program ("Segodnia," or "Today") came on at 7 p.m., the Channel Two news ("Vesti") at 8 p.m., and Channel One's "Vremya" at 9 p.m., followed by NTV's late evening news at 10 p.m. Viewers could compare coverage, and even some of the newspapers said that NTV's account was the correct version. In addition to being the target of criticism from government officials and members of Parliament, NTV came under considerable pressure to cancel coverage of such things as press conferences where the Russian government's policy was criticized; the pressure included threats of possibly closing down the station. It compromised on occasion, but didn't cancel its coverage. Its example appeared to encourage Channel Two's "Vesti," which began to cover the war more critically. Channel One remained faithful to the Russian government's position.

Several surveys taken in January 1995 indicated that NTV was increasing its share of viewership, and that the government's position on the war was unpopular with the Russian public. As the war dragged on, that public grew less and less interested in following it through television. However, two events in the spring of 1995—the Russian military's capture of the Chechnyan town of Samashki and subsequent (alleged) massacre of its inhabitants, and a Chechen military group's hostage-taking (2,000 hospital patients) in the Russian city of Budyonnovsk—rekindled viewer attention, and saw NTV and Channel Two furnishing the same accurate coverage that had marked their earlier efforts. Ellen Mickiewicz states that the breaking of the government monopoly on information "finally spelled the end of the Soviet media system." While that didn't mean an end to attempts by the Russian government to reassert control during perceived crises, it did mean that the government no longer could assume that it would be successful.[173]

While the government didn't reassert control in the parliamentary elections of 1995, it certainly attempted to provide the political party it favored—Our Home is Russia—with every advantage in airtime. The party received what Urban calls "unlimited free access" to state television, plus two million dollars for paid political spots—more than 600 times the television budget of the Communist Party (KPRF). Despite that, the latter took 22 percent of the vote, while the former received only 10 percent.[174] In addition, Vladimir Zhirinovsky was able to include anti-ethnic minority remarks in some of his campaign speeches, despite the fact that such remarks supposedly violated the law.[175] That would not be the last time.

The next election found the media again supportive of Yeltsin, although the circumstances were far different. Here, it was the presidential election of June-July 1996, and Yeltsin clearly was in a tight spot: visibly ill, lacking energy, sounding confused and uncertain at times, it must have seemed to many Russians as if it were time to replace him. His chief challengers were younger and more energetic, but also more overtly nationalistic, favoring a reassertion of Russia's power and glory. That carried with it the possibility of tighter controls over the media, which were often criticized for bringing too much American and European cultural influence into Russia. The state and private television services reacted quite predictably: they lined up behind Yeltsin and favored him in almost every available way. There was nothing that any of them could do about the legal requirement that all candidates would have the same amounts of free airtime on the state channels, and with no interference from the stations. The candidates also had the right to pay for airtime to advertise themselves, and most of them did so. However, the stations could, and did, ignore Yeltsin's unexpected absences from rallies and other campaign events, even though the strong likelihood that the president's physical condition was the cause of those absences would have been a very important campaign story.

As in the 1993 election, U.S. advisors were involved in developing

Yeltsin's campaign. They tended to play up their importance in advising the president; Russians close to the president tended to minimize their importance. Yeltsin appeared all over the country. From what one could see on television, he was generally vigorous and up on local situations, and looked and sounded fit enough for another term. His main opponent, the Communist Party's Gennadi Zyuganov, had plenty of airtime and was adept at using it, but one of his followers, Viktor Anpilov, was quite outspoken in his anti-Semitism, and the media emphasized it. (A video clip played on an interview program showed Anpilov saying that those who can't speak Russian properly should be removed from the TV screen, in favor of real Russians. "We see those Jewish faces and it insults us" was his closing remark on the clip. See Mickiewicz, "Changing Channels," 180.)

The television campaign itself was sometimes bizarre, particularly because of a candidate who had virtually no chance of winning the election, Vladimir Bryntsalov. He flaunted his wealth and engaged in stunts designed to attract viewer attention, although they can't have given the public much confidence that he would be either serious or dignified as a chief of state. He wanted the public to perceive him as athletic, so he went to a riding ring to demonstrate his skill, even though he had never ridden a horse. He looked anything but skillful. He also boasted of his sexual prowess, and had his wife Natasha pull down her pants and show her backside on TV.[176] He received a fraction of 1 percent of the first-round vote, so viewers were spared or deprived of seeing what she or he might display in the final round. On the last day of the final round, television did show Yeltsin in less than peak physical condition, when he appeared with Prime Minister Viktor Chernomyrdin to make a statement about the importance of voting. That was his first appearance in five days, and, according to Mickiewicz, he "looked alarmingly like the incapacitated leaders of the Soviet past," although Chernomyrdin said that it was only a cold, and that Yeltsin's grip had been as strong as ever. "Segodnia" ran a story about Zyuganov in which he voiced his concern about Yeltsin's health, but the anchorperson led off the story by saying that Zyuganov seemed to have "obsolete information."[177] Yeltsin won by 13 percentage points over Zyuganov.

The struggle between the Yeltsin administration and the Parliament continued. In September 1997, the Duma had its first reading of a new draft bill covering the regulation of radio and television, and approved it. A draft of amendments to the bill followed. Simultaneously, the Duma introduced a new bill on state control and support for govenment-operated broadcasting. It contained a provision that forbade advertising on the government-operated channels, which Yeltsin allegedly favored. However, a provision on the creation of an "Observation Council" could have served to bring those services under greater control by the communists in the Duma, according to *Rossiyskiye Vesti*.[178] That would have been enough in itself to ensure that Yeltsin would never sign it.

The following year brought a repeat performance: President and Duma stuck with positions that the other side could not accept. Even so, there were two significant changes in the system, the first engineered by the office of the President, the second the result of Russia's disastrous economic situation, and both occurred within a few weeks of one another. On July 27, 1998, then-Prime Minister Sergei Kiriyenko signed a decree reorganizing the All-Russian State Television and Radio Broadcasting Company (its Russian acronym is VGTRK), with the reorganization itself to take effect on January 1, 1999. The "new" company would include TV channels "Russia" and "Kultura," Radio Russia, the over 90 state TV and radio companies located in cities all across Russia, separate TV news, sports and telefilm services, and satellite, radio and television transmission services. The consolidation supposedly would lead to a more-efficient organization. Duma members protested that they had not been consulted on what they regarded as an illegal change (although reports concerning it had been circulating for weeks), and private broadcasters called the new enterprise "The Godfather," fearing that it would enable the government to charge stations astronomical prices for transmitting their signals, or even to cut off transmission services entirely if a station had displeased the government. Whether any of this would affect the Russian public TV service, ORT, was unclear, since the media baron Boris Berezovsky held a large number of its shares.[178a]

Controversy over the reorganization of VGTRK soon took a back seat to an even more pressing issue: the crumbing Russian economy. On August 17, the ruble was devalued to such an extent that virtually all sectors of the Russian economy had to cut their budgets drastically. Television was especially hard-hit, since both the public and private services were so heavily dependent on advertising revenue. There were announcements of cancellations or "indefinite postponements" of advertising contracts worth a total of $20–30 million— small by U.S. standards, but significant in Russia. Many program managers cut back on Russian productions and ordered even more Western imports, if they could convince the sellers that they could come up with the money for rentals. Media staffs were cut by as much as 30 to 50 percent. The satellite service NTV+ faced a $50 million loan repayment, with a subscriber base of only 200,000 and possible subscriber cancellations due to the financial crisis. The government had been cutting back on its payments to the various State broadcasting services for the past few years, and certainly was in no position to step in to fill the financial gap.

The situation at ORT in particular became almost farcical in mid-November. The station was served with a debt collection order and its cars and trucks were seized, preventing news staff from going out to cover stories. A news anchor reported the seizure, read a few news bulletins, and signed off after three minutes, replaced by a printed message for the remaining 12 minutes. It read: "You are watching ORT news." As ORT news director Sergei Dorenko remarked, the government was suing itself for debts it owed to itself. Moscow's chief bailiff promptly rescinded the order "in order to provide ORT with more time to arrange for repayment." The Interfax news agency stopped supplying its service to ORT because of debts. Even RTR, fully owned by the Russian government, had to take extreme measures, which, in addition to staff layoffs and voluntary service by senior staff, included cancellation of the popular (c. 10.5 million viewers per evening) U.S. import "Santa Barbara," because of falling advertising revenues. A group of women then picketed outside RTR in protest of the cancellation.[178b]

All of this led to widespread speculation on the future of Russian broadcasting. There seemed to be agreement that the Russian government would continue to support at least one national TV service and some radio services, and that a number of the regional and local governments would find ways to support their TV and radio services. Whether the national government would use reorganization of VGTRK to eliminate some of the competition for advertising revenue was an open question, although the political and economic power still possessed by media moguls such as Berezovsky and Gusinsky might be sufficient to ensure the continuation of their enterprises. Most observers thought that program standards would continue to decline, that there would be even more repeats and cutting back of broadcast hours, and probably more and cheaper Western programs. Some felt that there would be consolidations among the private companies, with perhaps no more than one or two remaining. A few even saw the crisis as positive development in terms of helping to rationalize a situation where there probably were too many services in the first place, with too much dependency on Western advertising, programming, and perhaps even styles of management: fewer stations, "leaner and meaner" approaches, and more reliance on Russian program material and Russian advertising might be a real improvement. However, a general absence of investment capital as 1998 came to a close did inspire confidence that Russian programs and ads would proliferate. (The Internews service provided translations of a wide range of media commentary on the crisis and its effect on Russian broadcasting in a lengthy mid-December 1998 file entitled "The Russian Media in Crisis," available through *http://www.internews.ru/crisis.*)

FINANCING

There are two principal means of financing the electronic media: government appropriations and advertising/sponsorship. Both, as indicated above, are less reliable than usual because of the 1998 financial crisis. Investment might be considered a third means, since most stations operate at a financial loss and must be kept afloat through repeated infusions of cash from investors such as Vladimir Gusinsky (Media-Most, which forms part of the Most Bank Group, and which holds controlling shares in NTV) and Boris Berezovsky (Logovaz, which owns a portion of TV-6 and ORT-TV). However, those investors clearly regard their electronic media properties as potential profit-makers through sales of advertising time. There also are satellite-delivered program services, which receive monthly subscriber payments, but the subscriber bases are far too small to be significant sources of income.

Even before the 1998 crisis, government appropriations had become considerably less reliable.[179] In 1996, for example, ORT-TV received almost nothing, allegedly because the Duma saw it as pro-Yeltsin (which it is), but also because it didn't want to finance two state channels (the other is RTR, whose appropriation was cut somewhat less, perhaps because it was perceived to be more independent). ORT then had to rely more heavily on advertising and outside investments; so did the former Ostankino national radio services, whose budget also was cut back sharply.[180] As rental charges for use of Ministry of Communication transmitters are very high, but must be paid (the Ministry has cut off transmission services to "defaulters" in some parts of the country),[181] investment in programming suffers.

Advertising rates vary a great deal. The larger national TV services such as ORT, RTR and NTV charge anywhere from $2,000 to $30,000 per minute, depending on the time of day, while the more regional services, such as TV-6 Moscow, charge in a range from a few to several thousand dollars a minute. There is very little regulation of advertising content. As a result, some quite unusual products and services are advertised in some rather unusual ways: a public service spot on AIDS prevention shows a cartoon figure with an outsized penis, and then a hand coming toward the figure and rolling a condom on the erect organ. Clairvoyants, witches and warlocks may advertise their services. A 1996 presidential campaign ad for Grigory Yavlinsky featured dancing babushkas (grandmothers) singing Russian rap.[182]

Ads appearing on the national networks tend to have a somewhat slick, urban-oriented appearance, which has caused some observers to wonder what their impact might be in rural Russia, where retail stores of any sort are scarce. Vasily Kisunko conjures up a scene where "a sensuous beauty appears on the screen swallowing something called Raffaello or Dove chocolate and murmurs in a sultry contralto, 'Now *that's* temptation!' What response could that possibly evoke besides a healthy feeling of resentment?" But he also acknowledges that TV ads seem to cause less suspicion than they did in the days of Soviet television, when viewers "always understood that the intent was to foist something old, shoddy or uninteresting on us."[183]

Such regulations as do exist for advertising are contained in the Russian Law on Advertising (1995), which gives the Federal Anti-Monopoly Committee control over advertising content, and which sets limits on amounts of advertising; for example, a given product may be advertised no more than twice an hour, for a maximum of two minutes. The advertising of alcoholic beverages and tobacco products—themselves something of a national problem—is forbidden, aside from beer. The Law on Advertising prohibits ads showing people drinking beer.[184] No advertising is allowed on children's or religious programs. Text ads superimposed across the bottom of the screen must take up no more than 7 percent of the screen surface. Ads cannot interrupt live programming. Stations must carry some "social advertising" (public service announcements), "within a limit of 5 percent of airtime per year." Sponsoring is legal.[185]

Although radio has seen little advertising revenue thus far, television appears to be growing in importance as an advertising vehicle. Estimates vary, but it may have attracted as much as $1 billion in 1996. That figure is quite remarkable when one considers the relative infancy of TV as an advertising medium, and the parlous state of the Russian economy. Most of the larger accounts are those of western firms such as Procter and Gamble, which allegedly spent $4 million on Russian TV advertising in February 1996 alone. A few Russian firms had been major advertisers until 1995; they were predominantly advertising "get-rich-quick" schemes, and the bottom fell out of that market with the 1994 collapse of MMM, a financial investment company which had operated a pyramid scheme.[186]

GOVERNANCE AND ADMINISTRATION—INTERNAL

There is no single administrative model for electronic media in Russia. The private services operate basically as businesses, and their administrators rarely have backgrounds in electronic media work. The public service stations by and large were headed by broadcasters in the early to mid 1990s, but a combination of semiprivatization and the growing influence of businesspeople in national, regional and local government has resulted in the appointment by governments of more administrators with business backgrounds. (RTR appears to have fared better than most others: although several chairs have been appointed and dismissed, all have been experienced and respected broadcasters. See European Institute, "Media Structures," in "Media in the CIS," 7.) The top government officials in regions and cities may be deeply involved in some of the radio and TV stations in their areas of jurisdiction: for example, the government of the Primorskii krai (Vladivostok region) is reported by the Glasnost Defence Foundation to exert close control over some of the stations and newspapers in the region, favoring them and disfavoring others.[187] Not all regions and cities feature such control; the Irkutsk region seems to be quite free of it, for whatever reason.[188]

Unlike many of the public service broadcasting organizations elsewhere in the industrialized world, Russian PSBs don't include citizen advisory boards as part of their administrative structures. (Prime Minister Chernomyrdin did appoint a "collegium of government representatives" to help supervise ORT in late 1997. One of Anatoly Chubais' aides and Yeltsin's daughter were among the members.)[189] Instead, much as in the Soviet era, they continue to rely heavily on audience mail, as well as on survey results. The private stations also rely on audience mail, as well as telephone calls, but the latter are more severely limited than they are in most industrialized nations, since only about 20 percent of all Russian households have telephones.

There are various associations of Russian broadcasters, including attempts to hold annual congresses of nongovernmental broadcasters. The dominant organization at present is the National Association of Telebroadcasters (NAT). It held a convention in Moscow in October 1997, complete with seminars, workshops and equipment exhibits. According to Eric Johnson of Internews, NAT is functioning more and more along the lines of the U.S. National Association of Broadcasters, as it attempts to represent the interests of the 500-700 (there are no perfectly reliable figures) private broadcasters in Russia at the federal level.[190]

Whatever attracts individuals to seek employment in electronic media operations, it isn't likely to be large salaries, although they're improving. Broadcast "personalities" may receive annual salaries in the tens and even hundreds of thousands of U.S. dollars, but most media staff are paid considerably less: several hundred U.S. dollars a month is not unusual, particularly in the smaller media markets. Such a wage would count for far more in Russia than it does in the west, to be sure, and the occupation does carry a certain amount of prestige.

GOVERNANCE AND ADMINISTRATION—EXTERNAL

National Government

As with all other stations and services requesting permission to broadcast within the Russian Federation, the most recently authorized stations—Moskovia, TV-Centre and Kultura—won their slots in the frequency spectrum through presidential decrees. There is no licensing through a process of competitive hearings, as is usually the case in industrialized nations. Instead, media operations are registered, with a right to appeal to the courts if registration is refused. Broadcast services also must obtain a license, according to the Russian Mass Media Act of 1991, but the repeated use of presidential decrees to create such services means that licensing can in effect be bypassed. As already noted, there is no Russian law that deals exclusively with electronic media. Instead, there are the Soviet and Russian Media Laws of 1990 and 1991; nearly 20 laws dealing with specific activities, e.g., the Law on State Secrets, or the Law on the Coverage of the Work of State Organs of Government in State Mass Media;[191] governmental orders, including a December 1994 order on the licensing of broadcasting; and the many presidential decrees. Thus, any electronic media operation is on shaky ground, and subject to removal from the airwaves with little notice (although a warning must be issued, and a court order must follow it), for reasons which may or may not be specified, and which may or may not make sense.[192] Nor does the Russian Supreme Court appear to be interested in interpreting the law in ways that might protect the electronic media and the public, as the German Supreme Court has done.[193]

Citizens do receive some protection *from* the media in Article 23 of the constitution, which protects a person's honor and reputation. It requires media organizations to print apologies in the same place or broadcast them at the same time as the original information. The burden of proof is on the media organization—the opposite of most western law, where the plaintiff is expected to provide proof that the media knew the information to be false, or were acting maliciously.[194]

Television companies are required by presidential order to cover all branches of government "in an equal amount," and a federal law concerning status of deputies (members of the Duma and of the Federation Council) requires state television (RTR) to provide deputies access to the airwaves. The Central Elections Commission issues regulations for each election, but ordinarily the state media are required to provide each candidate or party with a specified amount of free airtime. But election laws also require journalists to provide balanced coverage of elections, which obviously wasn't the case in the 1995 and 1996 elections.[195]

Attempts to pass a law specific to the electronic media have been thwarted in part by animosity between the Yeltsin administration and the Russian Parliament, but also in part by divisions within Parliament itself—in other words, much the same situation that characterized the battle over a new media law in the closing years of the Soviet Union. Such a law appeared in draft form in 1995,[196] but was vetoed by President Yeltsin, and in 1996, when it was vetoed by the Federation Council.[197] A new draft law came out in September 1997, and passed through a first reading in Parliament. It underwent revision, but by late 1998 there still was no media law approved by both Parliament and President. However, since it contains provision for direct and indirect involvement by the Duma in the regulatory process, Yeltsin and the Council are likely to continue to block its passage. (Particularly draft Article 31, which states that the Russian Federation Duma is to name five of the 15 members of the Federal Commission for Television and Radio, and is to confirm the President's nominee for Chair of the Commission. (See *http://www.internews.ras.ru/eng/russia_law.html*) Also, as Serge Robillard points out, the very composition of the Russian Federation, with its mixture of internal republics, territories, regions, cities and autonomous areas (89 of them alone!), makes it difficult to please enough of those constituencies so that laws can be passed, and especially laws establishing central regulatory authorities.[198]

The Federal Commission (or Service) for Television and Radio (FSTR), established in the Russian Media Law of 1991, is in theory the body through which anyone wishing to operate an electronic media service must seek a license, although the Ministry of Communications allocates the broadcast frequency to be used, if one is needed. The FSTR has an unusual feature when compared with regulatory agencies in other industrialized nations: each region of Russia has its own FSTR commission, which is responsible for recommending to the federal commission the issuance of licenses within the region. In theory, that could promote greater citizen involvement, since citizens might be able to voice their opinions on how well an applicant or a licensee would be likely to serve, or had been serving, its audiences. But hearings on licenses aren't public, and according to Svetlana Kolesnik, the local governmental administrations which have dominated many of the regional FSTRs have used their power to make life difficult for any licensee, would-be or existing, who isn't loyal to the administration in the community where the license will be held.[199]

By 1995, the FSTR had issued roughly 700 licenses for private services.

However, the Yeltsin administration has been quite willing to allow stations to come on air and to increase their transmission hours without having them go through the Commission, which makes it appear as if the right political connections count for more than does following the proper legal procedure. According to Robert Campbell, the decisions necessary to rationalize licensing procedures hadn't begun to take into account the economic factors involved, and he saw little indication of movement in that direction as of the early to mid 1990s.[200] That still appears to be the case.

Licenses ordinarily are valid for five years. However, each broadcaster must be able to show that there is an agreement to rent a transmitter, which usually means renting from the Ministry of Communications. A 1995 Federal Law on Communications indicates that the Ministry has the power to change the terms of the license, to suspend it or to extend it. Many stations came on air without licenses in the early 1990s, when it was fairly easy to do so (the Ministry wasn't all that vigilant in enforcing the law). As they've sought to become legal, a number of them have had to wait for years to obtain a license, as have some who would be coming on air for the first time.

The Federal Agency of Government Communication and Information (FAPSI), a subsection of the Presidential Security Service (PSS), is supposed to handle information gathering (classified information in particular) and analysis for the government,[201] but according to Michael Urban, it plays the role of overseer of state radio and television programming—a situation he finds particularly distressing because it so closely resembles the manner in which the Soviet government so often operated: by creating an "inner wheel of the Russian state."[202] Quite aside from FAPSI, the power to classify information as a "state secret" resides (by presidential decree, signed in February 1994) in nearly 40 ministries, departments, committees and services, including such an unlikely entry as the Ministry for Higher Education.[203] The ministries have great latitude in designating items as "state secrets," and may even use that as an excuse in the absence of a formal designation. As one example, in April 1996 two journalists from the TV news program "Vremechko" were imprisoned by guards when attempting to shoot film for an item about the building of a dacha (vacation cottage) for the head of the Russian Defense Ministry's Department of Ideological Training. They were told that the dacha was a "secret object," although there was no documentation produced to support the claim. They had to demagnetize their videotape, and then were released.[204]

Regional and Local Government

As noted just above, there is provision for some degree of involvement in regulation at regional and local levels, and some of those governments have been quick to take advantage of the influence that they might wield, as you'll see later on. Some of those governments also have established electronic media services. If the national government wanted to exercise jurisdiction over the regional and local governments, it could do so: the FSTR holds ultimate power. However, thanks to the vastness of the country, and the strongly ethnic character of many of the regions, media services operating there can't be easily supervised from a national level, and attempts to do so wouldn't always be supported by the local authorities. As Professor (of media law) Andrei Richter expressed it, "What we see today in the provinces of Russia is a Balkanization of media legislation, open or potential contradictions between federal and regional statutes with no clear way to resolve them under the current political climate. The violations of journalists' rights, restrictions of the freedoms of speech and the press are more common the further you go from Moscow."[204a]

PROGRAMMING

Philosophy

In the Soviet era, it was quite easy to describe the philosophy of broadcast operations, since they were all part of a single monopoly, and were all charged with the same set of responsibilities: to uphold the authority of government and the Communist Party, etc. Those responsibilities had begun to erode even before the breakup of the Soviet Union, but with few exceptions they essentially evaporated after it. Even the few exceptions appeared far less often. The authority of government was upheld much of the time by the state-controlled stations, but not necessarily by the privately owned services. There were expressions of pride in things Russian, but the schedules of many electronic media operations featured more and more programming imported from the west, especially during television's prime-time hours. Pressures for a return to greater emphasis on Russian-made programming seemed to have little effect until the mid-to-late 1990s, and even then there were few major changes in programming policies for most of the services. Instead, the policy of buying low (paying little for imported programs) and selling high (charging advertisers as much as possible, which in fact wasn't very much given the weakness of the Russian economy and the large numbers of competing stations in major markets) predominated, making most electronic media outlets more entertainment-oriented than they were in many Western industrialized nations.

Radio

The program schedules of most Russian radio stations bear considerable resemblance to those of private radio services throughout most of the industrialized world, with heavy emphasis on music, little coverage of news (stations such as Mayak and Moscow Echo are rare exceptions), and advertising commensurate with demand on the part of advertisers for it. Moscow's Radio Maximum advertises itself as the capital's "top rock" station, and certainly popular music stations dominate the airwaves in Moscow and other large cities. Some private stations (there are between 25 and 30 in Moscow) specialize in western music, others favor Russian artists. Radio Yunost specifically targets young people, and Radio Rossii Nostalzhi aims for an audience ranging from teenagers to those in their late 30s.[205]

The stations with the highest ratings throughout Russia are, as one would expect, the national services that existed in the Soviet era, chiefly Rossiya (nearly 25 percent of the audience throughout Russia) and Mayak. They and Radio 1 were part of Ostankino until the company was dissolved in October 1995. Mayak and Radio 1 were partially privatized in November 1995, once again (surprise!) by presidential decree.[206] There was a major reorganization in August 1997, with Rossiya moving over to Channel One, which Radio 1 had occupied. Radio 1 was dropped entirely, apparently because of low ratings (less than 3 percent). Mayak was merged with Radio Yunost (Youth), and they share Channel Two. Radio Orfei (Orpheus), a state-operated classical music station for the Moscow region, uses Channel Three within the region, while local stations use that channel elsewhere.[207] Rossiya presents a mixed lineup of news, public affairs and entertainment, including radio plays and some educational material, while Mayak specializes in news and public affairs, with some music.

Most of the regional radio stations that operated in the Soviet era have remained active, and continue to rely on Moscow's nationwide services for much of their programming, although many of them originate news and public affairs programming, and, where there are linguistic minorities in the audiences, broadcast in some of the minority languages. Communist Party head Gennadi Zyuganov claims that "left-wing and patriotic forces" run three radio stations in the country.[208] There are dozens of small-scale radio stations scattered around the country, but many of them operate in conjunction with cable TV transmission systems, and fill their schedules with relays of other services (some of them foreign), perhaps adding a few minutes per hour of local news.[209]

Television

As of mid-1998, Moscow residents clearly had the greatest variety of TV channels from which to choose: 10 terrestrial services, plus whatever cable and/or satellite channels come through subscription (or piracy). The terrestrial channels follow roughly similar patterns of scheduling. Up until November 1997, Tele-Expo and Channel 5 shared the fifth channel: the former broadcast (weekdays) from 7 a.m. to 1:30 p.m. and from 12:30 a.m. to 2:45 a.m., while the latter was on from 1:30 p.m. to 12:30 a.m. Most of the other channels sign on (weekdays) between 6 and 7 a.m. and run through until 1 to 2:30 a.m. REN-TV is on from early afternoon (precise times vary from day to day) until midnight-1 a.m. STS-8, an entertainment channel, signs on at 7 a.m. Tuesday through Friday, at 9:30 a.m. on Saturday and Sunday, and at 5 p.m. on Monday, and usually signs off by 2 a.m. MuzTV, an MTV-like service, broadcasts from 7 a.m. to 3 a.m. Tuesdays through Fridays, 9 a.m. to 3 a.m. Saturdays and Sundays, and 7 p.m. (!) to 3 a.m. Mondays. Schedules on channels in other parts of the country would be similar, but without the same variety of service.

ORT-TV and RTR were set up as networks from the beginning, and they have outlets throughout Russia, many of which originate their own programming for a few to several hours a day. The private stations such as NTV had to build their networks gradually, as new private stations came on air across the country, and none of those networks has caught up with either ORT or RTR yet, although NTV is coming closer. The local private stations sometimes have contracts with two or more of the Moscow-based stations, and some have proven to be fickle affiliates, dropping and adding contracts with little or no notice. As Sigal observes, "Stations ... feel little compulsion to stay with networks out of loyalty," and he goes on to describe how one local owner places a high premium on "flexibility," by which the owner appears to mean that he can opt in and out of network feeds quite freely.[210] However, the networks were attempting to tighten their control over their affiliates as of early 1998.[211]

Channel One leads off each weekday with its "Good Morning" show, modeled after U.S. and British TV breakfast shows. None of the other channels carries anything that resembles it. All channels carry newscasts from four to 14 times a day, although Moscow's TV-Centre and REN-TV offer only five-minute news summaries. There are several other kinds of information shows, such as Channel One's "Press-Express" (a summary of newspaper commentary). Many of the channels rely quite heavily on strip programming for the weekday late morning to late afternoon period; much of that programming is informational (talk shows, tele-shopping, business reports), but movies and serialized entertainment (Latin American and Spanish soap operas, U.S. series such as "Flipper" and "Dr. Quinn") also are prominent.

Children's programming is in short supply, but there's been a Russian version of "Sesame Street" ("Ulitsa Sesam," on NTV) since October 1996. It was developed over a five-year period and at a cost of $6 million, most of which came from the U.S. Agency for International Development and the Soros Foundation. The U.S.-based Children's Television Workshop, producers of the original "Sesame Street," worked with Russian staff to develop a version with more authentically Russian characters and settings, including an apartment house courtyard instead of the steps of a New York City brownstone residence. The characters, human and puppet, may make borscht instead of sandwiches, but associational learning techniques such as letters that materialize into birds with names beginning with those letters still characterize the program. There's also a lot of singing, often of old Russian folk songs. And of course there are group activities for the children on the show: usually simple things that involve drawing and coloring. Although the series began with just 60 percent of the programs made in Russia (the remaining 40 percent were dubbed U.S. episodes), the hope is to have an all-Russian series in the near future. However, even the Russian-produced episodes receive some criticism for being yet another evidence of a U.S. "cultural invasion."[212]

The channel with the most distinctive profile is NTV, which offers more informational programming than its competitors. It carries regular newscasts, sports news, news about the cinema, the entertainment industry, finance and business, etc. However, it switches to entertainment during the evenings, which brings it directly in competition with all other channels. The newscasts themselves, on NTV and elsewhere, feature less elaborate sets than do their U.S. equivalents, and the anchorpersons (as often female as male) are somewhat more formal. NTV's "Segodnia" has a daily "theme" segment, often focusing on an adversarial situation in one or another city or town in Russia, and pitting one group, e.g., ordinary townspeople, against another, e.g., the local military post. Those segments, and other material about events in Russia, usually are shot and reported by NTV staff (including stringers); most foreign material comes via satellite and has a Russian voice-over. Money is tight, and few networks can afford to station their own correspondents abroad.

Every channel has at least some U.S. entertainment shows, both new ("The Simpsons," "Santa Barbara") and old ("Dallas," "ALF," "Flipper"), as well as movies from the United States, Europe and the Far East (kung fu films from Hong Kong are quite popular). Aside from that—and imported programming takes up well over half of the airtime on most of the channels—a number of the Russian-produced shows would seem familiar in format to non-Russian viewers, especially the game and quiz shows and the talk shows. However, some of them have a more distinctive character, if not always a distinctively Russian character. One show even offered real gold as a prize.

The long-running satirical program "Kukli" ("Puppets") bears some resemblance to the BBC's "Spitting Image" or to France's "Les Guignols." Russian political and entertainment figures are mocked through puppets whose caricatured features are clearly recognizable as those of Yeltsin or any of various Russian pop culture stars. A November 1997 episode featured Yeltsin as Grand Inquisitor, à la the Spanish Inquisition; his "victim" was Anatoly Chubais, his recently demoted economics "czar," strapped flat on a circular stone, with a skeleton off to one side. A very elaborate set featured all sorts of ancient instruments of torture, as well as the clockworks of a bell tower. A pendulum with an enormous blade swung back and forth over Chubais' head; the blade dropped lower when the clockworks chimed, which they did to the tune of various songs with political associations. Several other puppet faces appeared to watch the proceedings. They were politicians such as Zhirinovsky, Lebed and others who were or had been opposed to or supportive of Yeltsin. Their comments, and Yeltsin's, all were along the lines of how difficult it was to survive (politically, not physically!) in Yeltsin's rapidly changing political merry-go-round.

Russian-produced sitcoms, such as "Funny Business, Family Business" and "Café Strawberry," usually feature minimal sets, and reportedly employ older, out-of-work actors, so as to cut costs. The humor sometimes centers around the problems of unemployment, quick-money scams and other plagues of present-day Russia, but also features stock characters recognizable to western sitcom audiences: bossy mothers-in-law, womanizers, stupid brothers, etc.[213]

Russian television also has the rough equivalent of U.S. "reality-based" shows such as "Rescue 911." However, the Russian programs—there were at least six on the schedule as of mid-summer 1997—are indeed "rough" equivalents, since they emphasize gory details to an extent that would be unacceptable in the United States, or in most other countries. "Road Patrol," on air since 1995, draws 20 percent of the audience to its daily morning broadcasts. What they see in each 10-minute program may include car accidents, murders and drug busts, most of them as filmed by the police. Mutilated bodies are not unusual, and body parts may be clearly distinguishable. NTV's morning show, "Kriminal," is a bit more sober, but not very reassuring to the public; a theft report on one episode ended on the pessimistic note of, "Now all the victims can do is to wait for the police to solve the crime. True, hope for that is weak." One of the shows, "Petrovka 38," actually is produced by the head of the Interior Ministry's Information Department; interestingly, it is the only show with a consistently positive image of the police.[214]

One interesting feature of "Kriminal" and some of the other reality shows goes back to the Soviet era, when television usually covered any criminal act as a complete package: This crime occurred, we caught the criminal, she or he has been tried and found guilty. But the Russian "reality" shows display a level of realism that their Soviet-era counterparts never managed. The lighting sometimes is awful, sound quality varies enormously, there are odd shooting angles and the accused criminals usually look stupid or stupefied. And, in an interesting twist on the theme "the criminal always loses," a Saturday night show, "Interception," gives contestants a chance to win a car by driving it through Moscow streets with the police (real ones) in hot pursuit. If they remain within the speed limit and inside a restricted zone and evade the police for 35 minutes, the car is theirs![215]

Talk shows along the lines of the U.S. "Larry King Live" (CNN) were almost unknown in the Soviet era, but several have appeared on Russian television. The host of "Chas Pik" ("Rush Hour"), Vladislav Listyev, was a member of the "Vzglyad" team, and developed a reputation for hard-hitting interviews. In fact, he was murdered in 1995, although probably not because of his interviewing: he had become executive director of Ostankino, and had stated that he supported a ban on advertising over the network. Since some of the advertising revenue probably had gone into the pockets of highly placed individuals (perhaps connected with the Russian Mafia), they may have wished to emphasize their displeasure (to put it mildly) over the ban.[216] One of the best-known TV personalities from the Soviet era, Vladimir Pozner, created his own talk show, as have other former journalists.

While Russian-produced sitcoms are recent arrivals in the program schedules, and may catch on with viewers, soap operas are quite plentiful but almost never Russian. There was one attempt in 1996, "Garachev and Others," but it lasted less than a year. The plot may have been too close to grim economic reality for many Russian viewers, since it dealt with the attempts of a Soviet-era manager to make his way forward in the new Russia.[217] Soap operas from Latin American countries were and are quite common, and highly popular. Kate Baldwin, in her Freudian analysis of Russian viewing of the Mexican soap opera "The Rich Also Cry," speculates that Russians may be attracted to the trashy aspects of the drama, using them to create a sort of identification between themselves and the rich-but-unhappy individuals who populate those programs.[218] But it also could be the sense of contrast the audience feels between its own often-drab surroundings and the colorful language, extreme displays of emotion, etc. of the usual Latin American soap opera.

Erotic shows are available in several forms. The erotic films which are shown late at night on several of the channels are closer to hard-core pornography than those displayed over terrestrial nonsubscription TV services in most other nations. Erotic talk shows are a recent addition to the schedule, and Yelena Khanga, the hostess of NTV's "About 'It,'" doesn't even live in Russia (she flies in, tapes a number of shows and returns to New York City). She is of mixed African-American, African and Polish ancestry, and grew up in the Soviet Union. She was hired by NTV partly because, according to NTV's executive producer, "blacks had a stronger sexual image in Russia," but also because he wanted to show that "not all Russians are blue-eyed and blond." (Nevertheless, Ms. Khanga was fitted with a blond wig for the show!) The show itself covers a wide range of topics, including open discussion of sexual practices and preferences, and that is very rare in Russia, where sex remains something of a taboo topic for public discussion, despite the many erotic movies on TV and videocassette. Ms. Khanga promotes the advisability of safe sex on every program, and tries to maintain a reasonably calm, nonvulgar atmosphere. She's been surprised that her guests have been as open as they have, and that studio audiences have been well-behaved.[219]

One of the more bizarre offerings on Russian TV is "The Lonely Hearts Club." It came on air in November 1996, and soon attracted the attention of Russian female viewers in particular, since it served chiefly as a means of linking "lonely bachelors" in the United States and elsewhere (including Russia itself) with (potentially) interested Russian women. Some bachelors (usually those in other countries) submit tapes of themselves, their houses, cars, etc., and speak about what they're looking for in a woman. Where the U.S. bachelors are concerned, the New Jersey-based producer of the show conducts "woman-on-the-street" interviews in order to generate sound bites of "assertive American career women," presumably so that Russian women can see for themselves what the American bachelors are *not* looking for. The show's Moscow producer operates a one-line "phone bank" in her apartment, and takes calls from viewers, some of whom want to talk chiefly about the bad qualities of Russian men. If a viewer wishes to receive the addresses of any of the bachelors, she most deposit the equivalent of $20 in the show's account at a state-owned savings bank. The operation appears to be legitimate, but there are a number of similar operations active through the Internet, CD-ROM, catalogs and "romance tours" which are not.[220]

Educational programs once were available over Channel 4, but when NTV was given rights to airtime on that channel, the educational services were cut back to three hours a day. Whether that was a significant loss is a matter of opinion: most of the programs were produced by independent services operating on minimal budgets, and the low ratings seemed to show it. When NTV was allowed to claim the entire channel in 1996, it cut back educational programming to one hour a day, and was planning to drop even that.[221]

THE AUDIENCE

Public opinion surveys have become much more common in Russia than they were in the Soviet Union, although regions outside the largest cities and their surrounding areas still tend to be very much neglected. The All-Russian Center for the Study of Public Opinion is something of an exception, as it attempts to carry out its surveys on a nationwide basis. One of its more interesting studies, a nationwide survey done in spring 1995, sought to assess public confidence in various institutions. The mass media (undifferentiated in the survey) did quite well when the categories of "full confidence" and "some confidence" were combined: 70 percent. The Orthodox Church and the army drew 58 and 56 percent on that basis. Using only the figures for "full confidence" produced a rather different result: 47 percent for the church, 21 percent for the mass media.[222]

The first of the western-style survey research firms, Russian Media Monitor, was established in January 1992. It was a joint venture involving the U.S. Gallup Poll's Morgan Gallup division, the U.S. advertising agency BBDO and the U.K.-based sponsorship firm Invizible Arts. Its initial surveys used 600 monthly face-to-face interviews and a daily diary; they measured amounts of viewing time, shows watched, advertising recall and believability of advertising. Entertainment programming from the United States ("Disney Presents," "Santa Barbara") came out on top; the average TV viewer watched for slightly less than 3 hours per day; and ads from the United States and western Europe got considerably better credibility ratings than did Russian advertising.[223]

The growth of market research and polling organizations since that time has been phenomenal: as of 1997, there were close to 100 of them. But there is no standard methodology, and some of the firms are of dubious quality. There is no reliable source of nationwide data, although Russian Research, a British company, has developed a respondent pool of 2,800 in European Russia (west of the Ural Mountains), and uses diaries to collect its data. Results from surveys conducted at about the same time can vary widely. Viewer diaries have been heavily used to gather data; however, the few firms using peoplemeters—Gallup Media chief among them—are beginning to attract more business, and one of the largest Russian media time sellers, Video International, now relies on Gallup's peoplemeter data for its nationwide sample, although it still uses Russian Research's daily diary panels for more detailed analyses of viewing in the regions.[224]

A Gallup media survey of regional media usage in eight Russian cities indicated that three out of four respondents watched television every day.[225] A

1995 survey of 22 Russian cities by the Public Opinion Foundation showed even higher figures: 86 percent of the respondents claimed to watch every day. That same survey indicated that a clear majority of viewers watch TV for two or more hours a day, that retirees and women were the heaviest viewers during the 9 a.m.-noon period, and that the post-11 p.m. programs drew a predominance of male and younger viewers.[226] Another survey (no identification of source) showed that ORT's "Vremya" was the most widely viewed newscast in Russia, although RTR's "Vesti" and NTV's "Segodnia" were as strong as or stronger than "Vremya" in some markets. As ORT had full national coverage and RTR and NTV didn't, "Vremya" was able to claim the overall lead. Much the same situation affected radio, where national stations (Radio Rossia, Mayak and Europa Plus) came out ahead of the competition, although survey results also indicated that, if local stations were taken as an aggregated category, they had the highest overall percentage of listeners: 41 percent.[227] In the Moscow area, where surveys of viewing are conducted weekly, ORT, RTR and NTV dominate the top 10 list, with the news programs "Vremya," "Novosti" (both ORT) and "Segodnia" (NTV), as well as the weekly news analysis "Itogi" (NTV) and the satirical "Kukli," in that list on most weeks. Sports, talk shows, game shows, interview programs and "Ulitsa Sesam" also do well among Moscow viewers.[228] Local TV stations receive high ratings in many parts of Russia, especially in those cities where there are strong TV news programs.[229]

MINORITIES AND THE MEDIA

Broadcasting in the Soviet Union featured many programs for and about minorities, and often in minority languages, even if they were heavily slanted toward emphasis on positive images of the minorities themselves, the vastly improved lives they now led under a Soviet government, and the friendly relations they enjoyed with each other and with the Russians who dominated the decision-making structures in most parts of the nation. That has not been a high priority for the Russian government, and the national radio and television services provide little coverage of minority affairs and cultures, whether in informational or entertainment formats. Minority-language services are quite common in many cities and towns throughout the Federation, but not in the largest cities, despite the fact that some minority groups are quite numerous there.

As I indicated earlier, there are Russians who don't wish to see identifiable minorities on television, which is the attitude that NTV's executive producer claimed to be challenging when he selected Yelena Khanga as hostess of "About 'It.'" However, there are no legal stipulations regarding representation of minorities or minority languages through the electronic media, and little apparent sentiment in the Duma to support any requirement along those lines in the current draft legislation. Such provisions are exceptionally rare in any nation's media legislation, but most industrialized nations make some effort, governmental and otherwise, to encourage and support minority ownership, program production, employment and general portrayal in and through the electronic media.

PROBLEM AREAS

Concentration of media ownership is a potential problem, but its dimensions are difficult to calculate. Criticism of media concentration in Germany focused on the possible "media monopoly" that could develop because so many print media owners had invested so heavily in private electronic media operations. The situation in Russia is quite different: here, the concentrations are occurring because a variety of financially powerful (and politically well-connected, as in Germany) non-print corporations are investing in media properties. Media-Most, an entertainment conglomerate, owns 51 percent of NTV and its satellite service, and has controlling interest in four cable TV superstations, radio station Echo Moscow, the newspaper Segodnia, the magazine Itogi and the publishing house Sem Dnei (also the title [it means "seven days"] of one of the most popular Russian weekly TV guides). Logovaz, Boris Berezovsky's conglomerate of car dealerships, real estate, an oil company and investments in banks, has an unspecified (but probably large) investment in TV-6, owns 8 percent of the shares of ORT-TV (and probably controls many more through various banks which hold stock in the network), and owns the newspaper *Nezavisimaya Gazeta* and the magazine *Ogonyok*. Gazprom, a huge gas company, owns 30 percent of NTV, a slightly smaller percentage of shares in the newspapers *Komsomolskaya Pravda* and *Trud,* and has investments in a few dozen regional newspapers and TV stations. Oneksim Bank (Russia's largest), has substantial shares in *Komsomolskaya Pravda*, the magazine *Literaturnaya Gazeta,* and (rumored) investments in regional newspapers and TV stations. Lukoil, the largest Russian oil company, owns shares in TV-6 and the newspaper *Izvestia.*[230]

How much influence the corporations actually wield is a matter of dispute. TV news and other informational programs criticize Communist political figures and a number of other Yeltsin opponents. The new private corporations owe much to the Yeltsin administration, and a return to some form of communism would not be in their interest, but the private broadcasters also feel that they would have much (perhaps everything) to lose if the Communists came to power, since Communists definitely do not favor private enterprise, especially where media are concerned. So are the broadcast criticisms of Communists made because of the particular self-interests of the media, or do they result from pressure applied by the corporations? Or perhaps both? Does a corporation such as Gazprom invest in a highly popular paper such as *Komsomolskaya Pravda* because, as *Izvestia*'s economics editor Mikhail Berger alleges, "at the right moment it can resist efforts by the Government or the Parliament to withdraw its privileges,"[231] or because it's a sound business investment in terms of its potential for increasing corporate profits?

There are some very overt cases of owners using media outlets to promote their own agendas, including election to public office. One wealthy owner of a TV station (Integral) and a radio station (Prospect) campaigned in 1995 for a seat in the Duma as a member of the Communist Party. His stations carried supportive advertising and broadcast many favorable stories about his campaign. He won and, in an interesting development, became the deputy chair of the Duma's Committee on Information Policy and Communication[232]—the committee that drafts laws concerning mass media and reviews related laws drafted by other committees.

The power of private media operations (and the businesses which own them) to influence the government received a test of sorts in the summer of 1997, when the government sold off 20 percent of the shares in Svyazinvest, a government-owned telecommunications investment company. It was quite widely predicted that Berezovsky or Gusinsky or both would end up with the shares, whether they submitted the highest bids or not. However, a holding company (Mustcom) for Onexim Bank, together with investment from the United States (George Soros) and Germany, made the highest bid and emerged victorious. That led ORT's (partially owned by Berezovsky) "Vremya" anchorperson to attack one of Yeltsin's ministers, Alfred Kokh (deputy prime minister and State Property Committee chair), for selling the stock to "people of dubious reputation." The Most group (which includes Media-Most) accused government spokesperson Boris Nemtsov (first deputy prime minister) of lying when he claimed that Beresovsky and Gusinsky wanted to buy the shares cheaply "by pulling strings." Still, the government stuck to its original decision, allegedly (according to *Kommersant Daily* correspondent Andrei Bagrov) because another first deputy prime minister, Anatoly Chubais, convinced enough powerful cabinet members to prevail upon Yeltsin to approve the highest bid, despite what Yeltsin's friends Berezovsky and Gusinsky might want.

That episode is an interesting illustration of power politics in media affairs. It is also a good case study in the Byzantine power politics of present-day Russia. Berezovsky established himself in the media business in part thanks to his personal relationship with Boris Yeltsin. In the 1996 Presidential Election, Berezovsky's media swung firmly behind Yeltsin. Perhaps as a reward for that service, Yeltsin appointed him as deputy secretary of the National Security Council. When Berezovsky protested the Svyazinvest decision, he directed his criticism at Chubais, but not at Yeltsin. However, Chubais and Nemtsov worked to get him dismissed from his government post. Yeltsin dismissed him in November 1997, but stated that it had been done at the instance of Chubais and Nemtsov, thus distancing himself from the decision![233]

Investigative reporting remains an uncertain element in Russian electronic media activity. It can quite literally be worth one's life to cover certain types of stories, especially those dealing with the Russian Mafia or possible political corruption. Oleg Slabynko, producer of the current affairs program "Moment Istiny," was murdered in his home by "unknown assailants" in January 1996, possibly because the program was about to feature allegations of corruption.[234] There was an early 1998 attempt to kill Yakov London, President of Novosibirsk TV company NTN-4, perhaps because the station showed the Martin Scorcese movie "The Last Temptation of Christ," which religious fundamentalists had vigorously opposed. But there were other rumors of criminal or political motivations.[235]

Quite aside from that, Russian reporters face a myriad of laws, orders and decrees which can be used by just about anyone in a position of power to withhold information. The "state secret" designation supposedly is balanced by the 1995 Law on Information, Informatization [*sic*], and the Protection of Information, which indicates what sorts of information cannot be classed as "state secrets." However, there's no specific mechanism for implementing that law. "Commercial secrets" is yet another designation that hinders reporters, since businesses can use it to forbid their staff from disclosing anything relating to the operation of the company, including such financial data as their own salaries.[236] Article 27 of the September 1997 draft Law states that freedom to broadcast is "incompatible with the distribution of ... programs which ... reveal information which is a governmental or other secret especially preserved by law."

There's also a Presidential Chamber for the Adjudication of Mass Media Disputes, created by a 1993 Yeltsin decree. It is supposed to resolve disputes between the mass media and society, including individuals; Pilugin and Kolesnik, using observer reports, indicate that it has functioned quite well in rendering sound decisions, but those "verdicts" carry no fines or other punishments.[237] However, media operations may distrust it because it's a governmental creation, which for some of them automatically raises questions concerning its freedom from bias.[238]

As if that were not enough, Russian reporters must be licensed, and licensing conditions vary from one local government to another, while the state has its own set of conditions. Journalists supposedly are protected by the 1991 Law on the Mass Media, which provides an "inviolable" list of reasons for the revocation of accreditation. The Russian government attempted to get around that provision in December 1994, when it issued a special order regarding the uneasy situations in the Chechen Republic and other areas in the Caucasus. The order gave a temporary press center the power to "revoke accreditation of journalists for disseminating untruthful information, [or] propaganda of a nationalistic or religious slant." The Constitutional Court ruled in June 1995 that the special order was unconstitutional.[239] Still, that gave the government six months during which to use the order as a way of coercing journalists.

Television's attempts to help the public to understand how investigative journalism might be practiced, and why it's so difficult for Russian journalists to do so, are virtually nil. RTR was ready to broadcast a program series, "The Fourth Estate," on the subject, with illustrations from Chechnya, from the case of a Russian journalist who spied in Italy for the Russian foreign intelligence service, and from Russian media accounts of terrorist activities. It was scheduled for broadcast at the end of June, but finally appeared in RTR's schedule for July 6, 1997. It never came on air. It was replaced by a "program" featuring a male announcer who read the program schedule and then listed famous people with July 6 birthdays. The major reasons for the cancellation appeared to center on the dissatisfaction or discomfort of RTR administrators, possibly prompted by government officials, with the Chechnya segment, although some informants also cited staff unhappiness with the fact that the series was financed by a Russian-American organization (Internews), since some staff felt that they could produce just as good a show, and with *Russian* money.[240]

The journalists themselves haven't always been the best advocates for increased freedom to report. The practice of "pocketbook journalism" (organizations and individuals paying for the broadcast of favorable stories about themselves and unfavorable stories about others) was quite widespread in the early 1990s, and still seems to be prevalent: in a May 1996 conference held in Moscow by the International Federation for Electoral Systems, 40 percent of the Russian journalists questioned about the existence of such practices said that they were "very likely" to occur, and an ex-editor of Sreda (a quarterly journal on the Russian media) observed that they occur not only because salaries are so low, but also because of a change in perception of what is ethical: " ... the ability to sell oneself has become valued, a point of pride, ... elevated to the rank of professional merit."[241] Moscow University professor of media studies Andrei Richter feels that five years ago most of his new students studied journalism "to seek the truth." They now seem more interested in making money and "express[ing] their opinion."[242] Floriana Fossato, a Radio Free Europe/Radio Liberty (RFE/RL) analyst of Russian media, feels that the practice is diminishing, but chiefly because the major broadcast services have become much more clearly identified in terms of their business and governmental affiliations, and their reporters and commentators are expected as a condition of employment to favor their employers and disfavor the employers' enemies.[243] The lure of advertising contracts also can be used as a lever to influence coverage: in one unspecified Russian city, the manager of a milk production plant was running against an experienced politician. The local TV station gave him favorable political advertising rates and positive treatment in its coverage of his candidacy. He won, and the station obtained a lucrative advertising contract from the plant.[244]

Piracy of video material from other countries and even within Russia seems to have been more of a problem several years ago than it is now. The state stations themselves have been guilty of that practice,[245] perhaps because the budgetary support they've received from the government through direct appropriations has been low (and is becoming lower). The private stations, especially those in more distant parts of the country, probably have felt that they could get away with piracy because enforcement of most legal strictures is spotty, and it usually isn't that difficult to bribe officials to not report the offense.

There is protection for copyright in Russia, which is a signatory to the Bern Convention. The Interagency Commission on Intellectual Property

Rights Enforcement, created in 1995, enforces it. Provisions in the Russian Federation Criminal Code allow for up to five years' imprisonment and confiscation of equipment. Whether enforcement of those provisions will be vigorous is doubtful, as noted. However, there are signs that many, perhaps most, stations don't need to use piracy as often or at all.[246] Many are seeing an increase in ad revenue and are finding new ways to produce local material at low cost, which may bring a decline in production quality but a rise in viewership because "it's ours."

The overall situation for women in and on the Russian electronic media may or may not be a problem. Certainly there are women in positions of power, such as the outspoken journalist from the Soviet era Bella Kurkova, who served as chair of St. Petersburg Channel 5 until 1995. The deputy prime minister in charge of the media is Valentina Ivanovna Matviyenko. The deputy chair of the FTSR's License Allocation Division is a woman. Knesiya Ponomareva is General Director of ORT. There are many female directors of radio and television stations around the country, although most are in smaller markets. Many Russian news anchors and reporters are women, although there's no specific evidence to indicate that the stories they report are more likely to be of special interest to women, or to display a female perspective on a given situation.

A leading correspondent for NTV, Irina Zaitseva, claimed in an interview that she worked for "Vremya" as a researcher and junior editor with no expectation of becoming a correspondent: "They tried not to take women as correspondents on account of their well-known lack of brains." But she managed to become one, and, because of her ability to get people to speak about their more personal, human sides, she became moderator for a popular NTV program entitled "Hero of the Day without His Tie" (a literal translation from the Russian; "At Home with ____ [name of guest]" would be a closer approximation). She visits her guests in their homes, goes out walking in the woods with them, etc. She seems able to bring her interviewees to poke fun at themselves, partly because of her nonthreatening, relaxed manner. She also sometimes manages to make some of them look overly self-important or ridiculous,[247] rather along the lines of U.S. TV newswoman Barbara Walters in her feistier days.

Because there's so little entertainment programming of the sitcom and drama variety produced for Russian television, it's difficult to evaluate the portrayal of women in those settings. For other entertainment program genres such as game, quiz and talk shows, women are frequent contestants and guests. The talk shows for women tend to emphasize trivial or sensational subject matter, but that's true of such shows throughout the industrialized world. Advertising that features women also tends to place them in the more stereotyped consumer roles, whether of "busybody" neighbors boasting about how much cleaner their homes are than those of their neighbors, thanks to Comet cleanser or of various helpful "aunts" such as Aunt Aysa, peddling "Ace" bleach.[248]

RELATIONS WITH OTHER MEDIA

The newspaper and magazine industries, which are deeply involved in German and Japanese electronic media, and increasingly involved in Dutch and French electronic media, have very little direct involvement in those media in Russia. Perhaps Russian print media owners are being cautious as investors in what could well be expensive and risky investments, but it probably has more to do with the overall economic weakness of the print industry in Russia: the skyrocketing costs of newsprint alone have forced most Russian newspapers to cut back their print runs and hike their prices, which has led to a drop in subscribers and therefore, advertisers.

Cross-ownership of media is perfectly legal in Russia, as is evident in the examples just cited under Problem Areas. Russian cross-ownership generally comes through banks, utilities or other non-media businesses. While those businesses certainly are interested in the potential profitability of their media acquisitions, they're at least as interested in the political influence and protection that they hope, and even expect, to receive. They may not be so pleased about the public prominence that their media ownership has brought them, and especially the accusations some of them face from Russian nationalists that their "Jewishness" (a number of the top corporate owners are Jewish) makes them less loyal Russians. A Moscow newspaper, *Sovetskaya Rossiya,* blasted Most Group's owner, Vladimir Gusinsky, for allowing the group's NTV channel to carry "The Last Temptation of Christ." The paper was "surprised" that Gusinsky would ignore the sensitivities of the Russian Orthodox church, but linked his decision to the fact that he was Jewish.[249]

The film industry faced serious financial problems during the Soviet era, thanks to the practice of running films on television soon after they had begun to appear in the cinema. That seriously reduced the box office take, and crippled the industry. Also, filmmakers were unable to protest any use that TV made of their work.[250] In Russia's more private enterprise-oriented approach, film production houses have had to become more cost-efficient, which includes working more closely with the expanding television industry. From the late 1980s to the late 1990s, film production dropped off between five- and sixfold, and cinema attendance fell by over twice that much.[251] As one film critic put it, "This decline is a reflection of the increased consumption of cinematic production through television, cable and video. ... Simple statistics show us that today's audiences refuse to see Russian, other CIS, or any other films ... in movie theaters, even if the films are considered remarkable."[252]

INTERNATIONAL COOPERATION

Up to the present, the Russian electronic media have been on the receiving end of a great deal of programming from abroad, most of it from the United States. Given the combination of a weak Russian economy (precluding development of a solid, reliable production capacity), and the difficulties faced by foreign companies wishing to set up joint ventures in Russia, outside investors probably will remain cautious, although Storyfirst Communications appears to be doing quite well; its TV service (STS) receives about 50 percent of its financial support from foreign companies.[253] Métromedia has a fairly large investment in wireless cable operations in several cities, and owns radio stations in Moscow and St. Petersburg.[254]

There's yet another factor that makes importing programs particularly attractive for Russia, provided that they're the right sorts of programs: those paid for by the exporter. Radio Liberty has paid for airtime on many Russian radio stations; so have various religious broadcasters, such as Robert Schuller, whose "Hour of Power" began to appear on Ostankino starting in June 1992. Ostankino received $5,000 a week for carrying the program[255]—a small sum by most standards, but welcome to the cash-starved Russian stations.

Although it isn't a cooperative activity, Media-Most's mid-1997 initiation of a satellite service to feed Russian-language programming to Russian speakers in Israel[256] certainly is international, and may be only the first in a set of like services, directed at the émigré Russian populations of such cities as New York and Paris.

A more unusual international venture was Mir, formed in 1993 by individuals and organizations from nine of the former Soviet republics. Its intent was to emphasize historical and cultural ties among nations, with the aim of promoting peaceful relations. But it depended on ORT for airtime (three hours a week), and it relied on official information from the nine republics for much of its material, which ran the risk of sounding and looking like Soviet-era propaganda. Mir went off the air on January 1, 1997, after ORT had decided not to renew its agreement with the service. The basis for the decision was interesting: allegedly poor program quality, which depressed ratings severely. Sergi Blagovolin, ORT's then-General Director, called the programs "archaic, dull and utterly commercialized." But as the agreement was "enshrined in law" (*Izvestia*'s claim), there was some anger over yet another unilateral action by the Russian government.[257]

THE NEW MEDIA

As noted earlier, VCRs began to appear in some numbers during the final decade of the Soviet Union. Present estimates vary widely, but they may be in anywhere from 10 to 20 percent of all Russian households, and they appear to be growing in popularity, especially as a way to view "how-to ..." tapes and feature films not available over the terrestrial TV services.

Cable television has existed since 1945 in the form of master antenna service to apartment houses, and since the 1960s as importer and distributor of distant signals, but it has enjoyed a much higher growth rate since the breakup of the U.S.S.R. That has been particularly true for Moscow, where the city government-owned cable system has obtained a virtual monopoly by "rigorous enforcement of laws against independent cable television studios" and as a result serves millions of Moscow residents.[258] There are an estimated 25 million cable households in the former Soviet Union, most of them in the Russian Federation. There are supposed to be monthly subscription fees of roughly $3, but few households pay them, and most cable company income results from sales of ad time. Up to the present, cable companies have averaged between 1,000 and 3,000 subscribers; there are very few large companies along the lines of Moscow City Cable. Program choice is limited to between seven and 11 channels in most systems.

However, there are major changes looming on the horizon. A major U.S. investor, Storyfirst Communications (San Francisco), set up the STS network at the end of 1996, and expected to have an audience reach of 80 million viewers by 1998. It delivers its digitally compressed satellite signal to local stations, which relay it to households, most of them living in apartment buildings. Meteor TV, a project of state broadcaster RTR, is working through both cable and satellite to bring a package of services (movies, sports, etc.) to viewers. NTV Plus is a Media-Most cable and satellite service, and has provided Russian and foreign film channels, plus sports.[259] It expects to add information, family, cartoon and culture channels over the next few years.

NTV Plus is a good example of the magnitude of investment required for such an undertaking. The first stage of the project was reported to cost $170-$180 million—a huge sum, given the state of the Russian economy. There had been hopes at one time that Rupert Murdoch would invest in the project, but he didn't, and Media-Most had to develop an alliance with Gazprom, which became a 30 percent shareholder in NTV. When the NTV Plus project was announced at a press conference in mid-1996, NTV's chief producer said that it should take no more than two years to recover the investment, primarily through subscriber fees of $8-$10 per month.[260] But the receiving and decoding unit would cost roughly $150, which is a large investment for a Russian household, so the projection may be overoptimistic.

There are two keys to success here: a strengthening economy, so that viewers will have enough disposable income to afford to subscribe, and decoders and distribution amplifiers installed in the apartment houses so that, in order to receive the services, they *must* subscribe. But the sheer cost of developing the services *and* paying for and installing the amplifiers and decoders means that the large corporations which already dominate private terrestrial television will also dominate cable and satellite, since they're the only ones capable of expending the necessary capital and possessing the experience in electronic media to manage the task. Their close connections with the Russian government should make it fairly simple for them to receive the necessary permission to move ahead.

Russia is served by a large number of satellites, many of them dating back to the Soviet era. Many of the more remote rural areas of Russia already receive television through satellite relays, but the system is old and usually provides only one or two channels. Given the high level of poverty in rural Russia, very few households could afford to subscribe to multichannel DBS services, and even in urban areas the cost and utility (limited alternative viewing provided) would make it a tough sell. Also, the investment would be massive, since the old satellites can't be converted to provide current DBS technology; the NTV Media-Most project noted just above indicates the high level of investment involved. Early figures show that Media-Most has about 10,000 households subscribing to NTV Plus.

The more mass-oriented applications of the Internet seem even farther off. As of late 1997, there were estimates of anywhere from 150,000 to 600,000 individuals on line in Russia,[261] many of them businesspeople. While there were websites operated by individuals, most of the Russian users were far more active as recipients of material rather than as originators of it. Many Russian newspapers have become involved with the Internet in a variety of ways, but other electronic media have done little with it so far. The growing number of "cybercafés" around the country may serve as "stations" of a sort, since some of their users clearly seem anxious to share their views on public issues with larger numbers of people,[262] but they lack central editorial direction (which perhaps is what makes them popular).

In 1997, the Russian National Press Institute established the Center for Cyberjournalism—a computer lab with Internet access. It enables journalists to acquire skills such as news-gathering through the Internet, communicating with the audience and preparation of on-line publications. There also is a radio channel called "SkyMAN" which serves the "cybercafés," and presumably individual Internet users in Russia.[263] However, interactive broadcast programs remain experimental, and their further development looks to be a relatively low priority.

CONCLUSION

Russian electronic media represent both continuity and change when compared with their nature and usage in the Soviet era. They have no explicit government-dictated role in reshaping society: they're far more open to the outside, and especially western, world; and their journalistic coverage of developments within the country is more complete and more critical. At the same time, they continue to reflect a considerable degree of subservience to government, and the accusations that they don't do enough to mirror "true" (mainstream, nonminority) Russian culture certainly could have been heard in Soviet times, although chiefly as an indication of distaste for programs featuring minorities. The more recent expressions of dislike for so much U.S. programming find stronger echoes in the Russia of Peter and Catherine the Great, who also were sometimes accused of opening the country up to too much western influence.

The factors chiefly responsible for the shaping of Russian electronic media are familiar enough: *politics* certainly plays a major role, just as it did in the U.S.S.R. But *economics* now is equally powerful, although it has a strongly political streak, in that some of the larger investors seem at least as interested in access to political power as they are in profits and losses. *Technology* has been important in promoting the rapid growth of the private sector, since it's much less expensive to put a station on the air now than it would have been 15 or 20 years ago. It well may become even more important if Russia's economy continues to improve and cable and DBS begin to offer substantially more channel choice.

Where Russian electronic media will go from here is difficult to say, but it isn't likely that the country will return to the media structure and philosophy that characterized the Soviet era. Too many people have become accustomed to a greater measure of frankness and openness, especially through NTV and Moscow Echo, and, somewhat less often, RTR. At the same time, the fact that so many people rely so heavily on television for their information makes that medium a particularly attractive target for pressure by the government, which has numerous ties to most of the Moscow-based stations. Unless the economic situation improves considerably, newspapers are unlikely to regain their former prominence, and cable and satellite services aren't yet available on a wide enough scale to serve as a useful alternative source of information, particularly on events taking place within Russia.

The increasing power of certain economic enterprises, banking and energy in particular, appears to be producing an interwoven alliance of government and big business. Banking and energy concerns have been the largest investors in television, and Michael Urban sees them as "suturing together a collection of state-private conglomerates that channel their 'interests' directly into the state organs, bypassing publics, parties and Parliament."[264] If the public perceives television in particular as less and less able to play a role independent of government, that might lead to demands for a restoration of the medium's "watchdog" role, but it also could either result in greater public apathy, or movement for more revolutionary change (which probably would not be more democratic).

Journalists by and large lack effective means for combating employer pressure, just as they do in many industrialized and other nations, but the problem may be especially severe in Russia, where journalists' wages are very low and opportunities for journalistic employment elsewhere largely absent. One critic, Alexei Pankin, also feels that the journalists aren't sufficiently professional in their approach, observing that " ... the fundamental evil is not in who owns the media, but in the journalists themselves, who are still ideologues rather than professionals."[265]

There may be mounting pressure on television and, to some extent, radio, to reduce or eliminate the "lewd" soap operas, talk shows and music, particularly the imported programming. Still, some of the TV stations have produced their own contributions along those lines, many of which seem far more explicit than what comes in from abroad.[266] Since the attacks on U.S. and other western programming shown over Russian television seem to have a base resting in part on the concept of "poison from the outside world," they probably are tied in with Russian nationalism, but that seems unlikely to excuse the Russian soft-porn shows from attack: there's a strong religious overtone to much of the nationalist criticism.

Whether that criticism ever could become sufficiently severe and widespread to lead to a takeover of government by a movement led by an Ayatollah Khomeini-like figure, with "purification" of the media as one of its objectives, seems a remote possibility, but continued economic hardship for the majority of the population might lead to desperate measures which could include increased "media-bashing." And certainly the current political opposition in Russia, led by the Communists and the ultranationalists, continues to plug away on the theme of "Russia for the Russians." Communist Party head Gennadi Zyuganov, interviewed just after the government had announced the creation of "Kultura," said that he was suspicious of the new service because it was to be headed by ex-Deputy Culture Minister Mikhail Shvydkoi, who had "tried to convince us to turn cultural valuables [art works taken by the Red Army as it invaded Germany] over to Germany." He also charged that "not a single [ethnic] Russian person" appeared on the five leading Russian TV networks.[267]

Urban contends that the tight financial circumstances faced by many Russians have led them to seek escape in the mass media, but in a somewhat different way from the more usual forms of "escapism" in industrialized societies. He states that "large segments of society seem keenly receptive to messages in which elements of the miraculous have been encoded," and cites as examples some of the foreign soap operas (many from Latin America and Mexico, often featuring characters rescued from difficult situations by various forms of deus ex machina) on Russian TV. He also sees it extending into real-life instances where something advertised on TV as the answer to one's economic prayers—investment schemes sure to make people rich almost instantly, such as Sergei Mavrodi's MMM[268]—turned out to be hollow promises, and deprived many viewers of the little savings they had.

Brian McNair is torn between optimism and pessimism regarding the future of the electronic media in Russia. He sees Russian television as "in limbo," somewhere between the Soviet system and a commercial system, and observes that "sooner rather than later, depending on the resolution of the political and economic crises afflicting the country as a whole, Russian television must stabilize. Whether it does so as a respected part of the European broadcasting system, or as an instrument to be exploited by criminal and authoritarian politicians, remains to be seen."[269] Monroe Price observes that, "Russian television is as much a continuation of Soviet television as it is a rupture from it."[270]

Shortly after the breakup of the Soviet Union, sociologist Anatoly Rakitov accurately speculated on the likely effects of a large decline in economic production: "Russia will be shaken by explosions of anarchy, by revolts and conflicts, hunger, epidemics, sociocultural disintegration, national-territorial conflicts. ..." He regarded "financial dictatorship," a "liberalization" of prices on goods and other economic moves as the only hope for a better future, and felt that the only way for Russia to achieve it was to move from a "disintegrating feudal-industrial civilization to an information-based civilization."[271] The electronic media could play important roles in that regard, as they've done in other industrialized nations, but it's open to question whether they will receive sufficient guarantees of stability, freedom to innovate and outside investment to enable them to do so. At the same time, they must be prepared to place greater distance between themselves and the government. The price may or may not be too high.

6 What's Comparable, What Isn't And What It May Mean

While the systems covered in the previous chapters represent differing national circumstances and approaches, there are several respects in which direct comparisons are both possible and meaningful. Those comparisons follow along the lines of earlier chapters; they also appear in various guises in other comparative studies of electronic media.[1] They have one common denominator: the interactions of electronic media institutions and society. Society may include governments, public interest groups, labor unions, linguistic minorities and more, but the fact remains that those media are social institutions first and foremost.

BASIC FACTORS

What do the experiences of the systems tell us about the relative importance of the six basic factors considered in chapter 1?

First, it seems evident that *geography* is somewhat less important than it was when broadcasting began, especially for large or exceptionally mountainous nations. The coming of communication satellites has made it possible (if expensive) to conceive of bringing electronic media services to every corner of a nation. That same development has implications in terms of signal spillover, and as a result it took a crowded area such as western Europe far longer to work out and implement a plan for satellite usage than it did for such large and relatively isolated nations as the Soviet Union, Canada and the United States.

Second, it has become more difficult to consider the factors in isolation. The development of more efficient means of communication—the Internet is only the latest example—itself has meant that nations have become increasingly interdependent, so issues of *culture, economy, politics and demography* have more and more supranational ramifications. The flow of goods between countries has increased; so has the flow of the labor force. Speakers of minority languages are becoming more and more aware of each other's experiences with the mass media around the world, particularly as *technology* makes it imaginable for them to have their own electronic media services.

Even if it weren't for the "internationalization" of those factors, there appears to be a growing interdependence among them on a national level. For example, if societies within nations are becoming increasingly pluralistic (probably with the help of the mass media), any decision taken to augment the level of electronic media service to those societies will have political implications (individual politicians usually are elected by collections of small to medium-sized interest groups) and economic implications (added services cost money, and who will pay? But added services also may bring more jobs and stimulate the economy), as well as very obvious demographic and cultural implications. And if certain groups seem to be getting more favorable treatment than others, or if certain groups seem to use the added services to separate themselves from the larger society, the implications for national unity are considerable. So are implications for the future of the nation-state, which we'll consider later.

But the *political* factor seems the most crucial. So many major changes have come about because of changes in political power—for instance, privatization in France and commercialization in Germany, Russia and the Netherlands—while lack of change in political power seems to have been accompanied by lack of notable change in programming, as in Gaullist France, in East Germany throughout most of the period of Communist rule, and in the Soviet Union before Gorbachev. However, changes in political power now appear to be declining in importance where changes in media policy are concerned: the Socialist Parties of the Netherlands, Germany and France have been increasingly well-disposed toward private enterprise in the 1990s, although they remain relatively strong defenders of public service broadcasting. There seems to be an economic motivation behind this: much of the public appears to want more choice in services, but doesn't want to pay for an expansion of PSBs through license fee increases, so private enterprise is the only apparent choice.

In fact, the *economic* factor often runs in tandem with the political factor (which is exactly what political economy theorists would expect, although they may have somewhat greater difficulty applying the theory to the actions of socialist governments, as in France, which have been favorable to the development of commercial media; that wasn't the expected pattern of political-economic behavior), as the more conservative parties in particular look upon electronic media technology (fiber-optic cable, satellites) and on the licensing of commercial stations as "engines" to drive the economy. But it's also possible that they look to commercial media as a way to reduce the overall level of attention paid to politics, and indeed many of the new commercial services offer little or even nothing in the way of news and current affairs. And then there's always speculation about television as the present-day equivalent of bread and circuses ...

MODELS

The models of communication systems covered in chapter 1 probably have lost some of their relevance with the passage of time: very few communist nations remain. The proliferation of electronic media in most industrialized nations has made it increasingly difficult to think in terms of models or even systems. Regulatory agencies find themselves with decreased powers. Is it still possible to consider those media in systematic terms?

I would argue that models do retain relevance, for two reasons: they provide a benchmark for measuring change over time; and they remind us of the fundamental purposes for which the media exist and to which they've been put. They may even help us to see where things seem to be heading, although I've never felt that comfortable entrusting too much predictive power to models.

If we look back to the 1920s, when radio was in its relative infancy, we find a widely varied mixture of systems in the industrialized nations, ranging from laissez-faire (the United States until the late 1920s) to social responsibility (Great Britain after 1926, with creation of the British Broadcasting Corporation) to communist (the Soviet Union by the late 1920s, once the government had centralized power). By the 1930s, fascist governments in Germany, Italy and Japan had harnessed the power of broadcasting to strengthen their own hold on power. Most other European nations had moved in the direction of monopolistic, social-responsibility systems. The United States remained a largely free-enterprise, commercially based system, but Canada and Australia had added public broadcast services to their already-existing commercial services.

After World War II, PSB-dominated systems were the rule within the industrialized nations, although the United States, Canada and Australia continued to feature robust commercial sectors. The development of television as a truly mass medium brought with it vastly increased costs of production, and a growing tendency to include advertising as a source of financial support for PSBs; sole reliance on annual license fees or government appropriations became rarer, and audience ratings more important. The greatest change, however, was in central and eastern Europe, where most nations came under communist rule, and their broadcast systems followed suit. That was reversed in the early 1990s following the collapse of communism in those nations and in the Soviet Union, although much in the Russian and other former Soviet republic systems (and in some central and eastern European countries) is reminiscent of communist days.

Meanwhile, the nations of western Europe moved in the direction of the free enterprise approach followed by the United States, encouraged in some instances by the Reagan administration's deregulatory policy of the early to mid-1980s. The European Community's (later, Union's) economically driven policy set forth in *Television Without Frontiers* helped to break the PSB-dominated monopoly structures, and led to some heavy soul-searching on the part of the PSBs as they sought new or reshaped roles in their altered circumstances. As of the late-1990s, there are no monopolies in any of the industrialized nations, and free enterprise-oriented models seem to be dominant in sheer numbers, if not necessarily in their influence on society. Social responsibility hasn't vanished, by any means, but it's in a much weakened position as a model. The communist model no longer exists in the "pure" form it enjoyed before the collapse of communism in the late 1980s to early 1990s (save in North Korea, Cuba, Laos and Vietnam, although small cracks are beginning to appear in the latter two; in any event, none of the four is an industrialized nation), but events in Russia and in many of the other former Soviet republics show that it isn't altogether dead just yet.

Whether the overall shift in dominant models will prove to be lasting is yet to be seen, but in a world of increasing electronic media choice, that seems quite likely. Social responsibility is likely to remain a factor of some importance in most systems, but it seems unlikely that it'll recover its former strength. Still, as we consider the emergence of various models over time, and of variations within each model, we realize that most of the industrialized nations have a wide variety of electronic media outlets, from "pirate" (unauthorized) stations—the anarchical end of the scale—to stations that serve chiefly as mouthpieces of the government in certain of the former Soviet republics—the authoritarian end of the scale. Some stations preach disrespect and even hatred toward certain "other" groups in a society; some preach tolerance and mutual understanding. Some are dominated by commercial advertising, while others carry no ads. There are specialized services of bewildering variety, some of them operated by ethnic and other minority groups which were unable to represent themselves through the electronic media as recently as a decade ago. If models are of decreasing importance, the underlying notions of the relationship between media outlet, government, economy and society represented by them continue to find expression in the experiences of that vast array of approaches.

GOVERNMENTS AND THE ELECTRONIC MEDIA

No government ever has been willing to give the electronic media a totally free hand. I stated in the first chapter that there are good technological reasons for this, chief among them the need to keep broadcast signals within the country and between countries reasonably interference free. Neither has any government permitted total freedom of speech over the electronic media, although there are differences in degree of freedom permitted. Sometimes those differences become very evident when we measure systems against one another, but sometimes the degree of freedom changes over time, almost imperceptibly, within a system.

Governmental Administrations

The ability and desire of governmental administrations (the ruling party or parties) to limit the degree of freedom of speech for the electronic media usually is thought of in what might be called traditional political terms: limits on criticism of the political party in power at a given moment, which usually extend to limits on criticism of the individuals exercising that power. Administrations often have influence over how much money a system (particularly a public service system) receives; they may grant tax breaks to media services; they sometimes appoint the chief administrators of public service systems; they usually appoint regulatory agencies that license and supervise the electronic media; and they usually have the right to address the public by means of those media. Thus, they have numerous ways of imposing limits on what the media can say about them, and of replying to criticisms of them made through the media. Those same limits may apply to other less obviously political forms of programming, as well: More than one administration (e.g., in the U.S.S.R., France, Germany) has imposed its moral standards on radio, TV, cable and the Internet, both to reinforce certain "desirable" (to the administration, at any rate) forms of moral behavior and to eliminate "undesirable" forms.

Certainly the most fundamental reason for administrations to be concerned over freedom of speech is the assumption, usually unquestioned, that the electronic media have a powerful influence on their audiences. That assumption not only has led certain administrations (Nazi, Soviet) to prevent and/or to encourage the broadcast of certain types of material, but also to intervene in a technological sense: encouraging the manufacture and distribution of certain types of receivers to ensure that the largest possible audience could be reached, but discouraging the ownership of other types of receivers that could pick up broadcasts from outside the country. The white South African government appears to have had the same objective in mind when it developed its Radio Bantu service for black South Africans on FM, since FM receivers could not pick up most broadcasts coming from the politically hostile "front-line" nations near South Africa. Such a policy may lead to short-term success, but it appears to be hard to sustain over the long haul.

That assumption concerning the power of the electronic media to influence society may need to be questioned as they offer a wider and wider range of program choice. Very few nations nowadays have just one radio service, and many nations, certainly in the industrially developed world, but sometimes in the developing world as well, have two or more television services. As soon as a choice is offered, it becomes possible for audience members to avoid what they consider uninteresting or threatening without turning off the set.

That in turn may mean that audience members have fewer and fewer programs that most of them have seen and that most of them can discuss among themselves or with the help of a discussion leader. Also, as systems expand the numbers of radio or television services, often they fill the increased airtime with imported material: music records and CDs in the case of radio, entertainment programs in the case of television, and international news services (Associated Press, World Television News) in the case of both. If that occurs, audience members have the opportunity to measure domestic programs against the imported material, and the former may suffer by comparison, especially if the administration has considerable influence over their nature and form. And if those audience members have ready access to and can understand broadcasts from neighboring countries, the problem may be compounded. Many administrations seem to have little skill in preparing messages so that they will be attractive to the mass audience.

But administrations often are skilled in preparing messages that the media themselves will understand. Theodore Roosevelt once noted that the presidency gave its occupant a "bully pulpit" from which to address the nation, but the pulpit needs an outlet, and the outlet usually is the mass media. If a national leader should consider any one of the mass media to be in need of a lecture itself, for whatever real or imagined offense, such a lecture also can be delivered through the mass media. Even if the offending media outlet refuses to carry the criticism, the other media usually will do so. President Nixon, acting through Vice President Spiro Agnew, berated the U.S. commercial TV networks for their alleged liberalism in 1969 and after; various Soviet Communist Party leaders and presidents criticized Soviet broadcasting for its alleged dullness; Prime Minister Helmut Schmidt of West Germany called for a weekly television-free day in a 1982 speech. In each of those instances, both the print and electronic media gave the messages widespread coverage. And if a medium or one of its members should refuse to provide the desired coverage, there are still other means available to bring (or to attempt to bring) it into line, as President Reagan's press secretary did when he told the Mutual Broadcasting System radio network that he was withholding the cooperation of the White House Press Office in retaliation for Mutual's decision to "jump the gun" in using advance-release material contained in a Reagan Saturday morning radio address.[2]

Administrations also appoint review or study committees in many nations, and this, too, becomes a means of bringing governmental influence to bear upon the electronic media, since administrations tend to appoint committee members who agree with a given government's political philosophy. Rarely is there much attempt to appoint a bi- or multipartisan committee, even though that could enhance the report's credibility. Also, administrations have a great capacity for ignoring those parts of a report that they don't like, as Mitterand's Socialist administration in France did with the Moinot Report in 1985 and as Thatcher's Conservative administration did with much of the Peacock Report on the financing of the broadcast media in 1986.

Legislatures

Legislatures, as we've seen, also can be a powerful source of influence. The French experiences of the 1960s and 1970s show that there are circumstances in which those challenges have little effect, but the U.S. Congress's success in preventing the Reagan administration from cutting annual budgetary appropriations for public broadcasting back to almost nothing in the 1980s tells us that checks and balances can work.

Legislative bodies often end up deciding how public broadcast systems are to be financed and in some cases decide how much money they will receive. We have seen several instances of how that power may be used or misused, once again with examples of both in France over the years. With the coming of the costly "new technologies" and the push for the privatization of broadcasting in many western European nations in the 1980s, the use of financial power took a slightly different turn: Some legislatures (e.g., the Netherlands, France, Great Britain) held down license fee increases while at the same time permitting and even sometimes encouraging private enterprise to enter the media field.

There are differing interpretations of why legislatures have acted in those ways; the usual explanation is that people (meaning the voters) are tired of paying higher and higher license fees, and legislators don't wish to risk upsetting them. Yet another explanation is that some legislators and some political parties believe that the media should allow for a wide diversity of presentational styles, program types, viewpoints and so on, and that commercial services will accomplish this more economically than will license-fee-based services (a prominent argument of some British Conservative Party politicians in the 1980s, which also appeared in the Peacock Committee report of 1986). Another is that license-fee-based systems seem by nature to be economically inefficient—a frequent argument of some of the parties in the Dutch Parliament. And still another explanation is that some legislators, especially those with conservative leanings, often feel that license-fee-based or annual appropriation-supported systems tend to favor a liberal or even leftist point of view; reducing or not increasing appropriations or fees may warn them to mend their ways, and encouraging private enterprise to establish services may better ensure expression of the conservative point of view. (Some West German media observers offered that as a major reason why the Christian Democrats opened up the electronic media to private enterprise in the mid-to-late 1980s.)

Most legislators, acting individually or collectively, are able to call upon media executives to account for their specific programming decisions. Certain individuals become quite famous as broadcast critics. Winston Churchill (grandson of the famous British prime minister) got a fair share of media attention in the mid-1980s by attacking the BBC for its broadcast of "pornographic" material. U.S. Senator Thomas Dodd became quite well-known as a critic of television violence in the 1960s. French Senator André Diligent became a prominent advocate of broadcast reform in the 1960s. However, such individuals seem to have little lasting impact on the medium.

If a number of legislators become involved, matters can be more serious. CBS television learned that in the 1960s and early 1970s when it had to spend considerable time and money defending its documentary programs, such as "Harvest of Shame" and "The Selling of the Pentagon," from attacks by various members of the U.S. Congress. Those attacks probably led CBS to schedule fewer documentaries, and perhaps to tone down those it did carry, although the network continued to attract congressional criticism into the 1980s, most notably with "The Uncounted Enemy—A Vietnam Deception." Many members of the British Parliament attacked the BBC in 1983 for its alleged "evenhandedness" in covering the Falklands War, when some of those members wanted a more partisan account. Several U.S. senators led a drive to curb "pornography on the Internet" through restrictive legislation in the mid-1990s.

But generally speaking, such instances of legislator disapproval don't result in fundamental changes in media law. Legislators seem content to rely on their expressions of disapproval to get media executives to think twice before acting in a similar fashion in the future, because they are aware that executives don't wish to spend time and money in legislative hearings, which also run the risk of generating unfavorable publicity. (The press in many countries often seems to love to expose the problems of its fellow mass medium; the electronic media rarely do the same to the press.)

Legislative bodies in many countries also appoint commissions to study broadcasting from time to time, usually in reaction to a crisis or problem. As the French experience shows, such commissions probably will have little impact upon broadcasting unless the political party in power wishes them to. The 1977 report of the Annan Committee in Great Britain, which contained a number of quite thoughtful and very interesting recommendations for the future of British broadcasting, had a limited impact on the system that eventually developed: The committee reported while the Labor government was in office, but the Parliament that finally acted on the report a few years later was dominated by the Conservative Party, which had its own agenda to promote.

There's another connection between legislators and electronic media—a symbiotic relationship of sorts: the former depend upon the latter to publicize their activities; the latter depend upon the former to keep government regulation from becoming too burdensome. According to some critics, that prevents either group from being terribly critical of the other, to the general public's loss. There may be some truth to that argument, although it's a rare year when there aren't at least a few legislative committee investigations of one or another aspect of the electronic media.

In most industrially developed nations, political advertising of any sort is rare, but many systems provide blocks of airtime for the use of political parties, which accept full responsibility for whatever their membership chooses to put on the air. (U.S. Vice President Al Gore strongly supported such a development in 1997, as he pushed the commercial television industry to accept that and other obligations as part of their "payment" for being allowed to gain access to high-definition TV [HDTV] frequencies free of charge.) And many systems, including U.S. commercial and public broadcasting, devote some airtime to political discussions in which politicians can be challenged by other politicians and/or by broadcast and press reporters. The politicians often are less free to present their points of view and their personalities without challenge than they are in the United States, and less likely to curry favor with broadcasters in hopes of receiving more favorable treatment. The communist systems were obvious exceptions, but then, their politicians didn't have to ask for favorable treatment—they simply assumed they'd get it.

The Judiciary

Anyone who is familiar with the role played by the judiciary in influencing U.S. electronic media may have been surprised to see so little indication of judicial influence in most other national systems. There are several possible explanations. For one thing, the United States probably is a more litigious society than are most others, so there's a greater likelihood that there will be legal cases involving stations. For another, there are large numbers of electronic media services in the United States, which itself increases the possibilities for legal cases. And for a third, the presence of a regulatory commission in charge of both licensing those services and supervising their output (admittedly in a very loose manner) is almost guaranteed to produce conflicts that must be resolved by the judicial system. The FCC is not a court of last resort, and communication lawyers and their clients are well aware of that. It's probably a combination of those three elements that produces the high degree of judicial involvement in the United States, since other countries have large numbers of independent stations (much of Europe, Australia, Canada, Japan and some of the Latin American nations), a few are quite litigious (India, Mexico) and many now have regulatory commissions.

When the judiciary does become involved in electronic media regulation in most countries, it's likely to be over a relatively limited range of issues: whether the government (usually the administration, but sometimes parliament) has the right to do something to or about those media, as has happened in Germany; or whether a service should or should not have carried a specific program, often on a broad political or societal issue (e.g., the Holocaust, news about a national election campaign). Questions of whether a specific service should or shouldn't be permitted to operate rarely arise, perhaps because so many regulatory systems operate on the assumption that, once a service is licensed or otherwise authorized, it will stay on the air forever (or at least as long as there's financial support for it). While there often is a system of periodic licensing, license renewals are almost certain.

Demands from members of special interest groups for airtime to reply to programs with which they disagree are about as rare. That may be because right of reply is built into the systems themselves, as in the Netherlands, or because there is a quasi-judicial body to handle such complaints, such as the

Broadcast Complaints Commission in Great Britain. There also seems to be less of a presumption in other countries than in the United States that the courts can and should serve as a means of publicizing one's cause, by which token courts in other countries rarely if ever handle cases involving advertising opposed by ecological groups (e.g., the 1971 case involving Friends of the Earth and the FCC) or demands for airtime to oppose government policy (e.g., the 1973 Business Executives Move for Peace in the Vietnam vs. CBS case).[3]

Such cases have become rare in the United States in the 1990s. That could be one result of deregulation in the 1980s, but it also could be due to the rapid expansion of electronic media outlets that deregulation and technology have produced: with so many outlets available (at least in and around cities), can't almost *any* group find one or two willing to carry its messages? That has happened in other parts of the world, as well. But the proliferation of outlets also makes it harder for such groups to attract audiences. Even those sympathetic to a group's cause may not know when or where its programs will be on air, unless the group has conducted a far better publicity campaign about its electronic efforts than most such groups manage to do.

Regulatory Agencies

Regulatory agency involvement in electronic media regulation at one time was as rare as judicial involvement, but it is increasing quite rapidly, in large part because of the growth of commercial services. However, some nations seem uncertain as to the mandate of a regulatory agency, how its members should be chosen, who should supervise it and so on. Lacking their own precedents, countries either establish an agency, give it a very loose mandate (and often a small budget) and hope that it'll work, or they turn to examples in other countries and model their commissions on those experiences.

Those few concrete examples themselves offer conflicting evidence of how a regulatory commission might be structured, but they seem to agree in certain respects: Such a commission should have a fairly sizable full-time staff which isn't subject to political appointment and should be headed by a small group of commissioners which is, but which should not contain more than a bare majority of commissioners associated with a given political party. A commission should have an annual governmental appropriation, although those using its services may be required to pay fees to help offset some of its costs. Its decisions must be a matter of public record and must be challengeable in courts of law. The licenses it awards are to be for specified periods and on specified terms and may be renewed. It determines its own procedures but is subject to the limitations of the law establishing it, which may be amended by the appropriate legislative body.

Thereafter, practices may differ quite widely. Canada's CRTC holds hearings for the initial licensing and subsequent license renewals in the community where the service is to be licensed; the Australian Broadcasting Tribunal (ABT) followed much the same practice, although its successor, the Australian Broadcasting Authority (ABA), is less active in that regard. The U.S.

FCC and the French CSA hold almost all such hearings in their respective national capitals. The FCC pays, or at least claims to pay, some attention to program content as a criterion for determining whether a service's license should be granted or renewed; the French CSA pays little attention to programming practices, aside from the amount of French-produced program content. The FCC has attempted to promote diversity of ownership in the media by (generally) refusing to grant a broadcast license to a corporation that owns a newspaper in the same city; the ABT and ABA, Great Britain's Independent Television Commission, Germany's *Landesmedienanstalten,* and many other such agencies, have renewed the licenses of many "same-city-newspaper-owned" services. The Canadian, Australian and French regulatory agencies all have requirements that promote the placement of Australian-, French- and Canadian-produced programs on the stations they license, but the FCC has no comparable requirement.

Those differences may be a reflection of cultural philosophies: Canada and Australia, for example, don't wish to be flooded by U.S. programs, which they fear will weaken their indigenous cultures. France has very strong feelings about promoting French culture. Differences also may stem from socio-economic philosophy: The FCC and the U.S. Department of Justice believe that diversity of expression may be hampered if newspapers also operate the broadcast stations in their cities, while newspapers are the dominant investors in private stations in Germany, Australia and Japan, including many stations in the newspapers' own communities. Regulators in those nations seem to feel that it's logical for the publishing industry to protect itself by investing in a potentially competitive medium, and besides, the publishing industry probably has a better notion than do most potential investors of how to manage a communications outlet successfully.

But some of the differences are difficult to explain in any rational way: Australia and Canada both are large nations, as is the United States, and yet the regulatory commissions in the first two manage to conduct hearings in the cities where the stations operate, whereas the U.S. FCC does not. If the airwaves are considered to be the public's property—the usual philosophical basis upon which governmental regulation of broadcasting rests—why not give the public the opportunity to comment on how well they think they will be served or are being served by a station and give them that opportunity in a fashion that makes it easy for them to comment? The answer may be that the process of licensing and renewal can be handled more efficiently if it all takes place in one location, and the taxpaying public saves money when a governmental agency can increase its efficiency, but that is not the answer given by the FCC. To the extent that there has been an answer, it has been that the public didn't seem all that interested in making its views known when the FCC conducted renewal hearings in Omaha and in Chicago in the early 1960s. As it takes some time for the public to become familiar with any new process (and perhaps to learn that its time will be well spent in using that process), it may not be surprising that public interest was low.

There are some fairly complex systems which do not feature regulatory agencies. Japan has a dual system, the private sector contains a fair number of independent stations and there is periodic relicensing. Yet the U.S. occupation authorities' introduction of an independent regulatory commission failed to take hold, and there has never been one since. Various Japanese broadcasters and critics of broadcasting have told me that the concept of such a commission is alien to the Japanese, which begs the question. A few of those broadcasters and critics have gone on to say that it is alien because the Japanese are an authority-loving (or at least authority-respecting) people and don't sense the need for a commission that, ideally at least, would be relatively free of influence from the government and the broadcasters and at the same time open to public input. As the Japanese system doesn't appear to be notably less democratic than other systems where a commission exists (except that investment in private stations is dominated by publishers, and except that politicians seem to be treated more respectfully and less critically than in some other systems), perhaps it proves that a regulatory commission is not absolutely necessary, but it also simply may prove that Japan is a singular case.

INTERNAL RELATIONSHIPS

The systems covered in previous chapters have shown that internal structures are two-layered for the making and transmission of programs, and the administration of the enterprise. Theoretically, one could dispense with administrators, at least those at the top, on the grounds that they don't contribute directly to the program production and transmission process, which after all is the essence of a media service. Some small stations take a step in this direction by not having any full-time senior administrators: Any individual who has administrative responsibilities also will have production or engineering duties. That's possible as long as the station not only is small but also has an uncomplicated program structure (an all-music station is an excellent example) and an uncomplicated financial support base. Many stations possess the former, but few the latter; except for radio stations financed by club or association members who themselves operate the station, virtually every type of financial support base requires accountability, whether to advertisers, the public, the legislative body or whatever else. And as soon as accountability enters the picture, top-level administrators seem to become indispensable, if only to provide that accountability and to keep the money flowing into the service so that the producers and engineers can function.

However, many of those administrators also have firsthand experience with program production and use that experience when working with program-makers. And if they do not have that experience, as often is the case with administrators appointed by governments, they soon begin to feel that they should take a more active role in the production process, if only to show that they mean to "run a tight ship" and to "keep on top of things." Such an approach may be necessary if they are to explain to the government officials who have appointed them, to the advertisers who support the operating costs, or to the public that listens and watches that they really know why programs look and sound as they do. In other words, many top administrators have a public relations function, and not only with the general public. It's a function that demands some degree of working knowledge of the programming process as well as a display of the ability to influence that process.

It would be difficult to discover whether one specific approach to the development and maintenance of a "good" internal relationship has been better than any other. "Good" for whom? Administrators? Producers? The financiers of the system? The audience? And might there not be at least occasional merit in having a "bad" (adversarial) internal relationship, on the assumption that such a relationship would cause all involved to keep on their toes, always watchful, so that any errors by one partner in the relationship surely would be detected by the others?

It seems more profitable to ask what the end product of the internal relationship should be, although even here it's a matter of perspective: Autocratic governments want strong and even absolute control from the top down, while democratic governments at least profess that they want (relative) freedom of expression for diverse opinions, cultures and so on. But most individuals connected in one way or another with the media do seem to agree on the need for systems to operate with reasonable fiscal efficiency, to be responsive to the wishes of listeners and viewers, to present programs with some degree of professionalism, especially in appearance, and to present them in an interesting manner.

That list looks almost too obvious to merit examination, but in fact the systems covered earlier and many more not mentioned in this book have had problems in one or more of those areas. "Fiscal efficiency" was a major issue for French broadcasting in the 1970s, and it's been a major justification for the appointment of certain committees to examine the BBC in the 1970s and 1980s. In contrast, I have heard many European media staff praise U.S. commercial and noncommercial services for fiscal efficiency, especially when compared with experiences in their own systems. Responsiveness to audiences certainly takes many forms, and no one system seems to follow precisely the same approach taken by any other, but French public broadcasting has often received low marks from critics for its responsiveness, while Japanese public broadcasting tends to get high marks. As for professionalism of appearance of programming, most systems exhibit high quality, but some, such as the Soviet system, seemed to take longer to reach that level than did others. And while "interesting" programs, much like beauty, are in the eye of the beholder, Soviet and French informational and U.S. educational programs have drawn more criticism along those lines than did similar British or German programs.

Are there differences in the internal relationships within the systems themselves that seem to promote greater satisfaction with the end product, at least for the audience? Set aside the question of whether we have fully adequate measures of public satisfaction, and examine such partial measures as public opinion surveys that explore public satisfaction with electronic media content; amounts and types of critical mail received by electronic and print media and by external supervisors and regulators; degree of public compliance with license fee payments where they exist; criticisms raised by the print media and by legislative bodies and by governmental administrations. Does any one system seem to come out on top?

The Japanese public system (NHK) seems to achieve the highest overall levels of public satisfaction by the above measures, although that in part may be a function of the allegedly traditional Japanese reluctance to criticize. It also may be because the NHK employs so many different approaches for assessing public satisfaction. It may or may not have much to do with internal relationships. The NHK appears to have much the same sort of internal structure as do other services, although unlike certain other systems (notably those in communist countries and, much of the time, the French system), politics is just one of several factors in the selection of most administrators. Nor are there any particularly strong unions within NHK, which might promote a more cooperative atmosphere. And finally, there is the legendary Japanese mode of group decision-making, which certainly is not followed as rigidly in the electronic media as it is in various industries, but which does stress the importance of cooperation.

If part of the Japanese experience stems from a cultural characteristic that probably will not exist in most other countries, part of it may be more universally applicable. The way in which administrators come to hold their positions seems to be an important factor in promoting greater trust and cooperation within the system and between the system and the press, the audience, the legislature and so on. BBC administrators seem to enjoy a fairly high degree of trust on the part of program producers, critics in the print media and political figures (although the last-named have ripped the BBC often enough for its alleged political imbalance). That may be because most of them rise through the ranks and usually have held several different positions in production and administration by the time they arrive at or near the top of the administrative pyramid. Thus, if a high-level BBC administrator makes an observation about program production, there's a fair likelihood that she or he does so because of firsthand experience. French PSB production staff ordinarily wouldn't expect a high-level administrator to know one end of the camera from the other and resent attempts by administrators to tell them how to produce programs.

The diversity of modes for assessment of public satisfaction that the NHK displays nearly are matched by the BBC, and German public broadcasting is not far behind. But what really matters in assessing the relationship between the internal organization of the system and public satisfaction with its product is how the system uses those modes. The NHK and the BBC both publish at least some results from their audience research studies, and both organizations hold a number of public meetings each year at which audience members are invited to express their opinions about broadcasting. The public then may believe that those results and opinions must play some role in the program decision-making process, and administrators occasionally make public statements to that effect. Still, the "reality" of program decision-making, from what I can determine, doesn't show that program producers attach much importance to those opinions and results.

Finally, the success or failure of any given form of internal administration is affected heavily by available resources—not just budget, important as that is, but also of top-quality personnel. If the government or other forms of private industry manage to siphon off the best electronic media talent for their own purposes as soon as it has exhibited its quality in those media, the quality of program output is bound to suffer. That happens with some frequency in Third World broadcast systems, where the best talent in broadcasting often is drawn into other branches of private industry or into government, sometimes because of money, but sometimes because of the insistence of top-level government officials that their needs come first. A promising program director soon may find her- or himself heading a branch of the Ministry of Agriculture.

RELATIONSHIPS BETWEEN PUBLICS AND MEDIA SYSTEMS

It should be clear by now that there is no single electronic media public, nor probably ever has been. Most systems have included certain structural provisions in their organizational makeup that at the least allow for some sort of general public input and which on occasion even strongly encourage it. A specific example of the former was the U.S.S.R.'s "letters from the audience" programs, and of the latter the Japanese NHK's coupling of annual license fee collection with a brief questionnaire on audience satisfaction with NHK broadcast services. Several systems include general advisory councils, usually for public services, but occasionally (Germany) for private ones. They are supposed to represent a broad spectrum of public opinion and reaction, although there's little that is representative about them.

Most electronic media staff realize that much of the energy they spend in dealing with the public in fact will be spent in dealing with specific interest groups or with individuals who think of themselves in group terms. Again, the systems covered in this book exhibit a number of ways of treating this situation. In some, the media take the initiative and appoint advisory councils or committees of experts that will consult with them on the most correct and/or best ways of preparing programs on religion, education or whatever the subject area might be. In others, the citizenry itself will take the initiative and will attempt to bring pressure to bear on the system in order to prompt more suitable (to the group in question, at any rate) programming.

Whether the citizens will be successful or not probably will depend upon how well organized they are and whether they can obtain coverage of their activities by other mass media, but it also may depend upon how impervious the system is to public criticism of that sort. In Japan, for example, the many protest campaigns launched by parents and teachers against "immoral" programming on Japanese commercial television by and large have failed, perhaps in part because the commercial system felt that it could ignore such pressures. That feeling probably has stemmed from the fact that commercial broadcasters had many "friends" in the Japanese Diet and from the fact that there is a very close link between the press and commercial broadcasting, making the former less likely to carry criticism of the latter. In France, the close links between the government and electronic media seem to have had much the same effect, and in Australia the financial ties between the press and commercial broadcasting also appear to have made it difficult for groups unhappy with one or another sort of commercial programming to obtain coverage of their grievances.

I mentioned in the previous section of this chapter that a few systems or parts of systems had managed to achieve fairly high levels of public satisfaction with their performance. We can take another perspective on that issue if we look at it from the standpoint of how the public, especially individual members of the public and specific interest groups, have sought to express their dissatisfaction, and how successful their efforts have been. It seems fair enough to conclude that the vast majority of the audience in most countries doesn't even think of expressing dissatisfaction with programming most of the time; it sits back and takes what it gets, sometimes with a bit of grumbling, seldom with anything worse. The most popular form of public expression of feelings throughout the world seems to be the letter, and the many media staff with whom I've discussed audience mail lead me to conclude that little of that mail expresses dissatisfaction. BBC and U.S. commercial network research division staff have confirmed that most letters are requests for more information about "stars," about how certain aspects of broadcasting work, and for revivals of old favorites no longer on air. And when critical comments do appear in letters, often they are so generally stated (e.g., "There's far too much sex/violence/sports/advertising on TV") that it's almost impossible to draw any firm conclusions from them.

Certainly there are other ways of expressing dissatisfaction, especially through groups, and some have proven to be quite adept at presenting their grievances. Certainly the National Viewer's and Listener's Association in Great Britain attracted a good deal of print (and some electronic) media attention in the early 1980s for its allegations of explicit sexual content on TV and found allies in the British Parliament (including Prime Minister Margaret Thatcher) to express its concerns in that body. The Campaign for Better Television appeared to have some success in convincing the British Parliament to place a requirement for more meaningful program standards in the 1990 Broadcasting Act. Certain religious organizations, especially in the United States and in Germany, have had similar success through similar channels, and some of those organizations also have their own publications through which they can work. Some of the "fringe" political parties or groups within larger political parties have carried out their protests in a similar fashion. In a few countries, especially Germany and to a lesser extent the Netherlands, such parties also have managed to place members within media organizations (usually PSBs), which at least has the potential for ensuring that the group's points of view will find their way into programming. Some social interest groups, such as gay rights groups, occasionally have employed that tactic in the United States, but also have worked through production houses to sensitize producers to their concerns.

All of those approaches can work some of the time. The major problem with them is that they take a lot of effort, they need money and they need continuity: Jefferson's dictum about eternal vigilance being the watchword of liberty can apply just as well to groups seeking to combat what they see as unfavorable or improper programming. In almost all instances, the money has to be raised by the groups themselves, although grants from various U.S. foundations helped to keep several citizens' groups alive in the 1970s, and there even was a proposal (never enacted) that the Federal Communications Commission cover certain legal costs associated with citizen group versus broadcaster cases brought before them.[4] Furthermore, the legal system of any given country may not encourage court cases from such groups. Even if it does, the legal assistance necessary in presenting a case itself is expensive. A few countries have provided something a bit less formidable and certainly less expensive for the presentation of such grievances, e.g., Great Britain's Broadcast Complaints Commission. But often such mechanisms have no true legal standing themselves, so that the media service suffers the ignominy of bad publicity, but nothing else. Regulatory commissions such as the CRTC, the Australian Broadcasting Authority and the FCC may be a bit less daunting and expensive than the courts, but not much.

There remains the type of council that isn't appointed by the broadcaster and that has some real power over the broadcasting organization, but there are few examples: Germany and some of the Dutch broadcast organizations, and to a lesser extent certain of the Scandinavian councils. Even here, as in the case of Germany, groups on the fringes of society in terms of their neglect or misrepresentation by the electronic media—guest workers, feminist organizations, the elderly—may lack formal representation. Also, such councils meet infrequently—four to six times a year is typical—so a group seeking to work through such a council may find that the specific grievance it expresses will be a few to several weeks old by the time the council next meets.

It isn't surprising that some groups dissatisfied with the electronic media have taken matters into their own hands and set up their own stations. French and Italian radio in the late 1970s and early 1980s probably furnish the largest number of examples, but most of the industrialized nations in the western world have had such operations. Sometimes they're legal, sometimes they're not. Always they take some time, money and effort. Some of the earlier efforts didn't last more than a few months, often because they had little or no support from the larger group of which they were a part.

The experience of certain French pirate radio stations operating on behalf of the workers in the late 1970s is instructive: Their staffs found that union officials often were suspicious of such efforts and preferred to work through the "tried and true" channels with which officials felt comfortable (meaning those that they could control).[5] Most of the Italian worker-oriented stations that operated in the late 1970s had disappeared by the early 1980s, bought out by commercial radio interests or devoid of sufficient financial support, and much the same happened to many of the French community-supported stations by the late 1980s. The call of the British government's Home Office for applications for community radio services in the spring of 1986 brought forth nothing from labor unions, even though some union figures (notably Arthur Scargill, head of the Coal Miners' Union) frequently criticized the BBC and IBA for "anti-union bias." Certain individuals deeply involved with community radio in Great Britain told me in September 1986 that that didn't surprise them, since union officials seemed to have little interest in expressing themselves through their own stations, or at least over stations that would operate more or less permanently.[6] However, the Coal Miners' Union and the Printers' Union each operated pirate stations during strikes in the mid-1980s. Also, a "Radical Communist," Gennadi Zyuganov, began a campaign to create a "worker's station" in Russia late in 1997.[7]

Some ethnic groups, notably blacks in Great Britain and the United States, Arabs in France, and some linguistic groups, notably Spanish in the United States, have had more success in organizing themselves and in getting services on the air or on cable, but that seems to have been largely because they constituted numerically viable groups as targets for advertising. However, starting in the mid-1970s, many of the western industrialized nations began to provide opportunities for minority groups to gain airtime through community radio services. A few, notably Australia, Canada and New Zealand, even provided continuing financial support for the development of ethnic radio and even TV stations. Minority-group protests, coupled with the support those protests received from religious and educational institutions (and, less often, mainstream broadcasters and politicians), seem to have been the chief motivators of those changes.[8]

Religious groups have enjoyed similar success in a number of countries: In the Netherlands, some of the broadcast societies are linked with religious organizations; in Norway and Sweden, the "närradio" channels in many towns and cities are dominated by them;[9] and there are many such stations in the United States and in various Latin American, African and Asian nations. But only the larger organizations, or at least wealthier ones, ordinarily can afford the cost of such a venture. A rather different situation confronts political groups; very few countries allow such groups to operate their own services (although many of them do so through "närradio" in Norway and Sweden),[10] while many countries make some provision for political party airtime on radio and TV. However, such arrangements usually exist only for the mainline political parties, and smaller parties rarely gain access.

The Scandinavian "närradio" services seem to have achieved the most satisfactory method for permitting a wide range of religious, political, ethnic and cultural groups to broadcast, since a group doesn't have to be wealthy to support its broadcast efforts, and since there are very few restrictions on what a group can say or do over radio. Still, it *is* radio, with all of the attendant restrictions on audience size and on types of programming. Access programs on TV are becoming more common now, especially in some of the German states, the United States and Canada, but the far higher cost of TV limits such utilization, even when some of those costs are subsidized. The Dutch "Migranttelevisie" service is severely handicapped by lack of financial support. Cable radio offers similar possibilities and limitations and has been utilized by a number of groups: Turks and other minorities in the Netherlands and Germany, African-Americans in the United States.[11]

Certainly the capacity of any broadcast system to accommodate all points of view as frequently as those holding those points of view would like is limited. Large and wealthy nations such as the United States clearly have faced such limitations, so it isn't surprising that smaller, less wealthy nations, especially if they have great sociocultural diversity and lots of geographic neighbors, may face even greater limitations. It is also quite clear that many groups in many countries don't want the full-time responsibility of running a station. Again, however, the "närradio" concept, at least as it is practiced in Sweden, allows groups to have their own broadcast outlets on very modest terms—as little as 15 minutes a week, if that's all they wish. But "närradio" cannot accommodate a group that doesn't want to broadcast on a recurring basis and yet might want to have access to airtime on an occasional basis, especially to reply to a broadcast it considers damaging to itself. No system anywhere guarantees that form of access, although the Netherlands comes fairly close with its quite liberal provision for airtime on the spur of the moment, and access channels on cable TV in many countries do the same.

RELATIONSHIPS AMONG THE MASS MEDIA

Most industrialized nations exhibit some degree of adversarial relationship between the press and electronic media. It may be because the press has been around longer and feels that it knows better, it may be because there is competition for advertising revenue, it may be because the electronic media are enormously popular and newspapers can count on some reader interest in them, especially if stories contain a hint of scandal. Even in countries where the press is a major investor in those media—Australia, Germany and Japan, certainly—newspapers don't hesitate to criticize broadcasting, although a given newspaper may spare its particular station or network. Some systems are set up so that the electronic media do not compete with newspapers for advertising, others feature restrictions on the degree of competition, and a few engage in head-on competition, but the press seems equally adversarial in all three conditions.

Perhaps that's just as well, since most systems aren't given to self-criticism. When it's present, it usually appears over public services, and not commercial ones. The BBC, the ZDF and several other European PSBs have had occasional televised meetings with one or another segment of the public, as did Great Britain's commercially supported ITA, and some of those meetings have been forums for rather sharp criticism of various program practices. Such broadcasts are not a regular occurrence in most systems, however; when they are, they usually appear on radio, which draws much less public attention. Great Britain's commercial Channel Four once had a weekly program featuring viewer observations on television. "Right to Reply" was edited from comments recorded by individuals in "video boxes" located in London, Manchester and Glasgow. (I visited all three locations in 1986. Rates of usage were low—three or four a day—and comments were general in nature. There also were a few exhibitionists, including sexual, but their contributions never appeared on "Right to Reply.") But viewers and listeners cannot demand such meetings or broadcasts, since they aren't required by law.

However, press criticism of the electronic media often is a regular feature in many European countries, where most of the nationally distributed newspapers carry critical columns daily. Not all such columns actually criticize the media, or at least not all of the time; many devote much of their space to describing upcoming programs, giving profiles of actors and directors and so on. Still, there is enough criticism that it appears to inspire the public to write letters to newspapers rather more frequently than is the case in the United States. Sometimes columnists actually call upon the public to write, usually in order to "save" some high-quality series from cancellation.

Whether this adversarial (some would claim healthily adversarial) stance on the part of the press will continue as program services expand and as the press itself gains more opportunities to invest financially in stations, cable and satellite services is another question. The fact that most of the industrialized nations have had relatively few electronic media services until quite recently has made it easier for the press to cover them, since most readers would be interested in and familiar with the programs, policies and personalities it was covering. That broad public familiarity is not so easy to assume any longer. And if the press becomes a colleague rather than an adversary, it probably will mean that at least some broadcast services—chiefly those owned by the papers and magazines—will be treated kindly, as often happens in Japan and in Australia. Furthermore, press treatment of major legislation affecting electronic media possibly could be influenced by press ownership of those media.

If parts of some systems are being "invaded" by the print media, those systems themselves are becoming more and more important in the life of the motion-picture industry, although not without complications (note France, Russia and Germany). Most of the industrially developed nations do not have large cinema industries, and television has had much the same effect on them as it has had on cinema in the United States: The industry keeps itself alive in large part by making films for TV, but also making some films in versions for TV and for the cinema, as Italy began to do in the mid-1980s.[12] We may assume that many of those made-for-TV films aren't the sort of work that filmmakers would undertake for the cinema, both in subject matter and in types of visual effects. However, it has been possible for certain film directors and writers to create major works of unquestioned artistic merit for television, as with Ingmar Bergman's "Fanny and Alexander" (much longer as shown on Swedish TV than the cinema version, and richer and probably more comprehensible in its story line, too), Rainer Fassbinder's "Berlin Alexanderplatz," and the two monumental ZDF-produced social history dramas, "Heimat" (1984) and "Die Zweite Heimat" (1992).

There's no reason why electronic media systems couldn't treat filmmaking as they have treated classical music for so many decades. Most of the major European PSBs, as well as Canada's CBC, Japan's NHK and Australia's ABC, have commissioned composers to write music of all sorts—chamber music, choral music, jazz, symphonies and so on. Furthermore, most of those systems have recorded that music and made it available to the record-buying public. Composers have had the creative freedom to write pretty much what they wish, and there's adequate rehearsal time to assure that their works will receive first-class performances. Some systems have commissioned films and have given producers the same creative freedom, but that hasn't yet become as frequent a practice as it has for music.

There also are cases where electronic media sign contracts with the film industry that establish both rental costs and conditions of usage, often including the provision that the media will show the film as it was shot, and won't edit it to the point where it becomes almost unrecognizable.[13] Some also set aside funds to assist various filmmaking projects. The German PSBs have done so, giving filmmakers the opportunity to make films that might offend most TV watchers and probably never will appear on that medium. (However, in 1987 the West German government did withdraw subsidies from two feature films on the grounds that they made fun of religious feelings.) The European Community's MEDIA fund also has assisted film productions, although the EU's modest financial support—MEDIA's budget for its second five-year term (1996-2001) is roughly $500 (ECU 400) million—limits the fund's impact. Furthermore, its top priorities seem to have become program production, distribution and training, with less support available for production development.[14]

The coming of *pay-TV* systems to many countries also has provided a financial shot in the arm for some domestic cinema industries. France's Canal Plus shows hundreds of feature-length movies each year, and is required by law to favor French-made films. That requirement has resulted in a marked increase in the annual production of French feature films, with Canal Plus' own film and TV production unit emerging as one of the giants of the French production industry. Quantity is no guarantee of quality, but at least it maintains domestic film production, and helps to ensure that pay-TV doesn't simply become another outlet for U.S.-produced material. Those industrialized nations which haven't yet done so might consider how pay-TV and the domestic cinema industry might assist each other (and presumably benefit the nation as a whole). Great Britain's Channel Four, although not a pay-TV channel, has shown that it's possible to invest in films ("My Beautiful Launderette," "Enchanted April") that turn a profit and can subsequently be shown on television. And finally, some of the most distinguished recent examples of single-episode dramas on U.S. television, a few of them shown in cinemas as well, have been produced for HBO, the dominant U.S. pay-TV channel.[15]

Mergers, acquisitions and cross-media investment have become much more common throughout the industrialized world since the mid-1980s, and show considerable potential for altering the media landscape. Media barons such as Kirch and Springer in Germany, Murdoch in several parts of Europe, North America and Australia, and Berlusconi in Italy, have commanded much attention, in part because of their sometimes colorful actions. But organizations such as Canal Plus, the Scandinavian Broadcasting System (partly financed by the U.S. ABC network), and Endemol in the Netherlands, if less noticeable, are no less active, and are becoming important participants in media systems outside their home countries. The media "empires" established in Germany, combining as they do both production and distribution outlets, and comprising both the print and electronic media, don't have the multinational reach of Canal Plus or of the SBS, but they may pose a greater threat to diversity of expression through the electronic media, simply because of the variety of media outlets over which they have influence.

REGULATION, COMMUNICATION POLICY AND THE "MEDIA EXPLOSION"

One of the greatest changes that came over most electronic media systems in the industrialized world during the 1980s was the need to take a fresh look at regulation in the light of the "media explosion." By the late 1970s, there already was widespread discussion of cable TV, DBS, and, in nations that had not considered them before, commercial broadcasting and local broadcasting. Often the press took a lively role in that debate, in part because the press was eager to invest in broadcasting. By the early 1980s, many of those services were reality or much closer to it, and nations now had to cope with demands for licenses. Choices had to be made where no one had thought about choices before.

The regulatory bodies that emerged often were ill-equipped at first to deal with the plethora of new services and applications that arose. Poorly financed and subject to political pressures (witness France's Haute Autorité), lacking a body of case law and experience to serve as a point of reference (the U.S. FCC had many years to "learn the ropes," first with radio, then television, then cable TV, whereas the Haute Autorité had to learn everything all at once), and with little by way of overall communications policy to guide them, no wonder that some of those bodies got off to a rocky start. Furthermore, participants in the new licensing game often were (and still are) well-connected politically, so regulatory bodies sometimes found themselves making perfectly sensible licensing decisions, which then had to be unmade because some politically powerful applicant wasn't happy with those decisions. (France furnished plenty of examples in the 1980s.)

Some of the regulatory agencies improved over time, particularly in France, and became both more precise in their use of regulatory power and less subject to political pressure. But the German, Russian and Dutch experiences show that determined, financially strong and politically powerful investors in the electronic media often can work their ways around the regulatory agencies, often by pulling the right political strings. The German practice of regulating through councils made up of representatives of society, commendable as it might be in its fundamental purpose of giving society some direct control over the electronic media, may have outlived its usefulness: the amateurs serving on the councils seem to be out of their league in regulating the kinds of professionals who have come to the fore over the past decade.

Finally, no regulatory body, whether new or old, will be able to affect the development of a well-integrated system unless there is the national will, chiefly as expressed by the national government, to formulate and maintain a communications policy that will bring about such a system. But long-range, all-embracing communications policies are rare items among the industrialized nations. If such policies could be developed, a regulatory body could do a great deal to make them become a reality. However, some nations (Great Britain, Germany) have headed in a different direction and have established separate regulatory bodies for various purposes. Great Britain has one body for commercial radio and another for commercial TV (including satellite and cable). The noncommercial BBC stands apart from either of those bodies. The German states have separate bodies for the PSBs and for commercial services. Such diffusion of responsibility is almost certain to make coordination of any sort of communications policy (if one even exists) difficult if not impossible.

In fact, the rapid growth of different sorts of electronic media throughout the industrialized world, much of it driven by commercial forces, makes it doubtful that most industrialized nations could now create an integrated communications policy. Opposition from the commercial forces themselves, together with the increased levels of support they've received from leading political parties on the right and on the left over the past 15 years, would be enormous. It's difficult to see how there could be a correspondingly powerful coalition of forces supporting such a policy. The Dutch Media Council (1988-present) perhaps represents the closest thing to an effective enforcement mechanism for a communications policy that aims to keep commercial and noncommercial sectors in some sort of balance, but expansion of cable TV's channel capacity and growth in popularity of DBS, if and when either or both occur (and there's nothing in the Dutch legal system to prevent that), would seem certain to alter that balance beyond recognition.

PAYING FOR THE MEDIA

As I indicated in the opening chapter, the electronic media have been financed in a wide variety of ways, ranging from the highly personal (one individual supporting one station) to the broadly national (license fees, subscription fees, annual appropriations) to the commercial (advertising, program sales, rental of studio facilities). Fees, appropriations and advertising still predominate. Traditionally, broadcast services were supported by one or another of those methods, but usually each type of service was financed by a single method. For example, public and private broadcasting in Japan, Great Britain and Australia were supported through mutually exclusive means: the public sector through license fees or annual appropriations, the private sector through advertising. In countries where broadcasting was a monopoly, such as the Soviet Union, financing often came in one form only, although a few monopolies (the Netherlands in 1967, France in 1968) moved from a single or dual financial source to a multiple-source system, usually adding advertising to license fee revenues.

With the advent of the "media explosion," there were increasing financial pressures on broadcasting, and especially on systems with a single financial source or with one major source and one quite minor source. Most of those problems arose in cases where the single source or the major source were provided or authorized by the national government—in other words, annual appropriations and license fees, which have either declined or failed to grow. Governments like to show the electorate that they try not to burden people with "added" expenses, in this case money to operate broadcasting. That makes them reluctant to increase license fees or to vote larger annual appropriations for broadcasting, perhaps in part because the print media (which often compete in the electronic media arena) are almost certain to make the public aware of any such increases. As costs for broadcasting often have risen more rapidly than has the annual rate of inflation, there have been increased tensions between some broadcast services (PSBs in particular) and their governments. Also, some governments, particularly those favoring private enterprise, feel that electronic media should be open to more participants, which will give more businesses a chance to make money and to stimulate the economy, and will cause PSBs to become more fiscally responsible. Since a number of conservative governments came to power in western Europe from the late 1970s to the late 1980s, pressures of that nature have increased. And finally, artists (writers, producers, performers, etc.) and politicians (usually from the parties in opposition) have seen some real or potential danger in PSBs relying too heavily on one source of income, since they might become artistically smug and narrow or might be open to greater political influence by the government of the day.

Those factors, acting singly or in combination, led to changes in the ways in which the electronic media receive their financial support in most industrialized nations. By the early 1990s, there were very few of those nations which had not experienced the introduction of private radio, private television, cable TV, DBS and pay-cable. Those "new media," usually supported through private enterprise, caused governments to become far more reluctant to raise license fees or to increase annual appropriations to pay for public broadcasting. And if investors were to become involved, they wanted to be sure that there would be a decent financial return on their investments. User fees were one approach, but many industrialized nations already had user-fee support in the form of license fees. That often forced private radio and TV to rely upon advertising as a major, if not sole, means of support, which in turn brought governments to reconsider their attitudes toward advertising, and particularly toward permissible amounts and types of it. Many of them (the Netherlands and Germany are good examples) had protected the press by not allowing broadcast advertising, or by permitting only small quantities, and occasionally by allowing ads for nationally marketed products and services only. A few even used some of the revenue from broadcast advertising to help newspapers supposedly harmed by its introduction. Governments also began to tell some of the PSBs to think the unthinkable: to introduce advertising in a service that never had done so and probably never thought it would or should! Some of the BBC's replies to the Peacock Committee's recommendations on advertising over BBC Radio 1 and Radio 2 were more like cries of outraged honor. PSBs that already carried limited amounts of advertising sometimes were directed or permitted to increase that total, as were Dutch broadcasters in 1985.

Governments often seem to reason that, if a new media service is to live or die on the basis of its ad revenue, then surely the PSBs won't suffer unduly if their audiences, too, must now receive their daily dose of commercials, or a larger dose than before. After all, that helps to keep the license fees or annual appropriations lower, and it may even help to stimulate the economy. However, the private broadcasters, cable operators and other competitors with the pre-existing services usually haven't welcomed that reasoning, since it would benefit them far more if those services weren't competing with them for ad revenue. But politically economically conservative governments often have taken the attitude that business enterprises should "compete on a level playing field," as U.S. President Ronald Reagan was fond of saying. Sometimes that philosophy has meant that governments have encouraged the old-line services to consider development of separate pay-TV services, DBS services, videocassette distribution, teletext and so on. All of that has driven the electronic media to become more and more competitive, with private and public services alike vying for ad revenue, sales of programs abroad, subscriber fees for special services (teletext, pay-TV, cable) and so on.

That competition for ad revenue can lead to an interesting balancing act. The government may decide to reduce or not raise the annual license fee that supports the nation's PSB—a political move that should please many voters. The PSB campaigns for some financial relief, and the government allows it to advertise or to increase advertising—an economic move that should please the PSB and perhaps advertisers, which may be able to drag the PSB and the commercial services into a price-cutting war. The commercial services, seeing their ad revenue reduced, campaign for increases in advertising time for themselves. If an increase is granted, there may or may not be an absolute increase in ad revenue. Meanwhile, the public finds that more and more of each program hour is consumed by advertising. Whether any of the actions taken in that chain of events really ends up serving anyone's interest (aside from advertisers—but they too may lose out if the public perceives the increased ad time as more "clutter," and pays less attention to the ads) is questionable.

That competition has the potential to drive the individual electronic media services to become more and more alike. To the extent that those services compete for the same sorts of audiences, it seems inevitable that there will be a greater degree of homogeneity in programming. Some of the older duopolies—Canada, Australia, Japan, Great Britain—continue to display a fairly high degree of programmatic differentiation between public and private broadcasting, although various British critics (Milton Schulman, Chris Dunkley) quickly claimed to see more "popularization" and "sensationalism" in the BBC's output as a result of the IBA's presence. As those duopolies break down in the course of the "media explosion," will that differentiation continue? Canada's PSB, the CBC, dropped most U.S. TV programs from its TV schedule in the mid-1990s, even as the government was cutting back on the CBC's annual appropriation. How much longer the CBC can sustain its differentiation (the private services rely heavily on U.S. programs, and Canada's cable and satellite services carry many U.S. channels) in the face of continuing cuts is an open question.

And as that competitive situation extends beyond national borders throughout the industrialized world (certainly a major goal of the European Union), so that cable and DBS services offer entire channels from systems in other nations, and videocassettes are available from many parts of the world, how are PSB services responding? With direct imitations of the imported material? With roughly similar but more specifically indigenous programming (German or Russian series based upon "Dallas" or "Santa Barbara," but with appropriately German or Russian settings, themes and topical references)?

That could be a very strong temptation, so long as programs were not too indigenous, because it would enable those national systems to compete in foreign markets themselves. That approach was encouraged in the European Community's 1984 report, *Television Without Frontiers.*[16] European broadcasters and their respective governments were urged to open national boundaries to trade in broadcast programming and advertising, just as nations in the Community were to open their borders to trade in produce such as apples and sheep. Still, apples and sheep feed the body, whereas electronic media feed (or can feed) the mind, and the Council of Europe—a larger group than the European Community (now Union), and more politically/culturally minded than economically driven—often has discussed the potential danger to national cultures if programs are allowed and encouraged to flow too freely between nations.

The Council's Fourth European Ministerial Conference on Mass Media Policy, held in Prague in December 1994, issued a strong declaration in support of public service broadcasting. The ministers decided "to safeguard the independence of public service broadcasting and to secure for it a safe and appropriate funding framework enabling it to fulfill its mission ..."[17] In 1996, a British member of the European Parliament, Carole Tongue, led an effort to win the European Union's support for the strengthening of EU member PSBs.

The effort eventually was successful, which was quite remarkable, given that the EU's overall policy with respect to broadcasting had been to deal with it predominantly in economic terms, with little differentiation between commercial and public services.

Even with Council and Union support, European (and other) public service broadcasters will never regain the dominance they had during the decades when they enjoyed monopoly or duopoly status. There's far more competition now, and its rate of growth shows little sign of slowing. Private terrestrial stations now exist in every European nation. Cable is well-established in Scandinavia, Germany, Switzerland, the Benelux nations and even central and eastern Europe, and is finally showing signs of significant growth in Great Britain and France. Direct-to-home satellite services have established solid footholds in Germany and Great Britain, and are establishing themselves in Scandinavia. Videocassette recorders are important in the overall media mixes of most European nations, but they're largely a matter of personal investment, whereas the establishment of cable and DBS services involves large sums of money and, on the user's end, continuing support through subscriber fees. Because many nations already had annual license fees, there were doubts at first that viewers would pay yet again for a further set of broadcast services, including some that they already could receive. The record of the past decade indicates that the doubters were wrong.

It's harder to explain why cable and/or DTH haven't taken off more rapidly in some of the economically strong industrialized nations, such as Japan, Great Britain, France, New Zealand and Australia. Perhaps they feel well satisfied with the services already available. Perhaps their citizens are more economically conservative. Perhaps they don't regard what they've come to know about the variety of programming available through cable or DBS as much of an alternative to what's already available. Perhaps they have very different ideas about how to spend their disposable income. (I often have wondered whether higher levels of unemployment and underemployment may bring households to continue to subscribe to services such as cable or DBS because they provide viewers with a wider variety of entertainment to fill empty hours and days. That might help to explain why so many of the central and eastern European nations, a number of them with quite high un- and underemployment, have experienced such rapid growth in cable and satellite subscriptions.) But there are no easy answers, which must make it difficult for investors in such media services to decide where to risk their investments!

Perhaps the greatest expression of concern over future patterns of financing centers on the simple question of who pays for what. If advertising becomes the dominant form of financial support, are the advertisers simply buying numbers of viewers—the more (and the more of the "right" sort), the better? And if license fees or annual appropriations remain an important form of support in some nations, will governments be willing to raise either of them enough to allow PSBs to provide the public with the increased range of services it may wish, so long as it doesn't have to pay too much more for the privilege? Despite the actions of the European Union and the Council of Europe in support of public broadcasting, there's nothing that compels any nation to fund PSBs at any specified level.

Put another way, if advertising dominates, will programming become almost entirely mass-oriented and as cheaply made or obtained as possible? If fees or appropriations dominate, will public broadcasting be able to change with the times, and will governments refrain from applying heavy political pressure on their programming? Would an ad-dominated system inevitably lead to heavy reliance on U.S. programming? Would a fee- or appropriations-dominated system inevitably lead to a preservation of the national culture?

In fact, there's nothing inevitable in either scenario. License fees haven't made Dutch broadcasting a model of cultural preservation, nor have the Dutch commercial services served as little more than pipelines for U.S. programs. In fact, the most popular Dutch commercial service, RTL-4, achieved that position by providing large amounts of Dutch-produced entertainment (much of it admittedly bearing a fairly strong resemblance to U.S. series). Nor has exclusive reliance upon advertising kept Japan's commercial services from producing most of their own material. Size of population and relative prosperity of the economy are important factors, of course, but so may be the high costs of the top-heavy administrations that seem to characterize so many of the appropriations- or fee-supported systems. And there are cases where ad-supported systems do produce programming that clearly isn't made for a mass audience. Great Britain's IBA was perhaps the best example of that. But the IBA and its successors, the ITC and the Radio Authority, rest on a foundation of governmental commitment to the idea of public service broadcasting, and the ITC didn't have any commercial competition until 1997. France's various private services, including the privatized TF1, appear to lack such a foundation, and as a result (and with the exception of certain interest group-operated radio stations) feature little but mass-oriented programming.

Many of the fee- or appropriations-supported systems now place greater emphasis on alternate means of financing, and especially on means other than advertising. (But most BBC and NHK staff seem to regard advertising as a form of prostitution, and Germany's ARD and ZDF keep it at arm's length, although that arm seems to have become shorter with the advent of strong competition from commercial services.) There is increased interest in (and necessity for?) selling various broadcast-related products, and not only programming: The BBC opened a retail store in London late in 1986. It deals exclusively in BBC publications and other retail products such as T-shirts and coffee mugs. Symbolic of the importance attached to the selling of BBC products was the hiring in 1986 of a director of BBC Enterprises (the sales arm of the BBC) for a salary very close to that of the BBC director general. A few public broadcasting services in the United States draw some 5-10 percent of their annual revenues from sales of retail products, and most public broadcasters throughout the world probably would rather sell themselves in that manner than through the sale of airtime, although most also would admit that doing so is almost certain to have its effects on creativity in program production. More and more of the PSBs also are developing specialized services for distribution via satellite, as well. In any event, it's no longer a matter of "business as usual" for most PSBs.[18]

PROGRAMMING PRACTICES AND ISSUES

It should be self-evident that the ultimate purpose of the electronic media is to distribute programming, but it's quite easy to lose sight of that purpose in the thicket of structural considerations that surrounds those media. It also may be easy to assume that, generically speaking, the program product will not vary a great deal from one country to another. If genres are defined with sufficient breadth, that is quite true: Every electronic media system (although not every service within a system) provides news and other informational programming and also provides entertainment. One can go a step further and state that every system provides national and international news, "serious" and "light" entertainment, programming intended particularly for adults, particularly for children, and so on. Every system also forbids certain sorts of program content: hard-core pornography, incitement to riot, material dangerous to children, promotion of violent overthrow of the national government. And there are some overall similarities in scheduling, especially in the placement of major newscasts and most of the more expensive entertainment programs in the prime-time hours, which may begin as early as 6 p.m. in some nations or time zones, and as late as 8 p.m. in others.

But there are some quite striking differences, as well, even among the systems covered in previous chapters. A very few, most of them public services, sign off on TV before or at midnight during the work week, while others, particularly commercial services, have extended their TV schedules to almost 24 hours a day. Financial resources play a role here, but so have political-sociological factors: Communist nations didn't want to have workers up too late at night! (Some of the more "radical" Islamic nations, such as Iran, appear to be similarly minded.) Although no public system in any industrialized nation fails to broadcast seven days a week,[19] certain political figures, such as former West German Chancellor Helmut Schmidt, have advocated "TV-free" days for the sake of social cohesion. And the broadcasting of TV programs for the general public during the morning hours came to most of western Europe only during the 1980s. Again, this was due in part to limited finances, but also to a feeling on the part of some broadcasters and of some government officials that the public shouldn't become too television-dependent.

Also, while various studies from the 1980s[20] indicated that percentages of time devoted to overall categories of programming on public TV services did not differ that much from country to country, there were some quite clear differences in relative popularity of various program categories and in the prominence of various sorts of story lines, whether fictional or factual. West German viewers seemed to favor quiz shows and crime dramas (Germany now has a cable and satellite channel which provides nothing *but* crime shows);

French viewers leaned toward variety shows; the Japanese prized newscasts and variety shows; Soviet audiences placed nature and geography shows at or near the top of the list. Increasing commercial competition changed those priorities in some cases, particularly the increasing popularity of quiz and game shows.[21]

Those national distinctions seem far less evident when one looks at top 10 ratings for various industrialized nations in the late 1990s. In most of them, sports, game shows, sitcoms, soap operas and perhaps a newscast or an informational program along the lines of the long-running CBS "60 Minutes" will appear regularly; rarely will a dramatic series other than a law enforcement-based program break into the list, and when it does, it's often a limited-run series of perhaps four to six episodes. Most or all of the top 10 shows are likely to be domestic productions; it's rare for an imported series to reach that level of popularity, even in the smaller industrialized nations such as the Netherlands.[22]

But ratings data show something else when examined over an extended period of time: just as in the United States, the more traditional, long-established services, public and private, are losing shares of audience to the newer services. Since most of the latter have been available on a widespread basis for only the past five to 10 years, we may assume that the erosion of audience shares for the "veteran" services will continue to drop. That has some potential social implications: fewer programs will serve as common denominators for society; viewers and listeners (including Internet users, small as their absolute numbers are at present) will be more easily capable of limiting their electronic media diets to material they find congenial and comfortable; and groups seeking to communicate their points of view and activities to larger audiences will have to publicize their programs far more effectively if they hope to make those audiences aware of those programs.

The content of similar program categories also can differ sharply from nation to nation. Most larger national systems present at least a few crime dramas, but the presentation of law enforcement officials, criminals, victims and so on shows considerable variation. German "krimis" shown on PSBs usually feature compassionate, rather slow-moving detectives, and we learn a fair amount about their private lives. The German commercial service "krimis" feature more violence and other forms of action, but remain on the whole less violence laden and slower paced than their U.S. counterparts. Japanese equivalents, most of them on commercial services, tend to be fast-moving, methodical and somewhat impersonal. The French version often features highly individualistic and somewhat quirky law enforcers. Overt violence was minimal on Soviet crime shows, but has long been high on Japanese series (where, however, the pain of the victim generally is far more evident than it is for crime shows anywhere else in the world), and is well-nigh overwhelming on Russian "reality-based" programs of the late 1990s. The few Dutch-produced crime shows wouldn't strike an American, and certainly not a Japanese, viewer as particularly violent, although there are complaints that those shown on commercial TV are becoming more so.

Quiz shows look at first to be cut from the same cloth, but closer examination reveals that monetary prizes were nonexistent on Soviet TV and started quite low on Russian TV, although the prizes (including real gold) are becoming grander as of the late 1990s. Japanese commercial TV's quiz shows are even noisier and more physically active than are the U.S. shows, and participants engage in "zany" stunts that their opposite numbers in the United States might be ashamed to undertake (some of the stunts are downright cruel). Dutch PSB quiz shows often feature considerable wit; the Dutch commercial TV versions are either based directly on U.S. shows or look as if they were, and prizes are a major attraction.

Situation comedies, which are increasing in popularity as a program genre in the western world, often have chosen rather different targets as the objects of humor: the problems of divorced mothers raising their children and holding down jobs (Germany), a grocer striving to function in an increasingly multiracial neighborhood (Great Britain), apartment dwellers trying to manage the everyday vexations of living in close proximity (the U.S.S.R.). The newer commercial services offer sitcoms that often seem closer to U.S. series, with silly or stupid teenagers, bumbling parents and improbable complications as their stock in trade. Soap operas, a fairly recent phenomenon in most western media systems, tend to resemble their U.S. counterparts more closely than do other program genres, with rather sensationalistic portrayal of such subjects as interracial homosexual relationships (New Zealand's "Shortland Street").

While most systems don't go to the lengths of the old Soviet system when it comes to "modeling," all systems seem to include (consciously or not) some "socializing" messages through their factual and fictional programming. Ethnic minorities, when they appear in TV situation comedies and dramas (which isn't often), rarely are the downtrodden or the rebellious; instead, they are either criminals (with little if any indication of what brought them to that state) or successful doctors, lawyers, judges and so on. Women often are portrayed in traditional roles, as nurses, teachers, secretaries, homemakers, although increasingly there are professional roles for them, as doctors, lawyers and government officials (but usually not as the characters around whom the plots revolve). Law enforcement officials seldom come across as incompetent or venal, although more and more of them are depicted as violence-prone, not to mention impervious to any lasting harm. Most drama and comedy programs have big-city settings, with city life depicted as enjoyable if one keeps one's eyes open for possible deception (or worse). A small-town or rural setting for a comedy or drama almost guarantees a celebration of the values of the simple, trusting, cooperative life, just as it almost guarantees at least a few quaint characters.

Factual programs also show some interesting similarities and differences. Most radio and TV newscasts feature rather brief (10 to 90 seconds) items, and newscasts from national services usually contain a mixture of national and international news. There also is some similarity in the nature of news coverage among western stations: more emphasis on "negative" than on "positive" items, more depiction of problems than solutions, failures than successes. The Soviet system displayed a higher percentage of domestic successes and capitalist world failures than did systems in the western world. Domestic coverage began to be more self-critical under President Gorbachev's policy of glasnost (openness) in the mid-1980s, but lost some of that openness in the early 1990s, shortly before the failed coup attempt. Television newscasts in the United States once appeared to include more items centering on individuals than did newscasts in other industrialized nations, but many of the European systems, especially their commercial services, appear to be including "personality" items more and more frequently, and many of the public and private European services, including Russia's, are placing increased emphasis on the personalities of the news presenters, more and more of whom are women.

Just why similarities and differences exist isn't easy to say. Some of the similarity in newscast content can be attributed to the dominance of a few major wire services (AP, Reuters, AFP) and a few major telefilm suppliers. Physical similarities between quiz shows in many countries is not always coincidental: Some of the popular quiz show formats are marketed throughout the world by companies mainly in the United States and Canada. Certain situation comedies, such as the BBC's "Man About the House," have been seen by producers in other nations, who have purchased the rights to use the overall plot line—in this case the U.S. sitcom "Three's Company." French TV producers bought the rights to make a French version of the U.S. situation comedy "Maude." Also, international markets in television programs have resulted in more foreign programs appearing on screens in a number of nations, especially following an expansion in the number of stations or cable outlets. Occasionally, some of the more successful imports spawn domestic imitations. Coproductions also have some impact upon the similar look of television from nation to nation.

As for differences, they may be a result of ideology (Soviet television's frequent depiction of World War II so that people wouldn't forget its horrible lessons), of legislation (bans in many nations on the depiction of what authorities consider pornographic or overly violent), or of quotas to keep imported programming to a minimum, which may have the dual advantage of promoting the national culture and of strengthening the country's program production industry. However, those quotas cannot ensure that programs produced within the nation won't bear some resemblance to programs produced abroad. Nor do the attempts of a few nations to reward quality productions (France and Australia both have employed such approaches) ensure the development of a truly national programmatic "language."

But there probably are differences in national tastes, as well. British audiences seem to have a greater appreciation for satire than do their American cousins. Germans will watch political discussions with far greater avidity than will French viewers. Soviet viewers had a love of the sentimental that went far beyond anything I have seen in western nations. Russian viewers adore the colorful and highly emotional Latin American soap operas, which haven't enjoyed much success in other parts of the industrialized world. "Tastes" aren't always synonymous with "popularity"; as noted earlier, German television's presentations of political discussions don't begin to receive ratings comparable to those for quiz shows or "krimis," but they do obtain high scores on appreciation index ratings. A careful analysis of those ratings might reveal some interesting demographic differences, to the point where certain programs would appeal particularly to the tastes of German men, British women, French teenagers and so on, but I've never seen a comparative analysis along those lines.

Although the major national public and commercial radio services throughout the industrialized world are becoming more and more homogeneous—almost every industrialized nation has at least a few around-the-clock services of pop music and brief newscasts—there still is quite a range of difference with this older medium, too. Most of the major European PSBs continue to program radio plays, both original and adapted, as they've done for decades, although the quantity of such productions is declining. Some of the PSBs still broadcast quiz shows: Several of those carried by the BBC are decidedly intellectual in content and have small but highly devoted audiences. Whether such "old-fashioned" services reflect national tastes is another question; my own feeling is that many of them are created by aging heads of service and producers for an aging audience, and that most listeners in their 40s or younger pay little if any attention to them. All of this may mean that they face the prospect of extinction, although certain program genres such as original radio drama may survive longer.

As for high-culture programs on television (usually public TV)—classical music, ballet, operas, tours of museums, transcriptions of classical literature—they rarely finished in any nation's top 10 programs for a given week even before commercial competition emerged, and many ended up in the bottom 10. Still, they often reached far more people than would see them in a theater or a concert hall over a period of many years or even a lifetime. They were part of a public service commitment that most PSB services sought to fulfill as part of their mandate to provide programming for all audiences, and perhaps to elevate public taste. Many PSBs became actively involved as commissioning agents for contemporary drama, music, ballet and other fine arts, created their own symphony orchestras, jazz and choral groups, and distributed their own recordings of the performances of those ensembles. Such programs, much like radio plays, have dwindled in number, in large part because they're expensive to produce and harder to justify to budget-conscious media administrators and government officials. But they live on, and they may be one of the few programming arenas in which the PSBs can readily distinguish themselves from the commercial competition. They also can contribute to the preservation and extension of the national culture, although many of them still seem to consider "national culture" far more in terms of mainstream culture than in terms of the increasingly multicultural societies that characterize most industrialized nations.

Already, some of the orchestras and ensembles have been dissolved, commissions for original works (plays, compositions) are fewer, and there's little likelihood that the trend will be reversed. Certainly the commercial services don't expect to assume any of those responsibilities, and regulatory agencies don't expect them to, either. Pressures to keep annual appropriations low or license fees from increasing make PSBs more "cost-per-audience member" conscious than ever, which makes it especially difficult to justify support for expensive and low-rated programs. Government officials sometimes wonder why the fans of high-culture programs shouldn't pay to receive them—an argument that's harder to refute now that so many industrialized nations have subscription fee and pay-TV services. But that argument ignores the fact that what the PSBs encouraged often became a part of the national culture, for all of the public to enjoy. As this particular PSB role shrinks, society itself runs the risk of becoming that much poorer in spirit.

Perhaps the greatest single change I've noted in European television over the more than 40 years that I've viewed it is the makeup of the prime-time schedule. My first exposure was to German, French and British television in 1956-57. The first two were public services monopolies, and the third had been a monopoly until 1955, when a commercial service (the ITA) came on air. Television schedules were abbreviated by today's standards: programming for the general public usually began in mid-to-late afternoon and often ended well before midnight. Programming during prime-time hours consisted of a mix of mass-appeal and minority-appeal shows, in line with the assumption (it was never a condition for licensing) by the PSBs themselves that they should serve both broad and narrow publics, and that the latter shouldn't always have to wait until the off-peak hours for "their" programs. In fact, showing narrow-appeal programs during prime-time hours might actually lead a broader public to learn about something new, interesting and perhaps worth pursuing.

The coming of commercial services in the 1980s changed that situation quite radically, and in two ways. By and large, the minority-appeal programs were displaced from their prime-time slots, and entertainment (and some informational) programming on the PSBs often acquired a more commercialized appearance: regional accents became fewer or less distinctly regional, physical action increased, laugh tracks began to appear, news anchors became more prominent and less formal, plots and characters became more generic.

There's no simple explanation for that change, but several elements probably played important roles in bringing it about: the PSBs had sometimes taken for granted the goodwill of audiences and politicians alike, perhaps seeming at times to pay too much attention to subjects and lifestyles that disturbed those groups and that the commercial services ignored or downplayed; some PSBs came to seem fiscally wasteful when compared with some of the leaner commercial services; certain PSB programs appeared increasingly formal and slow paced to audiences now accustomed to the action, informality and brevity that often were the hallmarks of commercial services. Meeting the challenge of those services probably helped to increase the "salability" of PSB programming in foreign markets, since more of it was "user-friendly" to their audiences: fewer "incomprehensible" accents, more familiar plot lines. Some of the PSBs even began to recover a bit of the ground they had lost to commercial services in the ratings wars. But their programming also became less and less of a reflection of what is distinctive about the national, regional and local cultures of their respective countries.[23]

Even with that homogenization, there appears to be increasing fractionalization of programming along geographic, linguistic and "community of interest" lines. The chief agents of that fractionalization have been local and regional radio and TV in many nations, cable TV and DBS in several, and VCRs and Internet in a few. Languages that were almost extinct or were beginning to fade from use—Occitan, Frisian, Sami, Maori, Welsh—have enjoyed something of a revival,[24] as have elements of regional and local cultures (folk music, storytelling). Local government officials and the people they serve are using the electronic media as channels through which they can exchange views, seek answers and ask questions, although often the process is slow to develop. However, for those nations where local broadcasting and cable are recent developments, the local services seem to be regarded more seriously by audiences than are similar services in North America. There, the development of network television soon caused most local radio stations to economize by turning to prerecorded music, sometimes delivered by prerecorded disc jockeys, and many of the local cable access services either disappeared or were cut back during periods of deregulation and economic recession. The rapid growth of Internet services and users in the United States may restore some of that local distinctiveness, even as it also encourages the formation of nationwide and worldwide "communities of mutual interests."

TOWARD AN "IDEAL" ELECTRONIC MEDIA SYSTEM

If it were possible to combine the best features of the systems covered in the previous chapters (perhaps extended to include the oft-noted British, Canadian, U.S., Japanese, and Australian systems), would it necessarily result in an ideal system? Given the highly public, mass-oriented nature of the medium, given the diversity of tastes likely to be exhibited by even one public in just one nation, and given the proliferation of electronic media services over the past decade (and, it would seem, on into the future), it probably isn't. But I believe that it *is* possible to extract from those features a clearer notion of what would be desirable goals for systems in general. In doing so, it will be necessary to consider *why* those goals are desirable, because that should help to focus a discussion of the role of the electronic media in society.

Governments and Electronic Media

Governments and media inevitably are linked, if only because news and other informational programs do and should cover governmental activities.

But because the electronic media offer such tremendous advantages (and therefore temptations) to government officials—immediacy, mass coverage, authoritativeness—it's necessary to keep an arm's-length relationship between those media and government. They should be able to function both as reporters of fact and as analysts and critics—roles that audiences in most industrialized nations have come to expect them to play. Governments should be able to challenge what they see as misinterpretations or errors, but preferably under conditions where the reporter, critic or analyst and a government official would confront one another directly, so that the audience can have the opportunity to reach its own conclusions on the truth. Few systems feature such a practice, and none that I know of has it as an ongoing function. If the government itself operates the system—and that is rarely the case any longer in the industrialized world—such a practice is unlikely to be established. If the system is supported entirely by advertising, the practice could only be established by law: It would be costly and time-consuming, it almost certainly wouldn't do well in the ratings, and it would be controversial. Commercial services surely would reject it for any or all of those reasons, and only a legal requirement could force them to carry it.

Governments also are likely to be supersensitive to what they perceive as public moods, and the electronic media need to have some protection on that front, as well. Sex and violence in the electronic media, including the Internet, have become hot topics every now and again in several countries, and it would be very tempting for a government to respond to public criticism by forcing the media to drop such material. Although media administrators certainly should be sensitive to public criticism, whether expressed through governmental bodies or by any other means, it doesn't follow that every breath of criticism deserves a programmatic response. However, if the government holds too much power over the media, their administrators might think twice before *not* responding, which can easily lead to a diet of inoffensive, noncontroversial, bland viewing and listening. It also could lead to the growth of illegal, unlicensed media outlets specializing in forbidden material.

If we assume that electronic media must be accountable to government on the grounds that most of them use a public resource—the airwaves(VCRs and Internet services do not; neither does cable, but it does use a great deal of material that it receives through the airwaves)—and that licensing of services is necessary to ensure that that resource be used in an orderly manner, we admit the need for some sort of regulatory body to see to it that, at the very least, those services using the airwaves stay on their assigned frequencies, and at their power limits. Otherwise, listening and viewing become chaotic experiences. All industrially developed nations also seem to agree on the need for governments to concern themselves with certain programmatic issues: incitement to riot, libel, hard-core pornography, positive portrayals of child abuse and other forms of criminal behavior. Self-regulation often covers such issues, but no nation relies entirely upon self-regulation to determine whether stations have violated norms, largely because those norms cover far more than the media and often are embodied in the law of the land. The courts can handle such cases; is there any need to create a specialized regulatory agency to do so, or to concern itself with other aspects of broadcasting?

As broadcasting and other electronic media (cable, VCR, DBS) expand throughout the industrialized world, the resultant volume of activity seems to justify the existence of regulatory agencies. Decisions must be made as to who among a number of competing applicants should be licensed and whether a licensee should continue to hold a license. Therefore, licensees must propose and maintain certain technical and (although there are exceptions)[25] programming standards. A specialized regulatory agency can make those decisions on the basis of a body of accumulated and expert knowledge and practice. The trick is to create an agency that will stand at the center of a triangle: media, government and the public. The agency must be open to input from each of the three, but not under the primary influence of any one of them.

An initial sticking point is budget. If an agency is funded through annual government appropriation, the government may "lean" on the agency by threatening to reduce its budget, as the U.S. Congress did with the Federal Trade Commission in the late 1970s. But a regulatory commission could be paid for by a combination of license-filing fee and frequency spectrum use fee, as the U.S. FCC has been in part.

A second problem is legislative authorization for such an agency. If a legislature chooses to circumscribe or otherwise influence the agency, it need only amend existing laws or pass new ones. If the experience of most industrialized nations is any guide, bi- or multipartisan politics generally will ensure that the law does not get bent out of shape. If there are no second or third political parties, and/or if a government is determined to have its way, the law will not provide much defense, anyway.

A third problem is avoiding undue political influence through the appointment process. Regulatory agencies usually are headed by a small body of commissioners, and governments usually appoint them. Appointments to the U.S. FCC are made with the assumption that partisan politics will play a role. The Communications Act of 1934 (as amended) specifies that no more than three of the five FCC commissioners will be affiliated with a given political party. The Dutch Media Authority's three commissioners each represent a different political party. But such assumptions need not govern appointments, and they seldom do for the BBC or NHK boards of governors, where nonpartisanship is more likely to be predominant. If the appointments were to be made for limited, nonrenewable terms, say seven years, and if commissioners were to be removable only for gross moral violations or criminal behavior, that could make their positions more secure at times of political change. It would be especially helpful if commissioners could be chosen on the basis of distinguished public service, which itself would serve as an indication of the importance of broadcast regulation.

A fourth problem is avoiding undue media industry influence, which can be exceptionally difficult in our present age of media barons, multinational industries and conglomerates. Electronic media staff sometimes are able to manipulate regulatory bodies because politicians and broadcasters find it in their mutual interest to have a "cozy" relationship, but also because media operations are in a good financial position to hire lawyers who understand the complexities of communications law and to hire former regulatory agency staff who understand the inner workings of the organization. If influence by politicians can be kept in line by the measures noted above, that would minimize the ability of the media to use them to influence the regulatory body. Higher pay should help to alleviate the second difficulty, as would the clearer writing of communications law, but that's part of a much larger problem regarding legal language.

A fifth problem is hearing the voice of the public. If the regulatory body sits in the capital city and doesn't hold hearings on-site, if communications law is complex, and if the public doesn't know much about what the body does and how the public best might interact with it, then the body won't be of much use to the public. The Canadian CRTC, the Australian Broadcasting Authority and the Russian Federal Radio and Television Service show that regulatory bodies can get out to the public; the U.S. FCC for a brief period in the 1970s developed booklets and an information hot line that helped the public understand, in clear and simple terms, how to present its concerns to the commission. If the regulatory body also were responsible for conducting audience research (quantitative and qualitative), as does the CRTC, that would give it increased public visibility and also a means of measuring the accuracy of media claims to provide a public service.

To sum up, the regulatory body would have to have a fair measure of independence from the government of the day, which probably would mean that its top officials should be selected through a bipartisan, multipartisan or nonpartisan process, albeit not through popular elections (media regulation isn't *that* important or vital as a public concern). Those officials should have a demonstrated interest in the media, although that interest needn't be highly sophisticated. They should be paid well enough and provided with enough staff support that private industry would not seem all that much more attractive after two or three years on the job. And they should be required to interact with the public in various ways: through licensing hearings (on-site wherever possible); through public meetings where general topics, such as violence on television, can be discussed; through commission and publication of research on public attitudes toward broadcasting; and through preparation and dissemination of publications that outline public rights with respect to broadcasting, cable or DBS. The airwaves are public property, and the public has certain rights over the manner in which they are used.

A regulatory body with the properties just listed, especially if it is a single regulatory body, should make it easier for those public rights to be upheld. Granted, a single regulatory body could end up being spread too thin, but if such a body were to deal *only* with issues of *program content* and were to leave technical matters to a separate body (as is the case in France), that should make the task more manageable. A number of the comments made to the European Commission of the EU on its 1998 report on convergence (see later), as well as observations contained in the Campaign for Quality Television's (U.K.) 1998 report "The Purposes of Broadcasting" advocate such a division of responsibilities, and underscore the need for the regulator of technical matters to ensure that there be wide access to transmission facilities for society.[25a]

Still, given the tremendous proliferation of electronic media services in so many industrialized nations, could any single agency expect, and be expected, to keep track of their activities on a continuing basis? Is it likely that economy-minded, antiregulatory governments would be ready and willing to authorize and appropriate the large amounts of money for such an agency, or would be bold enough to require that all licensed media operations pay high fees for the privilege of holding licenses? Those regulatory agencies which have been in existence for some time now seem to be less and less powerful, even when led by individuals who appear to be genuinely interested in reminding the electronic media, commercial and public, of their public services obligations (fewer and fewer) and responsibilities.[26]

If regulatory agencies dealing with program content were to be abolished altogether, as some advocate, such matters as the transmission of pornographic material or libelous statements could be handled by the courts (which in most industrialized nations already are overstretched). However, the abolition of regulatory agencies dealing exclusively with issues involving the electronic and other telecommunications media would seem to signify two things: first, that those media are *businesses* in much the same way that other manufacturers of "products" (programming) are businesses; and second, that the concept of the airwaves belonging to the public has little meaning any longer. Those two concepts have served as the foundation of virtually every electronic media regulatory agency throughout the world. Their near-universality alone should tell us that electronic media are not just businesses, but that they have special properties that make them strongly influential where society is concerned. And that should tell us that we abolish them at our peril.

Whether the various categories of electronic media should be held to identical sets of regulatory limitations and protections is another matter. Several industrialized nations, Germany for one, differentiate between public and commercial services, between terrestrial and cable/DBS services, between national and local services. Regulatory agencies in Great Britain, the Netherlands and Germany operate with "a lighter touch" where commercial services are concerned: those services ordinarily aren't expected to carry the sorts of minority-interest programs which PSBs commonly carry, and which usually result in low ratings, nor are they expected to exhibit high levels of diversity in their programming lineups. If PSBs are allowed to carry advertising, the commercial services usually are permitted to carry even more of it. And, with few exceptions (chiefly in the form of protection of children from harmful material), videocassette distribution and Internet services are free from many of the program content regulations governing cable and DBS services, which in turn are freer than terrestrial broadcasters; the latter often must observe tighter limits on violent or sexually explicit material before 9 p.m. than after that hour.

Most of those differences are based on two conditions: the relative degree of control that adults can exercise over children's access to programs; and the major sources of financial support for the services. Public broadcasting faces the prospect of the highest degree of control because it's easily accessible to children and because the public pays for the greater share of its budget, through license fees or annual appropriations covered by income taxes. Internet and VCRs fall at the other end of the scale because they involve a very high degree of individual choice, and therefore, responsibility.

Whatever the system of regulation, it seems appropriate in an ideal system that public broadcasting be required to provide material for audiences unserved by other electronic media. But it also seems appropriate that those other media, with the exception of Internet and VCRs, be held responsible for at least some amount of public service. That could be done through requirements of program time devoted to specific categories of service, as in FCC Chairman Reed Hundt's initiative to require U.S. commercial broadcasters to furnish three hours per week of children's educational programming;[27] through financial support furnished by the other media for the production of such programming on PSBs and community stations; through lower subscription cost or even free access to public service material (job banks, "help" services) available through cable, Internet, etc., for households meeting a specified low income requirement; or through promotion over their own services for specialized programming available on the public services.

Internal Relationships

Systems that draw their administrators largely from the ranks of staff members who have some knowledge of program production seem on the whole more likely to uphold high production standards than systems that do not. The German, British, and Japanese PSB experiences have shown at one and the same time a willingness to innovate and a resistance to immediately pick up on every trend that may appear elsewhere. The French, Soviet and Russian experiences, where nonbroadcasters frequently are appointed to top administrative posts for political reasons, often display an overall lack of innovation and an all-too-common openness to political influence. The U.S. experience, where top administrative staff more and more frequently come from the business world, shows a concentration on the "bottom line" (profitability) that makes a near fetish of high ratings and that imposes severe restraints on such unprofitable genres as nonserial/original prime-time drama, documentary and even news.

There *is* a danger of overreliance on production staff as administrators. They may become careless about budgeting for production, finding it hard to deny to others the financial resources they were accustomed to (or at least would like to have been accustomed to!). They may be particularly reluctant to impose limits on choice and presentation of subject matter, not wishing to interfere with the creativity of others any more than they would have wanted others to interfere with their creativity. And they may have become so accustomed to viewing the production process from a particular perspective that it's difficult for them to evaluate and accept fresh ideas, especially if the ideas come from outside the system.

There are ways of dealing with all of those potential problems. Periodical examination of data gathered on production costs within the system and from other systems, especially if it's presented to an advisory council as well as to the supervisory board of the operation, can serve as a reminder of careful budgetary practices. Some overall limits governing taste in programming can be developed by supervisory boards and advisory councils working together with producers, as the BBC has done in reviewing the treatment of violence on television. A system can impose time allotment patterns that provide the opportunity for producers working outside that system to display their work. The Dutch system achieves this through its provision of airtime for some very small groups, and the U.S. public broadcasting system has an annual program selection process that operates through the Station Programming Cooperative and that allows at least a few independent producers to gain access to the broadcast schedule, although not necessarily on terms that encourage creativity.[28] The Independent Broadcasting Authority's (U.K.) Channel Four provides considerable airtime for independent producers, in part through a Channel Four-managed production grants program. The Canadian CBC has had a roughly similar arrangement.[29] The Dutch system, as noted, has a dedicated fund for cultural programs. And, starting in 1987, the Conservative Party in Great Britain pressured the BBC and IBA to agree to obtain 25 percent of their domestic television production from independent producers; that is now a requirement under the 1991 Media Act.

If production staff make the most desirable administrators, it doesn't follow that they will automatically possess the needed administrative skills, or that they will see administration as a worthwhile pursuit. Ideally, some in-house training—both classroom and on-the-job—would precede an administrative appointment. Also, it would contribute tremendously to the attractiveness of an administrative post if producers could continue to maintain some direct involvement in production even after they had become administrators. That would help to ensure that the administrator-producer would retain some sense of the "real world" of production for which she or he was administratively responsible, and it would ease the transition back to production, should the administrator wish to return. If there is a relevant model here, it would be academic administration, where many professors-turned-administrators maintain their contact with teaching and research.

There's also the issue of union involvement with the electronic media. Unions representing media staff exist in most industrialized nations, and they've been an important element in some systems in terms of their ability to win reasonable working conditions for staff who might be particularly open to exploitation. They've also been successful in a few instances in calling the public's attention to government censorship of informational programming, especially in France and Great Britain. But unions are having a hard time surviving in an increasingly fractionalizing climate: With more and more private stations, community stations and cable operations appearing in the industrialized nations, those unions that have become quite accustomed to dealing with one or two national organizations are finding it difficult to gain a foothold in a situation involving dozens and even hundreds of services, many of them small and with modest economic resources. The overall free enterprise climate prevailing in Europe starting in the 1980s isn't very helpful to unions, either. They definitely have a place in the "ideal" broadcast system, but they will have to discover different negotiation tactics and exhibit greater flexibility in bargaining if they are to survive.

Relationships between Publics and Media Systems

I noted earlier in the chapter that the Japanese NHK probably has the highest level of audience satisfaction with its broadcast output. The NHK knows that because it asks the public about it regularly and in many different ways, and the act of asking itself seems to promote public confidence in the NHK as public servant. Frequent and scientifically sound qualitative and quantitative research is an absolute necessity here, and it doesn't seem to matter whether the research operation itself is housed within the system (as it is in the NHK and in the Netherlands' NOS) or whether it stands outside that system (as it does in part in Germany and Great Britain). If the research is scientifically sound and is conducted with some frequency and regularity, it will stand up to inspection.

However, the rapid growth of commercial services in most of Europe has meant that the predominant form of research—and the form in which the general public receives research data—is quantitative, and is limited to indicating audience size and demographics. The appeal is obvious: those data, presented in the simplified form of "Who's Number 1, 2, 3, etc.," are easy to understand and even fascinating to read, since most people like to follow contests. But that tells us nothing about quality of programs as perceived by the audience, or about how much audiences value the programs they watch. Data on the latter aren't difficult to collect, as the audience appreciation index approach used by many European PSBs illustrates: viewers use a 10-point scale or a "grading" system (A-F) to indicate their evaluations. The "size and demographics" model that is becoming more prevalent throughout the industrialized world makes it very difficult for a media organization to justify carrying more-specialized programs for smaller numbers of viewers, since it won't reflect the usually high degree of audience appreciation for such programs. And, since government officials seem more and more sensitive to the presence of ratings, that simplified model can also have its effect on increases in license fees or annual appropriations.

Advisory and externally appointed supervisory councils with "public" membership appear to play a moderately important role in providing a measure of public input. "Public" may not be a very accurate descriptive term, however, as most individuals who serve on such councils come from the middle- and upper-income ranges, have high school or university educations and tend to be active in community affairs. (The British call them "The Good and the Great!") Those with lower incomes, lower levels of formal education and relative absence of community involvement don't appear very often in council membership lists. Whether they should appear there is another question. Certainly they listen to radio and watch television, and certainly there are a good many of them. But identifying them is not always easy, and getting them to participate may be difficult. If people don't feel that their participation will have much effect on programming, it isn't likely that they'll volunteer to serve in the first place.

If stations were to publicize the existence of the councils, present their recommendations (or at least summaries of them), note specific staff reactions to them, and report on actions taken as a result of them, that might help to develop greater public confidence in the importance of councils. Few systems with councils do much to publicize them, especially through broadcasts, and some actually try to conceal the identities of council members from the general public, on the grounds that they don't want council members to be "pestered" by members of the general public who might wish to voice their opinions about programming. The VARA and VPRO broadcasting associations in the Dutch system at one time made a real effort to promote public involvement, although mainly on the part of their own members, but they said little about council recommendations or staff replies in their broadcasts. It shouldn't be all that difficult for producers to make attractive program material out of those recommendations and replies.

How to select council members isn't a simple issue. The German system, where councils are made up on the basis of lists of groups and organizations, appears to be a bit too rigid; it's hard to change council makeup as society changes. However, the idea of having groups choose their own representatives may make good sense, since it removes the possibility of selection bias on the part of the media organization. A council composed of representatives from more broadly defined groups, such as education, religion, the arts, the sciences, labor, management, ethnic minorities and others, would avoid the fractionation of the German system and its large numbers of council members. Eight to 10 such members should be enough. They then could form a screening committee to select a further five to seven members to be chosen on an at-large basis, from applications that individuals would submit to the council and in which they would indicate their backgrounds and their reasons for wishing to serve. As in the German model, an administrative committee could be chosen from within the council, leaving the council free to concentrate on programming issues (which obviously are of the most concern to the general public), while the administrative committee concerns itself with budgetary and structural issues. Such an approach may not be well-suited to a media system where there are dozens of stations, cable operations and so on within one locale, but in many of those situations, one council operating at each locale and funneling into regional councils which in turn would funnel into a national council should help to ensure that audience viewpoints would be given some attention at various levels of media activity. Again, the key to success would be the publicizing of council recommendations and media responses, along with the visible independence of councils.

Quite aside from whatever councils may or may not do, citizens may choose to operate electronic media services themselves: over shared transmitting facilities (Scandinavian "närradio"); over access cable radio and TV (Japan, much of North America, Europe); over community stations (Australia, New Zealand, Japan, Canada, the United States, parts of Europe); over illegal ("pirate") stations (parts of Europe, the United States); or through audio- and videocassette distribution. Decreasing costs of equipment, expansion of the frequency spectrum and an increasing degree of group activism starting in the late 1960s all have contributed to this development. Not every operation has been successful, even if "success" means nothing more than being able to stay on the air, but many of them have given media voices to groups that previously suffered neglect or misrepresentation through the media. Homosexuals, feminists, old people, all have found outlets, as have indigenous peoples, immigrant communities, guest workers and members of minor (and major) political parties.[30] Some minority groups active in the electronic media have formed international associations, such as the European Ethnic Broadcasting Association (1995). It seems reasonable to expect that any industrially developed nation should be able to authorize some form of direct citizen participation in broadcasting, whether on cable, on a shared frequency, at low power or whatever the circumstances may dictate. Technical limitations no longer can serve as an excuse for not doing so, nor can financial reasons.

Some nations may fear such services in terms of their potentially disruptive effects on society, as did Great Britain until the late 1980s and as did the European communist nations. That fear has some foundation. Stations have been involved in allegedly instigating riots and in preaching ethnic hatred, as were two Spanish-language radio stations in Miami, Florida, in 1965;[31] or a number of stations in Serbia, Bosnia and Croatia during the conflicts of the 1990s;[32] or Radio Maryja, a station operated by a Roman Catholic priest in Torun, Poland, which calls for politicians who favor liberalizing the law on abortion to have their heads shaved, and which carries anti-Semitic remarks.[33] But the greater fear may be that, with more minority-interest services available, the largest, most powerful, most influential of the old-line stations will feel justified in neglecting minority communities. Still, it would seem worth that risk to develop more diversity in broadcasting.

Programming Practices

The ideal media system should be capable of giving audiences what they want when they want it, but no system ever could be expected to manage such an enormous and costly task, even if there were some way of knowing what audiences really want or would want if they knew what was available or could be made available. Large as the task seems, however, many nations are far closer to meeting it than most observers would have thought possible a decade or so ago. The expansion of cable and VCRs, satellite delivery and the opening up of hitherto unused (for broadcasting) portions of the frequency spectrum have made a wide range of choices available to audiences in many industrialized nations.

Some of those added choices carry price tags for their users: subscription fees for cable and DBS services, rental costs for videocassettes, pay-per-view; others have not, although there are costs in the form of general income taxes or whatever advertising adds to the cost of a product or service. It's even possible to set up a computer program that can select a specific videotape from a collection, send the tape to a machine and start the machine. Theoretically, then, audiences could order specific programs at the time they wanted to see them. In practice, lack of multiple copies of programs keeps this from being feasible, at least for home viewing. (It could be quite practical for an educational institution; the Japanese University of the Air developed such a system in the mid-1980s.)

The promise of 500-or-more-channel systems delivered by satellite either as DBS or through cable now brings with it the ability to transmit repeats of program material at different times and on different days over a set of channels. HBO already provides such a service over some of the 200-channel satellite-delivered services in the United States, as do several direct-to-home satellite services. While it isn't video-on-demand, it comes closer than anything else except rental, which it bests on grounds of convenience.

Even if such a system were widely available, would it necessarily be in *society's* interests for audiences to have it? If one can accept the argument that society needs certain linkages, certain ties that bind it together, certain traditions in common, then there is something to be said for a media system in which larger numbers of people share some of the same programming at least some of the time. The idea of a shared experience receives attention each time a major event occurs: an assassination, a moon walk, a royal wedding, mass starvation, the death of the "people's princess" (Diana). But shared experiences occur far more commonly than that, although they may occur among hundreds of thousands rather than among hundreds of millions. The U.S. sociologist Harold Mendelsohn has spoken of the "social lubrication" factor in the mass media, and television in particular displays it quite strikingly. A character with a particular vocal mannerism appears in film or on TV and spawns instant imitation by millions. A politician notes the attraction a certain TV or movie character has for "the masses" and works that shared experience into her or his speeches, as with U.S. President Reagan's evocation of Rambo or Japanese Prime Minister Nakasone's reference to the "Oshin" spirit. We share in our recognition of certain plots, characters, events, and that knowledge serves as common ground, thus "lubricating" our conversation. Our opinions may differ, but they are unlikely to emerge unless we sense that we do have a shared recognition. ZDF's one-time controller of international affairs, Hans Kimmel, observed that, "It is important to have workers in the early morning busses or secretaries in coffee breaks share experiences of yesterday night's programming, and to have newspapers comment on it. There is a structurising effect of network programs which cannot be achieved through local programmes or by selling subscription movies or videodiscs."[34]

Quite aside from the uses of social lubrication, there's also the matter of exposure to the unknown. If audiences were able to call up exactly what they wanted when they wanted it, would they be likely to expose themselves to subjects that might be troubling or even downright provocative? Would they seek out programs that expose them to some completely unfamiliar subject? In 1984, Great Britain's BBC broadcast a very vivid and even shocking drama entitled "Threads." It dealt with the aftereffects of a nuclear attack, and it made the U.S. ABC network's "The Day After" (a 1983 telefilm about the aftermath of a nuclear missile strike on the Kansas City area) look mild by comparison.[35] But it touched off further discussion in Great Britain about nuclear warfare, and that discussion carried through to Parliament. If viewers had had a wealth of viewing opportunities on the evening in which "Threads" appeared, instead of four channels of television, would the program have achieved the impact that it did, given the large audience that had it as a common denominator and the large audience that did not see it but heard about it from friends or that read about it in newspapers and magazines? On a less serious note, many hobbies and sports have received tremendous boosts in popularity after appearing on "the tube." Championship snooker on British television led to a considerable expansion of snooker playing around the country, and championship darts on TV helped to revitalize an old pub sport.

How "good" any of this is for society is another question, but there should be little question about the need to achieve better understanding among groups within a given society and between societies and nations. Most industrialized nations, and many industrializing ones, either are multilingual and multiethnic or are headed in that direction. "Guest workers" and émigrés (many of them now permanent residents) from around the Mediterranean basin in many European nations; South Asians in many of the oil-rich nations of the Arab world; émigrés from southeast Asia, Africa and the Caribbean in North America and parts of western Europe; staff connected with multinational corporations, all have added to the cultural mix. However, that doesn't mean that they have contributed to that mix. They may or may not have been recognized by the mass media in those nations; they may or may not have had the opportunity to establish media outlets of their own. To the extent that they can achieve the latter, they at least are able to talk to themselves; to the extent that they can achieve the former, they might be better understood and more readily accepted by the mainstream population.[36]

Much the same can be said about minority groups within the indigenous society: Welsh, Breton, Sami and Frisian had been in Great Britain, France, Scandinavia and the Netherlands longer than, or as long as, the present majority population. Broadcast services in their languages were minimal until the late 1970s to early 1980s, and they rarely had the opportunity to address the majority culture in the majority language, either. It's doubtful that most mainstream British, French, Scandinavian or Dutch listeners and viewers understand their traditions and aspirations. How much more difficult would it be if the very limited coverage of those groups over the majority culture electronic media services were dropped because the groups now have their own outlets (as all of those do), and no matter that most of those outlets don't achieve anything like nationwide coverage. (Norway and Sweden both have brief periods of time for national services in Sami, mainly to reach Sami speakers living in the larger cities.) The Soviet broadcast system had one of the stronger records in that regard: Many minorities (rarely religious, and certainly not political) had airtime on national radio and television quite regularly, and broadcast about themselves in Russian so that at least Soviet viewers and listeners had the opportunity to learn more about them.[37]

Jurgen Habermas, renowned for his writings on the concept of the public sphere, has expressed his own concern over the possible limitations faced by members of a civil society when seeking to express themselves in "a public sphere dominated by the mass media." He wondered how realistic their chances were " ... in their competition with the political and economic invaders' media power, to bring about changes in the spectrum of values, topics, and reasons channeled by external influences, to open it up in an innovative way, and to screen it critically."[38]

The growth in access to the public sphere through the more traditional mass media remains limited, as I've already indicated. The spread of the Internet offers some prospects for increased access by minority groups, a number of which already are quite active. Thus far, its use seems to be chiefly as an *intra*group communication channel, which certainly is beneficial, but doesn't really address what Habermas and others have in mind when they speak of a "public sphere:" a place for *inter*group communication, a place where size or power (economic, political, religious, ethnic or whatever) does not determine whether a group may enter into dialogue with other groups. Certainly there is nothing to prevent individuals and groups using the Internet from reaching out to others, but there's little that facilitates such use. A proposal made by one Ted Ganchiff in January 1999 could do so: his TalkNetRadio (*http://www.talknetradio.com*) is set up "to allow any Internet user to create and broadcast original programming to listeners worldwide."[38a] Whether it will do so is yet to be seen, as is the possibility that it might inspire similar services.

Yet another dimension of this same question is programming by and for other audiences that may not be thought of as minorities but that certainly can be considered as such where the electronic media are concerned. While all industrialized nations have experienced a major shift of population from rural to urban areas in the 20th century, there still are sizable numbers of people living in rural areas, although many aren't connected with the rural economy. As communication channels proliferate, we should bear in mind that they don't automatically become available to everyone—quite a difference from past assumptions made in many nations, where a national broadcasting system was to be just that and *was* to provide universal service, expensive as it was to do so, and with programming of specific interest to just about every segment of the population. But cable TV poses problems: It isn't financially feasible to extend it to rural areas, especially in large nations with very uneven population distribution, such as Canada, Russia, Australia and the United States. Yet with cable available in urban areas and serving the majority of the population, there may be an increased tendency to prepare and distribute programs for that audience, and a converse tendency to neglect the tastes and interests of the rural audience, to the extent that they differ from those of the urban audience. The very same set of arguments can be used with respect to the urban poor.

An ideal system should see to it that such audiences are not neglected, at least from the standpoint of programs about them and of special interest to them. Such programs are part of the aforementioned fabric of society and thus form part of a nation's social cohesiveness. But an ideal system might well go one step further and make some of the new media services available to audiences that would find it prohibitively expensive to pay for their true costs. If the new media turn out to have special value to society as providers of information that the older broadcast services are unlikely to produce and transmit—specialized channels with information about city government, health services, etc.—perhaps subsidization is appropriate. That may be easier to do in a license-fee- or annual-appropriations-financed system than it is in an ad-supported one, since the cost of subsidization can be spread out through a relatively small per capita increase in fees or taxes, but it isn't unknown in private enterprise, where telephone services or costs of heating fuel may be subsidized for low-income households. Certainly it would be consonant with a *public* service philosophy.

When I wrote *Comparing Broadcast Systems* 10 years ago, I stated that teenagers also were a possibly unserved audience, although there was plenty of pop music on radio services that seemed intended especially for them. There were at the time a few broadcasters who had attempted to develop teen-oriented TV programs that were more than visualized top 40 hits, and one Australian Broadcasting Corporation weekly TV program called "Beatbox" employed teenagers as researchers and production personnel, set up the production unit in a "down-market" Sydney suburb (Parramatta) and covered some tough issues, such as race relations. It was expensive and controversial, but ABC continued to produce it anyway and was rewarded with a quite substantial increase in audience, although after two years ABC dropped it and turned to a rather different, less gritty, youth program.[39]

I had the strong impression at the time that the teenage audience was a mystery to most television staff and advertisers. An executive with the Dentsu advertising agency in Japan with whom I spoke in September 1985 felt that values to which young people would respond in TV commercials were unlikely to be very different from those of their parents and grandparents, despite the evidence of various surveys that the outlooks and aspirations of the two groups were quite different. Some producers told me that use of the music video style (rapid cuts, unusual camera angles, bizarre costumes, etc.) would get the message across. As the teenage audience was one of the smaller collective audiences in most industrialized nations, it may have been easy to ignore, and it wasn't that easy for most producers to understand.

Since then, especially with the growth of cable and DBS and their multitude of channel choices, young viewers have been somewhat better served, although the most visible sign of that service—and admittedly popular among those viewers—is MTV clones around much of the world. However, even those services no longer confine themselves to providing music videos; in many nations, they've branched out to include specialized news programs, discussion shows dealing with such thorny issues as drugs, premarital sex, parental abuse, and talk shows with adult guests who may receive something less than respectful treatment from the host and the audience. Some of the cable companies are carrying youth channels that are a real alternative to MTV, such as Great Britain's "Rapture."[40] Even a few of the older terrestrial services such as the Netherlands' NOS are becoming more involved: the NOS daily newscast for and about teenagers, "Jeugdjournal," features teenagers as consultants and makes a real effort to present major stories of the day from the standpoint of what that audience would find of particular interest. And many of the German public radio services have a "youth channel" in their lineups.

Where programming for *any* audience is concerned, there's still a need to maintain and even increase creativity in both content and style. The expansion of media outlets throughout much of the industrialized world carries with it the possibility that the cost of making or acquiring programs will become more and more important as competition between those outlets increases. That could carry with it the pressure not to spend much on programs that are costly to make and that don't attract large audiences. Program funds for the film industry of the sort described in the chapters on Germany and France could help to counteract such pressures. The second Carnegie Commission on U.S. Public Broadcasting proposed to safeguard creativity from various sorts of financial and political pressures by setting aside a budget for the Program Services Endowment that would award production grants to individuals and groups making proposals. The commission recommended entrusting such budgetary decisions to a committee made up of individuals who had had some experience with creativity in television,[41] radical as that might seem. (The U.S. Public Television Service introduced a much smaller fund for the encouragement of "creative" programming in 1986; it continues to this day.)

Creativity also might be aided through more emphasis on coproduction. Technological developments have made it relatively simple and inexpensive for media systems to share programs, and financial pressures (and perhaps some creative impulses) have encouraged some systems to agree to coproduce material that may not attract a large audience in any one nation, but can do so in several of them together. Some of the fruits of those collaborations have been mentioned earlier. They aren't always easy to arrange, and they run the risk of being weighted down by compromises (remember the old adage about too many cooks spoiling the broth) or by overreliance on a U.S. "model" of efficiency,[42] but at their best they will allow the participants to retain a fair degree of cultural integrity while opening themselves to the cultural visions of other systems, which should help to stimulate creativity and to advance the cause of international understanding. Finally, there's a need for the creative visions of both national services, with their capacity for uniting societies, and of specialized services to promote and exhibit the cultural diversity of nations in their multifaceted, particularized glory.

Paying for the "Ideal" System

Clearly it will take money, and a great deal of it, to make an ideal system become reality. The money to support the various parts of the system would come from a variety of sources: advertising, governmental appropriations, subscription fees, annual license fees (in nations that already have them) and various forms of voluntary contribution by individuals, groups and corporations. Supplemental services such as movie channels on cable would of course be paid for by the user. A mix of financial sources should help to guarantee that no one financial source becomes too powerful in dictating program content. It will be especially important, as I've suggested earlier in this chapter, that certain vital services be furnished to people who otherwise could not afford them: literacy lessons through radio or TV; programs featuring assistance to people who encounter problems in dealing with bureaucracies, whether governmental, educational, commercial or whatever; certain ethnic minority broadcasts, especially in minority languages. Those are examples of services that clearly are not just pure entertainment and that probably wouldn't attract advertising or even very much voluntary support because of the relative poverty of the particular audiences.

Such an approach to financing, and for that matter the rest of what I've proposed as part of the ideal system, rests on the assumption that the electronic media do have a public service role to play, that no single source of financing will prove adequate if they are to play that role for all of society, and that such a role is of great importance to society's development. Many examples demonstrate that the media can play a positive role in the political, cultural and social life of the nation, but many examples also demonstrate that they can be used negatively. The decentralization and diversification of electronic media that seems to be well under way in most industrialized nations can help to minimize the impact of the negative uses, but it will require some reconsideration of the structure and financing of those media if nations are to draw maximum benefit from them.

There's another possible approach to the financing of certain types of programming that may have more relevance in a multichannel world, although I know of only one instance where it has been proposed seriously. If increasing numbers of services don't want to carry certain categories of programming that they might consider too expensive and/or unattractive, but if there's a general obligation for every service to furnish a full range of programming, some of the services might be given the option of paying someone else to produce them, and perhaps even to carry them. When the U.S. FCC announced in the mid-1990s that it would require commercial broadcasters to carry three hours a week of educational programs for children, it considered at one point permitting stations to pay other stations to do so.[43] A roughly similar approach was suggested by some broadcasters and broadcast critics from Russia and the former Soviet republics in a 1996 conference, but for a very different program category and reason. They wondered whether newscasts could be better-insulated from government pressure if a number of broadcast outlets could pool the money they'd normally spend on producing news programs themselves, and use it to establish and support a news production service operated by journalists, which ostensibly would be freer to present the news without the government threatening to take away their licenses. Of course, the government would have to agree that the stations would be excused from responsibility for whatever was presented in each newscast, which is doubtful, but the idea itself certainly is novel.[44]

As that decentralization and diversification proceeds, there's another potential financial pitfall that awaits the ideal system. There has been widespread re-examination of telecommunications structures and policies over the past decade, with electronic media often lumped in with telephony, data transfer and other nonbroadcast communications services. That's led some politicians, advisors and officials to think of those media in terms of pricing structures and competition-enhancing regulation or deregulation. By that token, the media are quite apt to be evaluated in quantitative rather than qualitative terms, and "social benefit" may matter very little. If telecommunications policy-making treats each of the electronic media as "user services" to be paid for by the public, it's quite possible that their collective contributions to the broader political, social and cultural life of the nation will diminish.

TOWARD THE YEAR 2000

Electronic media systems throughout the industrialized world are in a period of rapid organizational, economic and programmatic change, and the pace of that change may even increase in years to come. Privatization, commercialization, cable, DBS, VCRs, Internet services and the development of low-cost equipment all have helped to break the monopolies once held by public service broadcast organizations in many nations. While *technology* has been a major factor in promoting change, so have *politics*, *economics*, and to a lesser extent, *culture* and *demography*. *Geography* may now be more influenced *by* that change than it exerts influence *on* change. But what matters far more in terms of the impact of the media on society and vice versa is the programming choices that will be available, and, from among those choices, which will find the greatest favor in the eyes and ears of the audience.

There seems little doubt that the sheer quantity of program material will increase considerably for most audience members, although it will take longer in Russia and in parts of central and eastern Europe than it will in most other parts of the industrialized world. Even there, however, increases are taking place rapidly enough, with the spread of VCRs in Russia and parts of central and eastern Europe, while cable and satellite are becoming well-established in Poland, Hungary and the Czech Republic.

There also seems little doubt that a substantial portion of that material will be "made in the U.S.A." Already, U.S.-made feature films dominate the videocassette market throughout most of the world. Sky Channel, the most widely distributed satellite-to-cable service in Europe (tens of millions of households as of the late 1990s), relies heavily upon syndicated material from U.S. commercial television. CNN and MSNBC appear on more and more European and Japanese screens, thanks to satellite distribution through DBS and cable.

But does all of this signify the death of the public service tradition, swept away by a tidal wave of inexpensive programming from the United States? Or deserted by PSB staff who no longer have the sense of vision of what could and should be, but instead are caught up in a bottom-line mentality that nips creativity in the bud? Those and other arguments are the core of a number of recent books that bemoan the passing of the public service tradition of Reith, Bredow, and others. (One of the most thoughtful of those books is Michael Tracey's *The Decline and Fall of Public Service Broadcasting,* published by Oxford University Press in 1998; it is the best summary of the historical roots of that tradition that I have read.) Does it signal the dominance of inexpensively operated, largely private, broadcast, cable and PBS operations, favored or encouraged by increasingly private-enterprise-oriented national governments and grinding out increasingly similar programs that are increasingly devoid of meaningful, challenging content?

I feel that it probably does not, although the PSB tradition certainly is undergoing change almost everywhere,[45] as those services seek out ways to reclaim a large enough share of the audience to justify public support through license fees, annual appropriations, listener and viewer contributions, etc. Interestingly, many of them have been quite successful, as the chapters on France, Germany and the Netherlands have indicated. And, while some of what they produce can be difficult to distinguish from commercial programming, the distinctions often strike me as meaningful, as I've indicated earlier in this chapter. Furthermore, there are signs that many of the PSBs are seeking to reach some hitherto underserved segments of the audience—older adults, émigrés, young people—with programming that either isn't available at all through commercial services, or is restricted to a very narrow range of genres, such as action-figure cartoons or music videos. Finally, some of the freshest, most innovative program material appearing these days comes from ethnic and community stations, video clubs, media centers, art institutes, almost all of them public, in that they're sustained by public funding of one sort or another.

Public service operations also are developing identities as suppliers of programming for other outlets: conventional broadcasting, specialized cable and DBS services, videocassette recordings, videotext, and informational material through the Internet. The most worrisome aspect of such a change is that some segments of the public, especially the poor or those living in physically remote areas, could be deprived of access to material available to them in the past, much of which they probably would continue to enjoy and to find helpful, and which even might be "good" for them (*pace* the BBC's Sir John Reith and his paternalistic views on the "mission" of broadcasting to improve the tastes of society!). I have suggested earlier in this chapter that some subsidization of services for "deprived" audiences might be part of an ideal system, although I'm not optimistic that most private enterprise-oriented governments would be ready to support such a move.

The "American tide" of programming is a different sort of concern. Several nations individually and the European Union collectively have set quotas designed to keep it under control, but they're becoming less and less effective as 50 percent or more of all households in many of those nations have VCRs and/or cable, and as commercial stations and networks spring up. Even if all of those services observed a quota limit, as not all do, there would still be more U.S. programming available to anyone wishing to seek it out (and in some cases pay for it) than there ever has been in the past. What's more, many of the newer services depend on inexpensive programming, much of it from the United States, for their very existence, and would have difficulty surviving without it, which in fact France's La Cinq could not.

As I've pointed out in several earlier chapters, U.S. programming has influenced programming in other systems in a variety of ways. It will continue to do so, for good or for ill. It simply is too large, inexpensive and popular a body of material not to. Furthermore, program-makers in other nations will be influenced in their own creative decision-making by the presence of that material, both as competition within their own countries and regions and as competition within the U.S. market itself, where cable operations and independent television stations are proving to be increasingly interested in purchasing foreign-made programming. (Note, for example, the dependency of the U.S. Arts and Entertainment cable service on that source.) And as industrialized nations have expanded the range of channel choice available to their citizens, they certainly have lessened the power of whatever claim could once have been made that electronic media systems are reflective of specific, unique national characteristics

Yet there are some interesting indications of how foreign viewers regard the greater availability of U.S. material. Feature films from the United States do very well in competition with videocassettes from elsewhere when it comes to sales and rentals of cassettes, but most European households make far heavier use of their VCRs for time-shifting of domestically available broadcasting than for playing rented or purchased cassettes. The satellite-to-cable services featuring the largest amount of U.S. material—Sky Channel, MTV, CNN—have rather low regular viewership. They appear to be especially attractive to young and/or unemployed or underemployed viewers. And even when certain domestically produced programs are based directly on U.S. series, as many game shows and sitcoms are, there still are respects in which they may reflect the domestic culture.

Despite the increasing availability of U.S. programming, the top 10 or even top 20 ratings lists of programs in nearly all of the major industrialized nations and in several of the smaller ones continue to show a clear predominance of the "homegrown" product, whether quiz shows, situation comedy, newscasts and current affairs, sports, or, less often, "serious" drama. Presuming that governments don't become too economy-minded where financial support for PSBs is concerned, and assuming that there are no serious economic recessions that might cripple a young and still-growing European commercial video production industry, that state of affairs should last. However, it will take greater cooperation among the various nation-states of Europe to create the larger market necessary to assure the economy of scale required to establish a strong counterweight to the U.S. product.

There remains one very large area of uncertainty: the effects of what could be called electronic convergence, meaning the inclusion of broadcasting, telephone and information technologies in one sphere of activity. Some media conglomerates already are moving in that direction, with Microsoft as a leading example if only because of the many warning flags that are hoisted with the corporation's every move in the direction of acquiring or developing a relationship with some other company already active in one or another of those enterprises. But the flags also are beginning to fly in Europe as I write, with European Union consideration of a major overhaul of regulation for that sphere of activity—an overhaul that could go far beyond the deregulatory policies of the Reagan administration.

Perhaps fittingly, the European Commission of the EU chose to release its 80-page report and policy recommendations—entitled "Towards an Information Society Approach"—through the Internet, in mid-December 1997. And perhaps ironically, it may have felt compelled to issue the report because of the "threat" of a Microsoft-dominated digital world, with (in the report's words) "our [Europe's] businesses and citizens ... left to travel in the slow lane of an information revolution which is being embraced by businesses, by users, and by governments around the world." Many of the concerns expressed in the report, such as the high cost of making telephone calls from one EU nation to another, are very real and very damaging to the growth of a more competitive (with the United States) European economy. But others bear directly on the issue of just how loose or how tight regulation of the sphere of activity should be, with "light" regulation as the preferred approach.

The question then becomes whether all elements included within the sphere should be regulated on the same basis, or whether there should be differential levels of regulation: very light for most of the "nonbroadcast" industries, somewhat heavier for commercially based broadcast-type services (especially the more widely available terrestrial services), heavier yet for the PSBs. One can find EU officials who argue for minimal regulation across the board as well as those who argue for differential levels, and even those who would require certain commercial services to contribute financially to the support of various parts of the European audiovisual industries, especially film, so that high-quality European program production will be strong enough to withstand the competition provided in the form of programming imported from the United States. But how easy will it be to require the financially powerful, politically well-connected enterprises commanding a converged cluster of technologies to follow such dictates, should they become part of official EU policy?

The European Commission of the EU gathered comments on its proposals over a five-month period, with those comments both gathered and shared throughout the Union and abroad through the Internet. It then prepared and released (in July 1998) a summary of the results of its public consultation. This "working document," which bore the lengthy title of "Summary of the Results of the Public Consultation on the Green Paper on the Convergence of the Telecommunications, Media and Information Technology Sectors: Areas for Further Reflection" (*http://www.ispo.cec.be/convergencegp/gpworkdoc.html*), drew still further public comments. All of this was to be followed by a Commission Communication with policy proposals at the end of 1998.

Very briefly, the initial report proved to be a typical EU document in that it dealt principally with the economic aspects of the issue an secondarily (a *distant* second) with cultural aspects. It proposed three models of regulation; the first of those—building upon current regulatory structures—drew the most support in public (chiefly government agencies, national commercial broadcasters and PSBs, and telecommunication enterprises, but with a number of community activists, academics and community broadcasters) comments. There was considerable concern about the prospect for overregulation of newly emerging communication technologies, and a number of suggestions along the line of "Don't apply the regulatory model for traditional broadcasting to the new media, or you'll stifle their growth."

The activists, academics, community broadcasters and PSBs were more apt to express their disappointment at the lack of attention to cultural considerations, and a number of comments centered around the need to provide the less-well-off and rural dwellers with reasonably equal access to the new media. There were expressions of concern over the possibility that costs of program reception might be driven up by setting a date for phasing out analog TV signals and thus forcing audience members to purchase digital receivers, whether they wanted the extra services that digital TV could provide or not. What that might also mean to programmers of limited financial means, minority groups of many sorts among them, can be guessed: unless they receive increased financial support from somewhere (and any subsidy drawn from user fees isn't likely to do the job), the conversion to digital transmission will prove too much for most of them, and several of those commenting saw this as the possible death knell for community broadcasting. Once the European Commission releases its final recommendations, and if, as seems likely, convergence is supported through those recommendations, and absent any substantial forms of subsidy for such groups, the electronic media could very well end up being less reflective of societies in their many facets than now is the case.[46]

THE NATION-STATE AND THE ELECTRONIC MEDIA

Whether nation-states in Europe and elsewhere will continue to maintain their dominant position as social-political-economic structures is itself an open question, given the political, economic and social pressures to both internationalize and localize. Philip Schlesinger provides an excellent summary of the viewpoints of several scholars (Anderson, Deutsch, Gellner, Giddens, Mackenzie, Pye and others) regarding communicative aspects of nationhood, and then goes on to discuss what he labels "collective identities in a changing Europe." Here he acknowledges the possibility of a blurring of national borders, but sees any change as limited, given the depth of historical memory for most European nation-states.[47]

Still, where the electronic media are concerned, internationalization has been a "hot topic" for more than two decades, and debates over media/cultural imperialism are one of the more visible indications of its presence. So are the activities of some of the more powerful "media barons," such as Murdoch and Berlusconi. And so, in a somewhat contradictory way, are the policies of the European Union, which has set limits on the importation of programming from outside the Union (but without a pan-European regulatory agency to enforce them), and simultaneously has sought to open the borders of its member nations in order to promote the free flow of programming within the EU. On the other end of the scale, geographic, linguistic and cultural localism have been encouraged by the opening up of the frequency spectrum, permitting the creation of more electronic media services; by technological change, especially in the form of higher-quality production equipment at lower and lower cost; and by a growing recognition of the importance of "microcultures" within and across nations—a recognition fueled to some extent by European Union, Council of Europe and United Nations declarations and policies supporting what the Union has labeled "subsidiarity."

Those challenges to the supremacy of the nation-state have been most visible in Europe up until now, perhaps because of its relative economic prosperity. Poorer regions such as Africa and Latin America rely quite heavily on imported programming (sometimes from one another in the case of Latin America) in part because there's no ready alternative, although the growing presence of communication satellites to serve that particular region makes it more and more possible for its nations to exchange programming with one another. In theory, that could help them to reduce their dependence on programs from outside Latin America, but those same satellites may also lead to the growth of cable and DBS services, which are minuscule at present.[48] Should that occur, "outside" programming could become more important than ever, at least to those households subscribing to cable or DBS. Those services are even less in evidence in Africa, but the higher overall level of poverty throughout most of the continent makes it necessary for Africa's existing electronic media services (most of them government-operated) to continue to rely on European (especially the former colonial powers, such as Great Britain and France) and U.S. programming to fill out TV schedules.

On the local end of the scale, Latin America has had community-level broadcast services for decades, but most of them are radio stations, and most of those are commercial services carrying little programming that is truly local. There are a few hundred community radio services in the region, and they feature minority languages and cultures, but most are low-powered and, because of their real or imagined disruptive effects on the larger society, subject to frequent shutdowns by the government. Sub-Saharan Africa has even more minority languages and cultures than does Latin America, but far fewer stations at the local level. Most of the national governments haven't encouraged their creation, probably in part because those governments have very modest and tight budgets. But the relative recency of independent nation-states in Africa also has meant that governments aren't anxious to encourage localism, since that might challenge the often-fragile national structure.

Still, if the electronic media aren't likely to weaken the nation-states of Africa or Latin America anytime soon, what is happening already in Europe may serve as predictor of what could happen in those two continents within a matter of decades, as transmitting and receiving equipment becomes even less expensive, more portable, easier to operate, and in the case of the Internet, difficult to exclude or regulate. Even in Europe, the nation-states remain quite strong, but the increasing ranges of choice available through radio, TV and Internet services allow for the growth of other than national loyalties, affiliations and affinities—the "communities of mutual interest" that can exist on a nongeographical basis. Stephen Kobrin states that "digitalization and the emergence of electronic media markets and electronic commerce may well render the very idea of geographic jurisdiction—and the singular, unambiguous territorial authority characteristic of the modern state system—problematic." He also observes of nongovernmental organizations such as Greenpeace and Amnesty International that "These transnational actors are now able to link interest groups directly in a large number of countries through telephone, fax and the Internet. They can share information widely and rapidly, develop a common transnational position on issues, publicize it broadly and effectively lobby both their respective national governments (as concerned citizens) and international organizations."[48a]

It's still too early to determine the extent to which the Internet and other "new media" may encourage such activities, or whether they could materially weaken the fabric of the nation-state, but that seems at least a possibility. Nor would the electronic media be likely to serve as the sole, or even major, cause of such weakening as may occur. They seem more likely to serve as catalytic agents, planting seeds of doubt, disaffection and indifference randomly and unconsciously, for the most part, until those seeds coalesce and national society fractionates, even if it never disappears.

THE EUROPEAN UNION AS SUPRANATIONAL MODEL?

The European Union already has had notable influence on the European electronic media landscape.[49] Media mergers sometimes have been forbidden, protectionist policies regarding national media have been successfully challenged, national markets have been opened up to electronic media from other EU members, and there even have been attempts to subsidize the development of electronic media programming which would have a pan-European character. Are other parts of the world likely to emulate the European example?

To answer that question, consider the dual nature of the EU's approach: economic and cultural. It's clear that the economic factor continues to predominate. Most EU actions regarding the electronic media are aimed at various forms of protectionism, supporting the free flow of media content and investment within the Union, opposing the free flow of media content and investment from outside. That hasn't taken the form of an outright ban on the right of individual EU members to erect barriers designed to protect certain aspects of the national way of life, for example against the advertising of condoms in EU nations where Catholicism is the national religion. Nor has it stopped certain nations, France in particular, from enacting regulations designed to favor the national production of programming. And if the Union should expand to include the nations of central Europe, where freedom of expression of political views at present is generally more restricted than it is within the EU, it's doubtful that the Union's legislative and judicial system would act to require comparable openness of those new members. That is an aspect of national sovereignty that the EU seems very reluctant to challenge.

If Europe, which is more homogeneous than are Asia or Africa, hasn't been able to establish a policy for governing media content, it isn't likely that those huge continents, or even segments within them, would wish or could manage to do so. Latin America is more homogenous in both culture and language, but mutual suspicions resulting in border skirmishes and cultural snobbery ("our Spanish is purer than your Spanish") make it unlikely that a true union of Latin American nations will emerge anytime soon, or that those nations will open their borders fully to one another's electronic media programs.

The economic aspect of EU electronic media policy, which has been pursued much more boldly by its member nations, might seem both attractive and applicable in other parts of the world. Various economic unions, alliances and other forms of cooperation already exist on most continents, and even between some of them. However, disputes among their members are frequent, the ability of individual nations to claim exemptions from various requirements is widespread, and enforcement mechanisms usually are absent or weak. They are not as advanced as is the European Union in the fundamentals of economic cooperation, and thus serve as poor foundations for cooperation and protectionism in the realm of the highly complex (being both economic and cultural entities) electronic media sphere.

There is another, far more modest approach. There had been a decades-long practice of exchange of programming among many western European nations before the European Union became involved in electronic media policies and practices in the early 1980s. The European Broadcasting Union, made up of the public broadcasting systems of the western European nations (most but not all of them EU members), began to promote program exchange of news and sports at the end of the 1940s. It also has promoted the exchange of ideas about all sorts of program genres—children's, religious, musical, etc.—that has helped to stimulate thinking about different ways to approach program production.[50] Its one great drawback in terms of achieving wider influence is that it hasn't reached out to include the newer commercial services, in part because some of its members regard those services as not functioning in the public service tradition, in part because the PSBs seem to enjoy the exclusivity—the "in-group" nature—of the EBU as they themselves have created it. While it's very likely that many commercial electronic media services wouldn't see themselves as profiting from EBU membership, there are others which seem to operate in the public service tradition at least some of the time, and might be encouraged to do so even more if they were welcomed as relative equals.

There are roughly similar associations in other parts of the world: the Arab States Broadcasting Union (ASBU), the Asian [and Pacific] Broadcasting Union (ABU), the Union of African Broadcasters (URTNA) and the Inter-american Broadcasting Union (AIR). None has developed the elaborate program exchange system or the forum for the exchange of ideas that characterize the EBU, although the ABU has done reasonably well. Huge economic disparities among the member nations, age-old animosities, national pride, technological barriers and other factors have stood in the way. Still, they might yet serve as models for the development of a heightened sense of public service among electronic media outlets in their respective geographical regions, particularly if they were ready to welcome at least some of the commercial services.

MOGULS, MERGERS AND MULTINATIONALS

There seems little doubt that the role of media conglomerates of various sorts, whether they're the result of the actions of media moguls, corporate mergers combining media and non-media holdings, multinational corporations or co-production ventures, will continue to grow. The scale of investment required to establish new media enterprises almost guarantees it. That doesn't mean that there won't be ample scope for low-budget media operations, as well, but those services will find it increasingly difficult to function at anything above a local or regional level. The national and international outlets will be priced beyond their reach, aside from whatever arrangements they may be able to make with the PSBs to carry some of their programming nationally, or through low-budget national and international "networks" such as the

Women's International News Gathering Service (WINGS) or American Indian Radio on Satellite (AIROS).[51] As Internet users grow in number, there also should be increased opportunities for groups to make their programming available to larger numbers of listeners and viewers nationally and internationally, but significant activity along those lines appears to be a hope for a more distant future.

Perhaps the most important implication of increased conglomerate activity will be the increasing homogenization of programming. It's obviously cheaper to make any product on the basis of "one size fits all," so long as enough customers will buy it. There are limits to that approach where the electronic media are concerned: it's hard to imagine a generic TV newscast that would be able to match the popularity of any given nation's own newscast. However, if the generic version is truly international in scope, and if it's updated frequently during any 24-hour period, it can attract a sizable and usually influential audience of government officials, businesspeople and other "movers and shakers." Certainly the BBC's World Service Television and Ted Turner's CNN International do so. If anything, the ability of such services to provide broad, current and trustworthy international news coverage should induce most national news services to concentrate even more of their time, money and effort on the coverage of regional and national developments, with coverage of international events usually limited to what would be of particular interest to the national audience (achievements and problems in former colonies, wars with potential spillover effects on the national economy, etc.).

But it is in the realm of entertainment programming where I would expect to find the greater potential influence of homogenization. In fact, there already are signs of that influence. Although I have yet to see a comparative study of changes in the character of a given genre (sitcoms, police and detective shows, soap operas, etc.) over the past 15 or so years, my own viewing in Europe, North America and Australia during that period leads me to conclude that programs in each genre *are* coming to look more and more alike, although differences still are detectable. The public service broadcast outlets appear to feature more of those differences than do their commercial counterparts, but even here the differences appear to be dwindling. The similarities among programs in any given genre will differ according to the nature of that genre, but often will take the form of "more action, less dialogue," plot lines involving "klutzy" family members and friends, "canned" laughter and applause. It is no accident that RTL-4 in the Netherlands and RTL Plus (now RTL) in Germany both produced versions of the soap opera "Good Times, Bad Times" at about the same time, or that the originator of the concept was an Australian company (Grundy) with a good sense of program content that might be acceptable to more than just one country.

How harmful any of that may be to society is another matter. Perhaps some of it has no discernible effect. It's still possible to speak of British humor, French style, German efficiency, U.S. spectacle, and have a good idea as well as numerous current program examples of what's meant by those terms.

Philip Schlesinger speaks of two distinct senses of the term "culture": as shared values, practices, beliefs, etc. of a social group; and as a commodity that is bought and sold, such as U.S. television programs, German automobiles, etc. He observes that there may be attempts to classify certain perceived qualitative dimensions of the latter, as for example when we speak of "high" and "low" culture when discussing movies, TV programs and other "commodified" cultural artifacts. But he regards such artifacts as far less fundamental to a social group's definition of itself than are the shared values, practices and beliefs.[52] Thus, he sees little possibility of fundamental challenge to social identity from U.S. sitcoms and the like.[53] And we must acknowledge that there are certain well-nigh universal values, such as triumph against the odds, delight in improbable reunions of long-lost friends and family members, "good" victorious over "evil" (with frequent disagreement over who belongs in which camp), compassion for those who suffer (so long as we don't see *too* much of it!), etc. We shouldn't be surprised to see those values appearing on the TV screens of nation after nation.

Some of those values may help to explain the relatively high international popularity of a given entertainment series such as "Dallas," "Baywatch" or some of the Mexican "telenovelas" (soap operas). The first two are U.S.-made, and depict lifestyles that seem larger than life to most Americans, so they must seem utterly exotic to non-American viewers.[54] But they also seem to attract viewers because they contribute to images of what at least some aspects of life in the United States "really" are like. The Mexican "telenovelas" may have a different sort of appeal, more akin to fairy tales where the rich and powerful mistreat and bully the poor ("Cinderella" is a fine example!), who in most cases eventually win out in small or big ways. (One of the few Japanese TV series to have some international popularity was the soap opera "Oshin," which centered around the theme of the eventual triumph of a poor, hardworking woman over all sorts of obstacles.) To the extent that such approaches to dramatic genres are becoming more universal, any "harm" may be more in the degree to which TV dramas in general will emphasize the exotic or fairy-tale approaches to the exclusion of plot lines that tell us something about the more usual experiences of society—both those that should be praised and valued and those that should be condemned and eradicated. There's a place for TV as "pure" entertainment, but there's also a place for TV as entertainment that educates and motivates, and it would be most unfortunate if the former (which seems to lend itself better to international distribution) were to marginalize the latter.

And finally, there's the issue of "national character." I find it interesting that, as national character becomes harder and harder to define in most industrialized nations and with many minorities becoming more numerous and more vocal, certain "leaders" (Gennadi Zyuganov, Jean-Marie Le Pen, Franz Schoenhuber, U.S. Senator Jesse Helms) who claim to represent the views of "mainstream national culture/character" are becoming more insistent upon the need for electronic media services to pay more attention to the "real" Russians, French, Germans, Americans, etc. I have argued elsewhere that a healthy society recognizes and celebrates its pluralism through the mass media, thereby strengthening its collective fabric.[55] Internationally distributed TV entertainment isn't well-suited to display societal diversity; it's far better suited to help viewers to forget about diversity, as it presents images of society with the sharp edges rounded off and the differences minimized or ignored. As with the argument for both TV as "pure" entertainment and TV as entertainment that also educates and motivates, it's the balance that matters.

THE ROLE OF THE PUBLIC BROADCASTING SERVICES

I have observed more than once that the public service broadcasters currently are going through what an old Chinese curse ("May you live in interesting times") might describe as *very* interesting times. While there appears at present to be something of a positive reversal of fortune in the form of Council of Europe and European Union declarations of support for PSBs, most of the PSBs in industrialized nations face uncertain futures. There's one exception: it *is* certain that the PSBs will never return to the days when they dominated their respective markets.[56]

Public service broadcasters will have to change in certain respects if they are to continue to play important roles. They will have to learn how to operate more economically, first and foremost. The presence of competition has highlighted just how expensive production had become in many of the PSB services. Yet the example of a Channel Four in Great Britain shows that it's possible to achieve high quality and originality on a smaller production budget. The financially slimmed-down U.S. Public Broadcasting Service also has managed to maintain its commitment to high-quality news and public affairs programming, as has its radio counterpart, National Public Radio.

As Internet broadcasting develops, more and more PSBs must be prepared to join those already involved (e.g., several of the German public stations, the BBC, PBS in the United States) and to provide both interactive and noninteractive material for carefully defined audience groups. That certainly does not mean the abandonment of broad-appeal programming—common-denominator programs still will have a role to play—but it would mean that there would be less of it.[56a]

The PSBs also may have to find more ways to allow the public to feel that it has a more specific influence on program decision-making. A public that senses that it's being listened to by PSB program decision-makers is more likely to invest its time in listening to and watching the public service, and perhaps less of it in the product of the competition. And such a public is less likely to resent increases in the annual license fee or in government appropriations for broadcasting. I've suggested that Japan's NHK may be something of a model in its utilization of several lines of contact with the public. It might also be helpful to the PSB cause if their staff members were in closer, more regular contact with primary and secondary schools, cultivating students and teachers alike by making their programming more readily available for use in supplementing the curriculum, and even working with schools at a local level to produce programs. That should serve to heighten the relevance of public service broadcasting, and could pay off in increased PSB listening and viewing by adults, both as they attend to their own children's programs and as the children themselves grow to adulthood.

Public broadcasters also could display their relevance to society more prominently if they were to develop more programming that commercial services would be unlikely to feature, such as programs for and about minority groups (recall the statement of the NOS Board of Management in Chapter 2), educational entertainment for young children (the BBC, NHK, the U.S. PBS and several other PSBs continue to be active in that genre, but French, German, Russian and other PSBs have decreased their commitments), programs about societies in other lands that are more penetrating than the picture postcard variety so common at present, and newscasts that present a clear alternative to the offerings of the commercial services, perhaps along the lines of the U.S. PBS TV's "News Hour with Jim Lehrer" (four or five feature stories in the hour), or, at a subnational level, KTCA-TV's (Minneapolis-St. Paul) "News-Night Minnesota" (five or six feature stories per half-hour). In short, the PSBs would do well to display themselves as even clearer alternatives to commercial services than most of them now do. And if they budget carefully, they can claim to be providing a true public service for the many viewers and listeners who cannot afford or do not have access to the many specialized cable and satellite channels that might furnish some of the sorts of programming just mentioned.

I would also hope that PSBs could continue their long-standing tradition of patrons to the arts, commissioning original plays, music, dance and other art forms. A few of the commercial services—the Independent Television Companies and Channel Four in Great Britain, HBO in the United States—have contributed along those same lines, especially with original drama, but there's little sign that their example is inspiring their commercial colleagues to follow suit. If the tradition is to live, it'll be up to the PSBs and their financiers: annual license fee payers, and governments through annual appropriations. The financiers will have to be convinced that the "patron of the arts" role truly is a *public* service, and not a service for the cultural elite alone. If the arts include classical music and jazz, ballet and boogie, plays by and about members of majority and minority groups, that should help to carry the argument.

And finally, in this increasingly multichannel world, the PSBs, but also community stations, Internet radio services and other noncommercial outlets will have to devote far more time, money and effort to identification and promotion of their offerings it they expect to reach any but their devoted followers.

ETHICAL ISSUES IN A MULTICHANNEL WORLD

During much of the history of broadcasting, it was common for broadcasters, commercial and public service alike, to speak of their obligations to serve the public. One of those obligations was ethical responsibility: acknowledgment that broadcasters held privileged positions (not everyone could afford to operate a station, and for those who could, not everyone could be licensed, since the frequency spectrum was a finite resource), and owed it to their audiences to present information that was accurate and balanced (if opinions were expressed at all) and to present entertainment that took account of what would be called "family values" in present-day terms, although as the decades have passed, the definition of that has become somewhat broader.

Once cable and multichannel services came along, the concept of a limited frequency spectrum became less and less of a limitation, and regulatory agencies relaxed or eliminated their former demands for balanced coverage. And, since households paid for cable and DBS services as a matter of individual choice, it was up to household members to determine what met their personal standards for family values. As a result, the range of opinions expressed, the nature of language used and the assortment of entertainment offered all have increased—more rapidly in some nations, more slowly in others. That has its positive and negative sides: breadth of choice overall, narrowness of focus per outlet. Many people and groups with little or no opportunity to see or hear, much less express themselves, through the electronic media in the "old days" have increasingly found themselves with a greater range of choice: cable radio and TV access channels; low-power (and occasionally high-power) radio stations; satellite-to-cable services featuring information and entertainment in their minority languages, from their former homelands, focused on their particular interests; Internet websites devoted to their particular causes and open to their participation.

Those are not always conditions that promote dialogue within the broader society. Taken to extremes, they could have the opposite effect: the promotion of group and individual interests to the point where they predominate, and there is no longer a broader society. That is where the issue of ethics arises. While it isn't likely that all administrators of electronic media outlets will ever agree on what constitutes ethical behavior, they should be able to agree on one element: the electronic media have the potential to affect the behavior of their audiences. Whatever regulatory agencies or laws may or may not demand, responsibility for recognizing and acting upon that potential rests with those administrators. A one-sided attack on an individual or group over a licensed electronic media outlet (individual distribution of videocassettes and messages over the Internet often are exempted because those activities often aren't licensed) should be weighed carefully before it ever airs. If it goes ahead, and if individuals or groups want to reply, it may be correct to state that the outlet doesn't have a legal obligation to provide reply time, and to tell them to find another outlet for the purpose. But it isn't ethical, and it certainly doesn't contribute to the existence of a healthy society.

Rather, it deepens the divisions that already seem threatening to societal cohesion. The expression of points of view, however strong and however repugnant, is basic to a democratic society, but the provision of opportunity for counterbalancing points of view is basic to a healthy society.[57]

A FEW COMPARATIVE WHYS

There's so much yet to be learned about the electronic media that it may seem foolhardy to suggest a few issues worthy of further attention. What I offer here is by way of illustration only. Hopefully it will serve as food for further thought (including the generation of more whys) and publication.

1. Why have so few media systems made much of a place for ethnic and linguistic minorities? I've provided some partial answers in earlier chapters, but we need deeper understanding of this phenomenon if we are to understand how that situation might be improved. It may have something to do with the degree to which a given mainstream society feels threatened by "outsiders." But it also could be a matter of the mainstream society being so self-centered (and perhaps being reinforced by the mass media in that respect) that nonmainstream societies either don't exist or surely would rather become mainstream themselves. Even so, the efforts to assist and promote minority media taking place in the Netherlands show us that it's possible to make progress.
2. Why have certain nations with strong public service broadcasting traditions seemed willing to lessen their commitments so rapidly (since the mid-1980s, for most of them) and dramatically? Was it because governments perceived public demand for a greater variety of services—a demand that could be met only through commercial operations? And if there was such a demand, was it driven primarily by discontent with what PSBs provided and did not provide, by visions of a much wider world of media services, by an overall increase in societal affluence and/or leisure time? Were the PSBs themselves unwilling to adjust to a changing society? Did the government itself wish to have other media voices available—especially voices that supported a more conservative political and economic agenda? There are hints of that in certain nations, but nothing approaching solid proof. If we had a better understanding of root causes, we should be in a better position to reverse the process.
3. Why are some nations willing to place public service obligations on the newer commercial media ventures, while others are not? And what impels governments to support some obligations and ignore others? In France, for example, obligations placed on the newer commercial ventures center around French program content. But how effectively can a nation expect to combat "cultural invasion" while at the same time

increasing the numbers of media outlets? In Germany, the existence of the PSBs appears to be guaranteed by law. Yet the Conservative government of Helmut Kohl seems to have acted both to favor private interests and to disfavor the PSBs. Could private interests have been favored *without* disfavoring the PSBs? Or was that a necessary step in asserting the primacy of economic considerations? Again, a clearer understanding should provide us with an indication of how the traditions of public service might be restored and revitalized.

The whys of any societally complex situation—and the electronic media certainly are societally complex—are never easy to uncover. But the more we ask and (partially) answer, the more we should expect to learn about the functioning of society in general.

A FINAL WORD ON BEHALF OF HISTORY ...

Throughout this book, I have attempted to provide both a schema and a rationale for the comparative evaluation of media systems: a schema for articulating the elements of those systems; and a rationale for the importance of those elements in making comparisons. That is where I feel there may be lasting value in my approach. But there's another dimension that I feel has great importance, and it runs through my descriptions and analyses of every system: history. I feel that one must regard the electronic media in a historical light. Given the turbulence of the media scene in the industrialized world over the decade following the publication of *Comparing Broadcast Systems,* I could have confined my study to that period, since it's been so diverse and rich in examples. But history offers many useful lessons, if we take the time and effort to note them.

We've seen how some governments, that of Nazi Germany in particular, managed to mobilize radio and turn it to their purposes, which was all the easier because the system already was centralized and monolithic (probably a good argument against a monolithic system; even the BBC in its early decades often was criticized for being too close to the government). We've seen how other governments sought with varying degrees of success to prevent broadcasting from providing reasonably balanced coverage of some controversial issues, as with France and the strikes of 1968, and how a number of those journalists refused to go along with the government, paid for their resistance with their jobs, but ultimately helped to create a less pressure-prone system. We've seen how the U.S.S.R. (and other communist systems) attempted to use the media to reshape society, and how rapidly most of that reshaping vanished following the demise of the Communist government. We've seen how some systems have decided to give high priority to displaying their own cultural heritages by imposing quotas on imported programming and subsidizing and/or commissioning the production of original films, radio plays, ballets, operas, jazz and classical music. We've also seen how nations have struggled to find the best (most painless?) ways to finance electronic media, and how most of them have turned increasingly to various forms of commercial support, in some cases with a degree of loss of national identity in programming. And we've seen instances where the electronic media have been used to challenge the very notion of national identity.

The issues underlying those experiences are bound to remain or to resurface, albeit in other forms. Solutions to them may proceed along different lines than were followed in the experiences covered here. However, history does have a way of repeating itself, and a fuller knowledge of how and why problems arose and how they were resolved (and, if we can discover it, how well) can only help us to approach such problems in the future with greater wisdom.

History shows us something else worth remembering: the uneven but never altogether absent conviction on the part of many electronic media staff, critics and—perhaps less often—public officials, that the media should do more than simply entertain. It's been rarer to find individuals who could see how education, information and entertainment could be presented in ways that were fresh and compelling, but again, there always have been some, in both the public and commercial sectors. Those individuals may see themselves as fighting a rear guard action today, defending a tradition of public service, a tradition of media artistry, a tradition (often hard-won) of responsible journalism.

The philosophy of "electronic media as telecommunications commodity" noted just above threatens those traditions. Not every tradition deserves to continue, of course. But every tradition deserves to be considered in light of what it has meant to society, and then re-examined to determine whether its diminution or disappearance would leave society the poorer. We can hope that those in charge of determining the future of the electronic media will understand what they are working with in light of what those media already have contributed to society. We can help them to understand by reminding them of media history.

Notes

CHAPTER 1. COMPARING ELECTRONIC MEDIA SYSTEMS

1. There are many books that present comparative studies, but relatively few that discuss what is involved in conducting such studies. One I've found particularly useful is Hans Keman, ed., *Comparative Politics: New Directions in Theory and Method* (Amsterdam: VU University Press, 1993). The essays it contains present a range of perspectives and subjects, and the prose is reasonably clear.

2. Philip Schlesinger, *Media, State and Nation* (London and Newbury Park, Calif.: Sage, 1991), offers a good critical summary of viewpoints on the subject, and the author adds several useful insights of his own.

3. For a detailed, if controversial, study of how British television portrayed union activities, especially in the course of union-management confrontations, see three books prepared by the Glasgow Media Group: *Bad News*; *More Bad News*; and *Really Bad News*. The first two were published by Routledge and Kegan Paul, London, 1976 and 1980; the third was published by Writers and Readers, London, 1982.

4. Certain observers (e.g., H. H. Wilson) have contended that economically conservative governments have supported and/or profit from the creation of commercial broadcasting because the advertising it carries gives audiences the feeling that the economy is healthy and things are running smoothly. See *Pressure Group: the Campaign for Commercial Television* (London: Secker & Warburg, 1961), 210-15.

5. Donald R. Browne, "Alternatives for Local and Regional Radio: Three Nordic Solutions," *Journal of Communication* 34, no. 1 (1984): 36-55; Timothy Tomlinson, "The Development of Local Religious Radio in Norway and Sweden" (Ph.D. diss., University of Minnesota, 1994).

6. Donald R. Browne, *Electronic Media and Indigenous Peoples: A Voice of Our Own?* (Ames, Iowa: Iowa State University Press, 1996).

7. John Davies, *Broadcasting in Wales* (Cardiff: BBC, 1995); William J. How-

ell, "Britain's Fourth Television Channel and the Welsh Language Controversy," *Journal of Broadcasting* 25, no. 2 (Spring 1981): 123-37.

8. George Codding Jr., and Anthony Rutkowski, *The International Telecommunications Union in a Changing World* (Dedham, Mass.: Artech House, 1982).

9. Fred Siebert et al., *Four Theories of the Press* (Urbana, Ill.: University of Illinois Press, 1963). William A. Hachten with Herva Hachten, *The World News Prism*, 4th ed. (Ames, Iowa: Iowa State University Press, 1996), proposes an interesting alternative view on press theories.

10. Erwin Krasnow, Lawrence Longley and Herb Terry, *The Politics of Broadcast Regulation,* 3rd ed. (New York: St. Martin's Press, 1982).

11. Hans Ehrmann, "The Media in Marxist Chile," *Performance* 3 (1972), 80-85; author's field observations, Santiago and Valdivia, Chile, 1977. Even Chile's "mild social responsibility" Frei government sometimes put stations off the air for "antigovernment" offenses, just as previous governments had done. Some lessons are hard to unlearn!

12. Louise Bourgault, *Mass Media in Sub-Saharan Africa* (Bloomington, Ind.: Indiana University Press, 1995), is a good introduction to the media policies and behaviors of most African nations. Douglas A. Boyd, *Broadcasting in the Arab World* (Ames, Iowa: Iowa State University Press, 1993), serves the same purpose for the Arab world. And Elizabeth Fox, ed., *The Politics of Latin American Media* (Newbury Park, Calif.: Sage, 1988), covers several of the Latin American nations, while Everett Dennis and Jon vanden Heuvel, *The Unfolding Lotus* (New York: Freedom Forum Media Studies Center, 1993), and Kenneth Donow, *East Asian Media* (Washington, D.C.: U.S. Information Agency, December 1995), offer brief but useful treatments of some of the Third World nations in Asia.

13. Meyer Weinberg, *TV in America: The Morality of Hard Cash* (New York: Ballantine, 1962).

14. Sydney Head, Christopher Sterling and Lemael Schofield, *Broadcasting in America*, 7th ed. (Boston: Houghton-Mifflin, 1995), 483-84.

15. That freedom was slow in coming to U.S. cable companies, whose user fees were regulated by the municipal governments which licensed them to operate locally. That continued until January 1987, when one portion of the Telecommunications Act of 1984 finally took effect. It took that power away from municipalities and gave it to the companies, many of which promptly began to raise fees, sometimes by spectacular amounts. That led to widespread public dissatisfaction, and pressure on the U.S. Congress to restore some control over cable rates. In 1992, Congress passed legislation turning cable user fee regulation over to the FCC, which had a difficult time deciding how to do the job. As of the late 1990s, some Republicans (and a few Democrats) are attempting to restore such power to the cable companies. Satellite-to-home services set their own fees.

16. Ellis Blaine, *Life With Aunty: Forty Years with the ABC* (Sydney: Methuen of Australia, 1977), chap. 8; Frank Peers, *The Public Eye: Television and the Politics of Canadian Broadcasting, 1952-1968* (Toronto: University of Toronto Press, 1979); Clement Semmler, *The ABC: Aunt Sally and the Sacred Cow* (Melbourne: Melbourne University Press, 1981); and Thomas Whiteside, "Annals of Television: Shaking the Tree," *The New Yorker,* 17 March 1975, pp. 41-91.

17. Personal visit to Channel 31, Melbourne, Australia, March 1996, and viewing of community TV in Sydney, Melbourne and Brisbane, February-March 1996.

18. Les Brown, *Television: The Business Behind the Box* (New York: Harcourt Brace Jovanovich, 1971), chap. 14.

19. Karen Siune and Wolfgang Truetzschler, eds., *Dynamics of Media Politics: Broadcast and Electronic Media in Western Europe* (London and Newbury Park, Calif.: Sage, 1992), 126.

20. Gayle Feldman, "Book Sales by Public Radio Raise Questions," *New York Times,* 26 August 1996, p. C7.

21. VCRs and the technology needed to produce one's own video programming actually seem to be dropping in price, as do certain types of sound equipment and low-power transmitters.

22. McQuail and Siune frame such forces as *actors,* but many of their actors are institutions, rather than individuals or groups. Their list is lengthy and detailed, and I find their consideration of *transnational* actors quite intriguing, as it ranges from professional to political to economic institutions. Denis McQuail and Karen Siune, eds., *New Media Politics: Comparative Perspectives in Western Europe* (London and Beverly Hills: Sage, 1986), chap. 2.

23. The IBA was replaced by two agencies in 1990: the ITC, which licenses and supervises all cable, satellite and commercial TV operations; and the Radio Council, which plays the same role for all forms of commercial radio. The ITC has continued the IBA's practice of also operating an internally appointed Complaints Review Committee.

24. Personal observations from two visits to the Commission's London offices, September 1989 and September 1990.

25. In a narrow (5-4 vote) and convoluted decision, the U.S. Supreme Court in July 1996 ruled that cable operators had the freedom to choose not to carry certain kinds of programming, primarily "indecent" speech and pornography. However, that freedom did *not* apply to the public access channels carried by most cable systems. For those channels, so the majority ruled, the utmost degree of freedom of speech should prevail. The roots of the concern over indecency in this case are outlined in Linda Greenhouse, "Court Wrestles With TV Indecency Issue," *New York Times,* 22 February 1996, p. A9.

26. Andrew Boyle, *Only the Wind Will Listen: Reith of the BBC* (London: Hutchinson, 1972).

27. Michael Tracey, *A Variety of Lives: Sir Hugh Green of the BBC* (London: Bodley Head, 1983).

28. Pamela Wilson, "NBC Television's 'Operation Frontal Lobes': Cultural Hegemony and Fifties Program Planning," *Historical Journal of Film, Radio and Television* 15 (1995): 83-104, provides some idea of Pat Weaver's approach to programming.

29. W. Veltroni, *Io e Berlusconi (e la RAI)* (Rome: Editione Riuniti, 1990); Jeremy Tunstall and Michael Palmer, *Media Moguls* (London and New York, Routledge, 1991).

30. Christopher H. Sterling and J. Michael Kittross, *Stay Tuned*, 2nd ed.

(Belmont, Calif.: Wadsworth, 1990), 434; Federal Reporter, 2nd series, *Writers Guild of America v. ABC* (670 F2d9) (St. Paul: West, 1979).

31. ACT ceased operation in 1992. Its leaders felt that the group had accomplished most of its goals, and in particular the passage by Congress of the Children's Television Act of 1990. It's also likely that the leadership, which had remained largely the same for 25 years, was worn out.

32. Frank Peers, *The Politics of Canadian Broadcasting, 1920-1951* (Toronto: University of Toronto Press, 1969), esp. 64-76.

33. "How Australia Fought for Mandatory Children's Programming ... and Won," *re:act* (U.S. Action for Children's Television magazine) 13, no. 1 (1984): 8.

34. Colin Shaw, former Director, Broadcasting Standards Council (U.K.), personal letter to author, 3 December 1997.

35. Willard Rowland, "The Illusion of Fulfillment: The Broadcast Reform Movement," *Journalism Monographs* 79 (December 1982) (Lexington, Ky.: Association for Education in Journalism and Mass Communication).

36. Barry Cole and Mal Oettinger, *Reluctant Regulators,* rev. ed. (Reading, Mass.: Addison-Wesley, 1978), 74-76.

37. Mark Armstrong, member, Australian Broadcasting Tribunal, conversation with author, Berlin, Germany, 1984. Mr. Armstrong indicated that, by 1984, the situation had improved considerably, and in my subsequent visits to Australia (1987, 1989, 1991) while the ABT still existed, I was able to confirm that assessment.

38. Jochen Zimmer, *Europas Fernsehen im Wandel: Probleme einer Europaeisierung von Ordnungspolitik und Programmen* (Frankfurt am Main: Peter Lang, 1993), is easily the most thorough account of Europe's many experiments with pan-European television, most of them short-term and very few of them successful.

39. S.C. Bryce, "Life Plus Seventy: The Extension of Copyright Terms in the European Union and Proposed Legislation in the United States," *Harvard International Law Journal* 37, no. 2: 169-83; Richard Collins, *Broadcasting and Audio-Visual Policy in the European Single Market* (London: John Libbey, 1994); Aaron Mowray, "The Internationalization of Audio-Visual Media and the European Community: A Study of Copyright Harmonization and the MEDIA Programme" (summa honors thesis [B.A.], University of Minnesota, 1997); Emmanuel Paraschos, *Media Law and Regulation in the European Union.* Ames: Iowa State University Press, 1998; Vincent Porter, *Beyond the Berne Convention: Copyright and Broadcasting in the Single European Market* (London: John Libbey, 1991).

40. Aaron Mowray, "Internationalization"; Anthony Weymoth and Bernard Lamizet, eds., *Markets and Myths: Forces for Change in the Media of Europe* (London and New York: Longman, 1996), chap. 7 under "The Europeanization of the Media."

41. Jeremy Tunstall, *The Media Are American: Anglo-American Media in the World* (New York: Columbia University Press, 1977).

42. Krasnow et al., *Politics,* chap. 1.

43. See "Communications Policies in ... (Ireland, Japan, etc.)" (Paris: UNESCO, various dates in the 1970s).

44. M.S. Gore, "The SITE Experience," *Reports and Papers on Mass Communication* 91 (Paris: UNESCO, 1983); Alfian [one name only] and Godwin Chu, eds., *Satellite Television in Indonesia* (Honolulu, Hawaii: Communications Institute, East-West Center, 1981).

45. Robert McChesney, *Telecommunications, Mass Media, and Democracy: The Battle for the Control of U.S. Broadcasting, 1928-1935* (New York: Oxford University Press, 1993), provides the most detailed account of public involvement, most of it by educators, in the development of the Communication Act of 1934.

46. Krasnow et al., *Politics,* chap. 6.

47. British historian A. J. P. Taylor points out that, when the BBC was created in the 1920s, "Conservatives liked authority; Labour disliked private enterprise," and argues that that is why both were comfortable with a monopoly structure. A. J. P. Taylor, *English History, 1914-1945* (London and New York: Oxford University Press, 1965), 233. But Conservative Party sentiment had changed somewhat by the early 1950s, when younger party members were able to break the monopoly with the passage of an act authorizing commercial broadcasting. H. H. Wilson, *Pressure Group: The Campaign for Commercial Television* (Princeton: Princeton University Press, 1961).

48. Kenneth Dyson and Peter Humphreys, eds., *Broadcasting and New Media Policies in Europe* (London and New York: Routledge, 1988), 11-12.

49. Where imported material is concerned, "protectionism" often is managed through quotas, sometimes covering all imported material, sometimes directed specifically at material from a given nation, usually the United States. Marit Bakke provides a good summary of such measures as they were in effect in Europe during the early to mid-1980s. Marit Bakke, "Culture at Stake," in McQuail and Siune, eds., *New Media Politics*, chap. 10.

50. In September 1996, U.S. cable TV giant TCI provoked those viewers devoted to the Lifetime Channel (a "female-oriented" service) by announcing that Lifetime would be discontinued in several TCI service areas. TCI officials expressed little sympathy with its disgruntled customers, and, since very few service areas feature competing cable providers, there wasn't much that protestors could do, aside from stopping their subscriptions and thus doing without cable altogether. Bill Carter, "TCI Plan to Cut Lifetime Angers Women's Groups," *New York Times,* 14 September 1996, p. 17.

51. Howard Kurtz, media reporter for the *Washington Post* and guest on "Talk of the Nation," National Public Radio, 12 September 1996.

52. Patrick Hughes, *British Broadcasting: Programmes and Power* (Bromley, Kent, U.K.: Chartwell-Bratt, 1981), 72-75.

53. Viewing of community TV services in Brisbane, Sydney, Adelaide and Melbourne, February and March 1996; visit to Channel 31, Melbourne, March 1996.

54. Sophie Chauchard-Smart, "Corporate Cool," *TV World* (April 1996): 89-90; Don Clark, "The Crucial Connection," *Wall Street Journal*, 20 March 1997, p. R8; Carl Franklin, "Lost in Cyberspace," *TV World* (April 1996): 83-85; and Sandy George, "The Soft Soap Treatment," *TV World* (October 1996): 30.

54a. "The Internet and Indigenous Groups," special issue of *Cultural Survival*

Quarterly 21, 4 (Winter 1998).

55. An excellent research topic. Serge Régourd has considered the phenomenon of imitative "help the police" shows, but hasn't traced the reasons for the multiplication. Serge Régourd, *La télévision des Européens* (Paris: La Documentation Française, 1992), 298-302.

56. Kaarle Nordenstreng and Tapio Varis, "Television Traffic—A One-way Street?" *Reports and Papers on Mass Communication* 70 (Paris: UNESCO, 1974); Thomas Guback and Tapio Varis, "Transnational Communication and Cultural Industries," *Reports and Papers on Mass Communication* 92 (Paris: UNESCO, 1982); Tapio Varis, "International Flow of Television Programs," *Reports and Papers on Mass Communication* 100 (Paris: UNESCO, 1985); Graham Chapman et al., *International Television Flow in Western Europe* (Cambridge, U.K.: Development Policy, 1986); *Import/Export: International Flow of Television Fiction* (Paris: UNESCO, 1990); and Preben Sepstrup and Anura Goonasekera, eds., *TV Transnationalization: Europe and Asia* (Paris: UNESCO, 1994).

57. Fred Fejes, *Imperialism, Media and the Good Neighbor* (Norwood, N.J.: Ablex, 1986); Kaarle Nordenstreng and Herbert Schiller, *National Sovereignty and International Communication* (Norwood, N.J.: Ablex, 1981); Herbert Schiller, *Communication and Cultural Domination* (White Plains, N.Y.: M.E. Sharpe, 1976); James Schwoch, *The American Radio Industry and Its Latin American Activities, 1900-1939* (Urbana, Ill.: University of Illinois Press, 1990); Alan Wells, *Picture Tube Imperialism?* (Maryknoll, N.J.: Orbis, 1972).

58. Canada's CBC-TV announced in December 1995 that it was dropping all U.S.-made programs from its schedule for the 1996-97 season. However, financial support for additional Canadian-made programming turned out to be almost nonexistent, and it wasn't until late in 1996 that the CBC did manage to trim most U.S. shows from the prime-time hours. "Canada: New Push for Non-US TV," *Minneapolis Star Tribune,* 11 September 1996, p. A7; Bernard Simon, "CBC Plan to Turn Off US TV Shows," *Financial Times* (London), 20 September 1996.

59. "India Retains Its Curbs on Foreign Media," *New York Times,* 13 August 1996, p. C6.

60. "Social Education Through Television," *Reports and Papers on Mass Communication* 38 (Paris: UNESCO, 1961), provides a description of the early uses of Indian television for social development.

61. Douglas Boyd, Joseph Straubhaar and John Lent, *The Videocassette Revolution* (New York: Longmans, 1989); Gladys Ganley and Oscar Ganley, *Global Political Fallout: The VCR's First Decade* (Norwood, N.J.: Ablex, 1987); Gladys Ganley, *The Political Fallout from Personal Media* (Norwood, N.J.: Ablex, 1992).

62. There are several books that deal with minorities and their portrayal through and activities in the electronic media. The following are among the more comprehensive: Donald R. Browne, *Electronic Media and Indigenous Peoples: a Voice of Our Own?* (Ames, Iowa: Iowa State University Press, 1996); Donald R. Browne, Charles Firestone and Ellen Mickiewicz, *Television/Radio News & Minorities* (Queenstown, Md.: The Aspen Institute, 1994); John Downing, *Radical Media* (Boston: South End Press, 1984); Claire Frachon and Marion Vargaftig, eds., *European Television: Immigrants and Ethnic Minorities* (London: John Libbey,

1995); Bruce Girard, ed., *A Passion for Radio* (Montréal: Black Rose, 1992); Charles Husband, ed., *A Richer Vision* (London: John Libbey, 1994); Clint Wilson and Felix Guttierez, *Race, Multiculturalism and the Media* (Thousand Oaks, Calif.: Sage, 1996).

CHAPTER 2. FRANCE

1. There are many books that provide a reasonably comprehensive picture of French government and society, among them Henry Ehrmann, *Politics in France,* 4th ed. (Boston: Little, Brown, 1982); Michel Crozier, *Strategies for Change: the Future of French Society* (Cambridge, Mass.: Massachusetts Institute of Technology Press, 1982); François Gougel and Alfred Grosser, *La politique en France,* nouvelle ed. (Paris: A. Colin, 1984); Martin Harrop, ed., *Power and Policy in Liberal Democracies* (Cambridge, U.K. and New York: Cambridge University Press, 1992); and Gordon Wright, *France in Modern Times,* 3rd ed. (New York: Norton, 1982). There are several books and book chapters about the media in France: Ekkehard Egge, *Die Insezenierung von Politik: Debatten mit Politikern im Franzoesischen Fernsehen, 1980-1990* (Rheinfelden: Schauble, 1991); Raymond Kuhn, *The Media in France* (London and New York: Routledge, 1995); Sheila Perry and Maire Cross, eds., *Voices of France: Social, Political and Cultural Identity* (London and Washington, D.C.: Pinter, 1997); Brian Rigby and Nicholas Hewitt, eds., *France and the Mass Media* (Basingstoke, U.K.: Macmillan, 1991); and Ruth Thomas, *Broadcasting and Democracy in France* (Bradford, U.K.: Bradford University Press, 1976). Several books (see Bibliography for full citations) contain useful chapters on French broadcasting: Robert Avery, 1993 (Vedel and Bourdon); Bertelsmann Foundation and European Institute for the Media, 1995 (Régourd); Kenneth Dyson and Peter Humphreys, 1988 (Simon); Walter Emery, 1969; Claire Frachon and Marion Vargaftig, 1995 (authors); Wolfgang Hoffmann-Riem, 1996 (author); International Institute of Communication, 1996 (Kuhn); Raymond Kuhn, 1986 (de Tarlé); Serge Robillard, 1995 (author); Alessandro Silj, 1992 (Jezequel and Pineau); Smith, Anthony, 1979 (Grosser); and Tony Weymouth and Bernard Lamizet, 1996 (Lamizet).

Of the many books in French that cover French broadcast history, the following strike me as most thorough and least opinionated: Jérome Bourdon, *Haute Fidélité: Pouvoir et Télévision, 1935-1994* (Paris: Seuil, 1994); Jérome Bourdon, *Histoire de la télévision sous DeGaulle* (Paris: Anthropos/INA, 1990); Christiane Brochand, *Histoire Genérale de la Radio et de la Télévision en France, Vol. 1, 1921-1944* (Paris: La Documentation Française, 1994); Elisabeth Cazenave and Caroline Ulmann-Mauriat, *Presse, radio et télévision en France: De 1631 à nos jours* (Paris: Hachette, 1994); Rene Duval, *L'Histoire de la Radio en France* (Paris: Alain Moreau, 1979); Cecile Meadel, *Histoire de la Radio des Années Trentes* (Paris: Anthropos/INA, 1994).

2. Roger Louis and Joseph Rovan, "Television and Teleclubs in Rural Communities," *Reports and Papers on Mass Communication* 16 (Paris: UNESCO, 1955).

3. The two most thorough sources of information on the struggles between the private stations and the PTT, as well as the struggles among the private stations, are Duval, *L'histoire,* and Brochand, *Histoire générale, Vol. 1*, 108-31.

4. Brochand, *Histoire générale,* 450-51 for politics and radio in the 1920s, 451 for the quotation (translation mine).

5. Brochand, *Histoire générale,* 437.

6. Gwyneth Jackaway, *Media at War: Radio's Challenge to the Newspapers, 1924-1939,* Westport, CT: Praeger, 1995.

7. Meadel, *Histoire,* 265-71; quotation on 266 (translation mine).

8. Meadel, *Histoire,* chap. 8.

9. Walter Emery, *National and International Systems of Broadcasting* (East Lansing, Mich.: Michigan State University Press, 1969), 242.

10. Meadel, *Histoire,* chap. 5-8, passim.

11. Duval, *L'Histoire,* 309-10.

12. Bourdon, *Haute Fidélité,* 27, notes that, even though the first director (head) of television was a journalist, he limited use of the medium to entertainment. He cites Thierry Kubler and Emmanuel Lemiuex, *Cognacq-Jay 1940: La télévision française sous l'Occupation* (Paris: Plume, 1990), 86, as his source.

13. Bourdon, *Haute Fidélité,* 24-29; Brochand, *Histoire générale,* 569-602; Kubler and Lemieux, *Cognacq-Jay 1940*; John Swift, *Adventures in Vision* (London: John Lehman, 1950), 113-16; *Historical Journal of Film, Radio and Television* article on German broadcasting in Paris (1994?).

14. Duval, *L'Histoire,* chap. 5.

15. François Mitterand, later to become president of France, served as minister of information during part of this period (July 1948 to October 1949). At the time 32 years of age, he apparently focused his attention on radio and had little interest in television. Bourdon, *Haute Fidélité,* 32. Bourdon doesn't say whether Mitterand had anything to do with keeping de Gaulle off the air.

16. Helène Eck, in Rigby and Hewitt, 132 and 144; Kuhn, *Media,* 90-91.

17. Eck, passim; Michael Scriven, *Sartre and the Media* (New York: St. Martin's Press, 1993), 72-90.

18. Thomas, *Broadcasting,* 8-9.

19. Etienne Lalou, *Regards neufs sur la télévision* (Paris: Editions du Seuil, 1957), 162.

20. Henri Spade, *Histoire d'amour de la télévision française* (Paris: Editions France-Empire, 1968), 127-28.

21. F.O. Giesbert, *François Mitterand* (Paris: Le Seuil, 1977), 103.

22. Pierre Descaves and A. J. V. Martin, *Un Siécle de Radio et de Télévision* (Paris: Les Productions de Paris, 1965), 92 (translation mine).

23. Roland Dhordain, *Le roman de la radio* (Paris: La Table Ronde, 1983), chap. 10.

24. Bourdon, *Histoire,* 283-96.

25. Antoine de Tarlé, in Smith, *Télévision*, 51. See also Bourdon, *Haute Fidelité,* 74-75, and Thomas, *Broadcasting,* 13.

26. Thomas, *Broadcasting,* 13.

27. Alain Peyrefitte, cited in Thierry Bombled, *Devine qui va parler ce soir?* (Paris: Syros, 1981), 28.

28. Cited in Bourdon, *Histoire,* 106. Bourdon cites as his source the transcripts of meetings of ORTF program committees, in the ORTF collection of the French National Archives, but provides no further details (translation mine). However, in his *Haute Fidelité,* 77, Bourdon cites the newspaper *Le Monde,* 4 May 1965.

29. Bourdon, *Histoire,* 87-90. Bourdon, in *Haute Fidelité,* 69-71, provides additional details on *Cinq Colonnes,* including the relative boldness of the show's producers in dealing with Algeria at all (rare on French TV in those days), but also noting (p. 71) the threats made by various ministries against it. He attributes the relative success of the show's producers in battling against censorship to the most important among their number, Pierre Lazareff. Lazareff also was manager of *France-Soir,* the only French daily at the time with circulation in excess of a million.

30. Phillip M. Williams, *The French Parliament, 1958-1967* (London: George Allen and Unwin, 1968), 91-93.

31. "Le debat, c'est moi," *The Economist,* 29 February 1964, pp. 77-78.

32. Genet (Janet Flanner), "Letter from Paris," *The New Yorker*, 1 June 1968, pp. 105-6.

33. Thomas, *Broadcasting,* 21.

34. Genet, "Letter from Paris," *The New Yorker,* 11 March 1967, pp. 151-52; see also Thomas, *Broadcasting,* 21.

35. "Rapport fait en conclusion des travaux de la Commission de Controle" [Diligent Report], *Journal Officiel,* Documents Senat no. 118 (13 April 1968).

36. Thomas, *Broadcasting,* 26.

37. The most thorough account of this period is in Comite d'Histoire de la Télévision, *Mai 1968 a l'ORTF* (Paris: La documentation Française, 1987).

38. "Un referendum de Télé-7-Jours," *Le Monde,* 31 July 1968, p. 9.

39. "M. Conte's Adresse aux Personnels de l'Office," *Le Monde,* 27 July 1972, p. 6.

40. Jean Paul Aymon, "Arthur Conte joue son va-tout," *L'Express,* 1-7 October 1972, p. 36.

41. "La crise de l'ORTF," *Le Monde,* 19 October 1973, p. 27; see also Nan Robertson, "Two Ousted in Paris on Radio-TV Issue," *The New York Times,* 24 October 1973, p. 5.

42. Arthur Conte, *Hommes Libres* (Paris: Plon, 1973).

43. "TV Talk by a Critic of Pompidou Barred," *The New York Times,* 28 November 1973, p. 6. Bourdon, *Haute Fidelité,* 141-47, provides a quite thorough account of this confrontation. He feels that Conte tried to "play the role of minister without having the rank" (p. 142) (translation mine).

44. Jean-Claude Sergeant, in Meryl Aldridge and Nicholas Hewitt, eds., *Controlling Broadcasting* (Manchester, U.K.: Manchester University Press, 1994), 233.

45. Thomas, *Broadcasting,* 99-101.

46. Jean Diwo, *Si Vous Avez Manqué le Debut* (Paris: Albin Michel, 1976),

264-65, cited by de Tarlé in Smith, *Television,* 61-62.

47. De Tarlé, in Smith, *Television,* 67.

48. Ibid., 64.

49. Francis Balle, "The French Broadcasting System: Public Service and Competition," *Studies in Broadcasting* [NHK Japan] 16 (1980): 102-3.

50. Bombled, *Devine,* esp. chap. 5; Claude Collin, *Ecoutez la vraie difference!* (Claix: la pensée sauvage, 1979); François Cazenave, *Les Radios Libres* (Paris: Presses Universitaires de France, 1980). Cazenave notes (p. 47) that there may have been a student-operated pirate station (Radio Campus) in or near Lille in 1969. Jean-Emmanuel Ray and Muriel Ray, *Corsaires des Ondes* (Paris: Les Editions du Cerf, 1978), 56, mention a Radio Halles that came on air in Paris in 1976, but furnish no details on it.

51. Caroline Pfaff, "Giscard Lowers Hammer on Pirate Socialist Station," *Advertising Age* (10 September 1979).

52. "Hunt Is on for the 'Witches' of French TV," *London Sunday Telegraph,* 21 June 1981, p. 11.

53. "France: New Broadcasting Law," *InterMedia* 10 (May 1982): 7-8.

54. Adelbert de Segonzac, "French Want to See 'Dallas' and 'Kojak,' Not Socialist Sermons," *Minneapolis Star,* 2 May 1982.

55. Brian Moynihan, "Paris Radios Rebel," *Times of London,* 16 December 1984, p. 22.

56. Bertelsmann, *Television,* 150.

57. Kuhn, *Media,* 206, feels that lobbying against cable on the part of the local press in various parts of the country was the chief reason for the medium's lack of success. The press was afraid that, sooner or later, cable would compete with it for advertising revenue.

58. Udayan Gupta, "French Socialist Government Shifts Telecommunications Policy," *Advertising Age* (3 November 1983): 17.

59. Simon, in Dyson and Humphries, *Broadcasting,* 169-74.

60. Kuhn, *Media,* 213-15.

61. Anne-Elizabeth Moutet, "Commercial Break for French TV," *The London Sunday Times,* 20 January 1985, p. 59.

62. "Channel 80," *The Economist,* 26 January 1985, p. 57.

63. *L'Empire Agite de la Radio-Télé* Les Dossiers de Canard, no. 8 (*Le Canard Enchainee,* September 1983), 61. Gougel and Grosser, *La politique,* 151, note a statement made by the newly appointed president of TF-1 in September 1983: "I have the advantage of being fairly close to the President of the Republic, and for that reason no one is going to impose anything, no matter what, on me." (Translation mine.)

64. Brian Moynihan, "French 'BBC' Plan Misfires as Politics Makes a Comeback," *Times of London,* 7 October 1984, p. 20.

65. Jean Belot, "La cote de Cotta," *Télérama* (12 September 1984): 40-41. The Haute Autorité also became involved in the controversy surrounding a 1985 documentary made for A2 about the World War II activities and present status of some French Communist Party members who were fighters during the Resistance (against Nazi rule of France). The Communist Party objected to the documentary,

the director general of A2 asked the HA to screen it before it was aired (and also asked a group of Resistance fighters to look at it), and then pulled it from the schedule. It aired several weeks later, with a Communist Party attack immediately preceding it and a debate following it. See Jane Kramer, "Letter From Europe," *The New Yorker*, 5 August 1985, pp. 52-57; for a more critical appraisal, see Marcel Ophuls, "Mitterand's Red Scare," *American Film* (December 1985): 34-37.

66. Georges Ridoux, "Private Television—the Brédin Report Proposals," *EBU Review* 36, no. 4 (July 1985): 61-63.

67. Michael Dobbs, "French Government Awards Its First Private TV Network," *Minneapolis Star Tribune*, 21 November 1985, p. 14A.

68. Philippe Belingard, "A New Legal Framework for Audiovisual Communication in France," *EBU Review* 37, no. 6 (November 1986): 23-27.

69. Bourdon, *Haute Fidélité*, 273.

70. "TF1 Looks to Hachette," *TV World* (March-April 1987): 6; see also Paul Michaud, "The Two-Horse Race to Buy TF1," same issue, 16-17.

71. Neil Watson, "Pluralism Underlies TF1 Decision," *The Hollywood Reporter*, 7 April 1987, p. I-1; "Surprise Winner for TF1 Network," *TV World* (May 1987): 8.

72. Neil Watson, "Bouygues-Maxwell Group Gets 50 Percent TF1," *The Hollywood Reporter*, 6 April 1987, pp. 1, 8.

73. Bourdon, *Haute Fidelité*, 277-78; "French Regulator Droit Indicted for Corruption," *Variety*, 2 June 1988, p. 16.

74. "France's CNCL Center of New Controversy," *Variety*, 2 November 1987, p. 8; Frank Eskenazi, "Radio Courtoisie a attrape la Bande par les cheveux," *Liberation*, 2 November 1987, p. 5; Georges Bonopera, "Les anomalies des radios 'muettes' de la bande FM," *Le Matin*, 2 November 1987, p. 2; Bruce Alderman, "French Broadcasting Watchdog CNCL Fighting for Its Political Life," *Variety*, 16 December 1987, p. 27; author's informal discussion with Antoine de Tarlé, Paris, September 1989.

75. Kuhn, *Media*, 215-16.

76. Alain Woodrow, "French Correction," *Broadcast* (U.K.), 21 April 1989, p. 37.

77. Bourdon, *Haute Fidélité*, 281-82.

78. Sergeant, in Aldridge and Hewitt, *Controlling*, 241. Sergeant goes on to indicate that Mitterand revived the proposal as part of a constitutional reform package in 1992, but it did not pass.

79. Peter de Selding, "But First We Have Sports," *Paris Passion* 64 (September 1989): 37.

80. Personal visits to the Nimes, Toulouse and Périgord stations in October 1995.

81. Conseil Supérieur de l'Audiovisuel, "Les Télévisions Locales en France: Situations et Perspectives" (Paris: CSA, November 1989), 35-36; Pia Farrell, "French Cablers Looking to Turn Corner on Profitability," *The Hollywood Reporter*, 8 January 1991, p. I-1.

82. Conseil Supérieur de l'Audiovisuel, *Rapport au Parlement* (Paris: CSA, March 1994), 162, notes that "local channels, far from developing, are perishing,"

and goes on to indicate that it (CSA) had recommended previously (1991) that local channels should be allowed to carry advertising. In fact, some do, but usually in the form of local businesses offsetting program costs in return for brief mentions of thanks on the air and in literature distributed by the cable service to its customers.

83. Bethany Haye and Neil Watson, "Posse of Euro Media Giants Finalizes TDF-1 Channel Bids," *The Hollywood Reporter,* 28 February 1989, pp. I-1, I-8; "Euro-Tycoons and the German Angle," *TV World* (March-April 1989): 38; Pia Farrell, "Losses of $40 Million Predicted for France's Faltering TDF," *The Hollywood Reporter,* 30 October 1990, p. I-1; Pia Farrell, "France Pulls Back from DBS project," *The Hollywood Reporter,* 28 November 1990, p. 4.

84. I visited such a station in Bayonne (southwestern France) in September 1989. After several years as a relatively successful community-oriented operation, infighting and loss of interest in working to keep the operation going led to its sale to a national network. The station had moved into a new building about a year before the sale, but the studios were useless after the sale, most of the offices likewise, and a part-time receptionist/secretary and two local salespeople were the only remaining occupants.

85. Pia Farrell, "French Anti-Quota Group Unravelling," *The Hollywood Reporter,* 24 April 1991, p. I-2.

86. Pia Farrell filed several articles on the travails of La Cinq for *The Hollywood Reporter*; see the issues of 16 December, p. 4; 18 December, p. 1; 20 December, p. 1; 23 December, p. 3; and 31 December, p. 1, all 1991; and 2 January, p. 1; 6 January, p. 3; 14 January, pp. 4, I-5; 3 February, p. 9; 4 February, p. 4; 13 February, p. 13; and 14 April, p. 4, all 1992. Also helpful is a brief but succinct account of the steps leading to La Cinq's demise in Cazenave and Ulmann-Mauriat, *Presse,* 205-8.

87. Vincent Canby, "Bidding Adieu to the Classic French Film," *The New York Times,* 9 June 1991, p. 15; Geraldine Fabrikant, "French TV Giant Turns Global," *The New York Times,* 20 June 1990, p. C1.

88. Roni Amelen, "Shoot to Kill," *TV World* (October 1992): 14.

89. Personal interview with Guillaume Sainteny, Paris, October 1995.

90. Adam Sage, "French Turn off Radios," *The Press* (Christchurch, New Zealand), 30 March 1996, p. 6.

91. Pia Farrell, "Antenne 2 Execs Say Net to Break Even by Dec. '92," *The Hollywood Reporter,* 24 December 1991, p. I-3.

92. A useful source of current figures for France and for other European nations is the *Cable and Satellite Yearbook,* published annually by the *Financial Times* (London). Also helpful (and more detailed) is the European Audiovisual Laboratory's *Statistical Yearbook,* published annually by the Laboratory (Strasbourg).

93. Yves-Marie Labé and Nicole Vulser, "Le rapport Missaka sûr l'audiovisuel publique critique sévèrement l'État," *Le Monde,* December 11, 1998, p. 1.

94. The major sources of this complex story were Marcel Machill and Niels Lutzhoeft, "Der französche Fernsehmarkt im digitalen Zeitalter," *Media Perspektiven* 3/98, 132-143, and articles appearing in the daily newspaper *Le Monde* in

1998, particularly the following (in order of appearance): Yves-Marie Labé and Nicole Vulser, "Mme Trautmann veut 'cantonner' les activités médias des groupes industriels," January 29, p. 19; "Point de vue" (a Statement by Trautmann), March 11, p. 1; Yves-Marie Labé, "Les chaînes publiques Françaises auront un financement pluriannuel," April 8, p. 20; "Télévision: les chaînes publiques regroupées," July 11, p. 1; "L'audiovisuel en panne de réforme," December 3, p. 1; "Les déconvenues d'un texte longtemps défendu par Lionel Jospin, December 3, p. 7; and "Le projet de loi sur l'audiovisuel est retardé de plusiers mois," December 3, p. 6.

95. There is a deposit fee of Fr 500 (about $85) for the set-top decoding box. Bertelsmann, *Television*, 160.

96. Ted Clark, "Disclose Setup on How Quality Affects Coin for French TV-AM," *Variety*, 21 July 1976, p. 40.

97. *L'empire agite*, 39.

98. "L'audiovisuel public devra realiser 616.6 millions de francs d'economies en 1997," *Le Monde*, 21 September 1996, p. 14.

99. *La Lettre CSA* 72 (September 1995): 9-11.

100. Bourdon, *Haute Fidelité*, 290-92; Pia Farrell, "French Networks to Combine Prod'n," *The Hollywood Reporter*, 24 April 1991, p. 4.

101. Roger Cohen, "Books Star on TV, but Only in France," *New York Times*, 10 September 1990, p. C7.

102. Frank J. Prial, "The World's Most Popular Book Show," *The New York Times Book Review*, 29 September 1985, p. 3.

103. In my October 1986 visit, some station staff at Radio France Melun and Radio France Cote d'Azûr did express some concern that the newly elected Conservative majority would cut back on funding for regional and local public radio, partly because Conservatives weren't regarded as all that "local-minded," partly because a few influential deputy ministers were seen as hostile toward Radio France and supportive of local commercial (private) broadcasting as sufficient to address local needs.

103a. Breton language and music supporters were sufficiently disturbed about the lack of air time for broadcasts of Celtic music and in Breton that they demonstrated quite noisely in front of one of two "offending" Radio France stations in Brittany in 1998. "Radio," *Le Monde*, March 21, 1998, p. 20.

104. *L'empire agite*, 29-34; Sophie Jouve, "French Video Market Anxieties," *TV World* (December 1983/January 1984): 46.

105. Pia Farrell, "Four More Years of Red Ink," *The Hollywood Reporter*, 9 July 1991, p. I-1; Pia Farrell, "Capital Improvements," *The Hollywood Reporter*, 18 February 1992, p. I-5.

106. Pia Farrell, "French TV Producers Must Merge to Survive, Study Says," *The Hollywood Reporter*, 14 July 1992, p. I-1.

107. Bertelsmann, *Television*, 166-67.

108. Franklin S. Haiman, *Citizen Access to the Media: A Cross-Cultural Analysis of Four Democratic Societies*, Institute for Modern Communications Research Monographs, no. 1 (Evanston, Ill.: Northwestern University, 1987), 17, indicates that there were only three instances of the use of right of reply during all of 1985 for all three public networks.

109. Dianna Geddes, "Setback to Eiffel Tower TV Role," *Times of London,* 14 December 1985, p. 6; Michael Field, "Dubbed Films Feared as France Gets 'ITV'," *Daily Telegraph* (London), 25 January 1986, p. 5; Paul Michaud, "Five's Rocky Road to Reception," *TV World* (February 1986): 38.

110. Bruce Alderman, "CLT Discussing TV-6's Takeover," *The Hollywood Reporter,* 10 February 1987, p. I-3.

111. Pia Farrell, "$10 Million TF1 Plagiarism Fine," *The Hollywood Reporter,* 12 March 1993, p. 4.

112. There are useful summaries of the activities of French electronic media regulatory agencies in Hoffmann-Riem, *Regulating,* chap.4; International Institute of Communications, *Media,* chap. 3; and Robillard, *Television,* chap. 10.

113. Georges Ridoux, "Audiovisual Communications in France," *EBU Review* 33, no. 6 (November 1982): 6-13.

114. Pierre Braillard, "From TV to Video and Videotext" (paper delivered at the annual conference of the International Institute of Communications, Tokyo, Japan, September 1985), 9.

115. Bruce Alderman, "1986 Radically Alters French TV," *The Hollywood Reporter,* 20 January 1987, p. I-8.

116. Stephane Just, "La Bataille de Paris," *Journal Antennes Broadcast* (September-October 1987): 8-11.

117. Bertelsmann, *Television,* 159.

118. The directive doesn't place an absolute prohibition on showing violent material; rather, the CSA looks at sheer quantity of violent scenes, along with duration of scene and intensity of violence depicted. (*CSA Monthly Report* 73 [October 1995]: 4.) Fines have ranged between 200,000 and 5 million francs; the latter is close to a million dollars (Bertelsmann, *Television,* 158).

119. Bertelsmann, *Television,* 143.

120. Jean-Claude Sergeant, "Government and Broadcast Media in France," in Meryl Aldridge and Nicholas Hewitt, *Controlling Broadcasting* (Manchester: Manchester University Press, 1994), 237-38.

121. Bertelsmann, *Television,* 156.

122. Marcel Machill, "The Impact of Radio Policy in an Area Defined by the Antagonistic Forces of Commercialization and Cultural Protection," *European Journal of Communication* 11, no. 3 (1996): 393-415.

123. Bertelsmann, *Television,* 153.

124. Hoffmann-Riem, *Regulating,* 181.

125. Hoffmann-Riem, *Regulating,* 181; Régourd, in Bertelsmann, *Television,* 157-58.

126. Robillard, *Television,* 73.

127. Bertelsmann, *Television,* 159.

128. Hoffmann-Riem, *Regulating,* 178.

129. Claudine Helmlinger, personal interview, Paris, September 1972.

130. Jean-Claude Petit, "Nous, Téléspectateurs, Exigéons Qualité et Choix," *La Vie,* 31 August 1989, p. 5.

131. Bertelsmann, *Television,* 167-68; "MTT: La voix des téléspectateurs," descriptive brochure published by MTT (Paris), 1995.

132. Jean-Claude Sergeant, in Aldridge and Hewitt, *Controlling,* 241.

133. "Canal Plus en Direct," *Canal+ Le Magazine des Abonnes* (October 1995): 25; Marlise Simmons, "A French Mother Fights TV Violence," *The New York Times,* 30 August 1993, p. A5.

134. Herve Bourges, "Violence et télévision," *Le Monde,* 28 September 1996.

135. Bertelsmann, *Television,* 170 (for both surveys).

136. George Ross, "French Labor and Economic Change," in Stephen S. Cohen and Peter A. Gourevitch, eds. *France in the Troubled World Economy* (Boston: Butterworth Scientific, 1982), 172.

137. Bourdon, *Haute Fidelité,* 292.

138. However, France 2 is required as a condition of licensing to produce and broadcast "programmes of a religious nature reflecting the main forms of worship practised in France" (Catholicism, Protestantism, Islam and Judaism) every Sunday morning, and at its own expense. (Bertelsmann, *Television,* 146-47) Also, a few dozen local radio stations around the country are operated by the Catholic Church.

139. Kelly, in Rigby and Hewitt, *France,* 29.

140. "All-News Radio Grows Rapidly in France," *The New York Times,* 17 December 1990, p. C12.

141. Bruce Alderman, "France Sets New Rule on La Cinq TV," *The Hollywood Reporter,* 3 February 1987, p. I-6.

142. Bill Grantham, "French Broadcasters Reacting Hot, Cool to Government Probe," *Variety,* 21 January 1987, p. 16.

143. Richard Bernstein, "TV Station at Center of Paris Storm," *The New York Times,* 22 June 1986, sec. 1, p. 3.

144. Bourdon, *Haute Fidelité,* 277; Joshua Jampol, "Ax Falls on TF1 Talk Show Host," *The Hollywood Reporter,* 6 October 1987, p. I-1.

145. My observations are based on my viewing of television and listening to radio in France during most of October 1995.

146. *Annuaire de la Radio* 97, Annex, 6-7.

147. Dhordain, *Le Roman,* 204, 210.

148. "Radio Agora Silenced," *InteRadio* (Newsletter of AMARC [World Association for Community Radio]) 7, no. 2 (1995): 3.

149. J.-R. Duchastellier, "L'Heure du Choix," *Journal Antennes Broadcast* 3 (September-October 1987): 16-17.

149a. François Chirot, "Les radios associatives veulent être réconnues d'utilité sociale," *Le Monde*, February 11, 1998, p. 17.

150. *Annuaire de la Radio* 97, Annex, 7.

151. French media critic Noel Mamére described the quiz show formats originating in the United States as products of "the garbage pails of Uncle Sam." (Noel Mamére, *La dictature de l'Audimat* [Paris: Editions La Découverte, 1988], 23.)

152. A phrase which itself was banned by the French Parliament in a 1994 law designed to rid the French language of Anglo-American words and expressions. Its preferred phrase—heures de grand écoute (lit. "hours of big listening")—was both clumsy and inappropriate, since TV is both a visual and an oral medium. In any case, the French Constitutional Council quickly ruled the ban il-

legal where radio and TV, public and private alike, were concerned. "French Council Eases Language Ban," *The New York Times,* 31 July 1994, p. 4; Alan Riding, "France's 'Mr. All-Good' Is Defeated by English," *The New York Times,* 7 August 1994, p. 4.

153. La Cinquieme's formal title is "The television [service] of knowledge, education, and employment." Little of its programming has to do directly with preparing people for employment, and some of the educational material draws criticism—for example, running "Rintintin" in its original English version so as to interest children in learning English. (Emmanuel Legrand, "Public Education," *TV World* (January/February 1995): 11.

154. Marie-Castille Mention, "Stars, Producers Defect from TF1," *The Hollywood Reporter,* 27 April 1987, p. 4, 13; Joshua Jampol, "TV Journalists Quit French Net," *The Hollywood Reporter,* 13 October 1987, p. I-1.

155. Program broadcast on M6, 4 October 1995, 8:40-10:30 p.m.

156. Emmanuel Legrand, "The Dark Horse," *TV World* (January-February 1995): 8.

157. Gaelle Canova-Lamarque et al., "France: Identity Crisis of Regional Television and Expansion of Local Television," in Miquel de Moragas Spa and Carmelo Garitaonandia, eds., *Decentralization in the Global Era* (London: John Libbey, 1995), chap. 4 (as the title indicates, this chapter also has a useful account of regional TV); "La Longue Marche des TV Locales Hértziennes," *Sonovision* 358 (April 1992): 23-34; Philippe Mounier, "Evolution"; personal visits to Télé-Toulouse (Toulouse), AquiTV (Périgord) and Télé-Bleue (Nimes), October 1995.

158. Jean-Jacques Bozonnet, "Le gouvernement se penche sûr la viabilité des télévisions locales," *Le Monde,* April 20, 1998, p. 21.

158a. Personal visits to local TV in Nimes, Sarlat, Toulouse and Epinal, October 1995.

159. "In France, Political Puppets May Upstage Real-Life Counterparts," *Minneapolis Star Tribune,* 4 May 1995, p. 5A.

160. "Riviere Esperance Flows from Mipcom to Mip-TV," *TV World* (March 1996): 32.

161. Stephen Crofts has an interesting analysis of why the Australian soap opera "Neighbours," dubbed and shown (over A2) as "Les voisins" in 1989, failed within seven months. Poor scheduling may have had something to do with its early demise, but Crofts offers a number of sociological speculations, including the discomfort felt by many French when confronted with unfamiliar settings and situations. Crofts, "Global Neighbors?," in Robert C. Allen, ed., *To Be Continued ... Soap Operas Around the World* (London and New York: Routledge,1995), 115-18.

162. The program descriptions come from France TV 5 (International) web site: http://www.tv5.ca.

163. Elisabeth Perrin (interviewer), "Repondez Monsieur le Producteur: Jean-Luc Azoulay," *Dernieres Nouvelles d'Alsace TV Magazine,* 2-8 October 1995, pp. 14-16.

164. Anne Cooper-Chen, *Games in the Global Village* (Bowling Green, Ohio: Bowling Green State University Popular Press, 1994), 208-11, provides a useful summary of French game shows up to 1993.

165. Gerard Pangon, "Jusqu'ou oseront-ils?," *Télérama* 2386 (4 October 1995): 79-80.

166. Jerome Garcin, "Putain de part de marché," *L'Evénement du jeudi* 20 (6 February 1992), pp. 89-93, cited in Hugh Dauncey, "French 'Reality Television': More Than a Matter of Taste?," *European Journal of Communication* 11, no. 1 (March 1996): 99. Dauncey sees the reality TV phenomenon as indicative of the general move in French TV toward a "demand-led, advertiser-dependent and audience ratings-driven free market" (p. 101).

167. "TV: l'Information Chez les Autres," *L'Express,* 25 February-3 March 1974, pp. 34-35.

168. Claude-Jean Bértrand, "A Critique of French Media," unpublished paper, March 1985, 12-15.

169. Pia Farrell, "French Anchor Indicted over Gifts," *The Hollywood Reporter,* 16 February 1993, p. I-5.

170. James M. Markham, "What's More Vulgar Than Money?," *The New York Times,* 1 March 1989, p. 4.

171. "Don't Touch That Dial," *Paris Passion* 64 (September 1989): 37.

171a. Sylvie Kerviel, "France 2 ose la réforme du 'JT,'" *Le Monde,* October 12-13, 1997.

172. Alan Tillier, "Bad News for Moonlighting French Anchors," *Hollywood Reporter,* 4-6 April 1997, p. 10.

173. Paul Michaud, "Ratings in from the Cold," *TV World* (February 1986): 35.

174. Bethany Haye, "French TV Ratings Service Braces for Nielson [*sic*] Arrival," *The Hollywood Reporter,* 3 January 1988, p. I-1; "Peoplemeters Signal Bow of New Gallic Ratings Era," *Variety,* 24 February 1988, p. 18.

175. Gun Akyuz, "Open Season," *TV World* (December 1997): 44.

176. (Senator) Jean Cluzel, "Presse: Bilan et Perspectives. Production Audiovisuelle: Une Priorité Absolu" (Paris: Les rapports du Senat, 1993-1994, no. 514), 74.

177. I listened to the station while in Toulouse in October 1995.

178. *Annuaire de la Radio 96-97* (Paris: Les editions Victor, 1997), B-17.

179. Machill, *French Radio,* 411.

180. Claire Frachon and Marion Vargaftig, eds., *European Television: Immigrants and Ethnic Minorities* (London: John Libbey, 1995), 145-48. See also Pascal Boucaud and Paul Stubbs, "Access to the Media and the Challenge to Cultural Racism in France," in Charles Husband, ed., *A Richer Vision* (London: John Libbey, 1994), chap. 4.

181. Alec Hargreaves and Dalila Mahdjoub, "Satellite Television Viewing among Ethnic Minorities in France," *European Journal of Communication* 12, no. 4 (December 1997): 459-77, contains much fascinating ethnographic data, including indications of a generational split in program preferences, with younger Muslim viewers wanting more "western" fare such as MTV and CNN, and even moving the satellite dish while their parents were away in order to see it, rather than the "home country" channels their parents favored.

182. Those observations are drawn from a variety of sources: Frachon and

Vargaftig, *European,* 135-58; conversations with French and North African attendees at the Second Conference on Public Broadcasting for a Multicultural Europe, Strasbourg, France, October 1995; and conversations with French and North African students at the University of Minnesota.

183. My observations are based on two separate visits to Alsace in October 1995. I witnessed much the same pride in a far more peculiar setting in August 1994, when I met a group of young Frenchmen in a pub in Dingle, Ireland. I began to describe some of my research on Basque language radio, and mentioned that several stations in the nearby Bordeaux region broadcast in Occitane. One of the group was amazed that anyone from outside the region would know about such broadcasts, and went on to express his great pride in speaking the language of his ancestors—which, he said, the broadcasts had helped to inspire him to learn.

184. Details on this activity were contained in an information packet prepared by the Association Dedans-dehors, and distributed from the Association's headquarters in Lyon (BP5017, 69245 Lyon cedex 05).

185. Donald R. Browne, *Electronic Media and Indigenous Peoples: A Voice of Our Own?* (Ames, Iowa: Iowa State University Press, 1996), 187.

186. Haiman, *Citizen Access,* 26-27. The author also provides (16-35) a concise account of procedures governing party political broadcasts and notes various allegations of abusive practices.

187. My observations are based on an examination of French TV guides for the month of October 1995, as well as on my viewing of French TV during most of that month.

188. Raymond Kuhn, ed., *The Politics of Broadcasting* (New York: St. Martin's Press, 1985), 76.

189. Paul Michaud, "The Midas Touch," *TV World* (May 1987): 103.

190. Alain Woodrow, "The French Correction," *Broadcast* (U.K.), 21 April 1989, pp. 38-39.

191. Roni Amelan, "Headliners: Jeanine Langlois-Glandier," *Broadcast* (U.K.), 15 April 1991, p. 8.

192. Birgitte Yallov, in Nick Jankowski, Ole Prehn and James Stappers, eds., *The People's Voice: Local Radio and Television in Europe* (London: John Libbey, 1992), 218.

193. A development actively encouraged by the French government: President Mitterand was largely responsible for the Council of Europe's "Eurimages" coproduction initiative in 1988-89. But lack of financial support limits its impact. Mario Hirsch and Vibeke Petersen, in Karen Siune and Wolfgang Truetzschler, eds., *Dynamics of Media Politics* (Newbury Park, Calif.: Sage, 1992), 50-52.

194. Jeff Kaye, "Italy's RAI on the Move; Link to France," *The Hollywood Reporter,* 10 April 1995, p. 7.

195. Kuhn, *Media,* passim (but esp. 135-37) provides a useful description of the many media activities of Hachette, Hersant and Havas.

196. Ted Clark, "Private TV Development Greenlight Sparks French Small-Screen Scene," *Variety,* 17 January 1986, pp. 32, 56.

197. Cluzel, "Presse," 18.

198. Cluzel, "Presse," 13.

199. Kuhn, *Media,* 104.

200. "French Feevee Net Can't Get Film Biz to OK Releases," *Variety,* 20 July 1983, pp. 89, 104.

201. Clark, "Private," 56.

202. "FR3—Dedicated to Quality Films," *Variety,* 28 March 1979, pp. 52, 64.

203. A useful source of information on developments in French cinema and television is the annual "Les chiffres cles de la télévision et du cinema—France 19__" (Paris: La Documentation Française, annual).

204. Tony Crawley, "Filmed in Comfyvision," *Paris Passion* 64 (September 1989): 44.

205. Véronique Cauhapé, "Les producteurs audiovisuel vont 'se battre' contre les conventions CSA-TF1-M 6," *Le Monde,* 24 September 1996.

206. Jochen Zimmer, *Europas Fernsehen im Wandel* (Frankfurt: Peter Lang, 1993), 254-57, provides a brief account of TV5, which has attracted little scholarly attention.

207. Ted Clark, "French Government Buys $500,000 Stake in Telefrance USA, Cable Feeder," *Variety,* 7 June 1978, pp. 52, 68.

208. Kaye, "Italy's RAI," p. 7.

209. "French Programme Exports Rise," *Broadcast* (U.K.) 20 (September 1996).

210. Douglas Boyd and John Benzies, "SOFIRAD: France's International Commercial Media Empire," *Journal of Communication* 33, no. 2 (1983): 56-69; personal interviews with SOFIRAD staff, Paris, September 1984.

211. Thomas, *Broadcasting,* 105.

212. Roland Dhordain, *Le Roman de la Radio* (Paris: La Table Ronde, 1983), 223-26.

213. Ross, in Cohen and Gourevitch, *France,* 172.

214. Kuhn, *Media,* 206.

215. "The Biarritz Network," *InterMedia* 13, nos. 4/5 (July-September 1985): 51.

216. Bill Grantham, "France Halts Plans for Hi-Tech Cable," *Variety,* 15 January 1987, p. 1.

217. Pia Farrell, "French Cablers Looking to Turn Corner on Profitability," *The Hollywood Reporter,* 8 January 1991, p. I-1.

218. Personal visit to Epinal, October 1995; discussions with staff of "Images Plus"; "Dossier de Presentation Images > Television (1995)" (presentational document prepared for potential advertisers, of whom there have been very few—the service's roughly $500,000 annual budget comes mostly from subscriber fees, some local sponsorship, and fees charged by Images Plus for video training courses and ad production).

219. Kuhn, *Media,* 220-28, concludes that a combination of political infighting and technological uncertainty sharply reduced any chances of success for DBS in France.

220. As of the end of March 1998, information about the Fair and IFI was available through the following website: http://www.fete-internet.fr. There was a mock trial held in connection with the Fair, where various individuals praised or

condemned the Net. "Dehumanization" was one of the more frequently leveled charges, and there were some fears of the Internet as a delivery belt for pornography. Radio and television devoted considerable coverage to the Fair, and France 3's weekly "Sur le Net" devoted an entire program to it.

221. "TPS and Renault Develop Interactive Ad," *screendigest* (December 1998): 285.

221a. Conseil d'État, *Internet et les Réseaux Numériques* (Paris: La Documentation Française, 1998).

222. Two particularly helpful sources on the subject of French cultural policy with respect to the electronic media are Cazenave and Ulmann-Mauriat, *Presse,* 210-13, and Marcel Machill, "Background to French Language Policy and Its Impact on the Media," *European Journal of Communication* 12, no. 4 (December 1997): 479-509.

223. Bill Grantham, "France Attempts to Halt Blurbs on TV Webs," *Variety,* 7 July 1987, p. 1.

224. Thiérry Védel and Jérome Bourdon, "French Public Service Broadcasting," in Robert Avery, ed., *Public Service Broadcasting in a Multicultural Environment* (New York: Longman, 1993), 50.

225. Jean-Claude Sergeant, "Government and Broadcast Media in France," in Meryl Aldridge and Nicholas Hewitt, eds., *Controlling Broadcasting* (Manchester: Manchester University Press, 1994), 241.

CHAPTER 3. THE NETHERLANDS

1. For general background information, see Arend Lijphart, *The Politics of Accommodation: Pluralism and Democracy in the Netherlands* (Berkeley: University of California Press, 1968); and Gerald Newton, *The Netherlands: A Historical and Cultural Survey, 1795-1977* (London: Ernest Benn, 1978). Kees van der Haak, *Broadcasting in the Netherlands* (London and Boston: Routledge and Kegan Paul, 1977), is a very useful, if dated, monograph. John L. Hiemstra, *Worldviews on the Air* (Lanham, Md.: University Press of America, 1997), is a fine source on the formative years of Dutch broadcasting. See also book chapters on the Netherlands: Wigbold, in Smith, *Television and Political Life* (1979); van der Haak, in Bertelsmann, *Television Requires Responsibility* (1995); McQuail, in Avery, *Public Service Broadcasting* (1993); Frachon and Vargaftig, *European Television* (1995); and Robillard, *Television in Europe* (1995).

2. Lijphart, *Politics,* 16-23, and Newton, *Netherlands,* 210-14, offer good explanations of societal tensions and of the concept of "pillars."

3. Marlise Simons, "Dutch Take 'Third Way' to Prosperity," *New York Times,* 16 June 1997, p. A6.

4. Van der Haak, *Broadcasting,* 7-8; P. Doorn and Y. Bommelje, *Ontkerkelijking en verzuiling: een onderzoek naar de invloed van kerken op publieke middelen in Nederland* (Utrecht: Humanistisch Verbond, 1987).

5. N. Tj. Swiestra, "The Birth of Broadcasting," *EBU Review* 114B (March 1969): 10-15.

6. Hiemstra, *Worldviews,* 113 (quotation from van der Deure of NCRV). Heimstra's work is based on many firsthand sources.

7. J. H. J. van der Heuvel, *Nationaal of Verzuild, de strijd om het Nederlandse omroepbestel in de periode 1923-1947* (Baarn: Ambo, 1976); Jan Wieten, "Television's False Dawn," *Gazette* 53, no. 3 (1994): 207-28.

8. J. De Boer, *Omroep en publiek in Nederland tot 1940* (Leiden: Sijthoff, 1946), 184.

9. Wigbold, in Smith, 196.

10. Newton, *Netherlands,* 121.

11. Dick Verkijk, *Radio Hilversum, 1940-1945* (Amsterdam: B. V. Uitgeverij Ardeiderpers, 1974); and Michael Crone, *Hilversum unter dem Hakenkreuz* (Munich: Saur, 1983), provide detailed accounts of Dutch broadcasting under the Nazis.

12. See Wigbold, in Smith, 197, for some interesting reflections on what a national system might have brought about.

13. Jan Wieten, "Radio Against Television: How Broadcasters Slowed Down the Introduction of Television in the Netherlands" (paper presented at the annual conference of the International Communication Association, Montréal, May 1997), is the source for much of the information about pre-World War II television in the Netherlands.

14. Lijphart, *Politics,* 183.

15. Karel Remes, "Prevention of Broadcasts Transmitted from Artificial Islands," *EBU Review* 90B (March 1965): 47-52, presents a detailed account of the legal maneuvers needed to authorize the invasion of TV Noordzee.

16. Lijphart, *Politics,* 59-67, indicates the direct links that existed at the time between the governing councils of the Dutch broadcasting organizations and the Dutch Parliament.

17. Wigbold, in Smith, 203-15, offers a detailed account of controversies over programming practices.

18. "Cable Television Pirates," *Broadcasting News from the Netherlands* 3 (1981): 5.

19. "U.S. Firms Irked by Dutch Pirates," *Wall Street Journal,* 21 September 1981.

20. Netherlands Scientific Council for Government Policy, *A Coherent Media Policy* (Den Haag: author, 1982).

21. Marit Bakke, in Denis McQuail and Karen Siune, eds., *New Media Politics: Comparative Perspectives in Western Europe* (Beverly Hills: Sage, 1986), 135.

22. "The 'Historic' Change Has Taken Place," *HilverSummary* (NOS) 4 (1989): 1.

23. Adam Dawtry, "Pubcaster Veronica Wins Stay of Execution," *The Hollywood Reporter,* 12 June 1990, p. I-4.

24. Sandra van Beek, "Dutch Pubcasters Plan to Reorganize," *The Hollywood Reporter,* 17 January 1991, pp. 44, 56.

25. Robert Allen, ed., *To Be Continued ... Soap Operas Around the World* (London: Routledge, 1995), 14; Hans Beerekamp, "New Channel Finds Dutch

Hungry for Home-Made Fare," *Variety,* 15 April 1991, p. M-106.

26. "Public Television in the Nineties," *HilverSummary* 1 (1991): 4-5.

27. "Broadcast, Broadcast, Narrowcast ... The Nineties!," *HilverSummary* 1 (1991): 1.

28. "Public Television in the Nineties," 4.

29. Beerekamp, M-106.

30. "Difficult Start for Independent Production Facilities Project," *HilverSummary* 1 (1989): 6-7.

31. "Regional Radio in the Netherlands," *HilverSummary* 2 (1988): 2-3.

32. "Public Radio Situation Worrying," *HilverSummary* 1 (199): 2-3; "Research into Media Habits of Migrant Children," *HilverSummary* 1 (1990): 3-4.

33. Dick Hussaarts, "Aandeel van het buitenland in omzet Endemol steeds groter," *De Telegraaf,* 23 October 1996.

34. Marlene Edmunds, "Endemol Practicing More German for News," *Variety,* 7-13 April 1997, p. 66; personal letter from Harrie Bos, NOS, 7 November 1997.

35. Matters could have been worse. TROS had often threatened to leave the pillar system, and the climate in 1994-95 produced many rumors that it was about to do so. It finally decided to remain with the pillars. That put an end to speculation that, if it did, the government would turn the third TV channel into a strictly commercial operation, since the remaining pillars wouldn't need it. Then-Minister of Culture Hedy d'Ancona had said as much in 1991 (Sandra van Beek, "Dutch Pubcaster May Go Private," *The Hollywood Reporter,* 11 June 1991, p. 13).

36. Noel van Bemmel, "RTL 5 maakt weinig kans als nieuweszender," *De Volkskrant,* 4 October 1996.

37. Jacques Geluk, "Het jij-nieuws van SBS 6 raakt kijker in het hart," *Arnhemse Courant,* 31 August 1996.

38. Commissie Publieke Omroep, *Terug naar het publiek* (Den Haag: author, 1996).

39. Mike Ackermans, "Nuis wil omroepen veel macht ontnehmen," *De Volkskrant,* 26 October 1996, p. 7.

40. Fokke Obbema, "EO-voorzitter verantwoordelijk voor Hilversumse revolutie," *De Volkskrant,* 26 September 1996; "Regerungsfracties zien wenig in NOS-plannen," *De Volkskrant,* 26 September 1996.

41. Denis McQuail, "Dutch Public Service Broadcasting," in Robert Avery, ed., *Public Service Broadcasting in a Multicultural Environment* (New York: Longman, 1993), 90-91.

42. Arnold Marseille, "Mediaraad: kijkgeld afschaffen," *De Gelderlander,* 18 May 1995; Remco Meijer, "Walter Etty: 'Publieke Omroep Achter Decoder,'" *Elsevier,* 21 September 1996.

43. Ruud Morees, Financial Director, STER, personal interview, Hilversum, October 1996.

44. Lidy Adlershoff, "Reclame-inkomsten STER op dieptepunt," *Adformatie,* 19 September 1996.

45. Henk Langerak, "Klap voor Ster," *Algemeen Dagblad,* 14 September 1996; "Omropeen moeten bezuinigen door minder reclame," *De Volkskrant,* 16 September 1996.

46. *De Nederlandse Reclame Code* (Dutch Advertising Code), Stichting Reclame Code, September 1996, 21-28.

47. Adriaan Hofland, VARA, personal interview, Hilversum, October 1996.

48. "Sponsorship Legally Regulated," *HilverSummary* (August 1994): 2, 3.

49. Van der Haak, in Bertelsmann, *Television,* 264-65.

50. Bill Third, "Progress Towards a More Liberated System," *TV World* (September 1981): 8.

51. Van Essen, "De kabelondernemer ..."

52. Henk Schutten, "Lanceren kanalen betaal-tv uitgesteld," *Het Parool,* 22 October 1996.

53. Raymond Snoddy and Andrew Jack, "Empire Builders Look to Spread the Pain," *Financial Times* (London), 9 September 1996.

54. Harrie Bos, head, Library Services, NOS, personal letter, 17 November 1997.

55. "Co-Production Fund," *HilverSummary* Special Edition (1993): 7.

56. "Long-term planning with a mission," *Hilversummary 3/4* (November 1998), 2-5; "Radical changes in Dutch media legislation," *HilverSummary 1* (March 1998,) 2-3.

56a. Van der Haak, *Broadcasting,* 47-48.

57. Harrie Bos, Documentation and Library Department, NOS, Hilversum, personal letter, 4 December 1987.

58. Freek Stoopendaal, VPRO, personal interview, Hilversum, October 1996.

59. Ibid.

60. Personal observation of VARA Annual Meeting, Hilversum, September 1972.

61. Hofland, interview, October 1996.

62. Van der Haak, *The Netherlands,* 267.

63. Kees van der Haak, NOS, personal conversation, Hilversum, October 1996.

64. "The Battles of Brinkman," *TV World* (February 1987): 44.

65. Kees van der Haak, "The Netherlands," in *Television Requires Responsibility* (Guetersloh, Germany: Bertelsmann Foundation and European Institute for the Media, 1995), 274. A report cited by van der Haak (p. 275) indicates that the Authority was not only very successful in freeing up the minister's time, but also brought far more consistency to decisions and a "tougher" image for the Media Act.

66. Van der Haak, "Netherlands," 275-76.

67. Serge Robillard, *Television in Europe: Regulatory Bodies* (London: John Libbey, 1995), 157-62; and Kees van der Haak, in Bertelsmann, *Television,* 274-76, provide fairly detailed descriptions of the duties and structure of the Authority.

68. Three excellent sources of information on local and regional broadcasting are Nick Jankowski and Anna-Lieke Mol, "Democratization of Communications and Local Radio in the Netherlands," in *RTV Theory and Practice Special Issue 3* (Belgrade: Radio Televizija Beograd, 1988), 97-121; Nick Jankowski, "The Netherlands: In Search of a Niche for Regional Television," in Miquel de Moragas Spa and Carmelo Garitaonandia, *Decentralization in the Global Era* (London: John

Libbey, 1995); and James Stappers et al., "The Netherlands: Emergence of a New Medium," in Nick Jankowski, Ole Prehn and James Stappers, eds., *The People's Voice* (London: John Libbey, 1992), 90-113.

69. The Council was displeased with what it saw as the overly leftist "tilt" of the station, and threatened to establish a second station, which would have a more "traditional" viewpoint. (Limburg is a strongly religious province.) And when Radio Limburg announced in December 1985 that it would broadcast a long report on Christmas Eve about leftist groups and their proposed activities for 1986, the station's broadcast council got the coordinator of regional programs at NOS to persuade the station to drop the program, at least on Christmas Eve. Staff members at STAD Radio (Amsterdam) and Radio Fryslan (Leeuwarden), my sources for those examples (personal visits, October 1986), clearly were disturbed by what they regarded as a threat to the independence of regional stations.

70. Stappers, "Netherlands," 96.

71. Gertjan van Schoonhoven, "Televisie over de heg," *Elsevier,* 21 September 1996, pp. 46-49.

72. Fred van Essen, "De kabelondernemer is geen bijbelse tollenaar," *DeGooien Eemlander,* 9 September 1996.

73. Bos, letter, 17 November 1997.

74. "Helping a Man to Kill Himself, As Shown on Dutch TV," *New York Times,* 13 November 1994, sec. 4, p. 7.

75. Van der Haak, in Bertelsmann, *Television,* 269-70.

76. "Dienstenbond tegen samenwerking NVJ met NVO," *De Journalist* (NVJ journal), 18 October 1996.

77. Wigbold, "Shaky," 223.

78. "NCRV: Television: A Quality Product," in *Broadcasting News From the Netherlands* (1985): 1, 5.

79. Wigbold, "Shaky," 207.

80. "Radio verliest terrein," *De Telegraaf,* 22 October 1996.

81. Personal visit to Radio Gelderland, Arnhem, October 1995.

82. Bos, letter, 17 November 1997.

83. Personal visit to Stadsomroep Arnhem, October 1995.

84. Arjan Peters, "'Zwarte sneeuw,' film de in stukjes wordt uitgezonden," *De Gelderlander,* 2 September 1996.

85. Tom H. A. van der Voort, "Radio and Television in the Dutch Open School," and Henk Jurgens, "The Open School—Present and Future," in *EBU Review* 33, no. 6 (November 1982): 25-29.

86. Anne van der Meiden, "Media Ethics and Media Morality in the Netherlands," in Thomas Cooper, ed., *Communication Ethics and Global Change* (New York: Longman, 1989), 89.

87. Bos, letter, 17 November 1997.

88. Hilde van den Bulck and Luc van Poecke, "National Language, Identity Formation, and Broadcasting," *European Journal of Communication* 11, no. 2 (June 1996): 228.

89. "NOS Audience Research," *Broadcasting News from the Netherlands* 1 (1987): 2.

90. Dick Wensink, "Kijkkunde," *VARA TV Magazine* 43 (26 October-1 November 1996): 66.

91. Letters from Bos, 4 September 1984 and 17 November 1997.

92. Rene Appel, "Bloed & buis," *VARA TV Magazine* 43 (26 October-1 November 1996): 6-9.

93. Ruud van der Schaft, "Kabelnetten moeten inspelen op wensen consument," *Kabelvisie* (September 1996). The figures are taken from a report by the Public Broadcasting Commission.

94. Aside from the works cited in this section, I have drawn much of my information on minorities and media in the Netherlands from visits to STOA (Utrecht, October 1996), Migrant TV (Amsterdam, September 1995), SALTO (Amsterdam, September 1995), and participation in the Second Assembly of the organization Public Broadcasting for A Multicultural Europe, Strassbourg, France, October 1995. I am particularly grateful to the head of STOA, Ed Klute, for his assistance.

95. "Harderwijk bekent kleur," and "Sound-Check," both in *Stoa-Magazine* 3, no. 3 (September 1995): 4-5, 7. STOA and OLON (the Association for Local Broadcasting), working together, have held workshops and published booklets to encourage local stations to work with minorities.

96. Gerard Reteig, Chief Editor of Migranttelevisie, transcript of press conference, Amsterdam, 29 August 1986. See Ineke Gooskens, "Experimenting with Minority Television in Amsterdam," in Jankowski, Prehn and Stappers, *Voice,* 225-34, for a more detailed discussion of the background to Migranttelevisie's creation and early years.

97. Personal interviews with Gerard Reteig and with Richard Troelstra (producer), "Migrant TV," Amsterdam, September 1995.

98. SALTO, *Jaarverslaag 1994* (Amsterdam: author, 1995), 50-51.

99. Bart Top and Monique Doppert, "Balance or Blunder: Recommendations for Reporting on Migrants" (Amsterdam: Working Group Migrants & the Media of the Netherlands Association of Journalists [NVJ], 1994).

100. STOA, "Allochtonen in Nederlands tv-dramas" (Utrecht: author, 1994), 18-20.

101. "Aanklacht moet leiden tot proefproces," *Meer Kleur in de Media* 3, no. 2 (October 1995): 4.

101a. "Long-term planning ..." *HilverSummary 3/4* (November 1998), 4.

102. Carl Bybee et al., "Determinants of Parental Guidance of Children's Television Viewing for a Special Subgroup: Mass Media Scholars," *Journal of Broadcasting* 26, no. 4 (1982): 697-710.

103. Tom H. A. van de Voort et al., "Determinants of Parental Guidance of Children's Television Viewing: A Dutch Replication Study" (paper presented at the annual conference of the International Communication Association, May 1991), 20.

104. Michael van Os, "Carlson: 'Op kinderen gerichte reclame wordt een hot issue,'" *Adformatie,* 10 October 1996.

105. Theo van Vugt, "Nederland pilot bij nieuwe aanval op kinderreklame," *Adformatie,* 10 October 1996.

106. "Reclame uit buitenland niet meer tegen te houden," *Adformatie,* 10 October 1996.

107. Van Vugt, "Nederland."

108. "Women in Dutch Broadcasting Seek to Contact Colleagues From Abroad," *Broadcasting News From the Netherlands* 2 (1984): 4.

109. "Allochtonen en vrouwen geen concurrenten," *Meer kleur in de media* 5 (December 1994): 2; "Fatima drinkt bier," *Meer kleur in de media* 4 (October 1994): 4.

110. "Beautiful or Bold," *HilverSummary* (May 1994): 3-6; "NOS Portrayal Department," *HilverSummary* (November 1998), 7.

111. Birgitte Yallov, "Women on the Air," in Jankowski, Prehn and Stappers, *Voice,* 218-19.

112. Bos, letter, 17 November 1997.

113. Ilse van der Velden, "Jeugd-Offensief," *VARA TV Magazine* (5-11 October 1996).

114. G. Cleveland Wilhoit and Harold De Bock, "'All in the Family' in Holland," *Journal of Communciations* 26, no. 4 (Winter 1976): 75-84.

115. Bos, letter, 17 November 1997.

116. Ibid.

117. "Briefly," *EBU Review* 37, no. 5 (September 1986): 22.

118. "Broadcasting and Culture in the Netherlands," *Broadcasting News from the Netherlands* 4 (1982): 2-3.

119. Bos, letter, 17 November 1997.

120. Piet Te Nuyl, "Sowing the Seeds of Pay TV," *InterMedia* 12, no. 1 (January 1984): 9-11.

121. James Fallon, "Netherlands Begins Project Testing Interactive Cable," *Multichannel News,* 8 December 1986, p. 28.

122. Paul Wessels, "Strijd om winkelen via Internet barst los," *NRC Handelsblad,* 9 September 1996.

123. Ruud van der Schaft, "Interaktieve tv bij Nozema," *AV Journaal,* 30 August 1996.

123a. "Europe ready for digital economy," *Eurecom,* 10, 4 (April 1998), 3.

124. Jaap Timmers, "Kijker kan zelf grasduinen in EO's Reality," *De Gooi- en Eemlander,* 9 September 1996.

125. Romana Abels, "Wie is God? op Internet," *Trouw,* 21 September 1996.

126. Bos, letter, 17 November 1997.

127. Jerome Schutijser, "De kijker zapt en wil geen video," *Algemeen Dagblad,* 28 September 1996; "Huurvideo: leuke avond voor leuke prijs," *Algemeen Dagblad,* 28 September 1996.

128. "Huurvideo."

129. "Filmnet Entangled," *Cable and Satellite Europe* (September 1986): 24.

130. Fred van Essen, "De kabelondernemer is geen bijbelse tollenaar," *De Gooi- en Eemlander,* 7 September 1996.

CHAPTER 4. GERMANY

1. General material on the two Germanies has been drawn largely from Michael L. G. Balfour, *Germany: The Tides of Power* (London and New York: Routledge, 1992); John Breuilly, *The State of Germany* (London and New York: Longman, 1992); Gordon Craig, *Germany 1866-1945* (New York: Oxford University Press, 1978); Mary Fulbrook, ed., *German History Since 1800* (New York: St. Martin's Press, 1997); Henry Kirsch, *The German Democratic Republic: The Search for Identity* (Boulder, Colo.: Westview Press, 1985); Golo Mann, *History of Germany Since 1789* (New York: Praeger, 1968); and Brian Reading, *The Fourth Reich* (London: Weidenfeld and Nicholson, 1995).

2. There are relatively few books in English that deal exclusively with the German electronic media, and none on its entire history. Vincent Porter and Suzanne Hasselbach, *Pluralism, Politics and the Marketplace: The Regulation of German Broadcasting* (London and New York: Routledge, 1991), mostly about the 1980s; and Arthur Williams, *Broadcasting and Democracy in West Germany* (Bradford: University of Bradford Press, 1976), which covers the period 1945-75, are the most comprehensive. Book chapters in English are quite plentiful (see Bibliography for full citations): Etzioni-Halevy, in author, 1987; Frachon and Vargaftig, in authors, 1995; Grosser, in Smith, 1979; Hickethier, in Weymouth and Lamizet, 1996; Hoffmann-Riem, "Germany," in author, 1996; Hofmann, "Germany," in Silj, *Television in Europe,* 1992; Kleinsteuber and Thomass, in de Moragas Spa and Garitaonandia, 1995; Robinson and Hildebrand, in Avery, 1993; Schulz, in Bertelsmann, 1995; Williams, in Kuhn, 1985. Hans Brack, *German Radio and Television: Organization and Economic Basis* (Geneva: European Broadcasting Union, EBU Monograph 6, 1972), is helpful on the subject of structure. There also are a few excellent books about mass media in Germany where the coverage of electronic media is quite thorough: Peter Humphreys, *Media and Media Policy in Germany,* rev. ed. (Oxford, U.K. and Providence, U.S.: Berg, 1994); John Sandford, *The Mass Media of the German-Speaking Countries* (London: Oswald Wolff, 1976). The most comprehensive German-language coverage for German broadcasting during the period 1919-45 is in Ansgar Diller, *Rundfunk im Dritten Reich* (Munich: Deutsche Taschenbuchverlag, 1980); Winfried Lerg, *Die Entstehung des Rundfunks in Deutschland* (Frankfurt: Knecht, 1965); Winfried Lerg, *Rundfunkpolitik in der Weimarer Republik* (Munich: Deutscher Taschenbuchverlag, 1980); Heinz Pohle, *Der Rundfunk als Instrument der Politik* (Hamburg: Hans Bredow Institut, 1955). The period 1945-79 receives careful examination in Hans Bausch, *Rundfunkpolitik Nach 1945* (Munich: Deutscher Taschenbuchverlag, 1980), 2 vols. Gitta Muhler-Achs, ed., *Bildersturm: Frauen in den Medien* (Munich: Verlag Frauenoffensiv, 1990), has several interesting chapters on women's professional experiences in the electronic media in West Germany. There's a fascinating article by Lore Walb, recounting her 30 years of service with the Bayerische Rundfunk, in Christa Schmerl, ed., *In die Presse geraten: Darstellung von Frauen in der Presse und Frauenarbeit in den Medien* (Cologne and Bonn: Boehlen Verlag, 1985). W. Arnold, ed., *Die Elektronischen Medien* (Heidelberg: R. von Decker & Co., 1984); and Hans Kleinstueber, *Rundfunkpolitik in der Bun-*

desrepublik (Opladen: Leske Verlag & Budrich GmbH, 1982), both are helpful in presenting the period just before the beginnings of commercial broadcasting. The early years of East German broadcasting get detailed if heavily biased treatment in Gerhard Walther, *Der Rundfunk in der Sowjetischen Besatzungszone Deutschlands* (Bonn: Deutscher Bundes-Verlag, 1961). Gunter Holzweissig, *Massenmedien in der DDR* (Berlin: Verlag Gebr. Holzapfel, 1989), is more up-to-date and less obviously biased. And finally, for readers of French, there are two books by Isabelle Bourgeois: *Radio et Télévision Publiques en Allemagne,* and *Radios et Télévisions Privées en Allemagne,* both published in Paris by CIRAC, in 1993 and in 1995.

3. Lerg, *Entstehung,* 197-201.

4. Pohle, *Rundfunk,* 140.

5. Eugen Hadamovsky, *Dein Rundfunk* (Munich: publisher unknown, 1934), 22.

6. Tangye Lean, *Voices in the Darkness* (London: Secker and Warburg, 1943), 20, quoting an unidentified source.

7. *Rundfunk in der Region* (Cologne: Verlag W. Kohlhammer, 1984), 211-16 and 267-76, offers some interesting accounts of regional radio in the Nazi era.

8. Henry Delfiner, *Vienna Broadcasts to Slovakia,* East European Monographs 7 (Boulder, Colo.: East European Quarterly, 1974).

9. Thierry Kubler, *Cognacq Jay 1940: La Télévision Française sous l'Occupation* (Paris: Editions Plume, Calman-Levy, 1990), deals with the Nazi-run television service in occupied Paris; John Swift, *Adventure in Vision* (London: John Lehman Ltd., 1950), 111-116, covers German use of television in Germany during World War II. There is also a highly useful collection of articles on German television from the 1920s, when it was experimental, to 1944, contained in *Historical Journal of Film, Radio and Television* 10, no. 2 (1990).

10. Hugh Trevor-Roper, ed. *Final Entries, 1945: The Diaries of Josef Goebbels* (New York: Putnam, 1978). There's an excellent example of Goebbels' dual behavior in the entry for 3 April 1945 (p. 305), where he expresses his dismay over the worsening situation but clearly feels that propaganda, especially a "pep talk" by Hitler, could help save the day. Hitler remained silent.

11. Sandford, *Mass Media,* 204.

12. Hofmann, "Germany," in Silj, *Television,* 526.

13. Kleinstuber, *Rundfunkpolitik,* 21. Humphreys, *Media,* 155-56, places this in the context of Adenauer's general "centralizing" ambition.

14. Bausch, *Rundfunkpolitik* 1, 252-57, also covered in Humphreys, *Media,* 148-49.

15. Gerard Braunthal, "Federalism in Germany—the Broadcasting Controversy," *Journal of Politics* 24, no. 3 (August 1962): 545-61.

16. Ibid.

17. Hofmann, "Germany," 530-31, discusses the implications of the court's decision.

18. Humphreys, *Media,* esp. 180-84; Williams, *Broadcasting,* 99-135.

19. Peter Grothe, *To Win the Minds of Men* (Palo Alto: Pacific Books, 1958),

111-13; personal viewing and listening to East German broadcasting, Berlin, June 1960.

20. As RIAS was an international station, supported jointly by the U.S. and West German governments and broadcasting from West Berlin primarily for listeners in East Berlin and East Germany, I do not cover its activities here. See Donald R. Browne, "History and Programming Policies of RIAS Berlin" (Ph.D. diss., University of Michigan, 1961); Donald R. Browne, *International Radio Broadcasting* (New York: Praeger, 1982), 132-35; and Donald R. Browne, "RIAS Berlin," in K.R.M. Short, ed. *Broadcasting over the Iron Curtain* (London: Croome-Helm, 1986), chap. 10.

21. *Contrast* (British film and TV magazine) (Autumn 1963): 40.

22. Douglas Boyd, "Broadcasting Between the Two Germanies," *Journalism Quarterly* 60, no. 2 (Summer 1983): 232-39; Fred Casmir, "Two Unusual East German Radio Stations," *Journal of Broadcasting* 12, no. 4 (Fall 1968): 323-26.

23. Lawrence Soley and John Nichols, *Clandestine International Broadcasting* (New York: Praeger, 1987), 74.

24. Bausch, *Rundfunkpolitik* 1, 630-37; Walter Mahle and Rolf Richter, *Communication Policies in the Federal Republic of Germany* (Paris: UNESCO, 1974), 65-71.

25. Bausch, *Rundfunkpolitik* 1, 630-37; Williams, *Broadcasting,* 113-19.

26. This highly complicated situation is covered in some detail in Humphreys, *Media,* 180-85.

27. Ibid., 236-38.

28. Ibid., 240.

29. Hans Bismark, *Neue Medientechnologie und grundgesetzliche Kommunikationsverfassung* (Berlin: Drucker und Humblot, 1982); Michael Schmidbauer and Paul Lohn, *Die Kabelprojekte in der Bundesrepublik Deutschland: Ein Handbuch* (Munich: K.G. Saur, 1983); Michael Schmidbauer, *Kabelfernsehen in der Bundesrepublik Deutschland: Die Interessen von Wirtschaft, Politik und Publikum* (Munich: K.G. Saur, 1982). Humphreys, *Media,* 193-285, presents a quite comprehensive picture of developments in cable.

30. Humphreys, *Media,* 234. Humphreys notes that the West German Publishers Federation had tried to develop much the same sort of system in 1981, but the venture, LUX-SAT, collapsed.

31. Ibid., 255-66; Hoffmann-Riem, *Regulating,* 120.

32. Bausch, *Rundfunkpolitik* 2, 951-65; Klaus Berg, "The 'Fourth Broadcasting Judgement' of the Federal Constitutional Court," *EBU Review* 38, no. 3 (May 1987): 37-43; Helmut Druck, "The End of an Era for German Broadcasting," *InterMedia* 8, no. 3 (May 1980): 13-17; Humphreys, *Media,* 180-85.

33. "East German Newscast Jumps," *Hollywood Reporter,* 6 November 1989, p. 1.

34. "Auf Wiedersehen, Herr Schnitzler," *TV World* (November-December 1989): 4.

35. Ron Holloway, "First Independent Station in East Germany Emerges," *Hollywood Reporter,* 28 August 1990, pp. I-1, I-8.

36. Ron Holloway, "German States Get New TV Stations," *Hollywood Reporter*, 6 July 1990, p. 1.

37. Holloway, "First," p. I-1.

38. Lawrence Gross, "Head Start for German Pubcasters," *Hollywood Reporter,* 6 November 1990, pp. 3, 94.

39. Lawrence Gross, "Kohl Earns Pubcasters Favor but Rest of Industry's Fury," *Hollywood Reporter,* 6 November 1990, pp. 3, 94.

40. Klaus Schoenbach and Beate Schneider, media researchers, Academy for Music and Theater, Hannover, Germany, conversations with author, Chicago, Illinois, 24 May 1991.

41. Ron Holloway, "New Stations Coming to Fruition," *Hollywood Reporter,* 18 June 1991, p. I-4.

42. Hans Juergen Bucher and Christian Schroeter, "Privat-rechtliche Hoerfunkprogramme," *Media Perspektiven* 8 (1990): 517-40.

43. Wolfgang Darschin and Bernward Frank, "Tendenzen im Zuschauerverhalten," *Media Perspektiven* 3 (1991): 188.

44. Ibid., 116, 123.

45. The two services were merged in the early 1990s, apparently in part as a response to political and public pressure to make better (more economical) use of public television's financial resources. The two satellite channels carried regular ARD and ZDF programming, for the most part, and most viewers already could receive it through terrestrial transmitters. The combined operation retains the title 3SAT, and includes Swiss and Austrian television public service programs.

46. HOT (Home Order Television) was established in October 1995 but at first was permitted only experimental status, and only in Munich and Nuremburg. German and European Union media law allows the broadcast of only one hour per day of home shopping transmissions. HOT's argument that it wasn't a broadcaster because it had no relevance to the influencing of public opinion didn't carry any weight at first. See Ridder, "Germany," in International Institute of Communications, *Media,* 78-79. Eventually, it was allowed to broadcast full time, and it was joined by a second such service, QVC Deutschland, in 1996.

47. Created in January 1997, and almost immediately in "hot water" with the German Association of Private Broadcasters (VPRT) because they claimed that it was yet another instance of "frequency stuffing," a process whereby PSBs allegedly create new services for cable in order to keep commercial broadcasters from filling the available slots. Andrew von Gamm, "Kinderkanal: Still Teething?," *TV World* (March 1997): 6.

48. Inge Grassle, *Der Europaische Fernseh-Kulturkanal ARTE: Deutsch-Franzoesische Medienpolitik zwischen europaeischem Anspruch und Nationaler Wirklichkeit* (Frankfurt and New York: Campus Verlag, 1995). While Arte is billed as "the European culture channel," the vast majority of its program material comes from ARD and ZDF on the German side, La Sept/Arte on the French side, with minor contributions from Swiss and Belgian PSBs. Most of the material consists of reruns.

49. "Hamburg: Frequenzstreit zwischen Deutschlandradio und Alternativfunk?," *Kirche und Rundfunk* 93 (26 November 1994): 21; "Privatfunk-Lobby at-

tackiert 'Frequenzfresser' Deutschlandradio," *Kirche und Rundfunk* 93 (26 November 1994): 21; personal visit to OK (Offene Kanaele) Radio, Hamburg, September 1995.

50. These observations are based on conversations I have had with media personnel and scholars during three visits to Germany in the 1990s. For the 1992 incidents, see Wilfried Ahrens, "Politicians Move to Restrict German B'caster Activities," *Hollywood Reporter,* 25 August 1992, p. I-1.

51. Hofmann, "Germany," 570. He sees a trend toward developing programs for export that will have a less distinctively German character, to enhance prospects for their sale abroad.

52. Not every state has agreed with the concept of subsidy, and in 1992 the Hessicher Rundfunk (Frankfurt) stated that it would no longer help to support the financially weak stations. (The total subsidy for 1992 was $135 million.) That drew criticism from other ARD state broadcasters, especially the wealthiest, WDR (Cologne), and eventually HR backed down. Wilfried Ahrens, "Public TV Channel ARD Facing Uncertain Future," *Hollywood Reporter,* 31 March 1992, p. I-5.

53. A good source of annual statistical information on fees, percentages of program categories carried by the various services, etc., is the periodical *Media Perspektiven's* annual "Basisdaten: Daten zur Mediensituation in Deutschland 199_."

54. "Urteil des Bundesverfassungsgerichts vom 22 Februar 1994," *Media Perspektiven—Dokumentation,* I/94. The court makes it abundantly clear that anyone possessing a set therefore has the *possibility* of watching the programs paid for by the fee, and cannot avoid paying it simply because he or she doesn't actually watch them. The court goes on to apply that logic to the "Kabelgroschen": the cable services supported by it are there to be used, whether one chooses to or not. See pp. 61-62.

55. Hofmann, "Germany," 526.

56. Humphreys, *Media,* 273, quoting from figures furnished through the European Institute for the Media.

57. Ibid.

58. Schulz, "Germany," in Bertelsmann, *Television,* 194.

59. Ibid.

60. Ibid. See also Hoffmann-Riem, "Germany," in author, *Regulating,* 139.

61. Wilfried Ahrens, "ARD, ZDF Fight for Advertising Deregulation," *Hollywood Reporter,* 23 September 1992, p. I-1.

62. Elke Baur, ... *und Frauen kommen vor* (Baden-Baden: E. Baur Verlag, 1980) (self-published, but interesting); Joachim Kotelmann and Lothar Mikos, *Fruehjahrsputz und Suedseezauber* (Baden-Baden: E. Baur Verlag, 1981), 59-77; Muehlen-Achs, *Bildersturm,* scattered references to advertising portrayals. Also author's personal observations.

63. Hans Mathias Kepplinger and Thomas Hartmann, *Stachel oder Feigenblatt?: Rundfunk- und Fernsehraete in der Bundesrepublik Deutschalnd: eine empirische Untersuchung* (Frankfurt: IMK, 1989), is a very thorough study of the councils and their problems.

64. Hoffmann-Riem, *Regulating,* 124.

65. "NDR Vizeintendant Sterling fristlos gekuendigt," *Kirche und Rundfunk* 60 (2 August 1995): 8.

66. Manfred Jenke, then Press Officer of the NDR, personal interview, Hamburg, September 1972.

67. "Versammlungsvorsitzender der LPR Hessen unter Protest zurueckgetreten," *Kirche und Rundfunk* 90 (16 November 1994): 19.

67a. "Staatsvertrag ueber den Suedwestrundfund," *Media Perspektiven: Dokumentation*1, 1997, 5-7.

68. Dirk Herkstroeter, "Die Entwicklung der Landesmediengesetze," *Rundfunk und Fernsehen* 42, no. 1 (1995): 60-81, covers the evolution of the media councils and the many differences they exhibit from state to state.

69. Schulz, "Germany," in Bertelsmann, *Television,* 206.

70. Klaus Schoenbach, Director of the Program in Journalism, Academy for Music and Theater, Hannover, Germany, personal interview, September 1995. I raised the question with Prof. Dr. Schoenbach because I had recently seen an episode from an RTL regional (for North Rhine-Westphalia) series entitled "10 for 11," broadcast from 11 to 11:30 p.m. An American musicologist who spoke excellent German gave an illustrated (with piano, but also with recorded excerpts) talk about Alban Berg's atonal opera "Wozzeck," linking it with modern film music. I couldn't understand why a commercial broadcast would want to carry such a program. The answer was that it wouldn't, but it had to! Hoffmann-Riem, *Regulating,* 133, notes a roughly similar requirement imposed on RTL Plus: to achieve somewhat better political balance (RTL Plus was regarded as conservative), it had to carry a "leftish" opinion program, "Spiegel TV." Conservatives attacked the program, but it did well enough to weather the attacks and remains on air.

71. Volker Lilienthal, "Die Gremienplage," Parts 1 and 2, *Kirche und Rundfunk* 61 and 64 (5 and 16 August 1995), offers a fairly detailed examination of some of the arguments. He includes examples of council members treating themselves to lavish "information-gathering" visits abroad and of political influence so endemic that one may wonder whether any council member *ever* arrives at a decision on other than political grounds.

72. Schulz, "Germany," in Bertelsmann, *Television,* 208.

73. It certainly is true that economic security for production staff can come with a high price tag. Yves Achille, *Les Télévisions Publiques en Quête d'Avenir* (Grenoble: Presses Universitaires de Grenoble, 1994), 194, cites an example from the Hessischer Rundfunk: a producer who has worked for more than 10 years, but then is terminated, will be paid her/his *full* salary until age 65.

74. Fritz Ossenbuhl, *Rechtsprobleme der Freien Mitarbeit im Rundfunk* (Frankfurt: Metzner [Beitraege zum Rundfunkrecht Heft 17], 1978), deals with legal protection for free-lance staff. A Federal Constitutional Court decision in 1982 gave employers somewhat more freedom to decide whether to hire, fire and retain free-lancers; see "Rundfunkfreiheit umfasst auch freie Auswahl der Programmarbeiter, *Media Perspektiven* (April 1982): 293-99.

75. Felicitas Merkel, *Rundfunk und Gewerkschaften in der Weimarer Republik und in der fruehen Nachkriegszeit* (Potsdam: Verlag fuer Berlin-Brandenburg, 1996).

76. One alleged (by the PTT) problem was finding a suitable frequency: West Germany had few broadcast frequencies available until 1986, both because the ARD stations took up so many frequencies, and also because German (and most other European) engineers were slow to reconsider spectrum use. Staff members at Radio 4 in Ludwigshafen told me in October 1986 that they felt that some of their requests for frequencies were handled slowly because of reasons just cited.

77. Porter and Hasselbach, *Pluralism,* 143, 186.

78. John Vinocur, "Television in West Germany Becomes Hot Political Issue," *New York Times,* 15 October 1979.

79. Evangelisch presse dienst (epd), "Kohl fuer ARD Strukturreform und gegen Gebuehren-erhoehung," *Kirche und Rundfunk* 9 (4 February 1995): 8-9; Uwe Kammann, "Wenn Chefsachen die Machtbalance aushebeln (sollen)," *Kirche und Rundfunk* 9 (4 February 1995): 3-4

80. Bausch, *Rundfunkpolitik* 2, 934-40.

81. Schulz, "Germany," in Bertelsmann, *Television,* 194.

82. Ibid., 250-61.

83. Mahle and Richter, *Communication,* 64.

84. Named for the Commission's founder, German President Richard von Weizsaecker. See Otfried Jarren and Gerhard Vowe, "Medienkritische Oeffentlichkeit als rundfunkpolitischer Akteur?," *Rundfunk und Fernsehen* 43, no. 1 (1995): 5-25, for a good summary of the Commission's conclusions and a fine analysis of the process by which its members arrived at them.

85. Barbara Eschenauer, "Audience Awareness and Audience Consumer Organizations: How Things Stand in Germany" (paper presented at the Second Conference of Public Broadcasting for a Multicultural Europe, Strasbourg, France, October 1995), 4.

86. Jo Groebel and Uli Gleich, *Gewaltprofil des deutschen Fernsehprogramms. Eine Analyse des Angebots privater und oeffentlich-rechtlicher Sender* (Opladen: Leske + Budrich, 1993).

87. Wilfried Ahrens, "Watchdog LFR Concerned about Violence on TV," *Hollywood Reporter,* 25 February 1992, p. I-4.

88. Holly Semetko and Klaus Schoenbach, *Germany's Unity Election* (Cresskill, N.J.: Hampton Press, 1993), provides a very complete description of political party use of television in an election.

89. Hoffmann-Riem, *Regulating,* 117.

90. Agreement on Broadcasting between the Federal States in United Germany, 31 August 1991, 3rd revision, 11 September 1996, Article 26, Sec. 2.

91. Schulz, "Germany," 190-91.

92. Those estimates are based on personal listening and viewing during five visits to Germany over the period 1986-96, and on examination of selected program guides from eight years during that period.

93. Personal visit and listening to Radio 4, October 1986; Walter Klingler and Elfriede Walendy, "Radio 4: kommerzielle Hoerfunkkonkurrenz in Rheinland-Pfalz," *Media Perspektiven* (July 1986): 444-55; Hansjoerg Bessler, "Lokaler Rundfunk—grosse Hoffnung, schlechte Aussichten," *Media Perspektiven* (November 1987): 725-32.

94. Otfried Jarren and Manfred Knoche, "Mit dem Hoerfunk ins Lokale," *Media Perspektiven* (March 1981): 188-203; Otfried Jarren and Peter Widlok, eds., *Lokalradio* (Berlin: Vistas Verlag, 1985); Hans J. Kleinstueber, *Radio—das unterschaetzte Medium* (Berlin: Vistas Verlag, 1997); personal visits to Kurpfalz Radio, Heidelberg, and Radio 4, Ludwigshafen, October 1986.

95. Ralph Weiss, "Von 'Lichterketten' zum 'Buergerkrieg,'" *Rundfunk und Fernsehen* 42, no. 2 (1994): 149-70.

96. Nuremburg's Radio Z drew a DM 10,000 ($6,500) fine for broadcasting a "Leatherseries" in June 1994, on the grounds that it "endangered" young listeners to hear some of the rough language and descriptions of activities. The station had been penalized earlier for broadcasting pornographic material. See "10,000 Mark Bussgeld fuer Radio Z," *Kirche und Rundfunk* 80 (12 October 1994): 20.

97. "Nichtkommerzielle Radios koennen kuenftig Gebuehrengelder bekommen," *Kirche und Rundfunk* 15 (28 February 1995): 11; "Ministerpraesidenten stimmen Gebuehrenerfoerderung freier Radios zu," *Kirche und Rundfunk* 21 (18 March 1995): 13.

98. Christof Busch, *Was Sie immer schoen ueber Freie Radios wissen wollten, aber nie zu fragen wagten!* (Frankfurt: Zweitausendeins Versand, 1981), 185-91.

99. B. U. Biere and H. Henne, eds., *Sprache in der Medien Nach 1945* (Tuebingen: Niemeyer, 1993).

100. Karl Karst, "Regionalsprache im Massenmedium," in *Rundfunk in der Region* (Cologne: Verlag W. Kohlhammer, 1984), 251-324.

101. A September 1995 episode of "Das RTL Magazin" that I watched led off with a story about famous German males who had problems with alcoholism; the subject was treated very seriously. The second story dealt with a German mass murderer, and was definitely sensational. The third story, on emergency automobile services available on the autobahn (expressway), again was very straightforward. The fourth, on prostitution in vacation spots frequented heavily by German tourists, decidedly was sensational, with frontal nudity and more. Interestingly, the locals blamed the Russian Mafia for setting up much of the business.

102. "Home Grown Humour," *TV World* (October 1996): 107.

103. "'Tatorte' und 'Polizeirufe' sollen weniger Gewalt enthalten," *Kirche und Rundfunk* 90 (16 November 1994): 17-18.

104. Alan Cowell, "Even if German TV Doesn't Blush, You Might," *New York Times*, 13 February 1997, p. A4.

105. "Germans Want Reality TV Ban," *Hollywood Reporter*, 23 February 1993, p. I-1.

106. "Meet Motzki: He's Vulgar, Racist, Has Germany Edgy," *Hollywood Reporter*, 23 February 1993, pp. I-1, I-8. The show's creator, Wolfgang Menge, also created "One Heart, One Soul," and with much the same hope: to get Germans to confront the sometimes unpleasant sides of themselves.

107. Georg Feil, *Zeitgeschichte im Deutschen Fernsehen* (Osnabruck: Fromm, 1974).

108. Guido Knopp, "Contemporary History on Zweites Deutsches Fernsehen," *EBU Review* 82, no. 2 (1987): 22-26; James Markham, "West German TV

Specials Spark Debate on Reconciliation with Nazi Era," *New York Times,* 24 April 1985, sec. 3, p. 17; Richard Crouter, "German People Deserve Credit for Confronting Their Painful Past," *Minneapolis Star Tribune,* 26 September 1992, p. 17A.

109. Personal viewing, Berlin, September 1995.

110. Udo Michael Krueger, "Kontinuitaet und Wandel im Programmangebot," *Media Perspektiven* 6 (1993): 246-66. His study appears in *Media Perspektiven* annually at about the same time (early to mid summer). Humphries, *Media,* 275-76, provides a brief summary of Krueger's study, and notes that another study, by members of the Euromedia Research Group, seems to confirm his findings. See Karen Siune and Wolfgang Treutzschler, eds., *Dynamics of Media Politics* (London and Newbury Park, Calif.: Sage, 1992), 75-100. Again, that study is based primarily on category of programming, and doesn't provide a closer analysis of quality of content—a time-consuming and highly subjective task, to be sure! Also, the study was undertaken at the beginning of 1991, before the commercial stations had become as fully competitive in terms of distribution as they would by 1993.

111. The leading German weekly news magazine, *Der Spiegel,* examined the newscasts of the "Big Four" in 1995, and felt that the private services did a better job in terms of clarity of story, separation of leading stories of the day and background reports, and illustration of points. They found that younger viewers in particular were drawn to the RTL Plus and SAT1 newscasts. "Blutige Bilder," *Der Spiegel,* 4 September 1995, pp. 61, 64.

112. Steven Kinzer, "Quiet Airwaves? Teen-Agers Say No," *New York Times,* 28 December 1991, p. 5.

113. Grothe, *To Win,* 97-98.

114. When I visited Dresden in October 1972, I shared a table at a restaurant with an East German who talked mostly about how he loved watching travelogues. He said he wished that he could travel outside the "socialist world," but what really made him angry was the fact that the Olympic Games were going on in Munich, less than 100 miles away; he could easily have afforded to go there, but getting permission to do so (unless one was an athlete, which he certainly wasn't!) was out of the question.

115. Hans-Dieter Kubler et al., *Kinderfernsehsendungen in der Bundesrepublik und in der DDR: eine vergleichende Analyse* (Tuebingen: Niemayer, 1981).

116. Gunter Holzweissig, *Massenmedien in der DDR* (Berlin: Verlag Gebr. Holzapfel, 1989), 120-21.

117. Hansjorg Bessler, *Hoerer-und Zuschauerforschung* (Munich, 1980), provides details of audience research in Germany through the late 1970s.

118. "Wir sehen uns nicht in Konkurrenz zur GfK," *BlickpunktFilm (Daily),* 17 October 1996, p. 3.

119. *Media Perspektiven Basisdaten: Daten zur Mediensituation in Deutschland, 1996* (Frankfurt: Media Perspektiven, 1996), 70.

120. Wolfgang Darschin and Bernward Frank, "Tendenzen im Zuschauerverhalten," *Media Perspektiven* (April 1997): 175.

121. Ibid., 179-81.

122. Earlier studies include F. Boeckelmann et al., *Werbefernsehkinder*

(Berlin: Speiss, 1979); Hertha Sturm et al., *Emotionale Wirkungen des Fernsehens—Jugendliche als Rezipienten* (Munich: Verlag Dokumentation, 1978).

123. Bessler, *Hoerer,* 314-20; Karsten Renckstorf and Lutz Roland, *Nachrichtensendungen in Fernsehen* (Berlin: Volker Spiess, 1980); Wilfried Sharf, *Nachrichten in Fernsehen der Bundesrepublik und der DDR* (Freiburg im Breisgau: Verlag Karl Alber, 1976).

124. T. Bruns and F. Marcinkowski, *Politische Information im Fernsehen: Ein Langsschrittstudie* (Opladen: Leske und Budrich, 1997).

125. Christine Holtz-Bacha, *Ablenkung oder Abkehr von der Politik?* (Opladen, 1990). I am indebted to Prof. Dr. Hoffmann-Riem for his assistance in pointing out this overall change.

126. "Bredow-Studie: Fernsehen kein Familienmedium mehr," *Kirche und Rundfunk* 80 (12 October 1994): 19.

127. "Trotz Grimme-Preis-Nominierung: 'Gletscherclan' abgesetzt," *Kirche und Rundfunk* 3 (14 January 1995): 18.

128. Christa Braumann, "Fernsehforschung zwischen Parteilichkeit und Objektivitaet: Zur Zuschauerforschung in der ehemaligen DDR," *Rundfunk und Fernsehen* 42, no. 4 (1994): 524-41, provides an insider view of how audience research had to be conducted in line with SED party policy.

129. Christa Oehme, Head, Audience Research, personal interview, Berlin (East Germany), September 1972.

130. Gerhard Gmel, Suzanne Deimling and Juergen Bortz, "Die Nutzung des Mediums Fernsehen in der DDR vor und nach die Wende," *Rundfunk und Fernsehen* 42, no. 4 (1994): 542-54.

131. Chief sources informing this section include my own viewing and visits in September-October 1995 to Offene Kanaele in Hamburg and Berlin, Sender Freies Berlin's "MultiKulti" radio service, ZDF's "Nachbarn" department (Mainz), and SDR's (Stuttgart) *Auslaenderredaktion,* plus Frachon and Vargaftig, "Germany," in authors, *European Television,* 159-80.

132. Berndt Fischer, head of "Nachbarn" staff, personal interview, Mainz, September 1995. Herr Fischer expressed his deep disappointment over ZDF's decision to cancel the program, which cost little to produce. I watched the final broadcast (October 1), at the end of which an announcer stated that viewers had just seen the last transmission, thanks to the decision of the ZDF administration to cancel the series.

132a. Christian Breunig, "Offener Fernseh—und Hoerfunkkanaele in Deutschland," *Media Perspektiven.* 5/98, 236.

133. Information provided by Uwe Krautenmacher, OK Hamburg, and Juergen Linke, OK Berlin, in personal interviews conducted in Hamburg and Berlin, September 1995.

134. The survey was undertaken by the Institute for Media Studies of the Technical University of Berlin. Its N was 306 respondents, 209 of whom had cable. Two respondents said that they listened to OK Radio on a regular (once or more a week) basis. As for OK-TV, 1.7 percent said that they listened daily, 7.6 percent several times a week, 11.6 percent several times a month, 43 percent seldom, and 36 percent never. Personal letter from Clement Schwendler, Institute for Media

Studies, 4 October 1995. Breunig, "Offene," 247, briefly cites survey, showing higher figures, but these are for both radio and TV, with no separate figures for radio.

135. Friedrich Voss, Director, SFB 4-MultiKulti, personal interview, Berlin, September 1995; Reinhard Buenger, "Offen fuer Neues," *agenda* 18 (March-April 1995): 46-47.

136. Volker Lilienthal, "Fremde Blick: Auslaender im Deutschen Fernsehen," two-part series in *Kirche und Rundfunk* 40 and 42 (24 and 31 May 1995): 5-9, 12-16.

137. Christof Butterwegge, "Mass Media, Immigrants, and Racism in Germany: A Contribution to an Ongoing Debate," *European Journal of Communications Research* 21 (1996): 203-20.

138. Martin Kilgus, SDR Auslaenderredaktion, personal interview, Stuttgart, October 1996.

139. Faruk Sen, "Medienkonsum und Medienverhalten der Tuerkischen Wohnbevoelkerung in der Bundesrepublik Deutschland," Essen: Zentrum fuer Tuerkeistudien, Universitat Essen, *ZfT aktuell* 31 (February 1995): 6-8.

140. Josef Eckhardt, "Nutzung und Bewertung von Radio-und Fernsehsendungen fuer Auslaender," *Media Perspektiven* 8 (1996): 460. The studies by Sen and Eckhardt, and by SDR (Stuttgart) on émigré viewing and listening habits ("SDR—Auslaenderbefragung 1993") showed that Turkish households in particular were listening far less to radio broadcasts in Turkish that were broadcast by ARD state stations; the declines from the beginning of the 1990s, when Turkish TV services became available in some number through satellite and cable, were very steep: a 1990 survey of émigrés in North Rhine-Westphalia showed "never listen" figures for Turks at 6 percent, but 1995 figures of 75 percent (Eckhardt, 452).

141. My observations are based on my viewing of the association's programs over cable channel 9 in Munich, October 1996, and on the association's substantial information packet.

142. Schulz, *Germany,* 209.

143. Kate Lacey, *Feminine Frequencies: Gender, German Radio, and the Public Sphere, 1923-1945* (Ann Arbor: University of Michigan Press, 1996).

144. Lore Walb, "Lehrstueck: Frauenrolle Aspekte einer Frauenfunkgeschichte zwischen 1945 und 1979" in Christiane Schmerle, ed., *In die Presse Geraten: Darstellung von Frauen in die Presse und Frauenarbeit in die Medien* (Cologne and Vienna: Boehlen Verlag, 1985), 215-48. The Strauss observation occurs on p. 240.

145. Information on the 1975 study and its aftermath comes from a chapter by von Boenningham in Gitta Muehlen-Achs, ed., *Bildersturm: Frauen in den Medien* (Munich: Verlag Frauenoffensive), 128-40; on the "Sour Pickle" award, from "'Saure Gurke 1994' fuer den NDR-Film 'Made in Hongkong,'" *Kirche und Rundfunk* 94 (30 November 1994): 15; and on the 1981 study from a chapter by Schaad in Muehlen-Achs, *Bildersturm,* 184-85. Further studies of various aspects of women in and on the electronic media can be found in Romy Froehlich and Christine Holz-Bacha, with Jutta Velte, *Frauen und Medien: eine Synopse der*

Deutschen Forschung (Opladen: Westdeutscher Verlag, 1995).

146. Anne Rose Katz, "Ganz Ohne Weiber Geht die Chose Nicht," in Muehlen-Achs, *Bildersturm,* 122, 127.

147. Annedore von Donop, Doris Hepp and Liane Jensen, "NOVA: Ein Nachrichten magazin von Frauen," in Muehlen-Achs, *Bildersturm,* 156-63. The *von* in the title is important, because it signifies a program *by* women—at the time a rare event, and not much more common today, at least on national television.

148. Wolfgang Hoffmann-Riem, note to author, 4 November 1997; Eva Lettenmeier, "Von Frauen und Reichweiten," *infosat* (the SAT-TV multimedia and online magazine) 115 (October 1997): 76; Jochen Zimmer, note to author, 4 November 1997.

149. Sandford, *Mass Media,* 81; Bausch, *Rundfunkpolitik* 2, 637-40.

150. Williams, *Broadcasting,* 131-33.

151. Grosser, "West Germany," in Smith, *Television,* 1979.

152. Anthony Smith, *The Politics of Information* (London: Macmillan, 1978), 54-73; Humphreys, *Media,* 189-90; Bausch, *Rundfunkpolitik* 2, 817-29.

153. Jochen Zimmer, note to author, 4 November 1997, indicates that the SPD has become far more pro-commercial in its media policy, although it remains more critical of media concentration and more positively disposed toward the PSBs than is the CDU.

154. "Falscher Mann" and "Unselige Verquickung," both in *Der Spiegel* 34, 21 August 1995, pp. 80-81.

155. Porter and Hasselbach, *Pluralism,* 124.

156. Even the highly successful Italian media baron Silvio Berlusconi could not crack this group. He was a major investor in Tele-5, which was supposed to be the third national commercial "mixed program" (as compared with "specialized program," e.g. all-sports or -news) service. But RTL Plus managed to keep Tele-5 from securing the number of land-based transmitters it would have needed to be successful (Hoffmann-Riem, *Regulating,* 156, note 7), and it was converted into the all-sports service, DSF, in 1992, with Thomas Kirch, son of Leo Kirch, as its single largest investor.

157. "Der Kampf um Schuerfrechte," *Der Spiegel* 35, 28 August 1995, p. 104; Nathaniel Nash, "A Dominant Force in European TV," *New York Times,* 28 August 1995, p. C1.

158. The U.S. entertainment industry magazine *Hollywood Reporter* published a lengthy and quite sycophantic tribute to Kirch and his company in 1992. Despite the absence of any truly critical appraisal, it contains a number of revealing insights on Kirch, especially on how he assembled the massive feature-film library that has been key to his success, and how he has leveraged it to build his "media empire." "The Player," *Hollywood Reporter,* special issue: Kirch Group Salute, 1992. More revealing yet is a document prepared by the Kirch Group and entitled "Perspektiven einer vorwaertsgerichteten Medienpolitik," reprinted in *Kirche und Rundfunk* 84 (26 October 1994): 23-26, which states that deregulation should be the dominant aspect of German media politics for the private sector, and denounces the existing council-based regulatory system as "worn out."

See also Martin Blaney, "Market Forces," *TV World* (October 1997): 71-72. There also is a book about Kirch: Michael Radtke, *Ausser Kontrolle—Die Medienmacht des Leo Kirch* (Munich: Edition Hans Empf, 1996).

158a. See "Vorbehalt von Springer," *Der Spiegel,* 50 (December 1998), p. 78.

159. Each year's edition of *Media Perspektiven Basisdaten* contains diagrams of the media holdings of the largest groups.

160. Hoffmann-Riem, *Regulating,* 123.

161. Porter and Hasselbach, *Pluralism,* 143.

162. Hoffmann-Riem, *Regulating,* 135-39, has an excellent description of the attempts made by the councils to prevent concentration of power, and the main reasons why those attempts have been unsuccessful, by and large. See also Humphreys, *Media,* 276-85. There is an annual summary of the activities of the "Big Four" and others: see Horst Roeper, "Formation deutscher Medienmultis 1996," *Media Perspektiven* 5/97 (April 1997): 226-55.

163. Frederick Stuedemann, "Telekom Silent on TV Network," *Financial Times,* 21 November 1997, p. 18; "Deutsche Telekom—Europe's number one in telecommunications," September 1998, available through the DT web site: *http://deutschetelekom.de/english/company/profile.*

164. Harald Keller, "Spiel mit dem Zuschauer," *Stuttgarter Nachrichten, Querschnitt* (weekend magazine), 30 September 1995, p. 2, notes Pro 7's attempt to rise in the ratings through more German production, and discusses its heavy production investment in a "psychological thriller," "Der Sandmann."

165. Itself something of an art. In 1992, one of the private channels acquired "Hogan's Heroes" and it attracted very few viewers. Kabel 1 (no longer in service) decided to try it again in mid-1997, and this time had the dubbers use heavy Bavarian and Swabian accents for the German characters, to make them more comical. Some of the story lines were revised, as well: discussion of a Nazi plan to blitz London became a bombardment of Britain with condoms, so that the Germans would win the war through birth control. Nazi salutes no longer were accompanied with "Heil Hitler," but with, "This is how high the cornflowers grow!" The series did much better in the ratings. Alan Cowell, "Hogan! Germans Need You," *New York Times,* 20 July 1997, sec. 4, p. 3.

166. "TV-Barometer," *HoerZu* 41 (16-22 September 1997): 105.

167. Isabelle Bourgeois, *Radio et Télévision Publiques en Allemagne* (Paris: CIRAC, 1993), 89, feels that the "star" system is far more prominent in French public and private television news programs than it is in Germany. Having watched a large number of French and German newscasts over the years, I would agree. But I would also observe that, although private television became important in both countries at about the same time, the introduction of private TV seemed to fuel the growth of the star system in France, but had far less effect in Germany. My best guess is that the Germans take the news far more seriously than do the French. Given the history of broadcast journalism in France, perhaps such a difference in attitudes wouldn't be surprising.

168. I watched both shows in October 1996. One of the odder skits on "Benissimo" featured Ben teaching viewers how to steal items from a department store. Obvious as he was, he didn't get caught.

169. *Mass Media in the Federal Republic of Germany* (Bonn: InterNationes, 1974), 28-30; Bausch, *Rundfunkpolitik* 2, 566-77.

170. "RTL wird Mitgesellschafter der Filmstiftung NRW," *epd-medien* 72 (17 September 1997): 8; "Einen Beitrag leisten," *epd medien* 74 (24 September 1997): 18.

171. Quoted in Billy Kocian, "Axing of Film Shows in Germany Rapped," *Hollywood Reporter,* 10 November 1987, p. I-10.

172. "Das Kino boomt: Faeddich?," *Journal fuer Deutschland* (Deutsche Bundesbahn) (October-November 1996): 18-19; "Werner Beinhart," *TV World* (May 1997): 29.

173. Bausch, *Rundfunkpolitik* 2, 874. Jan Tonnemacher, "The New Media in West Germany," *InterMedia* 10, no. 2 (March 1982): 18-26, indicates that there was very little public interest in cable at the time.

174. Bausch, *Rundfunkpolitik* 2, 878 (translation mine).

175. There are many articles on the digitalization issue. Here, in chronological order, are some that I found helpful. Martin Blaney, "Bouquets of Barbed Wire," *TV World* (October 1996): 103-4; Edmund Andrews, "German Media Giant Struggles," *New York Times,* 31 March 1997, p. C8; Candy Harper, "Germany's Rocky Road," *Cable World,* 7 April 1997, pp. 36, 40; Edmund Andrews, "Digital Pay TV in Germany," *New York Times,* 28 April 1997, p. C1; Edmund Andrews, "German Effort on Digital Moves Ahead," *New York Times,* 3 July 1997, p. C4.

176. *Media Perspektiven Basisdaten 1996,* 64, 65; *Media Perspektiven Basisdaten 1997,* 64.

177. *Media Perspektiven Basisdaten 1996,* 68, 69, where the source is listed simply as MA (96).

178. Ibid., 66.

178a. "Abonnenten ueberregionaler Onlinedienste 1997/1998," *Media Perspektiven* 8, 1998, 442; and "ARD/ZDF-Online-Studie 1998," *Media Perspektiven* 8, 1998, 423.

178b. "Welt im Blauraum," *Kirche und Rundfunk* 28 (12 April 1995): 7-8; "Wer nichts wird, wird virtuell," *Der Spiegel* 35, 26 August 1996, pp. 98-100.

179. Michael Krekeler, "Mit Radio auf Surfer-Fang," *Medien Bulletin* 10/96 (October 1996): 26-29.

180. Karl Ewald, Christoph Gscheidle and Christian Schroeter, "Professionalisierung und Spezialisierung im Onlinemedium," *Media Perspektiven* 10/98, 508-523.

181. Edmund Andrews, "German Judge Dismisses Criminal Charge Over Internet Link," *New York Times,* 1 July 1997, p. C7.

182. Ridder, *Media Perspektiven* 1996, 69-73, provides a summary of the contrasting positions, which were hotly debated during 1995.

183. Ibid., 72.

183a. Dieter Doerr, "Die KEK—ein taugliches Instrument zur Bekaempfung der Medienkonzentration?" *Media Perspektiven* 2/98, 54-60.

184. Bertelsmann would appear to be the strongest contender, particularly in light of the 1997 merger of its subsidiary UFA with the Companie Luxembour-

geoise de Television (CLT). Martin Blaney, "CLT-UFA Merger Buries Old Rivalries," *TV World* (March 1997): 10.

185. "Milliarden-grab," *Der Spiegel* 31, 28 July 1997, p. 64.

CHAPTER 5. THE SOVIET UNION AND RUSSIA

1. For general background on the Soviet Union, see Frederick Barghoorn and Thomas Remington, *Politics in the USSR,* 2nd ed. (Boston: Little, Brown, 1986); David Shipler, *Broken Idols, Solemn Dreams* (New York: Times Books, 1983); David MacKenzie and Michael Curran, *A History of Russia and the Soviet Union* (Homewood, Ill.: Dorsey Press, 1982). For background on the transition period and the Russian Republic, see Jerry Hough, *Democratization and Revolution in the USSR, 1985-1991* (Washington, D.C.: Brookings Institution, 1997); Anatoly Khazanov, *After the USSR: Ethnicity, Nationalism and Politics in the Commonwealth of Independent States* (Madison, Wis.: University of Wisconsin Press, 1995); Thomas Remington, ed., *Politics and the Soviet System* (London: Macmillan Press, 1989); David Remnick, *Resurrection: The Struggle for a New Russia* (New York: Random House, 1997); Michael Urban, *The Rebirth of Politics in Russia* (Cambridge, U.K.: Cambridge University Press, 1997); and Stephen White, Alex Pravda and Zvi Gitelman, *Developments in Russian & Post-Soviet Politics* (Durham, N.C.: Duke University Press, 1994). There are many books in English and a few in other languages about broadcasting and other mass media in the Soviet Union and Russia: Elena Androunas, *Soviet Media in Transition* (Westport, Conn.: Praeger, 1993), provides the perspective of one who was on the scene as the transition from U.S.S.R. to Russian Republic was taking place. Robert Campbell, *Soviet and Post-Soviet Telecommunications: An Industry Under Reform* (Boulder, Colo.: Westview Press, 1995), treats technological aspects of television as one element of telecommunications; Kristian Feigelson, *L'URSS et Sa Télévision* (Paris: Institut Nationale de l'Audiovisuel, 1990), has many examples of programming practices; Gladys Ganley, *Unglued Empire: The Soviet Experience With Communication Technologies* (Norwood, N.J.: Ablex, 1996), is quite thorough on the transition between the U.S.S.R. and the Russian Republic; Julian Graffy and Geoffrey Hoskins, eds., *Culture and the Media in the USSR Today* (New York: St. Martin's Press, 1989), has a number of contributions on programming in the last years of Soviet TV; Mark Hopkins, *The Mass Media in the Soviet Union* (New York: Pegasus, 1970), despite its age, is one of the best works on how ideology was integrated with the mass media. Yasha Lange, *Media in the CIS: a Study of the Political, Legislative and Socio-Economic Framework,* a report prepared for the European Commission by the European Institute for the Media (Brussels: The European Commission, May 1997), contains detailed synopses of media activity not only in Russia, but also in all of the other former Soviet republics. Ellen Mickiewicz has the longest and most solid scholarly track record in terms of politics and informational broadcasting, coupled with audience analysis: *Media and the Russian Public* (New York: Praeger, 1981); *Split Signals: Television and Politics*

in the Soviet Union (New York: Oxford University Press, 1988); and *Changing Channels: Television and the Struggle for Power in Russia* (New York: Oxford University Press, 1997). Brian McNair, *Glasnost, Perestroika and the Soviet Media* (London: Routledge, 1991), is very helpful on the Gorbachev era. Burton Paulu, *Radio and Television Broadcasting in Eastern Europe and the Soviet Union* (Minneapolis: University of Minnesota Press, 1974), is a servicable account of program types and decision-making. Reino Paasalinna, *Glasnost and Soviet Television* (Helsinki: YLE, 1995), emphasizes the policy conflicts of the Gorbachev era. Nicholas Pulagin and Svetlana Kolesnik, *Media Regulation in the Russian Federation,* 1997, accessible through website www.internews.ras.ru/report/media.html, has detailed treatment of regulatory structures and processes. Thomas Remington, *The Truth of Authority: Ideology and Communication in the Soviet Union* (Pittsburgh, Pa.: University of Pittsburgh Press, 1988), places the media in the broader context of political education and control. Paul Roth, *Die kommandierte oeffentliche Meinung* (Stuttgart: Seewald Verlag, 1982), provides translated (from Russian into German) extracts from various documents—proclamations, personal letters, etc.—relating to the development and use of the mass media in the Soviet Union. Scott Shane, *Dismantling Utopia: How Information Ended the Soviet Union* (Chicago: Ivan Dees, 1994), is a reporter's account of the "information revolution" in the Gorbachev years. Ivan Sigal, *A Survey of Russian Television,* prepared in April 1997 for USAID (Washington) and available through website www.internews.ras.ru/report/tv/index.html, furnishes a condensed guide to recent developments in Russian TV. Georgui Vatchnadze, (George Vachnadze for *Secrets of Journalism*), *Les Medias sous Gorbatchev* (Paris: Editions de l'Espace Europeen, 1991), and *Secrets of Journalism in Russia* (Commack, N.Y.: Nova Science Publishers, 1992), furnishes the viewpoint of a (Georgian) journalist turned academic, and is particularly useful on matters of censorship. See also Phillip Drummond, Richard Paterson and Janet Willis, eds., *National Identity in Europe: The Television Revolution* (London: British Film Institute, 1993), which has three interesting if brief chapters by Muratov, Sagalaev and Skillen on aspects of broadcast journalism under the Soviet and Russian governments.

2. Campbell, *Soviet,* esp. chap. 6.

3. Roth, *Die kommandierte,* 88, contains excerpts from a 19 May 1922 letter written by Lenin to Josef Stalin, in which Lenin stresses the advantages of radio in reaching not only illiterates, but also professors, particularly "our few Communist professors," so that the influence of bourgois professors could be minimized.

4. Thomas Guback and Stephen Hill, *The Beginning of Soviet Broadcasting and the Role of V. I. Lenin,* Journalism Monographs 26, December 1972. See also Peter Kenez, *The Birth of the Propaganda State: Soviet Methods of Mass Mobiliaztion, 1917-1929* (Cambridge and New York: Cambridge University Press, 1985), chap. 7, for a thorough description of various literacy training campaigns conducted in the U.S.S.R. during this early period. Kenez doesn't discuss the role of radio in such campaigns, but makes it clear that Soviet authorities injected specific political messages into the literacy lessons.

5. Paul Roth, "Der sowjetische Rundfunk, 1918-1945," *Rundfunk und Fernsehen* 2 (1974): 205.

6. Gayle Durham Hannah, *Soviet Information Networks* (Washington, D.C.: Georgetown University Center for Strategic and International Studies, 1977), 35-36, provides a more detailed account of the distinction between agitation and propaganda.

7. Hopkins, *Mass Media,* 74-75.

8. Alex Inkeles, *Public Opinion in Soviet Russia* (Cambridge, Mass.: Harvard University Press, 1950), 264-66.

9. *Govorit SSSR,* cited in *The Soviet Broadcasting System* (Washington, D.C.: FCC/Foreign Broadcast Information Service, 1944), 2.

10. Inkeles, *Public Opinion,* 272-73.

11. *Govorit SSSR,* 2.

12. Vsevelod Skorodumov, "On the History and Development of Broadcasting in the Soviet Union," Munich: Radio Liberty Dispatch, September 1973, 7.

13. *Monitoring Service Report of Soviet Home Broadcasts—15 June 1942* (Reading, U.K.: BBC Monitoring Service). Filed with BBC Written Archives Centre under E1/1264, Countries: U.S.S.R. Broadcasting in the U.S.S.R., A-Z, 1936-1952.

14. Skorodumov, "History," 10.

15. Hopkins, *Mass Media,* 263.

16. P. M. Box, *Radio and Television in the USSR* (Reading, U.K.: BBC Monitoring Service, 1 November 1951). Filed with BBC Written Archives Centre under E1/1274, Countries: Russia [*sic*] Radio Centre Moscow, File 1-2, 1945-1953.

17. Walter Z. Lacquer, "What the Russians See on TV," *The Reporter,* 29 October 1959, pp. 25-26, has a good description of Soviet TV programming in the late 1950s.

18. Hannah, *Soviet Information,* 28.

19. "Educational Television," *Komsomolskaya Pravda,* 11 April 1967.

20. Boris Firsov, "There Is No Average Viewer" (Munich: Radio Liberty Research Report, 1969).

21. Cited in David Powell, "Television in the USSR," *Public Opinion Quarterly* 39, no. 3 (Fall 1975): 295.

22. Robert J. Kaiser notes having seen a Soviet marshal read a text on the "Exposure of False Stories of the Great Patriotic War [World War II]" for 45 minutes, only occasionally looking up at the camera. Kaiser, *Russia* (New York: Atheneum, 1976), 240.

23. Dan Fisher, "Soviet TV," *Los Angeles Times,* 16 January 1979.

24. Konstantin Kusakov, head of the Drama Department (Television), Gosteleradio, personal interview, Moscow, September 1985.

25. L. N. Denisova, *Rural Russia: Economic, Social and Moral Crisis* (Commack, N.Y.: Nova Science Publishers, 1995), 103. Denisova uses official statistics, which may not be reliable.

26. Mickiewicz, *Split,* 60-68.

27. Robert L. Stevenson et al., "Soviet Media in the Age of Glasnost," in L. John Martin and Ray Heibert, *Current Issues in International Communication* (New York: Longman, 1990), 198-99. For an in-depth examination of "Vremya," see Mickiewicz, *Split Signals,* 1989.

28. James Dingley, "Soviet Television and *Glasnost,*" in Julian Graffy and Ge-

offrey Hosking, eds., *Culture and the Media in the USSR Today* (New York: St. Martin's Press, 1989), 6-25; Mickiewicz, *Changing*; Hedrick Smith, *The New Russians* (New York: Random House, 1990), 165-73.

29. James Dingley, "Soviet Television and *Glasnost*," in Graffy and Hoskins, *Culture*, 11.

30. Francis X. Clines, "His Show's a Hit, But Soviet TV Chief is Cancelled," *New York Times*, 17 May 1989, p. 5.

31. "Excerpts from Speeches at Soviet Communist Party Meeting in Moscow," *New York Times*, 28 April 1989, p. 6.

32. Fen Montaigne, "Changing Soviet TV," *Philadelphia Enquirer*, 27 December 1989, p. 1F.

33. Smith, *New*, 148-60; "How Leningrad's TV Affects the Whole," *TV World* (September 1989): 12.

34. Constantin Galskoy, "Coverage of RFE & RL in Soviet Media Since Cessation of Jamming," Munich: Radio Free Europe/Radio Liberty, Soviet Area Audience and Opinion Research, Report AR-7-89, December 1989, 4.

35. Francis X. Clines, "Scandal Erupts in Soviet Parliament," *New York Times*, 15 March 1990, p. A6.

36. Shane, *Dismantling*, 145-47.

37. Ibid., 147-48.

38. Bill Keller, "Did Moscow Incite Azerbaijanis?," *New York Times*, 19 February 1990, p. A6; Esther Fein, "Soviet Press Disrupted by Republic's Violence," *New York Times*, 19 February 1990, p. A4.

39. Smith, *New Russians*, 465.

40. Francis X. Clines, "Kremlin Troops Move in to Evict Lithuanian Aides," *New York Times*, 6 April 1990, p. 8.

41. Smith, *New Russians*, 153-54; Serge Schmemann, "Soviet TV Reflects the Kremlin's Grimmer Picture," *New York Times*, 8 February 1991, pp. A1, A4.

42. The process of doing so was exceptionally difficult and convoluted, as various deputies pushed and pulled to include or eliminate "liberal" or "conservative" provisions, and often they didn't even have drafts of the latest amendments available for their inspection. See Thomas Remington in Robert T. Huber and Donald R. Kelley, eds., *Perestroika-Era Politics* (Armonk, N.Y.: M. E. Sharpe, 1991), 186-94; Robert Sharlet, "Citizen and State," in Steven White, Alex Pravda and Zvi Gitelman, eds., *Developments in Russian and Post-Soviet Politics* (Durham, N.C.: Duke University Press, 1994), 116-18 and 123-24; and Elena Androunas, *Soviet Media*, 42-43.

43. Stephen E. Deane, "The Struggle for a USSR Press Law," *The Woodrow Wilson Center Report* 2, 3 (November 1990): 1-2.

44. Francis X. Clines, "Gorbachev Orders Change in Control Over TV and Radio," *New York Times*, 16 July 1990, p. 1.

45. Ibid.

46. Bill Keller, "Gorbachev Jeered at May Day Rally," *New York Times*, 2 May 1990, p. A4.

47. Mickiewicz, *Changing*, and Remington, *Truth*, 115-16, 151-55.

48. Ellen Mickiewicz, "Soviet TV Viewers Want Public Affairs," letter to the

editor, *New York Times,* 4 April 1991, p. A14.

49. Vera Tolz, "Recent Attempts to Curb *Glasnost,*" *Report on the USSR* 3, no. 9 (March 1991): 3.

50. Ibid., 4-5.

51. "World News," *Minneapolis Star Tribune,* 26 June 1991, p. 6A.

52. "New Broadcast Authority Replaces Gosteleradio," *World Broadcast News* (May 1991): 44; "International Bulletin," *World Broadcast News* (April 1990): 6; (May 1990): 6; (June 1990): 6.

53. Tolz, "Recent," 3-4.

54. The radio station of the Russian Federation, which also initiated its own six hour per day TV service, Russian Television (RTR) in May 1991. The inaugural broadcast contained satires poking fun at Gorbachev and criticizing the actions of Soviet military units in Armenia. "'Normal TV' Takes to Soviet Airwaves," *Hollywood Reporter,* 14 May 1991, pp. 1, 95.

55. Francis X. Clines, "Top Story on Soviet TV: Vote 'Da' on Referendum," *New York Times,* 8 March 1991, p. A3; Serge Schmemann, "Soviet Vote Becomes Test of Loyalties," *New York Times,* 16 March 1991, p. A1.

56. Schmemann, "Soviet TV Reflects," p. A1.

57. Mickiewicz, "Soviet TV Viewers," p. A14.

58. Bill Keller, "In Soviet Life, Thaw Becomes Chill," *New York Times,* 3 February 1991, p. A1.

59. "Index Index," *Index on Censorship* 20, no. 6 (1991): 41.

60. Ganley, *Unglued* (see index under Coup d'etat for page references), Mickiewicz, *Changing* (again, index under Coup attempt), and Shane, *Dismantling,* chap. 9, provide the most complete accounts of electronic media activity during this period.

61. Vatchnadze, *Secrets,* 303-4.

62. Sergei Korzoun, personal interview, Quebec City, Quebec, March 1992. As Ganley indicates, Moscow Echo was in trouble with Soviet authorities within months of its founding in August 1990, chiefly because of its criticism of Soviet policies in the Baltic republics, especially Lithuania. Ganley, *Unglued,* 118-19. Ganley discusses the station's coup activities on 170-71.

63. "Soviet 'TV of dictatorship' ousted," *Hollywood Reporter,* 30 August 1991, p. 6.

64. Skorodumov, "History," 8.

65. Paulu, *Radio,* 56.

66. Lyman Ostlund, "Russian Advertising: A New Concept," *Journal of Advertising Research* 13, no. 1 (February 1973): 13-14; Jeffrey Trachtenberg, "TV Advertising Russian Style," *Forbes,* 7 September 1987, pp. 107-8.

67. Hedrick Smith, *The Russians* (New York: Ballantine Books, 1976), 80-81.

68. Paul Lendvai, *The Bureaucracy of Truth* (Boulder, Colo.: Westview Press, 1981), chaps. 2 and 3, provides an interesting if quite tendentious account of limits placed on media reporting in various Communist nations. Information on coverage of Chernobyl came from Twin Cities Public Television's (KTCA-TV) monthly series "Channel Three Moscow," which included several excerpts of it; and from Jonathan Saunders, assistant director of the W. Averill Harriman Institute for the

Study of the Soviet Union, Columbia University, public lecture on "*Glasnost* and the Soviet Union," University of Minnesota, 24 April 1987.

69. James Oberg, *Uncovering Soviet Disasters* (New York: Random House, 1988).

70. Reino Paasilinna, *Glasnost and Soviet Television* (Helsinki: YLE, Research Report 5/1995), 103

71. Urban, *Rebirth,* 239.

72. That led to some rather odd decisions. For example, Glavlit determined that one couldn't name a pig "Proletarian" or "Pravda." Presumably that would have degraded those noble terms! See Paasilinna, *Glasnost*, 102.

73. Merle Fainsod, *Smolensk Under Soviet Rule* (New York: Vintage Books, 1963), contains a detailed description of Glavlit activities.

74. Urban, *Rebirth,* 78, indicates that the government "drastically reduced" the scope of Glavlit's powers in June 1986.

75. Hopkins, *Mass Media,* 123-28; Hannah, *Soviet,* 60-62; Ellen Mickiewicz, "Policy Issues in the Soviet Media System," in Erik P. Hoffmann, ed., *The Soviet Union in the 1980s* (New York: Academy of Political Scientists, 1984), 120-21; and Remington, *Truth,* chap. 4, provide descriptions of media decision-making processes.

76. Georgui Vatchnadze, *Les Medias Sous Gorbatchev* (Paris: Editions de l'Espace Europeen, 1991), 342-43 (translations mine). The third part of his book (pp. 333-402) contains numerous examples of censorship activities undertaken not only by Glavlit, but also by other Soviet agencies and individuals.

77. Herman Ermolaev, *Censorship in Soviet Literature, 1917-1991* (Lanham, Md.: Rowman & Littlefield, 1997), 226-30.

78. Androunas, *Soviet,* 50-52.

79. Remington, *Truth,* 31-35, discusses the place of the Department within the overall structure of the party, but says little about its specific activities.

80. Lendvai, *Bureaucracy,* 113-19. The major share of what the censor brought out is included in Jane L. Curry, ed. and trans., *The Black Book of Polish Censorship* (New York: Viking, 1984).

81. Leonard Finkelstein, "The System of Formal Censorship," in Martin Dewhirst and Robert Farrell, eds., *The Soviet Censorship* (Metuchen, N.J.: Scarecrow Press, 1973), 55-56.

82. Hopkins, *Mass Media,* 129-33.

83. Cited in Vatchnadze, *Secrets,* 176.

84. B. A. Grushin and L. A. Onikov, eds., "The Media in a Soviet Industrial City, Part 5," *Soviet Sociology* 21, no. 2 (Fall 1982): 31.

85. Ibid., 31-32.

86. In a September 1985 personal interview in Moscow, Professor Artemij Panfilov of the Moscow State University Faculty of Journalism noted that he had gotten his start in radio in the 1940s by working at a collective farm station. The studio could hold the control board operator, the interviewee and himself, but only if everyone remained standing! He added that facilities had improved a lot since then, but it was still possible to find "studios" similar to his.

87. Paulu, *Radio,* 164-66.

88. E. I. Tarshis, in "The Media in a Soviet Industrial City, Part 6," B. A. Grushin and L. A. Onikov, eds., *Soviet Sociology* 22, no. 3 (Winter 1983-84): 29.

89. Donald Shanor, *The Private War Against Soviet Censorship* (New York: St. Martin's Press, 1985), describes numerous unofficial and often illegal media activities in the U.S.S.R. See also Paulu, *Radio,* 48-49, and Skorodumov, "History," 11-13.

90. Vassily Aksyonov, "Selling Ideology—Not Beer," *Panorama* (May 1981): 74.

91. Kusakov, interview; Boris Kaplan, deputy head of Drama, personal interview, Moscow, September 1985.

92. "Soviet Dissident Recants on TV," *Minneapolis Tribune,* 8 April 1982, p. 13A.

93. Anatoli Daryalov, "Only a Sensation?," *Zhurnalist* 8 (1967), translated and published by Radio Liberty (Munich), undated but probably 1969.

94. Ellen Mickiewicz, "Soviet Viewers are Seeing More, Including News of the U.S.," *New York Times,* 22 February 1987, sec. 2, p. 29.

95. Iu. V. Arutiunian, "A Preliminary Ethnosociological Study of a Way of Life," *Soviet Sociology* 22, no. 4 (Spring 1984): 47.

96. A. Karasev, "What's Coming on 'Screen?'" *Sovetskaya Kultura,* 2 November 1982, describes a TV movie entitled "White Shaman," which portrays the conflict between a hunter who favors the Communist government and a rich shaman (religious leader) who represents the "decadent old order." See also Yaacov Ro'i, "The Task of Creating the New Soviet Man: Atheistic Propaganda in the Soviet Muslim Areas," *Soviet Studies* 36, no. 1 (January 1984): 26-44.

97. Leo Gruliow, "Russians Looking for Better Wedding Ceremony," *Minneapolis Tribune,* 10 June 1973, p. 22E.

98. Mickiewicz, *Media,* 48-49.

99. Kendall E. Bailes, "Soviet TV Comes of Age" (Munich: Radio Liberty Research Paper 24, 1968), 4.

100. David Wedgwood Benn, *Persuasion and Soviet Politics* (London: Blackwell, 1989), chap. 4; and Elizabeth Ann Weinberg, *The Development of Sociology in the Soviet Union* (London: Routledge and Kegan Paul, 1974), chaps. 1 and 2, are useful sources on this period.

101. Remington, *Truth,* 123-27.

102. Wedgwood Benn cites E. P. Prokhorov, ed., *Sotsiologiya zhurnalistiki* (Moscow: 1981) (no publisher indicated), 55, note 7, as his source for that date. Chap. 5 of Wedgwood Benn's book covers sociological research in the period from Stalin's death to Gorbachev's accession to power, and provides many interesting details on the efforts of Firsov, Grushin and other sociologists to develop more meaningful inquiries into public opinion.

103. Juri Zuzanek, *Work and Leisure in the Soviet Union* (New York: Praeger, 1980).

104. Paulu, *Radio,* 118.

105. Firsov, "Average."

106. David Powell, *The Soviet Television Audience: Viewing Patterns and Problems* (Washington, D.C.: U.S. Information Agency, Report R-16-75, November 1975), 9.

107. Zuzanek, *Work,* 95.

108. Mickiewicz, *Media,* esp. chaps. 2 and 8.

109. B. K. Alekseev, B. Z. Doktorow and B. M. Firsov, "The Study of Public Opinion: Experiences and Problems," *Soviet Sociology* 18, no. 4 (1980): 49.

110. Mickiewicz, *Media,* 25, 33; Zuzanek, *Work,* 320.

111. N. Rimashevskaia, "Current Problems of the Status of Women," *Soviet Sociology* 27, no. 1 (1988): 67.

112. See esp. Mickiewicz, "Policy Issues."

113. V. P. Volkov, head, Audience Research Department, Gosteleradio, personal interview, Moscow, September 1985. See also "Soviet Advances," *TV World* (March-April 1987): 22; and Mickiewicz, "Soviet Viewers."

114. Oleg T. Manaev, "A Dissenting Audience," *Soviet Sociology* 30, no. 3 (1991): 23-40. Quoted passages appear on p. 37 and p. 38.

115. Gail Lapidus, "Overview," in Andrei Melville and Gail Lapidus, eds., *The Glasnost Papers* (Boulder, Colo.: Westview Press, 1990), 23.

116. However, that equality varied a good deal over the first few decades of Communist rule. It did quite well during the 1920s, with encouragement of regional and local cultures and their languages. It suffered in the 1930s, as Stalin sought to centralize the nation and declared that Soviet cultures should be "national in form, socialist in content." The situation improved after his death in 1953, although Khrushchev was not all that well-disposed toward ethnic minorities, and certainly not toward religion. Gorbachev was somewhat better-disposed toward minorities. Zvi Gitelman, "Nationality and Ethnicity," in Steven White, Alex Pravda and Zvi Gitelman, eds., *Developments in Russian and Post-Soviet Politics* (Durham, N.C.: Duke University Press, 1994).

117. Henry Norr, "National Languages and Soviet Television: A Statistical Report," *Nationalities Papers* 13, no. 1 (1985): 84-105.

118. Ellen Mickiewicz and Dawn Plumb Jamison, "Ethnicity and Soviet Television News," *Journal of Communication* 41, no. 2 (1991): 150-61.

119. Anthony Adomovich, remarks contained in "What Is the Soviet Censorship?," in Dewhirst and Farrell, *The Soviet Censorship,* 19.

120. Regine Robin, *Socialist Realism: An Impossible Aesthetic* (Stanford, Calif.: Stanford University Press, 1992), chaps. 10 and 11, discusses the Soviet "hero" in some detail.

121. John Clews speaks of the "indicative-imperative" in communist propaganda messages: presenting the ideal—for example, a remarkable growth in collective farm productivity—as if it were real. The hope of the leadership was that, when people heard such reports and realized that they themselves weren't all that productive, they would redouble their efforts to do their "fair share" for society. Clews, *Communist Propaganda Techniques* (New York: Praeger, 1964). See also a discussion by Glowinski of Polish "newspeak," cited by Karol Jakubowicz in David Paletz et al., *Glasnost and After,* 24.

122. G. Shevelev, "Workers Grade," *Pravda,* 11 February 1982, p. 2. A 1985

survey conducted in Krasnoyarsk, Novosibirsk and Kemerovo showed that "workers and their families" criticized "Vremya" reporters for too often overlooking the human element in stories. V. P. Volkov, article in the *Soviet Radio and TV Guide*, translated and condensed by the BBC Monitoring Service under the title "Make It Better With a Letter," *TV World* (May 1986): 132.

123. Mickiewicz, *Changing*, 66-69.

124. Kusakov and Kaplan, personal interviews; "Soviet Advances," *TV World.*

125. Ellen Mickiewicz, "Feedback, Surveys, and Soviet Communication Theory," *Journal of Communication* 33, no. 2 (1983): 106.

126. N. Kirillova, "No Side-Stepping," *Soviet Sociology* 27, no. 1 (1988): 74.

127. L. N. Denisova, *Rural Russia: Economic, Social and Moral Crisis* (Commack, N.Y.: Nova Science Publishers, 1995).

128. Ibid., 131-32.

129. From annual exchange figures for 1976-85, reported in *Radio Television,* a periodical of the Organization for International Radio and Television, Prague, Czechoslovakia.

130. D. Lyubosvetov, "Announced By Radio ... ," *Pravda,* 13 December 1982.

131. Vadim Vernik, "Fighting for a Piece of the Big Screen," *Soviet Life* (August 1991): 60-62.

132. Serge Schmemann, "Back to the Russia of Peter the Great," *New York Times,* 25 November 1985, sec. 2, p. 1.

133. "Soviet SKS Unveils Western Co-Prods," *Hollywood Reporter,* 4 December 1990, pp. 1, 75.

134. T. Degtrioreva, "Intervision Convention," *Sovetskaya Kultura,* 7 October 1982.

135. "Soviet Advances," 22.

136. Shane, *Dismantling,* 26-28.

137. "TV Now and in the Future," *Televidenie Radio Vechany* (TV Guide), Moscow, 1 January 1985, p. 7.

138. Yushkiavitshus, Interview; "Eastern Promise," *Cable and Satellite Europe* (September 1986): 31.

139. Ganley, *Unglued,* 5. She adds that a number of western firms working in the U.S.S.R. used satellites for reliable telephone links, but that it wasn't easy for them to obtain government permission to do so (pp. 21-22).

140. Mickiewicz, *Split,* 16.

141. Sally Laird, "Videos, Pirates and the Underground: Soviet Union," *Index on Censorship* 3 (March 1986): 19-20; Douglas Boyd, "The Videocassette Recorder in the U.S.S.R. and Soviet-Bloc Countries," in Mark Levy, *The VCR Age: Home Video and Mass Communication* (Newbury Park, Calif.: Sage, 1989), chap. 14.

142. Reported in Andrew Rosenthal, "Soviets Reverse Field on Evils of Video," *Minneapolis Star Tribune,* 18 April 1984, p. 12C.

143. Mickiewicz, *Split,* 11-13, provides a useful account of videocassette activity in the early through mid 1980s, and notes that some individuals were fined or jailed for showing "pornographic" cassettes, Bruce Lee kung fu movies among them, to groups of paying customers.

144. Yushkiavitshus, Kusakov and Kaplan, personal interviews, September 1985.

145. Ganley, *Unglued,* indicates that the Russian Republic TV service produced tapes throughout the coup attempt and circulated them around the country, where some may have been shown over cable TV. Gerry Yandel, "Soviet Citizens Videotaping Crisis for U.S. Networks," *Atlanta Constitution,* 21 August 1991, notes that Atlanta-based CNN and other U.S. networks had distributed videocameras to Soviet citizens in various parts of the country earlier in 1991, as signs of disorder increased, and that tapes shot by some of those citizens were used by CNN and others.

146. Rex Malik, "Can the Soviet Union Survive Information Technology?" *InterMedia* 12, no. 3 (1984): 23. Ganley, *Unglued,* 31-32, agrees with Malik's gloomy assessment of the state of computer education in the Soviet Union, noting that most students who received instruction got it from training manuals, and not from hands-on experience.

147. Celestine Bohlen, "The Soviets Are Seeing the War At Home," *Washington Post National Weekly Edition,* 11 November 1985, pp. 16-17.

148. Gary Lee, "Gorbachev in Prime Time," *Washington Post National Weekly Edition,* 11 November 1985, p. 16.

149. *The Soviet Public and the War in Afghanistan* (Munich: Radio Liberty Research Report AR 4-85, June 1985), 21.

150. Cited in Peter Fraenkel, "In Spite of Babel," *The Linguist* 25, no. 3 (1986): 133.

151. Bill Keller, "A Steady Diet of Criticism Frazzles Nerves in Russia," *New York Times,* 8 March 1987, sec. 4, p. 3.

152. Androunas, *Soviet,* 134-38.

153. Bernard Weinraub, "Ready for Prime Time in Moscow," *The New York Times,* 22 January 1992, p. C1; "Western Exports Finding No Soviet Resistance," *Hollywood Reporter,* 21 July 1992, p. 13.

154. Brian McNair, "Television in Post-Soviet Russia: From Monolith to Mafia," *Media, Culture & Society* 18 (1996): 489-91.

155. Ibid., 498, note 3.

156. I doubt that those in charge of television in the other republics would agree with that sentiment. Monroe Price, *Television, the Public Sphere, and National Identity* (New York: Oxford University Press, 1995), 103-7, provides examples of the problems faced by Ukraine as it attempted to assert its electronic media independence while Channel One broadcasts remained accessible and popular there. It considered jamming Channel One, demanding that Channel One be closed down and its assets from Soviet days be divided among the republics, or working through a governing body representing all of the republics to force Channel One to be less biased against Ukraine. It and other republics finally agreed to stop contributing financially to Channel One, but also agreed not to charge Channel One for using its transmitters located within their boundaries.

157. Both quotations appear in McNair, "Television," 492. The translations are probably McNair's.

158. Ibid., 492-93; Daphne Skillen, "Afterword: Television in Russia and the

CIS since the coup," in Phillip Drummond, Richard Paterson and Janet Willis, *National Identity and Europe: The Television Revolution* (London: British Film Institute, 1993), 134-35.

159. McNair, "Television," 493-94; Mickiewicz, *Changing*, 123-26 and 135-38.

160. Mickiewicz, *Changing*, 140.

161. Ibid., 135-46, provides a fine account of the referendum. I saw a few of the referendum ads at the annual convention of the Speech Communication Association in November 1994, and was struck by their simplicity, in the sense that each emphasized a single point from a number of angles.

162. Ibid., 151-52.

163. Ibid., 146-64, furnishes an excellent summary of the role of television in the election. She notes that, although U.S. advisors were active in the Yeltsin group's campaign advertising, they remained under cover, for the most part. That cover was "blown" on one notable occcasion, when a U.S. advisor and funding from the U.S. Agency for International Development were linked with the possible use of U.S. government funds to support the TV ad campaign of the "Russia's Choice" Party (pp. 155-57).

164. The placard announcement appears in Urban, *Rebirth*, 289. Mickiewicz, *Changing*, 129-31, depicts Bragin as somewhat uncertain of what to do, sometimes for good reason and sometimes not, but ready to take credit for a "plan" to switch over to Channel Two.

165. Remnick, *Resurrection*, 73, states that Gaidar broadcast over radio station Moscow Echo. Mickiewicz, *Changing*, 132, places him at Channel Two. It's entirely possible that he spoke at both places.

166. For a description of the context and events of the revolt, see Michael Urban, *Rebirth*, 285-90; and, from a U.S. reporter's standpoint, Remnick, *Resurrection*, 56-83. Mickiewicz, *Changing*, 126-34, describes a situation in which confusion and the shifting of responsibility seemed to be the order of the day during the first few hours of the revolt where the Ostankino staff was concerned.

167. Monroe Price, *Television, the Public Sphere, and National Identity* (New York: Oxford University Press, 1995), 120-25.

168. Ibid., 124-5.

169. Mickiewicz, *Changing*, 229-30.

170. Price, *Television*, 123-24.

171. Vsevolod Vilchek, "'Ostankino' sredi drugikh," *Izvestia*, 4 February 1994, p. 9, cited in Mickiewicz, *Changing*, 232.

172. Andrei Zolotov, "Nationalist Gains Air Time in Television Coup," *Moscow Times*, 27 June 1997, cited in *Post-Soviet Media Law and Policy Newsletter* 38 (15 July 1997): pp. 2-3.

173. Mickiewicz, *Changing*, chap. 11, has the most detailed and authoritative treatment of TV's coverage of the war in Chechnya. Remnick, *Resurrection*, 260-91, has a partly personal account of the war. Mickiewicz also notes a situation involving the two leading presenters for the resurrected "Vzglyad," who in effect told viewers to disregard Gaidar's call to "take to the streets"; instead, they said, go to sleep and let the military forces (which still were standing on the sidelines,

waiting to see who would have the upper hand) do the dirty work. Both presenters were fired. Price, *Television,* 124, corraborates her assertion of the threats against NTV by the government.

174. Urban, *Rebirth,* 309. The author credits Andre Berezkin for the data on campaign spending.

175. Mickiewicz, *Changing*, 213.

176. The information on Bryntsalov's horsemanship comes from ibid., 183, and on the pants-dropping incident, from a report by U.S. National Public Radio's Moscow correspondent, Anne Garrels, on 11 June 1996.

177. Mickiewicz, *Changing,* 186.

178. *Rossiyskiye Vesti,* 16 January 1998, translated and published in *Post-Soviet Media Law and Policy Newsletter* 44 (1 March 1998): 3-4.

178a. "Reorganization of VGTRK," *Post-Soviet Media Law and Policy Newsletter,* 48-49 (September 1998), 1-9.

178b. Kathy Lally, "Russian powers pull media plug," *Baltimore Sun,* November 21, 1998, reprinted in *Post-Soviet Media Law and Policy Newsletter,* 51 (December 15, 1998), 2-3; "Interfax cuts news service to ORT," *ITAR-TASS news agency (World Service),* Moscow, December 2, 1998, reprinted in *Post-Soviet Media Law and Policy Newsletter,* 51 (December 15, 1998), 1; "Loss of TV Soap Has Russian Viewers in a Lather," *Times of London,* November 27, 1998.

179. Issue 44 of *Post-Soviet Media Law ...* , 6-9, also carries a lengthy 23 January 1998 article from *Novyye Izvestiya* on the economic situations and consequent political dealings surrounding various TV companies.

180. Ilya Nagibin states that the government's financial support for 1997 was only 5 percent of the printed budget for radio. Nagibin, "The State Has Three Radio Stations Left," *Kommersant Daily,* 5 August 1997, 3, translated and published in *Current Digest of the Post-Soviet Press* 49, 31 (1997).

181. Lange, "Media Structures," in *Media in the CIS,* 5.

182. Alessandra Stanley, "Russian Liberal Keeps Lines to Yeltsin Open," *New York Times,* 26 June 1996, p. A3.

183. Vasily Kisunko, "Commercial Without a Break," *Rossiiskiye Vesti,* 25 July 1997, p. 3. Text condensed, translated and published by *Current Digest of the Post-Soviet Press* 49, no. 31 (1997).

184. Nicholas Pilugin and Svetlana Kolesnik, "The Legal Basis of Media Regulation: Regulation of Advertising," in *Media Regulation in the Russian Federation,* report prepared (January 1997) for Radio Free Europe/Radio Liberty, available through website http://www.internews.ras.ru/report/media.

185. Sigal, "Advertising: Ad Brokers," in *Survey*, 4-5.

186. Sigal, *Survey,* sec. VIII (Advertising).

187. Lange, "Media Structures," in *Media in the CIS*, 12-13, available through website http://www.internews.ras.ru/books/media/russia.

188. Ibid., 13-14.

189. Alessandra Stanley, "Tycoon Purged from Kremlin as Reform Battle Heats Up," *New York Times,* 6 November 1997, p. A9.

190. E-mail message from Johnson, 28 October 1997.

191. Pilugin and Kolesnik, *Media,* is an excellent overall source of information on the regulation of Russian media. So is the *Post-Soviet Media Law and Policy Newsletter,* edited by Prof. Monroe E. Price and available through Prof. Price, Benjamin N. Cardozo School of Law, 55 Fifth Avenue, New York, NY 10003.

192. Krug and Price, "Russia," 187-88, illustrate the uncertain nature of licensing by using NTV's experiences as an example. The station had attempted to obtain airtime on Channel Four, which would bring it a potentially much larger audience. On 23 November 1993, Yeltsin signed a decree granting NTV's request, and then rescinded it a few hours later. Apparently Yeltsin's close followers were divided as to the merits of the request (and perhaps of the station itself). Yeltsin reissued the decree a month later, and this time the decision stuck. However, as Krug and Price indicate, at no time were any reasons for the decisions made public. They then observe, "Thus, while ownership pluralism is well established, the fate of individual broadcasters is political, rather than legal."

193. Peter Krug, "Constitutional Protection of Media Freedoms in Russia's Highest Courts," *Post-Soviet Media Law and Policy Newsletter* 34 (1996), cites several examples of the dubious protection afforded by the Constitutional Court and other courts.

194. Pilugin and Kolesnik, "The Legal Basis of Media Regulation: Right to Honor and Dignity," in *Media,* 51.

195. Ibid., 1, and "Election Coverage," 1.

196. Serge Robillard, "Russia," in author, *Television in Europe: Regulatory Bodies* (London: John Libbey, 1995), chap. 27, contains excerpts from the draft and some discussion of its provisions.

197. Natasha Malashenko, "Comparative Analysis of Independent Media Development in Post-Communist Russia and Ukraine" (M.A. thesis, Central European University, Budapest, Hungary, 1997), chap. 3, part 1, pp. 2-3.

198. Robillard, "Russia," 191.

199. Lange, "Legal and Regulatory Framework for the Media," in *Media in the CIS,* 5. There's some argument over whether the regional commissions of the FTSR are legal. The Chair of the FTSR Central Commission, Yassen Zassoursky (Dean of the Faculty of Journalism at Moscow State University), contends that the regional commissions are advisory to the central commission, but no licenses appear to be approved without the blessing of the regional commissions. Pilugin and Kolesnik, "Regulatory Issues: Licensing of Broadcast Media," in *Media,* 1-2.

200. Campbell, *Soviet,* 165-68.

201. Campbell, *Soviet,* 54, notes that FAPSI was created some months after the 1991 coup attempt, and that it took over some of the KGB information-gathering functions. However, he says nothing about control over radio and television programming. He does point out (p. 224) that it controls the certification of electronic eavesdropping equipment, and has used that power to block rival equipment, presumably so as to maintain government control over surveillance, much as in the Soviet era.

202. Urban, *Rebirth,* 297, 299. Urban cites an article in *Nezavisimaya Gazeta,* 23 February 1994, p. 2.

203. Valery Rudnev and Sergei Taranov, "President Vests Russian Bureaucracy with Right to Wield 'Top Secret' Stamp," *Izvestia,* 26 February 1994, pp. 1-4.

204. Cited in Lange, "Legal and Regulatory Framework for the Media," in *Media in the CIS,* 8.

204a. Andrei Richter, "Local Media Legislation in Russian Provinces: An Old and Winding Road," *Post-Soviet Law and Media Policy* 50 (December 1998), 39.

205. "The New Political Tele-Truncheon," *Nezavisimaya Gazeta,* 5 February 1998, translated and published in *Post-Soviet Media Law and Policy Newsletter* 44 (1 March 1998): 5-6.

206. Lange, "Media Structures," in *Media in the CIS*, 9-10, available at website www.internews.ras.ru/books/media/russia.html

207. Ilya Nagibin, "The State Has Three Radio Stations Left," *Kommersant Daily,* 5 August 1997, p. 3, translated and published in *Current Digest of the Post-Soviet Press* 49, no. 31 (1997).

208. "Leftists Begin Patriotic News Agency," press release (?) of 8 August 1997, transmitted by civilsoc@solar.rtd.utk.edu on 12 August 1997.

209. Pilugin and Kolesnik, "The Russian Media and Its [*sic*] Constraints: Broadcast Media," in *Media,* 2.

210. Sigal, "Networks and Network Channels: History," in *Survey,* 2.

211. Eric Johnson of Internews (johnson@internews.ras.ru) and John Bonar (john@rusmag.ru), Publishing Editor of *Marketing Russia,* had interesting e-mail observations on this subject on 26 January 1998.

212. Michael Specter, "In Creating Russia's 'Sesame Street,' 'D' Stands for Difficult," *New York Times,* 22 October 1996, p. B1.

213. Alessandra Stanley, "On Russian TV, Sincerest Form of Flattery," *New York Times,* 12 January 1997, pp. 1, 4.

214. Sarah Koenig, "True Crime, All Too True, on TV," *New York Times,* 24 July 1997, p. B1.

215. Daniel Williams, "On Moscow TV, Contestants Can Win a 'Stolen' Car," *Minneapolis Star Tribune,* 15 January 1998, p. E6, reprinted from the *Washington Post.*

216. "Russian TV Journalist Slain Gangland Style," *Minneapolis Star Tribune,* 2 March 1995, p. 17A. Sigal, "Advertising: Ad Brokers," in *Survey*, 2.

217. Sigal, "Advertising: Ad Brokers," in *Survey*, 4.

218. Kate Baldwin, "Montezuma's Revenge: Reading 'Los Ricos Tambien Lloran' in Russia," in Robert Allen, ed., *To Be Continued ... Soap Operas Around the World* (London and New York: Routledge, 1995), 285-300.

219. "Russians Tell All On Yelena's Sex Show," *Moscow News,* 4-10 September 1997, p. 12; Alessandra Stanley, "On Russian TV, Suddenly the Screen is Steamy," *New York Times,* 13 November 1997, p. A4.

220. Alessandra Stanley, "Valentines to Russia, Seeking Patient Brides," *New York Times,* 14 February 1997, pp. A1, A8. My comments on this and other shows also are based on viewing of videotapes made at my request by Internews (Moscow) in late November-early December 1997.

221. "NTV and Its Universities," *Rossiyskaya Gazeta* (Moscow), letter to the

editor, 25 September 1996, on website http://www.ctr.columbia.edu/vii/monroe/34fourteen.html; Sigal, "Government Television: Government Channels," in *Survey,* 7-8.

222. *Segodnya* (the newspaper, and not NTV's evening news program), 8 April 1995, p. 3, cited in Urban, *Rebirth*, 414, note 102.

223. Louise McElvogue, "'Disney' Tops in Russian Houses," *Hollywood Reporter,* 13 August 1992, p. 3.

224. Sigal, "Viewer Preference and Market Research: Market Research," in *Survey,* 1-4; "Who Will Ratings Depend On in 1999-2000?" available through http://www.internews.ru/crisis

225. Russian Public Relations Group, cited in Sigal, "The Role of Television in Russia: News Sources," in *Survey,* 1.

226. The Public Opinion Foundation, "Russian TV Atlas '22 Cities' Regional TV Monitor: Ratings of Local and National TV Channels and Stations" (Moscow: author, 1995), cited in Sigal, "Viewer Preference and Market Research: Viewer Habits and Preferences," in *Survey,* 1.

227. Unspecified research firm, cited in Sigal, "The Role of Television in Russia: News Sources," in *Survey,* 1.

228. Sigal, "Viewer Preference and Market Research: Viewer Habits and Preferences," in *Survey,* 2. Findings are based on survey data published in *Vestnik Televizionnoi Informatsii* 46-54 (November-December 1996).

229. Ibid., 3-4.

230. Information on the holdings of various corporations was drawn from "Commercial Groups' Control of Broadcasters, Press," *Argumenty i Fakty,* 24 April 1997, cited in *World Media* (BBC London) 18 (2 May 1997): 14-15; Michael R. Gordon, "Russian Media, Free of One Master, Greet Another," *New York Times,* 16 March 1997, p. 3; BBC Monitoring Service, "Russian Media Conglomerates," *World Media* 29 (18 July 1997): p. 3; and Alessandra Stanley, "A Russian's Rise From Car Dealer to Tycoon," *New York Times,* 14 June 1997, p. 3.

231. Gordon, "Russian Media," 3.

232. Lange, "Media Structures," in *Media in the CIS,* 2.

233. Andrei Bagrov, "Owners of ORT and NTV Lose First Battle," *Kommersant Daily,* 30 July 1997, pp. 1-2, translated in *Current Digest of the Post-Soviet Press* 49 no. 30 (1997): 5 and 14. There are several other media accounts of the episode in this issue of the *Digest;* Alessandra Stanley, "Tycoon Purged from Kremlin as Reform Battle Heats Up," *New York Times,* 6 November 1997, p. A9.)

234. *Open Media Research Institute Daily Digest,* 26 January 1996, cited in Brian McNair, "TV in Post-Soviet Russia," *Media Culture and Society* 18 (1996): 496.

235. "Has Yakov London 'Drained the Cup' ...? *Segodnya,* 16 January 1998, translated and published in *Post-Soviet Media Law and Policy Newsletter* 44 (1 March 1998).

236. Pilugin and Kolesnik, "The Legal Basis of Media Regulation: Rights and Duties of Journalists," in *Media,* 1.

237. Ibid., "The Legal Basis of Media Regulation: Adjudication," 1.

238. Kristians Rozenvalds, "Ethics Codes and Their Impact in the States of the Former Soviet Union" (paper written for the Aspen Institute, Washington, D.C., 30 April 1996), 1.

239. Pilugin and Kolesnik, "The Legal Basis of Media Regulation: Accreditation," in *Media,* 1-2.

240. Valerii Kichin, "The Fourth Estate Has Been Demoted to the Second Oldest Profession," *Obshaya Gazeta,* 8 July 1997, and "The Second Oldest Profession in the Country of the Victorious Criminal," *Obshaya Gazeta,* 19-26 June 1997; Sergei Nikodimov, "The Fourth Estate: Is Forbidden," *Kommersant Daily,* 8 July 1997; and Elena Rykovtseva, "At His Master's Call," *Moskovskaya Gazeta,* 6-13 July 1997. All are accessible through website www.internews.ras.ru/article/FourthEstate.html.

241. The IFES finding and the quotation both appear in Sigal, "The Role of Television in Russia: Paid Journalism," in *Survey,* 1.

242. "Where No News Is Bad News," *The Economist,* 20 September 1997, p. 60.

243. Floriana Fossato, personal e-mail message, 7 October 1997.

244. Spiridonov, cited in Sigal, "The Role of Television in Russia: Election Coverage," in *Survey,* 5.

245. Sigal, "Government Television: Local Government Television," in *Survey,* 2.

246. Sigal, "Legal and Regulatory Environment: Copyright Law," in *Survey,* 1-2.

247. Aleksi Filippov, "The First Lady of NTV," *Obshaya Gazeta,* 11-18 June 1997, accessible through website listed in note 240.

248. Kisunko, "Commercials."

249. *Sovetskaya Rossiya,* 15 January 1998, translated and published in *Post-Soviet Law and Policy Newsletter* 44 (1 March 1998): 10-12. The article accuses Gusinsky of playing "a leading role in the propaganda campaign against the national patriotic forces."

250. Vatchnadze, *Medias sous Gorbachev,* 349.

251. Peter Lisagor, a cinema specialist with the Moscow city government's cultural center, estimated that Moscow cinemas had as many as 100 million viewers per year during the Soviet era, but only 2 million as of 1995. He gave no sources for his estimates. The figures for numbers of films produced are from Kagan World Media, Ltd., *The Future of Media in Eastern Europe and Russia, 1997* (London: author, December 1996), 361. Both of the above are cited in Sigal, "The Role of Television in Russia: Entertainment Sources," in *Survey,* 1.

252. Ludmilla Pruner, "Kinovatr 1996: An End and a New Beginning," *The Russian Review* 56, no. 3 (1997): 294.

253. E-mail message from Eric Johnson, Internews (Moscow), 14 December 1997.

254. Lange, "Media Structures," in *Media in the CIS,* 3.

255. "Ex-Soviet 'Hour,'" *Hollywood Reporter,* 2 June 1992, p. 3.

256. BBC Monitoring, "Russian," 3.

257. Sarah Oates, "Broadcasting, Bullets and Ballots," *Television Quarterly* 27, no. 2 (1994): 83; "Russian Public TV's Dispute with Mir," *Izvestia,* 17 January

1997, available at website http://www.ctr.columbia.edu/vii/monroe/dispute.html (Vol. 37 of *Post-Soviet Media Law and Policy Newsletter).*

258. Peter Krug and Monroe Price, "Russia," in International Institute of Communications, *Media Ownership and Control in the Age of Convergence* (London: author, 1996), 176.

259. Anna Franklin, "Eastern Promise," *TV World* (June/July 1997): 28.

260. Ibid.; "Massive TV Project Launched," *Moscow News,* 20-26 June 1996, p. 7.

261. Michael Moran, "Russia + Internet = Net Profits?," filed for MSNBC (U.S. cable/satellite service), October 1997, and made available through Nicholas Pilugin (nwpilugin@glasnet.ru), 21 October 1997, indicates 150,000. Floriana Fossato, "Russia: Joining the Cybertimes, But Slowly," filed through johnson@internews.ras.ru, 23 October 1997, cites an estimate of 600,000 by the Russian Non-Profit Center for Internet Technologies.

262. Fossato, "Russia"; Michael Specter, "At This Site, Russian Nerds Get Together, Virtually," *New York Times,* 7 May 1997, p. A4; "What Is the Internet Café and Why Does Yekaterinburg Need It," accessible through website http://www.net-cafe.skyman.ru, summer 1997.

263. "Center for Cyberjournalism," is accessible through the website http://www.park.ru/INFO/info?w+new_world/centr_k_e.html, summer 1997.

264. Urban, *Rebirth*, 305.

265. Alexei Pankin, reply to the Andrei Fadin article "In Russia, Private Doesn't Mean Independent," distributed by e-mail (alexei@mdp.msk.ru), 9 October 1997.

266. "TV Groups Oppose On-Screen 'Violence and Sensuality,'" ITAR-Tass News Agency (World Service), Moscow, 2 February 1998, translated and published in *Post-Soviet Media Law and Policy Newsletter* 44 (1 March 1998): 6.

267. " ... and Russian TV," *RFE/RL Daily Digest,* 17 September 1997. The interview appeared in *Sovetskaya Rossiya,* 16 September 1997.

268. Urban, *Rebirth,* 411, note 55, observes that the TV commercials for MMM showed, in sequence, an ordinary and even somewhat simple man investing in Mavrodi's pyramid scheme and becoming so wealthy that he finally wins the hand of one of the most popular actresses on Russian TV at the time: Veronica Castro, the star of the Mexican soap opera, "The Rich Also Cry."

269. McNair, "TV in Post-Soviet Russia," 498.

270. Monroe Price, "*Glasnost* and Television," *Post-Soviet Law and Media Policy* 33/34 (1996).

271. Anatoly Rakitov, "Civilization, Culture, Technology, and the Market," *Russian Social Science Review* 34, no. 4 (1993): 93.

CHAPTER 6. WHAT'S COMPARABLE, WHAT ISN'T AND WHAT IT MAY MEAN

1. See Bibliography for a list of books involving comparisons of systems.

2. Ron Nessen, "Always on Saturday?" *The Washington Post Weekly,* 1 September 1986, p. 29.

3. For details on "Friends of the Earth," see Frank Kahn, *Documents of American Broadcasting,* 2nd ed. (New York: Appleton-Century-Crofts, 1973), 438-46. For details on "Business Executives ... ,: see Christopher Sterling and John M. Kittross, *Stay Tuned,* 2nd ed. (New York: Wadsworth, 1990), 428.

4. Barry Cole and Mal Oettinger, *Reluctant Regulators,* rev. ed. (New York: Appleton-Century-Crofts, 1978), chap. 5.

5. Claude Collin, *Ecoutez la vraie difference* (Claix: La pensée sauvage, 1979).

6. Simon Partridge, Community Radio Association, and Bevan Jones, Communications Officer, National Federation of Community Organizations, personal interviews, London, September 1986.

7. "Radio Station for 'Working Class,'" *Post-Soviet Media Law and Policy Newsletter* 32 (1996): 2.

8. Donald R. Browne, *Electronic Media and Indigenous Peoples: A Voice of Our Own?* (Ames, Iowa: Iowa State University Press, 1996), chap. 2.

9. Tim Tomlinson, "The Development of Local Religious Radio in Norway and Sweden" (Ph.D. diss., University of Minnesota, 1994).

10. Tomlinson, "Development."

11. Donald R. Browne, "The Snail's Shell: Electronic Media and Émigré Communities" (paper presented at annual conference of the Broadcast Education Association, Las Vegas, Nevada, April 1997).

12. Giovanni Grassi, "Italy: Strengthening Film and TV Alliances," *The Hollywood Reporter,* 17 April 1987, p. S-29.

13. As far back as 1985, an Italian Deputy to the European Parliament introduced a bill allowing film directors the right to say where and how to insert ads in their films. "Global Notes, Rome," *Electronic Media,* 4 November 1985, p. 20.

14. Aaron Mowray, "The Internationalization of Audio-Visual Media and the European Community: A Study of Copyright Harmonization and the MEDIA Programme" (summa honors thesis [B.A.], University of Minnesota, 1997), 43; *Communication from the [European] Commission: Audiovisual Policy Stimulating Dynamic Growth in the European Programme Industry* (MEDIA IIC1996-2000), COM (94) 523 final (Luxembourg: Office for Official Publications of the European Community, 8 February 1995).

15. Warren Berger, "At 25, Excellence and Big Budgets for a Late Bloomer," *New York Times,* 9 November 1997, sec. 3, p. 23.

16. Commission of the European Community, *Television Without Frontiers,* COM (84) 300 final (Brussels: author, 1984).

17. "The Public Service—a Factor in European Democracy," *EBU Diffusion Special* (a journal of the European Broadcasting Union) (February 1995): 9.

18. A particularly interesting source of speculation on the likely fate of PSBs in Europe and elsewhere is Anthony Weymouth and Bernard Lamizet, eds., *Markets and Myths: Forces for Change in the Media of Europe* (London and New York: Longman, 1996), chap. 7.

19. Iceland closed its public service for the month of July up until 1983, on the assumption that many Icelanders, including broadcast staff, would be (or would want to be) on vacation then. The service also observed a TV-free Thursday

until 1987. Broddason, in Ib Bondebjerg and Francesco Bono, eds., *Television in Scandinavia* (Luton, U.K.: University of Luton Press, John Libbey Media, 1996), 79.

20. UNESCO, *Three Weeks of Television: An International Comparative Study* (Paris: author, 1986), Document CC-81/WS/32; Horizons Media International, *Television Programming in Europe* (London: author, 1986).

21. Browne, *Comparing,* 387.

22. The most readily accessible source of data on top 10 programs in various nations is the British periodical *TV World.*

23. I have not yet seen a copy, but a book review of J. A. Coleman and B. Rollet, eds., *Television in Europe* (Exeter, U.K.: Intellect Press, 1997), would seem to confirm that view.

24. Browne, *Electronic.*

25. The auctioning of parts of the frequency spectrum to the highest bidder has become a more common practice during the 1990s: Great Britain, Australia, New Zealand and the United States all have done so. However, most of the frequencies auctioned are not used for broadcasting, and those that are won't necessarily be auctioned to the highest bidder: quality of service proposed can be a further criterion for the awarding of a license.

25a. "The Purposes of Broadcasting" (London: Campaign for Quality Television, 1998), pp. 17-18.

26. Reed Hundt, the FCC Chairman from 1993 to 1997, was such an individual. He was especially zealous regarding electronic media responsibilities toward children, and managed to win a few battles over that issue. Still, the U.S. electronic media landscape changed very little during his term of office.

27. How much "good" the requirement will do is another matter: Initial indications are that stations will try to avoid too heavy a commitment to the educational aspect by making programs as entertaining as possible, and sometimes by "rediscovering" the "educational" aspects of already-popular entertainment programs such as "Wheel of Fortune." See Lawrie Mifflin, "Media," *New York Times,* 10 February 1997, p. C8.

28. *A Public Trust: The Report of the Carnegie Commission on the Future of Public Broadcasting* (New York: Bantam Books, 1979), 155-57; Ralph Engleman, *Public Radio and Television in America: A Political History* (Thousand Oaks, Calif.: Sage, 1996).

29. Michael Rechtshaffen, "Verdict Out on Telefilm Fund," *Hollywood Reporter,* 19 May 1987, pp. I-1, I-8.

30. Browne, *Electronic*; Tony Dowmunt, ed., *Channels of Resistance* (London: British Film Institute, 1993); Claire Frachon and Marion Vargaftig, eds., *European Television: Immigrants and Ethnic Minorities* (London: John Libbey, 1995); Bruce Girard, ed., *A Passion for Radio* (Montréal: Black Rose, 1992); Charles Husband, ed., *A Greater Vision* (Paris: UNESCO, 1994); Peter Lewis and Jerry Booth, *The Invisible Medium: Public, Commercial and Community Radio* (Washington D.C.: Howard University Press, 1992); Steven H. Riggins, ed., *Ethnic Minority Media: An International Perspective* (Newbury Park, Calif.: Sage, 1992).

31. "FCC Fines WMIE For 'Incitement,'" *Radio-TV Daily,* 21 March 1965, p. 5.

32. Much has been written about the mutual hatred preached by various stations, most of them government-run, in Bosnia, Serbia and Crotia. A useful work in terms of both furnishing background and context for the situation and discussing the specific role of the broadcast media is Jasminka Udovicki and James Ridgeway, eds., *Yugoslavia's Ethnic Nightmare* (New York: Lawrence Hill Books, 1995). See especially chaps. 5 and 9.

33. Jane Perlez, "As a Priest Gives Poles Hate Radio, Rome Stirs," *New York Times,* 14 December 1997, sec. 1, p. 11.

34. Hans Kimmel, "Will Network Broadcasting Survive?" (paper delivered at the annual conference of the International Institute of Communciation, Helsinki, Finland, September 1982), 6.

35. BBC Broadcasting Research, "Threads and On the Eighth Day" (London: author, December 1984).

36. Browne, "The Snail's Shell."

37. What they learned was another matter: the official Soviet image of "We're all one happy family" certainly was underscored in those broadcasts, where there was no mention of the centuries-old animosities that Chechen, Ingush or any number of other Soviet minorities felt toward the Russians who had dominated them well before the birth of the Soviet Union—animosities borne of mass annihilations or deportations. The outbreaks of violence in the independence movements in Chechnya, Ingushetsia and elsewhere in the early to mid 1990s must have surprised a good many Russians.

38. Juergen Habermas, in Craig Calhoun, ed., *Habermas and the Public Sphere* (Cambridge, Mass.: Massachusetts Institute of Technology Press, 1992), 455.

38a. "TalkNetRadio.com Launches Registration Site for Do-It-Yourself Internet Radio," *Business Wire* (*http://www.businesswire.com*), January 5, 1999.

39. Michael Shrimpton, "'Beatbox': An ABC Television Initiative for Youth," *COMBROAD* (March 1987); personal conversations with 'Beatbox' production staff, Sydney, Australia, September 1987.

40. Jane Millichip, "Corralling the Neo-Young," *TV World* (October 1996): 33-34.

41. *A Public Trust,* 76-81.

42. Jane Millichip, "Forum on Fiction," *TV World* (April 1996): 56.

43. Lawrie Mifflin, "Can children get more educational programming without help from the F.C.C.?" *New York Times,* August 28, 1995, C7.

44. The conference of the Working Group on Principles and Paths for Democratic Media, which I attended in May 1996 at the Aspen Conference Center in Queenstown, Maryland, brought together a group of broadcasters, broadcast critics and academics from Russia, Kazakhstan, Lithuania, Scotland and the United States.

45. Perhaps least of all in Japan, where the NHK has shown little sign of being ready to engage in the "agonizing reappraisals" undertaken by PSBs almost everywhere else.

46. Note particularly the public comments of OLON, Carole Tongue and the Voice of the Listener and Viewer, all available through the same website cited for

the working document. The *Guardian's* (U.K.) on-line edition of 15 December 1997 contains an excellent article written by Simon Beavis and Chris Barrie—"Will the Men From Brussels Decide Our New Media Policy?"—on the implications of the report for British government policy-making.

47. Philip Schlesinger, *Media, State and Nation* (London and Newbury Park, Calif.: Sage, 1991), chaps. 8 and 9.

48. Luis Guilherme Duarte and Joseph Straubhaar, "The Emergence of a Regional Television Market in Latin America" (paper presented at Broadcast Education Association Annual Convention, April 1997).

48a. Stephen J. Kobrin, "Back to the Future: Neomedievalism and the Postmodern Digital Economy," *Journal of International Affairs,* 51, 2(Spring, 1998) p. 374 and p. 373 respectively. That entire issue of the Journal contains articles on the subject of the Internet's impact on the nation-state, mostly in terms of Internet effects on marketing.

49. Jochen Zimmer, *Europa's Fernsehen Im Wandel* (Frankfurt and New York: Peter Lang, 1993), is perhaps the best single source, not only on the development of European Union (Community) media policies, but also on the many failed attempts in Europe to develop various pan-European programming ventures.

50. Eugene Eugster, *Television Progamming Across National Boundaries: The EBU and OIRT Experience* (Dedham, Mass.: Artech, 1983); and Harold Fisher, "The EBU: Model for Regional Cooperation in Broadcasting," *Journalism Monographs* 68 (May 1980).

51. Browne, *Electronic,* 47.

52. This begs the question of how those shared values, beliefs and practices are formed, which I admit is not easy to discover. But to me there is a distinct possibility that simultaneous exposure over time on the part of members of a social group to cultural commodities such as TV programs from abroad could result in the acquisition of new values, etc., in part through the process of mutual reinforcement (continued discussions among group members of certain programs, for example).

53. Philip Schlesinger, "From Cultural Defence to Political Culture: Media, Politics and Collective Identity in the European Union," *Media, Culture and Society* 19, no. 3 (1997): 371-72.

54. "Dallas" certainly has received more attention in terms of its international impact than has any other U.S. TV entertainment series. See Ien Eng, *Watching Dallas* (London: Methuen, 1985); Tamar Liebes and Elihu Katz, *The Export of Meaning: Cross-Cultural Readings of Dallas* (New York: Oxford University Press, 1990); and Patrick Rossler, *Dallas und Schwarzwaldklinik* (Munich: R. Fischer, 1988).

55. Donald R. Browne, Ellen Mickiewicz and Charles Firestone, *Television/Radio News & Minorities* (Queenstown, Md.: The Aspen Institute, 1994), chap. 11.

56. "The Public Service: A Factor in European Democracy," *EBU diffusion special issue,* February 1995, 2-10. Dave Atkinson and Mark Raboy, eds., *Public Service Broadcasting: The Challenge of the 21st Century* (Paris: UNESCO, 1997),

and Michael Tracey, *The Decline and Fall of Public Service Broadcasting* (London and New York: Oxford University Press, 1998) are the latest (to date) in a number of works that deal with the uncertain future of PSBs. The former is unusual in that it takes into account the experiences of PSBs in nonindustrialized nations and regions such as India and Latin America. It also has two quite useful omnibus essays by the two editors.

56a. Rex Winsbury, "Public Service Broadcasting: looking to telecoms for a new vision of itself," *InterMedia* 26, 5 (December 1998), 24-27, offers some interesting suggestions on how PSBs might function in an "age of convergence."

57. There was an interesting proposal made by Jamie Wetzel, a former United Nations Human Rights Officer, in the U.S. magazine *Foreign Affairs* (Fall 1997). It called for units made up of portable "jamming" transmitters and their operators, to be sent out to areas where a "hate" broadcaster such as the Hutu-run "Radio-Television Libre des Mille Collines" in Rwanda was actively calling for the dispossession and even slaughter of a particular group (in this case, Tutsi, but also moderate Hutus). The U.N. unit would jam the broadcasts, presumably until the threat passed. But how would one know whether it had passed, or was simply staying off the air until the unit left? Wetzel's proposal was discussed by Jim Mann in "U.N. Hate-Radio Jamming Would Send Wrong Signal," *Los Angeles Times*, 3 December 1997, p. A5. How one would know whether the station had been rendered ineffective, or was simply staying off the air until the unit left, wasn't clear.

Bibliography

This bibliography consists of works in which comparisons are made between two or more electronic media systems. It should serve to provide anyone having interest in such comparisons with some guidance on approaches taken by others. Those wishing to consider my critical appraisal of most of the works cited below are invited to read my article "Comparing Electronic Media Across Cultures: Reflections in a Myopic Eye," *Journal of Broadcasting and Electronic Media* 40, no. 2 (Spring 1996): 265-80.

Achille, Y., and J. Ibanez-Bueno. *Les Télévisions Publiques en Quête d'Avenir* (Public TV in Search of Its Future). Grenoble: Presses Universitaires de Grenoble, 1994.

Aldridge, M., and N. Hewitt, eds. *Controlling Broadcasting: Access Policy and Practice in North America and Europe.* Manchester: Manchester University Press, 1994.

Allen, R. C., ed. *To Be Continued ... Soap Operas Around the World.* London and New York: Routledge, 1995.

Article 19. *Who Rules the Airwaves? Broadcasting in Africa.* London: author, 1995.

Atkinson, D., and M. Raboy, eds. *Public Service Broadcasting: The Challenges of the Twenty-first Century.* Paris: UNESCO, Reports and Papers on Mass Communication 111, 1997.

Avery, R., ed. *Public Service Broadcasting in a Multichannel Environment.* New York: Longman, 1993.

Baden, A. L. *Selected List of References on the Regulation and Control of Radio Broadcasting in the U.S. and Foreign Countries.* Washington, D.C.: Library of Congress, 1933.

Batson, L. G. *Radio Markets of the World.* (Separate volumes for 1928-29, 1930 and 1931.) Washington, D.C.: U.S. Government Printing Office, 1929-31.

Bebey, F. *La Radiodiffusion en Afrique Noire.* Issy-les-Moulineaux: Editions Saint-Paul, 1963.

Beidler-Wagner, F. W., et al. *The Educational Role of Broadcasting.* Paris: International Institute of Intellectual Cooperation, 1935.

Bertelsmann Foundation and European Institute for the Media, eds. *Television Requires Responsibility, Vol. 2: International Studies on the Structural Factors Ensuring Responsible Television.* Gutersloh: Bertelsmann Foundation Publishers, 1995.

Blumler, J., ed. *Television and the Public Interest: Vulnerable Values in West European Broadcasting.* London: Sage, 1992.

Blumler, J., and T. J. Nossiter, eds. *Broadcasting Finance in Transition: a Comparative Handbook.* New York: Oxford University Press, 1991.

Bombled, T. *Devine qui va parler ce soir: Petite Histoire des Radios Libres.* (Guess Who'll Be Speaking Tonight: A Little History of Free Radio.) Paris: Plon, 1981.

Bondebjerg, I., and F. Bono, eds. *Television in Scandinavia: History, Politics and Aesthetics.* Luton, U.K.: University of Luton Press/John Libbey Media, 1996.

Bourgault, L. *Mass Media in Sub-Saharan Africa.* Bloomington, Ind.: Indiana University Press, 1995.

Boyd, D. *Broadcasting in the Arab World.* Ames, Iowa: Iowa State University Press, 1983; rev. ed. 1993, 3rd ed., 1999.

Boyd, D., J. Straubhaar and J. Lent. *Videocassette Recorders in the Third World.* White Plains, N.Y.: Longman, 1989.

Browne, D. R. *Comparing Broadcast Systems: the Experiences of Six Industrialized Nations.* Ames, Iowa: Iowa State University Press, 1989.

———. *Electronic Media and Indigenous Peoples: A Voice of Their Own?* Ames, Iowa: Iowa State University Press, 1996.

———. *What's Local About Local Radio? A Cross-National Comparative Study.* London: Institute for International Communication (Occasional Monographs No. 1), 1988.

Bullinger, M., and F. Kubler, eds. *Rundfunkorganisation und Kommunikationsfreiheit.* Baden-Baden: Nomos, 1979.

Burrows, A. G. *Broadcasting Abroad.* Geneva: Union Internationale de Radiodiffusion, Information Series No. 7. Reprinted in slightly revised form in 1933 and 1934 through Chicago: National Council on Radio in Education; and Chicago: University of Chicago Press. The latter has a supplemental section on broadcasting in the Far East and South Pacific.

Busch, C. *Was Sie immer uber Freie Radios wissen wollten, aber nie zu fragen wagten!* (What You Always Wanted to Know about Free Radio, but Never Dared to Ask!). Frankfurt: Zweitausendeins Versand, 1981.

Caron, A. H., and P. Juneau. *Le Défi des Télévisions Nationales à l'Ere de la Mondialisation.* Montréal: Presses de l'Université de Montréal, 1992.

Casmir, F., ed. *Communication in Eastern Europe: The Role of History, Culture and Media in Contemporary Conflicts.* Mahwah, N.J.: Erlbaum, 1995.

Chiti-Batelli, A. *Mass Media e Societa Europea: La prospettiva federalista per una radio-televisione continentale.* Manduria: Lacaita editore, 1977.

Clark, N., and E. Riddell. *The Sky Barons.* London: Methuen, 1992.

Codding, G. A., Jr. *Broadcasting Without Barriers.* Paris: UNESCO, 1959.

Cohen, A., M. Levy, M. Gurevitch and I. Roeh. *Eurovision and the Globalization of Television News.* London: John Collins, 1995.

Cojean, A., and F. Askenazi. *FM: La Folle Histoire des Radios Libres.* Paris: Grasset, 1986.

Collins, R. *Broadcasting and Audio-Visual Policy in the European Single Market.* London: John Libbey, 1994.

———. *Culture, Communication, and National Identity: The Case of Canadian Television.* Toronto: University of Toronto Press, 1990.

———. *Satellite Television in Western Europe*, rev. ed. London: John Libbey, 1992.

Cooper-Chen, A. *Games in the Global Village: A 50 Nation Study of Entertainment Television.* Bowling Green, Ohio: Bowling Green University Popular Press, 1994.

Corcoran, F., and P. Preston, eds. *Democracy and Communication in the New Europe: Change and Continuity in East and West.* Creskill, N.J.: Hampton Press, 1995.

Crookes, P., and P. Vittet-Philippe. *Local Radio and Regional Development in Europe.* Manchester: European Institute for the Media, 1986.

Dahlgren, P. *Television and the Public Sphere.* Thousand Oaks, Calif.: Sage, 1995.

DeGourney, C., P. Musso and G. Pineau. *Télévisions Dechainees: La Dereglementation en Italie, en Grande Bretagne, et aux Etats-unis.* Paris: La Documentation Française, 1985.

Dibie, J-N. *Aid for Cinematographic and Audio-Visual Production in Europe.* London: John Libbey, 1993.

Dietrich, Charlotte. *Der Rundfunk in Afrika—Anfang der siebziger Jahre: Strukturen und Daten.* Salzburg: Instituts fur Publizistik und Kommunikationstheorie, Arbeitsberichte, Heft 3, 1976.

Dizard, W. *Television: A World View.* Syracuse: Syracuse University Press, 1966.

Donow, K. *East Asian Media: Television, Radio and Information Services in Eight Asia Markets.* Washington, D.C.: United States Information Agency, December 1995.

———. *European Media Markets: Commercial and Public Media in 15 Countries.* Washington, D.C.: National Association of Broadcasters, 1992.

Dowmunt, T., ed. *Channels of Resistance: Global Television and Local Empowerment.* London: British Film Institute, 1993.

Downing, J. *Internationalizing Media Theory: Transition, Power, Culture.* Thousand Oaks, Calif.: Sage, 1996.

———. *Radical Media: the Political Experience of Alternative Communication.* Boston: South End Books, 1984.

Drummond, P., R. Paterson and J. Willis, eds. *National Identity and Europe: The Television Revolution.* London: British Film Institute, 1993.

Dunnett, P. *The World Television Industry.* London and New York: Routledge, 1990.

Dyson, K., and P. J. Humphreys, eds. *The Politics of the Communications Revolution in Western Europe.* London: Frank Cass, 1986.

Emery, W. *National and International Systems of Broadcasting.* East Lansing: Michigan State University Press, 1969.

Etzioni-Halevy, E. *National Broadcasting Under Siege: A Comparative Study of Australia, Britain, Israel, and West Germany.* New York: St. Martin's Press, 1987.

Eugster, E. *Television Programming Across National Boundaries: The EBU and OIRT Experiences.* Dedham, Mass.: Artech House, 1983.

Fox, E. *Latin American Broadcasting: From Tango to Telenovela.* Luton, U.K.: University of Luton Press/John Libbey Media, 1997.

Fox, E., ed. *Media and Politics in Latin America.* Newbury Park, Calif.: Sage, 1988.

Frachon, C., and M. Vargaftig, eds. *European Television: Immigrants and Ethnic Minorities.* London: John Libbey, 1995.

French, D., and M. Richards, eds. *Contemporary Television: Eastern Perspectives.* Thousand Oaks, Calif.: Sage, 1996. "Eastern" here refers to Asia.

Ganley, G. *The Political Fallout from Personal Media.* Norwood, N.J.: Ablex, 1992.

Ganley, G., and O. Ganley. *Global Political Fallout: The VCR's First Decade.* Norwood, N.J.: Ablex, 1987.

German-Africa Society. *Commercial Radio in Africa.* Bonn: author, 1970.

Girard, B., ed. *A Passion for Radio: Radio Waves and Community.* Montréal and New York: Black Rose Books, 1992.

Green, T. *The Universal Eye: The World of Television.* New York: Stein & Day, 1972.

Groombridge, B., and J. Hay, eds. *The Price of Choice: Public Service Broadcasting in a Competitive European Marketplace.* London: John Libbey, 1995.

Gross, L. S., ed. *The International World of Electronic Media.* New York: McGraw-Hill, 1995.

Harte, J., ed. *Black People and the Media.* Warwick, U.K.: Warwick University Publications, 1988.

Hasebrink, U., F. Krotz, C. Matzen, H.-D. Schroeder and J. Simon. *Europaeisches Bildungsfernsehen: Strukture, Konzepte, Perspektiven.* Hamburg: Verlag Hans Bredow Institut, 1993.

Haslett, A. W. *Radio Around the World.* Cambridge, U.K.: Cambridge University Press, 1934.

Head, S. W. *World Broadcasting Systems: A Comparative Analysis.* Belmont, Calif.: Wadsworth Publishing Company, 1985.

———, ed. *Broadcasting in Africa: A Continental Survey of Radio and Television.* Philadelphia: Temple University Press, 1974.

Hilliard, R., and M. Keith. *Global Broadcasting Systems.* Newton, Mass.: Focal Press (Butterworth-Heinemann), 1996.

Hoffman-Riem, W. *Regulating Media: Licensing and Supervision of Broadcasting in Six Countries.* New York: Guilford, 1996.

Holznagel, Bernd. *Rundfunkrecht in Europa: Auf dem Weg zu einem Gemeinrecht europaeischer Rundfunkordnungen.* Tuebingen: Mohr, 1996.

Howell, W. S. *World Broadcasting in the Age of the Satellite.* Norwood, N.J.: Ablex, 1986.

Humphreys, P. J. *Mass Media and Media Policy in Western Europe.* Manchester, U.K. and New York: Manchester University Press and St. Martin's Press, 1996.

Husband, C., ed. *A Richer Vision: The Development of Ethnic Minority Media in Western Democracies.* London: John Libbey, 1994.

Huth, A. G. *La Radiodiffusion—Puissance Mondiale.* Paris: Les Documents Bleues No. 14, 1937; reprinted by New York: Arno Press, 1971.

———. *Radio Heute und Morgen.* Zurich: Universal Verlag, 1944.

———. *Radio Today: The Present State of Broadcasting in the World.* Geneva: Geneva Research Centre, 1942. (Also available through the periodical *Geneva Studies* [July 1942]: 1-160.)

Institut Panos. *Le Pluralisme Radiophonique en Afrique de l'Ouest.* Paris: L'Harmattan, 1993.

———. *Liberté pour les Radios Africaines.* Paris: L'Harmattan, 1994.

International Institute of Communication. *Media Ownership and Control in the Age of Convergence.* London: author, 1996.

Jamison, D. T., and E. G. McAnany. *Radio for Education and Development.* Beverly Hills: Sage, 1978.

Jankowski, N., O. Prehn and J. Stappers, eds. *The People's Voice: Local Radio and Television in Europe.* London: John Libbey, 1992.

Jongen, F., ed. *Medias et Service Publique.* Brussels: Bruylant, 1992.

Kaid, L. L., and C. Holz-Bacha, eds. *Political Advertising in Western Democracies: Parties & Candidates on Television.* Thousand Oaks, Calif.: Sage, 1995.

Kamalipour, Y. R., and H. Mowlana, eds. *Mass Media in the Middle East: A Comprehensive Handbook.* Westport, Conn.: Greenwood, 1994.

Katz, E., and G. Weddell. *Broadcasting and the Third World; Promise and Performance.* Cam-

bridge, Mass.: Harvard University Press, 1977.
Keune, R. *Electronic Media and the Third World: Exchange and Cooperation—or Condescension and Confrontation?*, 2nd ed. Bonn: Friedrich Ebert Stiftung, 1987.
Kleinstuber, H. J. *Radio: das unterschatzte Medium—Erfahrung mit nichtkommerzielen Lokalstationen in 15 Staaten.* Berlin: Vistas, 1991.
Kleinstuber, H. J., D. McQuail and K. Siune, eds. *Electronic Media and Politics in Western Europe.* Frankfurt: Campus Verlag, 1986.
Kopper, G., ed. *Europaeische Oeffentlichkeit: Entwicklungen von Strukturen und Theorie.* Berlin: Vistas, 1997.
Kuhn, R., ed. *The Politics of Broadcasting.* New York: St. Martin's Press, 1985.
Lafrance, J. P. *Les radios nouvelles dans le monde.* Paris: La Documentation Française, 1985.
Lange, Y. *Media in the CIS: A Study of Political, Legislative and Socio-Economic Framework.* Dusseldorf, Germany: European Institute for the Media, 1997. Covers Russia and the other former Soviet republics.
Lange, Y., and A. Palmer, eds. *Media and Elections.* Dusseldorf, Germany: European Institute for the Media, 1995.
Lee, C. C. *Media Imperialism Reconsidered: The Homogenization of Television Culture.* Beverly Hills: Sage, 1979.
Lent, J. A., ed. *Broadcasting in Asia and the Pacific: a Continental Survey of Radio and Television.* Philadelphia: Temple University Press, 1978.
Lewis, P. M., and J. Booth. *The Invisible Medium: Public, Commercial, and Community Radio.* Washington, D.C.: Howard University Press, 1990.
Lull, J., ed. *World Families Watch Television.* Newbury Park, Calif.: Sage, 1988.
Lunven, R., and T. Védel. *La Télévision de Demain.* Paris: A. Colin, 1992.
McCavitt, W., ed. *Broadcasting Around the World.* Blue Ridge Summit, Pa.: TAB Books, 1981.
McDaniel, D. O. *Broadcasting in the Malay World: Radio, Television, and Video in Brunei, Indonesia, Malaysia, and Singapore.* Norwood, N.J.: Ablex, 1994.
McLean, M., ed. *The Information Explosion: The New Electronic Media in Japan and Europe.* Westport, Conn.: Greenwood Press, 1985.
Michel, H., and A.-L. Angoulvent. *Les Télévisions en Europe.* Paris: Presses Universitaires de France, series Que Sais-je? No. 2719, 1992.
Mikos, L. *Es Wird Dein Leben! Familienserien im Fernsehen und im Alltag der Zuschauer* (It's Your Life! Family Serials on TV and in the Everyday Life of Viewers.) Munster, Germany: MAkS Publikationen, 1994.
Moragas Spa, M. de, and C. Garitaonandia, eds. *Decentralization in the Global Era: Television in the Regions, Nationalities and Small Countries of the European Union.* London: John Libbey, 1995.
Moschner, M. *Fernsehen in Lateinamerika.* Frankfurt: P. Lang, 1982.
Musso, P., ed. *Regions d'Europe et Télévision.* Paris: Editions Miroirs, 1991.
Namurois, A. *Structures and Organization of Broadcasting in the Framework of Radiocommunications.* Geneva: European Broadcasting Union, EBU Monograph No. 8, 1972.
Noam, E. *Television in Europe.* New York: Oxford, 1990. (Readers with an interest in comparative approaches to telecommunications should note four books authored or edited by Noam and others, all published by Oxford University Press: *Telecommunications in Europe* (1992); *Telecommunications in Latin America* (1998); *Telecommunications in the Pacific Basin* (1994); and *Telecommunications in western Asia and the Middle East* (1997).)

Paletz, D., et al., eds. *Glasnost and After: Media and Change in Central and Eastern Europe.* Creskill, N.J.: Hampton Press, 1995.

Paraschos, E. *Media Law and Regulation in the European Union.* Ames: Iowa State University Press, 1998.

Paulu, B. *Radio and Television Broadcasting in Eastern Europe.* Minneapolis: University of Minnesota Press, 1974.

———. *Radio and Television Broadcasting on the European Continent.* Minneapolis: University of Minnesota Press, 1967.

Pige, F. *La Télévision Dans le Monde—Organization Administrative et Financière.* Paris: Société Nationale des Entreprises de Presse, 1962.

Pilati, A., ed. *MIND: Media Industry in Europe.* London: John Libbey, 1993.

Porter, V. *Beyond the Berne Convention: Copyright, Broadcasting and the Single European Market.* London: John Libbey, 1991.

Price, M. *Television, The Public Sphere and National Identity.* New York: Oxford University Press, 1995.

Raboy, M. *Public Broadcasting for the 21st Century.* Luton, U.K.: University of Luton Press/John Libbey Media, 1996.

Régourd, S. *La Télévision des Européens.* Paris: La Documentation Française, 1992.

Renckstorf, K., ed. *Media Use as Social Action: A European Approach to Audience Studies.* London: John Libbey, 1995.

Riano, P., ed. *Women in Grassroots Communication.* Beverly Hills: Sage, 1994.

Riggins, S. H., ed. *Ethnic Minority Media: An International Perspective.* Beverly Hills: Sage, 1992.

Robillard, S. *Television in Europe: Regulatory Bodies.* London: John Libbey, 1995.

Rogers. E., and F. Balle. *The Media Revolution in America and in Western Europe.* Norwood, N.J.: Ablex, 1985.

Rosen, P. T., ed. *International Handbook of Broadcast Systems.* New York: Greenwood, 1988.

Sanchez-Taberno, A., et al. *Media Concentration in Europe: Commercial Enterprise and Public Policy.* Dusseldorf: European Institute for the Media, 1993.

Schramm, W. A. *Mass Media and National Development.* Paris: UNESCO, 1964.

Schutrumpf, E. D. *Broadcast Advertising in Asia, Africa, Australia, and Oceania.* Washington, D.C.: U.S. Government Printing Office, 1932.

Sepstrup, P. *Transnationalization of Television in Western Europe.* London: John Libbey, 1990.

Shaughnessy, H., and C. F. Cobo. *The Cultural Obligations of Broadcasting.* London: John Libbey, 1990.

Silj, A., ed. *The New Television in Europe.* London: John Libbey, 1992.

Siune, K., and W. Truetzchler, eds. *Dynamics of Media Politics: Broadcast and Electronic Media in Western Europe.* Newbury Park, Calif.: Sage, 1992.

Skidmore, T., ed. *Television, Politics and the Transition to Democracy in Latin America.* Washington, D.C.: Woodrow Wilson Center Press, 1993.

Smith, A. *The Age of Behemoths: the Globalization of Mass Media Firms.* New York: Priority Press, 1991.

———. *The Shadow in the Cave: The Broadcaster, His Audience, and the State.* Urbana: University of Illinois Press, 1973.

———. *Television and Political Life: Studies in Six European Countries.* New York: St. Martin's Press, 1979.

Statistical Yearbook 199X-199Y: Cinema, Television, Video and New Media in Europe (annual). Strasbourg, France: European Audiovisual Laboratory.

(La) Télévision Locale en Europe. Strasbourg, France: Acta, 1992.

(Les) Télévisions du Monde: Panorama dans 110 Pays. Paris: Editions Cerf Corlet, 1987.

Télévisions Francophones en Afrique. Paris: Eurekam, 1992.

Thede, N., and A. Ambrosi, eds. *Video the Changing World.* Montréal and New York: Black Rose Books, 1991.

Tracy, M. *The Decline and Fall of Public Service Broadcasting.* Oxford, UK and New York, NY: Oxford University Press, 1998.

Tudesq, A. J. *L'Afrique et ses Télévisions.* Paris: Institut Nationale de l'Audiovisuelle and Anthropos, 1992.

———. *La Radio en Afrique Noire.* Paris: Editions A. Pedoneris, 1983.

Tunstall, J. *The Media Are American: Anglo-American Media in the World.* New York: Columbia University Press, 1977.

Tunstall, J., and M. Palmer. *Liberating Communications: Policy Making in Britain and France.* London: Blackwell, 1990.

———. *Media Moguls.* London and New York: Routledge, 1991.

Tydeman, J., and E. Kelm. *New Media in Europe.* London: McGraw-Hill, 1986.

Ugboajah, F. *Mass Communication, Culture and Society in West Africa.* Oxford, U.K. and Detroit, Mich.: H. Zell; Gale Research, 1985.

United Nations Educational, Social and Cultural Organization (UNESCO). *Television: A World Survey.* New York: UNESCO Publications Center, 1953.

Vogel, A. *Rundfunk fur Alle: Burgerbeteiligung, Partizipation und zugangsoffene Sendeplatze in Horfunk und Fernsehen.* Berlin: Vistas Verlag, 1991.

Voss, H. *Rundfunk und Fernsehen in Afrika.* Koln: Verlag Deutscher Wirtschaftsdienst G.m.b.H., 1962.

Wedell, E. G., ed. *Making Broadcasting Useful: The African Experience.* Manchester: Manchester University Press, 1985.

Wedell, E. G., and P. Crookes. *Radio 2000: The Opportunities for Public and Private Radio Services in Europe.* Manchester: European Institute for the Media, 1991.

Wells, A., ed. *World Broadcasting: A Comparative View.* Norwood, N.J.: Ablex, 1996.

Weymouth, T., and B. Lamizet, eds. *Markets & Myths: Forces for Change in the European Media.* London and New York: Longman, 1996.

Whale, J. *The Half-Shut Eye: Television and Politics in Britain and America.* New York: St. Martin's Press, 1969.

Ziegler, D., and M. Asante. *Thunder and Silence: The Mass Media in Africa.* Trenton, N.J.: Africa World Press, 1992.

Zimmer, J. *Europas Fernsehen im Wandel: Probleme einer Europaisierung von Ordnungspolitik und Programmen.* (European Television in the Process of Change: Problems of Europeanization of Organizational Politics and Programming.) Frankfurt: Peter Lang, 1993.

Index